ENTREPRENEURSHIP

IN SUB-SAHARAN AFRICA

A Strategic Management Perspective

John O. Ogbor, Ph.D.

AuthorHouse™
1663 Liberty Drive, Suite 200
Bloomington, IN 47403
www.authorhouse.com
Phone: 1-800-839-8640

©2009 John O. Ogbor, Ph.D.

No part of this book may be reproduced, stored in a retrieval system, or transmitted by any means without the written permission of the author.

First published by AuthorHouse 3/24/2009

ISBN: 978-1-4389-3392-4 (sc)

Library of Congress Control Number: 2008911428

Printed in the United States of America
Bloomington, Indiana

This book is printed on acid-free paper.

ENTREPRENEURSHIP
IN SUB-SAHARAN AFRICA

A Strategic Management Perspective

John O. Ogbor Ph. D.

Published for

TECHNOLOGY & ALLIED
SERVICES, LTD

ABOUT THE AUTHOR

Professor John O. Ogbor is a management educator, researcher and consultant. His career in management and business education started at Lund University in Sweden where he obtained his MBA and Ph.D. degrees in management and worked as a research associate. Later, he taught at The Jesse H. Jones School of Business at Texas Southern University (both as an assistant professor and as associate professor of management) and served as the Director for the School's Honors' Program. He served as visiting distinguished professor at Illinois State University (1999-2000 academic-year). He joined American Intercontinental University as a Management Professor between 2004 and 2006. Professor Ogbor is presently serving as faculty mentor and Professor of Management at Northcentral University where he teaches doctorate programs in management. In addition to teaching and research, he has served on the chair of several doctorate dissertation committees.

He has published extensively in refereed journals including the *Journal of Management Studies*, the *Journal of Organizational Change Management* and *Cross Cultural Management: An International Journal*, His areas of research include: Entrepreneurship, Critical Theory and Management, The Global Economy; Corporate Culture and Strategic Leadership, Ethics and Corporate Governance. He is currently the Executive Director of Crown Institute for Management Development, where he assists for-profit and nonprofit organizations and business schools in developing competitive strategies, management and business curricula, accreditation management and entrepreneurial development. He has partnered with major Fortune 500 corporations in areas of strategic management, corporate culture renewal, and community-based education initiatives.

Outside of academia, Professor Ogbor is on the board of several nonprofit and faith-based organizations in the United States, Sweden and Africa. He is an ordained Pastor for World Prayer Ministries in Houston, Texas.

INTRODUCTION AND PREFACE

Education in entrepreneurship has found a secured niche in the business, management and economics curricula as the field is fast growing in the global economy. In a similar manner, entrepreneurship as a practice has become the focus of governmental policies, the mission of non-governmental organizations, and other entities interested in the promotion of economic development in a wide range of settings. Credit for this development belongs to many individuals and groups: (i) the entrepreneurs themselves, (ii) administrators of educational institutions who promote entrepreneurial education, (iii) governments that provide resources and infrastructures for entrepreneurial development and education, and (iv) students whose interest in entrepreneurial education has grown tremendously over the years.

Written with a focus on strategic management, *Entrepreneurship in Sub-Saharan Africa* is a comprehensive discussion of the most prominent issues in the management of entrepreneurial ventures. The book is written as a text in a management and business education and a reference or resource book for practicing and aspiring entrepreneurs in the context of a developing economy.

As has been documented in research and several other publication outlets, the importance of entrepreneurship in a nation's economic development cannot be over stated. From the perspective of economic development generally, and the economic empowerment of individuals in any given society, never before have so many nations and individuals realized that economic growth goes through the promotion of entrepreneurship. In recent time, the growing competitiveness of the Brazilian, Chinese, Indian and South African economies attest to the importance of entrepreneurial mindset as a powerful tool in competing in the global economy. Significantly, these four nations are able to exert their competitiveness and economic influence in the global economy through their investments in entrepreneurial key success factors. In these societies, entrepreneurship has been the cornerstone in the nexus of formal economic policies and actions.

In the developing countries of Sub-Saharan Africa however, the key sustenance of the economies is still to be found in the informal sector operated by individuals whose productivity is unaccounted for in the official description of national economic and development policies. For instance, research has shown that over seventy percent of the economic activity in Sub-Saharan Africa is located in the informal sectors outside of the organized public and private sectors! Unlike its counterparts in the more industrialized countries of North America, Western Europe and Southeast Asian countries, small businesses in the Sub-Saharan region have not been able to achieve two important goals: (i) transforming their societies and economies in order to compete effectively in the global economy, and (ii) transforming themselves from informal economic structure and survivalist mindset to that of an entrepreneurial one. The problem is that entrepreneurial development in Sub-Saharan Africa has been stranded in years of neglect as a result of the actions of policy makers and the academic community. This problem has its roots in two interrelated factors: (i) the context or environment of entrepreneurship (such as the economic, socio-cultural, financial, political, institutional, and infrastructural contexts), which is antithetical to entrepreneurial development and (ii) the underdeveloped managerial and organizational capabilities needed to manage small businesses. Arguably, combined with environmental constraints, lack of managerial capacity on the part of the African entrepreneur is the main reason why the sub-continent is lacking behind in global competitiveness.

One of the driving forces behind this book is the need to draw attention to the growing importance of entrepreneurial education as an important and timely management course in institutions of higher learning in Sub-Saharan Africa. Consequently, this book is written primarily for four groups of readership: (i) the academic community, (ii) the practitioners of entrepreneurship, (iii) the change agents of entrepreneurial and economic development, and (iv) the economy at large. For the purpose of simplicity, I will term these four groups, the stakeholders of entrepreneurial education in a developing country. These stakeholders are individuals or groups that have interest, claim, or *stake* in entrepreneurship in a particular nation or society. Their actions will influence how well entrepreneurship is promoted and encouraged, and how it can be beneficial to society.

The Academic Community: I am convinced from years of teaching and research that the academic community consisting of students, researchers and teachers of business management and economics has the unique responsibility to provide ideas that are essential for the economic development of societies. A textbook on entrepreneurship from a strategic management perspective is a step in the right direction. This book is written from the perceived need of the academic community. It contains theories of entrepreneurship, exercises, and cases suitable for classroom pedagogy. The practice of entrepreneurship and the techniques for the management of small businesses must be grounded in an educational context that is relevant and competitive; where teachers of entrepreneurship should have access to textbooks that address these issues; and researchers should be able to use a text that is grounded in the experience of developing countries. This book is useful as a text and a reference source in a management course or research in which the objective is to understand the meaning, importance and practice of entrepreneurship in the economic growth of a developing country. Contemporary issues in both entrepreneurship and strategic management within the context of Sub-Saharan Africa are used to engage and excite students, and lead them to theory grounded in entrepreneurial practice.

The Entrepreneurs and Small Business Owners: The second category of stakeholders consists of the individuals and groups of persons that practice entrepreneurship or manage their own business ventures, including those aspiring to become one. As will be shown in chapters three, four, and five of this book, small business owners in Sub-Saharan Africa face tremendous environmental constraints and management problems and for that reason, this book suggests strategies and other resources that can be helpful to the business owners and those individuals who consider themselves as prospective entrepreneurs. In Sub-Saharan Africa, for example, research indicates that there is a need for the development of entrepreneurial culture in the region. Business owners, especially those in Sub-Sahara African countries are good at setting up their own businesses, but they often fall short when it comes to the fundamental issue of managing growth and transition from small to large. The inability to transit from an informal economic agent and organization to a formal one is a major obstacle for the growth of viable entrepreneurship in Africa. For the practicing and aspiring entrepreneurs, therefore, there is an urgent need for a text with strategies that enhance entrepreneurial development and the management of small business in order to gain competitive advantage.

Policy Makers and Change Agents: The third group of stakeholders consists of policy makers and change agents of economic activities in a society or nation. As stakeholders of entrepreneurial and economic development, this group consists of economic policy makers (such as the agents of governments) legislators, governmental and non-governmental organizations (such as the World Bank, the International Monetary Fund, the International Labor Organization, etc), financial institutions (such as banks and other investor organizations), private investors and private enterprises, whose responsibility are, among others, the promotion of entrepreneurial development and economic growth in their countries. To these groups, this book is beneficial because it offers practical insights into how a business venture should be managed successfully.

The Economy at Large: Seeing entrepreneurship as a major driver of economic growth implies that many of the beneficiaries of entrepreneurial education are the society in general and its economy in particular. All economic participants, from producers to consumers, depend on innovative products and services. The operators within the so-called informal sectors depend on the policies of government to promote entrepreneurship. Governmental revenues and expenditures depend on activities undertaken by owners of business ventures. Large corporations depend on the economic activities in entrepreneurial firms as the later serve as sources of inputs. Small business owners provide employment for majority of people in the developing countries. In other words, for all intents and purposes, the level of entrepreneurial development in a nation's economy affects everyone.

THE DISTINCTIVE ADVANTAGE OF THIS TEXT

Undoubtedly, many books and articles have been written to address the importance of entrepreneurship in the developed and developing economies. Although, the book in your hand could be seen as one of the numerous texts in the entrepreneurship market, it has an edge over existing ones. First, it is developed for courses at both the undergraduate and the postgraduate levels in business and management studies with a focus on the African experience. Second, it is suitable both as a textbook to be used in institutions of higher education and as a reference book for practicing and prospective entrepreneurs, small business owners and economic change agents. The distinctive advantage of this book is summarized below:

(i) It examines the contexts under which entrepreneurship is practiced in Sub-Saharan Africa. In doing this, the book offers a discussion of the economic,

(ii) It examines the management and organizational constraints affecting the practice and performance of entrepreneurship in Sub-Saharan Africa.
(iii) It presents a strategic management perspective which helps the reader to understand the competitive nature of the chosen business environment and how to design appropriate competitive strategies.
(iv) It offers an extensive discussion of an ethical, stakeholder and social responsibility perspective in the management of small and entrepreneurial firms in the context of Sub-Saharan Africa.
(v) It provides cases that are uniquely localized for easy identification and familiarity with strategic issues, problems and solutions in Sub-Saharan Africa.
(vi) It offers strategies for preparing a business plan which is acceptable to potential investors.
(vii) It provides real life entrepreneurial experiences as case-in-point to illustrate the major themes of entrepreneurship and strategic management in the context of Sub-Saharan Africa.

THE STRUCTURE AND LOGIC OF THE BOOK

To achieve the above objectives, the contents of the book are structured in four parts. Each part contains several chapters with a focus on the major themes on entrepreneurial theory or practice from a strategic management perspective.

Part 1 is a *discourse* of entrepreneurship and examines the meaning and roles of entrepreneurship within the context of a nation's economic development. This first part also examines the various contexts or environments under which entrepreneurship is practiced in Sub-Saharan Africa. This part of the book consists of five chapters (chapters 1-5).

Chapter 1: The Meaning and Importance of Entrepreneurship
The chapter discusses the meaning and importance of entrepreneurship and small business in the context of economic development. It examines the nature of entrepreneurs and entrepreneurship, the conditions for entrepreneurship and the concept of innovation as it relates to the concept of entrepreneurship. In addition, the chapter examines the crucial differences between small business firms and entrepreneurial ventures. It argues that the concept of strategy is important for understanding the differences between an entrepreneur and a small business owner. Consequently, the entrepreneur is seen as a strategist. Furthermore, the importance of entrepreneurship in the context of Sub-Saharan Africa is examined.

Chapter 2: The Nature of Entrepreneurs: Characteristics, Profiles and Motives
In chapter 2, the characteristics of entrepreneurs are discussed with examples drawn from the experiences of successful entrepreneurs, including what they have in common and what makes them successful. The chapter also examines sources of business ideas and innovation, why people choose to be entrepreneurs and the drawbacks of becoming entrepreneurs. Chapter 2 is brought to a conclusion with a discourse of the African entrepreneur in terms of characteristics, profiles, motives and challenges.

Chapter 3: The Economic Environment: National, Regional and Global
The focus of chapter 3 is on the economic environment of entrepreneurship in Sub-Saharan Africa. Significantly, this chapter examines the economic environment and policies in the colonial and postcolonial eras; the economic policies adopted after independence and the nature of the economies in an environment of political instability and civil wars. A major economic policy that has had a profound impact on the economies of Sub-Saharan Africa is the policy of structural adjustment program. The chapter examines this policy in detail and explains its impact on the development of entrepreneurship. The nature of the global economy is also examined including the drivers of globalization: regional economic integration, information and communication technology, the multinational corporation and the shifting role of the nation-state. Among other things, this chapter examines the reasons why some countries were able to exploit global opportunities for the development of entrepreneurship and why others such as those in Africa could not.

Chapter 4: The Cultural, Financial, Political and Infrastructural Environment
In chapter 4 the socio-cultural environment of entrepreneurship is discussed with particular attention on how cultural values in Sub-Saharan Africa act as constraints to the development of entrepreneurship. Second, the financial and credit environment is examined in relation to the role of the formal and informal financial sectors, the role of microfinance institutions and the importance of public-private partnership in enterprise financing. Third, the political environment, including political risks, attitudes toward indigenous and foreign business ownership, the negative effects of bureaucratic corruption and governmental overregulation are examined in detail. Fourth, the infrastructural environment, including transportation facilities, energy supply, and information and communications technology (ICT) is discussed. In the context of entrepreneurial development, this chapter examines the inadequacies in the educational system, particularly entrepreneurial education, in Sub-Saharan Africa. Finally, the relationship between the informal sector and entrepreneurial development within the context of Sub-Saharan Africa is examined.

Chapter 5: The Management and Organization Context. The focus of chapter 5 is on management and organizational competencies as they relate to the management of entrepreneurial firms. Specifically, this chapter examines the set of management and organizational constraints facing entrepreneurs and small business owners in Sub-Saharan Africa. Issues examined in this chapter include the constraints of planning, the problem of managing growth and organizational transition, inability to manage human resources appropriately, the types of leadership and authority relations in Sub-Saharan Africa and how they affect entrepreneurship, marketing problems, the problems of ethics and corporate governance and issues of financial management.

Part 2 examines the concepts and principles of strategic management as they apply to the management of an entrepreneurial firm. This part consists of four chapters (chapters 6 - 9).

Chapter 6: The Principles of Strategic Management and Entrepreneurship
Following the strategic management perspective adopted in this book, chapter 6 discusses the principles of strategic management as applicable to the management of small businesses and entrepreneurial firms. The focus is to understand the relationship between strategic management and the entrepreneurial process. It explains why a small business must have a strategic-mindset in order to remain competitive in its chosen industry or business area. The chapter also examines different types and levels of strategies in a typical organization in a variety of environments. Finally, the chapter explains why and how a small business must create a competitive advantage in the market.

Chapter 7: Business Description, Vision, Mission, Values, and Firm Objectives
In chapter 7, the book discusses the first stage in the strategy-making process: business definition, vision, mission, and value statements, setting strategic and financial objectives and goals. This chapter is important in the sense that it gives the reader insight into why a prospective entrepreneur must first examine the reasons for going into business in the first place. It also provides the reader with tools on how to examine a business idea, what is been offered, the utility to be derived from the products or services to be offered and how these are to be offered. One of the highlights of this chapter is the explanation of the differences between a vision, mission, goals and objectives. In addition, the crucial differences between strategic and financial goals and objectives are examined.

Chapter 8: Industry and Competitive Analysis
The focus of chapter 8 is on how to analyze and understand a particular industry in which a firm intends to compete and to understand the nature of competition existing in that industry. The chapter provides tools useful for understanding the life cycle of an industry and/or market and how to formulate and implement appropriate competitive strategies in relation to the stage in which the industry finds itself in its life cycle. Third, the chapter discusses how to understand the key success factors in the industry chosen. It also discusses how to understand a company's strengths, weaknesses, opportunities and threats before making the crucial decision of whether or not to go into a business. Finally, the chapter examines how entrepreneurs can decide what their competitive advantage or core competencies are before making the crucial decision of launching a venture.

Chapter 9: Strategy Formulation for the Entrepreneurial Firm
Chapter 9 is about how entrepreneurs or small business owners can craft competitive strategies and the strategic options at their disposal in order to achieve a profitable business operation. The chapter examines the types of competitive strategies an entrepreneurial firm can use when entering the market for the first time and when it is

already a player in the market. Chapter 9 discusses the logic and advantages of offensive, defensive, cooperative, distribution, and location strategies for the purpose of the firm's competitive advantage. In addition, chapter eight examines innovative competitive strategies such as supply chain management, value chain management and networking as viable competitive strategies for the entrepreneurial firm.

Part 3 focuses on the different strategies available for the entrepreneurial firm and suggests strategies for designing them. This part of the book contains five chapters (chapters 10 – 14).

Chapter 10: Marketing Strategies for the Entrepreneurial Firm
The focus of chapter 10 is on the marketing strategies at the disposal of an entrepreneurial firm intending to be competitive in the market or industry it has chosen to stake its resources. The basic premise of this chapter is that entrepreneurs and small business owners are small players in an ocean of competition, swimming with the sharks – the big players in the industry. Secondly, small business owners and entrepreneurs are seen as fighting in a battlefield in which their resources are limited compared to those of the larger and well-equipped competitors. Therefore, in order to survive, the entrepreneurial firm must find a niche not currently satisfied by the big players. That is why this chapter discusses guerrilla-marketing tactics at the disposal of small business owners to create markets for their products and to gain market shares from the established big players in an industry. Important issues discussed in this chapter include how to build a guerrilla marketing strategy, how to identify the target markets for the small business, the role of market research in building a guerrilla-marketing plan and how to use guerrilla-marketing strategies.

Chapter 11: Growth and Organizational Strategies for the Entrepreneurial Firm
Chapter 11 discusses the strategies for managing the growth of an entrepreneurial firm. Since one of the problems facing entrepreneurial development in developing economies is that of managing growth, this chapter explains the factors that affect the growth of an entrepreneurial firm. It discusses how to find start-up partners, how to grow within a firm's current market, how to grow within an industry, how to manage diversification as a result of growth, how to organize the growth process, how to manage the organizational culture of the firm, how to develop a human resource policy, how to find and keep good employees, and how to train and develop employees. The chapter examines how to manage growth following a model known as the organizational life cycle and the types of strategies applicable to each stage in the cycle. This model consists of the different stages a firm passes through in the process of growth: the entrepreneurial (start-up) stage, the growth stage, the maturity stage, the decline stage and exit plans for an ailing business. Significantly, the chapter suggests competitive strategies suitable for a particular stage in the growth process. Finally, chapter 10 examines what an entrepreneur should do when things are not going well as he or she has originally planned by providing an exit strategy.

Chapter 12: Financial Strategies for the Entrepreneurial Firm
One of the often-stated reasons for business failures in Sub-Saharan Africa is financial mismanagement. Similarly, chapter 12 discusses the financial aspects of an entrepreneurial firm. Included in this chapter are discussions of how to put together an income statement, a balance sheet, a cash flow statement, and financial forecast and budgeting. The chapter also suggests strategies for securing finance for the business especially when one is seeking financial help from prospective investors. The ability to understand and prepare financial statements, budgets and balance sheets is seen as the corner stone for the success of a business venture. Strategies for doing this are one of the main purposes of this chapter.

Chapter 13: Ownership Strategies for the Entrepreneurial Firm
Chapter 13 examines the legal aspects of the business and discusses the advantages and disadvantages available to the business owner according to the legal form of business chosen. Similarly, the chapter examines the advantages and disadvantages of the sole proprietorship, joint partnership, a limited liability company or a publicly quoted company. In addition, the chapter examines the options opened to someone who intends to buy an existing business and how to evaluate it. Third, the idea of franchising, including its advantages and disadvantages are discussed. We know that choosing an attorney for the legality of a business is a difficult process and the chapter suggests steps to follow in choosing one.

Chapter 14: Ethics and Social Responsibility Strategies for the Entrepreneurial Firm
Chapter 14 examines the subject of ethics, social responsibility and stakeholder management in the context of an entrepreneurial firm. The main idea in this chapter is that the long-term profitability of a business depends on how it is run in an acceptable ethical business manner and how socially responsible a company behaved. The chapter examines the meaning of ethics in general, the meaning of business ethics, factors affecting entrepreneurial ethics, the demands of stakeholders of the entrepreneurial firm and ethical issues in managing the entrepreneurial firm. The chapter suggests an ethical decision-making model for the entrepreneur; shows the relationship between strategy, competition, ethics and social responsibility; and offers a model for developing a values-based organization.

Part 4 deals with how to implement the entrepreneurial ideas and the various strategies discussed in this book. This concluding part of the book is made up of chapter 15.

Chapter 15: Crafting a Competitive Business Plan
Chapter 15 is a synthesis of the discussions presented in chapters 6 to 14 as it deals with how to put everything together in a form of a business plan. The purpose of this chapter is thus to suggest strategies for crafting a winning business plan. Consequently, the chapter explains the purposes and functions of a business plan, the structure or content of a business plan and how to put one together.

ACKNOWLEDGMENTS

I have benefited immensely from the help of many people in the course of writing this book. My theoretical knowledge of entrepreneurship could not have been possible without the help of my colleagues and mentors at Lund University in Sweden and my students and colleagues at Texas Southern University, Illinois State University, Northcentral University and Grand Canyon University all in the USA. Undoubtedly, the comments and insightful criticism from my doctoral students and colleagues have helped me in refining my ideas in the process of writing this book.

I am blessed to have worked with terrific group of colleagues from the USA, Sweden, and Nigeria. Without them, this book would never have been written. I am particularly indebted to my mentors: the late Professor Kurt Kihlstedt and Professor Philippe Daudi (both of Lund University, Sweden); Professor Dale Fitzgibbons (of Illinois State University); and Professors Jean Ramsey and John Williams (both of Texas Southern University). To my friend and business partner, Mr. Ike Raphael, please accept my heartfelt gratitude for your generous support and encouragement. You and your family will experience divine blessing as you've sown into my life. To Samuel Ewurhie, I thank you for been there for me from the beginning. Your brotherly friendship has been a source of perseverance and sustenance. To Dr. Roseline Opara, Princess Mokolo, Innocent Ikhimokpa, Anita Okeke, Warren de Bourgeois, Dr. Jeff Ohanaja, Dr. Emmanuel Ogbeide, Bali Bukenya, and Kingsley Torru, I thank you all for been there for me when I needed you most. To Jacqueline Nichole Gaston, thank you for the excellent graphic work and your encouragement.

Special thanks to my family in Nigeria who have prayed for me, believed in me, and supported me in various ways: Elder Peter Ogbor, thank you for being there as a father; Daniel Ogbor, for your patience; Etiphrobome and Janet, for your motherly role; Young Abokitia, for your encouragement; and Theodore Ekperuo, for your immense support in Sweden and Nigeria in all these years.

To my children (Nathaniel, Jacqueline, Jeff and Michael), I say thank you all for your sacrifices. And to my wife, Felicia, I salute you for been there for your husband in spite of the storm.

I thank Pastor Joshua Amzat and his wife, Minister Jane Amzat of World Prayer Ministries in Houston, Texas for guiding me in my search for Jesus Christ and for enhancing my spiritual growth. To all the members of World Prayer Ministries, I am indebted to you for your love, prayers and fellowship, which have sustained me both mentally and spiritually in my period of reconciliation with Christ and in bringing this book to conclusion. You will also live to testify to the goodness and glory of our Lord.

All of the above individuals are of course absolved of any responsibility for the use to which I have put their help in the form of this book.

Houston, Texas, September 2008

Pastor John O. Ogbor, PhD.

CONTENTS

About the Author *vii*
Introduction and Preface *ix*
Structure and Logic of the Book *xii*
Acknowledgement *xvii*

Part One: Meaning and Context 1

Chapter 1: The Meaning and Importance of Entrepreneurship 2
Chapter Learning Objectives *2*
- 1-1: Introduction: The Nature of Entrepreneurship *3*
- 1-2: Entrepreneurs and Entrepreneurship *5*
- 1-3: Conditions for Entrepreneurship *8*
- 1-4: Innovation and Entrepreneurial Activities *10*
- 1-5: Differences between Small Business Firms and Entrepreneurial Ventures *14*
- 1-6: The Entrepreneur as a Strategist *20*
- 1-7: The Importance of Entrepreneurship in a Developing Country *21*
- 1-8: Chapter Summary *24*
- 1-9: Chapter Discussion Questions *26*
- 1-10: Case Study 1: Raymond Dokpesi and African Independent Television *27*

Chapter 2: The Nature of Entrepreneurs: Characteristics, Profiles and Motives 34
Chapter Learning Objectives *34*
- 2-1: Introduction: Searching for Entrepreneurial Profile *35*
- 2-2: Characteristics of Entrepreneurs *37*
- 2-3: Sources of Business Ideas *45*
- 2-4: Why Do People choose to be Entrepreneurs? *52*
- 2-5: The Drawbacks of becoming an Entrepreneur *66*
- 2-6: The Discourse of Entrepreneurship and the African Entrepreneur *68*
- 2-7: Chapter Summary *72*
- 2-8: Chapter Discussion Questions *73*
- 2-9: Case Study 2: Mike Adenuga and Globacom: Entrepreneurial Opportunities, Constraints and Strategies in a Developing Economy *74*

Chapter 3: The Economic Environment: National, Regional and Global 84
Chapter Learning Objectives *84*
- 3-1: Introduction: The Relevance of Economic Environment *85*
- 3-2: The Economic Environment in the Colonial Era *89*

3-3: The Economic Environment in the Post-Colonial Era *94*
3-4: Civil Breakdown and Economic Stagnation *100*
3-5: The Economic Policy of Structural Adjustment Program *101*
3-6: The Global Economy and Entrepreneurial Development *109*
3-7: Chapter Summary *131*
3-8: Chapter Discussion Questions *133*
3-9: Case Study 3: Ghana: Facing Opportunities and Challenges of a New Global Economic Order *134*

Chapter 4: The Cultural, Financial, Political and Infrastructural Environment *142*

Chapter Learning Objectives *142*
4-1: Introduction: The Need for a Contextual Perspective *143*
4-2: The Cultural Environment of Entrepreneurship *145*
4-3: The Financial and Credit Environment *153*
4-4: The Political Environment *163*
4-5: The Infrastructural Environment *172*
4-6: The Informal Sector *181*
4-7: Chapter Summary *188*
4-8: Chapter Discussion Questions *191*
4-9: Case Study 4: The Niger Delta, Politics of Oil and Underdevelopment *193*

Chapter 5: The Management and Organization Context *208*

Chapter Learning Objectives *208*
5-1: Introduction: Entrepreneurship and Management *209*
5-2: Planning for the Enterprise *212*
5-3: Organizational Challenge and Managing Growth *213*
5-4: The Challenge of Human Resource Management *219*
5-5: Leadership, Authority Relations and the Challenge of Employee Motivation *220*
5-6: Business Ethics and Social Responsibility *223*
5-7: Weak Corporate Governance and Poor Investment Opportunity *226*
5-8: Marketing Challenges *229*
5-9: The Challenge of Financial Management *231*
5-10: Poor Locational Decisions *233*
5-11: Chapter Summary *234*
5-12: Chapter Discussion Questions *236*
5-12: Case Study 5: Nollywood and the Challenges of Entrepreneurs and Entrepreneurship *237*

Part Two: Entrepreneurship from a Strategic Management Perspective

Chapter 6: Principles of Strategic Management and Entrepreneurship 248

Chapter Learning Objectives 248
- 6-1: Introduction: Strategy and Entrepreneurship 249
- 6-2: The Business Environment as a Battle Field 251
- 6-3: Firm's Competitive Advantage and its Strategy 253
- 6-4: Strategic Management as a Process 258
- 6-5: Levels of Strategies 261
- 6-6: Strategic Management Process and Entrepreneurial Ventures 268
- 6-7: Conditions for a Winning Strategy 271
- 6-8: Chapter Summary 272
- 6-9: Chapter Discussion Questions 274
- 6-10: Case Study 6: Entrepreneurial Strategies in a Developing Economy: The Dangote Group 275

Chapter 7: Business Description, Vision, Mission and Objectives 282

Chapter Learning Objectives 282
- 7-1: Introduction: The Importance of Vision, Mission and Objectives 283
- 7-2: What is a Business? 284
- 7-3: The Vision of a Firm 288
- 7-4: The Mission of a Firm 291
- 7-5: A Firm's Value Statement 302
- 7-6: Understanding a Firm's Objectives and Goals 304
- 7-7: Chapter Summary 307
- 7-8: Chapter Discussion Questions 308
- 7-9: Case Study 7: Ayodele's Slimmer's Club, Lagos 309

Chapter 8: Industry and Competitive Analysis 312

Chapter Learning Objectives 312
- 8-1: Introduction: The Power of Industry Knowledge 313
- 8-2: Understanding the Life Cycle of an Industry 315
- 8-3: Analyzing and Understanding the Industry Structure 319
- 8-4: Understanding Industry's Economic Features 320
- 8-5: Understanding the Nature of Competition in the Industry 321
- 8-6: Understanding Factors Driving Industry Change 326
- 8-7: Understanding the Industry's Key Success Factors 331
- 8-8: Understanding Firm's Competitive Position 332
- 8-9: Understanding a Firm's Resource Strengths and Weaknesses 333
- 8-10: Understanding Environmental Opportunities and Threats 339
- 8-11: Conducting a SWOT Analysis 343
- 8-12: Chapter Summary 345

8-13: Chapter Discussion Questions *346*
8-14: Case Study 8: The Nigerian Fast Food Industry *347*

Chapter 9: Strategy Formulation for the Entrepreneurial Firm *360*
Chapter Learning Objectives *360*
9-1: Introduction: Designing Appropriate Strategies *361*
9-2: Entry and Competitive Strategies *361*
9-3: Competitive Strategies for the New Venture *367*
9-3: Cooperative Strategies for the New Venture *369*
9-4: Offensive and Defensive strategies *373*
9-5: Distribution and Supply Chain Management Strategies *375*
9-6: The Value Chain and a Firm's Competitive Advantage *378*
9-7: Chapter Summary *384*
9-8: Chapter Discussion Questions *386*
9-9: Case Study 9: Abiodun Students' Impressions *387*

Part Three: Competitive Strategies for the Entrepreneurial Firm

Chapter 10: Marketing Strategies for the Entrepreneurial Firm *394*
Chapter Learning Objectives *394*
10-1: Introduction: The Customer as the Epicenter of Business *395*
10-2: Guerrilla Marketing Plan for the Entrepreneurial Firm *396*
10-3: Determining Customer Needs Through Market Research *399*
10-4: Conducting Market Research for the New Venture *403*
10-5: Identifying the Target Market *407*
10-6: Defining the Niche of a Firm *409*
10-7: Creating a Marketing Mix for Products and Services *412*
10-8: Promotional and Advertisement Strategies *426*
10-9: Chapter Summary *431*
10-10: Chapter Discussion Questions *433*
10-11: Case Study 10: Jide's Interiors: Developing a Promotional Strategy *434*

Chapter 11: Growth and Organizational Strategies for the Entrepreneurial Firm *440*
Chapter Learning Objectives *440*
11-1: Introduction: The Challenge of Managing Transition *441*
11-2: Finding Start-up Partners *443*
11-3: Identifying Factors that Affect Growth *446*
11-4: Growing in the Current Market *447*
11-5: Strategies for Diversifying Outside the Industry *450*
11-6: Organizing For Growth *454*
11-7: The Culture of a Company: Discovering the Soul of Your Business *455*

- 11-8: Developing a Human Resource Policy *458*
- 11-9: Recruiting the Right People *460*
- 11-10: Managing Growth and the Organizational Life Cycle *462*
- 11-11: New Forms of Organizational Structure *472*
- 11-12: The Exit Plan *475*
- 11-13: Chapter Summary *478*
- 11-14: Chapter Discussion Questions *480*
- 11-15: Case Study 11: Iyare's Furniture: Uncharted Organizational Relationships *481*

Chapter 12: Financial Strategies for the Entrepreneurial Firm *486*

Chapter Learning Objectives *486*
- 12-1: Introduction: The Importance of Financial Planning and Control *487*
- 12-2: Putting Together an Income Statement *488*
- 12-3: Putting Together a Balance Sheet *492*
- 12-4: Putting Together a Cash Flow Statement *499*
- 12-5: Forecasting and Budgeting *503*
- 12-6: The Master Budget *506*
- 12-7: Financing the Business *507*
- 12-8: Chapter Summary *514*
- 12-9: Chapter Discussion Questions *515*
- 12-10: Case Study 12: Projecting Cash Flows at Ajayi and Osunde Consulting (Nig) Ltd. *516*

Chapter 13: Ownership Strategies for the Entrepreneurial Firm *520*

Chapter Learning Objectives *520*
- 13-1: Introduction: Deciding on the Best Legal Form for the Business *521*
- 13-2: The Sole Proprietorship *522*
- 13-3: The Partnership *524*
- 13-4: The Limited Liability Company *527*
- 13-5: Buying an Existing Company *529*
- 13-6: Franchising *534*
- 13-7: The Nonprofit Organization *541*
- 13-8: Choosing an Attorney *542*
- 13-9: Chapter Summary *544*
- 13-10: Chapter Discussion Questions *545*
- 13-11: Case Study 13: Buying a Franchise: Look Before You Leap! *546*

Chapter 14: Ethics and Social Responsibility Strategies for the Entrepreneurial Firm *550*

Chapter Learning Objectives *550*
- 14-1: Introduction: Ethics, Social Responsibility and

        Business Competitiveness *551*
- 14-2: The Meaning of Ethics *553*
- 14-3: What is Business Ethics? *555*
- 14-4: Ethical Dilemma in Business Decisions *559*
- 14-5: Factors Shaping the Ethics of an Entrepreneurial Firm *562*
- 14-6: Ethical Issues in Business Practices *564*
- 14-7: A Model of Ethical Decision-Making *571*
- 14-8: Creating and Maintaining High Ethical Business Standards *575*
- 14-9: Strategy, Ethics and Social Responsibility *583*
- 14-8: The Stakeholders of the Entrepreneurial Firm and Its Social Responsibility *585*
- 14-10: Managing Stakeholder Relations and the Constructions of Organization Values *588*
- 14-11 Chapter Summary *590*
- 14-12 Chapter Discussion Questions *592*
- 14-13: Case Study 14: Foreign Exchange Malpractices: Why Perpetuators Cheat on Regulatory Authorities *593*

Part Four: Implementing Entrepreneurial Strategies

Chapter 15: Crafting a Competitive Business Plan *598*
    Chapter Learning Objectives *598*
- 15-1: Introduction: The Need for a Business Plan *599*
- 15-2: What is a Business Plan? *600*
- 15-3: Important Areas Where a Business Plan is Required *602*
- 15-4: Outline of a Business Plan *603*
- 15-5: Contents of a Business Plan *607*
- 15-6: Case Study 15: The Dilemma of Iya Joko's Moin Moin Business *627*

GLOSSARY *630*
ENDNOTES *646*
INDEX *676*

Part One: Entrepreneurship: Meaning & Context

Chapter 1: The Meaning and Importance of Entrepreneurship

Chapter 2: The Nature of Entrepreneurs: Characteristics, Profiles and Motives

Chapter 3: The Economic Environment: National, Regional and Global

Chapter 4: The Cultural, Financial, Political and Infrastructural Environment

Chapter 5: The Management and Organization Context

Chapter 1

THE MEANING AND IMPORTANCE OF ENTREPRENEURSHIP

The global trading system offers a potentially huge market for those goods and services which give Tanzania a comparative advantage. When properly developed, the SME (small and medium enterprise) sector will produce goods and services to compete on the global market and to be the basis of export-led growth ... Since 1986 Tanzania has been changing from a command economy to a free-market economy. This means that the private sector is expected to play a bigger role in driving the economy.
-The Government of Tanzania's Development Vision 2025 (May, 2005)

CHAPTER LEARNING OBJECTIVES
After studying this chapter, you should be able to:

1. Understand the meaning and importance of an entrepreneur and entrepreneurship.

2. Understand the differences between small business firms and entrepreneurial ventures.

3. Understand the conditions for entrepreneurship.

4. Understand the sources of innovation and entrepreneurial activities.

5. Understand the notion of an entrepreneur as a strategist.

6. Understand the importance of entrepreneurship in developing economies.

INTRODUCTION: THE NATURE OF ENTREPRENEURSHIP

Entrepreneurship is a process because it is the purposeful and organized search for change, conducted after systematic analysis of opportunities in the environment. Entrepreneurship is a philosophy precisely because it is the way one thinks, one acts and therefore it can exist in many situations be it business or government or in the field of education, science and technology or poverty alleviation. The process of entrepreneurship, according to Peter Drucker, is directing the use of resources to progressive activities rather than for administrative efficiencies. [1]

The industrial health of a society depends on the level of entrepreneurship existing in it. A country might remain backward not because of lack of natural resources or dearth of capital (as it is many times believed about Africa's situation), but because of lack of entrepreneurial talents or its inability to tap the latent entrepreneurial talents existing in that society. Entrepreneurs historically have altered the direction of national economies, industries or markets. The importance of entrepreneurship and innovation to any economy is like that of entrepreneurship in any community. Entrepreneurial activity and the resultant financial gain are always of benefit to a country.

Entrepreneurship begets and also injects entrepreneurship by starting a chain reaction when the entrepreneur continuously tries to improve the quality of existing goods and services and add new ones. For instance, when computers came into the market, there was continuous improvement in the models and their functions. Not only had this fostered the development of the software industry, computer and/or information education institutes, computer maintenance and stationery units, etc, but also other industries such as banking, education, travel, films, medical and legal transcriptions, business process outsourcing, etc. In this manner, by harnessing the entrepreneurial talents, a society comes out of economic backwardness to modern industrial culture. Sub-Saharan Africa needs entrepreneurs to capitalize on new opportunities and to create wealth and new jobs.

The idea behind the concept of entrepreneurship is about creating something "new" that has value. When an individual creates something new, the new creation is seen as an innovation. In the world of economic and business practices, the activity involved in the creation of something new is called "entrepreneurship." Entrepreneurship is simply about seeing an opportunity and acting on it on the basis of organizing the resources available to the entrepreneur or business owner.

Since there is no universally accepted definition of the concept of entrepreneurship, we will use the experience of BusyInternet located in Accra, Ghana to illustrate what we mean by the concept. BusyInternet was established as a result of business opportunities provided by the need for communication in a developing country: combining physical infrastructure with the social and business environment of the needs of entrepreneurs. In BusyInternet, although founded in New York, USA, the founders were able to understand that the developing countries of Africa provide huge opportunity for business development in the area of information and communication technology (ICT). As Mark Davis, one of the founders of BusyInternet rightly pointed out, "developing countries are the most information-inefficient places on earth, and if we can bring information to bear on local problems, we can make an enormous difference". [2]

There are business opportunities everywhere and the entrepreneur has to identify what opportunities matter. In all countries, entrepreneurs are perhaps the greatest mobilizers of resources, responsible for the generation of the majority of employment, the majority of wealth and much of the innovation. As we shall see in this chapter, the global economy has open doors for entrepreneurship to thrive.

One huge opportunity in Sub-Sahara Africa lies in the area of information and communications technology (ICT). That was the reason why the World Bank established *Infodev,* which is chartered to help developing countries maximize the impact of ICTs in combating poverty and promoting broad-based sustainable development. Entrepreneurial firm such as BusyInternet were able to understand this opportunity and got initial financial help from the World Bank. For example, BusyInternet got US$300,000 grant from *Infodev* to help it add operational support and technical assistance to the services it offers new companies. Mauritius, for example, identified ICT as having the potential to sustain economic development and the country is promoting the ICT sector as a new economic pillar. Consequently, entrepreneurial firms such as the Mauritius ICT Incubator Center were started to provide services such as outsourcing activities and assist in the growing interest of foreign investors in the local market. In South Africa, *the Bodibeng Technology Incubator* was also founded to take part in the growing opportunity provided by the need for industries and individuals to get connected worldwide.

In Sub-Saharan Africa, as in other parts and regions of the world, entrepreneurship has become a buzzword in the study and practice of management, business and economic development. For the past two decades, entrepreneurship has been viewed as the driver of economic growth. Furthermore, entrepreneurship has been recognized as a process, which is more than just starting and running a business. The importance of entrepreneurship as the engine behind economic development in the global economy has made the subject an exciting field of study. Research indicates that individuals who study entrepreneurship are three to four times more likely to start a business, and will earn 20 to 30 percent more than students studying in other fields. [3]

To understand the field of entrepreneurship better, it is essential to note one particular point: Entrepreneurship is more than just risk-taking. It is very much about an opportunistic mind-set and spirit. It is about having a vision, a mission, an idea and sets of goals and the ability to pursue them in a strategic manner. It is the ability to see opportunities where others cannot and the ability to act on such opportunities. In a nutshell, entrepreneurship is about risk-taking, understanding the existence of opportunities, generating ideas and implementing them.

ENTREPRENEURS AND ENTREPRENEURSHIP

The words *entrepreneur* and *entrepreneurship* have become so messy and so difficult to define as many people claim to be entrepreneurs and others are excluded from belonging to what others have come to see as a "privileged group." John Ogbor points out how the term "entrepreneurship" has been overused, misused, abused, and tacked onto practically anything and everything from owing a business to holding a particular view of the world.[4] In particular, Ogbor argues that the concept of entrepreneurship must be understood from the perspective in which it was originally and historically produced. Originally, entrepreneurship is simply about the destruction of existing pattern of business behavior and creating something new by capitalizing on an existing opportunity. For example, the founders of BusyInternet in Ghana created something new (that is, innovation) that has not existed in Ghana. There was a need. The need was that countries in developing part of the world were looking for technology incubation centers and BusyInternet came up with a cyber business center in Ghana's capital, Accra.

The perspective taken in this book is that entrepreneurship is more than having and managing a business. It is about managing the business *strategically and being innovative*. Following the idea of an entrepreneur as an innovator, Joseph Schumpeter, one of the most influential writers in this field, explains the concept of entrepreneur in terms of the functions he or she provides in the following manner:

> The function of the entrepreneur is to reform or revolutionize the pattern of production by exploiting an invention or, more generally, an untried technological method of producing a new commodity or producing an old one in a new way, opening a new source of supply of materials or a new outlet for products, by organizing a new industry.[5]

A person who creates and delivers a value in an economic system, either in the informal or the organized sectors of the economy, can be seen as an entrepreneur whenever that activity is undertaken strategically. Although, entrepreneurs come in an amazing variety of types and styles, there is one very important distinguishing factor, and that is *innovation, which is the successful exploitation of new ideas*. Robert Hisrich, Michael Peters and Dean Shepherd explain the concept of innovation and its relationship to entrepreneurship as follows:

> Indeed, innovation, the act of producing something new, is one of the most difficult tasks for the entrepreneur. It takes not only the ability to create and conceptualize but also the ability to understand all the forces at work in the environment. The newness can consist of anything from a new product to a new distribution system to a method for developing a new organizational structure.[6]

Entrepreneurs are also a unique type (or breed) of individuals. They do not believe in the way things are; they disrupt the status quo. The reason is that the ventures entrepreneurs create "disrupt" (or change) the way things are conventionally done in the economy. Entrepreneurs create *value* in the marketplace in an innovative way. For example, although Andrew Carnegie (one of the greatest entrepreneurs of all time) did not invent the steel, he introduced "manufacturing innovation" which lowered the price of steel, affecting virtually every aspect of life. His innovation reduced the cost of rails from US$160 a ton in 1875 to US$17 by 1890. [7] Although Michael Dell did not invent the personal computer (PC), he was able to revolutionize the industry by innovating on the industry's value-chain: "process innovation" – changes in the things (products/services) that an organization offers. [8]

Who exactly are those individuals we call entrepreneurs and who practice entrepreneurship? In simple terms, an *entrepreneur* is someone who identifies an opportunity in an economic system, assembles the resources necessary to successfully exploit that opportunity and creates and delivers a value in an economic system. These resources include financial, human, technology, and organization. In a similar manner, *entrepreneurship* can be defined *as the process of combining scarce resources in new ways to respond to opportunities or provide solutions to a problem.*

An individual can operate a venture in any type of an industry and be classified as an entrepreneur if he or she possesses certain characteristics and runs the business in certain ways such as assuming the risks involved in running the venture. Entrepreneurs like to do things that excite the world, bend the rules of the game a little bit, and make us look at something in an entirely new way. They are opportunistic, finding new possibilities to improve on existing products or services at every turn. In other words, the essence of entrepreneurship is creativity, innovation, and change. It is about "creative destruction" - the ability to create something new from what has not been there or from the existing products or services in the marketplace.

Michael Dell and Dell Computers Corp. illustrate vividly the idea of entrepreneurship as creative destruction – creating something new from the existing ways of doing things. [9] Born in 1965, Michael Dell is the upstart in the very competitive microcomputer market, where many of the more established firms such as IBM, Hewlett-Packard, Compaq, etc., have had difficulties or failed. Michael Dell dropped out of school in 1984 at age 19 and took $1,000 of his savings to launch PCs Limited, which he later renamed Dell Computer Corporation. His business idea was to use innovative mail-order marketing to reach his customers. It was here that Dell faced his first hurdle: where to find a source of machines. Initially, he decided to buy IBM computers on the gray market because IBM would not allow its dealers to sell PCs to anyone intending to resell them. However, this was not sufficient to meet his customers' needs, so Dell again resorted to his creativity, realizing that many dealers often carried a large inventory of hardware, much of which they could not sell. Dell knocked on the doors of these retailers and offered to buy their surplus at a cost. He then modified the PCS with graphics cards and hard discs and sold them by direct marketing.

In 1996 the company began selling computers over the Internet, and by 2000 Internet sales had reached $50 million per day. In 2001 Dell reached number one in global market share for the PC market, and in 2002 U.S. consumers selected the company as their number one computer systems provider. Revenue for the fiscal year 2003 surpassed $35 billion, with approximately 40,000 employees around the globe.

Dell's success in Internet commerce has become a model that many other firms in the PC market continue to emulate. Today the Dell website receives more than one billion page requests per quarter at 80 country sites in 28 languages/dialects and 26 currencies. It also ranks among the top 60 on the Fortune 500 list. Michael Dell is now worth well over $11 billion, ranking him in the top 20 list of the richest people in the world.

Michael Dell's idea of business venturing reveals an intriguing yet simple approach in finding a niche and marketing products or services in ways that reduce cost thereby affordable to the consumer. Michael Dell's niche and innovativeness was to eliminate dealers and distributors and work hard to meet customer needs through quality service. Dell's competitive strategy was simple yet aggressive in trying to position the company as a lower-priced, assemble-to-order, direct-response business. Dell's innovation was not in designing new PCs, but lies in how to market PCs. To be sure, Dell's future will continue to involve one marketing challenge after another as other firms begin to imitate its success with similar direct-marketing and internet strategies.

There are many strategies a company can adopt to remain competitive through innovative practices. As Dells' case illustrates, these practices can include alternative marketing or distribution strategies, provision of extra services, and other means through which a firm can reduce the costs associated with the length of the value chain. By first understanding the industry and assessing the needs of the market, the entrepreneur can decide which marketing or distribution strategy is suitable for his her competitiveness.

The basis of a society's economic growth and competitiveness lies in its capacity to innovate, create, and change existing ways in which things are done. That is where the importance of entrepreneurship comes in within the context of economic growth. Entrepreneurship is also important for economic growth precisely because most innovations are not carried out in large corporations, but in small entrepreneurial firms. Few examples are perhaps noteworthy here.

In Sub-Saharan Africa, for example, there are individuals who have successfully performed the entrepreneurial role of innovation by destroying and creating something new. A good example is the founder of DAAL Communications, Nigeria Limited, Chief Raymond Dokpesi, who started African Independent Television from the scratch. Olorogun Michael Ibru, (the chairman of Ibru Organization, one of the largest corporations in Sub-Saharan Africa) also began as an entrepreneur with only one fishing boat in the fish business. Michael Ibru's vision was to make fish available to every Nigerian household – even though fishing was one of Nigeria's major agricultural activities. He saw an opportunity in the fishing industry because the pattern of economic development in Nigeria was skewing the fishing industry and his mission was to provide imported frozen fish. He also knew that the fish producing communities in Nigeria would be placed in a position of fish-importing economy. The point I am trying to stress here is that innovations that spur economic development come from individuals and entrepreneurial firms most of the time. How these start-up companies were able to grow to the giant status they now occupy in their respective industries is a lesson worth learning.

CONDITION FOR ENTREPRENEURSHIP

In this age of global competition and the spread of the imperatives of the free enterprise system, Sub-Saharan African countries have found themselves cut in the tail end of the benefits of globalization. Gone are the days in which the state *per se* is expected to provide the impetus for economic growth. Entrepreneurship, as the engine for economic growth, has been accepted in all economies, both developed and developing. There are many factors accounting for the importance of entrepreneurship and we will call these "the drivers of entrepreneurship" or the conditions for entrepreneurship.

The first driver of entrepreneurship is the *reduced role of the state*. First, we live in an era in which individual initiatives promote economic growth as long as the necessary infrastructures are put in place. In other words, the role of the state has been reduced to that of a provider of institutional and infrastructural environment for the growth of individual entrepreneurial initiatives. That is the reason why entrepreneurship is flourishing in many parts of the world, especially in the developed and emerging economies. The developed countries and a number of the emerging economies understand that the government alone cannot provide the impetus for economic growth. They also understand that innovations and the competitiveness of their national economies rely on individual initiatives. Furthermore, the industrialized nations know that the growth of their economies cannot be placed on the prerogatives of the large corporations *per se*. Consequently, they have developed economic policies that encourage the promotion of entrepreneurship.

A second driver of entrepreneurial initiatives is derived from the *forces of globalization, technological advancement, information and communication technology, and the imperatives of market forces*. For example, the interplay of market forces such as trade deregulation, trade liberalization, and the removal of protectionist policies and technological advances have removed the power of monopoly from hitherto inefficient state bureaucracies. Kenichi Ohmae describes this process as follow:

> What has eaten them (national boundaries) away is the persistent, ever speedier flow of information – information that governments previously monopolized, cooking it up as they saw fit and redistributing in forms of their own devising. Their monopoly of knowledge about things happening around the world enabled them to fool, mislead, or control the people because only the governments possessed real facts in anything like real time. [10]

As a result of these forces, individual are now in control of their economic destiny – an entrepreneur in China does not require a visa to do business with his or her suppliers in the United States. Similarly, the resilience and competitiveness of national economies have increasingly been put at the mercy of individual entrepreneurs and small business owners.

A third force driving individuals and society towards entrepreneurship is *corporate downsizing*. The practice of cutting down the number of employees in corporations (downsizing), rightsizing and cross border mergers in companies' attempt to remain competitive have produced many corporate castoffs and dropouts. These individuals have consequently become an important source of entrepreneurial activity.

A fourth driver of entrepreneurship is *changes in economic and political ideologies*. Eastern European countries, China, Vietnam, and many others whose economies were state-controlled and centrally planned have now become the fertile ground for entrepreneurial activities. Not long ago, China was an isolated, centrally planned economy. While Japan and Asia's "tiger economies" were booming, China's economy was stagnating. China's solution to its problems was to invest in entrepreneurial development, revived its communist policies by injecting it with a heavy dose of capitalism. Today, the growth of the Chinese economy is enormous and growing by double digits. In the year 2005, China exported US$202 billion more to the U.S. than it imported, accounting for a quarter of the U.S. trade deficit. The imperatives of market forces tend to produce the spirit of entrepreneurship among individuals in these countries.[11]

A fifth driver of entrepreneurial activities or a condition promoting entrepreneurship can be found in *social transformation*. Over the years, the growth of entrepreneurships has occurred in nations and regions where there are fundamental shifts in the status quo such as change in economic ideologies and policies, changes in demographics and changes in attitudes to life. Successful entrepreneurs see changes in the environment as opportunities rather than threats.

Entrepreneurs are not gamblers, as some would prefer to term them, because in their businesses, they assess their options and choose their course of action based on their probability of success. They are not afraid to fail because they tend to measure their real success by how many times they learn from their mistakes and go on to try again.

There is a Yiddish folk saying that "*Experience is what we call the accumulation of our mistakes.*" Many entrepreneurs succeeded because they have gained a stockpile of experience from their mistakes. Most importantly, they were able to learn from those mistakes. Today's culture is quite different from what we had fifty years ago, as more people are becoming more adventurous, risk embracing, and individualistic. Society has transformed itself from a predominantly agrarian and bureaucratic one to the one that fosters and encourages radical changes and innovation. In fact, because people are more curious, they are more driven to challenge the status quo.

To understand the emergence and importance of entrepreneurship in our present society, it is equally important to recognize that we are all living in a global economy that is fast changing. Similarly, adapting to changes can be risky in spite of the opportunities, which come along with changes. Finding any aspect of life that is not risky or in a state of change in any society is difficult these days. Especially in the world of business and economic development, change is constant. We see the manifestations of change in companies going in and out of business, customers changing their loyalty every day, secured jobs disappearing overnight (as in General Motors getting rid of about 12,000 workers in 2005) and replaced by jobs that never existed before, technology changing the way we do things in every aspect of our lives, and businesses turning to outsourcing as a way of reducing the cost of labor. We live in an era that is somehow temporal and at the same time exciting.

The era of globalization and the Internet age is exciting because if you are not afraid of change and know how to deal with it, you will discover a whole lot of opportunities.

Thus, change can be horrifying if one is not prepared for it and exciting if one prepares for it. Dealing with change is one of the important things entrepreneurs do best. They thrive on it because they know that with change comes opportunity. Those kinds of opportunities are among the many reasons to think about developing the entrepreneurial spirit and mindset. For, as Alexis de Tocqueville once said, "America is a land of wonders in which everything is in constant motion and every change seems an improvement." No wonder, societies that embrace change as inevitable become the breeding ground for entrepreneurial activities.

In today's dynamic global economy, individuals are becoming more entrepreneurial because technology is expanding, especially in transportation and communication, governments are removing trade restrictions, institutions are providing services to ease the conduct of business, consumers know about and want foreign goods, competition has become more global, political relationships have improved among major economic powers and society in general is undergoing rapid and dynamic change. The point is that these changes carry along with them opportunities and threats. Those with entrepreneurial mindset are either able to exploit these opportunities or turn these threats to opportunities.

INNOVATION AND ENTREPRENEURIAL ACTIVITIES

Any attempt to understand the concepts of entrepreneur and entrepreneurship must invariably begin with the concept of innovation. First, the word "innovation" comes from Latin *in* and *novare* – to make something new, to change. The concept of innovation is intricately tied to the activities that are entrepreneurial in nature. In other words, any understanding of the concept of entrepreneurship must follow an understanding of the concept of innovation. Peter Drucker, in his book, *The Essential of Drucker*, puts it this way: "An enterprise, whether a business or any other institution, that does not innovate and does not engage in entrepreneurship will not survive long."

In economic terms, innovation, according to Peter Drucker, is "provision of different economic satisfaction." The most productive innovation, according to Drucker, is a different product or service creating a new potential of satisfaction, rather than an improvement.[12] Innovation may result in a lower price, a new or better product, a new convenience, or the definition of a new entrant. There is what is popularly called "process innovation", which comes from changes in the ways in which products/services are created and delivered. There is also what is called "position innovation", which comes from changes in the context in which the product/service are introduced. There is also "paradigm innovation", which comes from changes in the underlying mental models which frame what the organization does.[13]

Innovation may be finding new uses for old products. Internet service is not new in the developed countries. However, when the founders of BusyInternet café in Ghana launched their business, they found new markets for an existing product or service. In a similar manner, DVD is not new in the developed markets but when Nigerian movie-makers use DVD to produce and market their films directly to the consumers, they found a new use and market for DVDs. Innovation, according to Drucker, is not invention in the technical sense. It is social and economic innovation that matters in the context of entrepreneurship and economic growth. Entrepreneurs convert society's needs into opportunities for profitable business.

Innovations can spring from a variety of sources for the purpose of entrepreneurship. As Drucker points out, the organization's own unexpected successes and unexpected failures, the unexpected successes and failures of a firm's competitor can provide opportunities for innovation and entrepreneurial activities.[1] For our purpose here, we can identify three types of innovations and entrepreneurial activities.

New concept/new business: The Pioneer.

The classic entrepreneur is seen as an individual who develops a new product or a new idea and builds a business around it – *product innovation*. This requires a substantial amount of creativity and ability to see patterns and trends before they are evident to the general public. The business concept may be so new and revolutionary that it may create an entirely new industry. Examples of creative entrepreneurs include Steven Jobs, one of the founders of Apple Computers, and Bill Gates, founder of Microsoft. Most people would agree that these innovative business people are true entrepreneurs. Because they are the first to come out with a new product or service, theirs is extremely a difficult task because the innovator must be ready to mobilize resources massively to turn the innovation into a profitable venture. Entrepreneurs who come with new concepts and create new businesses are termed "creative innovators" because they actually come with something new.

To be first also demands substantial and continuing efforts to retain a leadership position; otherwise, all one has done is create a market for a competitor. According to Peter Drucker, the innovator has to run even harder now that he has leadership than he ran before and to continue his innovative efforts on a very large scale. The research budget must be higher after the innovation has successfully been accomplished than it was before. New uses have to be found; new customers must be identified, and persuaded to try the new materials. Above all, the entrepreneur who has succeeded in being "the first" has to make his or her product or service obsolete before a competitor can do it. Finally, the entrepreneur who comes first with a new product or service has to be the one who systematically cuts the price of his own products, services or process. To keep prices high simply holds an umbrella over potential competitors and encourages them.

In Nigeria, the owner of *Ayodele's Slimmer's Club*, Isaac Ayodele, saw a niche in the business of slimming. He came up with natural herbs where those who have arthritis are healed. His business concept grew out of the need for customers to prevent obesity in Nigeria, which was seen as a health problem in many developing countries. This is an example of what Drucker terms "creative innovation". By developing herbal medicines for curing obesity, Isaac Ayodele also created a new market, which has become an industry. Product innovation has been a key driving force in the emergence of many industries such as prescription drugs, the personal computer, digital cameras, video games, etc. Product innovations tend to alter the pattern of competition in an industry. Successful new product introductions strengthen the market positions of the innovating companies, usually at the expense of companies that stick with their old products or are slow to follow with their own versions of the new product.

Existing concept/new business: Creative imitation

There are also individuals who start new businesses based on existing concepts, products or practices. For example, if someone opens a convenience food store, the idea is not new and the founder may not be described as one who brought in a new concept or product but the business may be innovative if the person revolutionizes the way the product or concept is used. Peter Drucker terms this, "creative imitation." The creative imitator looks at products or services from the viewpoint of the customer. Creative imitation starts out with markets rather than with products, and with customers rather than with producers. Creative imitators do not succeed just by taking away customers from the pioneers who have first introduced a new product or service; they serve markets the pioneers have created but do not adequately service. Creative imitation satisfies a demand that already exists rather than creating one. Thompson, Strickland and Gamble, in their book, *Crafting and Executing Strategy*, suggest that advances in technology can dramatically alter an industry's landscape, making it possible to produce new and better products at lower costs and opening up whole new industry frontiers.[15] Innovations that occur in existing concepts or products can dramatically change entire industries such as communication. For instance, Voice over Internet Protocol (VoIP) technology has spawned low-cost, Internet-based phone networks that are stealing large numbers of customers away from traditional telephone companies worldwide (whose higher cost technology depends on hard-wired connections via overhead and underground telephone lines).

The creative imitator exploits the success of others. He does not invent a product or service; he perfects and positions it. In the form in which it has been introduced, it lacks something. It may be additional product features. It may be segmentation of product or services so that slightly different versions fit slightly different markets. It might be proper positioning of the product in the market. Or creative imitation supplies something that is still lacking.

It should be pointed out, however, that individuals who engage in this type of activity seldom do so without some change being introduced. This change can take several forms: from outright cloning of an existing product (e.g., Compaq Computer, which was a clone of an IBM PC) to adding new services to existing products or concepts (e.g., hotels try to compete by offering customer loyalty programs). The likelihood of a business succeeding if it is patterned exactly after one that already exists is remote. Therefore, most entrepreneurs who start a business to compete with those that already exist do so in the hope that theirs will offer something new or better. Creating a new business for existing concepts is born out of creativity. Before the advent of Mr. Bigg's in Nigeria, the concept of fast food is not new. Nigerians were used to such fast food products such as meat pies, "gala," etc. However, Mr. Biggs, owned by UACN, made fast food a new concept by providing services that cater for not only the working parents but also for those on the move and the *generation Y* in Nigeria. Larry Ettah, managing director of Nigeria's pioneer fast food chain, Mr. Biggs, says that "With a population of about 12 million people (that is, the population of the city of Lagos), including several families, where husbands and wives are workers, people have become strapped for time. They rely on quick service restaurants, providing quick meals."[16] A new business can thus be added to an exiting concept by adding some features including new distribution strategies, location advantage, and customer service. We call all these entrepreneurial activities because there are changes involved.

It is noteworthy that this type of entrepreneurship – creative imitation is more profound in the emerging and developing economies where their socio-economic conditions placed aspiring entrepreneurs in the position of late-starters. The growth of generic drug industry perhaps illustrates the position of the emerging economies in terms of "creative imitation." There has been much progress in the production of generic drugs. Brazil has an extensive generic drugs industry that enables the government to supply antiretroviral AIDS drugs free of charge to whoever needs them. In India, local pharmaceutical companies produce both generic and the raw materials and chemicals used in their manufacture. The raw materials are often exported to major companies for the production of their brand-named drugs. With the help of expertise from Brazil, India and Thailand, a number of African countries, including Ghana, Mozambique, Tanzania, Uganda, Zambia and Zimbabwe are taking the first steps to set up their own generic drug plants.

BusinessDay in Nigeria was not a pioneer of quality business news in the world. However, through the newspaper's partnership with the *Financial Times* of London, it was able to revolutionize the coverage and presentation of business news in Nigeria both in content and in quality. This is a classic example of position innovation. The founders of *BusinessDay* newspaper changed the face of business journalism in Nigeria not because they pioneered or invented it. With partnership with world renowned business paper (*The Financial Times* of London); the management of *BusinessDay* was able to provide more business reporting and analysis with a global and current coverage.

Innovating on the value chain

There is a value chain in any industry. The value chain is the route a product or service passes through from production to the final consumer or end-user. The value chain of a company is embedded in a larger system of activities within a particular industry that includes the value chain of suppliers and the value chains of whatever distribution channels it uses in getting its product or service to the end-users. An entrepreneur can innovate in anyone of the activities in the value chain in order to remain competitive.

For example, entrepreneurs can become successful by introducing new ways to *market or distribute* their products. When firms introduce new marketing innovations, they can spark a burst of buyer interests, widen industry demand, increase product differentiation, and lower unit costs – any or all of which can alter the competitive positions of rival firms and force the revision of their strategies. Online marketing is shaking up competition in all types of products and services across a wide range of industries by redefining the value chain of many business activities.

Dell Computer Corp. revolutionized the PC industry through innovation in marketing and distribution strategies. Prior to venturing into the PC business, the industry was dominated by PC giants such as IBM, Hewlett-Packard and Compaq. In 1984, at the age of 19, Michael Dell invested $1,000 of his own money and founded Dell Computer with a simple vision and business concept – that personal computers (PCs) could be built to order and sold directly to customers. Michael Dell believed his approach to the PC business had two advantages: (i) bypassing distributors and retail dealers eliminated the markups of resellers, and (ii) building to order greatly reduced the costs and risks associated with carrying large stocks of parts, components, and finished goods. Within 15 years of starting his made-to-order computer business in 1984, Michael Dell turned Dell Computer into an US$18 billion international company. In the first quarter of 2001, Dell Computer became the world's No. 1 PC maker, surpassing Compaq for the top spot. Marketing and distribution innovations have also shaken up the educational sector in a dramatic way. Today, traditional colleges and universities are facing stiff competition from institutions delivering courses through online. Increasing number of music artists are marketing their recordings at their own Web sites rather than entering into contracts with recording studios that distribute through online and brick-and-mortal music retailers.

The success of this approach is predicated on one factor, and that is how industry leaders see quality. According to Peter Drucker, "quality" in a product or service is not what the supplier puts in; it is what the customer gets out and is willing to pay for. A product is not "quality" because it is hard to make and costs a lot of money, as manufacturers typically believe. That is incompetence. Customers pay only for what is of use to them and gives value. Nothing else constitutes "quality." In fact, this explains the domination of Nollywood movies in the Nigerian movie industry. Nigerian moviemakers were able to conquer the home market by producing movies that are directly marketed to the consumers. Quality to the consumers is how these movies satisfied their wants and been able to afford them.

DIFFERENCES BETWEEN SMALL BUSINESS FIRMS AND ENTREPRENEURIAL VENTURES

Although entrepreneurial potential exist in all parts of the global economy, differences exist, which can best be explained by a combination of factors such as current level of economic development, national government policies and previous experience with a market economy. Similarly, different countries and economies accord different meanings to the nature of entrepreneurship and entrepreneurial activities. As will be examined in this section, the definition and meaning of a small business or an entrepreneurial venture is contextually situated because social, political, and economic conditions influence what a country considers as a small business firm and an entrepreneurial venture. Secondly, the nature of entrepreneurial firm and small business varies according to the researcher's theoretical perspective and the yardstick chosen for measuring these firms.

Defining a Small Business

Before we attempt a discussion of the differences between a small business firm and an entrepreneurial venture it is important that we examine what constitutes a small business in different parts of the world. As in most developed countries, developing nations, for policy reasons, make a clear distinction between micro-, small-, and medium-sized enterprises (SMEs) on the one hand, and SMEs and large enterprise on the other. In some cases, the acronym, SMME is used to describe the category of small- micro- and medium-sized enterprise. In essence, the three criteria that are generally applied by governments to define micro-, small, and medium-sized enterprises are: (i) capital investment in plant and machineries, (ii) number of workers employed, and (iii) volume of production and turnover of business.

According to the European Union, a medium-sized enterprise has less than 250 employees, over €50 million in turnover and/or €43 million in total balance sheet assets. A small-sized enterprise has fewer than 50 employees, less than €10 million in turnover and less than €10 million in total balance sheet. Finally, a micro-enterprise has less than 10 employees and less than €2 million in turnover and total balance sheet.

The United Nations International Development Organization (UNIDO) provides two types of definitions each for developing countries and industrialized countries. For developing countries, UNIDO sees a large firm as having more than 100 employees; medium firms are those with 20-99 employees; small firms have between 5-19 employees and micro enterprises are firms with less than 5 employees. For industrialized countries, (according to UNIDO), a large firm employs more than 500 employees; a medium firm employs between 100 and 499 workers; a small firm has lesser than 99 employees. For the industrial nations, there are no micro firms.[17]

Particularly in Sub-Saharan Africa, small- and medium-scale enterprises (SMEs) are a very heterogeneous group. They include a wide variety of firms—village handicraft makers, small machine shops, restaurants, furniture manufacturers, agricultural ventures, and computer software firms—that possess a wide range of sophistication and skills, and operate in very different markets and social environments. Their owners may or may not be poor. Some are dynamic, innovative, and growth-oriented; others are traditional "lifestyle" enterprises that are satisfied to remain small.

Micro enterprises are normally family businesses or self-employed persons operating in the semi-formal and informal sectors; most have little chance of growing into larger scale firms, accessing bank finance, or becoming internationally competitive. Serving them often requires distinct institutions and instruments, such as the group-based lending methodologies used by some micro finance institutions. In contrast, SMEs usually operate in the formal sector of the economy, employ mainly wage-earning workers, and participate more fully in organized markets. SME access to formal finance is a desirable possibility, and SMEs are more likely than micro enterprises to grow and become competitive in domestic and international markets.[18]

Some Country Definitions

The meaning of a small business is somehow arbitrarily provided without a clear demarcation of what constitutes a small business and a medium-sized one. This is especially true in the developing countries where such definitions often ignore the distinction between firms in the informal sector and those in the organized sector. Thus, the World Bank uses the acronym; SMMEs (small, micro and medium-sized enterprises) to describe what in the developed economies are normally referred to as small businesses. In addition, many development organizations such as the World Bank, the International Monetary Fund (IMF) and the International Labor Organization (ILO) include economic activities in the informal sector in their description of small businesses in the developing parts of the world.[19]

The Nigerian authorities, like their counterparts elsewhere in Sub-Saharan Africa have consistently worked on this definition, which seems to include all actors in the informal economy, most of whom are engaged in survivalist activities such as casual workers and home-based workers. Thus, the Central Bank of Nigeria says that "A small and medium enterprise is defined as any enterprise with a maximum asset base of 500 million Nigerian Naira (about US$3.8 million as at 2005) - excluding land and working capital, and with no lower or upper limit of staff."[20]

In South Africa, SMMEs are defined and classified in terms of turnover, gross asset value and number of employees in differentiating between micro, very small, small, medium and large-sized enterprises. A *micro enterprise* in South Africa is a firm that employs up to 5 workers, with turnover of SAR0.02 million (US$0-30,000) and gross asset value at SAR0-0.1 million (US$0-15,000). A *very small enterprise* in South Africa is a firm that employs up to 20 workers, with turnover of up to SAR6 million (up to US$0.9 million) and gross asset value at up to SAR2 million (up to US$0.3 million). A *small enterprise* employs up to 50 workers, with turnover up to SAR32 million (up to US$4.5 million) and gross asset value at up to SAR6 million (up to US$0.9 million). A *medium-sized enterprise* employs over 200 workers, with turnover of up to SAR5-64 million (up to US$9 million) and gross asset value at up to SAR5-23 million (US$3.3 million). A *large enterprise* employs over 200 workers, with turn over of over SAR64 million (over US$9 million) and gross asset value of over SAR23 million (over US$3.3 million). In the case of South Africa, the US$ equivalent are approximate and based on the exchange rate as at April 2004.[21]

In Ghana, the Ghana Statistical Service (GSS) considers firms with less than 10 employees as small-scale enterprises and their counterparts with more than 10 employees as medium and large-sized enterprises. In addition, the Ghanaian authorities use the criteria of assets to define small and medium-sized enterprises. For example, the National Board of Small Scale Industries (NBSSI) in Ghana applies both the "fixed asset and number of employees" criteria. It defines a Small Scale Enterprise as one with not more than 9 workers, has plant and machinery (excluding land, buildings and vehicles) not exceeding 10 million Cedis (US$9506, using 1994 exchange rate). The Ghana Enterprise Development Commission (GEDC) on the other hand, uses a 10 million Cedis upper limit definition for plant and machinery.[22]

In Malawi, the official definition of enterprise sizes dates back to 1992 and based on the three criteria of (i) the level of capital investment, (ii) number of employees and (iii) turnover. An enterprise is defined as small scale if it satisfies any two of the following three criteria: it has a capital investment of US$2,000 - US$55,000, employing 5 - 20 people and with a turnover of up to US$110,000 (using 1992 official exchange rate). For manufacturing enterprises, capital investment is taken to mean the cost of plant and machinery, including working capital and the cost of land and buildings.[23]

In spite of these country differences in definitions, micro-, small- or medium-sized enterprises have certain roles in common: (i) they mobilize funds which otherwise would have been idle, (ii) they have been recognized as a seed-bed for indigenous entrepreneurship, (iii) they are labor intensive, employing more labor per unit of capital than large enterprises, (iv) they promote indigenous technological know-how, (v) they are able to compete (but behind protective barriers), (vi) they use mainly local resources, thus have less foreign exchange requirements, (vii) they cater for the needs of the poor, (viii) they adapt easily to customer requirements (flexible specialization), (ix) they act as intermediaries between consumers and large-scale corporations, and (x) they are the mainstay of developing economies particularly in terms of employment.

Despite these global common features, countries do not use the same definitions for classifying their small business sector for obvious reasons. Also, a universal definition does not appear feasible nor desirable as these diversities in definitions in use depend on the purposes these are required to serve according to the policies of the respective countries or governments. Furthermore, the diversities in definitions make it easier for each national government to target macro-level policies for specific group of enterprises.

Our immediate concern in this book is not to further engage the reader in the battle for operational definitions about what constitute a small business firm across nations. Whatever the size or market capitalization of the firm, we are concerned with how it can be managed from the perspective of entrepreneurship, following a strategic management process. In this context, size plays a lesser significant role in our attempt to understand the differences between an entrepreneurial firm and a small business venture. A small business firm can have two to twenty or even ninety employees, but that is an insufficient value as a measure of its entrepreneurial potential. What matters is the manner in which small enterprises can be organized to produce some of the benefits associated with entrepreneurial firms both at the level of the individual entrepreneur and the society at large. We can do this by examining what constitutes an entrepreneurial firm and how different it is from a micro, small or medium-sized enterprise.

The Entrepreneurial Firm

An entrepreneurial firm is an *innovative* firm that follows an entrepreneurial process. This process consists of:

Identifying and evaluating business opportunity: An entrepreneurial firm, unlike a small business venture establishes mechanisms that identify opportunities. Such a firm must also look for new ways of doing things and niches for new products. Some writers have indicated that although most entrepreneurs do not have formal mechanisms for identifying business opportunities, some sources are often fruitful; consumers and business associates, members of the distribution system, and technical people.[24] The path towards innovation, which is crucial to the entrepreneurial firm, is a continuous identification and evaluation of business opportunities.

Developing a business plan: For an entrepreneurial firm, a good business plan must be developed in order to exploit the defined opportunity. As we shall show in chapter fifteen, a business plan serves as the road map for managing the business venture. A good business plan is essential to developing the plans needed to exploit an opportunity and determining the resources required, obtaining those resources, and successfully managing the resulting venture.

Determining resources: The entrepreneurial process must include the determination of resources needed for addressing the opportunity. This process starts with an appraisal of the entrepreneur's present resources. The next step is acquiring the needed resources in a timely manner. Unlike a small business venture, an entrepreneurial firm assesses the risks associated with insufficient or inappropriate resources. In addition, the entrepreneurial firm also identifies the strengths of existing resources, identifying resource gaps and developing access to needed resources.

Developing management system: An entrepreneurial firm, unlike a small business venture, develops an understanding of key variables for success, identifying existing and potential problems, implementing control systems and developing growth strategy. Other crucial variables include, but not limited to, a clear marketing, financial, operational and organizational strategy. In addition, an entrepreneurial firm establishes a control system in order to quickly identify and resolve any problem.

Managing the entrepreneurial transition: One of the major differences between a small business and an entrepreneurial firm is in the process and ability to manage challenges as the firm grows. Managing a firm's transition requires an examination of different management and leadership styles, including appropriate organizational structures. A management style that is appropriate for a small business at the time of its inception might be irrelevant as the business grows.

From the above description, it is possible to define an entrepreneurial firm as:

> *An innovative firm that identifies and evaluates an opportunity, develops a business plan, determines the resources for addressing the opportunity, determines the key variables for success, develops appropriate strategies, implements the business plan, establishes a control system and develops plans for managing growth.*

The key word in the above definition is innovation. The firm, to be entrepreneurial, must have a different product or service creating a new potential of satisfaction. This innovation is possible when the firm identifies and evaluates opportunities and responds to them in a purposeful and systematic manner. In the world of entrepreneurs, opportunities can come in various forms: offering lower prices, better quality, better products, new convenience, etc. In fact, entrepreneurial firms are those firms that are able to convert society's needs into opportunities for profitable business. In other words, innovation begins with the analysis of opportunities.

Although the terms "small business firm" and "entrepreneurial venture" may at times overlap considerably, they are different in many fundamental aspects. First, the small business firm, like the entrepreneurial venture, may be independently owned and operated. However, unlike the entrepreneurial firm, many small businesses are managed without a clear *strategic orientation*. Thus, whatever terminology we use to describe a small business and entrepreneurial one, the fundamental difference is in the degree to which they are managed strategically and the extent to which they respond to the need for creativity and competitiveness in their chosen industry. For example, a once thriving business can find itself driven out of its domain by more aggressive entrepreneurial firms whose owners adopt successful competitive strategies.

Second, like the entrepreneurial firm, a small business may not be dominant in its field or industry. But unlike the entrepreneurial firm, many small businesses do not engage in *innovative practices*. Thus, although micro- and small-sized businesses represent the vast majority of all businesses in developing countries, they are not the *prime source* of innovation in the economy. Their operators cannot be regarded as entrepreneurs precisely because they are mostly motivated by necessity and lack the defining elements of the entrepreneurial spirit. The entrepreneurial venture, in contrast to a small business one, is any business whose goals are profitability and growth and that can be characterized by innovative strategic practices. A small business flows with the tide, while an entrepreneurial firm changes the way the tide is moving! Innovation occurs when changes occur in the way the tide is moving. To be successful, an entrepreneurial firm must try to change the rule of the game, that is, to be creative and to be innovative.

A third important difference between a small business and an entrepreneurial one is their relative *emphasis on growth*. Many small businesses tend to remain small and geographically bound because they remain in the local community from where their original target market started. Although most small businesses have the potential to grow and innovate and become entrepreneurial ventures, their founders typically do not want to do that. Many micro and small enterprises are set up to cater for self or personal needs. These business ventures, although they serve as source of employment in the society, nevertheless remain mired in survivalist activities as a result of an absence of entrepreneurial insight.

Whereas the entrepreneurial firm strives for growth opportunities and takes into consideration the management of the growth process, small businesses tend to remain small without any clear strategy for growth. In entrepreneurship, growth can come in a variety of forms such as growth in sales, growth in profit, growth in product line, growth in the structure of the business or growth in the number of employees. The ability to manage the transition from small to large defines success in entrepreneurship.

A fourth area where entrepreneurial venture is different from a small business firm is in the emphasis on *searching for opportunities in situations of dynamic change and the ability to thrive on change.* Unlike small business firms, entrepreneurial ventures are often associated with "momentary innovation," the idea of changing the value and satisfaction obtained from resources by the consumer at a particular point in time. The kind of innovation that really differentiates the entrepreneur from the general small business owner is "systematic innovation," which, according to Peter Drucker, is the purposeful, organized and constant search for changes, and the systematic analysis of the opportunities such changes might offer for economic or social innovation. Innovations that come from entrepreneurship, according to Peter Drucker, are much more than one-time invention because the entrepreneur must consistently search for, respond to, and exploit change. Entrepreneurs are those individuals who see change as not only normal but as provider of opportunities.[25]

Entrepreneurial ventures, unlike small business firms, are driven by opportunity because their owners see opportunities where others do not. Similarly, the entrepreneurial venture strives to satisfy a need that is not being served, or create a new product or technology that changes the way things are done. Entrepreneurial ventures, unlike small business ones, are creative and find ways to innovate in every aspect of the business, from the product or service, to marketing and distribution, to novel strategies of competition. Entrepreneurial firms change the economic environment of the marketplace in which they exist. And, unlike small business firms, entrepreneurial ventures seek to grow the businesses and exploit opportunity to the fullest. Remember once again that entrepreneurs do not sit and wait passively for opportunities; they search for it proactively. As General George S. Patton once said about his army, *"Opportunities do not come to those who wait. They are captured by those who attack."* This logic equally applies to the entrepreneur. The entrepreneur is someone who continually seeks areas of opportunities in the environment in which the business is located.

THE ENTREPRENEUR AS A STRATEGIST

From the above discussion, it is possible to see an entrepreneur as someone who creates a new business in the face of risk and uncertainty for the purpose of achieving his or her vision, turning this vision into a mission, concretely stating the strategic and financial goals of the firm, knows the strategies necessary to achieve the goals and knows how to implement the strategies and evaluate their outcomes. In fact, the entrepreneur is the ultimate strategist.

Contrary to conventional wisdom, business strategists do not only reside in large corporations, they are equally important in small business firms. They are the individuals who are most responsible for the success or failure of an organization, whether small or large. Entrepreneurs, as strategists, help a firm gather, analyze, and organize information. They track industry and competitive trends, develop forecasting models and scenario analyses, evaluate business performance, spot emerging market opportunities, identify business threats, and develop creative action plans.

In line with the perspective adopted in this book, we must be able to differentiate a small business owner from an entrepreneur because the whole essence of managing a business competitively and successfully depends on how we view an enterprise from these two perspectives and the relative emphasis we place on them: the business-owner and the entrepreneur. To do this, I believe that an understanding of the principles of strategic management and how it relates to the subject of entrepreneurship is an important point of departure.

A **strategic entrepreneur,** as against a small business owner, is thus someone who is a strategist. He or she makes all the strategic as well as operational decisions. To be a strategist as well as an entrepreneur, unlike the small business owner, one must (i) develop a basic business idea, a vision, mission and objectives, (ii) scan and assess the external environment, (iii) assess internal factors, (iv) analyze the strategic factors in light of his or her weaknesses, strengths, opportunities, and threats, (v) decide to or not to establish a business in light of the strategic factors, (vi) generate a business plan, that is, specifying how the idea will be transformed into reality, (vii) implement the business plan, and (viii) evaluate the implemented business plan.

The **small business owner**, on the other hand, is someone who starts a business undertaking and remains small without a clear plan for growth. Some of the characteristics of a small business owner are (i) running a business with lack of experience, (ii) running a business by people with management incompetence, (iii) poor financial management and control, (iv) failure to develop a strategic business plan and (v) inability to make the entrepreneurial transition. As this book will indicate, these are some of the reasons why we have high rate of failures among those who start their own businesses. It is also worth mentioning that the problem of high failure rate among business start-ups is not peculiar to small business owners in the developing countries: it is a worldwide phenomenon. However, as a result of constraints peculiar to Sub-Saharan Africa, the rate of business failure in the region is much higher compared to other parts of the world. The context in which the failure rate occurs in Sub-Saharan Africa is the subject of chapters 3 to 5 of this book.

THE IMPORTANCE OF ENTREPRENEURSHIP IN A DEVELOPING COUNTRY

While it may be true that by almost any measure the United States of America has the most vibrant entrepreneurship of any of the world's economy, by no means does it have a monopoly. The advantages of widespread entrepreneurial activity have not gone unnoticed by economic planners in other countries around the world, and recent years have seen the initiation of many programs to encourage small business formation in many other countries. The wave of interest in entrepreneurship has made its way around the world and this interest has been particularly strong among countries in the developing world for several reasons. In this section, we discuss the importance of entrepreneurship in developing countries, with particular reference to Sub-Saharan Africa.

First, small and medium-sized businesses are the engine of any economy, as they are seen as the "launching pad" for entrepreneurship, business innovation and economic growth. Entrepreneurial ventures is the wheel with which an economy is driven because the large-sized companies, the multinational companies and the public sector have not been able to sustain the livelihood of the majority of the populace in the developing countries.

Second, entrepreneurial development in developing countries (as in the industrialized nations) is important because small business provides the basis upon which large corporations thrive. By acting as suppliers and distributors to the larger companies, small businesses play a significant role in the economies of developing nations through a linkage effect. Small businesses in many nations have always played the role as the link between large companies that produce and the consumers. In many economies, the linkage between the large-scale producers and the consumers goes through individual small business operators. By providing an enabling environment in which small businesses can act as the conduit between producers and consumers, the role of entrepreneurs in the process of economic development can be enhanced.

Third, because of financial and budgetary constraints, the public sector has been unable to make major investments capable of achieving economic growth in the developing countries. As new innovations and investments come from enterprises created through individual initiatives, the role of entrepreneurial firms has taken a new importance in developing economies. Because public enterprises in developing countries have not been able to spur entrepreneurial development (as a result of bureaucratic, political, cultural, and other institutional and historical reasons), individual initiatives in entrepreneurship should be seen as the answer to the challenges of economic development in the less- and underdeveloped economies. As Peter Drucker points out, "what we need is an entrepreneurial society in which innovation and entrepreneurship are normal, steady, and continual."[26]

Fourth, we are now living in an era of privatization, "downsizing" and "rightsizing" in the global economy where many of the world's large corporations and the public sector continue to engage in massive layoffs of employees, dramatically cutting the number of managers and workers on their payrolls. This trend has all but destroyed the long-standing notion of job security in large corporations and in the public sector. In Sub-Saharan Africa, for example, privatization of public enterprises has seen a rise in the trend of "downsizing". The closure of state-owned enterprises and their eventual privatization in line with the policies of structural adjustment program has produced massive unemployment in these countries. The fact is that, more than in the developed industrialized nations of the world, developing countries need entrepreneurs and new businesses precisely because the public sector cannot provide the economic bases upon which to achieve economic growth.

For example, the privatization drive, which started in the early 1990s, made the Government of Uganda relinquish its position as the number one employer. According to research, The Civil and Public Service reforms in Uganda downsized the public service, reducing staff employed by central government from 320,000 in 1990 to 191,324 in March 2001, a reduction of 40.9 percent. As a result, tens of thousands of retrenched civil servants joined the private sector as small-scale business owners. This led to the mushrooming of small-scale business enterprises, most of which employed fewer than five persons and as many as 90 percent of the non-farm private sector workers. Since then, the number of small-scale businesses in Uganda has grown from 800,000 in 1995 to about 2,000,000 in 2002. These businesses serve about 6,000,000 people at business and household levels of the 26.3 million people in the country. [27]

The trend in downsizing has created a more significant philosophical change or value re-orientation among African countries. Starting from the structural adjustment period in Sub-Saharan Africa in the early eighties, a new era brought in a shift in attitude and ideological orientation. To many governments in the developing countries, massive bureaucracies and socialist oriented economic ideologies can no longer guarantee job security. As the case of Tanzania clearly showed, it was during this time that the governments of Sub-Saharan Africa countries, like their counterparts in other countries, began to formulate policies that help to disengage economic activities from the public sector.[28] Similarly, the masses in these countries saw this as an opportunity to go into business and as an opportunity to create their own economic destiny, and the opportunity to reap impressive profits without depending on a downsizing economy.

A fifth importance of entrepreneurship in the developing countries is that entrepreneurial firms do serve as a source of income for national governments. In most economies (developed, emerging, transition, and developing ones), tax is a major source of state revenues for national development. However, in Sub-Saharan Africa, for example, the contribution of tax to total revenue is still lower than desired. In situation in which formal entrepreneurial firms are not promoted, there is the likelihood of the growth of a parallel or informal sector. Because the informal sector is unregulated, there is a loss of tax revenues to the state. Empirical studies indicate that an increase of the informal economy leads to reduced state revenues, which in turn reduce the quality and quantity of publicly provided goods and services.[29] Ultimately, this can lead to an increase in the tax rates for firms and individuals in the official sector, quite often combined with a deterioration in the quality of the public goods (such as the public infrastructure) and of the administration, with the consequence of even stronger incentives to participate in the informal economy.

Since governments are always in need of funds for the development of public utilities, the development of the informal sector and the small and medium-sized business sector can serve as a source of government income. Development and growth of local entrepreneurs in the area of manufacturing can also help in the conservation of a nation's scarce foreign exchange, which can then be used for more national pressing issues.

Finally, the development of the informal sector can help in the process of structuring the economy in ways that reduce the negative incidences of that sector, such as bribery and corruption, the use of child labor, environment degradation, health hazard, and urban overpopulation. In countries with poorly constructed, inefficient, and non self-enforcing constitutional rules, the informal sector is usually quite pervasive. In such countries, the rules that regulate socio-political interaction, have failed to adequately constrain the activities of the underground economy. As a result, state intervention in private exchange is equally pervasive. On the other hand, excessive regulation of economic activities creates many opportunities for rent seeking, including bureaucratic corruption.

CHAPTER SUMMARY

The function of the entrepreneur is to reform or revolutionize the pattern of production by exploiting an invention or, more generally, an untried technological method of producing a new commodity or producing an old one in a new way, opening a new source of supply of materials or a new outlet for products, by organizing a new industry.

An entrepreneur is someone who identifies an opportunity in an economic system, assembles the resources necessary to successfully exploit that opportunity and creates and delivers a value in an economic system. These resources include financial, human, technology, and organization.

Entrepreneurship can be defined as the process of combining scarce resources in new ways to respond to opportunities or provide solutions to a problem.

The conditions for entrepreneurship are (i) the reduced role of the state, (ii) forces of globalization, (iii) information and communication technology, (iv) corporate and public sector downsizing, (v) the imperatives of market forces (vi) changes in economic and political ideologies, and (vii) social transformation.

Innovation is provision of different economic satisfaction. The most productive innovation is a different product or service creating a new potential of satisfaction, rather than an improvement.

Innovation may result in a lower price, a new or better product, a new convenience, or the definition of a new entrant. Innovation may be finding new uses for old products.

Three types of innovation are (i) new concepts and new business, where the entrepreneur is seen as a pioneer of a new product or service and creates a new market and business for it, (ii) existing concept and new business, where the strategy is that of creative imitation. Creative imitation satisfies a demand that already exists rather than creating one, and (iii) innovating on the value chain in which the strategy is to innovate in anyone activity of the value chain to remain competitive.

The three criteria that are generally applied by governments to define micro-, small, and medium-sized enterprises are: (i) capital investment in plant and machineries, (ii) number of workers employed, and (iii) volume of production and turnover of business.

The role of micro-, small- or medium-sized enterprises are (i) they mobilize funds which otherwise would have been idle, (ii) they have been recognized as a seed-bed for indigenous entrepreneurship, (iii) they are labor intensive, employing more labor per unit of capital than large enterprises, (iv) they promote indigenous technological know-how, (v) they are able to compete (but behind protective barriers), (vi) they use mainly local resources, thus have less foreign exchange requirements, (vii) they cater for the needs of the poor, (viii) they adapt easily to customer requirements (flexible specialization), (ix) they act as intermediaries between consumers and large-scale corporations, and (x) they are the mainstay of developing economies particularly in terms of employment.

The entrepreneurial process in an entrepreneurial firm consists of (i) identifying and evaluating business opportunity, (ii) developing a business plan, (iii) determining resources, (vi) developing a management system, and (v) managing the entrepreneurial transition.

An entrepreneurial firm is defined as an innovative firm that identifies and evaluates an opportunity, develops a business plan, determines the resources for addressing the opportunity, determines the key variables for success, develops appropriate strategies, implements the business plan, establishes a control system and develops plans for managing growth.

Opportunities come in various forms: offering lower prices, better quality, better products, new convenience, etc. Entrepreneurial firms are those firms that are able to convert society's needs into opportunities for profitable business. Innovation begins with the analysis of opportunities.

The differences between a small business firm and an entrepreneurial venture are (i) emphasis on strategic orientation, (ii) emphasis on innovation, (iii) emphasis on growth and the management of growth and (iv) emphasis on searching for opportunities in situations of dynamic change and the ability to thrive on change.

An entrepreneur is some who (i) develops a basic business idea, a vision, mission and objectives, (ii) scan and assess the external environment, (iii) assess internal factors, (iv) analyze the strategic factors in light of his or her weaknesses, strengths, opportunities, and threats, (v) decide to or not to establish a business in light of the strategic factors, (vi) generate a business plan, that is, specifying how the idea will be transformed into reality, (vii) implement the business plan, and (viii) evaluate the implemented business plan.

An entrepreneur is a strategist because he or she creates a new business in the face of risk and uncertainty for the purpose of achieving his or her vision, turning this vision into a mission, concretely stating the strategic and financial goals of the firm, knows the strategies necessary to achieve the goals and knows how to implement the strategies and evaluate their outcomes.

The small business owner is someone who starts a business undertaking and remains small without a clear plan for growth. Some of the characteristics of a small business owner are (i) running a business with lack of experience, (ii) running a business by people with management incompetence, (iii) poor financial control, (vi) failure to develop a strategic business plan and (v) inability to make the entrepreneurial transition.

A major difference between a small business and an entrepreneurial firm is that small businesses typically do not have a strategy and are not dominant in their field while the entrepreneurial company pursues profitability and growth and typically has an innovative strategy.

The importance and roles of entrepreneurship in developing countries are: (i) entrepreneurship is the engine for economic growth and source of innovation, (ii) small businesses and entrepreneurial firms provide the basis upon which large corporations thrive, (iii) entrepreneurship provides major investments capable of achieving economic growth in the developing countries, (iv) small businesses and entrepreneurial ventures provide employment, (v) entrepreneurship in the developing countries serve as a source of income for national governments.

CHAPTER DISCUSSION QUESTIONS

1. In your opinion, do you think that developing countries present opportunities for the growth of entrepreneurship? Please explain the basis upon which you base your opinion.

2. In your view, what are the conditions for entrepreneurship?

3. What is innovation? List and explain the sources of innovation with particular examples from the developing countries.

4. What are the roles of micro-, small-, and medium-sized enterprises in developing countries?

5. Describe the entrepreneurial process.

6. What are the major differences between a small business and an entrepreneurial venture?

7. Who is an entrepreneur?

8. Why do we consider an entrepreneur a strategist?

9. Who is a small business owner?

10. What are the major roles of entrepreneurship in developing economies?

CASE STUDY 1: RAYMOND DOKPESI AND AFRICAN INDEPENDENT TELEVISION[30]

Raymond Dokpesi pioneered ownership of private radio and television stations in Nigeria. He also blazed the trail in providing round-the-clock broadcasting and placing a Nigerian TV station on satellite. On February 25, 2008, Raymond Dokpesi, founder and Chairman of Daar Communications opened another epoch in the broadcasting industry when he took DAAR Communications to the capital market. With the public offering the company planned to raise N13.5 billion (US$ 112.5 million) through the capital market.

His admirers usually liken him to the American media mogul, Ted Turner, the founder of the renowned 24 hours global news television station, Cable News Network. But while his African Independent Television, AIT, may not have attained the same status as CNN which prides itself as the world leader, Raymond Dokpesi's exploits in the Nigerian broadcasting industry make the comparison with Turner a deserved inspirational model. When local entrepreneurs were wary of putting their money in radio and TV businesses, he took the plunge. Today, there are more than 20 stations of either side. He wouldn't stop there. Even when government television stations were penny-pinching on 24-hour relay, believing it was not feasible, Dokpesi took his AIT to the stretch; keeping willing viewers awake all night. Now, at least five TV stations, public and private, have cued in.

One would think he was done with his pioneering strides. No. The next thing was to actualize the dream of putting AIT on cable, an idea that was conceptually built into the birth of DAAR Communications. As expected, some rival concerns have gone satellite. For these rivals, there will, very soon, be a new catching-up game to do on DAAR. Ever so venturesome, Dokpesi concluded plans to take the premier private broadcasting station to the capital market. If the credit would not be taken away from him, Dokpesi sure sets the pace on the local broadcast front.

And to think that the adventurous broadcasting entrepreneur trained as a maritime engineer. So why the drift? As he once said in an interview, the interest developed while involved in a political campaign tour, which took him round nearly all the local government areas of Nigeria. While gallivanting, he discovered a dire lack of information and entertainment broadcast channels in most of the local government areas. Because these facilities were not there, the residents could not but be winking in the dark.

Born on 25 October 1951 at Ibadan, Oyo State, Dokpesi was not born with a silver spoon. But by dint of hard work and a daring spirit, coupled with some elements of luck, he was able to pull himself up by the bootstraps. In one instance when he was offered admission as one of the pioneer students of the then Midwest Institute of Technology, raising the initial 10 pounds sterling required as deposit for tuition fees was an uphill task for his parents. While struggling to raise the fees, fortune smiled on him with a Nigerian Ports Authority scholarship to study maritime engineering in a Polish university. He emerged with a first class Bachelor of Science degree in the discipline, and went on to add a Masters and a Doctorate degree in the same field. Well-equipped academically, he settled down to a teaching career as an Assistant Lecturer at University of Gdansk, Poland, and was aspiring to become a professor before he met Chief Olusegun Obasanjo who talked him into returning home. Back home, in 1978, he joined the Ministry of Transport, on grade level 12, and was deployed to the Nigerian Ports Authority.

It was at NPA that Dokpesi began to flourish, rising to become a General Manager when Alhaji Bamanga Tukur, who would become his mentor, was Managing Director. He resigned from the civil service in 1984. It was, however, his business association with the trio of Chief M.K.O. Abiola, General Shehu Musa Yar'Adua and Alhaji Tukur with whom he set up the African Ocean Lines that thrust him into prominence. He resigned from the partnership in 1989 to go solo.

The liberalization of the Nigerian broadcasting industry which allowed private ownership of radio and television stations in the early 1990s enabled Raymond Dokpesi, a trained marine engineer, to venture into the broadcasting business. In the early 1990's, as a result of the historic National Broadcasting Commission decree, Nigerian media was dominated by the government only. Information was only made possible from government owned broadcasting firms. However, the Head of State then General Babangida issued a decree, which allowed private broadcasting in Nigeria. After this decree came the first private television network in Nigeria, Africa Independent Television (AIT). AIT was pioneered by Dr. Raymond Dokpesi, and was also Africa's first satellite TV station.

In spite of the lack of an established private sector broadcast platform from whose experiences he can lean on, Dokpesi nevertheless established DAAR Communications to pioneer radio and television broadcasting in Nigeria. The company opened a new chapter in the history of broadcasting in Nigeria when Ray Power 100.5, its FM radio station, hit the airwaves of Lagos and adjoining states briefly in December 1993 on test transmission, as the country's first privately-owned radio station. The station went off air few weeks later to resume full transmission on 16, August 1994.

For many radio listeners, especially in the south western part of the country, programs from the new station was a refreshing experience from the fares being dished out from the government-owned radio stations they had been used to. The clarity, broad program content and exciting presenters in no time turned the new station into the darling of radio audience in the region. These were complemented by the round-the-clock broadcasting mode introduced by Raypower. The radio station thus became the first to do 24 hours broadcasting in Nigeria. To many listeners and other cynics in the industry, the idea of a radio station doing all-night programming sounded crazy. Many wondered who would be listening to a radio station at odd hours of the night or very early in the morning when they were supposed to be in bed. But the idea soon caught on and it is to the credit of Dokpesi that, today, most of the privately owned radio stations are available on the dial 24 hours.

He would replicate that in television when he launched the African Independent Television in 1996, which also has the distinction of being Nigeria's first privately owned television service.

Through Dokpesi's investment in latest transmission technology, the signals of Raypower and AIT are received in many countries in Africa. AIT has also made a statement with its live telecasts. Many Nigerians have come to rely on the AIT for coverage, especially for transmission of important sports, political and corporate events. For example, Nigerians were able to watch live the debate on the failed third term bid of former President Olusegun Obasanjo on the floor of the National Assembly in their living rooms. The broadcasting company was also in the thick of the campaign for the 2007 elections as it transmitted live images from campaign grounds of political parties across the country.

Having operated radio and television services for about 15 years, Dokpesi is taking his pioneering proclivity to the next level. Soon, DAAR Communications will become a public firm. Dokpesi says this is imperative given the wide-scale acceptance of the company by Nigerians. But more importantly, broadcasting, he argues, has become quite expensive the world over, beyond the scope of an individual undertaking if it is to be done the right way. "The time is now, the time is right to bring DAAR Communications to the doorsteps of every Nigerian in ownership. The radio and television stations have become the people's; it has outgrown one individual. The time has come when all Nigerians should be able to own a station or stations that can represent, promote, project and defend their interests at all times. So, shares of DAAR Communications will be made available to the Nigerian interested public to take over. I have done my best as an individual. It is now left for the rest of Nigeria to show confidence and improve on it," Dokpesi said.

DAAR Communications will float a N75 billion (about US$625 million) Initial Public Offer, IPO, on the floor of the Nigerian Stock Exchange after a Completion Board scheduled for sometime this month. As AIT expands in ownership, it will also be expanding its operations to cover local, regional and global events round the clock and in greater detail.

DAAR has sent some staff on training abroad to prepare them for the new challenges, while some experts will be brought into the country to train its employees. "We have arranged other training courses for reporters to get better acquainted with digital equipment and the digital space. The company will also employ workers outside the shores of Nigeria if there is need to do so," its chairman discloses.

DAAR Communications has been investing in new digital equipment to facilitate its emergence as a powerhouse in the broadcasting industry. "In three months we have acquired N400 million worth of fresh content. We are coming up with an expansion program, bringing AIT to the doorsteps of people terrestrially from 20 locations across the country. We have AIT International, Europe and Africa as well as National coming up. We have $25 million investment coming on interactive television. We have passed our offer to stockbrokers to look at. The idea is that you should also be able to watch television on your mobile phones and your laptop and we have all the equipment for that," he enthuses.

The ultimate goal, the broadcasting mogul contends, is to give Nigerians in particular and Africans generally a strong voice in the global broadcasting space. "We want to be able to promote and project Nigerians, and indeed, the rest of Africa globally. And in doing this, we believe that we need to give them accurate, reliable and dependable information. We want to be able to give our artistes, our own graduates of Mass Communication, a clean ground where they can compete with their talents across the world; give them the opportunity to be able to grow as well as catch up with the rest of the world," Dokpesi, who is the only son of his mother's 13 children, declares.

While relating the advent of television services into Africa, he notes that Nigeria was at the forefront with WNBS and WNTV, which were established in 1959. Nigerian television stations, he added started color transmission around 1977 during the Festival of Arts and Culture, popularly known as FESTAC, while South Africa started in 1995. But the former apartheid enclave has since left Nigeria behind in adoption of new technological developments in the broadcasting industry. For example, Dokpesi reveals, it will become mandatory in South Africa by 1 September 2007 for all television stations to broadcast on digital platforms. Some service-providers in that country have also been test-running their mobile television. "But Nigeria, the giant of Africa is not yet prepared. And that is why we want to be able to bring Nigeria to the forefront in television broadcasting, to regain the lost ground in the area of technology and even to start building equipment for the industry in the next few years," he says.

Dokpesi's doggedness has seen DAAR Communications, especially its television arm, stand its ground in the face of not a few adversities. On many occasions, it had played host to members of the security agencies. And recently, bulldozers of the Federal Capital Territory descended on the company's office in Abuja and demolished some structures for alleged violation of building approval plan.

The AIT chairman describes the demolition in which he claims the company lost equipment worth over N2 billion as most unfair. DAAR Communications, he maintains, had invested an undisclosed millions of naira to provide infrastructure in the area which was hitherto neglected. Dokpesi supported his claim that the demolition did not have anything to do with the company's encroachment on other people's land in the area or violation of approved building plans, by providing relevant documents to the press. Rather, he insists that the demolition is more of a political vendetta for the role the broadcasting organization played in the defeat of the infamous tenure elongation project of the former administration.

"I am confident to say that we submitted building plans to the Federal Capital Authority in the year 2002. It was very glaring that there was no problem until April 2006 when the third term came up. About that time, my country home was set ablaze by unknown persons. On May 15th 2006, the eve of the collapse of the third term bid, after I had been called by very high personalities in Nigeria who mounted pressure on me to remove my cameras from the National Assembly and I refused, I was told there and then that there would be dire consequences. It was on that 15th after an earlier meeting on the 14th and AIT continued with the transmission that Malam Nasir el-Rufai approved the demolition of AIT property. When I asked for reasons, they said it had to do with building plans. We were invited for a meeting on the 5th of July, my colleagues went to attend the meeting at FCDA because they said because of my status and so on, I should not come myself and I said 'fine'. So I asked the Executive Director as he was then, to lead the delegation to the meeting. There are laws, there are rules, but when on the 17th April DAAR Communications showed the documentary which was critical of President Obasanjo and Malam Nasir el-Rufai, Rufai called one Mr. Ezeamaka to go and resuscitate the memo of the demolition," Dokpesi laments.

The first threat to DAAR Communication came in 2000 when a consortium of banks led by Union Bank which provided Dokpesi funds for its take-off attempted a take-over and put it in receivership for failure to honor its financial obligations to them when due.

The accompanying crisis forced the station off the air for some months. Dokpesi speaks of how the comeback was hinged on "a little bit of restructuring of its equity structure."

DAAR Communications' Abuja office was also at a time completely gutted by a mysterious fire with all the company's equipment consumed in the inferno. Some reporters of the broadcasting outfit have also in the past had brushes with law enforcement agencies. There was also a time the company was so hard up it could not pay its workers for many months.

Dokpesi believes these tragedies are a price DAAR Communications has to pay for being a pioneer in the private segment of the industry. "It is most unfortunate that pioneers have to sacrifice a lot in other to allow those that come thereafter to be able to prosper and develop. The challenges we have had are simply based on the fact that we believe that the truth must be told and reported. We are holding tenaciously to the provisions of section 22 of the Nigerian Constitution of 1979 and also keeping in line with the ethics of the profession. People often ask me, 'why do you want to show the other side of the story if it will bring you troubles? Why do you want to report labor protest?' But that is what is important to the well being of all Nigerians; there is the need to know. Information, it is said, is power, and it is good to make information available to each and every individual so that he can determine his own destiny, rather than to a clique coming together to say this must be the situation. And if every individual is provided the required information, let him toe the line that he deems fit. This is a simple fact. AIT has never shown anything that is not supported by pictures, but to say that we should not look at the other side will be below the professional standard expected in modern day journalism," he insists.

Case Discussion Questions

1. In this chapter, it is pointed out that the idea behind the concept of entrepreneurship is embarking on activities that make a difference. How does this concept or idea relate to the activities of Raymond Dokpesi, DAAR Communications Limited and his African Independent Television?

2. To understand the field of entrepreneurship better, it is essential to note one particular point: Entrepreneurship is more than just risk-taking. It is very much about an opportunistic mind-set and spirit. It is about having a vision, a mission and sets of goals and the ability to pursue those goals in a strategic manner. It is about innovation and it is the ability to see opportunities where others cannot and the ability to act on such opportunities. Explain the entrepreneurial actions of Raymond Dokpesi and his business ventures in the context of these statements.

3. Is Raymond Dokpesi an entrepreneur or a businessman? Support your position by explaining the differences between an entrepreneur and a businessman. Give reasons why you think he is an entrepreneur or a businessman.

4. We have noted in this chapter that one of the drivers of entrepreneurial initiatives and activities is derived from the forces of globalization, technological advancement, information and communication technology, and the imperatives of market forces such as privatization and deregulation. In your opinion, explain how these forces contributed to the entrepreneurial initiatives and activities of Raymond Dokpesi and his AIT and DAAR ventures.

5. Discuss the importance of Raymond Dokpesi's entrepreneurial activities in a developing country such as Nigeria?

Chapter 2

ENTREPRENEURS: CHARACTERISTICS, PROFILES AND MOTIVES

"Ignore the conventional wisdom. If everybody else is doing it one way, there's a good chance you can find your niche by going in exactly the opposite direction. But be prepared for a lot of folks to wave you down and tell you you're headed the wrong way" (Sam Walton, founder of Wal-Mart, the World's largest retailer).

CHAPTER LEARNING OBJECTIVES
After studying this chapter, you should be able to:

1. Understand the characteristics and profiles of entrepreneurs.

2. Understand the sources of business ideas and innovations.

3. Understand the reasons why people choose to become entrepreneurs.

4. Understand the drawbacks of becoming an entrepreneur.

5. Understand the nature of African entrepreneur and entrepreneurship in relation to the discourse of entrepreneurship.

INTRODUCTION: SEARCHING FOR ENTREPRENEURIAL PROFILE

Any attempt at establishing an entrepreneurial profile that fits all categories of entrepreneurs is futile. The futility in this enterprise is borne out of the diversity in the subject. Entrepreneurs come in variety of forms, characteristics, behaviors and motives. What drives one to become an entrepreneurial is psychologically, socially, economically and politically informed. Having established this point, we can nevertheless attempt an exploration of some of the recognized and endearing characteristics of entrepreneurs in the discourse of entrepreneurship. Later in this chapter, we will situate the African entrepreneur in the context of the discourse.

In the previous chapter we examined some of the factors that drive entrepreneurship: demographic and economic factors, technological advancements, E-commerce and the Internet, global opportunities, corporate downsizing etc. As we pointed out, these changes create entrepreneurial opportunities in an environment. Although changes in the society create opportunities, not everyone respond to them with an entrepreneurial mindset. Secondly, where entrepreneurs see opportunities, others may see threats. In other words, some people are more driven to be entrepreneurs than others. The history and case studies of many successful entrepreneurs appropriately depict the point that entrepreneurs are those who identify opportunity where others see threats. Entrepreneurs think and behave differently than nonentrepreneurs. What set entrepreneurs apart from the general public is the subject of this chapter.

Entrepreneurs have a mindset different from nonentrepreneurs. An entrepreneurial mindset involves the ability to rapidly sense, act, and mobilize, even under certain uncertain conditions.[1] Common among entrepreneurs is their ability to identify opportunities where others see only threats. Successful entrepreneurs know when and how to transit through the entrepreneurial process and managing the growth of the organization, how to secure the necessary finance to enter into promising areas of business, and how to diversify from one base to the other. Successful entrepreneurs, especially those that have created conglomerates, have the mindset to identify an idea or opportunity with the right strategic fit and to identify the resources necessary to take advantage of the opportunity.

One thing that has become increasingly clear is that entrepreneurship will be the defining business trend of this century. Whether one starts as a small fish trading company such as the Ibrus, a bank such as Jim Oviah or a business school such as Pat Utomi, entrepreneurship will be the focal point for economic growth in any context. The culture of the present business world is significantly different from the ones experienced by the generation of traders in the post-colonial era in several ways. Particularly among first generation entrepreneurs in Africa, there were limited opportunities for entrepreneurship and those who venture into it were those who capitalized on opportunities afforded either by indigenization policies or through shifts in economic policies. Presently, the business culture has become laissez-faire and organizations are drifting toward a trend that emphasizes focus, psychological stamina, risk tolerance, self-reliance and individuality. People are asking themselves, from Internet wiz kids, marketing gurus, film producers, writers to evangelicals: "What can I do that's crazy and bizarre to draw attention to myself and get in the spotlight"? Discouraged with their prospects in the corporate world and civil service and propelled by a willingness to take a chance at controlling their own destinies, more young people are choosing entrepreneurship as their primary career path. Increasing numbers of women have realized that the best way to break the "glass ceiling" that prevents them from rising to the top of many organizations is to start their own businesses. Social taboos on certain professions (such as film acting and production) have been shattered and given new meaning. Globalization has also produced what can be termed as "melting pot" of diverse cultures in countries that were formally monolithic in culture. Thus, many people that have been economically marginalized have found economic freedom through business ownership. Religion, itself, is not immune from the powerful influence of entrepreneurship. People are no more shying away from questioning their deeply felt beliefs. Thus, in order to attract the disenchanted, more churches are using business innovative strategies to remain competitive in a highly fragmented religious environment.[2]

We live in an era that encourages individual thinker, with a level of endurance and interest in pushing one beyond the limits previously set by orthodoxy. In Africa, the new generation entrepreneurs are playing the game in accordance with the rules: educated, opportunistic, strategic leadership, resolve to reshape society through philanthropy, focus, etc. Examples include Patrick Utomi (BusinessDay), Jim Ovhia (Zenith Bank), Strive Masiyiwa (Econet), among others. Unlike first generation entrepreneurs, the present ones are emerging without the help of state patronage. The present culture encourages individuals to embrace risk, stand out with confidence and embrace social and economic obstacles with a new sense of individuality that is today's business world. Thus, if one follows the evolutionary pattern of today's business world, it is possible to predict with a degree of certainty that more entrepreneurs will be produced than people seeking safety from employees in large organizations. This trend is based on the increasing role of technology in societies, the globalization of the means of production, the rise of a global monolithic consumption pattern, re-definition of work ethics and ethos and the increasingly growing importance of individualism. The consequences of these actions are that (i) more organizations are resorting to outsourcing than in hiring and (ii) more employees are resorting to freelancing than in hiring. We live in a world of entrepreneurs.

So, what drives entrepreneurs to work so hard with no guarantee of success? What are the forces that push them to risk so much and to make so many sacrifices in an attempt to achieve a vision, a dream or a mission? Why are entrepreneurs willing to give up the security of a steady paycheck working for someone else to become the last person to be paid in the management of their own businesses? This chapter examines and provides answers to these and other questions. We will start by examining the characteristics of entrepreneurs.

CHARACTERISTICS AND PROFILES OF ENTREPRENEURS

The characteristics of an entrepreneur have been the object and subject of much research dealing with the phenomenon of entrepreneurship. In much of the research and literature, the idea that entrepreneurs have special characteristics that distinguish them from nonentrepreneurs has been extensively discussed. Many studies believe that entrepreneurs have special personality traits and the men (and women) who follow the difficult road of entrepreneurship are by necessity seen as a special breed.[3] As Jon Goodman rightly points out, whether entrepreneurial tendencies exist at birth or are developed as a person matures; certain traits are usually evident in those who enjoy success as entrepreneurs.[4] The following is a description of the most widely accepted characteristics found in a typical entrepreneur.

A Need to Create Value

Some entrepreneurs are driven by the need to create value. The entrepreneur creates value by serving a market need that can come from one of four possible sources: (i) *the meeting of a new or increasing demand* for a particular product or service within a specific market niche; (ii) *product differentiation by quality*, whereby a particular product or service is of a positively different or unique quality that makes it more valuable to a particular market need than existing products or services; (iii) *product differentiation by service*, whereby the service associated with a particular product makes it superior in value to any possible alternative; and (iv) *undercutting of price*, which is to say, having the lowest price, although many question whether price is a form of value creation that an entrepreneur can sustainable maintained.

More than anything else, it seems that the need to create value is the underlying motivation for going into business. This need may be borne out of a vision, a dream or purpose or a life philosophy. For instance, Raymond Dokpesi says that his motivation to go into broadcasting was born when he discovered a dire lack of information and entertainment broadcast channels in most of the local government areas while undertaking a political campaign. Because these facilities were not there, the residents could not but be winking in the dark. Raymond Dokpesi has a vision and a mission: To give Nigerians in particular and Africans generally a strong voice in the global broadcasting space. "We want to be able to promote and project Nigerians, and indeed, the rest of Africa globally. And in doing this, we believe that we need to give them accurate, reliable and dependable information. We want to be able to give our artistes, our own graduates of Mass Communication, a clean ground where they can compete with their talents across the world; give them the opportunity to be able to grow as well as catch up with the rest of the world." Many Nigerians have come to rely on the AIT for coverage, especially for transmission of important sports, political and corporate events.

Passion for the Business

The entrepreneur must have more than a casual interest in the business because there will be many hurdles and obstacles to be overcome. If there is no passion, or consuming interest, the business will not succeed. Steven Jobs, cofounder of Apple Computer, stated that Apple Computer succeeded not because it was a good idea but because it was "built from the heart." Having the passion to do what one wants to do defines the degree of success in the entrepreneurial venture. Walt Disney, the founder of The Walt Disney Co. has a passion for curiosity and cartoon characters in his early age. Through this passion, he created Mickey Mouse, which has become the most popular cartoon figure in the world and transformed the Disney Co. into one of the largest organization in the world. Walt Disney said that his passion for curiosity led to his innovativeness. "Curiosity keeps leading us down new paths," Disney said.[5]

A business venture, for most entrepreneurs, is a journey, not a destination. However, knowing the direction one is heading and why seems to be a common component of entrepreneurial success. For example, Abdul Wasiu Sanusi, the founder and publisher of *The Mark Newspaper* in Damaturu, Nigeria stated that it was through his passion for journalism and news reporting that he developed from college years that prompted him to open his newspaper business.[6] Some people become entrepreneurs because they love what they are doing. Because entrepreneurs love what they do, they are ready to put in long hours when everyone else is asleep and they are ready to work for many years without pay. Sam Walton (the founder of Wal-Mart, world's largest retailer) puts it this way: "if you love your work, you'll be out there every day trying to do it the best you possibly can, and pretty soon everybody around will catch the passion from you – like a fever."

Tenacity Despite Obstacles and Failure

Beverly Sills once said that "You may be disappointed if you fail, but you are doomed if you don't try." Many successful entrepreneurs were confronted with adversaries in some periods of their lives. Their success is rooted in their ability to turn adversaries and setbacks into success through a positive attitude, persistence and determination. Because of the hurdles and obstacles that must be overcome, the entrepreneur must be consistently persistent. Many successful entrepreneurs succeeded only after they had failed several times. It has been stated, "Successful entrepreneurs don't have failures. They have learning experiences." Entrepreneurs see difficulties as opportunities to learn from mistakes. In fact, one of the most enduring traits inherent in successful entrepreneurs is their refusal to accept failure. Oprah Winfrey said "There is no such thing as failure in my life. I just don't believe in it."

CASE IN POINT: SAM WALTON: LEARNING FROM FAILURE[7]

Sam Walton, the founder of Wal-Mart (World's largest company) felt sick to his stomach. It was 1950, and he had just spent five years turning his first store – a five-and-dime Ben Franklin franchise in Newport, Ark. – from a dying money-loser into the most profitable Ben Franklin in the six-state region.

Now he had to sell it.

His landlord refused to renew his five-year lease, because he wanted to give the now-thriving business to his son. Walton had nowhere else to move the store in Newport. So he sold it.

"It really was like a nightmare," Walton wrote in his 1992 autobiography, Sam Walton: *Made in America*. "I had built the best variety store in the whole region and worked hard in the community – done everything right – and now I was being kicked out of town."

Walton (1918-92) called it the low point of his business life. But he didn't dwell on his misfortune. Instead, he moved his wife, Helen, and their four small children to Bentonville, Ark., and bought a new store. Learning from his bitter experience, he secured a 99-year lease.

"I had to pick myself up and get on with it, do it all over again, only even better this time," he wrote.

Do it better he did. That new store was the start of what became the biggest retailer in the world – Wal-Mart Stores Inc.

Turning setbacks into opportunities was just one of the many things Sam Walton did to build his retail empire, which reached the $100 billion annual-sales mark in 1997. In five years, that number more than doubled to $218 billion. Wal-Mart changed the face of retailing. As of 2003, the company operates more than 4,000 stores worldwide. In 1999, with 1,140,000 associates, Wal-Mart became the largest private employer in the world.

Many individuals who experienced failure at one point in their entrepreneurial journey became the founders of many of the large corporations we have today. In addition to Sam Walton, Walt Disney went bankrupt three times before he made his first successful film. Henry Ford, the founder of Ford Motors, the third largest car manufacturer in the world, failed twice. They would never have been successful if they had given up easily. Most importantly, successful entrepreneurs have the strength to endure obstacles and other forms of difficulties. They have in them the spirit of tenacity to overcome threats and obstacles that may come across their ways.

Obstacles do not deter entrepreneurs because they have the tenacity and doggedness to keep them going. For example, Raymond Dokpesi's doggedness saw DAAR Communications, especially its television arm stand its ground in the face of not a few adversities. For example, the company's offices in Abuja, the Federal capital of Nigeria were demolished loosing equipment worth over N2 billion. Another adversity to DAAR Communication came in 2000 when a consortium of banks led by Union Bank which provided Dokpesi funds for its take-off attempted a take-over and put it in receivership for failure to honor its financial obligations to them when due. The accompanying crisis forced the station off the air for some months. Dokpesi speaks of how the comeback was hinged on "a little bit of restructuring of its equity structure." DAAR Communications' Abuja office was also at a time completely gutted by a mysterious fire with all the company's equipment consumed in the inferno. Some reporters of the broadcasting outfit have also in the past been arrested by law enforcement agencies for reporting news that did sit well with the government. And there was also a time the company was so hard up it could not pay its workers for many months. These tragedies did not make him quit: they strengthen his resolve to succeed. Raymond Dokpesi saw these tragedies as the price DAAR Communications has to pay for being a pioneer in the private segment of the industry. "It is most unfortunate that pioneers have to sacrifice a lot in other to allow those that come thereafter to be able to prosper and develop. The challenges we have had are simply based on the fact that we believe that the truth must be told and reported", he said.

Entrepreneurs must have the perseverance to succeed in their entrepreneurial initiatives and businesses. Because the start-up process is likely to be affected by setbacks of various kinds, persistence is required for success in the venturing process. In perseverance, entrepreneurs can see obstacles as opportunities. For instance, A. P. Giannini, the founder of Bank of America (the second largest commercial bank in the U.S.) says that, "I thrive on obstacles, particularly obstacles placed in my way by narrow-gauged competitors and their political friends."

Confidence

Individuals who possess self-confidence feel that they can meet the challenges, which confront them. They have a sense of mastery over the types of problems that they might encounter. Studies show that successful entrepreneurs tend to be self-reliant individuals who see the problems in launching a new venture but believe in their own ability to overcome them. Entrepreneurs are confident in their abilities and the business concept. They believe they have the ability to accomplish whatever they set out to do. This confidence is not unfounded, however. Often, they have an in-depth knowledge of the market and the industry and they have conducted months (and sometimes years) of research. It is common for entrepreneurs to learn an industry while working for someone else. This allows them to gain knowledge and learn from mistakes before striking out on their own.

Aliko Dangote, who controls the Dangote Group with annual revenue of $1.255 billion in 2005, exemplifies the entrepreneur with confidence. This confidence was manifested in his belief in the opportunity that the Nigerian, and indeed the African continent present for entrepreneurship:

"I believe in Nigeria. I believe there is always going to be Nigeria. My faith and belief in this country is unshakeable. …The importance of Nigeria is the market. The population is there. The money is there. It is just a matter of having good entrepreneurs who can push this thing forward… We are not a company that is owned by government. People are still doing business in troubled areas like Congo. In fact, Congo is one of the best countries to invest in. During the war in Liberia, people were still doing business. A friend of mine opened a flour mills six months ago in Cote D'Ivoire".

With confidence, entrepreneurs are able to recognize opportunities where others only see failure. Secondly, entrepreneurs are self-confident when they are in control of what they are doing and working alone. They tackle problems immediately with confidence and are persistent in their pursuit of their objectives. Most are at their best in the face of adversity, since they thrive on their own self-confidence

High Need for Achievement

Psychologists recognize that people differ in their need for achievement. Individuals with a low need for achievement are those who seem to be contented with their present state of affairs or status. On the other hand, individuals with a high need for achievement like to compete with some standard of excellence and prefer to be personally responsible for their own assigned tasks. Thus, entrepreneurs differ from nonentrepreneurs on the basis of how they view the need for achievement as a motivating factor in everyday life.

A leading figure in the study of achievement motivation is David McClelland, who discovered a positive correlation between the need for achievement and entrepreneurial activity.[8] In other words, those who become entrepreneurs have, on the average, a higher need for achievement than do members of the general population. This drive for achievement is reflected in the ambitious individuals who start new business ventures and then guide them in their growth. In some families, such entrepreneurial drive is evident at a very early stage. For example, sometimes a child takes a paper route, subcontracts it to a younger brother or sister, and then tries another venture. Also, some college students take over or start various types of student-related business or businesses that can be operated while pursuing an academic program. In particular, researchers David McClelland and David Winter provide evidence that the most economically developed societies are those that place high value on the need to achieve. For them, the need for achievement is a catalyst for competition, and competition is one of the drivers of entrepreneurship and economic development.[9]

Identifying and Capitalizing on Opportunities

Society today is dotted with opportunities as a result of globalization, the Internet age, economic policies of deregulation, socio-cultural and other demographic changes. The interesting aspect of these changes is that they come along with opportunities and threats and those who are able to see opportunities in them have been able to capitalize on them. Entrepreneurs that are successful are those who identify an opportunity and act on it. It is not enough to be goal-oriented to become an entrepreneur. Neither is it enough to be creative to become one. And certainly it is not enough to be self-confident. All these attributes must be applied in a situation where an opportunity arises and the ability to capitalize on that very opportunity.

From an entrepreneurial point of view, opportunity identification and evaluation are often very demanding and demands a certain level of creativity. As Robert Hisrich, Michael Peters and Dean Shepherd appropriately stated, most good business opportunities do not suddenly appear, but rather result from an entrepreneur's alertness to possibilities or, in some cases, the establishment of mechanisms that identify potential opportunities.[10] That is why entrepreneurs are seen as those individuals who are able to identify an opportunity, establish the means for exploiting the opportunity and acting on it. Thus, many successful entrepreneurs do not believe in luck. They see opportunities in areas where others don't. Oprah Winfrey insists, "I don't believe in luck. I think luck is preparation meeting opportunity."

Mr. Patrice Motsepe, a South African lawyer who was born in the township of Soweto took full advantage of the Black Economic Empowerment laws of South Africa that require mining firms to be over a quarter black-owned. He moved from being the first black partner at Bowman Gilfillan law firm in Johannesburg to running a mining contract firm after Apartheid collapsed. He bought several unprofitable gold mines and turned them round. His African Rainbow Minerals now has annual sales of $875 million. Today, Patrice Motsepe is South Africa's richest Blackman with a fortune, according to Forbes worth US$2.4 billion.

Whereas a number of people see their secured employment as an opportunity to make a decent living, others see theirs as a stepping-stone to launch their business ventures. As we shall see in this chapter, this is the route many successful African entrepreneurs had followed. Likewise, most people see the loss of their jobs as a failure in life while others see it as an opportunity or a call to move to something greater in life. Successful entrepreneurs assume a strategic perspective in searching for and responding to opportunities – they see and identify business opportunities whenever there is a change in the environment. They have convictions in their abilities; they critically identify and acknowledge their strengths and weaknesses. They also look after possible threats in their environments. For example, Raymond Dokpesi saw the liberalization of the Nigerian broadcasting industry, which allowed private ownership of radio and television stations in the early 1990s as an opportunity. Although there were no established private sector broadcast platform from whose experiences he can draw from, Dokpesi nevertheless took the risk and established DAAR Communications to pioneer radio and television broadcasting in Nigeria. The ban on the importation of frozen fish provides the Ibru Organization to venture into fishing directly.

Willingness to Take Risks

Entrepreneurs are seen as risk-taking individuals who take action to pursue opportunities in situations others may fail to recognize as such, or may even view as problems or threats. The risks that entrepreneurs take in starting and/or operating their own businesses are varied. For our purpose here, four areas that may pose risks for the entrepreneur can be identified:

(i) Financial risk: Entrepreneurs invest their savings and guarantee their bank loans.

(ii) Career risk: Entrepreneurs who fail may find it difficult to find employment afterward.
(iii) Family risk: The entrepreneur's spouse and children may suffer from inattention and the emotional stress of coping with a business failure.
(iv) Psychic risk: The entrepreneur may be identified so closely with a venture that he or she takes business failure as a personal failure.

Some early researchers in the field of entrepreneurship have pointed out that individuals with a high need for achievement also have moderate risk-taking propensities.[11] As pointed out by Robert Hisrich, Michael Peters and Dean Shepherd, in most discussion of entrepreneurship, three types of entrepreneurial behavior are predominant and include: (i) initiative taking, (ii) the organizing and reorganizing of social and economic mechanisms to turn resources and situations to practical account, and (iii) the acceptance of risk or failure.[12] Although the notion of risk-taking is intimately related to entrepreneurial undertaking, most successful entrepreneurs tend to prefer risky situations in which they can exert some control on the outcome in contrast to gambling situations in which the outcome depends on pure luck. In particular, entrepreneurs do not take unnecessary risks; they venture into situations that they can reasonably predict the outcome.

When we say that entrepreneurs are risk takers, what is really meant is that entrepreneurs are those individuals who take calculated risks. Ray Kroc, the founder of McDonald's Inc. exemplifies what we call a risk-taker. For example, in 1967 when economists were predicting a recession in the U.S. economy, most businesses began to plan cutbacks in their investments and constructions. Ray Kroc however, ordered expansion in his business to proceed. Reflecting on that incidence, he wrote: "Hell's bells, when times are bad is when you want to build. Why wait for things to pick up so everything will cost you more. If a location is good enough to buy, we want to build on it right away and be in there before the competition." As for his aptitude for risk-taking: Ray Kroc puts it this way: "You're not going to get it free, and you have to take risks. I don't mean daredevil risks. But you have to take risks, and in some case you must go for broke. If you believe in something, you've got to be in it to the end of your toes. Taking reasonable risk is part of the challenge."

Apathy towards Bureaucracy

The history of successful entrepreneurs is replete with stories of men and women who are allergic to a bureaucratic culture. To them, a bureaucratic culture not only stifles risk-taking, it also hinders innovative ideas and creativity, which are crucial for entrepreneurship. Organizations have cultures that the employees perceive as either inhibitive or enabling in their effort to be innovative. An organization with a bureaucratic culture values formality, rules, standard operating procedures, hierarchical coordination of activities and the maintenance of the status quo. Members of an organization with a bureaucratic culture are made to place value in standardized goods and services. There is no room for individual opportunistic behavior. Employees in a bureaucratic culture see change as a threat rather than opportunity. Consequently, there is no room for creativity. It's no wonder that most innovations come from small entrepreneurial firms and not large organizations.

Entrepreneurs are usually individuals with a sense of vision, mission and optimism. A bureaucratic culture is antithetical to optimism. Robert Noyce, Intel co-founder left his employer to establish Intel because his employing organization failed to provide room for innovative ideas. He said, "Optimism is essential ingredient for innovation. How else can the individual welcome change over security, adventure over staying in safe places." Innovation, Noyce pointed out, "cannot be mandated anymore than a baseball coach can demand that the next batter hit a homerun. He can, however, assemble a good team, encourage his players and play the odds."[13]

CASE IN POINT: STRIVE MASIYIWA[14]

Strive Masiyiwa (aka "Bill Gates of Africa") is a Zimbabwean businessman and cell phone pioneer, founding Econet Wireless. He was born in what was Southern Rhodesia in 1961. He went to High school in Scotland and gained a degree in Electrical and Electronic Engineering (Cum Laude) at the University of Wales. He returned to newly independent Zimbabwe in 1984, where he took a job with the state-owned telephone company. But he grew frustrated with the bureaucracy and formed his own engineering company. He applied for the country's first mobile-phone license yet had to fight all the way to the Supreme Court before he could connect his first subscribers in 1998.

His privately held company, Econet Wireless, generates revenue of more than $300 million a year, making it one of Africa's five largest telecom companies. Econet's operation includes cellular and fixed-line businesses in Zimbabwe, Burundi, Lesotho and Botswana. The company also owns a 3G license in New Zealand. In New Zealand Econet launched that country's third GSM network. He also owns a cellular licence in Kenya and launched the network in that country.

He was also the publisher of the Daily News, Zimbabwe's only independent daily newspaper, shut down by the government in late 2003.

In 2002 he was named to *Time Magazine's Global Business Influentials List*. He is also known as the Bill Gates of Africa, on account of his business and entrepreneurial savvy. He is a workaholic who has bucket loads of guts and passion to achieve his goals notwithstanding anything standing in his way.

Entrepreneurs are rarely slaves to convention. They do not allow themselves to be limited to the traditional way of doing things and they are not afraid to confront the unknown.

Thus, persons with entrepreneurial mindset are more likely to think and act in environments of high uncertainty than the average person. Entrepreneurial organizations that are successful are those that seek and exploit opportunities in dynamic environments that are characterized by rapid, substantial, and discontinuous change. Successful entrepreneurs believe that opportunities rarely come from stable, predictable and tightly controlled bureaucratic environments. Coupled with this apathy to a bureaucratic environment, those with entrepreneurial mindset are individuals with the cognitive ability to recognize opportunities in a dynamic and unpredictable environment.

SOURCES OF BUSINESS IDEAS

The concept of entrepreneurship is intimately related to the idea of innovation as discussed in chapter one. However, to be innovative, prospective entrepreneurs must have reliable and adequate sources of business ideas. The question then becomes: where do entrepreneurs get their business ideas? As we will examine in this section, business ideas can come from five major sources such as experience, existing businesses, changes in demographics and life styles, changes in industry structure, and unfilled niches in the market.

Experience and Goodwill as a Source of Business Idea and Innovation

Entrepreneurial ideas can originate from the experience one gained while working with someone else. The founders of Compaq Computer in Houston, Texas developed their ideas while working for IBM. The founders of Nigeria's *Tell* Magazine developed their ideas while working for *Newswatch* Magazine. Mrs. Modupe Fasusi, the founder and CEO of Human Services Limited, a business and management consulting firm specializing in medium and large-scale firms, got her innovative idea from the experience she gained while working for Unilever Nigeria Limited, Nigerian Industrial Development Bank, and Accenture, among other organizations. Through her experience with these organizations, not only was she able to learn a lot, she was able to create her own network of customers.

In a research conducted in the U.S. concerning the source of business and innovative ideas, nearly half (43 percent of the people responding to the survey) reported that they got their business idea from the experience they gained while working in the same industry or profession.[15] For these entrepreneurs, the move into their own business was not complicated by the task of getting to know who is who and what is in the industry. They know how things operate, and they typically had a network of contacts, which is very important in the start of a new business. The years of being in the industry provided the entrepreneurs insights into unfilled needs and how those needs translated into opportunities for new business.

CASE IN POINT: JAMES MAKAWA AND THE AFRICAN CHANNEL, CAPITALIZING ON EXPERIENCE[16]

Co-founder of The Africa Channel and originally from Zimbabwe, Mr. Makawa is one of the few executives from Sub-Saharan Africa to have enjoyed a successful career in both local and network television in the United States. For more than 10 years, Mr. Makawa worked as a local news reporter and anchor with leading local stations before joining NBC News as a correspondent in New York and Chicago.

Mr. Makawa returned to South Africa and co-founded the African Barter Company (ABC), in partnership with Grey Advertising Worldwide. ABC was the first barter syndication company ever launched in Africa. Mr. Makawa cleared hundreds of hours on TV stations across the continent reaching an audience topping 150 million. In 2000, Mr. Makawa co-founded the African Broadcast Network, a pan African network of television stations with affiliates in 18 countries throughout Sub-Saharan Africa. As ABN's executive vice president for program acquisition and distribution, Mr. Makawa acquired programming from such U.S. program suppliers as NBC, CBS, MGM, Columbia Tri-Star, Endemol and Paramount. During his tenure with the African Broadcast Network, Mr. Makawa also served as a member of the Board.

The importance of industry experience as a source of ideas for new businesses leads to the conclusion that the most promising preparation for an entrepreneur may be a conventional job. In addition to providing the means to discover opportunities upon which to start a business, this approach has the advantage of being much more forgiving of mistakes arising from inexperience. Mistakes are never welcome, even in a well-established business, but they are far more serious for a new business and can threaten its very existence. It should not come as a surprise that those individuals who learned what it takes to succeed while working for somebody else founded many of our most successful business organizations.

The importance of experience is clearly manifested among the brand of successful entrepreneurs in Africa. Among Nigeria's early and pioneer industrialists (Chief T. Odetola, Sanusi Dantata, Isiyaku Rabiu) and second-generation (e.g., Michael Ibru, Chief E. C. Iwuanyanwu, Onwuka Kalu) entrepreneurs, a background in trading from the established foreign-owned trading houses (e.g., UAC, John Holt) was crucial. Many entrepreneurs, according to Tom Forrest, "especially in Igboland, emerge from a background of apprenticeship and trade. As their enterprises have grown so they have raised their level of managerial, organizational and technical experience on the job and employment of expertise from outside."[17]

Getting Ideas from Existing Businesses

The second source of business ideas is about "innovating" on something that is already in the market. As noted in chapter one, some entrepreneurs make use of "creative imitation" as a strategy whereby the entrepreneur does something else that has already been done. In this case, finding a new use for an existing product is another example of innovation. Many entrepreneurs believed that they see someone else trying it, and they figured they could do better. Entrepreneurial firms, as pointed out earlier are those firms that capitalize on opportunities. These opportunities can come from the ability of new firms to add something new to what is offered in the market. This idea is in keeping with the confidence level enjoyed by many entrepreneurs; they feel that their abilities and perseverance will give them the edge to succeed at something that others are already engaged in. Entrepreneurs believe that they can do a better job of serving customers in an existing market by adding something new.

An entrepreneur can succeed by simply innovating on existing businesses through the application of new technology, customer service, quality and marketing innovations. The idea of innovating on an existing concept is far from imitation. Rather, this is an attempt to do something new from an existing product, production process, marketing, distribution, etc. offered by someone else. Many entrepreneurs go into business because of perceived dissatisfaction with something that is currently on the market. Thomas Golisano, the founder of Paychecx Inc. puts it this way" "You don't always have to be the pioneer. You just have to eventually do it better than everyone else." One may decide to start a school and offer a course of study that other schools are not offering (such as the Lagos Business School). Or, a publisher of a newspaper may decide to add something that other news organizations are not providing. For example, we see this in the case of the *Daily Sun* in Nigeria. The newspaper declares itself as "Nigeria's King of the Tabloids" because its existence is based on "capturing the unpredictable and unexpected rhythms of life and existence, the daily heartbeat of humanity in lucid and crisp prose." In essence, The *Daily Sun* is bringing something new into the Nigerian news industry. In each of these examples, the idea is to add something of value to an existing business or concept.

Unfilled Niche in the Consumer Marketplace

Many entrepreneurs have the ability to recognize an opportunity and turn it into a business. In a market-driven economy, customer needs and wants are in the most part created by entrepreneurs themselves who then develop something new and desirable by the customer. A need is created when one is able to find a niche that has been unfulfilled. Before the advent of the word processor, most people seemed to be satisfied using their typing machine but then with the introduction of the PC into the typing business, a need is created for word processing machines. Many entrepreneurs go into their own venture because they have found an unfilled niche in the consumer market place, which gave them the idea to start their business. Satisfying an unfilled niche must not always arise from the introduction of new products into the market entirely. In many cases, available products and services might not be able to satisfy all the needs a product or service can provide. An entrepreneur, being an opportunist, looks for those unsatisfied needs.

CASE IN POINT: HOW IFEANYI MUOKWUE FINDS HIS NICHE[18]

For Ifeanyi Muokwue, the President General of National Association of Nigerian Investors and Innovators, the dwindling fortune of his trading business in the 80s turned out to be his financial breakthrough. It led him into researches whose results are used by over 30 manufacturing industries today. And he is smiling to the bank.

As a trader between 1979 and 1984, Muokwue seemed to be on the right track and making a success of life. But this success did not last as his trading business took a noose dive, propelling him to search for alternatives or be cut out of existence. "When my trading business was going down drastically, I started thinking of what to do, how to do it and where to go. What came into my mind was going into manufacturing but the big question was; 'which area?' I started to research into various raw materials for the manufacturing sector".

Kerosene-Powered Pressing Iron

Today, Muokwue is a happy man in all respect, following the successful results of his painstaking efforts in researches. He has converted the ubiquitous red sand/laterite into a raw material that is used by paint industries. Secondly, the outcome of his research will gladden the hearts of tailors, drycleaners and others who rely on the National Electric Power Authority (NEPA) for power for their electric pressing irons. Muokwue has invented a pressing iron that is powered by kerosine which means that the vagaries of electricity supply will no more affect the businesses of those who hitherto relied on NEPA in this direction. But that is not all. The used vehicle cars tires that are dumped here are precious raw materials for Muokwue. He has been able to convert them to carbon-black that are used by manufacturers of shoe soles, floor mats, dyes, eye pencils, polish, etc.

Those who have known starch to be a by-product of mostly cassava would be surprised to see a synthetic starch on display in shops that was produced not from cassava but from drilling plates. With Muokwue, gum Arabic has become glue. And the synergic effects of his researches are the numerous industries that are making use of the results of their raw materials. According to him "I have created over 30 factories that are making use of the various inventions."

Standardization

He does not go to any scientific or technical laboratories to test his inventions. And this may be unconnected with the politics of standardization in Nigeria. "The markets", he insists, "are the testing grounds" for his products. He pointed out that "A product passes a test when you supply it to the market and it is not returned to you and, instead, more of it is ordered for ... when you supply a product like my carbon black to a company and they tested, used it and found out that it is working and they place order for it. If it is not working they won't buy it, no matter what." Though he has not taken any of his inventions to the Standards Organization of Nigeria for seal of approval and quality, he maintained that "it is the SON's right to come to us and have our products examined and tested as it is a government agency. And we are ready any day any time."

The Banks Are Luring Me

Muokwue claims that over 30 identified factories are making use of his inventions and that is why, today, he is a millionaire who is lured by banks despite starting with a borrowed paltry sum of N350 just to start his business over a decade ago. He pointed out that "if I started with just N350 and today I have lands and properties all over and have published eleven books. If the products are not widely patronized, I wouldn't have been as successful as I am. It is the sales from these products that I sponsor other voluntary works."

Changes in Demographics and Lifestyles

As we noticed in a previous section, social, cultural and demographic changes come with both opportunities and threats. In every way, most nations are much different today than they were two decades ago, and the future promises even greater changes. In every corner of the world, these changes and trends are shaping the way we live, work, produce, and consume. New trends are creating a different type of consumer and, consequently, a need for different products and different services. Changes in population's size, age structure, composition, employment, level of education, and income can create opportunities for innovation. Particularly for individuals with entrepreneurial mindset, these changes have brought along new business opportunities and ideas for innovation.

CASE IN POINT: HOW STEERS FAST FOOD FOUND ITS NICHE IN "WORKING PEOPLE"[19]

Its is not easy for a fast food outfit to join the market in Nigeria and find a foothold in a crowded market that has established names and brands. But Steers Fast Food, one of the rare names in the business in Lagos has been battling effectively with the big names and at last has secured a place for itself.

When the new CEO, Anietie Aoko joined the group after her sojourn abroad, she knew she had a tough task moving the business forward especially with a foreign background as Steers is originally a South African brand name. But the assessment of the CEO is that the business has been breaking new grounds and pulling its weight, while also seeing competition as just a part of life and business success.

"We have our specialty in burgers, beef burgers, chicken burgers, rose and pastries, vegetable salad, chicken salad, fried chicken and chips, jollof rice. We also do cakes, ice cream, bread of different types, meat and fish pies, our interior decorations are quite different from other fast food outlets. As a matter of fact, it has not been easy contending with the influx of customers from morning to late in the late night. I am about to introduce a television advertisement, but there is a particular program that is coming up very soon where Steers will advertise regularly on television and we are hoping that will increase our patronage. Already we have radio jingles that have been on for a very long time now and with our posters and handbills every where, which we have been using to create more awareness and that has helped us tremendously, we also have an internet system were people get to know the latest happening in Steers.

Cornering the working class

"Our targeted customers are the working people, and because it is located around Toyin Street in Ikeja where you have lots of working people who regularly come to have their breakfast and lunch and also so many private schools that parents normally bring their children to, so these groups constitute our real targeted customers. During holidays, children come here for recreation because of the beautiful nature of the place, you know children cannot do without ice cream, burger, chicken and chips and meat pies.

"I will say that our burgers and our lamps chops, all other fast food in Lagos, do chicken and chips, jollof rice, rice and stew, fried rice but we have that uniqueness of doing burgers deliciously. As a matter of fact foreigners come from Victoria Island, Ikoyi and other far distance area to come and eat our special burgers that cannot be found in any fast food in Lagos".

Great potentials

You see in this very place we have the capacity to do so many great things because we have great ideas, but one area of marketing that we have not be able to perfect is breakfast, we serve a very good continental breakfast and I am about to introduce Nigerian breakfast as well, so one is expected to serve breakfast to all the staff in major offices in this environment efficiently. We have the capability to serve up to at least 2,000 (Two thousand) people a day because we have the space and facilities people come, in almost every minute as a matter of fact, there is no idle moment for our staff.

Small and Medium Enterprise (SME) scheme from the bank has been our major financial back-bone in this business and we are still going to use their facilities and the profit we are making to expand our business in the near future, and we have well educated and highly placed people as directors in this business that brought in 60 percent of their money as working capital while the SME provided the remaining 40 per cent and so far both the directors, staff, management and the banks through the SME are well impressed about the general performance.

Tough competition

[The competition is] very competitive indeed, you can see that there are quite a number of fast food outlets, some of them even have up to six or seven outlets, even more than that within Lagos environs, but as I said earlier on, from our unique selling point, no matter where we go, just for the fact that we sell something very different, we have our customers, we have people who are loyal to us, who come here specifically for something different they cannot get anywhere.

As I said, our burgers and ice cream rank among the best in town. I really can't say there is much achieved because if this interview was to be held a month after today, because what I can tell you as the achievements I would have made here, is that I am about to introduce Nigerian food into Steers and you know Nigerians like to eat their own food, although some of them still like changes, so if you have a place where you can offer them varieties of both foreign and Nigerian foods, then you have a strong selling point. Anybody can come in with a crowd of people, those that want to eat foreign food in Nigeria will have it, as long as the taste is very good and in a very decent environment like ours.

As the case of *Steers Fast Food* has shown, an individual with entrepreneurial mindset is able to identify business opportunities wherever there are changes in the population of a society. Although the fast food sector in Nigeria is highly fragmented and overly competitive, Steers Fast Food is able to compete because societal changes has produced more working people and parents who now have their breakfast and lunch close to where they work. Secondly, in order for Steers Fast Food to remain competitive in the niche provided by "working people", the company embarked on a series of innovative practices such as technology (presence in web), creative advertising, and providing customers with "something different they cannot get anywhere."

In a similar manner, Funmilayo Akande started a company called Kids Express to shuttle children and teenagers to private schools, doctor and dental appointments, lessons, and extracurricular activities. With the trend to dual careers, parents are no longer always available to provide personal transportation for their own children and needed such a service. For Ms. Akande, these changes in demographics provided an opportunity. The popularity of *Mr. Biggs'* and other fast food restaurants in the developing countries (such as Ghana and Nigeria) is also due primarily to changing demographics and eating habits among the populace. The growth of the herbal health care industry in Africa mirrors a growing shift towards individual consciousness about obesity and other forms of health problems that can be cured using herbal products.

Changes in Industry or Market Structure

From an historical perspective, first-generation entrepreneurs in Nigeria (and indeed Africa) embraced the opportunities brought about by shift in political power and economic nationalism after independence. The shift in ownership structure created firms in distributorship, licensed buying agencies, government loans, board membership of foreign companies and parastatals, which encouraged patterns of accumulation. An industry emerges when there are changes in an economy. In a similar manner, new businesses are created when there are fundamental shifts in an already existing industry or market structure. Particularly in the developing economies, trade liberalization and deregulation brought forth new markets that were easily exploited by individuals with entrepreneurial insight. The deregulation of the communications industry in many parts of the developing countries, for example, witnessed innovative products and services that were not hitherto provided by the governments of these countries. Changes in the educational sector also brought in innovative educational packages in the form of private educational organizations. Changes in the broadcast industry also witnessed the emergence of private television companies with innovative broadcast ideas. When new governmental policies or regulations are brought to bear on existing industries, opportunities are also presented to those who can detect and capitalize on them. Changes in the global economy must also be seen as providing business ideas and as source of innovation. The expansion of Nigerian banks into African financial markets is an example of how industries react to opportunities in the global economy.

WHY DO PEOPLE CHOOSE TO BE ENTREPRENEURS

There are several reasons why individuals choose to become entrepreneurs. In the world of entrepreneurs, one thing is to have an entrepreneurial mindset (characteristics) and it is entirely a different thing to want to become an entrepreneur (motive). Conversely, although one may want to become an entrepreneur, it is totally a different thing to have what it takes to be one. In other words, we should be able to differentiate entrepreneurial characteristics from entrepreneurial motives. In a global and technologically driven economy characterized by uncertainties, corporate downsizing, business opportunities and a culture of individualism, it is not surprising that many people are always looking for ways to become owners of their own businesses. In this section, we will examine some of the reasons why many people would want to be an entrepreneur. Many terms have been used to describe the reasons why people choose to become entrepreneurs. Some authors term the reasons as the rewards of entrepreneurship, while others term this as the motivation behind entrepreneurship.

The Opportunity to be Self-Employed

Some people want to start their own businesses simply because they find it hard to work for their current employers. This group of would-be business owners or entrepreneurs really wants to be on their own and they want to leave the safety of paid employment to start their own business. Other people would want to start their own businesses because they want the freedom to come and go from the place of work. The implication here is that if you are your own boss, you must understand that you are the first person at work and the last person to leave. Not only must the routine work get done, but also special projects such as repairs, construction, maintenance, or special order, which may demand that you work evenings, weekends, and even holidays.

CASE IN POINT: TAIWO OGUNDE LEFT LEVENTIS GROUP TO ON HIS OWN[20]

Ten years ago, Mr. Taiwo Ogunde left the "certain" world of paid employment, as an engineer, for the "uncertain" terrain of self-employment. Today, he is the chief executive officer of Noble Technologies Limited, Ibadan, where he manufactures freezers and ice-block making machines. His other products include bottle chillers and recreation equipment.

Ogunde told Saturday Sun that his company's foray into the world of recreation equipment was "to make Nigerians learn to relax. The government is trying to promote tourism and we are trying to assist the government." While enumerating the advantages the locally made machines have over imported versions he said they are cheaper and easily maintained since the makers are easily accessible, adding that the only imported component of the machines – electric motors – are easily available on the shelf. According to Ogunde, all plastic parts are made with thermoforming machines used in making plastic parts and this contributes to a cost reduction of up to 50 per cent achieved by the company.

Various organizations and individuals have attested to the high quality of the machines produced by the company. Trans Amusement Park, one of the renowned recreational parks in the country, hosted one of the machines for about three months during Eid-el kabir and Christmas festivals in 2002.

Among the various machines being produced by the company are Rock 'n' Roll, Funky Basket Circle, Dragon Boat, Pony Train, Space Station, Jumping Star, Flying Chair and North Pole, among others. Ogunde who said his company's products were well adapted to the Nigerian climate added that there was built-in protection against voltage fluctuations, outages and power surges. All those attributes, he claimed, are not found in imported products because they were made in a part of the world where power outage, fluctuations and surges are seldom experienced. The materials used in the construction are also treated to withstand corrosion encountered by cooling equipment after being in use for sometime, he said.

Ogunde founded Noble Technologies Limited in 1999, 12 years after graduating from University of Nigeria, Nsukka (UNN) in 1986. He joined the Nigerian Machine Tools (NMT), Osogbo, Osun State in 1989 and got involved in spare parts manufacturing where he had "to examine the parts, take measurements and produce a drawing from the part." He had to leave NMT in 1991 because many of the industries, the clients patronizing NMT, were dying off or at best operating epileptically making him to review plans about his career and future.

From NMT he went over to Leventis Group at its Frigolux plant in Ibadan as the maintenance engineer. He later became the project and design manager, a position in which he faced a lot of challenges and surmounted all. One of these challenges was when he was asked to lead a team of engineers to produce freezers for the use of the Nigerian Bottling Company in Nigerian Stadia, during Nigeria "99, something he successfully did. He credited his training in France and Britain in 1992 when he was to be made the project and design engineer to the success so far achieved. During the training he was exposed to how to make fast freezing ice making machines and many other ones.

As indicated in this case Mr. Taiwo Ogunde left the secured job at Leventis to become his own boss. Most importantly, he has a vision and a mission, which were to make Nigerians learn how to relax. He could not realize this mission while working for someone else. Secondly, he saw the idea of the government in promoting tourism as an opportunity where he could realize his vision and mission.

The Opportunity to Make Money

Many people in today's market-driven economy would like to make a lot of money, and this is a reason why they go into business. Although individuals are *pulled* toward entrepreneurship because of financial incentives, the financial return of any business must compensate its owner for investing his or her personal time (a salary equivalent) and personal savings (an interest and/or dividend equivalent) in the business before any reasonable profits are realized. Maybe one found him or herself working so hard for someone else and not making the money that he or she thinks is financially worthwhile. That person would like to start a business earning what he or she thinks is the worth of the "sacrifice". There are those would-be entrepreneurs who possess an extremely strong interest in financial rewards. For this group, this drive for profit continues to motivate entrepreneurs even after they achieve their original profit goals. That is why we see some entrepreneurs floating their "successful" business in the stock market. However, there are also those for whom profits are primarily a way of "keeping score." Such entrepreneurs may spend their profit on themselves or give it away, although most of them are not satisfied unless they make a "reasonable" profit. Indeed, some profit is necessary for survival because a firm that continues to lose money eventually becomes insolvent.

The Opportunity to be Innovative, Creative and Find Self-expression

The idea that one can do a better job, do it faster, or cheaper, or improve, enhance, modify, or find a way to be more efficient and effective is often the stimulus that leads some people to the eventual launching of a new venture. A state of dissatisfaction in a person's current job often results in a decision to launch a new venture. Many would-be entrepreneurs know their creative and innovative potentials and they have found out that working for someone or being trapped in a bureaucratic organization inhibits their creative talents and potentials. Overtime, these people become frustrated in doing what they are asked to do by their employing organizations without actually moving out of the box. The only outlet for such people is to establish their own ventures where they can fully tap into their potentials. This is valid as long as the prospective entrepreneur does not get lost in this creativity syndrome to the exclusion of such mundane things as paperwork and management. Although the marketplace rewards creativity, the ability to manage and market an entrepreneur's innovation and new creation is crucial to the success of the business that has been established. Lavern S. Urlacher suggests, "Free enterprise is constantly looking for the proverbial better mouse trap."[21] A unique product or service that is difficult to duplicate can leave a business in a niche by itself. If cash inflow is adequate and expenses are controlled, this type of business has a good chance of success. The key to success here is often the implementation of good management practices, which entails some degree of discipline and the maintenance of good records.

The Opportunity to be in Control in Making Decisions

Related to the above discussion is the desire to be independent, to be in control and the ability to make your own decisions. We know that the world over, *independence* has become a fashionable term that encompasses nearly all spheres of life. Most people would agree that the exercise of ones' independence comes from his or work life. We also know that some of our problems arise from frustrations in the workplace. For some of us, this frustration leads us to look for avenues in which we can be independent, that is, having control of our own lives. But one must also remember that all small business owners must be responsible for the decision-making, whether they enjoy it or not.

The need to be independent must also be balanced with a preparedness to take responsibilities. The entrepreneur will be held responsible even if he or she fails to make decisions. Failure to make decision or act on critical information can be the worst decision of all. The desire to own a business for purpose of controlling your own responsibility and making your decisions can be a valid reason if the desire stems from dissatisfaction of the way your employers or the marketplace are currently meeting a need. This may also inspire a sense of personal confidence that you can do a better job. If your skills, training, and experience exceed your current level of responsibilities, you may be ready to the entrepreneurial way alone. Success will depend on how well you really are equipped to handle those responsibilities, as well as your response to the many variables over which you have no control.

Preparing for Retirement and Part-Time Entrepreneurs

Another factor that pushes people towards establishing their own businesses is the decision about what to do when one reaches the age of retirement. Another reason is to try ones business idea while enjoying the safety of being employed. There are those employees who have reached their retirement age and still believe that they have something left in them to give to society irrespective of how the society defines their competency according to their age. Thus some people choose to run a business as a way to prepare for their ultimate retirement, not the one prescribed by their employers, and not just in the sense of having something to occupy their time, but in the sense of preparing financially for retirement. Some members of this group tend to run their businesses on a part-time basis, such as teaching in a university as part-time lecturers while others establish their own schools as a place where they can make use of their teaching talents after their retirement. In the medical field, it's not uncommon to see fully employed medical doctors operating their own clinics in preparation for retirement.

Starting a part-time business has become a popular gateway to entrepreneurship as part-time entrepreneurs can have the best of both worlds.[22] Part-time entrepreneurs can ease into business for themselves without sacrificing the security of a steady paycheck and employment benefits. A major advantage of going into business part-time is the lower risk in case the venture flops. Many part-time business owners are "testing the entrepreneurial waters" to see whether their business ideas are feasible and whether they enjoy being self-employed. As they grow, many part-time enterprises absorb more of the entrepreneur's resources until they become full-time businesses.

The Opportunity to Achieve a Satisfying Way of life

Many entrepreneurs frequently speak of the personal satisfaction they experience in managing their own businesses. Some even refer to their businesses as "fun." Part of the enjoyment may derive from the need for independence described above, but some of it also apparently comes from the peculiar nature of the business, the entrepreneur's role in the business, the entrepreneur's opportunities to be of service, and what the entrepreneur gets as part of his or her hobby or recreational activity while satisfying his or her most important life desire and earning some money doing it. Thus some people, such as hobbyists, go into a business, which involves a product or service that has a special interest for them. In some type of businesses, especially those owned by retirees, owner-managers find that they can devote more attention to home and family obligations. Occasionally, couples are able to share business responsibilities and to enjoy spending time together at work as well as at home.

Although such arrangements may also involve family conflict, many successful family endeavors - such as the joint operation of a school, an Internet café shop or a restaurant are not uncommon.

CASE IN POINT: WHEN BIODUN LEFT BANKING FOR ART, PEOPLE THOUGHT HE WAS MAD[23]

A pastime, which once put a rascally boy into trouble, has today brought him fame and success. Biodun Omolayo was so taken by art, from childhood that he once drew a caricature of his head-teacher at St. Andrew's Primary School, Owo, Ondo State and landed in a fix. For his naughtiness, the teacher asked him to buy a pack of chalk for every class in the school. While in primary 6, Omolayo, in Ibadan with his uncle, did the unthinkable at Agbowo villa, near a railway line. It was a new building. On the wet cement, the boy used charcoal to sketch images. "I was seeing people riding horses and everything. I just kept tracing. Before I knew it, the whole wall was covered with drawings", he recalled. When he was arrested by the workman and accused of "destroying" the building, the boy looked lost. To him, he saw images and traced. Today, the zeal for art and the inspiration have not left him. Although he tried to dump his first love, the goddess of arts keeps following him about. Eventually, he had to abandon his managerial seat in top ranking bank to return to art.

Divine Arrangement
"Before, I used to say it was by accident that I went into banking. But now I knew better. I call it divine arrangement. Banking would have been the last profession I would have loved to go into. I remember an experience, when I was in Ibadan Polytechnic, doing my A'level GCE. There was a bank on campus. Once, robbers came there and were shooting. They held the bank manager and customers hostage. When I looked into the bank, I said"
"Jesus! These people are really going through a lot of risk. I will never work in a bank." My love had always been art and when I went to the university I was given admission to study Fine Art. We were supposed to be the pioneer students at the University of Ilorin. When we got there in 1983 we were told the programme could not take off. The option was either you won't get admission or you come for Performing. So Professor Zulu Sofola, very wonderful woman, called me and said, 'look you came to study Fine Art, that the programme has not taken off. I will advice you to come in for Performing Art, by the time you move in, you'll realize that the line of demarcation is very thin. There are some things you even do together'". Eventually, he took the Prof's advice and has not regretted it once.

Enters Banking
Omolayo never had banking training. He just saw an advert inviting fresh graduates for interview and applied. At the interview, when he was asked what an artist was looking for in banking, he told the panel that the world was a stage for every person to perform his best. Somehow, he got the job – as a banking officer. Then, he tasked himself, buying all the banking and economics books he could come by. When he resumed, he understudied the experts without them knowing. Soon, no one believed he had not studied banking in school. After a brilliant career that took him through FSB International Bank, North/South Bank and New Prudential Mortgage Finance, Omolayo, like the chicken, returned home to roost. Tired of petty jealousy and boardroom politics, he just quit one day. And almost everyone thought he was mad, except his wife and uncle.

Encouraged
"My uncle was the only one that encouraged me and said look if this is what you want to do you have to be focused, you don't have to look back. It's going to be tough initially but if you insist this is what you want, plan your life the way you want to do it. Others said, 'this guy is crazy or something is wrong.' Some even said, 'you can be doing business and still stay in the banking business.' At that point, I wasn't thinking the way they were thinking. The way I was thinking was, I'm tired of this thing. Let me just go to this (art) area." He left and formed Specifics Ventures Limited in 1992, devoted to visual arts, interior decorations and designs.

Bank Influence
But what are the things he learnt in the banking industry that has influenced his work now as an artist?

"How to do my business. You see, so many people are into business and don't even keep record. But you have to be accountable even to yourself. Because one day some people will want to look at books and records. How have you been performing? Like now, if you are a small-scale industry you want to go to the bank and say I need facilities. They would ask how you've been running your cash flow. Let's see how you have been carrying your money. And again, in marketing there is what we call packaging. And that packaging is not just the product; you don't package just the product. You could package yourself – looking good and dressing well.

Now, I'm able to enter some offices without intimidation. If I walk into any bank, you would have taken for granted maybe this guy is from another bank or whatever and I will have free access to get in there. And by the time I get in there what I want to discuss is artwork, painting and whatever. Some of them will be surprised. Then the next question is, are you the one painting them? Are you sure you are the one painting them? I have that access, because of what I have learned in the banking industry. That is, to comport yourself, package yourself and dress very well. And then, even how to manage money is part of it. Because if I have any fund I don't see it as mine, it is the business fund. Like I'm here, I pay myself salary; I don't just spend money anyhow. I went through a lot of training even in management. Like now, every Monday we have a meeting to draw the programme for the week, set the target for everybody. Customer service is part of what I learnt in the banking industry. It is very, very important. If you don't know how to service your customer very well, you will lose that customer. And I have been imparting that knowledge.

Networking
Another thing Omolayo learnt in banking is what he calls networking. "The people I knew in the banking, some are still there. So today, if I just get to a place, I will just realize that I know about two or three people there. Today in Citizens International Bank, if you go to their head office you'll see my paintings there. I have done some work for Intercontinental Bank on Toyin Street. I handled their calendar, twice. In Kaduna branch, I have my paintings there. Idumota, Apapa, I have my paintings there. Because when I get to that area I feel very comfortable, I don't feel intimidated by anybody.

A focused Entrepreneur
Omolayo says he's much focused. And to enhance his success, he enrolled at Yaba College of Technology to study Fine Art (his pet dream), Design, Graphics, Printing and Publishing. "My going to Yaba Tech to do that programme was part of the plans I set for myself. Look if you want to make it in this area, you need to go to school. Go back to school and study the thing you loved so much so that if you were talking tomorrow, they wouldn't say you don't know what you are saying. You need a corporate cover. You need a body, where they can locate you; oh! He finished from here. That was why I went to finish that programme. It's part of the success story. I'm successful as far as that one is concerned. I said I want to set up something of my own. I want to turn this business into a kind of outfit that even other artists could come and know that this is how a business should be done. Not just because I'm an artist I just paint and sit out there leaving everything like that. I want to do it like a business, comfort myself, do the right way I'm supposed to do. Even, provide job for other people who are not even artists. And it's happening now. So, I think I'm successful and I'm happy. Being successful means you are happy with what you are doing or with yourself.

The Opportunity to Give Back to Society

Although it may be true that financial reward is one of the motivating factors pushing people toward entrepreneurship, there is apple evidence that for most successful entrepreneurs, going into business has nothing to with being rich financially. There is something very intriguing about entrepreneurs who are successful and that's their need to give back to society and their devotion to the community. For these individuals, setting up a business and making a lot of money is not their ultimate vision. Rather, they have the belief that money is a tool to be used for the common good. The need to give back to society is exemplified in the person of Andrew Carnegie, the founder of Carnegie Steel Co. and the man who revolutionized the steel industry. Although, he is well known for his innovative ideas and for what he has built, he was also known for what he has given away to society. Carnegie believed that the wealthy had a moral obligation to act as stewards for society. "The man who dies rich dies disgraced," he said.

The Need to Succeed Against all Odds and a Passion for "Revenge"

Many successful entrepreneurs are driven by a passion for revenge. Coupled with the need for revenge is the need to turn adversaries into strengths. Sometimes many successful entrepreneurs take their business as a personal crusade to right some thing they perceived as evil; they see it as a way of proving something to society.

Sam Walton talked about his nightmare when he was forced out of business in 1950 as a result of his landlord's refusal to renew his five-year lease. At the time, Walton had just spent five years turning the first store from a dying money-loser into the most profitable store in the region. His landlord wanted to give the now-thriving business to his son and Walton had no where else to move the store. So he sold it. He wrote that he "had to pick myself up and get on with it, do it all over again, only even better this time". In 1969, Sam Walton opened a Wal-Mart store close to the same spot where the first stayed was located and was run by his former landlord's son. He competed with it and while the Wal-Mart store thrived, the store run by the son of his landlord went out of business.

When Ray Kroc, the founder of McDonald's had a problem with his partner, buying him out put a severe strain on his company's resources. Rather than get irritated by it, Kroc chose to look on the upside. He later wrote "Perhaps without that adversity I might not have been able to persevere later on when my financial burdens were redoubled. I learned then how to keep problems from crushing me."

CASE IN POINT: BANK OF AMERICA'S A. P. GIANNINI: HIS FOCUS ON ORDNARY PEOPLE HELPED BUILD A FINANCIAL GOLIATH[24]

Amadeo Peter Giannini (1870-1949) knew what it was to be a workingman, to get up early every morning and come home late at night, bone-weary. The problem: None of his fellow board members at Columbus Savings & Loan in San Francisco did. He joined the board in 1902 but soon found himself at loggerheads with the other directors. As a one-time laborer, Giannini wanted the savings and loan to market services for ordinary people who were struggling to make something of their lives. He saw an untapped market. The other directors, however, were more concerned with the carriage trade, the traditional and almost exclusive market for banks. After two years of struggling to have his views heard, Giannini decided he couldn't take it anymore and resigned.

"I'll start my own bank," he declared.

He set up a shop almost immediately. His determination led to the Bank of Italy, later the Bank of America, which at one time was the largest bank in the world.

"It's no use ... to decide what's going to happen unless you have the courage of your convictions, he said. "Many a brilliant idea has been lost because the man who dreamed it lacked the spunk or the spine to put it across. It doesn't matter if you don't always hit the exact bull's-eye. The other rings in the targets score points, too," he wrote.

Giannini was born in San Jose, California, the son of immigrants from Genoa, Italy. When Amadeo was 7, his father died. His mother remarried, and the family moved to San Francisco.

Amadeo was 12 years old when he went to work in his stepfather's produce business. He had to rise in the wee hours of the morning, well before school, and go to the San Francisco docks to await shipments. It was far from wasted time, though. He used the time he waited to think about his future and how he wanted to approach it. Even at this young age, Giannini was already developing what was to become the prevailing philosophy of his business life.

"I decided that a man who wants to reach the top must keep his record clear. He cannot do anything of which he is ashamed or that might bob up at some future time to embarrass him. I also concluded that you had to set up a mark to shoot at. Decide what you want – and then go after it, hammer and tongs," he wrote.

Although a quick learner, Giannini quit school at 14 to work full time for his stepfather. He understood that to learn the ways of business, he needed to get firsthand experience he wasn't getting in the classroom. Soon he was traveling up and down the California coast meeting with farmers. Although young, he knew to succeed he had to be straightforward with them or they wouldn't deal with him. He offered honest deals, good prices and respectful treatment, and he stood by his word.

His reputation – and the company's business – grew. His stepfather made him a full partner by the time he was 19. Just a dozen years later, the business had grown enough that Giannini sold his interest to employees with the intention of retiring. However, the following year he joined the board of Columbus Savings and Loan. When he decided to start his own bank, Giannini borrowed US$150,000 from his stepfather and 10 friends and opened the first branch of the Bank of Italy. It occupied a converted saloon across the street from Columbus Savings. He didn't think of problems that sprang up as barriers. He looked at them as inspirations that spurred him on.

"I thrive on obstacles, "he said in 1923, "particularly obstacles placed in my way by narrow-gauged competitors and their political friend."

From the beginning, Giannini showed a willingness to defy conventional wisdom. While banks at the time considered it unethical to solicit business, Giannini went door-to-door to convince prospective depositors of the soundness of his venture.

For Giannini, doing good was good for business and he developed a passion for giving back to society, perhaps as a way of waging personal crusade to help society with his wealth. After the 1906 San Francisco earthquake and the fire, Giannini discovered his call.

"At the time of the fire, I was trying to make money for myself. But the fire cured me of that," he said.

He made it his life mission to use the power of banking to help others. In 1921 he opened a women's banking department. Though the prevailing wisdom in the industry was "Never loan money on anything that eats," he helped finance California's dairy, sheep and beef industries. Under his leadership, the institution became the state's largest agricultural lender.

The need to succeed against all odds is typical among entrepreneurs who are of the minority group or are severely disadvantaged as a result of their ethnic or gender backgrounds. For instance, the growth of women entrepreneurs can be traced to women's attempt to break the "glass ceiling" that prevents them from rising to the top of many organizations. Like women, minorities cite discrimination and access to decent paying jobs as the principal reasons for going into their own businesses.

Johnson H. Johnson, the founder of Johnson Publishing Co. and *Ebony* magazine, wrote in his autobiography *Succeeding Against the Odds*, "Because my mother made such great sacrifices for me, I didn't just want to succeed for my self. I wanted to succeed for her." Although Johnson had to overcome severe racial and economic barriers to achieve success, he said he found "there are some advantages to disadvantages." Being poor, he said, made me run scared. It made vow never to go back to welfare, never to go back to poverty. It drives me even today. Some days when I don't feel like getting up, all I have to think about is welfare and humiliation, and I get up early and rush to work."[25]

In a similar manner, Oprah's entrepreneurial drive is informed by her desire to make sure that what has happened to her in her teenage life does not happen to any child and she summed this up in her declared mission:

> "A part of my mission in life now is to encourage every other child who has been abused to tell. You tell, and if they don't believe you, you keep telling. You tell everybody until somebody listens to you…I don't want another child to be afraid of saying, 'This is what happened to me'."[26]

CASE IN POINT: DETERMINATION TO SURVIVE LED TO A BUSINESS IN PAINTING[27]

At 26, Ogechika Mildness Nwosu has seen the turmoil of life, starting from her family to her school days and beyond. But the one which seemed to have pushed her to take the extreme decision of choosing house painting and welding - rare occupations for women - was her encounter with her immediate boss in a company, where she was denied confirmation from a casual worker to permanent staff because she refused to "use what she has (her body) to get what she wanted."

This led to her resignation from the job. But to keep body and soul together, Mildness decided to take the bull by the horns to equip herself with the necessary skills not minding whether they are masculine. She chose to become a house painter cum welder, perhaps, to use her skills to get what she wants rather than her body.

In this interview, Miss Nwosu told Daily Sun how hard life has been for a lady who is determined to survive without falling prey to bosses with amorous intentions.

Background
I am Ogechika Mildness Nwosu. I was born some 26 years ago to the family of Mr. Josiah Nwosu from Oboro, Ikwuano Local Government Area in Abia State. I am the last child in the family of two boys and four girls. I was born when my parents were already old. In fact, according to them, they never expected me, but I came after all. And that was why my mother fondly called me, Agaezichiheogeme, meaning 'would one tell God what to do?'

Education
Although the family was not so rich, my mother struggled to ensure we got the basic education. But despite her efforts, none of my elder sisters completed primary education;

rather they preferred getting married. I am the only person that completed secondary education in the family, and that was in 2000 at St. Gabriel's Catholic School, Mokola, Ibadan in Oyo State. After the secondary education, I secured admission into University of Benin to read Psychology.

Problems

My elder brothers and sisters did not support my university education. They felt I would lord it over them if I became a graduate. For this reason, they refused to assist me in completing my admission requirements. They even convinced our father to stop assisting me and asked him to persuade me to get married. My father listened to them, seized all my documents and frustrated me out of the university.

In dismay, I left my family in Ibadan and moved to Lagos to stay with an auntie (name withheld) who is my mother's sister. She promised to send me back to school after settling my problem with my family. But instead of keeping her words, I realized that all she needed from me was to become her house girl. She did not talk of sending me to school again, but would rather tell me that I would serve in the house of God. What she meant by that, I could not discern.

My relationship with her later went sour when my mother fell sick in Ibadan and I needed to see her. I asked her for some money to buy one or two things for my mother, but she failed to oblige. But I managed to travel to Ibadan to see my mum.

Search for survival

When I returned to Lagos, I felt it wise to look for something to do to overcome poverty. So, I started searching for a job. I heard of an auditioning being organized by Zeb Ejiro Production for a home video, and I went to meet him. I did not succeed in picking a role in the production but Ejiro offered me a job as his office assistant. That development gave me the opportunity to participate in other auditions both in Ejiro's company and in other film organizations. I succeed in getting a role in Royal Tears, a soap opera written by Pius Okugbere and produced by Black Gold Productions. I played the role of a goddess there. I also participated in Face in the Mirror, a home video where I played the role of a waitress.

Why I left the movie industry

I love acting but could not cope with one of its demands. I found out the industry is too corrupt for my liking. I had discovered in some cases, I scaled through in the auditioning but was not allowed to take part in the production at the end of the day. And anytime I raised eyebrows, the producer or the director would tell me 'you have not paid your dues.'

It was easy for me to pick a role in Royal Tears because the producer is a devoted Christian who respects his personality. And my success in Face in the Mirror came because the producer's wife was a part of the business and would follow the crew to every location. So, she never gave her husband any chance to mess around. But for other producers that came my way, I failed, mainly because I refused to pay their said 'dues'. When the pressure was becoming too much for me and I discovered that I could not cope with the amorous demands of most producers, I left the industry.

Stint with Julius Berger
After the movie industry, I joined Julius Berger Construction Company as a clinic assistant, a job I did for a while before I joined another company for a better pay. I started as a casual worker on the ground that after a brief period of probation I would be converted to a permanent staff. But after working for some months without getting the confirmation, and when I noticed that all my mates in the company had gotten their confirmation/conversion letters, I asked my immediate boss one day why my case was different. And he said to me, "why are you behaving like a kid? You should know the right thing to do, you better use what you have to get what you want… It would only cost you offering me a timeout and the next day you will cease from being a casual worker."

On hearing this trash, I went home weeping and I never went back there. I was at home for a while thinking of what to do as there was no help from anywhere. I was forced to look for another job, and my search took me to many building construction sites in Lagos. I did menial jobs like helping builders with blocks, water, sand and cement. It was while on this job that a passionate bricklayer, who admired my courage, introduced me to Canada site at Odogunyo, in the outskirts of Lagos where a bigger construction was going on then. That was 2002.

The vision
At Canada site, I also worked as a laborer, but I developed interest in house painting and welding work after watching the workers. The site was a complex one, which exposed me to many fields in building construction. And when the contractor in charge of the place noticed my interest, he opted to help me realize my dreams. He took me as an apprentice in his company – Shola Steel Fabrication Company Ltd at Iyase Street, Ketu, Lagos. It was there I learnt the art of house painting and welding. I graduated as an iron erector/painter. I can now paint any type of building, no matter the height. I can as well work comfortably in any construction site, erecting iron and welding them properly. I can do such work on church buildings, factories, private buildings and perhaps bridges.

Expertise
When I see any house or object to be painted, I can help the client by suggesting the suitable/matching colors for the building. This suggestion may be based on the weather condition of the area where the house is located as well as the dominant color in the area. But in all, the ultimate choice lies with the client. I can as well, after taking the measurement of the building, tell you the number of tins of paints the whole building will consume. I equally assist my clients in buying the required paints to avoid imitation and half-measures. For special colors, I can mix different colors of paints to get secondary and tertiary colors based on the need at hand. This I do when the needed color is not in the market.

How hard is the way?
Being a painter or an erector/welder is not hard, though it depends on how you see it. There is no means of survival that is a bed of roses. Even those we call women of easy virtue are exposed to great risks and dangers. To cut the story short, I chose to be a

painter/welder because I want to survive and make a living myself. I don't want to remain a burden to anybody. I know there are other ways of survival which may seem easier, but I wouldn't want to mess around with people who would want to go to bed with me before I could get favor from them. Although no where is totally free from such an evil because some people compromise. Even some of those who would want to offer you jobs may still want to toast you, but I think I am very free with my job. I have my skills and expertise, which no body can take away from me except God. So, if any man calls me for a job and begins to talk cock and bull stories, I simply leave him and go my way. But I must tell you, I am very much free with my job.

Rich?
(Smiles) I am comfortable. I have my handset to receive phone calls from prospective clients who will make me rich. I maintain my comfortable apartment and I know that my dream car is still cooling its engine at the factory, (laughter).

Relationship
Still single and searching for Mr. Right, though not in a hurry. The truth is that I love to carry children, and I would love to carry my own children. O yes! Some men may be scared because of my kind of job, but I believe that the scared man is not my better half. When my man comes, he will love me for who I am. He will cherish my work.

Ambition
To establish a reputable company that will handle any kind of construction work, especially in iron construction and painting. And to settle down with my family at the right time.

For many entrepreneurs, adversity teaches them a great deal about survival skills. Being free from fear of failure seems to be a great motivating factor for entrepreneurial success. The case of Ms. Mildness Nwosu illustrates this point clearly. It also shows that the need for survival as an entrepreneur is prevalent across cultures. Whether we are talking about how Oprah Winfrey turned adversity into opportunity, how Johnson built Johnson and Johnson out fear of being pushed into a welfare system or how Ms. Nwosu found her painting business for fear of being used by unscrupulous male bosses, many successful entrepreneurs found their businesses out of the need to survive a difficult situation.

Other Precipitating Events

Benjamin Disraeli (British Prime minister, 1868 and 1874-1880) once pointed out that "Man is not the creature of circumstances. Circumstances are the creatures of men." Sometimes this statement can apply to entrepreneurs who respond to circumstances in their environment. Many potential entrepreneurs never take the fateful step of launching their own business ventures. Rather, situations, sometimes beyond their control, forced them to become entrepreneurs. Precipitating events such as job termination or unexpected opportunities stimulate some of those who actually make the move. Getting fired is only one of many types of unforeseen circumstances which may serve as a catalyst in "taking the plunge" as an entrepreneur. Divorce may force a hitherto fulltime housewife into making use of her experience (such as child caring) by setting up a daycare center. A relative may suggest that an individual leaves a salaried position and take over a family business or other small firm. For example, Medina Salawudeen, the founder and managing director of *Medaaz Nigeria Limited*, a yogurt-producing firm, started the business with only N1,000 as start-up capital in 1996, and today the business is worth N40 million. The precipitating event that led her to start the business was job termination: Faced with a job loss at Nigeria Printing and Minting Company Limited, NPMCL, in 1996 because she was married to a co-employee, Salawudeen decided to venture into entrepreneurship. In line with her resolve, she began trying her hands on local yogurt production.[28]

CASE IN POINT: MOBOLAJI STARTED CARD MAKING AS A RESULT OF POVERTY. NOW HE EMPLOYS GRADUATES[29]

A school dropout who ventured into card making out of necessity just to keep body and soul together is now an employer of labor including graduates and undergraduates alike.

Mobolaji Samuel Idowu, a 31-year-old says the economic situation in the country made him to go into the genre of arts called painting, though he intended to further his school certificate program.

"The economic situation of the country made me to go into art, but I still have plans to go back to school for a university degree. I had plans to study Economics because I wanted to be a banker."

How I started
The Osun State born artist disclosed that he discovered he had the talent very early in life and was able to practice it while in secondary school. "I knew I had this talent of card painting in me, and I went into it in secondary school, then I used to do cards for my friends and they would ask me how I knew the art of card making. I always told them it was a talent. But what really made me to go into it full time was hardship. There was no money to further my education, but I have never for one day learnt how to make cards and nor any formal training on card making. It is just a talent and inspiration from God. The designs I used in my cards come as a vision to me, it could be while I am eating or taking my bath. It would keep coming until I design the cards."

How Expensive
It depends on the type of card the customer wants, we have different kinds of cards, and some are as cheap as N50. If customer approaches me for cards, I have an album I show to them and they choose from them. There are some I have to carve out names from wood and scan pictures; some I use velvet or cardboard papers, depending on the amount the person is paying. I also make banners for churches and tutorial houses".

It pays my bills
Idowu revealed that he made a lot of money from his chosen profession and could pay salaries of graduates if he so wishes. "Being an artist has helped me a lot, even some degree holders cannot make as much as I am making from it in a month or week. The demand is so high that some times I have to sleep in the office to satisfy my customers. Card making is seasonal, demand of cards are high anytime there is a festival in town. I have more than 15 boys working for me. 10 of them are undergraduates of University of Lagos, Delta State University and University of Benin.

Mobolaji's case indicates that circumstances can bring out the entrepreneurial spirit in you. Poverty is one of those circumstances.

THE DRAWBACKS OF BECOMING AN ENTREPRENEUR

Each year thousands of new businesses are born. Each new business owner has a dream that his or her idea will work out and that all dreams will come true. As we noticed in the foregoing discussions, people start businesses for many different reasons. However, there are numerous stories and publications regarding failure rates in entrepreneurship. Going into business is not all bed of roses; there are challenges, disadvantages and several drawbacks. For the prospective entrepreneur, it is important that the motivation to start a business stems from the right reasons and that the wrong reasons can be identified and avoided. The following are some of the drawbacks that an entrepreneur can encounter.

Loss of Freedom

If having free time is the reason for having a business, the prospective business owner must think twice. Having your own free time as the reason for owing your own business is not probably the best choice for those prospective business owners and entrepreneurs. As an entrepreneur, there is no free time and one of the reasons for business failure is that many entrepreneurs are not willing to work hard enough. When you have your own business, you are probably (and most likely) the first person at work and the last person to leave. Not only must the routine work get done, but also special projects such as repairs, construction, maintenance, or special order, which may demand that you work evenings, weekends, and even holidays. Consequently, one of the drawbacks of entrepreneurship is the possible loss of your freedom. As pointed out in a preceding section, the need to be free must also be accompanied by the readiness to take responsibility for the business decisions and actions.

Loss of Independence

Related to the above issue is your possible loss of independence as soon as you are on your own. For some people, one of the reasons for going into business is the need for independence. Some say that they want to be their own boss because they find it difficult to work for someone else. But the reality is that going into your own business venture may actually cause you some of your independence and many persons will become your boss. As the owner of your own business, you will be forced to work with various groups of people, including those you do not like. Not only that your customers will be your boss, so too will your suppliers, distributors, banker and/or other creditors. You will sacrifice your independence or freedom at the altar of customer satisfaction. In fact, you have no freedom because you are at the mercy of so many people trying to get a piece of your service such as customers, suppliers, the regulatory agencies, the labor union, and even your competitors. In management, we call these groups your stakeholders. These stakeholders have a stake in your company; they are your bosses. If you fail to satisfy customers, your revenue source will dry up. You must deal with employees if you have any. You must deal with governmental agencies and many others. Under these conditions, the idea of you becoming your own boss becomes an illusion.

Financial Constraints

Another drawback of becoming an entrepreneur is the problem and challenges associated with financial constrains. Not everyone who becomes an entrepreneur instantly becomes a millionaire. The reality is that the fortune of many successful entrepreneurs such as Bill Gates, Michael Dell, Oprah Winfrey, Aliko Dangote, Michael Adenuga and Michael Ibru of Nigeria does not reflect the myth of instant riches commonly ascribed to entrepreneurs. Going into business because you want to be a millionaire can actually become the wrong motive especially during the initial years. If you have your money and you want to make more money, think seriously about the reasons for going into business discussed in the preceding section. To be rich in financial terms, there are easier ways to make money than starting a business. For example, you can put your money in the stock market, long-term, and watch it grow as you relax. This does not mean that you cannot become a millionaire by becoming an entrepreneur. To go into business just to make money is not something customers will accept. As the owner, you must remember that you are not only the last one to go home at night but is usually the last one to get paid. Everybody else demands to get paid first. While you were employed, your monthly salary is guaranteed and secured. As a small business owner just starting, there is a high degree of uncertainty in your finances and your earnings. In other words, you will be faced with financial constraints.

Some have even pointed out that making a great deal of money in the initial years of venturing into a business does not augur well for the growth of the business as an entrepreneurial firm. Steve Case, the founder of AOL, the online empire struggled financially in the initial years before making the company a success. Referring to the innovative ideas that drove AOL to success, Frank Caufield, a venture capitalist, noted "Steve had the advantage of not having any money, so there were a lot of innovative approaches."[30]

One important thing to remember here is that most people who own their own business do so for more than just monetary gain. They are looking for personal satisfaction. They may serve a community need, do something they like, or enjoy the personal independence of being an entrepreneur. As a prospective entrepreneur, one must have knowledge of the financial constraints especially during the early stage of launching the business.

THE DISCOURSE ON ENTREPRENEURSHIP AND THE AFRICAN ENTREPRENEUR

What then has the discourse on entrepreneurship got to say about the African entrepreneur? Over the years, entrepreneurship in Sub-Saharan Africa has received increased attention both in research and in practice. Studies have covered areas such as the contexts of entrepreneurship as it relates to Africa. On the other hand, there are numerous studies that have examined the micro aspect of the subject of entrepreneurship in Sub-Saharan Africa, focusing on issues such as the personality characteristics and motives of the African entrepreneur. In this section, the discussion will be on the micro issues – examining what the existing research says about the characteristics of the African entrepreneur. We shall leave the contextual side for the chapters that follow.

The research on entrepreneurship in Sub-Saharan Africa has linked several personality traits or characteristics of entrepreneurs to entrepreneurial success in Africa.[31] As in the discourse generally, debate continues as to whether psychological variables, socio-demographic factors or external factors are the best determinants of entrepreneurial behavior and performance in Sub-Saharan Africa.[32] For example, Samuel Buame observed that in Ghana, individual characteristics are not sufficient to explain the nature of entrepreneurial success or failure. In particular, the researcher calls attention to the importance of institutional factors (context) in explaining entrepreneurial behavior.[33] Keyser and associates, however, have shown empirically that "psychological factors may be more important than socio-demographic ones."[34] LeVine used McClelland's need for achievement theory to differentiate the various Nigerian ethnic groups in terms of their entrepreneurial effectiveness. Consistent with historical experiences, achievement scores were highest for the Ibo, lowest for the Hausa, with the Yoruba being in between.[35]

Perhaps the strongest empirical evidence in support of the efficacy of individual traits as predictors of entrepreneurial success comes from the Giessen-Amsterdam studies by Frese and his associates. In a series of studies of five African countries (Tanzania, Uganda, Zambia, Zimbabwe, and South Africa), the researchers concluded that psychological variables such as personal initiative, innovativeness, entrepreneurial orientation, and autonomy differentiated successful from less successful entrepreneurs. The central argument of these studies is that the actions of the entrepreneur, influenced by his or her personal attributes, explain differences in reaction to the environment. The conclusion of these studies is that psychological variables are important predictors of micro business firms.[36]

The problem of high failure rates among small-scale firms in Sub-Saharan Africa has also been given increased attention in the extant research on African entrepreneurship. First, it recognized that most of the small firms in Sub-Saharan Africa are located in the informal sector dominated by commerce (trading, vendors). Because of the dominance of informal activities, productivity and the capacity to innovate, to introduce new technology, and to manage strategically are not forthcoming in the African context. As Moses Kiggundu rightly pointed out, in Sub-Saharan Africa, there is no shortage of entrepreneurs or people willing to take risks to start business activities. However, most of these business activities are very small one-person operations mostly in the easy-to-enter trading and service sector, which is also the least profitable. These categories of businesses provide only a limited range of services or products, and do not innovate either by way of new products/services or markets. The more the macroeconomic conditions worsen, the more of these micro enterprises open up because they are predominantly a push type.[37] For these reasons, many of Sub-Sahara African small businesses have not been able to exploit the opportunities offered in the global economy. In particular, shifts in the macro economy such as changes in economic policies, change in governments, etc, are capable of disrupting the viability of these small-scale enterprises. The likelihood for the high failure rates is further pronounced in the absence of managerial capabilities to manage firms against macroeconomic imbalances such as inflation, foreign exchange instability, privatization or indigenization policies, etc.

Other studies have examined the relationship between African entrepreneurs or business owners to the socio-cultural, political and institutional context and concluded that most businesses in Sub-Saharan Africa suffer as a result of neglect, extended social and family obligations and extra-firm demands. In particular, Buame and Kallon concluded that social and family relations disadvantaged entrepreneurs in West Africa.[38] One researcher, M. Dia, provides a positive interpretation of the effects of social status, social relations and social transfers for African entrepreneurship. According to Dia, African institutional failures result in entrepreneurial failure. Consequently, social relations and social capital are seen as some of the necessary conditions for the growth of African entrepreneurship.[39] In a similar manner, Kennedy's study of capitalism in the Sudan concluded that entrepreneurs consolidate social relations and social status through intermarriages between wealthy families, business partnerships between immigrants and local entrepreneurs, political contributions to business-friendly political parties or regimes, and maintaining close business and personal ties. On this basis, the researcher recommends that African entrepreneurs need to enhance their social skills to navigate through complex, dynamic, and often interrelated family and social relations so as to advance the commercial interests of their businesses.[40]

Another category of factors accounting for the success or failure of African entrepreneurship is the external environment within which both the entrepreneur and the firm exist and operate. Many of these studies focus on factors such as local and national politics, the quality of public administration and governmental institutions, socio-cultural variables, the nature of the market, the rule of law, regional and global economy and the prevailing industrial relations. According to these studies, the individual characteristics or traits of an entrepreneur would interact with the macroenvironmental factors to determine the success or failure of entrepreneurship. Significantly, although an enabling environment for entrepreneurial development is necessary, it is not sufficient by itself, to sustain changes in entrepreneurial behavior and firm performance. These macroenvironmental factors must be linked with personal characteristics or traits of the individual entrepreneur.[41]

In general some studies concluded that within the context of Sub-Saharan Africa, government policies, attitudes, overall quality of public administration and service to entrepreneurship, or lack thereof are the causes for entrepreneurial problems in Africa. Some researchers assert that the African business climate is less favorable than other regions, which compete with Africa for trade and investment. Taxation, security of property rights, and the regulation of trade and other commercial activities are more restrictive in Africa than other globalizing regions.[42] Both Samuel Buame and K. M. Kallon reported that public attitudes and societal values in Ghana and Sierra Leone respectively are not supportive of the underlying values of capitalism in general and entrepreneurship in particular.[43]

The dilemma faced by the African entrepreneur is illustrated in the concepts of Kalabule and Magendo, which literally translate to informal illicit business activities. As explained by Moses Kiggundu, Kalabule (Ghana) and Magendo (Uganda) are two societal practices, which refer to illicit, improper, or illegal business conduct. They are used to criminalize entrepreneurial activities in order to allow those in positions of control and influence to make quick and illegal money.[44] According to Buame, Kalabule ruled in Ghana in the 1990s, and during that time, no commercial law, no banking law, no company law, and no laws of ethics were in force. Lawlessness and corruption characterized the environment under which economic and social activities were undertaken and affected persons and groups in different occupations including taxi drivers, managers, police officers, military personnel, teachers and public servants. In addition to undermining the legal framework and the national integrity and regulatory system, both Kalabule and Magendo undermine trust and confidence among the entrepreneurs, which form a critical part of the foundation for private enterprise.[45] Practically every African country has its own version of corruption, bribery and other forms of lawlessness at great cost to the entrepreneurs, the general economy, public administration, and the wider society.

Another area of research on the characteristics of the African entrepreneur examines the demographic profile. According to this research, various personal demographic variables appear to differentiate successful from less successful entrepreneurs in Africa, as they do elsewhere.[46] Earlier studies found that successful African entrepreneurs tended to be male, middle-aged, married with a number of children, and more educated than the general population. For example, Benedict found that the growth and success of family entrepreneurs was dependent upon a strong authoritarian father and a closely knit family structure, with wives and children willing to submit to the father's rule.[47] Other studies indicate that female entrepreneurs experience more operational and strategic impediment to success than their male counterparts and male-owned firms grew faster than those owned by women. Yet other surveys report higher rates of female entrepreneurial participation, both as owners and employees. For example, Mead and Liedholm report female ownership participation rates of 48 percent and employees of 44 percent.[48] This is particularly the case for the micro and small enterprises (MSEs), employing very few if any people and generating little or no income for the owners.[49]

Several researchers have found the predictive validity of demographic variables to be unstable over time.[50] One important reason for this is that societal values, norms and practices are changing to the effect that the cultural taboos that have precluded the African woman from becoming an entrepreneur are gradually fading away. Secondly, education and the forces of globalization have provided the typical African woman entrepreneurial opportunities denied their predecessors. Thirdly, the drive and impetus for entrepreneurship have now shifted to the younger African generation with Western education and business exposure. Significantly, the importance attached to age and traditional wisdom as a prerequisite for economic independence has now given way to such entrepreneurial qualities as innovativeness, drive and risk-taking.

In the area of motives behind entrepreneurship, some studies have shown that the African entrepreneurs cite higher social status and wider social relationships in their respective communities as one of the reasons they chose becoming business owners.[51] In a study of the motives of entrepreneur in South Africa one researcher, B. C. Mitchell, reports that both men and women entrepreneurs were found to be primarily motivated by the need for independence, need for material incentives and the need for achievement. Male entrepreneurs in comparison to females were more motivated by the need to provide family security and to make a difference in the business. Female entrepreneurs, more than males, were motivated by the need to keep learning and the need for more money to survive.[52]

In a study on the determinants of small business growth constraints in a sub-Saharan African economy, John Okpara and Pamela Wynn, observed that 75 percent of their respondents said they went into business because they wanted to be rich (make money), 63 percent wanted to be their own boss (independence), and 50 percent wanted to enjoy a satisfying life (personal satisfaction). Other reasons were continuing a tradition, the availability of a market, the success of others, no other options, fighting poverty, professional inclination, and a requirement for limited capital.[53]

One important feature of successful African entrepreneurs, as rightly pointed out by Tom Forrest, is the practice wherein a small enterprise, usually a trading firm, is the progenitor of other companies, which may eventually form a diversified group.[54] The most prominent examples of this type of corporate conglomeration are the Ibru organization and the Dangote Group of Companies. In the context of a developing economy, it is rare to see any highly successful entrepreneur, especially in Nigeria, without some form of diversification into unrelated business lines. Although, some have argued against this type of entrepreneurship, African entrepreneurs with the financial resources argue that they are investing their resources in and responding to the emerging business opportunities that can only be found in a developing economy.[55]

The norm among African entrepreneurs is to start as a trading outfit and then diversify into unrelated areas and sector of the economy as the business grows. The impulse to diversify into unrelated fields among larger enterprises has been explained as partly the result of strategies designed to spread and reduce risk and minimize unavoidable losses. Sub-Saharan Africa, particularly Nigeria, is a high-risk environment emanating from economic instability, political uncertainty and from inconsistent and unpredictable changes in government policies. General responses to risk include a reluctance to commit funds to long-term investment in fixed assets, which acts as a deterrent to manufacture and the reluctance to give up trading activities. Further impetus is given to diversification by the adoption of strategies that allow flexible responses. However, as Tom Forrest puts it, some firms diversified as a result of perceived profit opportunities in industry that turn out to be short term as a competing enterprises rushed to enter similar lines of business.[56]

CHAPTER SUMMARY

The characteristics of the individual entrepreneur are (i) passion for the business, (ii) tenacity despite failure, (iii) confidence, (iv) high need for achievement, and (v) the willingness to take risks.

There are three types of entrepreneurial activities: (i) new concept/new business, (ii) existing concept/new business, and (iii) existing concept/existing business.

Sources of business ideas and innovation include: (i) experience, (ii) innovating on existing businesses, (iii) unfilled niche in the consumer marketplace, (iv) changes in demographics and lifestyles, and (v) changes in industry or market structure.

The reasons why people choose to be entrepreneurs are: (i) the opportunity to be one's own boss, (ii) opportunity to make money, (iii) opportunity to be innovative, creative and find self-expression, (iv) opportunity to be in control and in making decisions, (v) preparation for retirement, (vi) opportunity to achieve a satisfying way of life, and (vii) other precipitating events such as when one got fired from the job.

Some of the drawbacks of becoming an entrepreneur are: (i) loss of freedom, (ii) loss of independence, and (ii) financial constraints.

Entrepreneurial success in Africa is linked with personal characteristics of the entrepreneur and external environment.

In Sub-Saharan Africa, psychological variables such as personal initiative, innovativeness, entrepreneurial orientation, and autonomy differentiated successful from less successful entrepreneurs.

Most of the small firms in Sub-Saharan Africa are located in the informal sector, and as result, productivity and the capacity to innovate, to introduce new technology, and to manage strategically are absence.

Many businesses in Sub-Saharan Africa suffer as a result of neglect, extended social and family obligations and extra-firm demands.

Social relations and social capital are seen as some of the necessary conditions for the growth of African entrepreneurship.

In Sub-Saharan Africa, government policies, attitudes, overall quality of public administration and service to entrepreneurship are seen as some of the causes for entrepreneurial problems.

Illicit, improper, or illegal business conducts; including lawlessness and corruption negatively affect the growth of private enterprise and entrepreneurship in Sub-Saharan Africa.

Until recently, successful African entrepreneurs tended to be male, middle-aged, married with a number of children, and more educated that the general population.

Female entrepreneurs tend to experience more operational and strategic impediment to success than their male counterparts and male-owned firms grew faster than those owned by women. Female ownership participation rates are higher for the micro and small enterprises (SMEs), employing very few if any people and generating little or no income for the owners.

There is a demographic shift in entrepreneurial undertaking in Sub-Saharan Africa as a result of education, the forces of globalization, western education and business exposure and the diminishing importance of age and traditional wisdom.

CHAPTER DISCUSSION QUESTIONS

1. What are the characteristics of entrepreneurs discussed in this chapter?

2. Discuss the types of entrepreneurs and entrepreneurial activities discussed in this chapter.

3. Discuss the various sources of business ideas available to a prospective entrepreneur.

4. Why do you think that many people in our society want to become entrepreneurs?

5. What are the drawbacks of embarking on entrepreneurship?

6. In your opinion, do you think the African entrepreneur is different from the global entrepreneur in terms of characteristics, attitudes and motives?

CASE STUDY 2: MIKE ADENUGA AND GLOBACOM: ENTREPRENUERIAL OPPORTUNITIES, CONSTRAINTS AND STRATEGIES IN A DEVELOPING ECONOMY[57]

Michael Adenuga was born on April 29, 1953 in the city of Ibadan. He attended the Ibadan Grammar School, in Oyo State for his secondary education and studied Business Administration at Northwestern State University, Alva, Oklahoma in the United States. He also earned a Masters degree at Pace University, New York, majoring in Business Administration with emphasis on Marketing. His experience in the United States of America in search of education has also revealed the entrepreneurial acumen in him. Even though the young Adenuga came from a relatively comfortable background, he was said to have paid his way through school with money got from driving taxi cabs and working as security guard at several times while in the United States.

As far as entrepreneurial initiatives are concerned, Adenuga is certainly no new kid on the block. He is reputed to have distinguished himself in the business of importation at the young age of 22. Ever since that time, Mike Adenuga has left an indelible imprint on the Nigerian business scene. At age 26, Adenuga had already become a millionaire with connections in high places. With his unique flair for risks and sheer tenacity of purpose, in no time he started reaping profits in billions. In addition to Globacom, he owns Equitorial Trust Bank and Consolidated Oil, which carries out crude oil drilling, refining and marketing.

The name of Mike Adenuga as a successful businessman and an accomplished entrepreneur came when his company, Consolidated Oil became the first indigenous company to strike crude in December of 1991. After that he ventured into the telecommunications sector. With his Communications Investment Limited, CIL, he was issued a conditional license in 1999 and frequencies to operate the Global System of Mobile Communications (GSM). The Federal Government of Nigeria later revoked the license. Again, when in 2002, the government, through the Nigerian Communications Commission (NCC), organized new auction for the GSM license, Communications Investment Limited participated and was one of the four that won the bid. Mike Adenuga paid the US$20 million mandatory deposit. However, in the process of effecting the release of the balance payment of US$265 million, the company was adjudged to have failed to pay within stipulated time. CIL lost both the license and the US$20 million deposit. Mike Adenuga later went on to bid for the Second National Operator (SNO) licence, and deposited another US$20 million. This time, his perseverance and tenacity paid off. He won the bid in August 2002 through his Globacom Limited. The SNO has a wider range of operations as Globacom has the right to operate as a national carrier, operate digital mobile lines, serve as international gateway for telecommunications in the country and operate fixed wireless access phones.

The Nigerian Telecommunications Market and Globacom

Communication without doubt is a major driver of any economy. Emerging trends in socio-economic growth shows a high premium being placed on information and communication technology (ICT) by homes, organizations, and nations. Nigeria is not left out in this race for rapid development as the nation's economy has been subjected to years of economic reversal via mismanagement and especially corruption. The Nigerian telecommunications sector was grossly underdeveloped before the sector was deregulated under the military regime of General Ibrahim Babangida in 1992 with the establishment of a regulatory body, the Nigerian Communication Commission (NCC). Between that period and 2001, the NCC has issued various licenses to private telecommunications operator. These include 7 fixed telephony providers that have activated 90,000 lines, 35 Internet service providers with a customer base of about 17,000. Several VSAT service providers are in operation, and have improved financial intermediation by providing on-line banking services to most banks in Nigeria. These licenses allowed private telephone operators (PTOs), to roll out both fixed wireless telephone lines and analogue mobile phones. The return of democracy in 1999 paved the way for the granting of GSM license to 3 service providers: MTN, Nigeria, ECONET Wireless, Nigeria and NITEL Plc in 2001.

Brief History

The journey to success in Nigeria's telecommunication milieu has been long and tortuous. Telecommunication facilities in Nigeria were first established in 1886 by the colonial administration. At independence in 1960, with a population of roughly 40 million people, the country only had about 18,724 phone lines for use. This translated to a tele-density of about 0.5 telephone lines per 1,000 people. The telephone network consisted of 121 exchanges of which 116 were of the manual (magneto) type and only 5 were automatic.

Between 1960 and 1985, the telecommunication sector consisted of the Department of Posts and Telecommunications (P&T) in charge of the internal network and a limited liability company, the Nigerian External Telecommunication (NET) Limited, responsible for the external telecommunications services. NET provided the gateway to the outside world. The installed switching capacity at the end of 1985 was about 200,000 lines as against the planned target of about 460,000. All the exchanges were analogue. Telephone penetration remained poor equaling 1 telephone line to 440 inhabitants, well below the target of 1 telephone line to 100 inhabitants recommended by ITU for developing countries. The quality of service was largely unsatisfactory. The telephone system was unreliable, congested, expensive and customer unfriendly.

Arising from the foregoing, in January 1985, the erstwhile Posts and Telecommunications Department was split into Postal and Telecommunications Divisions. The latter was merged with NET to form Nigerian Telecommunications Limited (NITEL), a limited liability company. The main objective of establishing NITEL was to harmonize the planning and co-ordination of the internal and external telecommunications services, rationalize investments in telecommunications development and provide accessible, efficient and affordable services.

Almost 43 years down the line, the Nigerian Telecommunication Plc, NITEL had roughly half a million lines available to over 120 million Nigerians. NITEL the only national carrier had a monopoly on the sector and was synonymous with epileptic services and bad management. On assumption of office on May 29, 1999 the President Olusegun Obasanjo administration swung to gear to make a reality the complete deregulation of the telecom sector, most especially the much touted granting of licenses to GSM service providers and setting in motion the privatization of NITEL. This proactive approach by the government to the telecom sector made it possible for over 2.5 million Nigerians to clutch GSM phones.

Effect of GSM & Employment Creation

In 2001, telecommunications companies doing business in Nigeria are set to make a fortune with the launch of digital GSM cellular services in the country. In less than three weeks of operations, the two private mobile networks licensed to run the services say they have already attained the one-year target set for them by the Nigerian Communication Commission, (NCC).

MTN's chief executive Karel Pienaar told the BBC's World Business Report that they forecast one million connections for the entire market - all three operators - by March of 2002. The third company licensed to operate GSM services, Nigeria's State telecom company, NITEL, is anticipating higher subscriptions when it starts business because its tariffs will be lower than those of the two private companies. The number of mobile phone subscribers is expected to grow hugely in the coming years.

"It is predicted that within the next five years there will be between six and 10 million mobile subscribers in Nigeria," says Dave Imoko, Public Affairs manager of the NCC. Such high projections mean good business for the companies producing GSM phone sets and accessories. Samsung, Siemens, Ericsson, Alcatel, Nokia, Motorola, Mitsubishi and Sagem have been licensed by the NCC to sell their products in the lucrative Nigerian market. Hundreds of local businessmen are signing up as distributors and retailers.

With a population of 140 million, which is about one sixth of Africa's population, Nigeria is the largest telecommunications market in the continent. This huge business opportunity however remained untapped until 2001. Before now, the country relied on less than 500,000 landlines provided by NITEL. With only one person in 250 owning a phone, Nigeria has one of the lowest "tele-densities" in the world. Theft of expensive copper cables and corruption by NITEL staff made the expansion of the telephone network impossible. The problem was further compounded by reluctance of past governments to commit public fund to telecommunications, which was a government monopoly.

But now, the government of President Olusegun Obasanjo has liberalized the sector in an effort to attract the much needed funding from the private sector. The private telecommunications operators say they are willing to inject the money. According to the BBC, the companies seem to mean big business with their numerous billboards lining major highways. Nigerians are already dreaming of how things will change for the better in a Nigeria where everybody clutches a mobile phone. The economy is likely to witness the most significant impact of the network.

"We are excited at the roll out of the GSM network in Nigeria because we know this is a giant stride," says Imoko. "The new system will certainly help the economy grow as development economists have agreed that a percentage increase in a nation's telecommunications network usually leads to a significant growth in the overall economy itself," says Tayo Ekundayo, NITEL's Public Relations General Manager.

Doing business without telephone was a nightmare for millions of Nigerians. Many have to travel long distances wasting time and money for business transactions, which could easily have been done by a phone call. As a matter of fact, the GSM service providers have completely changed the tempo of the Nigerian business terrain by creating countless opportunities for small and medium businesses in franchises, dealerships, retailer-ships and value added services within the GSM market. The duo of MTN and Econet Wireless have caused employment explosion both directly and indirectly. Over 2.5 million Nigerians had, at this time, a convenient way of communication; this development greatly affected positively the country's business environment.

Enter Globacom and Mike Adenuga

This scenario was further spiced when the NCC granted a license for Second National Operator (SNO) to Globacom, Nigeria on August 12, 2002. The motive is to create an alternative network to the government owned NITEL, whose service is nothing to write home about. Globacom paid the mandatory 20 million dollars for the license before the August 30, 2002 deadline. The license involves the following:

- National Carrier Services;
- Digital/Mobile Services;
- Long Distance Communication; and
- Fixed Wireless Access Service.

Obligation to be met by Globacom includes the provision of 150,000 digital lines on its mobile network and 100,000 fixed line network within first 12 months of operation. In trying to meet the challenges of its predecessors in the GSM industry, Globacom signed interconnectivity agreement with MTN Nigeria and appointed over 350 dealers nationwide. On Friday 29th August 2003, Globacom rolled out their services in Abuja, Nigeria's Federal Capital City, FCT. True to their earlier promise, they introduced a per second billing system with a tariff of 80 kobo per second for the pay-as-go subscribers.

In the year 2007, Globacom reached a subscriber base of 15 million with over 12 million active subscriber-base. With this development, Globacom established its second position in the Nigerian market holding strongly to over 35 percent share of the entire Nigerian subscriber market and warming to take over market leadership in the shortest possible time.

To do this, the company according to its chief operating officer, Mr. Mohammed Jameel, is installing a capacity for over 30 million subscribers by the end of the year by adding over 150 base stations every week around the country and will have installed additional 750 base stations to its 3000 existing stations by the end of the year. According to Jameel, the equipment for achieving this phenomenal growth is already in the country and so has gone beyond mere wishes to the level of concrete reality.

The company also announced that at its current growth rate, it will soon hit 18 million subscribers and that will confer on its market leadership of the telecom sector in Nigeria in terms of subscriber base. As at October of 2007, Globacom has invested over US $3 billion since 2003 and has given direct employment to over 2500 people. And to ensure steady development of the network, it signed a US$1 billion equipment supply agreement with Alcatel of France and Huawei of China, covering Mobile, Fixed and Submarine Optical Fiber Cable linking Nigeria and the United Kingdom, with a dedicated link to the U.S.

On the gateway business, Globacom is one of the largest carriers of voice traffic in Africa carrying over 2 billion international minutes annually. At the local scene, Glo is the gateway for most network operators in Nigeria and the surrounding African countries and has built strategic partnerships with 43 Tier One Carriers (35 TDM and 8 VoIP) with a total of 618 E1s. Telcos like AT&T, BT, France Telecom, and Sprint use Glo to connect to their customers in Africa.

The company's international roaming services involve 193 networks in 98 countries and provide services on voice, SMS, GPRS roaming and BlackBerry services. It also provides bulk sale of bandwidth and offers access to 804 networks in 174 countries via International SMS.

Globacom is the first operator in West Africa to launch Gateway switches outside of Africa to carry International Voice Traffic and this accounts for its easy connection to all the big time players like BT, FT, MCI, Belgacom, ARBINET, etc. Apart from the UK, Globacom has also established points of presence in France, Germany and the U.S. with five state-of-the-art Gateway switches in Nigeria – three in Lagos and one each in Abuja and Port Harcourt. It also plans additional Points of Presence in Singapore, Hong Kong, UAE and Australia. The company says its submarine cable has reached Senegal from UK and work will soon begin on the Lagos Senegal route to link both cables. The fast paced growth of Globacom saw it winning a GSM licence recently in Benin Republic.

Globacom's growth in Nigeria has been phenomenal. Starting two years behind other operators in Nigeria, the network has become the fastest growing in Africa and the Middle East region and is the third fastest growing network in the world.

Mike Adenuga's Spirit of Entrepreneurship and Style of Management

Mike Adenuga is said to be the most successful indigenous entrepreneur in Africa. Ibrahim Babangida, a former Nigerian Military President, once described Globacom and Mike Adenuga in the following terms: "One thing stands out uniquely about it: it is the brain of a Nigerian. He is really trying to make it the leading telecommunication outfit, not only in Nigeria but also in Africa. Adenuga is a very serious businessman. And he is not a flamboyant businessman who goes to sleep, folds his arms, saying his business is doing well. No, he works very hard. I think he is worthy of emulation."

One thing that is well known in Mike Adenuga's business is that many people saw him as been able to break the monopoly of foreign owned business in crucial sectors of the African economy. Professor Wole Soyinka, the Nigerian Nobel Laureate, describes his endorsement of Globacom and Mike Adenuga as follows: "Monopoly being enjoyed in the business then by some operators who are from outside the country was scandalous. And Globacom being a Nigerian brand, owned by a Nigerian who loves a challenge, I decided to support him."

Although he has made giant strides in several business categories, Nigerians would probably remember him more for his timely intervention in the telecommunications arena, where he seems to hold the aces that determine the pace of play. Globacom historic introduction of Per Second Billing and subsequent crashing of SIM price did not only skew the GSM equation in its favor but has continued to hold a lot of implications for the fledgling Nigerian telecommunications sector. As a result of his vision, drive and ambition, Globacom has been adjudged the fastest-growing telecoms operations in Africa and the third fastest in the world, with an active subscriber base currently in excess of 11 million within just 3 years of operation.

Adenuga has a management style of employing highly qualified Indians to man his business. Mohammed Jameel, an Indian who is the Chief Operating Officer of Globacom recalls his first impressions of his boss: "Two, three days after joining Globacom, he called me to his office. The first day I met him, he was very quiet. And I didn't want to say anything. I just watched him. Of course, a lot of my colleagues were there. I was very impressed with him. He was planning to launch the brand Globacom. I saw in him a lot of passion. I saw in him a lot of commitment. I saw in him a lot of vision. He wanted the brand to succeed. And the kind of figures he was talking about in terms of subscribers, putting in infrastructure did really surprise me. At the first meeting I was convinced that the brand is going to make a revolution in telecommunication in the market."

Mohammed Jameel also describes Mike Adenuga as a "very successful entrepreneur who can turn any venture into good. He is a very, very aggressive manager. He is a very target-oriented manager. He is a manager who has a huge vision. He always thinks big. If you are hearing him for the first time, you would think this man is just joking. But he is not joking. Whatever he says, he is determined to achieve it. He is very passionate about whatever you do with the business you do for the brand. Even things like branding the street, he goes into the details to get things right. And he doesn't take instant or spontaneous decisions. He has to think it across. He doesn't take decisions on his own. He respects the views of others. He calls all of us and gives us the opportunity to air our views, share our thoughts, share our ideas. He also makes his own inputs to the whole issue and we end up coming up with a collective decision. So that it's not one man's decision. It's a decision of the group. So we put our thoughts, cook it on the table and we are sure that what comes out is an excellent dish. He is a manager who respects collective decisions and he lends his ears and mind to whatever is being talked about, irrespective of whether it is the COO or the person employed in the customer service."

The Entrepreneur and Company with a Difference

Though a late entrant into Nigeria's hugely lucrative telecommunication sector, Mike Adenuga has within a short time grown Globacom to become Nigeria's second national operator behind MTN Nigeria Communication Limited, and with over 15 million subscribers and market reputation as Nigeria's fastest growing mobile service provider, Globacom and the Michael Adenuga (MA) Group are set to make a difference in Africa's business environment.

The Michael Adenuga (MA) Group consists of Conoil, a downstream oil operations outfit, Consolidated Oil, an oil exploration and exploitation firm and Equitorial Trust Bank, in addition to stakes and interests in construction and real estate firms. Although there are several other Nigerian companies and entrepreneurs that have interests in key sectors in the Nigerian economy, the difference between the MA Group and some of these entrepreneurs and their businesses may be that whereas these entrepreneurs have remained inward looking, concentrating their operations within Nigeria, the MA Group has forayed abroad in search of other financial conquests and has emerged as Nigeria's first global corporation.

There are at least two reasons why Nigerian indigenous entrepreneurs and companies have not been prominent in foreign markets. In particular, some observers have attributed the absence to lack of vision and management skills especially on a global level on the part of the entrepreneurs. Another reason may be the fact that some of these enterprises are run as sole proprietorships (one man businesses) with their success relying solely on the life or death of their founders. Thus, it is not uncommon that the children of some of these old-school entrepreneurs are still not able to carry on with the family business tradition when the sage passes on, thus creating a "here today gone tomorrow" business legacy.

In the context of Nigerian entrepreneurship, the MA Group and Globacom, in particular are making a difference by venturing into the global market. In 2006, the MA Group announced that it plans to invest US$700 million from a war chest of US$1 billion in the lucrative Indian economy. This is a first for a Nigerian company in terms of outward investment. By so doing MA group would join other corporate and technology global corporations that have since established their presence in the Indian sub-continent.

While this move may be good news to the Indian people, economy and government in terms of job creation, it may not be such a good news to the Nigerian government who would really wish that the Adenugas invested their money in other sectors in the Nigerian economy, in line with its current efforts to attract foreign direct investments (FDIs), which has not really picked up as hoped by the government, despite the economic reforms already in place. According to Mustapha Bello, the Chief Executive of the Nigerian Investment Promotion Commission (NIPC), FDI inflows into Nigeria between June 1999 and July 2005 sadly stands at US$35 billion, "the FDI inflows were not only in the oil and gas sector but also in the telecoms, ICT, manufacturing and services sectors", he said.

India has become the green pasture for those seeking low-cost labor in the high-tech industry and the MA Group is joining other global corporations in locating a part of their production facilities in the Indian sub-continent. Because of Indian's attractiveness, the MA group has over 150 Indians to work in its Nigerian facilities. In an official statement, the group said it has initially planned to focus its investments in the telecom sector in

India and then move on to other sunrise sectors over a period of time. "We are a cash-rich company keen on foraying into India, as the telecom market there is booming", the group said in a statement. The MA group also said that it is not averse to investing in call centers, banking and petroleum sectors in India. Investing in these sectors will allow it leverage on its experiences from operating in similar sectors in Nigeria. The group also plans to make India the Asian hub of their manpower needs for telecom.

Although the group is expanding to India, it has, through its Globacom brand, kept faith with the Nigerian economy. The group has invested over US$3 billion in Nigeria and creating thousands of jobs for Nigerians. In a form of symbiotic relationship, Nigerians have also kept faith with them, it is the Nigerian customers that have helped them eclipse Econet/V-Mobile in terms of subscription, and even continue to patronize them as they keep hot on the heels of MTN in the quest to become Nigeria's leading mobile telephony provider. The Nigerian customers have been drawn towards Globacom by their sense of patriotism and have adopted Globacom as their own ("our own brand").

Awards and Recognitions

Mike Adenuga has been recognized for many of his philanthropic initiatives. He single-handedly bankrolled a foreign coach for Nigeria's national soccer team and he has assumed the sole sponsorship of the annual Confederation of African Football (CAF) Awards. President Kufuor of Ghana recently crowned Adenuga as Africa's No. 1 businessman. According to the President, "When you talk about business in Africa, you talk about Adenuga. He has within a short time left his footprint on different areas of business including banking, oil, aviation, real estate and telecommunications". The President pointed out that he is "particularly impressed with what he (Adenuga) has done in Globacom. In just a little over three years, Adenuga has made Globacom a force, not only in Nigeria but also in Africa's telecommunications landscape. We are happy with what they have achieved in Nigeria and look forward to having them replicate that success in Ghana."

In August of 2007, Mike Adenuga was named the African Telecoms Entrepreneur of the year for his courageous and rapid investment in the telecoms sector. The recognition was given at the 2007 maiden African Telecoms Award event held in Lagos and witnessed by eminent Africans such as Nobel Laureate, Prof. Wole Soyinka, former president of The Gambia, Mr. Dauda Jawara, and eminent professor of African History, Prof. Molefe Kete Asante. At the event, which also featured the 2007 edition of the Nigerian Telecom Awards, Globacom's Chief Operating Officer, Mr. Mohamed Jameel, received the Telecom personality of the Year, Glo BlackBerry was adjudged the product of the year and Globacom received the West African Telecom Company of the Year. Organizers of the award said, Mike Adenuga is admired for his courage and never-say-die attitude. According to the award citation, "Adenuga saw a new window of opportunity in the National Operator License, which was going to give him the GSM license, (which he had earlier lost through CIL), a fixed and fixed-wireless license, a gateway license and an online license. He went for it and won. His competitors had gone miles ahead; but again, the attribute of courage came in. He plunged in and is currently setting the pace in many areas of operation." Globacom, as a company, was praised for its backbone deployment along the West Coast of Africa to the United Kingdom, a facility, which on completion, will drop tariffs and improve total communications connectivity in the sub-region.

The Confederation of African Football, CAF has awarded Adenuga the title of "the Pillar of Sports in Africa" for his strong support for African Football at both national and continental levels. In Nigeria, President Olusegun Obasanjo has honored Mike Adenuga with the National Award of the Officer of the Order of the Niger (OON).

Case Discussion Questions

1. In your opinion, how innovative are Mike Adenuga's ideas and entrepreneurial initiatives? How would you classify and describe the types of innovations attributed to him and Globacom?

2. How would you describe his entrepreneurial spirit and management styles in comparison to what is conventionally associated with the typical African businessman?

3. What is your opinion about Globacom's expansion into the Indian Sub-continent? As an entrepreneurial organization competing in a globalized market what are the advantages and implications of an Indian adventure?

4. It is often said that entrepreneurs re-invent the ways things are done; they challenge the status quo; they break the rules; and they change the way societies and economies are organized by introducing new products and ideas. How would you place Mike Adenuga and Globacom in the context of this statement?

5. What lessons, if any, do you think other entrepreneurs and business owners in Africa could learn from Mike Adenuga, Globacom and the MA Group?

Chapter 3

THE ECONOMIC ENVIRONMENT: NATIONAL, REGIONAL AND GLOBAL

You do not choose to become global. The market chooses for you; it forces your hand" (Alain Gomez, CEO, Thompson SA)

CHAPTER LEARNING OBJECTIVES
After studying this chapter, you should be able to:

1. Understand the economic environment under which entrepreneurship is practiced in Sub-Saharan Africa.

2. Understand the economic policies and pattern of economic and entrepreneurial development in the colonial and post-colonial eras.

3. Understand the political economy of Sub-Saharan Africa and the impact of economic ideologies on the development of entrepreneurship in the region.

4. Understand the impact of the policies of structural adjustment programs on entrepreneurial development in Sub-Saharan Africa.

5. Understand the drivers and forces of globalization (regional trade blocs, information and communication technology and multinational and transnational corporation) and their impact on the development of entrepreneurship in Sub-Saharan Africa.

6. Understand the changing role of the nation-state and the basis for its competitive advantage through entrepreneurship.

INTRODUCTION: THE RELEVANCE OF THE ECONOMIC ENVIRONMENT

Whatever opportunities or threats the global economy may have presented to countries in the world, taking advantage of these depends on each country's definition of its strategic advantage, its economic policies and ideologies, its development and entrepreneurial policies and the manner in which they are implemented. For all intent, the nature of the economic environment (such as economic policies and ideologies) is crucial for the development of entrepreneurship. That is why South Africa is developing economically and socially while its neighbor, Zimbabwe, is economically and socially bankrupt.

To be sure, both countries have so much in common, at least in the historical context. First, they were under apartheid regimes: Zimbabwe was under white rule when it was known as Rhodesia. The country achieved its independence from white domination in 1982. South Africa, too, was under apartheid until it gained its freedom in 1994. Both countries are situated in Southern Africa. In a similar vein, both countries have been provided with opportunities and threats arising from the global economy. More telling is the difference in their reactions to opportunities created in a globalized economy, their growth and entrepreneurial development policies and the manner in which these policies have been implemented. Why would two countries with so much in common – historically, culturally and geographically – exhibit such wide differences in economic and entrepreneurial development?

Zimbabwe, once a vibrant and diversified economy, had been a hope for Africa's future. Known today as Africa's worst basket-case economy, Zimbabwe provides an excellent case study of an economy gone seriously bad thanks to political and economic mismanagement. In terms of statistics, Zimbabwe's plight is pretty much immeasurable. As at April of 2008, the rate of inflation is more than 1000 percent and unemployment rate in excess of 80 percent. After 28 years under Robert Mugabe, emotive terminology such as utter despair and desperate destitution describe the situation in Zimbabwe better than any maths and statistics can ever do. After one of the most despotic regimes in the history of Africa, Zimbabwe's human capital and economic resources have been massively depleted. Out of a population of estimated 13 million people, millions of those able to do so have fled to seek better lives abroad and to provide for relatives back in Zimbabwe, living the maimed and the wounded in utter despair.[1]

The agricultural situation that was once the fountain of entrepreneurship and economic growth is in dire straits. Looted by Mr. Robert Mugabe's cronies during the early 2000s from white farmers, the country's most productive grain and tobacco farms have been either actively wrecked or sadly neglected. Farm failures have hampered the nation's ability both to feed its people and earn foreign currency. More than eight out of 10 people survive on less than US$2 per day and almost half the population suffers from malnutrition.[2] In many ways it seems obvious that Zimbabwe's current economic difficulties are linked to specific government policy decisions. For example, the policy of land seizures as a nationalization policy and the chaotic disruption on the farms is likely the main reason the staple maize production fell by three-quarters. This impacted rural incomes, exports, and food security.[3] Political crisis combined with abandonment of sensible economic policy also closed off most of the aid support from donor countries and organizations. The misguided economic policies also scared away most foreign investments and chased much of the talented workforce out of the country. While many of these actions appear economically rational, they may be explained as products of political ideology. It can hardly be a coincidence that the economy began its precipitous fall just as the ruling party unleashed a wave of political violence and repression directed against a rising opposition movement. Most noticeably, the forcible appropriation of commercial farm seems calculated to undermine the financial and popular support for the opposition.[4]

Zimbabwe's vision of economic growth is anchored on a policy of nationalization in the midst of globalization. Zimbabwe, in spite of its poverty, has the potential to compete in the global economy. For example, Zimbabwe possesses the world's second-largest deposits of platinum at a time when world prices are soaring. This would normally be counted as a good fortune in terms of the country's competitiveness in the global economy. But because of Zimbabwe's economic policies, this resource has been turned into another misfortune in its process of development. Following its nationalization zeal, the government announced that 51 percent of all foreign mining shareholdings would have to be transferred to the government, half of them without compensation. Prior to the government's decision, many international mining corporations have been contemplating investing in the country's platinum industry. However, the government's decision brought these plans to an abrupt halt. The cash-starved Zimbabwean's authorities are unlikely to be able to finance their share of the investment, which is necessary to boost production, while mining companies cannot afford to shoulder all the costs for 49 percent of the returns. Operating in Zimbabwe is already difficult enough – with inflation raging above 1000 percent, the worst in Sub-Saharan Africa, an unrealistic official exchange rate and crippling shortages of fuel and other basic infrastructure.[5] One of the consequences of all these actions is the death of the spirit of entrepreneurship.

South Africa has benefited from opportunities in the global economy. In 1994, the country's first democratically elected government inherited a distorted, under performing economy, based on a system that had deprived the majority of the population of education and economic opportunities. Since the end of apartheid, the South African authorities have not only stabilized the economy, they have also improved fiscal management. Secondly, the public sector has been slimmed; public debt has also been cut while trade and exchange controls have been gradually deregulated and liberalized. Since 2003, the economy has grown by an average of 3.4 percent, against a dismal 1 percent during the last 13 years of apartheid. Inflation, since 2003, has been kept within a 3-6 percent span.

In the month of September 2005, the International Monetary Fund gave South Africa a thumbs-up in its annual review of the country's economic performance. South Africa's Gross National Product (GDP) is growing quite fast (by 3.7 percent in 2004). The rand (South Africa's currency) has recovered from its 2001 depression, and foreign exchange reserves are strong. The international financial community has confidence in South Africa's economic policies and pattern of growth. The international business community also has high confidence in the country's economic policies. For example, in the month of July 2005, Barclays Bank of England finalized its US$4.7 billion investment in ABSA, one of South Africa's main banks; and in August, Standard and Poor's upgraded the country's credit rating, a few months after Moody's.[6]

South Africa was able to achieve this economic feat through a policy of development that actively reacted to the dynamics of the global economy. To do this, the country developed what it called "economic building blocks" which include (i) the development of skills, (ii) promotion of entrepreneurial and business activity, (iii) infrastructure development, (iv) the importance of technology, and (v) the role of government. The South African government pointed out "The realities of globalization are that if we are to be successful as a country, we need to have high levels of skills so that we can compete with other industrializing and developed countries. The days of competing on the basis of having natural resources and inexpensive labor are over. While natural resources continue to remain a significant part of our economy, such resources are finite and rapidly fluctuating commodity prices make reliance on this sector unsustainable in the long term."

The South African government believes that entrepreneurial development is the key to success in competing in the global economy. As a policy initiative, the government points out that "given the structural changes that are taking place in big businesses at a global level, small businesses have proven that they are increasingly an important part of any economy, be it in a first-world or developing country. Part of the success of small business-driven economies is that they are able to create an economic environment that is more robust and dynamic as well as create more employment opportunities."[7]

The nature of entrepreneurship in a society is, above all, a product of economic circumstances and factors. Thus, although this book is about how to formulate and implement appropriate strategies at the firm level, it is crucial that we first examine the economic factors under which such strategies are formulated and implemented. The economic environment in the context of national, regional and global arenas provides the opportunities or threats that entrepreneurs must respond. Significantly, it is naïve to examine entrepreneurship in isolation of the wider economic environment under which entrepreneurial actions are made meaningful. National, regional and global economies have profound impact on the success or failure of entrepreneurial strategies both at the micro- and macro-levels.

The economic and developmental process in Sub-Saharan Africa over the past ten decades may be explained along a process of series of economic events that have historical significance. In short, what Africans, and indeed the rest of the world are experiencing today in terms of economic growth and the competitiveness of their national economies has, very largely, been the product of economic history. Historically, many nations have passed through different stages of economic development in terms of economic policies adopted within a particular era in their developmental processes. Most importantly, mistakes learned from past economic policies have been used as guides for the formulation and implementation of future economic policies. The experience of development from the transitional and emerging economies (e.g., Eastern Europe, China, Brazil, India and South Africa) indicates that these nations have experimented on various forms of economic and political models. In this regard, it seems appropriate to examine the pattern and context of economic development in Sub-Saharan Africa and how these impacted entrepreneurial development.

Perhaps the story of Zimbabwe and South Africa shares some features with Charles Dickens' description of revolutionary France as the best of times and worst of times in terms of the paths of economic development followed by these two nations. The simultaneous extremes of these two nations seemed particularly indicative of how economic policies shape economic and entrepreneurial development. As the above chapter prologue indicates, the key determinants in a country's competitiveness rest on the economic policies adopted by that country in relation to their responses to forces shaping the global economy. Most importantly, the story of Zimbabwe and South Africa indicates how economic policies in a particular country reflect the strategies that country adopted to deal with circumstances thrust upon it by history.

Reflecting on its colonial experience, Sub-Saharan Africa is particularly vulnerable to the factors that shape global competition. As late starters, Sub-Saharan Africa does not have the first-mover advantages enjoyed by her colonizers and the industrialized nations. For this reason, the economic experience of these countries must also be placed within the context of history beginning from the colonial and post-colonial regimes against the background of the development of indigenous entrepreneurship. After independence, many Sub-Sahara African countries had placed their hope on self-reliance and economically independence from colonial rulers. However, this hope had turned to despair as political instability and civil unrest engulfed most part of Africa. In some other contexts, many African governments such as the government of Tanzania experimented on a variety of development models with dire consequences for the development of indigenous entrepreneurs. This chapter examines the nature of such crises and their impacts on the process of economic development and entrepreneurship.

The majority of Sub-Sahara African nations place heavy reliance on monoproducts and the exportation of commodities the prices of which are determined by forces in the global economy. Despite the presence of abundant natural resources in countries such as Angola, Cameroon, Gabon, Nigeria, the Democratic Republic of Congo, Sub-Saharan Africa still remains one of the poorest regions in the world in terms of both economic and human development. Now, it is essential to examine what development policies have been adopted to compete in a global system of exchange where certain policies favor some countries and inhibit the growth of other countries' economies. For this reason, the policies of structural adjustment programs and their impact on entrepreneurial development are examined in this chapter.

In a global economy in which the role of the nation-state as providers of employment and economic activities have increasingly diminished, the role of small businesses and entrepreneurial ventures as engines of economic growth in developing countries has long been brought to the fore in the discourse of economic growth. A vibrant private sector in the context of developing countries relies most exclusively on the creation of business ventures by entrepreneurs and small business owners as long as there is the necessary macroeconomic, sociopolitical, regulatory and institutional environment. Such an environment is, in turn, affected by forces in the global economy. In other words, any discussion of entrepreneurial development including the role of the nation-state must be done with reference to the phenomenon of globalization.

As pointed out in chapter one, globalization brings opportunities and benefits. These opportunities and benefits, some would argue, are not fairly distributed. Others would see globalization as unbalanced and unequal, a historical process that benefits some and hurt others. It is true that some countries have succeeded in traversing, to a greater or lesser degree, the gap between developing and developed. Although, higher rates of economic growth and poverty reduction in East Asia, notably in China, and to a lesser extent in India and a few countries in other parts of the world (e.g., Brazil), cannot only be attributed to globalization, as many other factors were involved, the successful exploitation of global economic opportunities played an important role.[8] This is the difference between Zimbabwe and South Africa in the chapter's prologue.

Both developed and emerging economies have used a variety of devices to protect themselves from the competitive forces in the global economy while they increased national capacity for competitiveness. For the developed and emerging economies, opening up to the global economy without that capacity is a recipe for deindustrialization, as uncompetitive enterprises fail. Meanwhile, in other parts of the world, notably in Sub-Saharan Africa, growth has been low and poverty increasing. The questions to be asked in this context are: Why is it that some countries were able to weather the globalization wave and others were unable? Why is it that some countries were able to exploit global opportunities for the development of entrepreneurship and others could not? This chapter examines these questions through a review of the economic policies and ideologies adopted in Sub-Saharan Africa.

THE ECONOMIC ENVIRONMENT IN THE COLONIAL ERA

For a start, European colonial governments left Africa with a mounting economic crisis that had been the end product of eighty years of colonial rule. During the colonial era, the typical African economies, such as they were, had been conditioned towards exporting cheap agricultural raw materials and unprocessed minerals to Europe and in return importing relatively expensive manufactured goods. There had been little or no attempt to develop African economic self-sufficiency, for that would have defeated the purpose of Europe's colonial adventure as an industrial processing center for the colonies. Not only were the nature of the products, but also the "term of trade" determined by Europe at the expense of African economic interests. Prices for Africa's export commodities were controlled in the developed economies of Europe and North America. Although, a detailed discussion of economic policies and activities in Sub-Saharan Africa during the colonial era is beyond the scope of this book, a brief examination of how colonial economic policies affected entrepreneurial development in the region is in order here.

Prior to colonial administration, parts of Sub-Saharan Africa were also linked to international trading circuits. For instance, Swahili Arab traders plied small vessels along the coasts of East Africa, establishing trading ports in Zanzibar and Mozambique and exporting ivory and gold. Camel caravans moved across the Sahara into the Sahel and Savannah regions, and large canoes made their way up and down the navigable African rivers. Yet the very different geography between southern, northern and the Sahel regions of Africa made transport much more difficult and impeded trade links. Furthermore,

Africa's western coast and the interior were almost completely cut off from significant outside contacts. As Oliver and Atmore's history of the African Middle Ages notes, in 1400, "there was no maritime traffic anywhere between southern Morocco and the Limpopo, and for those living between these points the ocean marked the end of the world."[9] It was not until the arrival of Europeans and the marked acceleration of the slave trade that Africa's many small, regional trading networks were finally linked into a continent-wide system in the late 18th century. Yet for another hundred years, until the demand for Africa's industrial raw materials rose in the mid-19th century, neither production nor trade grew in a sustained manner.

Colonialism brought intense competition and often-brutal suppression for indigenous traders in the Sub-Saharan region. In the 17th century, Portuguese efforts to capture the gold and ivory trade in Sub-Saharan Africa greatly reduced the activities of the Arabs who had traded along the east coast and also kept local groups from taking their place. As colonial trading enterprises penetrated further into the interior of Africa, they used their exclusive charters, greater access to capital, and the protection of colonial authorities to force African competition out of business. In Nigeria in the 1880s, for example, Ja Ja of Opobo, a successful indigenous trader, with some several thousand employees, was moving into direct export of palm oil to Europe when he was deposed and exiled by the British. Likewise, in Southern Africa, "Africans wishing to enter commerce were severely restricted in order to protect European commercial interests."[10] In the early colonial period, these moves kept most indigenous African entrepreneurs from accumulating capital on any significant scale.

The first modern factories in Sub-Saharan Africa were established in Kenya and other places in the first two decades of the 20th century. Nigeria appears to have established its first modern factories only in the 1920s. In many other areas such as Côte d'Ivoire, John Rapley notes that industrial development was almost nonexistent "until after the Second World War, and even then it was limited until the postcolonial period".[11] Entrepreneurs in Côte d'Ivoire, Ghana (then the Gold Coast) and Nigeria tended to focus on plantation agriculture, and diversify into services (transport, money lending) and real estate. After World War II, as African countries moved closer to independence, some colonial authorities began to implement import substitution policies. For example, in the 1950s, Nigerian authorities raised tariff levels on some classes of imports, thereby encouraging local production to which only companies of colonial origin could take part. But in general, policies to stimulate domestic industry would wait until after independence.

During this period, foreign indigenes (such as Indians and Lebanese immigrants who first settled in Africa) acted as local entrepreneurs. For example, Indian immigrants began to arrive in significant numbers in Mauritius in 1834 as laborers in the sugar plantations, and came to the rest of Africa as traders throughout the 19th century, settling primarily in Southern and East Africa. By the 1930s, some Indian firms like Chellarams, a Sindhi Indian trading company with branches in Southeast Asia, the UK, the Middle East, the West Indies, and West Africa, and the Chandaria Group, with subsidiaries in Kenya, Nigeria and elsewhere, had become the key players in the sub-continent's economy. The Lebanese came predominantly to West Africa, arriving in Nigeria in the mid-1890s, where they became traders and transporters.

As the colonial period came to a close, indigenous African entrepreneurs remained concentrated in the service sector: trade, transport, real estate, and construction, where some amassed considerable investment. Others set up mills, bakeries, and other light industries but very rarely on any significant scale. Thus, in Sub-Saharan Africa, it was non-indigenous entrepreneurs who had accumulated the networks, capital, and business skills, and who had the global linkages necessary to begin the transition from commerce to modern manufacturing. In Nigeria, for example, European capital first began to shift into larger-scale, import-substitution manufacturing after 1957 as a defensive reaction to new tariffs on imports. Kenyan Indians ("Asians") who had started out in commerce and banking in the late 19th century, slowly moved into manufacturing in the 1920s. By the 1950s, they were producing on a large and diversified scale, and by the mid-1980s, one study concluded that "Kenyan manufacturing industry is almost exclusively owned by multinational corporations, Kenyan Asians, or government parastatals; Africans own very few medium or large-sized manufacturing firms."[12]

Ethnicity became an important political issue in region, as colonial governments reconsidered economic development policies and strategies in the post World War II period. After independence, pressure grew for the new leadership to intervene to create opportunities for indigenous capital. A number of African countries, such as Kenya and Nigeria, attempted to promote indigenous African business by new licensing requirements and regulations that pressured Lebanese and Indian entrepreneurs to vacate trading and small-scale services (leaving these for African entrepreneurs), and move their capital into more sophisticated manufacturing. Some, like Uganda under Idi Amin Dada, expelled their Asian population.

It is possible to say that under colonial rule, modern economic activities, for various reasons were controlled either by European multinational trade companies or Indian/Lebanese trade houses. This was the period in which European merchants sought commodities for which a market could be found in the European countries. In Sub-Saharan Africa, the search for raw materials as inputs for the production of goods was the main attraction of European merchant traders, while Asian merchant houses were selling goods to the more affluent in Africa. Palm products, rubber products, cocoa, and cotton goods were some of the main exports from the African countries for sometime; then followed by other raw materials which could be used as industrial inputs in Europe. In practice, this implies that European merchants bought up crops grown by peasants in response to cash incentives, encouraging more to turn over production for the European markets. Thus, the future of Sub-Saharan Africa as primary exporting colonial outposts began to take shape when Britain, France, Holland, and Portugal turned toward a development-minded colonialism – the desire to expand empire resources while legitimizing colonial rule.

The pattern of economic activity then followed closely with the British, French, Dutch, and Portuguese perception of the strategic usefulness of the economies of the colonial territories in terms of foreign trade in which colonial merchant houses played a predominant role. In East Africa, West Africa and other Dutch and Portuguese colonies elsewhere in Africa, the role of the colonies was mainly seen as that of primary producers for the advanced manufacturing industries located in Europe. At the same time to facilitate trade, a modern infrastructure had to be built up, with ports and harbor facilities to link the area with the European economy, and railways and roads built to connect various producing areas in the hinterland.

As trade expanded, some sections of the indigenous population in Sub-Saharan Africa increased their income and began to participate in the distribution economy mainly serving as middlemen between peasant producers and the European exporting companies. The home market in the colonies also began to grow, as the need for manufactured imports from Europe tended to rise. The colonial administration and Asian trading houses welcomed this development, but never committed itself to developing manufacturing industry in these colonies. For the colonial and Asian multinational trading firms, it was more lucrative to import cheaper and better-made foreign manufactured goods than to finance the local production of the colonies' substitutes.

Meanwhile, some indigenes in the colonies were able to accumulate capital, albeit on a limited scale, whether in agriculture, petty trading or such fields as road maintenance and transportation. However, the local businessmen or would-be entrepreneurs were not able to go into industrial production or manufacturing, mainly because they lacked adequate capital, technical know-how and management skills or the civil service held more promise than in industry. Frederick Cooper uses the experience of cocoa farmers in Ghana and Nigeria to illustrate how the African agrarian capitalist skewed the industry in favor of trade and employment in the civil service. Starting in the late nineteenth century in southern Gold Coast (now Ghana) and in the early twentieth century in southwestern Nigeria, cocoa production created differentials of wealth. "The wealthy planter cultivated supporters as well as crops, sponsored ceremonies, and otherwise strove to turn wealth into prestige. Rather than push agrarian capitalism to its extreme, the wealthiest planters were more likely to invest excess profits outside, in starting trading or transport companies or insuring their children's access to education and then to positions in the civil service."[13]

In any case, had they opted for local industrial production, African indigenous wealthy farmers would have to face a very stiff competition from imported products, the supply of which was controlled by the large foreign companies, with more large pool of financial, technical and superior psychological resources. For the locals, returns on capital were higher in other fields where the risks were minimal such as in petty trading and other artisan professions. Similarly, there was little scope for the growth of local entrepreneurs in the manufacturing sector outside such limited areas as government employment. It should be pointed out, however, that for the most part, economic activity was patterned along the production of food and raw materials for the home market and commodity goods for the colonial markets. The nexus of this international trade was made possible by the activities of the colonial "global trade houses" (such as John Holt, United African Companies, etc) and small-scale artisan-type workshops and petty traders located in the colonies.

Thus the economy of Sub-Saharan Africa under colonial era represented a type of dependent colonial capitalism dominated by the territorial British, French and Dutch companies concerned principally with marketing the region's primary products. However, the preservation of the peasantry and the modest prosperity of the colonial local bureaucrats, together with other developments made possible the constitution of a national petty bourgeoisie within the framework of this export-dependent African economy. Although the African national bourgeoisie itself was incapable of entering into the productive sector for reasons mentioned earlier, it nevertheless did seek outlets in fields, which promised to be profitable although not sought after by the foreign companies. The areas, which held promise, included local trade, building construction and other artisan-related occupation such as carpentry, and in the more professional ones such as legal services.

Meanwhile, a large part of the population was becoming more capitalist conscious: it produced raw materials for the colonial market, it was familiar with the monetary incentives, it wanted to consume more and many of the things it wanted to consume had to be imported. Both the major exports and most of the manufactured imports passed through the hands of the foreign companies. But there was a trickle-down effect, which was to the benefit of the more educated ones, of export producers and others concerned with the modern trading sector. In this way, individual acquisitive desires and strategies induced by market forces grew up alongside the traditional occupation and tended to predominate as the modern sector grew.

Those sections with more access to the "benefits" of the foreign trading companies, in turn, became addicted to consuming manufactured imported goods and regarded them as superior to, and more desirable than, traditional products or home-produced substitutes. In such an economic environment, it is hardly surprising to see a lack of investment in the local production of consumer goods. Significantly, as foreign concerns made large profits and failed to use them for industrial investments in the colonies, so also did some indigenes who increased their money returns and accumulated capital had little incentive to invest in local production or manufacturing. Consequently, the role of the colonies as primary producers of cash crop seemed to accord with those expectations and was further encouraged to proceed in this direction indefinitely.[14]

At the same time, as more effort was put into cash-crop production and laboring in the mines, subsistence cultivation for Africa's basic food was neglected. By the 1950s, Africa had become a net importer of food. In other words, Africans on average were producing or growing less than half of their own consumption needs. The growing level of urban unemployment heightened the crisis of demand exceeding supply of food. From the late 1940s and early 1950s more and more people migrated to the towns in a desperate attempt to escape increasing rural poverty as a result of the abandonment of subsistence mode of economic activities.

Another legacy from the colonial period was Africa's transport system, which was totally inadequate for the region's internal development. In Sub-Saharan Africa during the era of colonialism, most of the railways had been built around the turn of the century to ease the export of the region's raw materials to Europe. By independence they were badly in need of repair and simply linked a country's mines or main source of cash crops to the sea. Roads were poorly developed and most of the policies regarding Africa's roads and rail networks showed no concern for a country's internal economic development. Furthermore, there were virtually no regional road or rail links to help promote trade between one African country and another, unless as a route from a land-locked country to the sea. Telecommunications were the same. Internal rural networks were almost nonexistent, and it was easier to telephone from Africa to Europe than it was to telephone from one African city to another.

Thus, in addition to economic and trade policies that worked against local economic and entrepreneurial development, the infrastructures needed for indigenous entrepreneurship were conspicuously lacking.

ECONOMIC AND ENTREPRENEURIAL DEVELOPMENT IN THE POSTCOLONIAL ERA

At independence, the founding fathers of the African nations were committed to a policy of industrialization wherein the government was expected to play a major role in the process of industrialization and economic development. It seemed to have been accepted as a matter of fact and, indeed, principle, that the government should be responsible for developing the infrastructure and the public utilities upon which industrial growth depends. More importantly, because of the dearth of private capital, it is then obvious that investment must come from government (public) sources. Herein lays the socialist economic development ideologies in Tanzania (under Julius Nyerere), Ghana (under Kwame Nkrumah), Zimbabwe (under Robert Mugabe), Mozambique (under Samora Michel) and a host of other countries. In accordance with this socialist/communist developmental ideology and policy, it was seen as necessary for the new independent governments to indigenize economic activities that were formally under the control of the colonial administrators and foreign owned multinational companies.

For example, aside from being committed to a policy of industrialization, newly independent African nations had the desire to provide public utilities using indigenous capital. In Nigerian, for example, this period witnessed the growth of public enterprises such as the Nigerian Electric Power Authority (NEPA), Nigerian Ports Authority (NPA), the Nigerian Railway Corporation (NRC), etc. Because of lack of local financial sources, the postcolonial governments had to rely almost entirely on state funding as the engine of economic growth. As a result of limited resources at its disposal (apart from agricultural export), the state was not in a financial position to fund viable economic activities.

In this type of economic environment it was almost impossible for the development of indigenous entrepreneurs. Three reasons can be adduced to this. First, there was a lack of sufficient capital base from which local entrepreneurs could be developed. Second, there was the grip of the international corporations on the postcolonial economies at this time. Third, the majority of the indigenes in postcolonial Africa were ill prepared to play the role of local entrepreneurs or managers of industry. It could be argued that during this period, the national bourgeoisie has the mentality of men of affairs, not captains of industry. The elite were those drawn from the colonial civil service sector, insufficiently prepared to assume the role of entrepreneurs. Whatever businessmen and women Africa was able to produce during this era, they essentially were raised in the agricultural sector and were made to be engaged in the cultivation of products that serve as raw materials such as cocoa, rubber, cotton, palm produce, cotton, etc which were supplied to the multinational corporations and shipped overseas for processing. With the exception of very few who ventured into trading (e.g., the Ibrus and the Odetolas of Nigeria), African indigenous capitalists were restricted to farming for the production of agricultural raw materials for export to the European factories.

Thus, at independence, African governments found themselves struggling with and generally failing to overcome the problems of uneven development and the export-oriented economies, which they had inherited from colonial regimes. The expectation in Africa and the euphoria that followed the struggle for independence was that African leaders who championed the course for independence would and should be able to develop courses of actions that would justify the reason for achieving independence. Thus, African leaders were determined to chart a new course of action – one based on inward looking development approach. This philosophy and strategy is aptly captured in Tanzania's *Ujamaa*.

Tanzania's Ujamaa Economic Policy of Development

In Tanzania, for example, it was Julius Nyerere who tried to chart a bold new course and to try to take African development in an entirely new direction. It began in February 1967 with what is known as the Arusha Declaration. In it, Nyerere laid down the principles by which he sought to reverse the trend of African development based upon European model of capitalist industrialization. For Tanzania, and indeed Sub-Saharan Africa, the early years of independence had shown that the adopted European model depended upon huge foreign investment. This increased African indebtedness, in effect continuing to drain African wealth in the direction of the developed capitalist economies of Western Europe and North America. At the same time, as Africa grew poorer and less able to feed itself, private greed was increasing class-division within African society. Julius Nyerere, like other like-minded African rulers such as Kwame Nkrumah of Ghana, was determined to end this "fattening of the elite".

Nyerere's vision of a future Tanzania was of a prosperous, self-reliant and classless society. He called it "African socialism". The idea had evolved among African nationalist leaders of the 1950s as a reaction to what is then perceived as the capitalist exploitation of colonial rule. Nyerere claimed that Africans had no need to be taught the principles of European socialism evolved by Marx and others in nineteenth-century Europe. With a rather idealistic view of pre-colonial African history, Nyerere argued that "traditional" African Village society operated on its own socialist principles of communal cooperation.

Tanzanian socialism was to be based on local resources rather than imported, high-technology industrialization. The country's main banks and foreign-owned capitalist companies were to be "nationalized", that is, taken over by the state on behalf of the people. A "Leadership Code" banned political leaders from accumulating private wealth. The main emphasis of government was to be rural development, leading to self-reliance.

Nyerere proposed the gathering-together of Tanzanian's mass of small remote rural settlements into larger, more effective villages. This would make it easier for government to provide better roads and rural markets combined with agricultural advice and improved technology. Better water, health, and education facilities could also be provided more efficiently to larger, centralized villages. The policy was known as *Ujamaa*, variously translated as "family hood", "self-help" or "mutual cooperation". It was based upon the ancient African tradition of family and clan self-help at times of communal need such as harvest or the clearing of new land. A vital aspect of *Ujamaa* was thus the promotion of the "African socialist" principles of communal labor for the benefit of the community.

Applied to the new large villages it would, Nyerere believed, increase agricultural productivity, enabling communally cultivated fields to produce a surplus for sale to the towns or for export. At the same time, the socialist principles of *Ujamaa* would ensure that greater rural prosperity would be communally shared. This would avoid the sharp divisions of wealth between the masses and the few, which had been a characteristic of colonial and early independence economic and development policy.

However appealing the theory of *Ujamaa*, Tanzania's economic and development policy had a built-in contradiction. It was self-imposed from above. Most importantly, the peasants were reluctant to give up the personal security of private ownership of plots for the sake of communal ones. When persuasion failed to work, government turned to compulsory "villagization". They were helped by severe drought in 1973-74, which persuaded many villagers that a move was worth a try. Between 1973 and 1976 some five million people were moved into *Ujamaa* villages. There were 8000 such villages by 1977.

As a form of economic development, the problems with which the policy was confronted were numerous. One of such problems is the overwhelming bureaucracy that could support such a policy because compulsory villagization, controlled by urban bureaucrats, was sometimes oppressive and often inefficient. Another problem was that of infrastructure. Peasants were sometimes moved before roads, markets and public welfare facilities in new villages were ready. There followed severe shortages of basic commodities such as paraffin, soap and sugar. Government and party officials portrayed peasants as backward and ignorant, not to understand and accept the advantages of villagization. But peasants understood only too well. Levels of production on communal lands in *Ujamaa* villages were not noticeably higher than overall peasant production previously. Some families had been moved off good farming land on to poorer ones. The new agricultural "experts" did not necessarily understand the motivation behind peasant productivity. By the 1980s peasant knowledge and experience were gaining greater respect. Government was forced to ease up on the rigid dogma of the early 1970s. Non-communal individual peasant farmers were allowed to continue, some becoming prosperous petty-capitalists, growing cash for export.

On a regional scale, Tanzania, in the 1980s, remained one of the poorest countries in Africa. It had huge foreign debts and was still dependent upon exporting agricultural raw materials such as coffee, cotton, sisal, etc at prices controlled outside Africa, in exchange for increasingly expensive manufactured imports. But unlike several other countries in the Sub-Saharan Africa region, Tanzania avoided the massive accumulation of landless rural poverty, which characterized its nationally more prosperous neighbor Kenya. And Tanzania had succeeded in providing the mass of rural people with vastly improved welfare service: clean water and free health and education facilities.

Ghana, Nkrumah's Socialism and Political Instability

Ghana, like Tanzania, is a former colony of the British Empire. At independence the country began with a rich mix of agricultural resources in the form cocoa, significant gold and foreign-currency reserves, strong British legal and political institutions, and similar educational systems. But unlike Tanzania that had a stable political environment under Julius Nyerere, the political history of Ghana, including its political economy is a study of instability, political crisis and followed a tortuous path beset with frequent change of government, military coups and abandonment of development policies until early 1990.

Ghana became independent on March 6, 1957, with Kwame Nkrumah as the first prime minister. It was the first nation in black Africa to come out of colonial rule. On July 1, 1960, Ghana became a republic with Nkrumah winning the presidential election that year. He was influenced by socialist ideologies while he was a student in England. By 1961, dissatisfied with the British model of development philosophy based on capitalism, Nkrumah started to lean more toward socialism by calling for greater state participation in the economy and a move towards socialism.

Nkrumah had also wanted Ghana to play a leading role in Africa's liberation from colonial domination. He was an advocate of revolutionary movements that, he thought, would lead to the creation of a United States of Africa, that is, a continental government. For Nkrumah, Ghana, with its enormous untapped resources, was to be the "Black Star of Africa." Thus, on the domestic front, massive government expenditures on road building, mass education, and health services were adjudged important if Ghana were to play its leading role in "Africa's liberation from colonial domination." As a spokesman for the newly independent Africa, Nkrumah wanted the region to develop its own style of government, suited to its special circumstances. To achieve this, vast sums were spent on mega projects. Anthony Baah notes that immediately after independence, "the development strategies in Africa had one goal - human development. This was to be achieved within long and medium term development frameworks whose objectives were to eradicate the colonial structure that had been imposed on African economies, speed up economic growth and to improve living standards of the people. The key feature of African development initiatives in the 1960s was the important role the state played. The state allocated to itself a central role in the development process - building social and economic infrastructure and providing social services to the impoverished people of the continent".[15]

Nkrumah, just like Julius Nyerere and other postcolonial African leaders, believed that the most effective way to develop Africa and Africans was to involve the state in economic activities in order to ensure that there was fairness in the distribution of the benefits from national income and growth. The new states, therefore, invested heavily in social services, particularly education and health. Huge investments also went into the building of economic infrastructure such as roads, ports, communications facilities and factories. Anthony Baah notes that in Ghana, the number of primary schools increased from 154 360 in 1951 to 481 500 in 1961 (211.9 percent); middle schools increased from 66 175 to 160 000(141.7 percent); secondary and technical schools increased from 3 559 to 19 143 (437.8 percent); teacher training colleges from 1916 to 4552 (137.5 percent). In 1951 there were only 208 university students in Ghana. In 1951 the number had increased to 1 204 (478.8 percent increase). In the health sector, number of hospital beds increased from 2 368 in 1951 to 6 155 (160 percent increase); rural and urban clinics increased from 1 to 30; doctors and dentists from 156 to 500 (220.5 percent increase). There were similar investments in transport, communications and electricity. Another feature of the development initiatives in the 1960s was the import substitution strategy which ensured adequate protection of local industries and employment."[16]

In order to reduce the dependence of Africa on the colonial powers, i.e. to gain economic independence, import substitution strategy (ISI) became the key element of the development strategies across Africa. This needed a massive support for the industrial sector. In Ghana, under Nkrumah's seven-year development plan, 62 percent of all investments were to go to the social services sector while 38 percent was to go directly to the "productive sector". In trade, African states controlled substantial proportion of imports of consumer goods and exports. In Ghana, the state controlled 41 percent of imports and over 60 percent of exports (mainly cocoa, gold and timber).

When foreign currency reserves were exhausted as a result of massive investments in social infrastructure, Nkrumah resorted to deficit financing and foreign borrowing. He was criticized for paying little attention to Ghana or for wasting national resources in supporting his pan-African adventures. By the mid-1960s Ghana had a huge debt with rising inflation of about 26 percent in 1965 and economic mismanagement.[17] By the late 1960s, the momentum of Ghana's development had slowed down considerably attributing this partly to "over-investment" in the social sector and corruption.[18]

As in other parts of Sub-Saharan Africa, state monopoly also has its toll on the nascent Ghanaian economy. In Ghana, as in most Sub-Saharan Africa, where so many people live off the land, agricultural development is crucial. The state's intervention in agricultural activities was through the agricultural marketing board—a statutory monopoly that bought farmers' crops at controlled prices and resold them either at home or abroad. The prices paid to farmers were kept artificially low, on the assumption that farmers ignored price signals. Between 1963 and 1979 the price of consumer goods went up by a factor of twenty-two in Ghana while those in neighboring countries went up by a factor of thirty-six. But the price paid by the cocoa marketing board to Ghana's farmers went up just six fold. In real terms, therefore, the returns to cocoa farmers vanished. The country's supposedly price-insensitive farmers responded by switching to production of other crops for subsistence, and exports of cocoa collapsed.[19]

In Ghana, as in most other developing countries in Sub-Saharan Africa, the explanations of economic failure take on two distinct schools of thought: the orthodox school which views the problems as product of faulty economic policies and economic mismanagement and the conspiracy school of thought which seeks to explain the crises as a product of western government's efforts to undermine the growth of Africa's economies. Thus, Clive Crook explains, "As economic troubles mounted, he (Nkrumah) nationalized companies and followed with capital repression. Under his regime capital flew abroad, and people with skills and money did the same. The kleptocrats (government officials who steal large amounts) ran the country into the ground."[20]

However, as Anthony Baah suggests, "What is ignored is the negative and long lasting effect of the cold war on Africa which became one of the battle grounds for the cold war immediately after independence. The West realized that more and more African countries were likely to follow the human-centered path of economic and social development, which had proved to be remarkably successful particularly in Ghana, Zambia and Tanzania. The Western powers saw this rapid development, via the socialist oriented policies, as a threat to the free market ideology. They, therefore, sought to interfere in African political affairs through their secret agencies and in economic affairs through international institutions … the objective of this strategy (West) was not to help Africa to develop but it was in the strategic interest of the West. Having all the new African states on their side was a good strategy during the cold war. The long-term objective was to undermine state participation in economic activities in Africa. Knowing that indigenous Africans could not takeover the major economic activities (because of lack of entrepreneurship skills and credit), the pullout of African states from economic activities would pave the way for the giant western multinationals to take over these enterprises. This strategy worked very well, unfortunately."[21]

Whatever the explanation, however, the set of economic crises that befall Ghana triggered a wave of military coups in the country, which was to be replicated in other neighboring African countries – notable in Nigeria. One thing though is certain, "the heavy financial burdens (in Ghana) set off increasing opposition to Nkrumah from within his own political party, the CP. When Nkrumah visited China in 1966, the military, led by General Ankrah, staged a coup d'état and overthrew the CPP government. It was the beginning of a number of coups that would plague Ghana for years to come. Once the military intervened in 1966, it created a culture that made it easier for subsequent military coups to occur. Nkrumah and the military charted a course for Ghana that would make it hard for future leaders to change direction and help the country to develop economically."[22]

Frequent interventions by the military in Ghana's politics did not generate an environment of political certainty and policy continuity needed to attract and retain private foreign capital and skills. Since Ghana has low domestic savings rate, it needed private direct foreign investments to help sustain the growth of its economy. A history of instability has not helped in attracting the type of direct investments by foreign investors that require heavy initial outlays, such as in manufacturing. In common with many other countries in Sub-Saharan Africa, Ghana suffered from serious post-colonial political instability, experiencing nine changes of government and four military coups in the 26 years between 1957 and 1983. Although Ghana, unlike other African countries, managed to avoid much of the violence that has been associated with political instability, the country has not followed continuity in economic policies as a result of political crisis.

Another explanation for Ghana's economic woes in the late 1960s and early 70s was its immigration policy. According to Benjamin Asare and Alan Wong, liberal immigration policies in Ghana until 1969 had led to large numbers of foreign nationals residing in Ghana. In 1960, it was estimated that about one-eighth of the population was of foreign origin, with the largest numbers coming from African nations like Togo, Burkina, and Nigeria.[23] Consequently, at independence, it was not surprising to find that the business class in Ghana and elsewhere in Africa was composed largely of foreign nationals, especially from India, England, Lebanon, and Syria. As non-citizens, it was not unusual for them to repatriate much of their profits to their countries of origin.

Concerned about the dominant role played by non-nationals in commerce, the Ghanaian government passed the Ghanaian Business Promotion Act that excluded non-Ghanaians from certain categories of business and restricted the conditions under which non-Ghanaians could carry on business. The government of Kofi Busia, concerned about the overwhelming influence of foreign nationals (Asians, Lebanese, Syrians, and Europeans) in the retail-trading sector dating back to colonial times, made a drastic move by requiring all retail trading concerns, whose capital outlay did not exceed half a million *cedis*, to be reserved for Ghanaians. This move was followed by an "alien compliance order" which forced all aliens without proper documentation to leave the country within two weeks. This led to an exodus of African laborers from neighboring countries, leading to a near collapse of the cocoa industry due to labor shortages.

Although some indigenous groups in Ghana were involved in gold trading, Ghanaians generally did not have much experience in modern commerce. After independence, Ghanaians not only lacked a distinct and sizable business class, they also lacked domestic capital. Ghana had to turn to and depend more on external capital and technical know-how to help develop its economy. As in other African countries during this period, much of the external capital came in the form of borrowing. This situation deepened the economic crisis in Ghana with a widening external deficit.

CIVIL BREAKDOWN AND ECONOMIC STAGNATION

It would be impossible to understand the pattern of economic and entrepreneurial development in Sub-Saharan Africa without understanding the economic environment, which emerged from political crises, civil wars and the institutionalization of military rule that befall the sub-continent.

Unlike in Tanzania, Zambia, Kenya, Botswana and Senegal, where there was a long period of political stability after independence, many African countries experienced political crises and civil wars that affected economic and entrepreneurial development in a negative way. From November 1965 coup followed coup with frightening regularity in Africa, taking in Nigeria and Ghana in early 1966, Sierra Leone, Liberia, Democratic Republic of Congo in the eighties and early nineties. By the early 1970s military rule had become a serious African political and economic option and it remained the most frequent means for change of government through the 1970s and late 1990s.

From a historical perspective, the political crises with which African countries were confronted can be traced in part to the legacy of the political landscape inherited from the European colonizers, and in part by the perceived failure on the part of the politicians to deliver what was promised to the masses during the agitation for independence. Importantly, the dream for economic growth was seen by the masses as paramount and the inability to achieve this dream was blamed on the corrupt practices of the African politician. Also, the perceived inequalities among ethnic and social groups were a source for the political crises. These developments and the resulting political and economic crises became the fertile ground for the production and perpetuation of military regimes in the region. In particular, the coups that occurred in Africa in the 1960s can be seen as reactions against inefficient and corrupt civilian regimes. As such most coups against civilian regimes were initially welcome. At least until they got into power the military were known to be well disciplined and usually free of corruption.

It should not be concluded from the above that the military in Sub-Saharan Africa was necessarily a positive force for African economic and entrepreneurial development. Military rulers were just as likely to be corrupt and tyrannical as their civilian counterparts. For example, the demise of the Ugandan economy in this period was based on the tyrannical force of Idi Amin. The year 1979 saw the downfall of three of Africa's most corrupt and tyrannical regimes, that of General "Emperor" Jean-Bedel Bokassa of the

Central African Republic (1966-1979), Field-Marshal Idi Amin of Uganda (1971-79) and civilian president dictator Francisco Marcias Nguema of Equatorial Guinea (1968-79). Bokassa squandered huge sums of his poor country's revenue upon himself and his friends, including his own notorious imperial coronation and his gifts of diamonds to the president of France. Idi Amin, Marcias Nguema and Sani Abacha of Nigeria were responsible for the torture and death of untold thousands of real and imagined opponents of their brutal dictatorial regimes and the looting of state finances for the perpetration of dictatorial tendencies. Idi Amin's military regime is generally credited with having looted and destroying what was once regarded as one of Africa's most thriving, agriculturally based economies. Uganda's "economic war" of 1973 was a starting point of a period of intense economic destabilization and mismanagement. In Tanzania, the war with Idi Amin in 1978 (born out of clash of ideologies) and the country' leadership political ideology which defended the basic features of economic system based on socialism was responsible for that country's economic problem. In Mozambique, faulty Marxist economic ideology coupled with guerrilla warfare and conflicts with neighboring South Africa created an economic and political crisis. The resulting process of Mozambique's economic development was the gradual withdrawal of the peasantry from the planned economy towards subsistence production or black marketeering. In Zambia, unsettled political problems in neighboring countries led to transport problems occasioned by the closure of the southern route and negatively affected the country's export-import trade. Internal hostilities in Somalia, Sudan, Eritrea and Ethiopia led to an influx of refugees and a complete breakdown in civil order and economic institutions. In addition to these crises were natural disasters, including prolonged droughts and excessive rains and social crisis in the form of accelerating growth in urban population, bribery and corruption. In such an environment, it is hardly surprising that the economies failed to grow and entrepreneurship failed to emerge.

THE ECONOMIC POLICY OF STRUCTURAL ADJUSTMENT

Without doubt, one of the most profound economic policies that have shaped entrepreneurship and economic development in Sub-Saharan Africa is that of structural adjustment program. A Structural Adjustment Program is a program of economic development and restructuring consisting of economic policies which countries must follow in order to qualify for new World Bank and International Monetary Fund (IMF) loans and help them make debt repayments on the older debts owed to commercial banks, governments and the World Bank. Although SAPs are designed for individual countries, they have common guiding principles and features which include export-led growth; privatization and liberalization; devaluation of national currencies against the dollar; lifting of import- and export restrictions; removal of price controls and state subsidies; and the efficiency of the free market.

Reflecting the economic crises in Africa such as decline in growth rates since 1973, fallen food production per capita, rising rates of inflation and unemployment, widening deficits on current accounts of balance of payments, it was time for new economic policies of development in the region. Between the late seventies and early eighties, most of Sub-

Sahara African countries have become import-dependent and major parts of their imports were paid for by loans and grants provided by Western donor countries and organizations.[24]

According to reports from the World Bank, real per capita GDP in Sub-Saharan Africa fell by about 25 percent between 1980 and 1988; industrial growth rates have been very low or negative, as industries dependent on scarce foreign exchange for imported inputs have had to close down. Foreign exchange has become scarce, as export revenues have declined. The resultant increases in balance of payments deficits led to recourse to further borrowing. Economic growth, which averaged about 5 percent during 1974-1976, fell to about 2 percent during the period 1977-1979. Accordingly, during this period per capita real income declined. Total short- and long-term liabilities of Sub-Saharan Africa increased from US$38.5 billion in 1978 to US$80 billion in 1984, representing 30 percent and 50 percent respectively of the region's total GNP. Total debt service increased from US$6.4 billion in 1983 to US$7.9 billion in 1984, while the debt service ration of 21.6 percent in 1984 rose to an average of 50 percent in 1987 for the region as a whole.[25]

Faced with these crises, Sub-Saharan Africa, in particular, and developing countries in general had two policy options. They could both curtail imports and impose restrictive fiscal and monetary measures, thereby impeding growth and development or they could finance the widening account deficits through more external borrowing. Unable, and sometimes unwilling to adopt the first option, many of these countries had to rely on the second option. However, they could not borrow funds in the world's private financial markets without first asking the International Monetary Fund (IMF) for assistance. Typically, debtor countries must deal with the IMF before a consortium of international banks will agree to refinance or defer existing loan schedules. Relying on the IMF implies submission to policy and economic adjustment and stabilization programs of IMF, the conditions of which are tantamount to the first policy option. Thus, access to international finance implies acceptance of IMF's conditions, otherwise known as "fund conditionalities."

IMF conditionalities simply means the conditions – generally relating to macroeconomic policies – which countries have to meet to qualify for international loans as a way of ensuring that borrowed resources are used to assist balance of payment adjustment; as a way of encouraging private capital inflows; as a way of retaining scarce IMF resources; as a mechanism for counter-cyclical world economic management. Furthermore, these conditions are packaged in policy instruments called structural adjustment program (SAP) and are provided by the World Bank and the International Monetary Fund. Briefly, a structural adjustment includes the following policies:

1. *Liberalization and deregulation of the economy and trade in order to open markets for international competition*: Liberalization is the removal of or reduction in the trade practices that thwart free flow of goods and services from one nation to another. It includes dismantling of tariff (such as duties, surcharges, and export subsidies) as well as non-tariff barriers (such as licensing regulations, quotas, and arbitrary standards). Deregulation, on the other hand, entails reduction or elimination of specific governmental rules and regulations that apply to private business

including removal of regulations that prevented the private sector from competing with a nationalized monopoly.

The rationale behind trade liberalization is thus: Opening up to external markets would ensure better allocation of resources and promote the orientation of investments towards exporting sectors which had previously been held back by development strategies focused on domestic markets; causing considerable distortions in the functioning of the laws of the market in the developing countries. This rationale rests upon the assumption that protective measures applied since the 1960s led to misallocation of scarce resources and weak growth and productivity in those economies. Trade liberalization should therefore correct these distortions and promote optimal allocation of resources and investments in the developing countries. It would also revive economic growth and enable developing economies to play a more competitive role in a globalized world.

Trade liberalization, deregulation and removal of controls are another area in the adjustment policies. For example, it is assumed that agricultural production has suffered as a result of low agricultural producer prices imposed by a system of price control. The IMF also believed that many of the bureaucratic control apparatuses needed to define and monitor price controls imposed substantial costs on society. Furthermore, it is claimed that dismantling the price control system would also eliminate the need for government subsidies to parastatals and the incidence of black marketing. Export promotion in which poor and developing countries are required to export more of their primary products in order to raise enough money to pay off their debts in a timely manner was also promoted by various liberalization and deregulation policies.

2. *Interest rate policy:* From the point of view of IMF and the World Bank, economic growth depends largely on the level of domestic capital formation. In this regard, IMF focuses on policies that it believes can improve domestic savings and encourage private sector investment. One instrument for achieving this objective is to follow a high interest rate policy objective. A higher rate of interest is supposed also to reduce the level of investment expenditures, by increasing the cost of capital funds in the market, and by so doing eventually reduce domestic inflation. Similarly, higher interest rates are supposed to increase the return on savings and thus encourage the population to save a larger proportion of their incomes. Monetary austerity was also recommended in order to tighten up the money supply to increase internal interest rates to whatever heights needed to stabilize the value of the local currency.

3. *Foreign exchange policy such as currency devaluation:* The IMF had increasingly worked on the premise that since developing countries' rate of inflation had been greater than the rate of inflation among the countries' trading partners; their currencies should be devalued to compensate for the differences in the inflation rates. The assumption was that an inappropriate exchange rate, defined as overvalued rate, generates cost-price distortions that have a negative effect on the consumption-investment mix as well as on the export-import mix and tends to

reduce the profitability of export and import competitive activities in the economy. Thus, it was assumed that devaluation of local currencies in Sub-Saharan Africa would have a positive effect on the balance of payments, discourage the parallel market in foreign exchange, reduce leakages through smuggling, restore government's budgetary balance and have a favorable impact on the local manufacturing sector.

4. *Privatization of public enterprises*: Privatization is a process that entails the reduction of the role of the government in asset ownership and service delivery and a corresponding increase in the role of the private sector. A central theme underlying privatization is the general distrust of the public sector to manage commercial enterprises. A general supposition among proponents of privatization is that, everything else being equal, a private actor will be a better manager of a commercial entity than the public sector. It is often argued therefore that the government can be more effective as a facilitator than a provider of basic services. Privatization is commonly associated with full divestiture (complete transfer of a public enterprise to a private actor).

Minimizing the role of the state in the provision of basic social infrastructure is seen by the IMF as solution to the problem of excessive expansionary impact of fiscal policies in developing countries. The public sector in the developing countries is seen as incurring substantial loss, which is borne directly or indirectly by the central government budget. From the point of view of the World Bank and the IMF, financial stability can be restored through (i) control of the government deficit through curbs on spending, especially in areas of social services and food subsidies, and (ii) control of wage increases, in particular assuring that such increases are at rates less than inflation.

The public sector is also seen as incapable of promoting gross domestic development, at least in the context of developing nations. Privatizing public enterprises is seen as a way of restoring financial stability. This could be achieved through the sale of public enterprises to private holders in order to establish competitive market conditions. This would also ensure a rational possible allocation of resources to activities, which are internationally competitive, and which could thus become the basis for sustained export-led growth for the economy.

Impact of Structural Adjustment Program on Economic and Entrepreneurial Development

Such economic reforms as discussed above have been a mixed blessing for the development of indigenous entrepreneurship. A study on structural adjustment program reforms in five countries (Ghana, Malawi, Mali, Senegal, and Tanzania) indicates that the possible effects on the operation of small enterprises include greater access to imported inputs, a shift in relative prices in favor of domestic inputs (which small enterprises tend to use more intensively than larger firms) and less restrictive business regulation.[26] In spite these positive effects, most analysts have argued that the structural adjustment programs have had a negative effects on the growth of developing countries economy and hampered indigenous entrepreneurial development.

First, the policies of trade liberalization and deregulation came into being because of the perceived notion that protectionism serves as barrier to free trade. Protectionism, as against deregulation is seen as a form of isolationism and subsidizing industries that could otherwise not compete fairly against others. As good as this may sound, it has been noted that deregulation, among other things, stifles domestically grown industries as multinational corporations are more likely to have the resources to out compete local ones. This is precisely the case of the dairy industry in Nigeria and the fate of many local industries in Sub-Saharan Africa under structural adjustment program.[27]

From a historical perspective, protecting and nurturing young industries has been a positive step in a country's attempt to promote economic growth. In the 19th century, industries were protected as core or metropolis countries were industrializing. Yilmaz Akyüz looks at length at how tariffs have been historically used in positive ways for industrialization and how the rich nations are now "kicking away that ladder" that helped them progress, and making poor countries abandon such practices. Akyüz suggests that: "Compared with the historical experience of mature and newly industrialized countries, trade policy in developing countries today appears to be unduly liberal ..."[28]

Thus, several researchers have argued that one of the reasons why the economy of Sub-Saharan African countries have worsened after the adoption of structural adjustment programs is to be found in the policies of trade liberalization and deregulation. Specifically, it is argued that rapid trade liberalization in Africa has not been reciprocated in terms of better access to markets for African producers. Furthermore, massive subsidies afforded to agricultural producers in advanced countries and other forms of protection have hindered Africa's efforts to upgrade capacities and invest in local production. Nor have African exporters been helped by the exchange rate misalignments and instability (created by deregulation) that have often followed moves towards capital account liberalization.[29]

The aggressive manner in which trade liberalization, deregulation and privatization was pursued in many developing and emerging economies was also faulty precisely because the existing social and macroeconomic environments were either ill prepared or unsuitable for such abrupt and drastic socioeconomic changes. As a consequence, trade liberalization and deregulation bred a chaotic economic and business environment where local producers and entrepreneurs found themselves at a disadvantaged competitive position in the global economy.

The policy of export promotion in which poor and developing countries are required by the World Bank and the International Monetary Fund to export more of their primary products is recommended as a policy instrument that would help these countries raise foreign exchange which is necessary for the repayment of their debts. However, some observers have argued that this policy has worsened the competitive position of developing and poor nations and deepened their dependency on the Western economies. One author, J. W. Smith explains the logic of this dependence in the following words:

> "If a society spends one hundred dollars to manufacture a product within its borders, the money that is used to pay for materials, labor and other costs moves through the economy as each recipient spends it. Due to this multiplier effect, a hundred dollars worth of primary production can add several hundred dollars to the Gross National Product (GNP) of that country. If money is spent in another country, circulation of that money is within the exporting country. This is the reason *an industrialized product-exporting/commodity-importing country is wealthy and an undeveloped product-importing/commodity-exporting country is poor*"[30] [Emphasis Added].

Smith suggested that developed countries grow rich by selling capital-intensive products for a high price and buying labor-intensive products for a low price. This imbalance of trade expands the gap between rich and poor. The wealthy sell products to be consumed, not tools to produce. This maintains the monopolization of the tools of production, and assures a continued market for the product.[31]

Thus, one of the effects of structural adjustment is that developing countries must increase their exports. Usually commodities and raw materials are exported. But as Smith noted above, developing countries lose out when they export commodities (which are cheaper than finished products) and are denied or effectively blocked from industrial capital and real technology transfer, and import finished products (which are more expensive due to the added labor to make the product from those commodities and other resources). This leads to less circulation of money in their own economy and a smaller multiplier effect. Yet, this is not new. Historically, this has been a partial reason for dependent economies and poor nations to remain perpetually dependent on the dictates of the economies of the developed nations. This was also the role forced upon former countries under colonial rule. In today's more globalized economy, we see the less developed economies finding themselves in the same uneven pattern of trade: export commodities to west and import finished products from the West. Richard Robbins describes this relationship as a form of *unequal trade*:

> "At first glance it may seem that the growth in development of export goods such as coffee, cotton, sugar, and lumber, would be beneficial to the exporting country, since it brings in revenue. In fact, it represents a type of exploitation called **unequal exchange**. A country that exports raw or unprocessed materials may gain currency for their sale, but they lose it if they import processed goods. The reason is that processed goods—goods that require additional labor—are more costly. Thus a country that exports lumber but does not have the capacity to process it must then re-import it in the form of finished lumber products, at a cost that is greater than the price it received for the raw product. The country that processes the materials gets the added revenue contributed by its laborers."[32]

The economic assumptions of the World Bank and the International Monetary Fund had been premised on the logic that exporting commodities and resources would favorably help developing countries earn foreign exchange with which to pay off debts and keep currencies stable. However, partly due to the price war, which can induce a situation where developing countries produce more of raw materials, commodity prices have always dropped in the world market relative to prices paid for manufactured products. In addition, Celine Tan argues that falling commodity prices have meant that large increases in export volume by commodity producers have not translated into greater export revenues, leading to severely declining terms of trade for many commodity producing countries. For example, when the purchasing power of a country's exports declines, the country is unable to purchase imported goods and services necessary for its sustenance.

Secondly, the country that exports commodities is unable to generate enough income for the implementation of sustainable development programs. A vast majority of Sub-Sahara African countries depend on commodities as a main source of revenue. Primary commodities account for about half of the export revenues of developing countries and many developing countries continue to rely heavily on one or two primary commodities for the bulk of their export earnings.[33] Furthermore, a fall in commodity prices has also led to a build-up of unsustainable debt. The consequence of all these is that Sub-Saharan Africa, for the most part, has remained a consumer of manufactured products in the West. An economic environment that encourages commodity export rather than manufactured goods is hardly an environment for the growth of indigenous entrepreneurship.

In a nutshell, the above research seems to suggest that what the IMF, the World Bank and the developed countries recommended as solutions to the problems of developing countries is contrary to what they had adopted in the process of their economic development. As J. W. Smith notes, every rich nation today has developed because in the past their governments took major responsibility to promote economic growth. There was also a lot of protectionism and intervention in technology transfer. There was an attempt to provide some sort of equality, education, health, and other services to help enhance the nation. The industrialized nations have understood that some forms of protection allows capital to remain within the economy, and hence via a multiplier effect, help enhance the economy. Yet, as seen in the structural adjustment policies, the developing nations are effectively being forced to cut back these very same provisions that have helped the developed countries to prosper in the past.[34]

Indeed, some analysts have argued that Western countries have used the excuse of debt restructuring and debt forgiveness to further restructure the global economy in a direction that favors the rich countries and further perpetuate the inequality that has existed in the global system of exchange. Thus Susan George suggests, "Debt is an efficient tool. It ensures access to other peoples' raw materials and infrastructure on the cheapest possible terms. Dozens of countries must compete for shrinking export markets and can export only a limited range of products because of Northern protectionism and their lack of cash to invest in diversification. Market saturation ensues, reducing exporters' income to a bare minimum while the North enjoys huge savings. The IMF cannot seem to understand that investing in a healthy, well-fed, literate population is the most intelligent economic choice a country can make."[35]

The policy measure that requires developing countries to depend more and more on primary commodities is also seen as detrimental to the development of indigenous entrepreneurship. According to critics, the type of trade that Sub-Saharan Africa needs is one that promotes a diversification of its economic base in order to weather through economic storms, not to depend on single commodity exports. Matthew Lockwood is worth quoting in regards to how this phenomenon aptly applies to Africa:

> "What Africa needs is to shake off its dependence on primary commodity exports, a problem underlying not only its marginalization from world trade but also its chronic debt problems. Many countries rely today on as narrow a range of agricultural and mineral products as they did 30 years ago, and suffer the consequences of inexorably declining export earnings. Again, the campaigners' remedy — to improve market access for African exports to Europe and America — is wide off the mark."[36]

Another area where structural adjustment programs are seen to have hampered economic and entrepreneurial development in Sub-Saharan Africa is the program's abandonment of the social infrastructure and human resources needed for socio-economic development. Although, Sub-Saharan Africa was asked to spend on average 50 percent of its total GNP on debt servicing, essential investments in health, education and other infrastructure such as electricity and transportation were conspicuously neglected. In short there was a frightening decay in the key success factors needed for global competition. While insisting on pushing weak African economies into markets where they were unable to compete with the might of the international private sector, the World Bank and IMF was also requiring these countries to reduce state support and protection for social and economic sectors, these policies further undermined the economic development of African countries.

One researcher, Ann-Louise Colgan argues "even more significantly, the policies of the World Bank and IMF have impeded Africa's development by undermining Africa's health. Their free market perspective has failed to consider health an integral component of an economic growth and human development strategy." Instead, the policies of these institutions have caused deterioration in health and in health care services across the African continent."[37]

In summary, the effects of structural adjustment programs on entrepreneurial development were ambiguous in most developing countries. In Nigeria, for example, the structural adjustment program initiated by the Ibrahim Babangida regime in 1986 not only reinforced a culture of foreign-import-dependent economy, it also perpetuated it. The policy measures that were introduced to open up the economy, to move toward a more prominent role for the private sector, and the withdrawal of the state from direct service provision created an environment of lawless business practices. Through structural adjustment, Nigerians were provided with the opportunity for entrepreneurship in a midst of an import-dependent economy. This opportunity witnessed a massive growth in economic activities especially in the housing sector.

Significantly, the economic policies of structural adjustment program reinforced the growing power of businessmen who were neither entrepreneurs nor innovators, but traders serving as middlemen between producers in foreign markets (e.g., Europe and Asia) and consumers in Sub-Saharan Africa, smugglers of foreign made goods and traders involved in foreign currency speculation. Structural adjustment program did not discourage black marketeering; it reinforced and institutionalized the practice. Whatever foreign exchange earnings that was made available from exportation of agricultural commodities to businessmen; it was used for the importation of foreign made good to the detriment of home-manufactured substitutes. In other words, the development of the economies of Sub-Saharan Africa under structural adjustment period found itself in the worst form of laissez - faire development and economic policy. In Nigeria, in particular, trade was liberalized without due consideration to the protection of home industries. Criminality attained its highest peak as a form of business practice and the nation became a taboo in terms of foreign investment.

THE GLOBAL ECONOMY AND ENTREPRENEURIAL DEVELOPMENT

We are moving away from a world in which national economies were once seen as relatively self-contained entities, isolated from each other by barriers to cross-border trade and investment; by distance, time zones, and language; and by national differences in government regulation, culture, political ideologies and business practices. And we are moving toward a world in which barriers to cross–border trade and investment are tumbling; perceived distance is shrinking due to advances in transportation and telecommunications technology; material culture is starting to look similar the world over; and national economies are merging into an interdependent global economic system. The process by which this is occurring is commonly referred to as globalization. Similarly, we will call this period "globalization era." The era of globalization is the ongoing period in which the state of a nation's economy is based on worldwide interdependence of resource supplies, product markets, and business competition. In this book we see globalization as *a process of interaction and integration among the people, companies, and governments of different nations, a process driven by international trade and investment and aided by information technology.*

Although globalization is not new phenomenon and has been an historical process, the era beginning from the mid eighties has witnessed a fundamental shift in the pattern of economic development with considerable impact on entrepreneurship and its role in economic development. Various developments in the global economy have created opportunities for the growth of entrepreneurship. This is especially true for national governments and individuals who are able to seize the opportunities presented by the process of globalization. Although various developments in the global economy have created opportunities for the growth of entrepreneurship, some of these have also hindered entrepreneurial initiatives in a number of countries.

The major global factors driving entrepreneurial development in this era are (i) expanded cross-national cooperation and the formation of regional trade blocs; (ii) the preeminence of information technology, global communication, the Internet boom and the emergence of the World Wide Web; (iii) MNEs and the growing trend in the outsourcing of means of production by major global and multinational corporations; and (iv) the diminishing role of the nation-state. In Sub-Saharan Africa, these factors have either provided opportunities or threats in the development of indigenous entrepreneurs.

Globalization, Regional Trade Blocs and Entrepreneurship

Rapid and increasing globalization of markets has facilitated the formation of regional trade blocs and has forced smaller companies to enter international markets. **Regional trade blocs** are intergovernmental associations that manage and promote trade activities for specific regions of the world. In order to appreciate the relationship between globalization, emergence of regional trade blocs and their impact on entrepreneurship in developing countries, it is perhaps important to look at this phenomenon from a global perspective, drawing on examples from the experience of the European Union, North America and Southeast Asian countries. From a comparative perspective, we will then examine the nature and impact of trade blocs in Sub-Saharan Africa.

Early manifestations of the trend in the formation of regional trade blocs in reaction to globalization were the formal integration of some European countries into the Single European Market in 1992, the formation of the Association of Southeast Asian Nations (ASEAN) in 1967 and the formation of North American Free Trade Agreement (NAFTA) in 1993. As a result of global competition among countries on the one hand and corporations, on the other, governments are increasingly realizing that their own country's competitive interests can best be enhanced by cooperating with other countries in the same regions through treaties and agreements. Although geographic proximity is one of the important reasons for regional integration, common historical, cultural and economic development backgrounds and policies have increasingly played an important role. For example, countries want to ensure that companies headquartered within their borders are not disadvantaged by foreign-country policies. Thus, such countries join international organizations and enter into treaties and agreements with other countries on a variety of commercial activities, such as transportation and trade. Another reason is that high real-interest rates in one country can attract funds from countries in which interest rates are lower, which can disrupt economic conditions in the latter countries because there will be a shortage of funds available for investment. For the benefits for local companies, governments also enter into regional trade blocs for the acquisition of resources. In addition to facilitating free trade among countries in an economic bloc, many groups have developed strategies to enhance the competitiveness of their entrepreneurial firms in the global economy.

The largest and the most comprehensive of the regional economic groups is the European Union, which has moved toward a single market since the passage of the Single European Act of 1987. Among other things, the act included the elimination of the remaining barriers to a free market. Today, the European Union accounts for a fifth of world trade, a common currency (the euro), 27 member countries with a population of over 460 million in 2007, a combined gross national product (GNP) of about US$12 trillion and per capita income of US$32,900 (2007 estimate). The European Union is the foremost regional economic bloc when it comes to promoting entrepreneurship. For example, in 2002, the European Economic and Social Committee of the European Union recommended the establishment of a special statute for the promotion of entrepreneurship. The Union recognized that: "Small enterprises must not stay outside the globalized world economy. Just like bigger enterprises they should be able to follow international strategies affording them maximum development." As a consequence, the

Union created a "European Statute for SMEs" which, is aimed at "promoting entrepreneurship and the creation of new activities, in addition to being an incentive to cross-border partnerships within the single market."[38]

The European Union also recognized that small entrepreneurs in general and women-led businesses in particular, perceive the issue of "finance" as one of the main barriers to start up and to lead their companies to growth. This is why the Entrepreneurship Action Plan adopted in February 2004 by the European Union has collaborated with member states in the areas where the needs of women entrepreneurs are not yet met, namely access to finance and networking.[39]

The North American Free Trade Association (NAFTA) is another major trade bloc comprising the United States, Canada and Mexico with a population of about 430 million in 2007 and a combined gross domestic product (GDP) of over US$15 trillion in 2007, with per capita income of US$29,945. Through the North American Free Trade Agreement (NAFTA), tariff and nontariff barriers between the U.S., Canada and Mexico have been eliminated, trade rules between the three countries have been harmonized and restrictions on services and foreign investment among the three countries have been liberalized. Although there are economic pros and cons in NAFTA as in any trade agreement, over the 10 years since NAFTA was implemented, U.S. companies invested an average of $12 billion per year in Mexico. Mexico's per capita income rose to $6,230 in 2003, compared with only $1,100 in China, and was higher than in any other country in Latin America, including Brazil. Mexico's economy is now the ninth largest in the world, up from number 15 when NAFTA was signed.[40]

Through NAFTA and other trade agreements, many companies have set up their production plants in Mexico in order to get access to Mexico's cheap labor and its proximity to the U.S. market. The establishment of production facilities in Mexico, especially in industries such as automobile and electronics, has also seen an increase in local entrepreneurship acting as intermediaries in these industries' value chain. In general, trade among the United States, Canada and Mexico more than doubled from $291 billion in 1993 to $678 billion in 2002, while foreign direct investment by the three countries in one another increased during the same period from $120 billion to $310 billion. While Mexico and Canada are aware of the overwhelming importance of the United States to their economies, the United States has Mexico and Canada as its first and second largest trading partners. The United States exports nearly four times more to Mexico and Canada than to China and Japan, and 75 percent more than to the European Union. Moreover, Canada and Mexico are the sources of 36 per cent of all U.S. energy imports.[41] Specifically, U.S. businesses have experienced a dramatic upsurge in exports to Mexico – from $41.6 billion in 1993 to $97.4 billion in 2003, which is a rise of 134 per cent. Consumers, again along with many businesses, experienced benefits from a 246 percent rise in imports (from $39.9 billion to $138.1 billion) from Mexico. Total trade (export plus imports) between the U.S. and Mexico grew by 189 percent - from $81.5 billion to $235.5 billion. Interestingly, that growth in total trade with Mexico from 1993 to 2003 was almost three times faster than overall U.S. economic growth.[42]

The Association of South East Asian Nations (ASEAN) is another regional trade bloc with a combined gross domestic product of US$2,172billion, per capita income of US$4,044 and large market with over 550 million people. As in other trade associations, the goal of ASEAN is to promote cooperation in many areas, including industry and trade through the development of entrepreneurship.

Thus, the ASEAN Economic Ministers at its 36th meeting on September of 2004 in Jakarta, Indonesia adopted the ASEAN Policy Blueprint for SME Development (APBSD).[43] ASEAN, as a regional trade group, recognized that "small and medium enterprises (SMEs) including micro-enterprises form the backbone of the economy in ASEAN member countries. They (SMES) are the largest source of domestic employment across all economic sectors, in both rural and urban areas. The SME sector also provides opportunities for women and the young to participate in the economic development of the country. A strong, dynamic and efficient SME sector will ensure the sustainable economic development." Thus, ASEAN governments recognized that the "encouragement and promotion of competitive and innovative SMEs is necessary in contributing to greater economic growth of the ASEAN region."

ASEAN also acknowledged that the "SME sector in ASEAN is confronted with a wide-range of structural, fiscal and non-fiscal issues and challenges, such as limited access to finance, technology and market. There are also insufficient entrepreneurial spirit and management skills among ASEAN SMEs. These problems are compounded with the lack of information, compliance to standards and certification and an enabling business environment. In addition, the new trend of conducting business utilizing information and communication technology (ICT) as well as the outsourcing and networking strategies adopted by large enterprises and multinational companies (MNCs) require SMEs to undertake proactive measures to ensure their business sustainability."

In particular, ASEAN governments stressed the fact that unlike large enterprises, SMEs are more agile and adaptable to changes in the business environment. They agreed that "Concerted actions and development programs in partnership with donor agencies undertaken by the ASEAN SME Working Group in enhancing the capacity of SMEs will ensure a more progressive SME sector towards the overall economic growth of the ASEAN region."

They recognized that greater competition, rapid technological advances, more demanding market requirements, and constant changes in consumer demands require SMEs to be innovative and creative in order to face the challenges of the global market. ASEAN governments also agreed that the "formation of SME-based clusters, and inter-firm networks and linkages within ASEAN will create further business opportunities for SME entrepreneurs in the region. Therefore, there is a need to create and promote a conducive business environment for SME development where both Government and the private sector assume synergistic and complementary roles." They also stressed the role of the governments in the process of entrepreneurial development, pointing out, "The Government acts as a facilitator, while SMEs themselves are the engine of growth. Collaborative SME development programs within public-private partnership framework will ensure the continued economic growth in the region."

In outlining the framework for SME development in the ASEAN region, the mission of the APBSD was formulated to include: (a) to develop and sustain a culture of entrepreneurship and innovation within the SME sector in the region; (b) to assist and ensure that ASEAN SMEs become and remain learning, dynamic and outward-looking enterprises; and (c) to encourage collaboration and networking among SMEs within ASEAN as well as with business enterprises outside the region.

The objectives of the APBSD are to (a) accelerate the pace of SME development, optimizing on the diversities of member countries; (b) enhance the competitiveness and dynamism of ASEAN resource development and skills, finance as well as technology; (c) strengthen the resilience of ASEAN SMEs to better withstand adverse macroeconomic and financial difficulties, as well as the challenges of a more liberalized trading environment; and (d) increase the contribution of ASEAN SMEs to the ASEAN region.

The Global Economy and the Benefits of Trade Blocs

In the context of regional trade blocs and economic integration, economic and entrepreneurial growth is impacted in a profound way. First, economic integration resulting from regional trade blocs creates trade. Such effects are the shifting of resources from inefficient to efficient companies as trade barriers fall. Production shifts to more efficient producers for reasons of comparative advantage, allowing consumers access to more goods at a lower price than would have been possible without integration. Companies that are protected in their domestic markets face real problems when the barriers are eliminated and they attempt to compete with more efficient producers. The strategic implication is that companies that might not have been able to export to other countries – even though they might be more efficient than producers in that country – are now able to export when the barriers come down. Thus, there will be a demand for their products, and the demand for the protected, less efficient products will fall. Regional trade blocs and economic integration can result to trade diversion. Trade diversion occurs when trade shifts to countries in the group at the expense of trade with countries not in the group, even though nonmember companies might be more efficient in the absence of trade barriers.

Integration also results in the overall growth in the market and companies within that group through economies of scale as firms can produce more cheaply. Another important effect is the increase in efficiency due to increase competition. This is especially true in the apparel and furniture industries in Mexico. When NAFTA was created, many apparel and furniture manufacturing companies left the United States and Canadian to Mexico. The Mexican textile industry brought jobs back from Asia countries like Malaysia and Singapore as labor rates increase and U.S. textile firms set up operations in Mexico to supply both the Mexican and U.S. apparel markets. The transfer of knowledge and technology to the Mexican textile industry by U.S. firms led to a multiplier effect thus making the Mexican textile industry more competitive in the world market.

Closer trade and economic association among countries are likely to stimulate multiple-country entrepreneurial activity. In the European Union and NAFTA settings, entrepreneurs have emerged as major "change agents" taking advantage of new combinations to open new markets, provide new sources of supply, suggest new methods of production, and in some cases stimulate the reorganization of entire industries. Such opportunities are expected to emerge as global entrepreneurship creates larger, more efficient productive bases, new sources of comparative advantage, and the increased international competitiveness of firms in regional trade blocs.

Regional Integration and the Experience of Sub-Saharan Africa

Although regional integration is increasingly recognized as the viable space within which small economies can better organize themselves to survive economically in a highly competitive world, Sub-Saharan Africa has been lacking in the formation of viable regional trade blocs. Although the launch of the African Union (AU) and the New Partnership for Africa's Development (NEPAD) have given new impetus to the integration process, political instability in the region has made the development of a viable trade bloc almost impossible.

A factor crucial to the success of any economic integration and development process in Sub-Saharan Africa is a peaceful political environment. As we discuss in the next chapter, economic growth can only materialize within an environment of peace, security and stability. The poor economic performance of the Sub-Saharan region and the slow pace of regional integration are in part the result of civil unrest, conflict and war in several of the countries of the region.

The Economic Community of West African States (ECOWAS)

The largest of the trade blocs in Sub-Saharan Africa is ECOWAS, the Economic Community of West African States, which was established on 28 May 1975 to promote cooperation and integration among West African countries. It was initially made up of the following sixteen (16) member States: Benin, Burkina Faso, Cape Verde, Côte d'Ivoire, The Gambia, Ghana, Guinea, Guinea Bissau, Liberia, Mali, Mauritania, Niger, Nigeria, Senegal, Sierra Leone and Togo. Following the withdrawal of Mauritania in 2001 there are now fifteen (15) Member Stares making up the community.

The mission of ECOWAS is to promote co-operation and development in all spheres of economic activity through the removal of all forms of trade barriers and obstacles to the free movement of persons, goods and services, as well as the harmonizing of regional sector policies. The main objective is to establish a large West African common market and create a monetary union.

ECOWAS Member States occupy a surface area of 1.5 million km2, representing 17 percent of the total surface area of the continent. The population of West Africa, which grows at an annual rate of 2.67 percent, was estimated at 261.13 million in 2006. Nigeria is the most populous country in the region with a population of 134.38 million (51.5 percent of the region's total population). It is followed by Ghana, which has an estimated population of 22.56 million, representing 8.6 percent of the total population of the region.

ECOWAS is the most populous regional economic community or bloc in Africa. A distinct economic sub group known as UEMOA also exists within the community. This sub group, which comprises eight countries, is a monetary and customs union with a common currency, the CFA franc. The countries are Benin, Burkina Faso, Côte d'Ivoire, Guinea Bissau, Mali, Niger, Senegal and Togo. The seven remaining countries in

ECOWAS have each their own national currencies. This group accounts for 75 percent of the region's GDP and 70 percent of its population.

Of this seven, five of them namely, Gambia, Ghana, Guinea, Nigeria and Sierra Leone are actively preparing to establish a second common currency (West African Monetary Zone, WAMZ) in December 2009 within the framework of the ECOWAS monetary cooperation program. On the basis of the performance of the countries relative to the ECOWAS macro economic convergence criteria, the two monetary zones are expected to merge after 2009 to form a single currency. However, a new impetus has been added to this monetary project with the recent directive by the ECOWAS Authority of Heads of State and Government that the ECOWAS Commission in consultation with the Ministers of Finance and the Governors of Central Banks of member states should fast-track the common currency project with a view to attaining a single currency in 2009.

Average GDP per capita was US$680 dollars US$ in 2006 compared with 600 dollars in 2005, a 13.3 percent progression. However, this average masks a number of disparities: Cape Verde continues to lead the pack with 2 689 dollars per capita GDP in 2006. Côte d'Ivoire with 947 dollars, Nigeria with 808 dollars and Senegal with 774 dollars had higher than average rates. The lowest rates were observed in Guinea Bissau (192 US dollars) and Liberia (198 dollars). Real GDP growth rate in the ECOWAS region was 5.7 percent in 2006 as against 6 percent in 2005. This decline was due to the increase in the oil bill and the persistent socio-political crises some member countries are experiencing. In 2006, all the countries of the region recorded varying levels of growth: 4.0 percent for Côte d'Ivoire, Guinea, Guinea Bissau, Niger, Senegal and Togo and above 5 percent for Burkina Faso, Cape Verde, The Gambia, Ghana, Liberia, Nigeria and Sierra Leone.

The external debt burden of the region declined from 40.0 percent of GDP in 2005 to 30.9 percent of GDP in 2006, thanks to sound macroeconomic management by the countries and the measures taken by the international community to reduce the debt burden of some member countries.

About 60 percent of the GDP was derived from the economic activities of the region namely, agriculture in the primary sector (24.2 percent), mines and quarries in the secondary sector (19.3 percent) and trade in the tertiary sector (15.7 percent). With respect to the primary sector, agriculture accounts for 79 percent. Some of the cash crops cultivated in the region such as coffee; cocoa, and cotton fetch substantial foreign exchange to Member States. However, the prices of such cash crops fluctuate in an unpredictable manner, as the countries have no say in the fixing of the prices. The main cash crops cultivated in the ECOWAS region are coffee, cocoa (Côte d'Ivoire, Ghana, Nigeria and Togo) and cotton (Benin, Burkina Faso).

In the secondary sector, mines and quarries account for 61 percent of all activities in the region. However its importance varies from one Member State to another. In Nigeria crude oil production accounts for 84 percent of its secondary economic activity, whilst mining in Liberia represents 53 percent of secondary economic activity. The reason for the average performance of Liberia can be traced to the embargo placed by the United Nations on diamond and other products from Liberia. In ECOWAS countries the main products of the extractive industries are crude oil (Nigeria, Côte d'Ivoire), diamond (Guinea, Liberia and Sierra Leone) and gold (Burkina Faso, Ghana, Guinea, Mali, and Niger).

In the ECOWAS region, the tertiary sector is dominant, heterogeneous and with activities related mainly to trade, transport, non-trade services of public administrations, and duties on goods. Also massively present is the informal sector, which is considered as the last resort of the unemployed and the vulnerable, particularly women and young job-seekers. With respect to the tertiary sector, trade is the most dominant activity, and represents about 42 percent of the contribution of the sector.

Also, the volume of intra regional trade is low. In 2004 it accounted for about 11 percent of the total trade of the region. The figures confirm the assumption according to which the informal sector of the region is dynamic and robust given that it accounts for a significant proportion of the unofficial trade of the region.

East African Community (EAC)

The East African Community (EAC) is a customs union in East Africa, consisting of Kenya, Uganda and Tanzania and was originally founded in 1967, but was disbanded in 1977 as a result of political and social crises in the region. In January 2001, at a ceremony held in the Tanzanian city of Arusha, which is also its headquarters, the EAC was revived. The new EAC treaty paved the way for an economic and, ultimately, a political union of the three countries. A further treaty signed in March 2004 set up a customs union, which commenced on 1 January, 2005. EAC has a combined Gross Domestic Product (GDP) of US$34.2billion with 95 million people. As at November of 2006, Kenya was ranking high in terms of economic growth with US dollars 16.2 billion, population of 32.8 million people and per capita of US dollars 485, followed by Tanzania with GDP of US$ 10.3 billion, population of 35 million and per capita of US$ 288. Uganda ranked third in the list with GDP of US$7.9 billion, population of 26.7 million people and per capita of US$ 292.

From a historical perspective, Kenya, Tanzania and Uganda have had some form of cooperation dating back to the early 20th century, including the Customs Union between Kenya and Uganda in 1917, which the then Tanganyika joined in 1927, the East African High Commission (1948-1961), the East African Common Services Organisation (1961-1967) and the East African Community (1967-1977).

In 1977, the East African Community collapsed after ten years, amid disagreements caused by dictatorship under Idi Amin in Uganda, socialism in Tanzania, and capitalism in Kenya, and the three member states lost over sixty years of co-operation and the benefits of economies of scale. Each of the former member states had to embark, at great expense and at lower efficiency, upon the establishment of services and industries that had previously been provided at the regional level.

The EAC made such political and economic sense that it was inevitable that its revival would be touted once the political climate in the region stabilized. Thus, Presidents Moi of Kenya, Mwinyi of Tanzania, and Museveni of Uganda signed the Treaty for East African Co-operation in Arusha, Tanzania, on November 30, 1993, and established a Tri-partite Commission for Co-operation. A process of re-integration was embarked on, involving tripartite programs of co-operation in political, economic, social and cultural fields, research and technology, defence, security, legal and judicial affairs. The East African Community was finally revived on 30 November 1999, when the Treaty for its re-establishment was signed. It came into force on 7 July 2000, twenty-three years after the total collapse of the defunct erstwhile Community and its organs.

The Southern African Development Community (SADC)

The Southern African Development Community (SADC) is a regional trade organization presently with fourteen members: Angola, Botswana, The Democratic Republic of the Congo, Lesotho, Madagascar, Malawi, Mauritius, Mozambique, Namibia, South Africa, Swaziland, Tanzania, Zambia and Zimbabwe. The aim of SADC is to promote Southern Africa regional cooperation in economic development. Presently, the region has a population of about 234 million, a combined Gross National Product (GDP) of US$737 billion and per capita income of US$3,152. The forerunner of SADC was the Southern Africa Development Coordination Conference (SADCC), which was formed in Lusaka, Zambia, on 1 April 1980, following the adoption of the Lusaka Declaration (entitled *Southern Africa: Towards Economic Liberation*) by the nine founding member states. The Declaration and Treaty establishing the Community, which replaced the Coordination Conference, was signed at the Summit of Heads of State or Government on 17 August 1992, in Windhoek, Namibia.

The main aims of SADC are, among others: (i) To harmonize the political and socio-economic policies and plans of the member states; (ii) To mobilize the people of the region and their institutions to take initiatives to develop economic, social and cultural ties across the region, and to participate fully in the implementation of the programs and projects of the SADC; (iii) To create appropriate institutions and mechanisms for the mobilization of requisite resources for the implementation of the programs and the operations of the SADC and its institutions; (iv) To develop policies aimed at the progressive elimination of obstacles to free movement of capital and labor, goods and services, and of the peoples of the region generally among member states; (v) To promote the development of human resources; and (vi) To promote the development, transfer and mastery of technology.

The SADC has, as of August 2001, restructured and adopted a centralized approach in running the integration and development of its 14 member countries. The aim of decentralizing or internationalizing the sectors was for SADC to guide and coordinate regional policies and programs on a country-by-country basis.

Already some member countries are emerging as continental leaders in terms of macroeconomic policies and poverty reduction strategies as well as institution building and these are: Botswana, Mauritius, Namibia and South Africa. In terms of the economic performance within the Region, Angola is leading the way with a 13.8 percent growth rate, followed by Mozambique with 8 percent and Tanzania with 6.2 percent. Improvements in growth rates have also been witnessed in Lesotho, Namibia and South Africa. On the Public Index Rankings, as contained in the Global Competitiveness Report, four of SADC's member states ranked among the top ten, with Botswana ranking first. The three others are South Africa, Mauritius and Tanzania.

Economic Constraints among the Sub-Saharan Africa's Trade Blocs

As in other developing countries, the bulk of the financial resources of the ECOWAS, EAC, SADC and other countries in Sub-Saharan Africa are derived from export revenue from commodities such as coffee, cocoa, cotton, coffee, tea, petroleum, phosphate and bauxite. With the exception of South Africa and a few other countries in Sub-Saharan Africa, an additional source is external funding in the form of loans and official development assistance. As a result, the performance of Sub-Saharan economies is heavily dependent on the external environment and, in particular, economic growth in the developed countries. Although many countries in other regional trade blocs are cooperating to reduce trade barriers among themselves, Sub-Saharan Africa, as producers of primary commodities, has become less competitive because primary commodity exports have become much less important as a viable source of trade. Consequently, the low price of raw materials in the global market negatively affected the growth of Sub-Saharan economies. These developments had repercussions on African countries, which are already weakened by the lack of economic diversification, the external debt burden, deteriorating terms of trade, persistent conflict, and spread of infectious diseases such as HIV/AIDS, malaria and tuberculosis.

Thus, many of the benefits commonly associated with regional trade blocs and the rationale for economic integration seem to be elusive in the context of Sub-Saharan Africa. Specifically in the case of Sub-Saharan Africa, experience has indeed shown that economic cooperation and integration do not prosper in an environment that is politically unstable and socially insecure. Peace and security are therefore pre-requisites for a balanced economic development and advancement as they largely determine the direction and pace of economic and political reforms of a country. Apart from political instability and other forms of social crises, the inability to have major regional trade blocs in Sub-Saharan Africa derives, in part, from the fact that African countries have been struggling to establish a political identity, and the different trade associations or blocs have political as well as economic underpinnings. Second, the markets in Sub-Saharan Africa, with the notable exception of South Africa, are underdeveloped, making trade liberalization a relatively minor contributor to economic growth in the region. Third, most African countries rely on trade links with former colonial powers than with each other, so intra-regional trade is not significant. This is particularly the case among Francophone and English-speaking West African countries.

I undertook the discussion in this section to reveal the relationship between the growing need for regional trade blocs as a response to increased global competition and the impact on economic and entrepreneurial development. From a global perspective, the historical and political development of the European Union and the economic objectives of NAFTA, ASEAN and other regional trade blocs indicate this relationship. From a comparative perspective, however, Sub-Saharan Africa is yet to benefit economically from the advantages commonly associated with regional trade blocs. In this section, some of the reasons behind this failure have been identified.

More significantly, although Africa has a long track record in regional integration initiatives, the results have been by and large rather disappointing. What Sub-Saharan Africa needs first is the establishment of viable political systems that encourage collective initiatives, which in turn would lead to the achievement of sustainable economic integration. Today 60 percent of world trade takes place within regional trade blocs. Large markets matter, especially for small economies and for least developed countries, because they create new investment opportunities, enhance the production of tradable commodities, and encourage the flow of foreign direct investment which could serve as the basis for local entrepreneurial initiatives.

For Sub-Saharan Africa, regional integration may provide an opportunity to pool resources, reduce costs and improve capacities in trade. Economics aside, issues and challenges that can be more effectively addressed through regional approaches include HIV/AIDS and other infectious diseases, riparian issues and environmental questions. While an African regional bloc as effective as the European Union or ASEAN may not be possible now, regional approaches accompanied by domestic reforms could provide a valuable avenue towards an effective response to globalization.

As pointed out in this chapter, globalization is an historical inevitability, a point in man's socio-historical development that keeps generating its own logic and as such cannot end. I pointed out that an inevitable offshoot of the process of globalization is the emergence of regional trading blocs. An ever-increasing proportion of trade is taking place between regional blocs as well as between trans-national companies. Thus, regional trade associations or agreements will continue to be a form of response to competitive pressures occasioned by globalization. In fact, the formation of regional trade blocs has become a historical replacement for empires. In one way or the other, regional trade blocs have become insulating capsules against the vagaries of globalization. Customs unions and common markets are able to create conditions for absorbing the shocks of globalization. To this end, Sub-Saharan Africa has no choice, therefore, but to speed the process of sub-regional and regional integration, for, globalization is not a passing phenomenon.

Globalization, ICT and Entrepreneurship

We have noted in a previous section that globalization is partly driven by information and communication technology (ICT). Thus, synonymous with the era of globalization is what has been commonly referred to as "the information age", the "digital age" or "ICT revolution." The rapid spread of the use of information and communication technology (ICT) is both an outcome and a determinant of the process of globalization, which has manifested itself in accelerated movement of goods, services, factors of production and technology across national boundaries. This development has, in turn, impacted the growth of entrepreneurial firms in many fundamental ways.

To start with, information and communication technology (ICT) is a generic term covering computers, broadcasting, telecommunications, data networks and related components, which are being increasingly applied in diverse uses. It can be defined as the totality of the electronic means to collect, store, process and present information to the end-users in support of their activities, and consists of computer systems, data communication systems, knowledge systems, office systems and consumer electronics.

Economic globalization arises out of the interaction between market- and technology-related factors as well as economic policies at the national and international levels. Market-related factors (such as increased competition for resources, greater engagement in international trade and enhanced efforts to attract foreign direct investment) have all been assisted by technological and information-related improvements. The growing role of multinational enterprises (MNEs) and transnational corporations (TNCs) in both the production and service sectors in practically every country is the result of information technology. This has put competitive pressure on home country firms, exerting an inordinate influence on the existing pattern of specialization.

As a result of information technology, financial innovations have led to lower transaction costs and the development of new financial institutions and instruments, as well as dramatic growth in cross-border financial transactions. For example, attempt to integrate the Ghana and Nigeria Stock Exchanges in 2007 is seen as the first step to the full integration of capital markets of member countries of the West Africa Monetary Zone (WAMZ). Integration through improved information technology is seen as a necessary mechanism to facilitate transaction process through improvement in market infrastructure and the security settlement system to promote online real time payment. Through information and communication technology, the integration of the region's financial markets is also seen as necessary for the capital market in the sub-region to fully participate in the global market.

In terms of technology-related factors, the componentization of production, facilitated by advancements in both manufacturing technologies and ICT, has led to lower costs and the dramatic shortening of economic distances. New communication technologies have facilitated the international diffusion of new production, marketing and organization technologies at low costs, allowing faster and cheaper movements of goods and services. At the same time, systematic rationalization of procedures and documentation for international trade, together with a wider and easier dissemination of prices of traded goods, has contributed to the convergence of market prices, resulting in fewer distinct markets.

In the context of the global economy, there are four dimensions of the positive impact of ICT on economic growth and the development of entrepreneurship. First, ICT allows process innovation (new ways of doing old things), which increases productivity and creates new value added. Second, innovative economic activities (new ways of doing new things) may be generated. Third, ICT represents a new factor of production along with land, labor and capital, which can lead to economic restructuring. Finally, it represents a new means of organizing activities through its synergies with other technologies. The recent advances to smaller, faster and cheaper ICT had led to a considerable decline in the cost-to-performance ratio of its application, which raises productivity. The potential for growth has been expanded by the use of ICT to promote more efficient utilization of inputs such as energy, raw materials and land. Some new applications of ICT have made production processes more flexible. With the facility to pay closer attention to customer tastes and preferences, producers have increased the value added of their products, and improved their quality.

Advances in telecommunications enable enterprises, which are geographically separated, to communicate both within a country and across borders. As indicated by the Indian ICT industry, the growing decentralization and globalization of many industries provide new opportunities for developing countries to participate in regional and global economic ventures. The organizational changes and decentralization options made possible by ICT can facilitate a better spatial distribution of economic activities, especially those industrial operations that have been centralized in large cities. Timely and detailed information about markets, point-of-sale information, and electronic linkages to clients and distributors have enhanced the capability to provide tailor-made products and services to consumers and create market niches.

Information and communication technology has revolutionized the marketing systems for widely traded standardized goods through the diffusion of market-determined prices instantaneously around the world. Entrepreneurial firms, small and medium-sized enterprises and even smaller-scale producers have the opportunity to become an integral part of the marketing chain as they can have access on a real-time basis through mobile phones, Internet etc. to the prices of their products on national and international markets. This has reduced the potential for the exploitation of these producers and enhanced their bargaining position with traders. Local traders have the means to become better equipped to compete with international trading firms, enhancing their competitiveness in marketing products as well.

New applications of ICT are profoundly changing the service sector. In particular, the nature and structure of financial, insurance, marketing, distribution, tourism and travel businesses have been transformed by the improvements in the speed, reliability and cost of manipulating vast quantities of information related to financial, inventory and sales transactions. At the same time, providers of services, traditionally small and decentralized, are being linked nationally and globally through the use of communication technology.

In the developing countries, the application of ICT is being used to improve the economic efficiency of the banking and financial sector, both to provide services to clients more conveniently and rapidly and to permit financial intermediaries to evaluate more correctly the investment preferences of savers while managing more effectively the risks inherent in global investment portfolios.

In the medium term there is the potential for enormous economic benefits from a broader and more integrated use of ICT in socio-economic development. In the developing economies, with new forms of application becoming available at decreasing costs, there has been a shift from quantitative to qualitative growth and reinforcement of efforts to promote a better distribution of income. The impact is, however, crucially dependent on the capacity to disperse ICT capabilities across a broad range of economic activities and income groups.

ICT and Entrepreneurship in Sub-Saharan Africa

In examining ICT and entrepreneurial development in Sub-Saharan Africa, attention has increasingly been drawn to the abysmal position occupied by the region in what is generally known as the global digital divide. To be sure, global digital divide (GDD) defines the distance between those with global access to information and those who do not. The digital divide is the gap between those with regular, effective access to digital technology and those without. Digital divide results from the socio-economic difference between communities that in turn affects their access to digital information mainly but not exclusively through the Internet.[44]

In Sub-Saharan Africa, the digital divide is still at its most extreme where the use of information and communication technologies is still at a very early stage of development compared to other regions of the world. The United Nation Status Report on ICT in Africa estimates that of the approximately 816 million people in Africa in 2001, only 1 in 4 have radio (205m), 1 in 13 have a TV (62m), 1 in 35 have a mobile phone (24m), 1 in 40 have a fixed line (20m), 1 in 130 have a PC (5.9m), 1 in 160 use the Internet (5m), and 1 in 400 have pay-TV (2m).[45]

Several studies have suggested that bridging the global digital divide would benefit Sub-Saharan Africa by (i) providing better means of communication; (ii) integrating economic activities (specially Agro-business which represents 80 percent of African economic activities); (iii) making public services more efficient (usually named as E-Government, E-Health, E-education, etc.); (iv) improve infrastructure and productivity; and (v) improving democracy and participation mechanisms.[46]

The United Nations ICT Task Force identified the obstacles facing the development of ICT in Sub-Saharan Africa to include the following:

(i) ICT growth tends to be concentrated only in big cities;
(ii) Lack of transport networks to install ICT infrastructure;
(iii) Low-education and "brain drain";
(iv) Political and economic instability; and
(v) Capital scarcity and lack of entrepreneurship promotion.[47]

As a result of these constraints, information and communication technology, within the context of Sub-Saharan Africa, has not contributed to the development of entrepreneurship when compared to other regions in the global economy. One of the reasons has been that, not until recently, African governments have invested very little in expanding the already decaying infrastructures upon which an ICT environment can be developed.

In spite of the above difficulties, there are over 100 million cell phone users in Africa in 2006, compared to just 1 million a decade ago.[48] Cell phones are being used for everything from simple banking services to comparing commodity prices in different markets. Yet, for Sub-Saharan Africa to fully benefit from information and communication technologies (ICT), investment in broadband Internet and other robust information technology is necessary. For firms in traditionally marginalized and disadvantaged areas, the Internet can be especially valuable, because it can override the distance factor and provide opportunities to connect to worldwide markets.

Information and communication technology, as defined earlier, is more than cell phones and Internet services. It embraces all forms and tools of modern communication technologies. Building capacity for ICT requires investments in physical infrastructure (such as fiber optic-cable), in the human capital necessary to operate these systems, and in government regulatory agencies. These investments are likely to yield economic growth and improve living standards. Unlike most parts of the global economy, African governments still face the challenge of how to make it easier for technologically-minded entrepreneurs to capitalize on ICT and to build a foundation for long-term economic growth in Africa.

Globalization, MNEs and Entrepreneurship

Under the force of globalization, the nature, direction and content of international trade are changing and have increasingly transcended national borders. One of the reasons is that a small number of multinational enterprises (MNEs) and transnational corporations (TNCs) have come to dominate worldwide production and distribution of goods and services, operating more and more outside the control of nation-states. In this section, we will use the two terms, MNE and TNC to describe *a company that has an integrated global philosophy encompassing both domestic and overseas operations*. A multinational enterprise is sometimes used synonymously with a multinational corporation. As an ever-increasing proportion of trade is taking place between regional blocks so is that trade occurring between multinational enterprises. Globalization pressures have also led to an increase foreign competition and have made companies to expand their businesses into international or global markets.

To remain successful in the competitive global economy a firm needs to grow. In mature markets such as North America, Europe, and Japan many firms and their products and services are having difficulties maintaining a rate of growth that satisfies stockholders. Given the intense competition in the global economy, where the big eat the small and the fast eat the slow, any competitive advantage, be it new technology, a new product, new know-how, increased market share, or a new market can make a huge difference. The successful corporations got that way by being innovative, taking risks and more importantly, opening new markets in foreign countries. The pressure to open new markets is what drives multinational enterprises to invest in other countries, especially in countries where there are no markets for their goods or services.

The presence of companies in other countries can take several forms and the most prominent of these is through direct investments in their host countries. Thus, the presence of multinational enterprises in other countries has been seen as a vehicle for the development of local entrepreneurs. This occurs either through their linkage effects in the local economy or through the provision of human and financial resources needed for the development of local entrepreneurs. Although multinational enterprises are driven to overseas because of increased competition in home countries, when they shop the globe for possible investment locations, local capabilities are among the key variables influencing their decisions.

In terms of economic and entrepreneurial growth arising from foreign direct investment, the experience of Sub-Saharan Africa can be compared with that of Southeast Asian countries. First, recalling that globalization is an historical process dating back to centuries, Southeast Asia was well integrated into Asian and European maritime trading networks several centuries before maritime trade reached most of Sub-Saharan Africa. This historical integration with more advanced economies has led to a positive development of local entrepreneurship in Southeast Asia than in Sub-Saharan Africa. Thus, and as appropriately described by Deborah Bräutigam, unlike Sub-Saharan Africa, Southeast Asia has had contacts with foreign enterprises much longer. The lower cost and greater ease of maritime trade meant that traders in Southeast Asia could develop business skills, be exposed to outside innovations, and accumulate significant capital much earlier than was possible for many in Sub-Saharan Africa. As part of this maritime mobility, waves of Chinese immigrants settled in Southeast Asia and were to become significant elements in the area's economic development, producing, as it were, a pool of local entrepreneurs.[49]

Second, significant import-substitution industrialization began in Southeast Asia in the late 19th century, three or more decades before any significant modern industrial development occurred in Sub-Saharan Africa, giving Asian entrepreneurs and workers a longer history of experience with industrialization. Third, proximity to Japan served as a powerful catalyst for entrepreneurial development in Southeast Asia. As a result of cultural similarities and geographical proximity, Japanese firms appear to be much more likely to enter into joint ventures in manufacturing with domestic firms, and at a lower level of technology than western firms. African entrepreneurs had no similar, "appropriate" catalyst. Direct foreign investments in Africa are still much more in mining, petroleum, and other primary commodity extraction ventures. Fifth, unlike, Sub-Saharan Africa, Southeast Asian countries have put in place appropriate economic policies that have attracted direct foreign direct investments from multinational enterprise.[50] In effect, the negative trend in the development of local entrepreneurship in Sub-Saharan Africa can be partly explained in terms of the unavailability of sizable number of multinational enterprises in the region.

The presence of multinational enterprises in a region has positive effects on that region's economic growth and the development of local entrepreneurs. The relationship between MNEs direct investment and entrepreneurial development is manifested in several forms: the links between the local economy as purchasers of production inputs, networks and clusters that provide information, assistance and examples, stimulate innovation and transfer knowledge, technology and skills. The absence of multinational enterprises in Sub-Saharan Africa, with the notable exception of South Africa, has meant that Africa has lagged behind in accessing such linkages, networks and sources of innovation needed as a base for the development of local entrepreneurs that are globally competitive.

One of the benefits of the presence of transnational corporations in a developing or emerging economy is the creation of industry clusters, which serve as an industrial environment for the development of local entrepreneurs. Thus, clusters of enterprises in similar or related industries can be found throughout Southeast Asia and in many parts of the globe. As pointed out by C. C. Edordu, president of African Export-Import Bank, in the countries where successes in economic growth and entrepreneurial development have been achieved, industrial clusters have been used as deliberate policy instruments.[51] Michael Porter, who is widely regarded as the pioneer of cluster model in economic policy-making and industry competitiveness, defines industrial clusters as, *"geographic concentrations of interconnected companies, specialized suppliers, service providers, firms in related industries and associated institutions in particular fields that compete but also cooperate"*.[52]

Clusters encompass an array of linked industries and other entities important to competition. They include, for example, suppliers of specialized inputs such as components, machinery, and services, and providers of specialized infrastructure. Clusters also often extend downstream to channels and customers and laterally to manufacturers of complementary products and to companies in industries related by skills, technologies, or common inputs. Many clusters include governmental and other institutions – such as universities, standard-setting agencies, think tanks, vocational training providers, and trade associations – that provide specialized training, education, information, research, and technical support. Michael Porter highlights these clusters as an important component of "competitive advantage", arguing that when industries are geographically concentrated, domestic rivalries are magnified, and rivalry is a potent force that goads entrepreneurs into keeping up with their neighbors. In the context of Southeast Asia, this explains the innovativeness in the electronic industry in East Asian countries. For developing economies, in general, the advantages of clustering are many and include:

(i)   The opportunity it gives local firms to increase the expertise available to them by locating among a cluster of other firms.

(ii) Possibility it provides to local companies to draw upon others with complementary skills to bid for large pieces of work which each of the individual firms would have been unable to do on their own.

(iii) Improved access to financing given the opportunity clusters provide for identifying credible entrepreneur and financing opportunities.

(iv) Economies of scale created through specialization within each firm, by joint purchase of raw materials at lower unit costs, and by joint marketing.

(v)   The ability of clusters to attract infrastructure, as well as professional and other services from innovative companies, and

(vi) The ability to achieve lower transaction costs through sharing information about market demand, reliable sources of technology and equipment, or supplies; equipment sharing; access to working capital; subcontracting opportunities; informal technical assistance, etc.

The policy of industrial clusters, as a tool for economic and entrepreneurial development, has not yet been promoted in the Sub-Saharan region due, in part, to past policies that have worked against foreign direct investment from multinational enterprises. South Africa is an exception with its policy of developing industrial clusters as exemplified by the Durban Auto Cluster (see case in point).

CASE IN POINT: THE DURBAN AUTO CLUSTER: A CASE OF TNC-SME LINKAGES IN SOUTH AFRICA[53]

In Sub-Saharan Africa, attention is increasingly been drawn to creating industry clusters where transnational corporations can exist in an environment that promotes the development of local entrepreneurs through linkage formation. In South Africa, the importance of industry clusters as a bedrock for local entrepreneurship is illustrated in the Durban Auto Cluster. Existing in an automotive sector, which is a globalized production system, the Durban Auto Cluster (DAC) is dominated by large OEMs (Own Equipment Manufacturer) and component producing transnational corporations and local firms.

The Durban Auto Cluster (DAC) emerged in a context of considerable policy adjustment in South Africa. Post 1994 trade liberalization in South Africa saw a dramatic reduction in tariff barriers, including high import tariffs on the importation of both vehicles and automotive components. Despite the commitment to trade liberalization by the South African Department of Trade and Industry (DTI), there was also a commitment, on the part of the government, to avoid potential pitfalls of de-industrialization from rapid tariff adjustments and so a program known as the Motor Industry Development Program (MIDP) was formulated together with key industry stakeholders. The MIDP sought to encourage consolidation of domestic production around the output of a reduced range of vehicles (for each OEM) allowing for export scale production of these vehicles.

Through exporting these vehicles the OEMs would then be entitled to earn duty credits to import a considerable greater range of models from production sites in other parts of the globe. These policy adjustments were deemed favorable to the OEMs and they began, one-by-one, to systematically take advantage of an opportunity to build South Africa into their global operations when previously South African production activities had either been under license operation or been viewed as somewhat marginal.

The impact of these national policy adjustments secured very substantial FDI commitments. Initially it was the German OEMs that moved to comprehensively reposition production of BMW, Volkswagen (VW) and Daimler (later Daimler-Chrysler). This was followed by major U.S. and Japanese-based OEMs. During these nationally driven processes, the Department of Trade and Industry made a number of attempts to initiate a country-wide cluster process to attempt to more effectively bind in components producers into the policy process.

Although, the Durban Auto Clusters evolved from an initial university research-firm partnership benchmarking exercise, it latter grew into a policy project with national government support. From the university-firm partnership, the exercise was subsequently supported by grants from the DTI's and Industry's Sectoral Partnership Fund, Competitiveness Fund, and Workplace Challenge Programme – all initiatives aimed at encouraging individual or collectives of firms to upgrade their performance. From these activities the KwaZulu-Natal Benchmarking Club was formed in 1998 as a firm-driven cooperative venture, supported in part by government grants, to get firms to consistently evaluate their relative performance in terms of both meeting customer demands and against competitor manufacturing process activities and to then share ideas on how to use such information to upgrade their performance. The process created a special-purpose organization to carry out the facilitation activities and perform domestic and international benchmarks.

Participants in DAC could chose between levels of involvement. Some firms chose to participate purely in information sharing activities. Firms can also access programs such as training sessions or collective logistics negotiations. In general, firms participated not only to get access to useful information, but also because they found they could use the information and resources to make better decisions in the workplace. Beyond the formal processes of interaction, participating firms also benefit from informal networking.

In terms of the work of DAC, it has been the Supplier Development Working Group that has had the most significant impact on relationships between the TNCs (inside and outside of the DAC) and SMEs (which make up the majority of the DAC membership). In an industry with relatively high barriers to entry and increasingly sophisticated accreditation and technology management process, the working group programs have enabled smaller firms to familiarize themselves with first-tier and OEM requirements and to share knowledge on how best to meet the requirements.

The impact of the collaborative work between the transnational firms (OEMs and component producers) and local firms witnessed improved performance overtime against international benchmarks and increased the competitiveness of local firms in the global auto industry. Second, the impact of DAC process and the general policy environment has also been a positive one in terms of employment and investment by local firms. Third, the environment in which this linkage activity has been made possible has been considerably influenced by national governments' programs to encourage small business development and in particular greater participation by black entrepreneurs in key sectors of the economy. This has, for instance, resulted in some of the major OEMs requiring their supplier development divisions make particular efforts to increase procurement from SMEs, and in particular black-owned SMEs.

This pressure to change has begun to feed through the supply chain and also encouraged components suppliers to examine opportunities to spin-off or outsource various supply activities to existing SMEs or to support the creation of new ones. The DAC has provided a very effective, accessible and consistent form of support for such processes. Both domestic and foreign-owned firms have been able to make use of its processes and formed ways of developing relationships and learning than might otherwise have been difficult without the "spill-over" effects of knowledge sharing in the DAC.

The Nation-State, Competitive Advantage and Entrepreneurial Development

The era of globalization has also brought in a new way of thinking about the role of the nation-state. To be sure, *a nation-state refers to a single or multiple nationalities joined together in a formal political union.* The nation-state determines an official language(s), a system of law, manages a currency system, uses a bureaucracy to order elements of society, and fosters loyalties to abstract entities like "Nigeria", United States", "United Kingdom", etc. As pointed out in the foregoing sections, this is the era in which many nations have altered their philosophical directions and changed their economic assumptions. As old ideas are cast aside, new leaders have emerged while old leaders have decided to think about economic development in new ways. The changes in politics, culture, increase in and expansion of information technology, liberalization of cross-border trade and resource movements, growing consumer pressures and expanded cross-national economic and political cooperation are visible in the many sudden and outright reversals of the conventional wisdom which says that the state has the absolute right to play a large role in the life of its citizens. In fact, the era of globalization has witnessed a shrinking role of the state in terms of economic development.

Gone are the days when many countries considered themselves as autonomous, self-contained, and self-sufficient entities when it comes to the production, distribution, and consumption of goods and services. Many people would agree that today we all compete in a global economy based on worldwide interdependence of resource supplies, product or service markets, and business competition in which every country or nation-state depends on another nation-state for the exchange of goods and services. We have seen how governments have increasingly realized that cooperating with other countries through treaties and agreements in order to gain reciprocal advantages can enhance their own countries' interest.

In the global economy, every nation has a role to play in ensuring that it is not left behind in the quest for economic growth. In most instances, the role of the state and its competitiveness in the global marketplace depend on the availability of its factor endowment and how it uses this to create competitive advantage (that is, to compete with other nations). Importantly, traditional factor endowments such as land and abundant raw materials have become obsolete as many countries are creating their own factor endowments through investment in infrastructures that promote investments from global corporations. One reason is that today's products are no more national, but universal, because they rely on so many different technologies or inputs that are scattered across the globe. For a product, such as a PC to get to the consumer, its production occurs in many countries where the resources needed for its production are located. A country that provides such a resource has a factor endowment. A factor endowment is a nation's positioning factor of production such as skilled labor or the infrastructure necessary to compete in the global economy. South Africa, for example, realized that its factor endowment lies in the country's institutional framework upon which small businesses play a significant role in entrepreneurial development.[54]

Multinational enterprises from the developed countries are now locating their production facilities outside of their home countries such as in India and other Southeast Asian countries. This is particularly true not only in labor-intensive industries (such as the textile industry) but also in technological-driven ones (such as computer hard- and software as well as in information and communications technology). Many industries that utilize information technology are now locating their production facilities in China as well as in India where direct investments in these countries have promoted the development of local industries with local entrepreneurs taking charge of the process of production and exportation of these products to the developed countries. Other hitherto desert countries are now redirecting the conduct of international business to their shores through the provision of infrastructures such as modern ports and communication technology as in the United Arab Emirates. In order to remain competitive many countries are trying to attract investments by offering a factor of production. What a country has to offer in order to be competitive in the global economy is that country's factor endowment.

Every nation has something unique which distinguishes it from other nations. A *factor endowment* is the extent to which a country is endowed with such resources as land, labor, capital, raw materials, technology, infrastructure, etc. As John Ogbor has pointed out, the global economy is a terrain for the competitiveness of nations and their economies. It represents an arena through which the Darwinian doctrine of the survival of the fittest is manifested. Those nations that are able to survive in this global competition are those that are able to develop a unique competence through entrepreneurship. It is this uniqueness that forms the basis for a nation's competitive advantage.[55]

Thus, with regard to the globalization of the means of production, companies are increasingly dispersing parts of their production process to different locations around the globe to take advantage of national differences in the cost and quality of factors of production such as labor, energy, land, technology, infrastructure, and capital. The objective is to lower costs, boost profits, and to be competitive in the global economy. *The relationship between the globalization of the means of production and entrepreneurial development in a nation is the trickle down effect or multiplier effect that such production facilities have in those countries that have invested in infrastructures.*

As a source of competitive advantage among nations, some countries are more supportive than others in terms of entrepreneurial development. For instance, from Eastern European countries to Brazil, Chile, and South Africa, entrepreneurial ventures have been seen as the road towards the building of successful free market economies. New entrepreneurial ventures are emerging daily with the support of governmental efforts in these countries. Unfortunately, not every country makes it easy to start a new venture. Some countries such as Zimbabwe are still ingrained in the old ways of thinking about development, while others, such as Somalia and Sudan, are still involved in the politics of ethnic cleansing. Still others are trapped in the old ways of doing things with cultural and institutional aversion to the risk taking so necessary to entrepreneurship. In other countries, the pervasive practice of depending on government employment is so ingrained that people do not like to take the initiatives to venture into establishing their own business. However, the greatest obstacle lies in the inability of the nation-state to support entrepreneurial development through the provision of an enabling environment necessary for economic growth.

Some of the factors driving entrepreneurship in the global economy are beyond the control of individual initiatives. The drivers of entrepreneurship such as national trade policies, foreign exchange policies, global market opportunities, availability of entrepreneurial education, provision of necessary infrastructure, security, acceptable interest rates, e-commerce and the emergence of the World Wide Web fall within the domain of national governments and global market conditions. Hence the developed and industrialized nations of the world today are those that have responded to and provided the conditions necessary for entrepreneurial development. The developed countries represent those with large concentration of small businesses, not large organizations *per se*.

The global era has also witnessed a re-evaluation of development strategies in many developing countries in Sub-Saharan Africa as they try to support entrepreneurial development through varieties of incentives. These include direct financial support, the building of infrastructure, provision of an enabling environment for the growth of indigenous small businesses and entrepreneurs, and most importantly, appropriate socioeconomic and political ideology, including a sound ethical and regulatory environment. In Nigeria, for example, there is a program called "The Small & Medium Scale Equity Investment Scheme (SMIEIS). The program was introduced to provide equity financing for small and medium scale enterprises. Through the SMIEIS program, banks in Nigeria are required to provide 10 percent of their profit before tax as equity investment in small enterprises in order to jump-start small and medium-scale entrepreneurs. In South Africa, the Small Enterprise Development Agency (SEDA) was established to promote cooperation between service providers that form part of the country's small and medium sized enterprise promotion strategy. The Government of Ghana has established the Ghana Investment Promotion Centre for the purpose of stimulating private sector investments.

Private initiatives are also being utilized in the provision of infrastructures needed for entrepreneurial development. As we noted earlier, in Sub-Saharan Africa, various forms of communication assistance and applications of information technology are being used for the purpose of promoting entrepreneurship. Indeed availability of the ICT infrastructure (connectivity, computers, cell phones, etc) has been one of the ways in which governments, in partnership with private initiatives, are using technology to help African entrepreneurs.

The aspect of developing the human capacity to leverage these technologies, capacity to harness technological efficiencies within the entrepreneurs' proposed and existing businesses, capacity to gain an edge over their competition, capacity to reach wider markets, capacity to position these businesses in favorable light for financial institution to have confidence in financing them, have become the main focus of many governments in Sub-Saharan Africa. Specifically in Sub-Saharan Africa, the diminishing role of the state has also led to an interest in a private-public partnership in which various stakeholders are identifying specific demand driven human capacity needs in bridging the divide between technology and entrepreneurial development.

We can deduce from the foregoing discussion that many African nations have been developing strategies for the promotion of entrepreneurship in response to the various forces of globalization discussed in this chapter. However, in spite of these efforts, entrepreneurial development is still been hampered by some inbuilt institutional factors prior to the era of globalization. These are: (i) an import-dependent economy, (ii) the absence of policy measures that could spark the growth of entrepreneurship, (iii) the aversion of the African business environment by foreign investors due to the dual problem of fraud and insecurity, (v) lack of infrastructures (such as electricity supply, information and communication technology, inadequate transport services, inadequate water supply, etc, (v) inconsistencies in policy formulation and implementation due to a pervasive bureaucratic culture, and (6) political crises and social unrest in many countries in the Sub-Saharan region.

CHAPTER SUMMARY

Historically, all nations have gone through different stages of economic development in terms of economic policies adopted within a particular era in their developmental processes.

The development of African economies can be discussed under five different eras: the colonial, postcolonial, political and economic instability, structural adjustment, and globalization era.

In the colonial era, economic and entrepreneurial development followed a pattern of exporting cheap agricultural raw materials and unprocessed minerals to Europe and importing relatively expensive manufactured goods from the colonial metropolis. The absence of infrastructure and a base for manufacturing hindered the development of local industry and indigenous entrepreneurship in Africa.

In the postcolonial era, African nations were committed to a policy of industrialization where the government was expected to play a major role in the process of industrialization and economic development. Because of problems inherited from colonial administrators and absence of capital, economic and entrepreneurial development was fundamentally hampered.

In the era of political crises and civil wars, economic development was significantly disrupted leading to economic stagnation. This era in many African countries, also witnessed massive corruption and looting of state resources by the military leaders. These developments compounded the economic and social problems that were already in existence.

The structural adjustment era witnessed the introduction of massive economic adjustment programs in Africa. In order to alleviate the debt burden in many African countries, governments were required to restructure their economies by the combined forces of the World Bank and the International Monetary Fund. Structural adjustment program failed to promote economic growth and entrepreneurial development. African countries were using major portion of their GNP in the repayment of debts. Trade and economic liberalization and deregulation opened up African economies for international goods without local investments.

The era of globalization is seen as the ongoing period in which the state of a nation's economy is based on worldwide interdependence of resource supplies, product markets, and business competition.

The major global factors driving entrepreneurial development in this era are (i) expanded cross-national cooperation and the formation of regional trade blocs; (ii) the preeminence of information technology, global communication, the Internet boom and the emergence of the World Wide Web; (iii) MNEs and the growing trend in the outsourcing of means of production by major global and multinational corporations; and (iv) the diminishing role of the nation-state.

As late starters, Sub-Saharan Africa is confronted with numerous problems such as increased competition from subsidized imported goods, protectionist policies in the developed economies and the inability for African countries to take opportunities in the global market.

An industrial cluster is a geographic concentrations of interconnected companies, specialized suppliers, service providers, firms in related industries and associated institutions in particular fields that compete but also cooperate.

Nations compete in a global economy based on worldwide interdependence of resource supplies, product or service markets, and business competition in which every country depends on another for the exchange of goods and services.

A country must have a competitive advantage and a factor endowment in order to compete effectively in the global economy.

A factor endowment is a nation's positioning factors of production such as skilled labor or the infrastructure necessary to compete in the global economy. A factor endowment is what a country brings to the global economy. A factor endowment is the extent to which a country is endowed with such resources as land, labor, capital, raw materials, technology, infrastructure, energy, etc.

The relationship between the globalization of the means of production and entrepreneurial development in a nation is the trickle down or multiplier effect that such production facilities have in those countries that have invested in production facilities.

Some of the factors driving entrepreneurship in the global economy are: national trade policies, foreign exchange policies, international trade relations, the availability of entrepreneurial education, infrastructure, security, laws, interest rates policies, and the existence of an enabling entrepreneurial environment.

In Sub-Saharan Africa, entrepreneurial development is hampered by (i) an import-dependent economy, (ii) the absence of policy measures that could spark the growth of entrepreneurship, (iii) the aversion of the African business environment by foreign investors due to the dual problem of fraud and security, (iv) lack of infrastructures (such as electricity supply, information and communication technology, inadequate transport services, inadequate water supply, etc, (v) inconsistencies in policy formulation and implementation due to a bureaucratic culture that has pervaded the various arms of governments, and (vi) political crises and social unrest in many countries in the Sub-Saharan region.

CHAPTER DISCUSSION QUESTIONS

1. What are the main features of economic activities during the colonial era? What are the consequences of these in terms of entrepreneurial and economic development?

2. What problems or factors inhibited the development of local entrepreneurs in colonial and postcolonial eras in Sub-Saharan Africa?

3. Discuss some of the reasons why Sub-Sahara African leaders decided to look inward for economic development in the postcolonial era? What are the consequences of these policies for economic development?

4. On what African tradition was the policy of "Ujamaa" based? What are the underlying aspects of the theory of "Ujamaa"? Why did "Ujamaa" failed to achieve its objectives? What went wrong with Ujamaa?

5. What are the causes of political instability, civil unrest, military rule, and economic crises in Sub-Saharan Africa between the late seventies and early nineties? What are their consequences in terms of economic and entrepreneurial development?

6. What is a structural adjustment program? From an historical perspective, what do you think gave rise to the adoption and implementation of structural adjustment programs in Sub-Saharan Africa? What went wrong with the

program? In your opinion, how did the policies of an adjustment program affect economic and entrepreneurial development in Sub-Saharan Africa?

7. What is globalization? What are the forces of globalization and what are the forces driving entrepreneurship in the era of globalization? What problems confront African economies in the era of globalization?

8. Name and describe the three important regional trade blocs in Sub-Saharan Africa. What are the problems confronting the formation and competitiveness of African regional trade blocs in the global economy?

9. What is information and communication technology (ICT)? Why is ICT important for the development of entrepreneurship? Should Sub-Sahara African governments focus on expanding low-cost technologies that are easily adopted in both rural and urban areas, such as mobile phones, or on expanding more robust ICT services, such as Broadband and fiber-optic cable, that require heavy infrastructure investment? What is the most effective way for the governments of Sub-Saharan Africa to demonstrate the potential benefits of ICT adoption and usage to firms?

10. What is a multinational enterprise and why is an MNE important for the development of local entrepreneurship?

11. What is an industry cluster and why are they important for the development of entrepreneurship in developing country?

12. What do you understand by the term "factor endowment"? Pick a country of your choice and discuss its factor endowment. How is the country using its factor endowment(s) as means of competition in the global economy?

13. What incentives are developing countries applying in supporting entrepreneurial development? Provide an example from one country.

CASE STUDY 3: GHANA: FACING OPPORTUNITIES AND CHALLENGES OF A NEW GLOBAL ECONOMIC ORDER[56]

Advances in information technology – from computing to communications – have created a new global economic order. Especially in this era of IT-driven globalization, no country can hope to compete globally without having a solid information technology base. With pressures on natural resources growing, any path towards higher living standards for the world's poor depends partly on advances in appropriate technologies. Innovations across a range of fields, from energy to medicine to food production, are essential for global competitiveness. But information technology, broadly construed, remains the most likely area from which poor countries can learn from rich ones

– and pioneer themselves. Many developing countries have now come to realize the importance of information technology as an important key factor in global competition.

The world economy is experiencing the effects of rapid globalization and liberalization as well as the impact of the emerging information age. This information age is bringing about a new global economic order to be dominated by information and knowledge-based economies (IKEs). Most African countries, including Ghana, are facing new challenges to their socio-economic development process as a result of this globalization process and the impact of the emerging new information age. This emerging information age characterized by information and communication technologies (ICTs) and the extraordinary increase in the spread of knowledge has given birth to a new era: that of knowledge and information. These technologies are offering even less developed agricultural countries like Ghana the opportunity to transform their economies and accelerate their socio-economic development process towards an information and knowledge-based economy

There is no doubt that the information and knowledge-based economy is the economy of the future and the challenge facing African countries including Ghana relate to how they should go about formulating and implementing appropriated integrated ICT-led socio-economic development policies and plans that could aid the process of moving their countries to be included in the new global economic order.

For Ghana to transform itself from the vagaries of the old economy to the new one, several obstacles have to be overcome. Ghana has a population of 19.9 million (2001). The literacy rate for people aged 15 years and over is 72.6 percent. According to the World Bank, however, 44.8 percent earns less than US$1 a day in 2001. The GDP per capita is US$372 (2000). According to Bridges.org, power failures are common. Limited availability of, and costly ICT infrastructure is a problem for businesses in Ghana. There were 1.82 telephones per 100 people in 2001, with tele-density skewed in favor of large cities. As in most African countries, mobile phones are gaining in popularity. According to the International Telecommunications Union, there were 102,000 mobile phone subscribers in Ghana by 2000. The cost of a mobile phone call was US$0.90 per minute (peak hours) and US$0.72 per minute (off peak) in 2001. According to ITU World Telecommunication Development Report, there were 235 Internet hosts; and a computer density of 0.33 in 2001. Internet access is expensive overall: between US$6 and US$50 per month – not including phone charges – depending on the ISP and the type of service provided. Ghana is politically and economically stable with little corruption and danger and overall considered to be a good place to do business. Liberalization and privatization of the ICT and telecommunications sectors have been carried out in an environment of political stability. There is a small but active population of Ghanaian expatriates returning to Ghana with business knowledge from the US and Europe, which are an important part of the growing ICT business scene in Ghana.

Ghana still faces some obstacles when it comes to the use of information technology for entrepreneurial development. According to Bridges.org, Ghana's small-to-medium sized businesses have a shortage of people trained in appropriate ICT skills, which is holding back economic development in this sector. The skills shortage can be traced to the universities. Until recently, students who graduated with a computer science degree in Ghana had spent minimal time actually working on a computer as part of their studies. As in many countries in Sub-Saharan Africa, the graduates might have learned old-fashioned computer languages like Fortran or Cobol that are no longer needed in the marketplace, or even learned coding on paper. Often those with computer science degrees need six to 12 months training after they leave university in order to be functional using their computer skills in a job. While both the ICT curriculum and the ratio of student to computer have improved in secondary and higher education settings, the lack of high-end ICT skilled people in the job market remains a major problem.

Response of Ghanaian Government

Governments worldwide have recognized the crucial role that they can play in socio-economic development. In this respect, a number of countries in both the developing and developed world are designing economic policies that will accelerate the process of transforming their economies into information and knowledge-based economies. Developed countries including the United States, European countries, Australia, Japan and emerging economies of Brazil, Chile, India, Singapore, Malaysia, Thailand, South Korea, China and Vietnam have policies and plans in place to accelerate their development process through the development, deployment and exploitation of ICTs. A number of African countries such as Mauritius and South Africa have also formulated and implemented comprehensive ICT policies in the context of entrepreneurial development. Following this trend, the Ghanaian government recognized that the country must put in place the relevant policies and corresponding action plans to address the challenges of globalization and the information age. Such policies and action plans are needed to move Ghana from its predominantly subsistence agriculture dominated economy into an information and knowledge-base one – the economy of the future.

In response to the need to fast track the development of IT and the infusion of information technology into all spheres of national development the government of Ghana set up an Information Technology team to speed up the development of that sector. The government also revamped the Ministry of Communication and added additional responsibility of Information Technology to it. The ministry is now called Ministry of Communication and Information Technology.

In Ghana, several projects have been set up to provide ICT resources and training directly to locally-based local entrepreneurs who are attempting to start or expand a business of their own. Some of these projects are private sector driven, while others are the results of public and private sector partnership. A good example of a private sector commercially driven outfit is BusyInternet, which provides local businesses with a central location for information and ICT-related services. These services include ICT-enabled office space, conference facilities, a cyber cafe, digital copy center, and wireless capability. They also work as an advocate for ICT-related entrepreneurial activities and in promoting the use of ICT in business endeavors. Also in Ghana, the solar-powered Asante Akim Multipurpose Community Tele-center (AAMCT), provides secure "e-commerce/digital culture solutions" for local businesses and additional services to support outsourcing, small business support, self-employment, and entrepreneurship. Another ICT-support organization in Ghana is Geekcorps, a non-profit organization that assists businesses in developing countries with information technology. Geekcorps' volunteers help small businesses with IT training and computer networks.

From Commodity Export to Knowledge Export

The emergence of ICT as an important investment tool for economic development is a new approach to entrepreneurial development in the country. Since independence, Ghana has depended on traditional exports like cocoa and gold, which due to the manipulation on the international market are no more yielding the desired revenue. Encouraged by the performance of India in the area of IT, the Ghanaian government is persuading the private sector to create the Sub-Saharan version of Bangalore in Ghana in order for Ghana to ascend her gateway status. Thus, policy makers in Ghana have initiated and sought cooperation between Ghanaian and Indian governments in the area of IT development. Consequently, the Indian government has unveiled plans to help Ghana open IT training centers in selected parts of the country to train the youth. If that materializes many Ghanaian youth could graduate from Internet users to IT experts, which is the vision of the government. The Minister of Communication and Information Technology, Felix Owusu Agyapong during one of the IT conferences, disclosed that software development is one of the important options his ministry is seriously considering. He said the ministry has plans to establish computer assembling plants as soon as practicable. In line with the cooperation between Indian government and Ghana, India has assisted Ghana with $2 million and technical know-how in setting up an ICT Centre in Ghana. The Centre – India-Ghana Kofi Annan Centre of Excellence in ICT – has been highly successful in conducting training courses in ICT and showcasing India not only in Ghana, but also in other ECOWAS countries.

Ghana, like India, has come to realize that there is a significant, unexploited opportunity to increase export of services in Ghana as a result of two major trends:

➢ The new, digital economy which now facilitates the marketing and delivery of services-on-line; and
➢ The trend within developed countries to contract-out or outsource non-core functions to developing countries.

Thus, the vision of Ghanaian authorities is to promote the export of professional and technical services (accounting, project management, public relations, legal counseling, etc.) by small and medium enterprises (SMEs) to the West Africa sub-region and beyond. According to authorities, potentials exist among professionals within SMEs in Ghana to export services especially to clients within the sub-region. By so doing, the country is reducing its heavy dependence on the export of commodity products such as cocoa, timber, and mineral resources—as the mainstays of its economy. As in other parts of Sub-Saharan Africa, the often-volatile nature of the world market price of these products made the economy very vulnerable to fluctuations in the prices of export commodities.

ICT, The New Economy and Entrepreneurial Development

As Matthew Clarke rightly noted, there is an optimistic view that the convergence of globalization and advances in information and communication technology, has resulted in a 'new' world economy, especially for the developing countries. Within such a new economy, knowledge replaces traditional productivity input as the primary driver of economic growth. There is optimism that such an economy offers great hope for developing countries. In order to participate in this new economy, governments in the developing countries are putting in place appropriate government policies that include improving access levels and quality of telecommunication and electricity infrastructure, education and providing both direct and indirect support to encourage local firms to become engaged with the global economy. Specifically, the new economy is replacing the old one that was based on exportation of commodities.

Information and communications technologies (ICTs) are powerful tools for income generation in developing countries and they have become the necessary tool for participating in the new economy. One country that has recognized the importance of information technology as a tool for global competition is Ghana. Ghana is one of the countries in the Sub-Saharan-Africa region where the increasing use of Internet is an indication of the reality that the digital age is gradually catching on in the continent. As in many other developing countries, Ghana realized that information technology is the key for economic and entrepreneurial development. With ICT, Ghana no longer relies exclusively on the exportation of commodities. In fact, with the embrace of ICT, Ghana is at the verge of replacing its dependence on commodity export (features of the "old" economy) to information technology and knowledge-base economy (the "new economic order). Specifically, with the new information technology in Ghana, young entrepreneurs are now in the business of exporting locally made products (other than commodities such as cocoa) to the West.

The BBC tells of Linda Yaa Ampah, a clothes designer and entrepreneur who exported $40,000 worth of stock to Africans living in the United States in 2003. She was advised to get an e-mail address after handing out international mobile phone numbers to American customers at a fashion show in Accra.

"I went to an Internet cafe and I couldn't believe it when I realized I could get an address for free," she says, adding that she had little knowledge of computers and presumed e-mail accounts were very expensive. A few years later, Linda employs an army of 50 tailors to meet her orders and attributes her success to her humble hotmail account.

"Americans are wary of long distance telephone calls," she says, but perfectly happy to e-mail their orders. 70 percent of her business is now generated through e-mail from the US.

"The Internet is beautiful, easy and clear," she says, "I wouldn't have got nearly so far without it."

In addition to such financial success stories, there are also many intangible benefits of the Internet for developing countries. There is the empowerment that comes from being able to research any subject and the increased knowledge of the wider world, helping poor people become what development agencies call "information rich". Besides the promotion of local entrepreneurs, ICT is also creating jobs in Ghana as many Western countries are now outsourcing in Accra. Frank Schooster, chairman of Global Response, a US firm which runs customer contact centers says that Accra has already played host to its flagship outsourcing company for three years, watching it grow from just 65 employees to more than 1,300. Analysts are of the opinion that with the outsourcing market expected to grow to $234 billion by 2004, even a tiny share of that industry could be revolutionary for many of Africa's stagnating economies. And Ghana is preparing itself to reap from this opportunity. The ease with which Ghanaians, including Linda have embraced this new digital revolution called Internet is quite phenomenal in this West African country. Ghana, it is argued, became the first country in West Africa to establish local Internet service in 1994. Eight years on the country has been cited by the Wall Street Journal as one of the five 'Silicon nations' to watch in terms of "connectivity, information security, human capital, business climate and priority by government to technology."

The experience of Ghana sums up the reality that the digital age is gradually catching on with the Ghanaian and African public. All over the major towns and cities of Ghana Internet cafes are sprouting like beans. Incidentally, the 2001 UNDP Human Development Report used the level of investment in technology to assess a country's level of human development. On that score, Ghana is placed 119 among the medium human development group ahead of Lesotho, Kenya, Cameroon, Nigeria, Senegal, Togo, Djibouti, Sudan, Mauritania, Tanzania, Uganda, Zambia, Côte d'Ivoire etc. The report underscored the fact that not all countries need to be on the cutting edge of global technological advancement, but in the network age every country needs the capacity to understand and adapt global technologies for local needs.

The IT industry in Ghana received a major boost on November 23, 2001, when BusyInternet Ghana, described as Africa's largest information technology center, was opened in Accra. The facility is a joint venture between Ghanaian and American investors. Mark Davies, founder and Chief Executive Officer of BusyInternet International, which holds majority shares, disclosed that the company decided to use Ghana as a launching pad to reach the rest of Africa because of the human capital he found in the IT industry in Ghana. "I firmly believe that Ghana is poised to become one of the first true cybernation of Africa," Davies said during the commissioning of the facility. It was during the commissioning of the facility that Davies spotted Jamal (a young school boy) sending a message that popped up on his uncle's mobile phone in London a few seconds later. Jamal's exploits on the Internet, according to Davies, erased his initial concerns about how interested Ghanaians could be in the new digital revolution.

One of the high points for Ghana is the extent to which BusyInternet International tapped local technology. According to Davies, the world-class software on which BusyInternet Ghana is currently operating was developed in Ghana by SOFT, entirely Ghanaian owned software company. This achievement by SOFT and other local software companies operating in Ghana has convinced many experts that IT can contribute significantly to Ghana's foreign exchange earnings. Ken Ofori-Atta, a financial analyst and Chairman of Databank Financial Services, one of two local part owners of the facility thinks Ghana has the human capital to become an exporter of IT. "Ghana stands on the threshold of changing the country's export mix with high value added services which are in high demand globally", Ofori-Atta told the large crowd that witnessed the commissioning.

Overcoming Obstacles

But all has not been smooth sailing with the digital revolution evolving in Ghana. For instance, at the computer science department of the Kwame Nkrumah University of Science and Technology, there are only 30 computers for the 100 students in that class. Worse still, most of the computers have not been serviced since they were installed and are not connected to the Internet. Thus, some of the computer science graduates who recently passed out of the school probably had never used an Internet while in school. This depressing situation probably compelled the school authorities to appeal to the University of Pennsylvania in the United Sates of America to come to the school's aid. Following a request for technical solutions and support, Hewlett Packard, as a part of its digital village program to bridge digital divide through e-inclusion, decided to assist the university. Spearheaded by Ghanaian and US education and affiliate institutions, Hewlett Packard plans to provide fifteen resource centers linked to a high-speed digital subscriber line and connected to Ghana Telecom over the next two years at the university. According to a release from the local partners of Hewlett Packard, the training will include web-based and online course generations, as well as the preparation and delivery of lectures, seminars and continuous education programs via video and tele-conferencing.

Many foreign investors believe that if Ghana permitted Internet calls, the desperately poor country could become a hub of call centers for companies in the West, a high-tech development path cut by India. "If they can export digital goods and services ... they can easily compete with India and other places," says Jim Moore, an expert on Internet development at Harvard Law School. "A relatively modest market share can do a lot for these countries because they are so poor."

The government of Ghana, like those in other Sub-Saharan countries, has a vested interest in protecting the revenue of the state telephone company. It hasn't ruled out Internet calls but is taking its time to study the matter. "Nobody knows whether voice transmission across the Internet is legal or not," says Mr. Davies, whose plans are on hold while the government ponders the legal issues. In the meantime, risk takers in Ghana are plunging ahead and daring the government to stop them. And the unlucky among them end up in jail. BusyInternet's founder, Mark Davies, a US Internet entrepreneur, sees its Internet cafe as an "enabling environment" - a place where smart people can come together. Mr. Davies said, "In a place like Accra it is very difficult for young entrepreneurs to find the right tools, not only in terms of hardware to start a high tech business, but also the social environment. If you are looking to be an entrepreneur, the most important thing is sharing ideas with other people with similar interests."

Analysts believe that for entrepreneurs in Ghana, and indeed in the developing countries to participate in the new economy and to benefit fully from ICT, certain obstacles need to be overcome. Professor Jophus Anamuah-Mensah of the University of Education, Ghana argues that most small and medium-sized enterprises in Ghana and Sub-Saharan Africa operate in non-electronic environments, where laborious manual methods are employed. Record keeping and data processing in such environment certainly are inefficient and less effective, making the running of such businesses less cost-effective. Activities such as operational management, client-customer communications and transactions, product packaging, advertisement, delivery and product improvement suffer from such deficiencies, since marketing, inventory, management and financial controls, administration, planning and budgeting, and accounting systems may not be properly organized. Organizational structures of such third world SMEs, says Professor Mensah, "are generally flat, as there are very few levels of management hierarchy. SMEs are mostly financed through resources of their owners, in a few cases through bank loans and in rare situations shareholders' funds or a combination of theses sources". Given these features of third world SMEs, the questions become: How does local development of digital inclusion impact on their operations? What type of ICTs should be adopted for such businesses? How could the deployment of such ICTs be sustained? These are important questions that designers of ICT-mediated systems for SMEs must address, if small and medium-sized business owners in developing countries are to meet the demands and needs of such businesses.

Case Discussion Questions

1. Based on the forces of globalization, as discussed in this chapter, why in your opinion, do you think Ghana recognized IT as the key success factor for entrepreneurial development and economic growth?

2. As in India, how can the IT sector in Ghana contribute to the foreign exchange earnings of developing countries in Sub-Saharan Africa?

3. What are the problems facing the development of the IT industry in developing countries such as Ghana?

4. As an entrepreneur, what are the benefits of a good IT environment in a developing country such as Ghana?

Chapter 4

THE CULTURAL, FINANCIAL, POLITICAL AND INFRASTRUCTURAL ENVIRONMENT

Alice said, "Would you please tell me which way to go from here?" The Cat said, "That depends on where you want to go." (Lewis Carroll in Alice in Wonderland)

CHAPTER LEARNING OBJECTIVES
After studying this chapter, you should be able to:

1. Understand the socio-cultural context under which entrepreneurship is practiced in Sub-Saharan Africa.

2. Understand the financial and credit environment of small businesses in Sub-Saharan Africa.

3. Understand the relationship between the informal sector and the development of entrepreneurship in Sub-Saharan Africa.

4. Understand the political and regulatory environment of entrepreneurship in Sub-Saharan Africa.

5. Understand the infrastructural environment and how it impacts the development of entrepreneurship.

INTRODUCTION: THE NEED FOR A CONTEXTUAL PERSPECTIVE

In the preceding chapter, we examined the economic environment of entrepreneurship in Sub-Saharan Africa. In it we discussed economic policies in the national and regional context. We also examined how forces shaping the global economy impact entrepreneurial development. In this chapter, we will continue with the same theme, albeit with a focus on a different subject: the cultural, financial, political and infrastructural environments of entrepreneurship in Sub-Saharan Africa. It is worth reiterating that although this book is about formulating and implementing appropriate strategies for the entrepreneurial firm, it is important that we examine the contexts in which such strategies are formulated and implemented. In other words, an understanding of the context of strategy making is important in order to understand the particular environmental constraints that will impact the development of local entrepreneurship. Secondly, both long-term and short-term strategies to guard against business failure cannot be developed without an adequate understanding of the environment under which the strategies are formulated and implemented.

Thus, chapter four is contextual because it examines the subject of entrepreneurship in the context of Sub-Saharan Africa. By *context*, the book refers to the totality of surrounding conditions influencing the practice and performance of entrepreneurship in Sub-Saharan Africa. Thus, *context* is used here to denote a condition having some bearing on entrepreneurship; a determining or modifying factor. From the perspective of this chapter, the subject of entrepreneurship in Sub-Saharan Africa cannot be adequately understood without considering the specific conditions in Africa that determine the possibility of entrepreneurial practice and success. In this chapter, these conditions include: (i) the socio-cultural, (ii) the financial, (iii) the political, (iv) the infrastructural, and (v) informal conditions. In chapter five, we will examine the management and organizational conditions influencing the practice and performance of entrepreneurship in Sub-Saharan Africa.

Entrepreneurship is both a social and an economic phenomenon and as such it is not immune to social and cultural forces in the environment in which it is practiced. There are many socio-cultural factors or attitudes that affect the development of entrepreneurship in a society. For example, cultural attitudes towards risk-taking can be a barrier to entrepreneurial development. In some cultures, creativity and innovation, which are the necessary conditions for entrepreneurship, are not always valued traits. Many developing countries have social systems that create a culture of dependence, while shunning risk-taking. Cultural or social interpretations of gender roles can also have a decisive factor on entrepreneurial development. The culture of imitation and of believing on fate as against that of strategic planning, attitudes towards wealth accumulation and cultural orientation towards achievement are among the cultural barriers to entrepreneurial development.

The financial and credit environment is one of the most crucial factors facilitating or inhibiting the development of entrepreneurship in any society. In the developing countries, a major stumbling block for many potential entrepreneurs at the lowest end of the economic spectrum is lack of access to the credit or seed funding necessary to start a business. In addition to lack of initial funding, entrepreneurs who are confronted with growth potentials or in a period of transition usually face difficulties raising investment capital. In order to understand the relationship between the financial environment and entrepreneurial development, this chapter examines the formal and informal financial sectors and how they relate to enterprise financing.

The political environment in a society cannot be ignored in a discussion of entrepreneurship especially in the context of Sub-Saharan Africa. One of the barriers to sustainable economic and entrepreneurial development in the context of a nation's political environment is the set of political risks and instability, which are pervasive in many developing countries. Political risk is the chance that political decisions, events, or conditions in a country will affect the economic and business environment in ways that lead investors and other economic agents to lose some or all of the value of their investment or be forced to accept a lower than projected and anticipated rate of return. Either through political ideologies inherited from the experience of colonialism, bureaucratic corruption, the persistence of totalitarian political system, religious fundamentalism or the urge to promote nationalistic development policies, many countries in Sub-Saharan Africa have experienced various forms of political instability that has adversely affected the development of entrepreneurship. Thus, issues of political risks as they affect entrepreneurial development in Sub-Saharan Africa are examined in this chapter. In addition to political risks arising from political instability and crisis, the nature of the political culture may also act in ways that are unfavorable to indigenous and non-indigenous ownership of business ventures.

The manner in which economic activities are regulated in a society also affects the performance of business ventures. Research indicates that, particularly in Sub-Saharan Africa, over-regulation of economic activities has had negative impact on the development of entrepreneurship. Another consequence of over-regulation is that businesses in the formal sector are driven into the underground, informal sector of the economy. The reasons for- and consequences of economic over-regulation in Sub-Saharan Africa, and its implications for the development of entrepreneurship are examined in this chapter.

Research dealing with the phenomenon of economic development in Sub-Saharan Africa has shown that one of the reasons for the poor performance of the economies of Sub-Saharan Africa is the nature of the region's political system, which produces and reinforces a culture of bribery and bureaucratic corruption. In particular, the pervasive role of government in business decisions, the underdeveloped legal system and weak enforcement, and the material temptations of an emerging capitalist society inspire extensive corruption in many parts of Sub-Saharan Africa. Similarly, the chapter examines the effects of bureaucratic corruption on entrepreneurial development and economic growth in Sub-Saharan Africa.

Apart from the existence of an enabling political environment, the availability of basic infrastructure in a society is a condition for the growth of entrepreneurship. Quite often, the barriers to starting and maintaining a business come down to simple, yet often insurmountable factors, such as lack of transportation facilities (roads, railways, sea- and airports), lack or inadequate supply of energy (electricity and gas), inadequate water supply, inadequate or underdeveloped telecommunication infrastructure and poor educational facilities. In this chapter, we examine the nature of the infrastructural environment in Sub-Saharan Africa and how it impacts on the development and growth of entrepreneurship in the region.

As we observed in chapter three, the availability of information and communication technology (ICT) has become an important tool for entrepreneurial activity especially in commercial undertakings. Increasingly, ICT has become a tool for improving the way companies do what they do, as it is a tool for improving the delivery of social services like healthcare, education, and government-to-citizen programs. While ICT may not seem like a central concern when supporting entrepreneurs that need a good business plan and seed funding more than they need a computer, the reality is that long-standing view in today's information society requires that most micro-, small- and medium-sized enterprises have some level of ICT use integrated into their businesses. An entrepreneur who uses ICT appropriately and effectively can run a more efficient business and reach markets that were previously unimaginable. Thus, lack of appropriate ICT environment can serve as a barrier to the competitiveness of entrepreneurial firms. For this reason, this chapter examines the ICT environment and how it has impacted on entrepreneurial development in Sub-Saharan Africa.

An additional barrier to the development of entrepreneurship is the overarching mindset that entrepreneurship cannot be taught, that it is a creative and innovative way of thinking that comes inherently to some people and not to others. While it is true that some individuals are gifted with creativity to develop new ways of doing things, creativity alone is not sufficient. Ideas must be matched with basic skills and an understanding of business practices. It is indisputable that business skills and competencies are things that can be taught to help aspiring entrepreneurs create successful businesses. In this chapter, we examine the nature of entrepreneurial education in Sub-Saharan Africa and its impact on the development of entrepreneurship.

In the last section of the chapter, the relationship between the informal sector, entrepreneurship and economic development is examined. In this section, the informal sector is seen as a product of institutionalized practices, values and norms. The discussion then draws attention to why the informal sector actively coexists with the formal sector in Sub-Sahara African economies and the consequences of this co-existence in terms of entrepreneurial development.

THE CULTURAL ENVIRONMENT OF ENTREPRENEURSHIP

Entrepreneurship is both a social and an economic phenomenon. As a result, it cannot be studied in a social vacuum. An understanding of what promotes or hinders entrepreneurship in a society demands that we examine the socio-cultural environment under which it is practiced. By cultural environment, this book refers to the social and cultural practices, patterns of normative behavior, attitudes, values and belief systems that influence and shape the behavior of people in a society. Although they are commonly referred to as economic agents, entrepreneurs or business owners are humans. As humans, they are always caught in web of cultural practices that they must spin. These cultural practices, which are grounded in the social and cultural belief systems peculiar to a given society, can either promote or inhibit entrepreneurial development.[1]

Situating entrepreneurship within a cultural context is important because it allows us to understand the relationship between cultural practices and entrepreneurship and the constraints such cultural practices may have on the development of entrepreneurship. The discussion in this section is articulated in a structure with a focus on, but not limited to (i) cultural attitudes towards risk-taking, innovation and entrepreneurial development; (ii) cultural attitudes toward change, innovation, wealth creation and its use; (iii) the relationship between culture and the development of an entrepreneurial enabling environment; and (iv) the relationship between gendered cultural practices and entrepreneurial development. We will begin by examining the concept of culture and its place in entrepreneurial studies and practices.

The Concept of Culture and Entrepreneurship

Culture comprises an entire set of social norms and responses that condition people's behavior; it is acquired and inculcated, a set of rules and behavior patterns that an individual learns but does not inherit at birth. Studies in social anthropology indicate that culture *"denotes an historically transmitted patterns of meanings embodied in symbols, a system of inherited conceptions expressed in symbolic forms by means of which men communicate, perpetuate, and develop their knowledge about and attitudes toward life."*[2] In short, culture enables people to make sense of their world. Knowledge of the concept of culture is imperative for understanding human behavior and how it affects the motives for entrepreneurship. It is important because certain questions as to why some people, social groups or nations are more entrepreneurial than others and what motivates people towards business entry and self-employment have been answered with reference to the role played by cultural values.

Although profit has been traditionally seen as one of the motives for entrepreneurship across cultures, as emphasized by several economists, the desire to take risk and the motive to advance ones' spirit of adventure have been explained as aspects of a society's culture and other institutional arrangements.[3] In several studies, it has been shown that an entrepreneur may be driven not only by economic motives but also by psychological motives such as the desire to innovate and create new products; religious and existential motives as ways of finding and making meaning of lives. Research has also indicated that such psychological, social and existential motives are fundamentally shaped by environmental factors, including cultural value systems, attitudes, religious beliefs and ideologies. Prominent in this literature was research conducted mostly by psychologists and sociologists reported in McClelland (1961) who sought to measure "need for achievement," understand its determinants, and establish what links, if any, there were to economic performance and entrepreneurship. For instance, although the psychological and sociological theories of entrepreneurial supply have individual personality as their common focus of study, research has also indicated that these constructs are shaped by particular social cultural practices, including religion.[4]

In this context, entrepreneurial behavior is seen as resulting from attitudes, which in turn are affected by the socio-cultural environment (institutionalized rules and practices, parental guidance, religion, belonging to marginal groups etc.). In certain socio-cultural settings, some individuals may have no other option but to choose self-employment. This is an argument that is frequently advanced in the context of minority and immigrant entrepreneurship. Even here, culture has been seen to play a major role. Although it is argued that minorities and immigrants opt for self-employment in order to avoid racial or ethnic discrimination in the host country's labor market, which forces them to accept low-paid jobs and blocks upward mobility, the pattern of entrepreneurial activities and the management of immigrant firms have been seen to be influenced by cultural value systems. Similarly, it has been shown that some ethnic groups may have a cultural propensity towards entrepreneurship than others.[5] In a variety of studies, it has been shown that culture and ethnicity affect attitude towards entrepreneurship and some cultures produce individuals with higher propensities for entrepreneurial activity than others.[6]

Over the past decade, culture-related entrepreneurship studies have examined cognition, entrepreneur's perceptions of the environment and associated strategic orientations, social interventions designed to encourage entrepreneurship and national cultural characteristics, which influence the practice of entrepreneurship.

Cultural Value Dimensions and Entrepreneurship

Geert Hofstede defines culture as "a collective programming of the mind which distinguishes the members of one group or category of people from another."[7] In other words, culture is regarded as a collective phenomenon that is shaped by individuals' social environment, not their genes and in turn shapes attitudes and behaviors. From this perspective, cultural differences are the result of national, regional, ethnic, social class, religious, gender, and language variations. Values are held to be a critical feature of culture and cultural distinctiveness.

Geert Hofstede's research and subsequent ones show how national culture affects workplace values and entrepreneurship across a range of countries. Frequently studied dimensions of culture in the context of managerial practices and entrepreneurship are individualism-collectivism, uncertainty avoidance and time orientation.[8] In general, researchers have shown that entrepreneurship is facilitated by cultures that are high in individualism, weak in uncertainty avoidance, low in power-distance, high in masculinity and have long-term orientation. Similarly, the greater the cultural distance from these ideal types, the lower the average individual and aggregate levels of entrepreneurship.[9]

Uncertainty Avoidance and Entrepreneurship

One of the dimensions of culture identified in Hofstede's research is "uncertainty avoidance", which is the extent to which the members of a culture feel threatened by ambiguous or unknown situations. This dimension reflects the way the culture or society sees ambiguity and try to avoid ambiguous situations. Differences in uncertainty avoidance imply differences in motivational patterns toward entrepreneurship, especially the motive for going into business and the management of a business venture. Similarly, weak uncertainty avoidance cultures tend not to avoid ambiguous situations and are often prepared to engage in risky behavior in order to reduce ambiguities and uncertainties.

One example of how uncertainty avoidance is manifested in a culture is the manner in which entrepreneurship is viewed and the importance attached to entrepreneurism in a society. For example, the weak uncertainty avoidance cultural value, which characterizes the culture of the United States, implies that people are willing to take risks. This propensity for risk-taking pushes people to venture out to start and run their own business. Similarly, cultures that breed entrepreneurs are normally associated with entrepreneurial traits such as high tolerance for ambiguous, ever-changing situations, which are the typical environment in which entrepreneurs most often thrive. Thus, many studies have shown and predicted that self-employment (which is one of the reasons for entrepreneurship) is more often chosen in countries where people were dissatisfied with their lives, not in countries with a higher tolerance for the unknown.[10] In weak uncertainty avoidance cultures, there are fewer employed people and more self-employed individuals.

The cultural value of weak uncertainty avoidance also breeds a culture of individuals that are future oriented. Hence, entrepreneurs in a weak uncertainty avoidance society have a well-defined sense of searching for opportunities. Here, most people tend to look ahead and are less concerned with what was done yesterday than with what might be done tomorrow. The predominant view of man in a weak uncertainty avoidance culture is that of a person who is a *master-of-destiny*. Individuals holding this viewpoint believe that they can substantially influence the future, that they can control their destiny and that, through hard work, they can make things happen. Entrepreneurial and strategic planning in such cultures is feasible because individuals are willing to work to achieve well-defined objectives and goals that come from a mission statement and a vision of the *future direction* of the firm. Consequently, people tend to have a propensity to develop and introduce radical innovation in cultures that value and reward behaviors associated with weak uncertainty avoidance.[11] The major lesson in weak uncertainty cultures is that: (i) life is paved with challenges; (ii) man assumes responsibility with every free choice; (iii) existence cannot in anyway be justified by inactivity and shirking of responsibility; (iv) in order to better conduct one's life, imagination and creative effort must always be in control; and (v) imagination and creative effort will definitely remain in control provided they are transformed into behavioral automatisms.[12]

In contrast to weak uncertainty avoidance cultures are the ones that strongly avoid uncertainty and ambiguity. In such cultures, each day is accepted as it comes and people are not likely to show risk-taking and other future-directed activities that are commonly associated with entrepreneurial behavior. In many societies, including numerous African and Middle East cultures, a *fatalistic* viewpoint, or "determinism," is part of the cultural fabric. Individuals influenced by this viewpoint believe that they cannot control their destiny, that God or some supernatural forces have predetermined their existence and willed what they are to do during their lives.

At the extreme, strong uncertainty avoidance societies are dominated by beliefs that are antithetical to planning for the future. Rational planning is either seen as foolish or dangerous because the correct approach is to live in existing systems, react in terms of one's experience, and not to try to change them by means of some scientific or rational means. As Max Weber pointed out, a rational economic ethos would not develop in such cultures owing to their belief in fatalism, excessive ritualism and reliance on supernatural.

Planning and implementing entrepreneurial activities in these cultures is therefore difficult.[13]

In every culture, the attitudes and responses toward creativity and rationality are sustained by the prevailing system of values. They are learnt very early, when one is young. In a culture that privileges rationality over fatalism, the prevailing values which are inculcated in the mind are those that show life as a challenge and an endless test in the face of which imagination and constant effort are essential. Creative anticipation and initiative are, in this regard, the best strategies and the best modalities for action. A culture that is predisposed to fate imposes upon itself detachment, fatalism and inactivity as the ideal modalities for conducting one's life. Here, an attitude towards risk-taking is seen as dangerous. As pointed out by Kabeya Tshikuku, fatalism strips existence of the freedom of choice and its corollary, namely responsibility for one's acts. In this context, inactivity means the absence of commitment and rejection of all effort.[14] An entrepreneurial undertaking is less likely to thrive in a situation that privileges inactivity and self-detachment.

Culture, Innovation and Entrepreneurship

Another cultural dimension in Hofstede's study is *long- versus short-term orientation*. Long-term orientation (LTO) stands for the fostering of virtues oriented toward future rewards – in particular, perseverance and thrift. Its opposite pole is short-term orientation, which stands for the fostering of virtues related to the past and present – in particular, respect for traditions and fulfilling social obligations. In a series of studies conducted by Hofstede, the Eastern and Western cultures are seen to be predominantly long-term oriented while African and Middle Eastern cultures are classified under a category of regions with short-term orientation. In fact, the result of consequent studies indicates that short-term thinking prevails in Sub-Saharan Africa.[15] It should be noted, as Hofstede rightly pointed out, that these value scores do not imply that all Africans are short-time thinkers, nor all Westerners are long-term thinkers. But they do mean that these ways of thinking are sufficiently general to affect common behavior patterns and entrepreneurship.

In long-term oriented cultures, it has been shown that perseverance and sustained efforts toward slow results is the norm in occupational activities. In addition, thrift (being sparing with resources), a willingness to subordinate oneself for a purpose, respect for circumstances and a concern with adaptiveness which are attributes associated with entrepreneurship are predominant in long-term oriented cultures. Long-term orientation, in combination with weak uncertainty avoidance, has been associated with potential for innovation, which in turn, is associated with generation of new ideas.[16]

In the Western cultures where long-term orientation is the norm, there is emphasis on strategic planning for the allocation of scarce resources for the future growth of a business venture. The role of strategic planning is crucial in this context for it is geared towards answering questions that provide answers to the future direction of the business: Where does the business need to go from here? What new or different customer groups and customer needs it should endeavor to satisfy in the future? What market position it should be staking out in the future? What changes in business make-up should be anticipated? Specifically, emphasis on the future direction of the business, which is the cornerstone of strategic management and successful entrepreneurship, is a drive in long-term oriented cultures. Essentially, the entrepreneur's expectations for the future would influence the types and amount of resources assembled, as would the location of the venture relative to needed resources. Together, these would influence early performance.

In short-term oriented cultures, there is a prevailing belief that efforts in business or entrepreneurial activity should be geared towards the realization of immediate results; there is social pressure toward spending; respect for traditions; concern with personal stability; and concern with social and status obligations. In Hofstede's study, Sub-Saharan Africa is classified among the regions of the world that score highest in short-term orientation, indicating that short-term thinking prevails with a positive attitude towards the past as against the future.[17]

It is hardly surprising that African countries which rate high on short-term value orientation are more likely to value and prioritize fatalism, submission to the supernatural, conspicuous social consumption, and inability to plan strategically. Here, excessive ritualism and reliance on magic or supernatural prevail. Having a different time orientation (orientation towards the past as against the future), being disinclined to be future-directed and motivated, are complex socio-cultural issues that do not necessarily auger well with the demands of entrepreneurship.[18]

Risk-Aversion and the Culture of Imitation

Weak uncertainty avoidance in combination with long-term orientation is associated with the potential for risk-taking and innovation. Conversely, a culture that is short-term oriented and strong in uncertainty avoidance will be risk-averse. Risk aversion is antithetical to innovation and when excessively pursued breeds a culture of imitation. Short-term oriented cultures, because they value the status quo, are predisposed toward personal stability and if this attribute is overstressed, it could discourage the initiative, risk-seeking, and changeability required of entrepreneurs in quickly developing new products and changing markets.

In the context of Sub-Saharan Africa, the prevalence of short-term thinking means that there is less of a prevailing sense of urgency and more acceptance of the status quo. In a context where community harmony is paramount and where traditions are reverend, the acceptance of new ideas, change and progress that threaten culturally sanctioned ways of life is avoided. As such, any innovative ideas for developing business that do not conform to indigenous cultural norms are hardly tolerated by the community and may be suppressed. The result is the emergence and perpetuation of a culture of imitation.

In chapters one and two of this book, the importance of innovation and creativity was stressed as the necessary condition for and precursor to entrepreneurship. From the perspective of strategic management, a major characteristic of entrepreneurship is creativity and/or innovation, not imitation. While imitation is the habit of repeating what others have done (expressed in the saying, "monkey see, monkey do"), creativity and innovation imply the habit of doing something in a novel way. Innovation is about finding a better way of doing things as the basis for a new venture. This is the classic pattern of entrepreneurship.

In many parts of Sub-Saharan Africa, the concept of innovation, which is very crucial to entrepreneurship and economic development, is almost non-existent precisely because many who venture into new businesses imitate what others are already doing in the marketplace without adding something new. Similarly, the culture of imitation which is predominant among African business owners has been partly explained against the background of indigenous cultural practices that privilege the status quo rather than change. For example, in a study of the characteristics and problems of small-scale manufacturing in Kenya, researchers find out that one of the primary weaknesses of entrepreneurial development is that the businesses they surveyed "produce products which were copies of others in the industry".[19] In a similar manner, Retha Scheepers argues, "most new and established businesses in South Africa employ strategies of imitation and not differentiation".[20]

Cultural Values and Entrepreneurial Environment

There is every tendency that certain cultural values in a society breed environments that are conducive to entrepreneurship. In particular, we would expect social institutions, industry characteristics, and behaviors to reflect and reinforce a culture's value systems. For example, differences in culture influence a society's legal system, which will in turn influence the level and intensity of entrepreneurial activities. Of great relevance here is the legal and institutional protection of intellectual property rights, which will influence investments in innovation. Similarly, it has been suggested that patterns of values and beliefs will vary systematically with variations in industrial structure. For example, countries or regions with greater industrial concentration would be expected to positively influence the presence of values and infrastructure supportive of entrepreneurship by increasing the propensity of this type of activity.[21]

The degree to which cultural values affect entrepreneurial environment can be understood when seen in the context of the cultural values attached to achievement orientation versus ascriptive orientation. Thus, cultures that are high on the achievement end of this dimension value competition, assertiveness and materialism. Whether competing as individuals or as members of a group (i.e., individualistic versus collectivist), achievement-oriented cultures value winning and the rewards that accompany success. Similarly, one would expect entrepreneurship to emerge from an environment that encourages competition, assertiveness and materialism. In highly achievement-oriented cultures, social status is largely derived from a person's achievements. In highly ascription-oriented cultures, on the other hand, social status is largely derived from personal attributes such as age, experience, social connections, or gender.

Another cultural dimension is that of universalism versus particularism (universalistic cultural orientation versus particularistic cultural orientation). In a *universalistic cultural orientation*, people believe they can develop rules and standards that can be reasonably applied to everyone in every situation. They tend to use contracts, formal systems, and procedures to convey what they expect from others. In a *particularistic cultural orientation*, people develop their expectations of others based on their personal relationships with them and their trust in them rather than on rules.

There is one particular difference between universalistic (or achievement-oriented) and particularistic (or ascriptive oriented) cultures in terms of which the rule of law is applied and its consequence for economic growth and entrepreneurship. In the universalistic/achievement-oriented society, laws and rights are supposed to be the same for all members and applied indiscriminately to every one on the basis of a universalistic principle. In the particularistic/ascriptive-oriented society, however, laws and rights may differ from one category of people to another on the basis of the principle of particularism. In particularistic cultures, where individuals are recognized on the basis of mostly primordial attachments to, for example, particular political orientations or the family background or ethnic segment to which they are born, the rule of law which is fundamental to maintaining justice, equity and property rights is fundamentally weak. In such a situation, favoritism, bribery and corruption, cronyism, etc prevail and are unsupportive to individual entrepreneurial initiatives.[22]

A conceptual rationale for the relationship between national culture and national firm-formation rates is that culture influences the supportiveness of the environment so as to make it more conducive and legitimate to form a new business.[23] It may also be the case that culture influences the psychological characteristics of individuals within the population so as to create a larger supply of potential entrepreneurs.[24] Thus, culture is important because it influences the motives, values, and beliefs of individuals.

Culture and Gendered Entrepreneurial Practices

Gender differences and its associated inequality, including their manifestation in economic activities have been explained against a backdrop of a cultural value orientation that privileges masculinity over femininity. Specifically in particularistic- and ascriptive-oriented cultures, sex roles in society are clearly defined and it is accepted that men should dominate in society.[25]

In Sub-Saharan Africa, socio-cultural norms, which have perpetuated gender inequality in social roles and economic opportunity, are seen as some of the obstacles to entrepreneurial development in the region. The gendered dimensions of the cultural, social and institutional environment in Sub-Saharan Africa are reflected in a number of gender-specific constraints in Africa. For example, property laws impose constraints on women, who do not always have the rights to acquire and own property. This limits their ability to have access to needed capital for business development as they lack property to use as collateral. This applies also to the labor policies when they lead to discrimination in employment and benefits.

Constraints resulting from gendered property laws and the practice of confinement due to some religious practices can also impede women to make connections or networks that will become valuable in business development. Cultural values may conflict with women entrepreneurs' need for freedom of movement and socializing with men. This is clearly observed in several countries around the world where women, due to religious practices and other socio-culturally imposed sanctions, cannot travel outside their homes or transact businesses without their husbands' consent. In some countries in Sub-Saharan Africa, civil codes as well as traditional and family laws discriminate against women in terms of money and ownership of property. The land ownership systems and registration acts, inheritance laws, credit laws, marriage and divorce laws, commercial codes, agricultural acts, privatization and investment laws are examples of practices that are reflective of the socio-cultural, institutional, politico-legal and regulatory environments that impede women entrepreneurial efforts and aspirations to become key economic players.

Women entrepreneurs tend to face constraints resulting from gender roles and responsibilities; occupational segregation; internal constraints; and cultural values. In the face of modernization, the typical African woman is now placed in a position to fulfill the dual role of a breadwinner and a homemaker. Similarly, attempts at reconciling work and family responsibilities are seen as constraints to the development of their entrepreneurial initiatives. In particular, women's more demanding role in the family relative to men's also affect their entrepreneurial ability by reducing the time, energy and concentration levels they can apply to their roles as economic agents. The amount of time they have available for business activity is limited by the time necessary to care for the family. Household responsibilities make them risk averse, while societal perceptions affect their treatment when they step beyond their perceived boundaries, limiting their access to the resources required for successful entrepreneurship.

Thus, despite the growing recognition of the importance of African women's contributions to economic growth and their dominance of certain sectors, particularly agriculture and textiles, women generally remain either marginalized, shut out of the formal economy, or constrained due to lack of access to capital. For example, most specialized financing provided for women to date has been at the micro level. Furthermore, private equity funds created to provide capital to SMEs in general are very few, and even fewer for women-owned SMEs.

THE FINANCIAL AND CREDIT ENVIRONMENT

In the context of entrepreneurial development in Sub-Saharan Africa, most studies conclude that financial difficulties, i.e., the lack of access to and cost of finance, remain a difficult constraint on credit or seed funding necessary to start a business and expansion for small-scale business ventures. In particular, it is not uncommon for small businesses to have insufficient working capital for day-to-day operations. For many enterprises the potential for growth takes the demand for capital beyond the limits of self-finance, and such needs for additional finance are not easily met from the banks as a result of the nature of the financial and credit environment in Sub-Saharan Africa. In general, small-scale enterprises in Sub-Saharan Africa lack access to finance and credit facilities and this constraint has been seen as one of the greatest barriers to the development of entrepreneurship in the region.

In order to understand the nature of the financial constraint, it is appropriate to examine the financial and credit environment in Sub-Saharan Africa as it impacts on enterprise financing and entrepreneurial development. To do this, this section examines the formal and informal financial sectors and how they relate to enterprise financing. In the context of Sub-Saharan Africa, a discussion of enterprise finance is not complete without an examination of the role of microfinance and microfinance institutions in enterprise financing. Consequently, this section looks into the role of microfinance in the process of entrepreneurial development with particular attention to the micro- and macro constraints in the system. An emerging area of interest in enterprise finance in the context of developing countries is the role of public sector partnership with non-governmental organizations and the private sector. This section examines the mechanism of this partnership with particular reference to the provision of micro-finance for the marginalized group with entrepreneurial spirit in the developing countries.

The Formal Financial Sector

In most countries, access to bank finance in the form of loans and credit facilities is seen as one of the major instruments for the promotion of enterprises and entrepreneurship. This, of course, presupposes a situation where there is the existence of sound financial and banking systems and appropriate conditions favoring access to finance by business owners. In any given situation, banks will not extend credit without assurances that borrowers are creditworthy and that it will be possible to recover the debt if there is a default. For example, aspiring entrepreneurs with promising business opportunities cannot obtain loans if the bank does not have enough information on the value of the property and the credit history of the borrower – and if the legal system does not protect creditors. A number of studies have indicated that lack of access to bank credit facility by business owners is undoubtedly the most serious constraint in enterprise or entrepreneurial development in Sub-Saharan Africa. Similarly, many observers have concluded that obtaining credit from the formal financial sector in Sub-Saharan Africa involves a lot of frustration and likely rejection and few aspiring entrepreneurs or small business owners bother to seek credit from the formal financial sector.[26]

To understand the relationship between the financial sector, enterprising financing and entrepreneurship in Sub-Saharan Africa, it is essential that we understand the nature and constraints confronting the financial and banking sector. The literature on the formal financial sector or markets in Sub-Saharan Africa illustrates periods in which governments exerted strict control on the one hand, and deregulation, on the other. In both instances, micro- and small-scale firms did not benefit from the formal financial sector enterprise financing.[27] As a result of macroeconomic instability, structural economic change, political instability and civil strife, economic and especially financial transactions in Sub-Saharan Africa have been conducted in highly uncertain and volatile environments, which have profoundly engendered more volatile returns to investment and income streams than in other parts of the world.

In the late seventies and early eighties, the governments of Sub-Saharan Africa were pursuing what economists termed as "interventionist financial policies". In particular, governments played a major role in determining credit flows through a system of subsidies, interest-rate ceilings, policy-based credit allocation, high reserve requirements, and restricting entry into banking and capital account transactions. These fiscal policies were justified on the need for government to actively play a controlling role in economic development. For example, a low interest rate policy was perceived as one of key instruments for promoting private investment, while direct credit allocation was regarded as a means of redistributing resources and building a broad-based, diversified economy. Thus, years of low interest rates combined with excessive expansionary monetary policies and huge deficits in government budgets led to negative real interest rates and adverse effect on the level of domestic capital formation.

The monetary policy adopted, especial prior to the liberalization of financial markets in pre-structural adjustment era, often involved excessive restriction and control and proved counterproductive, resulting in financial "repression" and hindered the development of financial institutions. Commercial viability was largely prevented by the dictates of government policy objectives and political goals. Undoubtedly, this history of political interference in the operations of banks seriously impaired their capacity to handle risks. In particular, and as a result of the volatility in the macroeconomic environment in response to the drastic changes and externally induced shocks, banks in Sub-Saharan Africa were ill-prepared to develop the capacity for risk assessment and for monitoring loan portfolios. Many studies describe this period as the era of banking crises in Sub-Saharan Africa and traced these to a combination of macroeconomic and policy environments, the structure of the financial market and the conduct of the banks.[28]

Thus, the inherent weaknesses of financial institutions resulting from exposure to high systemic risks was compounded by poor risk analysis, excessive political pressure on lending decisions, and limited opportunities for asset divestiture. The general quality of banks' portfolios deteriorated sharply in the 1980s, when the fiscal and balance-of-payments crises crippled the economies of Sub-Saharan Africa. For example, the World Bank estimated that loan-loss ratios in Sub-Saharan Africa during the early eighties ranged from 40 percent to 60 percent, with the portfolios of banks in some countries consisting of more than 90 percent bad debts.[29]

Against this record and the need for access to external borrowing and stabilization loans, the International Monetary Fund (IMF) and the World Bank argued that interventionist policies were responsible for the poor performance of financial institutions. Consequently, many Sub-Saharan African countries adopted a policy reform, which targeted the financial sector through the instruments of liberalization and deregulation of interest rates. The result of these policy instruments pointed to failure in the financial markets in several Sub-Sahara African countries.

Specifically, starting from 1982, the period of liberalization and deregulation of the financial sectors in Africa witnessed the introduction of market-oriented economic policies embodied in a structural adjustment program. As discussed in chapter three, the policy of structural adjustment program has had a profound effect on the financial markets and thus on their ability to play the role of enterprise financier. In particular, the banking sector during this period witnessed macroeconomic volatility (e.g., volatility in growth and interest and inflation rates), which caused banks to be particularly vulnerable as they attempted to alter the relationship between the values of bank assets and liabilities. Second, lending booms and surges in capital flows prompted banks to lend excessively and unwisely creating a crisis as the bubble bursts. Third, the mismatch between assets and liabilities produced loan loss and increased risk of bank fragility. Fourth, inadequate preparation for financial liberalization increased the danger of the banking crisis. Fifth, stabilization programs, such as politically induced privatization, and loose controls on connected lending hurt the profitability and efficiency of banks. Sixth, weaknesses in the accounting, disclosure, and legal framework adversely affected bank performance. Finally, the deregulation of exchange rate regime undermined bank soundness through its impact on vulnerability to speculative attack, a downward adjustment in the real value of bank capital and its negative effect in enterprise financing that eschewed investment in the productive base of the economies. In addition, savings mobilization was not actively pursued and private sector investment was not encouraged. There was neither active liquidity and liability management nor any incentive to increase efficiency, often resulting in increased costs for financial managemen.[30]

Microeconomic deficiencies, notably poor management practices such as connected lending have also been seen as some of the causes for banking failures in the region. Either through management inefficiency or lack of appropriate infrastructure and government regulation, the prevailing microeconomic environment induced by deregulation discouraged banks from investing in information capital, crucial for the development of financial systems. In dealing with the risks of private borrowers, banks were burdened by problems caused by costly and imperfect information – adverse selection, moral hazard and contract enforcement. In particular, the absence of appropriate financial infrastructure was a major constraint for greater access to finance. For example, agencies such as credit bureaus that compile and distribute credit and personal information to creditors and for helping financial institutions expand their lending to individual customers and small- and medium-sized enterprises were conspicuously non-existent. As a result, lending to individual customers and smaller businesses has been time consuming, expensive and risky.[31]

In general, results show that simply shifting policy from financial control to financial deregulation and liberalization could not address the fundamental problems facing the region's financial sector. Especially in Nigeria, where poorly designed reform was undertaken, deregulation measures led to crisis and eventual collapse of the financial system, necessitating policy reversals. In particular, about 60 percent of the total loans and advances of Nigerian banks were non-performing. As a result, their capital and reserves were negative in an amount of N8.4 billion (about US$1000 million) in 1994.[32]

Several studies have illustrated the extent and impact of these crises in several Sub-Sahara African countries, and concluded that most of the roots of the crises are endemic in character, resulting to incidences of non-performing loans which can be seen as bedrock for enterprise financing. For instance, the share of non-performing loans in total banking system loans reached 50 percent or more in Benin, Cameroon, Côte d'Ivoire, Guinea, Senegal, Tanzania, and Uganda, while it was almost as high in Nigeria where 45 percent of bank loans outstanding were non-performing at end-1992 and Ghana where about 40 percent of bank credit to non-government borrowers was non-performing in June 1993 estimated at less than 20 percent of total financial sector asset.[33]

Although some countries experienced positive changes in financial performance under the program of structural adjustment, banks' balance sheets remained precarious, as their portfolios were continuously dominated by an extremely high incidence of non-performing loans and excess liquidity. In particular, only in Kenya was the result somewhat better, with non-performing assets in June 1993 estimated at less than 20 percent of total financial sector assets.[34] Apart from managerial deficiencies and externally imposed policy uncertainty and credibility, banking operations were severely constrained by the institutional environment, which restricted banks' risk management and their ability to improve their operational practice.

Although some innovative instruments and products were developed to reach untapped segments of the financial market, lack of infrastructure and adverse institutional framework rendered such efforts unproductive. Similarly, bank loan portfolios did not experience any significant changes. As a result of ill-defined property rights, absence of credit information registries or credit bureaus, lack of acceptable collaterals, political patronage and other institutional and socio-cultural factors, banks' preferred loan composition continued to be heavily weighted against micro- and small-scale enterprises.

The Formal Financial Sector and Enterprise Financing

The above development has had a negative effect on enterprise financing in Sub-Saharan Africa. As far as small enterprise finance is concerned, banks perceive small borrowers as more risky, and they often charge them higher interest and use collateral requirements as credit rationing devise. On the other hand, banks concentrate on lending to larger (often public) enterprises, whose performance is not necessarily rigorously screened and monitored. There are a number of reasons why banks refused to lend to small-scale enterprises. One reason is that the foreclosure of collateral property is difficult in view of the ambiguities surrounding property rights in many Sub-Saharan countries. Banks in Sub-Saharan Africa do not have access to sufficient information to arrange state-guaranteed loans for borrowers who have not willfully defaulted. Nor is there an effective mechanism for banks to enforce repayment on willfully defaulted borrowers. Thus, banks generally incur high default-risk costs, as loan repayment rates continue to be poor.

Significantly, the aftermath of liberalization and deregulation in many Sub-Sahara African countries witnessed the emergence and growth of non-bank financial institutions, including semi-formal institutions. There were mortgage, usurious moneylenders, leasing and venture capital schemes that were mainly interested in financing trade and other commercial activities, where a quick profit is assured. The entrants of quazi-banking institutions in many Sub-Saharan Africa countries (especially in Nigeria) in the 1980s and early 1990s also saw some institutions engaging in "pyramid schemes" to meet growing credit demands, risking severe liquidity crises and, eventually, collapse of the financial sector. Although financial deregulation was meant to ease enterprise financing, macroeconomic volatility, lending booms, loose controls, the high interest rates and other malpractices in the financial sector including microeconomic deficiencies remain the central problem in terms of enterprise financing.

In Sub-Sahara African countries, some of these problems came into being because (i) financial deregulation took place before adequate prudential regulation was put in place; (ii) financial deregulation, competition, and innovation outstripped the capacity of banks to manage risks prudently; (iii) weak internal governance of banks left the banking system vulnerable to macroeconomic shocks; (iv) weak and insolvent financial institutions were allowed to continue operations, thus weakening the entire financial systems; and (v) declining business profits, together with excessive corporate indebtedness led to deterioration in asset quality.

In Sub-Saharan Africa, the internal shortcomings of the formal financial system, such as inadequate supervisory and regulatory provision, are compounded by poor legal mechanisms for contract enforcement, inappropriate incentive environments and restricted flows of information, increasing the level of risk associated with lending. Differences in confronting the increased risk affect transaction costs. Furthermore, the financial products and services offered by formal institutions do not easily match those required by potential borrowers and savers, i.e., operators of micro- and small-sized enterprises.

The Informal Financial Sector

Entrepreneurs and small business owners in the Sub-Sahara African region have limited access to financial resources due to a number of factors as noted in the preceding discussion. In the absence of formal sector credit facilities, informal sources have become increasingly active within the economic environment of many developing countries. To be sure, the *informal financial sector* includes non-formal financial activities and transactions that are undertaken in and by such institutions as credit unions, savings and credit co-operatives; less formalized, smaller-scale group arrangements such as savings groups, mutual aid associations, non-rotating savings and credit associations (SCAs), rotating savings and credit associations (ROSCAs); commercial lenders such as individual savings (*esusu*) collectors, estate-owners, landlords, traders, shopkeepers, and professional and non-professional money lenders; friends, relatives and business associates among whom transactions take place on a non-commercial basis.

Most importantly, the inability of loan applicants to be collaterally compliance imposes restrictions to the formal sources. Within the array of small-scale business financing, informal credit sectors are thus most popular. Collateral-free lending, proximity, timely delivery, and flexibility in loan transactions are some of the attractive features of informal credit. A small business owner who is basically skewed out from formal finance market would more or less demand informal loans or credits, as sources of institutional credit are highly elusive to them. But the dominance of informal finance with a lack of market-based small business and entrepreneurial finance has negative implications for entrepreneurial growth, including high rate of interest from informal sector moneylenders.

Informal financial transactions can be grouped into non-commercial, such as transactions between relatives and friends or small-scale group arrangements, and commercial, conducted by single collectors, estate-owners, landlords, traders or moneylenders. In Sub-Saharan Africa, most informal financial agents and institutions tend to specialize in either lending or savings mobilization. In any case, those engaging in both activities provide a members-only service in terms of loans or any other form of credit facility. In the West African countries, the main activity of savings collectors is mobilizing savings through periodical (daily, weekly or monthly) collection of small amounts of savings at markets or other workplaces, though they occasionally extend credit to their clients in flexible terms, mainly to finance the working capital needs of traders.

The informal financial intermediation occurs both in the rural and urban areas with middlemen or traders acting as intermediaries between producers and consumers. Traders operate among producers in rural areas and consumers in the urban centers, offering supplier's credit or an advance payment against future purchases. Middlemen, operating inter-linked credit lines, do not ask for collateral but enter into agreements (e.g., with farmers) to purchase all output over an agreed period. Imputed interest on these types of arrangement can be as high as 50 percent. In addition to middlemen acting as intermediaries between farmers and loan givers, there are also moneylenders who provide financial assistance to business owners. Operating at high interest rates, moneylenders are considered "lenders of last resort." They lend from profits generated by other economic activities, such as agriculture and real estate development, and re-invest the returns from lending into these activities.

It is worth noting that these informal financial markets have developed mechanisms for coping with the constraints inherent in imperfect information, property rights, collateral and insolvency regulation and enforcement laws. These mechanisms operate within socially and geographically confined community settings, and are firmly rooted in social codes and norms. Thus, they are anchored in institutional set-ups, tested over many decades, if not centuries. Informal lenders rely less on collateral than on social pressure, reputation and personal knowledge of borrowers or interlinked credit contracts for screening, monitoring and contract enforcement. The use of these methods for client selection reduces the risk of dealing with small borrowers, who remain high-risk for formal lending institutions. Informal lenders are used for cash flow, and liquidity management for consumption smoothing by small-scale borrowers and savers, albeit on a limited scale.[35]

The liabilities of the informal financial sector are limited to deposits from specific groups of people or to the surplus income of the lender. Saving cycles are typically very short: weekly, fortnightly and monthly contributions are very popular in schemes operating among traders, market women and other self-employed people. Savings collectors are relied upon primarily for security, and savings are returned to the depositors within the shortest possible time. Therefore, despite the potential of informal agents as deposit mobilizers, they have never played a key role in financial intermediation in Sub-Saharan Africa. The effective lending rates charged are often too high for these funds to be used as a regular source of working capital. Moreover, while many informal financial services grew along with demand, they face difficulties in moving beyond their mode of operation. Compared with other developing regions (e.g., Southeast Asia and Latin America), informal financial operations in Sub-Saharan Africa remain confined to traditional forms of economic activities, without transforming into more dynamic and entrepreneurial modes.[36]

The Role of Microfinance in Entrepreneurial Development

Microfinance refers to the provision of financial services to low-income clients, including the self-employed.[37] In addition, microfinance means providing very poor families with very small loans (microcredit) to help them engage in productive activities or grow their small business ventures. Over time, microfinance has come to include a broader range of services (credit, savings, insurance, etc.) as people have come to realize that the poor that lack access to traditional formal financial institutions require a variety of financial products. Traditionally, microfinance was focused on providing a very standardized credit product. The poor, just like anyone else, need a diverse range of financial instruments to be able to build assets, stabilize consumption and protect themselves against risks. The term also refers to the practice of sustainably delivering those services. More broadly, it refers to a movement that envisions "a world in which as many poor and near-poor households as possible have permanent access to an appropriate range of high quality financial services, including not just credit but also savings, insurance, and fund transfers."[38]

Theoretically, microfinance encompasses any financial service used by poor people, including those they access in the informal economy, such as loans from a village moneylender. In practice however, the term is usually only used to refer to institutions and enterprises whose goals include both profitability and reducing the poverty of their clients. Microfinance institutions provide macrocredit. In the context of micro- and small-scale businesses, Microcredit is the extension of very small loans to small business owners or entrepreneurs and who are not considered *bankable*. These individuals lack collateral, steady employment and a verifiable credit history and therefore cannot meet even the most minimal qualifications to gain access to traditional credit. Microcredit is a part of microfinance, which is the provision of a wider range of financial services to the very poor.

Microcredit came to prominence in the 1980s, although early experiments date back 30 years in Bangladesh, Brazil and a few other countries. The important difference of microcredit was that it avoided the pitfalls of an earlier generation of targeted development lending, by insisting on repayment, by charging interest rates that could cover the costs of credit delivery, and by focusing on client groups whose alternative source of credit was the informal sector. Emphasis shifted from rapid disbursement of subsidized loans to prop up targeted sectors towards the building up of local, sustainable institutions to serve the poor. Microcredit has largely been a private (non-profit) sector initiative that avoided becoming overtly political, and as a consequence, has outperformed virtually all other forms of development lending.

Traditionally, banks have usually not provided financial services to clients with little or no cash income. Banks must incur substantial costs to managing a client account, regardless of how small the sums of money involved. In addition, most poor people have few assets that can be secured by a bank as collateral. As documented extensively by Hernando de Soto and others, even if they happen to own land in the developing world, they may not have effective title to it. This means that the bank will have little recourse against defaulting borrowers. In other words, those that are not bankable have no access to credit facilities from the formal banking and other lending institutions.[39]

Because of these difficulties, when poor people borrow they often visit their relatives or the ubiquitous local moneylender, whose interest rates can be very high. An analysis of 28 studies of informal money-lending rates in 14 countries in Asia, Latin America and Africa concluded that 76 percent of moneylender rates exceed 10 percent a month, including 22 percent that exceed 100 percent a month. Moneylenders usually charge higher rates to poorer borrowers than to less poor ones.[40] While moneylenders are often demonized and accused of usury, their services are convenient and fast, and they can be very flexible when borrowers run into problems. Hopes of quickly putting them out of business have proven unrealistic, even in places where microfinance institutions are very active.

The importance of microfinance for entrepreneurial and small business development in the developing world has its origin in the founders of the microcredit movement in the 1970s (such as Muhammad Yunus) who have tested practices and built institutions designed to bring the kinds of livelihood opportunities and risk management tools that financial services provide to the doorsteps of poor people.[41] With the success of Grameen Bank (which now serves over 7 million poor Bangladeshi women), many developing countries have replicated the microfinance and microcredit model as a way of providing needed finance for poor as investment capital and especially for those who have no practical access to formal sector finance.

For aspiring business owners who could not met credit requirements from the traditional banks, access to credit, insurance, and other financial services that are provided by microfinance institutions, helps to cope with the everyday financial crises they face. For struggling business owners, microfinance can smooth transactions and significantly reduce the need to sell assets (such as lands, inventories, etc) to meet basic financing needs. Access to credit allows poor people to take advantage of economic opportunities. While increased earnings are by no means automatic, struggling business owners have overwhelmingly demonstrated that reliable sources of credit provide a fundamental basis for planning and expanding business activities.

Public-private Partnership in Micro Financing

Private sector participation in micro enterprise financing has become more crucial in the context of developing countries. In the Sub-Saharan Africa region, most of the credit institutions established to provide micro-financing have not been able to make a significant impact due to several operational deficiencies among which are gross inadequacies in staffing, organization and management as well as poor loan notable in the area of microfinance. For several reasons, such as institutional, political and social, the policy of financing or providing cheap credit to small business owners for the purpose of entrepreneurial development in developing economies through formal financial intermediaries has not achieved desirable objectives. Secondly, lack of financial resources has made it increasingly difficult for governments in Sub-Saharan Africa to provide needed funds for the development of micro-enterprises. In cases where such institutions were created such as "The People's Bank" in Nigeria, political patronage, bureaucratic corruption and gross inefficiency, have rendered them powerless in providing adequate finance for enterprise development.

Against this background, many observers have argued that entrepreneurship and certain types of entrepreneurial support activities can best be achieved through partnership between the public and private sectors in a collaborative manner otherwise known as public-private partnership (PPP). Such partnerships can address complex issues in a country's economic development including, but not limited to, providing finances or credit facilities to under-financed business owners in developing countries. In the context of socio-economic development, the public and private sectors often rely on each other's expertise and resources, which is a case for public-private partnerships. For its part, the private sector can contribute finance, technology, manufacturing skills, training and other entrepreneurial initiatives.

In recent years, many countries in Sub-Saharan Africa have made significant advances in entrepreneurial development through increased collaboration with donor agencies and multinational corporations. These developments are in response to the fact that supporting micro enterprises at the local level has placed a major burden in the national budgets of developing countries. In addition to financial constraints, several countries face a very serious shortage of experienced middle and upper-level managers in both the public and the private sectors. In many countries, these problems are being met in a more organized manner through the efforts of the United Nations, multinational enterprises (such as Microsoft, Hewlett-Packard, Shell), NOGs, multilateral agencies, donor countries and assistance of technical staff from multinational corporations. The shortage of private sector management and especially entrepreneurial skills and experience is potentially a much more serious obstacle in many developing countries' quest for economic growth.

Evidence from many countries in Sub-Saharan Africa indicates that considerable advantages in socio-economic development can be gained from strengthening private participation in public decision-making and development policies. For example, in Botswana, a gradual process of increased dialogue between business associations and the public sector has resulted in a remarkable (and unusual) growth of mutual trust and partnership, with benefits in policy coherence, transparency and accountability.[42] The ultimate objective of PPPs is to promote greater trust among local stakeholders and other partners in the development process, thus facilitating good governance and the strengthening of local communities and of the local private sector.

The potential benefits of PPPs are perhaps best recognized in the area of business development and access to needed finance. Examples from Mozambique and Zambia show how useful the PPPs mechanism was in providing loan-guarantee schemes and microcredit at below-market rates to farmers and small businessmen who normally would not have any access to credit.[43] In Kenya, for example, KIVA-Action Now Kenya is a local Non Governmental Organization whose mission is to facilitate the establishment of enterprise development activities in the areas of microfinance and entrepreneurship. In many parts of Sub-Saharan Africa, private organizations and other stakeholders supporting governments' programs under Public Private Partnership (PPP) initiatives have built an enduring and sustainable microfinance sub-sector. Example from Botswana shows the useful role of PPPs in a more mature economic environment, with established business associations and government overcoming initial suspicions and even hostility over a long period of growing dialogue and increasing mutual trust, to the benefit of the economy as a whole.[44]

THE POLITICAL ENVIRONMENT

The political environment of a nation includes all laws, the political system, system of government, government agencies, and lobbying groups that influence or restrict individuals or organizations in the society. The political environment also consists of the *political culture* and political ideology, which is the general political philosophy or belief system prevailing in society. The interest in the political environment in the context of entrepreneurship is that the political environment, with its culture, ideologies, and system, influences the legislations and government rules and regulations under which a firm operates. An understanding of a country's political environment in terms of how it affects business and organizations entails an understanding of that country's political culture.

The interest in understanding the political context in a given society lies in the belief that the political environment or culture may not support the range of conditions necessary to produce an entrepreneurial culture. Specifically, an understanding of the political environment and culture enables us to understand how laws, political systems, political actions, attitude, beliefs and ideologies affect the conduct of a business enterprise. As in Zimbabwe and South Africa respectively, entrepreneurial action may fail in one country on account of the political system or culture and likewise it may succeed in another country on account of its different political culture. The political context or environment under which business is conducted plays a significant role in the success of entrepreneurial development. Accordingly, the political system and culture of a nation affects its economic policies and business practices to the degree to which it promotes or discourages risks faced by investors. In this section, we will examine the issues of political risks and instability, how the prevailing political culture undermines indigenous entrepreneurship, how the politics of privatization, indigenization and prejudice against non-indigene entrepreneurs skews the development of entrepreneurship in Sub-Saharan Africa. In addition, the consequences of excessive regulation and bribery and bureaucratic corruption on entrepreneurial development are examined.

Political Risks and Instability

In chapter three it was pointed out that the development and growth of entrepreneurship in a nation is also a product of foreign investments flowing into that country. Particularly in several countries in Sub-Saharan Africa, the period following post-independence has witnessed various forms of political instability and economic crisis that resulted to the outflow of investment finances. Even in the year 2008, we have witnessed how political crisis in Kenya has undermined that country's efforts in economic development. The instability and unrest that followed the country's election led to the destruction of business enterprises and the flight of investment capital from the hitherto politically stable nation. In any country, foreign direct investment facilitates the development of entrepreneurship through the transfer of technology and management resources that are not available in the local economy. Second, the multiplier- and linkage effects of foreign direct investment in a developing country such as increase market competition, productivity growth, human resource development, product and process innovation and greater consumer choice are some of key drivers of entrepreneurial activities. These benefits are, however, not available in an environment that is politically volatile and unstable, beset by confrontations and various types of risks.

Although there are many sources and kinds of risks, it is worthwhile highlighting those risks that may arise from policy actions of national governments. An example of such a risk is *political risk*. Political risk has been defined as the chance that political decisions, events, or conditions in a country will negatively affect the profitability or sustainability of a firm's investment. It is the likelihood that political actions will affect the business environment in ways that lead investors and owners to lose some or all of the value of their investment or be forced to accept a lower than projected rate of return.[45]

Political risk is seen here in terms of loss of control over ownership or loss of benefits of business enterprise by actions that are political in nature. This concept of political risk includes and also concentrates on the unwanted consequences of government actions. Other occurrences of a political nature that adversely affect the conduct of business are also termed as political risks – these are political events or constraints imposed at the specific industry or specific firm level. The political events typically are changes in government or heads of state accompanied by violence, riots, arson and destruction of private and public properties. Constraints on the firm typically encompass expropriation (the surrender of a claim to exclusive property and the act of dispossessing a person or entity of ownership or propriety rights usually by the government), restrictions on remittance of profits, discriminatory taxation, and out right closure of business enterprises.[46]

More specifically, the effects of government instability, socio-economic conditions, internal and external conflict, corruption, militarism and militant regimes, religious fundamentalism and tensions, breakdown of law and order, ethnic tensions, democratic unaccountability, the quality of bureaucracy, and negative attitudes toward foreign-owned enterprises constitute a nation's political risk. A number of these political risk components are also linked to the quality of political institutions. Above all, the quality of the bureaucracy is closely associated with the institutional strength of a particular country. Likewise, ensuring law and order and reducing corruption levels are important determinants (and effects) of high-quality institutions. They constitute relevant sub-components of an overall assessment of what constitute investment and business climate. Other examples of political risk include acts of terrorism; the threat of violence, or other harmful acts committed for political or ideological goals.

So defined, political risk tends to be greater in countries experiencing social unrest and disorder and in countries where the underlying nature of the fabric of society is characterized with competing demands and recognition. In many parts of Sub-Saharan Africa, the prevalence of civil wars, political and social unrests resulting from the political culture are the causes of instances of underdevelopment. Examples include the Democratic Republic of the Congo, Liberia, Sierra Leone, Rwanda, Somalia, Sudan, Zimbabwe, Kenya, etc.

It is common knowledge that when a country's political system presents a risk, potential foreign investors avert that country because foreign investors seek to invest their resources in areas where they are assured of return on their investments. This situation appropriately depicts the experience of the Niger-Delta area of Nigeria. Political risk, in this context, involves not only the degree of political stability or forms of government prevailing in a nation or region, but other governmental policies such as nationalization and the political will of host government to protect the interest of foreign investors.

Political instability and social unrest typically find expression in strikes, demonstrations, various forms of terrorism, the taking of expatriates as hostages, and other forms of violent conflict. Such unrest is more likely to be found in developing countries where the composition of the population contains more than one ethnic nationality, in countries where competing political ideologies and religious beliefs are battling for political and economic recognition and control (examples include Somalia, Sudan, Nigeria, Rwanda), in countries where economic mismanagement has created high inflation and falling standards of living, in countries where the rulers and the elite live in opulence and the masses become envious of them. Surely, these characterizations fit perfectly into the political culture of several countries in Sub-Saharan Africa. Other political risks associated with the business environment in developing countries include the confiscation of the assets of foreign-owned enterprises for political reasons, political violence and the restrictions in repatriation of foreign exchange earnings to home countries of foreign-own enterprises.

The Political System and Indigenous Entrepreneurship

In the context of Sub-Saharan Africa, many studies have referred to a form of hostility towards indigenous firms. An entrepreneur or business owner who happened to belong to the "wrong" political party is seen as a threat to those in political power. A "wrong" political party, in this context, is an opposition party. The political culture in several African countries is such that there is harmful prejudice against businesses owned by those in the opposition political parties. And it is not uncommon that such businesses are confronted with severe threats of dissolution from the ruling political party. As Kabeya Tshikuku elaborately pointed out, the threat comes from three sides: (i) from the existing politico-legal system; (ii) from the old colonial monopolies; and (iii) from the local socio-cultural system.[47]

Especially, an enterprise belonging to a member of the opposition political party is hardly recognized as having a legal personality different from that of its indigenous founder (or manager): the minor offences of the individual in the deepest recesses of his private life are often turned into abominable crimes of the enterprise in its relations with the authorities. As Kabeya Tshikuku suggests, any suspicion of "treason" against the owner (or the manager) can be a sufficient reason for torpedoing the activities of the enterprise or for holding its assets to ransom and fragmenting, amputating or confiscating them. On any pretext and without risk, African governments sometimes clearly and categorically refuse to honor their commitments towards the local enterprises. This pernicious result may be obtained through a legal procedure, through quazi- and pseudo tribunals, by a very sustained media lynching or simulated violence by the political police.

Taking advantage of the public's lack of sympathy for capitalist enterprises, some organized individuals and groups can destabilize with impunity a local enterprise in various ways: a wildcat strike manipulated from outside and with nothing at stake for the strikers, a complete sabotage of the facilities and equipment of an enterprise by its own workers, a mock trial in court leading to a verdict of bankruptcy or a condemnation to a sum beyond the corporate assets, an arbitrary decision of a husband against his wife who is the head of an enterprise, legal action involving succession directed against a widow who is the proprietress of an enterprise, settlement of the succession among several heirs after the death of a parent who is the proprietor of an enterprise, settlement of a conflict of interests between the indigenous partners of an enterprise, etc. In all these cases and many other similar ones, enterprises established and run by indigenes are dissolved amidst widespread indifference, their assets are shared, their facilities are sold off, their capital is swallowed up in consumption, their workers are forced into unemployment, their claims and debts are written off, and their dream of conquest fades. With the death of each enterprise, the whole of society returns to square one, which is underdevelopment.

The result in this depressing climate, according to Kabeya Tshikuku, is fivefold: (i) reconversion of indigenous enterprises into precarious businesses operating in the underground of the informal sector; (ii) cautious and non dynamic behavior of nationals considering the establishment of enterprises; (iii) an impressive number of bankrupt or abandoned indigenous enterprises; (iv) a disturbing number of indigenous enterprises that never survive their founders; and (v) scarcity of institutions for the supervision, financing and promotion of enterprises – small and medium – established and owned by natives.[48]

The Political System and Non-Indigenous Entrepreneurship

Not only is the political system and culture in several Sub-Sahara African countries antithetical to indigenous entrepreneurship, they also work in ways that inhibit the development of non-indigenous entrepreneurial initiatives. Perceived prejudice against foreign-owned firms and other forms of business undertakings in Sub-Saharan Africa can be traced back to post-independence era when African governments were eager to develop a truly indigenous basis of production through indigenization and nationalization policies. To be sure, indigenization policy is a government policy that aims at the wholesale take-over of enterprises or a policy of linking government supervision in the extent of expatriate or foreign participation in various economic activities.

The argument in favor of indigenization and against foreign ownership seems straightforward: "The apparent foreign domination of the private sector in Africa could lead to highly undesirable results, both socially and politically. On the social front, foreign ownership perpetuates capital flight and diminishes the income redistribution milieu, negatively affecting the social safety net. As the gap between the rich and the poor grows – mostly in favor of the foreign business owners, domestic political tension grows which dampens the climate for promoting private sector environment."[49]

It is not difficult to see how such an attitude works against entrepreneurship in a region in need of foreign investment capital, skills and other forms of resources for the promotion of entrepreneurship and economic development. The policy of indigenization, while encouraging local participants tends to deprive foreign-ownership of economic activities. One of the problems here is that privatized organizations are left in the hands of ill-prepared indigenes in the name of indigenization. Thus, as Papa Thiam points out, this naïve approaches to private sector development have contributed to propagate a new rent seeking culture, notably in Sub-Saharan Africa.[50] Papa Thiam has argued that, in the wake of the promotion of indigenous ownership to support private sector led growth, civil servants that were more exposed to trade management by government and to the provision of public goods, were given economic dominions (import quotas, monopoly, etc.) overnight and became major "private sector actors" and government partners in public-private policy dialogue. In numerous cases, the collusion of interest between government and that "emerging private sector" contributed to blurring the lines between politics, entrepreneurial ventures and public governance. This situation contributed to erode the foundations for building de-politicized states that are indispensable to consolidate democratic governance and promote entrepreneurial opportunities for all. In most countries in Sub-Saharan Africa, ideological approaches to "indigenizing" private sector resulted in the spoliation of foreign entrepreneurs, whose enterprises were overnight, "transferred" to inexperienced domestic operators and managers close to political power, often without due indemnification. In the majority of cases, as Papa Thiam points out, the local beneficiaries got episodically rich while the related enterprises collapsed. Not only did this contribute to gradually dismantle the country economic fabric, but also the foundations for a more conducive business environment and entrepreneurship were also durably destroyed.[51]

Ironically, the policies of indigenization and nationalization as a viable instrument for transferring ownership of industry to the indigenous groups did not promote entrepreneurial development. Rather, the prevailing political culture, attitudes and reflexes helped worked against any attempt aimed at promoting indigenous entrepreneurship with contribution from foreign-led resources. In addition to political reasons, lack of financial resources, management and technological capabilities of a large part of would be indigenous investors limits their ability to engage in ways that sustain the viability of such enterprises once they have been disengaged from non-indigenous ownership and management.

To fully appreciate the import of government attitudes to non-indigene entrepreneurs and their concomitant implication for economic development, the experience of Zimbabwe and South Africa is illustrative of the general theme of our discussion here.[52] After gaining independence, Zimbabwe, under Robert Mugabe, started a phase of disqualification of a sizeable minority of its entrepreneurial and middle class – the white farmers. Some farmlands were taken away from them in favor of an embryonic group of black farmers. The entrepreneurial capacity of the "whites" (in terms of cultural values, attitudes, reflexes, financial assets and networks of cooperation) was therefore gradually extinguished. The political elite and rulers deliberately chose to rebuild this capacity from scratch, in the social and racial group that had spent a miserable century confined to tiny and unproductive lands.

This policy has a price, basically in terms of decline in entrepreneurial and economic activities. With the disappearance of white farms came the disappearance of large incomes from agricultural exports (about 450 million US dollars a year), hundreds of thousands of jobs, precious financial and commercial networks, industrial and production facilities and equipment, and other advantages necessary for Zimbabwe to develop economically and to compete strategically in the global economy. To this cost should be added the loss of expertise and the progress already achieved in terms of entrepreneurial culture as well as the unavoidable expenditure for the cultural and technical development of the embryonic group of new entrepreneurs.

From another point of view, this Zimbabwean policy is not an act of gratuitous malice. It is meant to be a brave and reasonable gamble with the future. By redistributing landed property to a broader section of the population, the leaders perhaps hope to save from idleness the unused land in white compounds, to diffuse the resentment and social antagonism which are responsible for some of the inertia in the area of economic initiative, and to involve the black majority of the country in the culture of responsibility for economic progress. But a gamble is a gamble and the result is what we see in Zimbabwe today – a case of failed nation – economically, politically and socially.

The case of Zimbabwe is not an isolated one. Under Mobutu Sese Sekou, the economy of Congo Kinshasa completely collapsed as a result of the so-called "zairinization policy". In this indigenization policy, farms and enterprises taken away from foreigners for the benefit of ethnic kinsmen, clients and allies of the Kinshasa regime ended up being totally liquidated amid general indifference and irresponsibility, and even with vengeful applause from the majority of domestic opinion. In Uganda under Idi Amin Dada, a similar suicidal development took place with the nationalization during the 1970s of enterprises and farms belonging to a dynamic Indo-Pakistani diaspora that had been living in the country for decades. Examples of privatization and indigenization policies ending in catastrophic decline in the economies are legion in the Sub-Saharan region.

The Regulatory Environment and Entrepreneurial Development

Economies differ significantly in the way in which they regulate the entry of new businesses. In some economies the process is straightforward and affordable. In others, the procedures associated with business registration are so burdensome and cumbersome that entrepreneurs have to bribe officials to speed up the process or they would rather run their businesses informally. Consequently, the growth of the informal sector in the developing countries has been attributed to the consequences of over regulation in Sub-Saharan Africa. In one study, the World Bank concluded that cumbersome entry procedures are associated with more corruption, particularly in developing countries. As explained by the World Bank study, each procedure is a point of contact—an opportunity to extract a bribe. In particular, the study indicates that burdensome entry regulations do not increase the quality of products; neither do they make working environments safer. Rather, they hold back private investment; push more people into the informal economy, increase consumer prices, and fuel corruption.[53] Other researchers have concluded that in Sub-Saharan Africa the biggest problems facing the development of entrepreneurship are corruption, which is rooted in the culture of excessive regulation, tax regulations and high taxes.[54]

There is nothing inherently wrong when a country regulates the conduct of business. Laws relating to business practices (such as contractual obligations) must be adhered to in order to achieve an environment conducive for business and economic growth. In the case of Sub-Saharan Africa, however, regulation has created more obstacles and bottlenecks than necessary when it comes to the development of entrepreneurship. From a comparative perspective, regulation in the developed countries follows series of logical responses to the need of ensuring rational economic development without stifling the conduct of economic and business activities. In the experience of the developed countries, regulation fulfills the task of essential controls of business without imposing an unnecessary burden on entrepreneurs. In these countries, high levels of human capital in the public administration, and the use of modern technology, minimize the regulatory burden on businesses. In addition, market-forces are allowed to act as regulatory mechanism, allowing competition to act as a substitute for regulation. By combining simple regulation with good definition and protection of property rights, the developed countries have achieved what many developing countries have been trying to achieve in decades: having government regulators serve as public servants, not public masters whose existence derives from bribery, corruption and kickbacks.

As pointed out by Brett Schaefer, a government can greatly facilitate economic growth by enforcing an impartial and reliable rule of law. A rule of law with these characteristics serves as the supporting structure of an economy, without which it cannot operate efficiently. It ensures entrepreneurs that (i) policies will have lasting power and can be changed only through transparent, widely recognized procedures, permitting an environment conducive to long-term investment; (ii) the rules will apply equally to all rather than exempting some or being subject to change at the behest of the powerful; and (iii) they will have legal recourse if policies unlawfully affect their activities, thereby reducing the risk of investments. On the other hand, an arbitrary, overly onerous, or poorly enforced rule of law can prove a very strong deterrent to growth by creating opportunities for corruption or increasing the costs of complying with the law to the point where economic activity is discouraged or leaves the formal sector.[55] In other words, governments must be cautious that efforts to create and maintain a secure environment for economic activity do not become excessive and thereby impede such activity.

The Effects of Bureaucratic Corruption and Bribery on Entrepreneurial Development

Although a number of factors account for the negative economic and entrepreneurial growth rate in Sub-Saharan Africa as discussed in this chapter, bureaucratic corruption has also played a decisive role. Bureaucratic corruption is the misuse of the power of public office for personal gain in breach of laws that govern public servants and moral principles.[56] In its basic form, bureaucratic corruption takes place when a government official demands and accepts bribes or kickbacks in performance of normal duties called for by the office. Bribery, on the other hand, is the practice of offering something (usually money) in order to gain an illicit advantage. Bribery, which can be direct cash payments, gifts, or the promise of reciprocity in future transactions, is usually paid either: to gain access to scarce government services or to avoid the cost of government service. In less common instances, bribery may be paid to deny rivals access to a government service or to impose inordinate cost on such rivals.[57] Others see corruption (in Africa) as the "outright theft, embezzlement of funds or other appropriation of state property, nepotism and the granting of favors to personal acquaintances, and the abuse of public authority and position to exact payments and privileges."[58]

Bureaucratic corruption, as the misuse of office by government functionaries is relatively common in areas of public procurement, revenue collection, land zoning, government appointments and contracts, licensing and permits. According to John Ifediora, bribery and corruption are readily executed through anyone of the following activities: (i) The civil servant receives from a private contractor a fixed percentage of awarded government contracts; (ii) Police or other law enforcement agents use the threat of sanctions to extort bribes in lieu of official fees or taxes; (iii) Customs agents insist on payments above the official rates or side payments before providing requisite services to both importers and exporters; (iv) Civil servants award large contracts to companies owned by relatives or partners, and in return receive an agreed upon fee or lavish hospitality; and (v) Officials responsible for permits and licenses demand extra payment for services ordinarily called for by their office.[59]

As pointed out by S. T. Akindele, most of the corruptions in Africa, and especially in Nigeria, are actually initiated by the office holders with few initiations by non-office holders. Generally, such office holders may, by virtue of the symbolism of their office or official duties sometimes use delaying tactics in inducing their clients into offering bribes before performing their duties. These tactics include phrases (in Yoruba Language) like "Kosi iwe" meaning, "no working paper", "Kosi oga nile" meaning, "the Boss is not in." In a detailed analysis of corruption and its problem in Nigeria, Akindele argues thus: "These tactics which have their types in other Nigerian (ethnic) languages and among other ethnic groups in Nigeria and Africa are euphemisms for luring the (usually unsuspecting initial) clients into giving bribes or kick-backs in Nigeria. However, with time, this development seemed to have become understandable to Nigerians and, Africans depending on the issue or issues at stake to the extent that, any time the corruptor mentions such phrases, the corruptee automatically knows what to do. The danger of this, is that, even though, the corruptees have the legitimate rights for the benefits at stake they are manacled into offering bribe in one way or the other to the officials before the later would respond. Even, in most cases, the victims are not successful in getting the desired benefits after such unreceipted transactions."[60]

The author continues: "Although the policemen are mostly notorious for this in Nigeria, because of the enormous discretion of enforcement of laws given to them, it has spread like the bush fire into various sectors of the nation's political landscape. For example, the issuance of Nigerian Passport, import licenses, vehicle licenses, submission of contract tenders, contract awards, application for employment and so many other things or benefits that should be normally obtained without tensions and nightmarish experiences, have fallen and continue to fall victims to these retrogressive, antidevelopment, and, corrupt tactics. It is mostly disturbing in that, to the perpetrators, nothing seems to be wrong with this, since to them and, a preponderant majority of the ignorant populace, it is getting their "eto", "obi", "kolanut" meaning "right" or "dues" in the course of performing their duties in total disregard of the fact that they are actually paid for doing the job in the first place."[61] Many studies have documented the effects of bribery and corruption on economic development.[62] In a developing context such as Sub-Saharan Africa with inadequate or poorly formed socio-political structures and weak economic and legal institutions, the consequences of bureaucratic corruption are particularly disastrous. In terms of investment, James Wolfensohn (a former World Bank President), in reference to corruption, suggests that, "Investors today... (prefer) to move their money to where the risks of corruption are less pronounced."[63] In addition to undermining the legal framework, national integrity, and regulatory system, corruption also undermines the trust and confidence of business owners. In particular, corruption has a negative impact on the scale, form and growth rate of private sector development. It has both direct and indirect consequences for the conduct of business. At the macro economic level, the consequences include:[64]

> Corruption helps *distort the market* by redirecting economic activity from one sector to another. In so doing, corruption destroys the structure and pattern of economic development and reduces the efficiency of economic activity.
> Corruption has fiscal, budgetary and debt effects which collectively damage the economy and make private sector development very difficult. In its extreme form, corruption destroys economies and makes business activity impossible.

At the level of the individual business or corporation, corruption is damaging in the following ways:

> It raises the costs of doing business
> It increases the risks and uncertainties of doing business
> It discourages and reduces investment in general and capital investment in particular
> It creates unfair competition
> It diverts resources away from productive investment
> It complicates and delays business transactions
> It deters entrepreneurs from starting up businesses

In developing and transition economies, much private sector activity arises from the privatization processes, which transferred state assets into private hands and turned pubic monopolies into private monopolies. These transfers are frequently associated with large-scale corruption and the newly enriched business leaders are able to exploit illegitimately acquired power at the expense of their business rivals.

Corruption undermines the efficiency of markets and the competitiveness of producers and suppliers. Where corruption occurs in international trade, it can undermine local companies by encouraging governments to buy from overseas. Where there is corruption, which enables importers to avoid customs duties and import taxes, the competitiveness of domestic companies is thereby eroded and they are likely to fail.

Private sector development flourishes when investment prospects are favorable and when entrepreneurs can minimize their costs and decrease their uncertainties. Corruption reduces the incentives and increases the costs and risks of doing business.

INFRASTRUCTURE AND ENTREPRENEURIAL DEVELOPMENT

As we have noted in this chapter, although the personal characteristics of individual entrepreneurs play a decisive role on the success and/or failure of the entrepreneurial firm, the influence of environmental factors is decisive in the degree to which entrepreneurs exploit their individual characteristics. One of those environmental factors is the availability of infrastructures such as transportation, energy, information and communication technology, water and availability of entrepreneurial education. In other words, we can distinguish between the personal resources of the entrepreneur and the environmental resources. The environmental resources – the infrastructures – must complement the strategic resources of the individual entrepreneur before successful entrepreneurial activities can be realized. In the existing research on economic development and entrepreneurship in Sub-Saharan Africa, quality of infrastructure has been identified as the dominant explanatory factor in both manufacturing and the competitiveness of entrepreneurial firms. For example, enterprise-level surveys conducted in several countries show that infrastructure costs and problems of unreliability rank high among issues of concern to businesses.[65]

The term *infrastructure* is used here to denote the facilities, structures, associated equipments, services, and institutional arrangements that facilitate the production and flow of goods and services between individuals, firms, and governments. Infrastructure therefore includes: public utilities, such as energy, telecommunications, water supply, sanitation, sewage and waste disposal; public works, such as irrigation systems, schools, housing and hospitals; transport systems, such as roads, railways, ports, waterways and airports; and educational facilities. In this era of global competition, the economic activities of any nation, including the impetus for private investment, depend on the totality of these basic physical infrastructures for the production and delivery of goods and services. For our purpose, four sets of infrastructure will be examined: transportation, energy, information and communication technology (ICT), and education. Where necessary, reference will be made to other types of infrastructure such as water and security in the course of the discussion. First, we discuss the relationship between infrastructure, entrepreneurship and economic development.

The Relationship between Infrastructure, Entrepreneurship and Economic Development

The infrastructure that a nation brings to bear on economic and entrepreneurial development consists of many activities such as the basic structures and facilities needed by the country to function efficiently and productively. According to the World Development Report 2006, the infrastructure capacity grows in concert with economic output. A 1 percent increase in the stock of infrastructure is associated with a 1 percent increase in GDP across countries.[66]

The relationship between infrastructure, entrepreneurship and economic development and the associated benefits are as follow:

(i) Infrastructure stimulates entrepreneurial activity and is a prerequisite for economic and social development.
(ii) Infrastructure services reduce poverty through health and educational improvements.
(iii) Infrastructure reduces the transaction costs associated with manufacturing, especially in the developing countries.
(iv) Infrastructure facilities create employment opportunities.
(v) Infrastructure contributes to technological development and provides an opportunity for technological learning.
(vi) Infrastructure services act as intermediate inputs into production.
(vii) The availability of infrastructure attracts firms to certain locations, which creates agglomeration economies and reduces production and transactions costs, and
(viii) Investments in infrastructure services are essential for the development of viable economic enterprises.

In the context of Sub-Saharan Africa, the underdeveloped infrastructural systems have been seen as one of the greatest obstacle to entrepreneurial and economic development. Indeed, in most Sub-Sahara African countries, the infrastructure costs borne by business owners increase their total costs by about 50 percent. For instance, Limão and Venables have established that poor infrastructure accounts for 40 percent of transport costs for coastal economies and 60 percent for landlocked countries.[67]

Although poor governance, political system, financial difficulties and cultural practices are some of the major obstacles to investment that come to mind, private sector participants usually point to inadequate infrastructure, especially in the transport and energy sectors, as a major bottleneck. Some have suggested that when machines cannot be powered and products cannot get to market, pro-business reforms are unlikely to succeed. Without underestimating the importance of good governance and availability of finance, most business owners in Sub-Saharan Africa agree that developing and improving access to infrastructure in Africa can promote investment and growth. In a situation where prospective entrepreneurs are made to add the costs of providing for their own energy supply, construct roads, provide pipe borne water and security, the overhead cost is transferred to the final consumer. Under this situation, it is hardly surprising that most business owners in Sub-Saharan Africa would rather engage in commercial activities (importing goods) than committing resources in local manufacturing. As will be indicated later in this discussion, for a developing country to develop economically, it must adopt policies that promote local production rather than the promotion of unrestrained policies that favor importation even when the imports are easily produced locally. One consequence of such a policy is that the entrepreneurial spirit needed for economic growth hardly thrives in an import-dependent economy.

Transport Infrastructure

For our purpose here, transport infrastructure refers to roads, railways, bridges, tunnels, ports (for maritime and inland water transport), airports, urban transport infrastructure (mass transit systems), dry ports and inland container depots (intermodal infrastructure). The importance of an efficient transport system in both developing and developed countries cannot be overemphasized, especially in terms of its relationship with economic growth. According to the World Bank, employment in transport, storage and communications ranges between 2.5 and 11.5 percent of total paid employment. Demand for freight and passenger transport, particularly by road, has typically grown 1.5 to 2 times faster than GDP in most developing and transition countries. Public investment in transport typically accounts for 2.0 to 2.5 percent of GDP. Landlocked countries face logistics costs that are, on average, 50 percent higher than those of countries with access to the sea. Consequently, many governments have assigned transport an important role as a key to economic development and integration into the world economy.[68]

The qualitative provision of basic transportation services such as railways, road transport, seaports and air transport is inevitable for the development of entrepreneurship. In Sub-Saharan Africa, however, the poor state of the transportation system has been a major infrastructural constraint hindering the development of entrepreneurship in the region. Various studies have concluded that transport costs are the most important component of trade costs in Sub-Saharan Africa. Specifically, some researchers found empirical evidence that countries with lower transport costs have had faster manufactured export and overall economic growth during the last three decades than countries with higher transport cost. For countries in Africa, the reduction in manufacturing activities due to transport costs could be much more severe, as many countries in the continent are landlocked. Similarly, some researchers have found that landlocked countries' transport costs are up to 50 percent higher than those of coastal countries. Landlocked countries may lose the equivalent of up to 40 percent of the export on high transport costs.[69]

Transport volumes in Sub-Saharan Africa, with the notable exception of South Africa, remain much less than those in other developing countries. Roads and railways laid down by European colonial powers were often cheaply constructed, with the prime purpose of transporting raw materials from mines and farm regions to the coast for shipping to the mother country. After decades of underinvestment, existing railways are generally run-down and unreliable; roads are insufficient, mostly unpaved and often impassable in the rainy season; ports are often substandard; and container terminals short of capacity. Consequently, deficient transport facilities are a significant factor in Africa's poor economic performance and a constraint to internal trade. Unlike other parts of the developing world, few railway lines have been built since independence in Sub-Saharan Africa, and governments have generally failed to meet the cost of managing and maintaining the existing ones.

Transportation costs in Africa are the highest of any region in the world. With landlocked countries having to figure in transport costs of up to 75 percent of the value of their exports, the continent faces extreme challenges to produce locally and to compete in global markets. Transport related impediments make it extremely difficult to deliver goods to the market at competitive prices. The problem of excessive costs extends beyond land transport into clearance at ports. For example, it costs about the same to clear a 20-foot container through the port of Dakar as it does to ship the same container from Dakar to a north European port. Shipping a car from Japan to Abidjan costs $1,500 but shipping the same car from Abidjan to Addis Ababa would cost $5,000. Delays at ports are another problem. It is estimated that every day spent in customs adds 0.8 percent to the cost of goods. Africa has the longest delays among the regions of the world. Customs delays in the whole of Africa average 11.4 days; while in Sub-Saharan Africa the delays average 12.1 days. For individual countries the delays range from 14 days in Uganda to as high as 30 in Ethiopia compared to an average delay of 3.4 days in Western Europe.[70] On the other hand, excessive bureaucratic bottlenecks, high insurance costs, cumbersome customs' procedures and outright corruption by public servants using bribes, official and unofficial checkpoints escalate transport costs in Africa.

In a study conducted by Wim Naudé and Marianne Matthee, at least five reasons why African countries face high transport costs are provided and include (i) distance, (ii) being landlocked, (iii) insufficient economies of scale in production, (iv) lack of sufficient investment in transport infrastructure, and (v) flawed trade and transport policies.[71]

The Energy Sector and the Development of Entrepreneurship

The availability and reliability of energy supply such as electricity is a prerequisite for the development of entrepreneurship and sustained economic growth. Although nature has endowed the African continent with the widest-possible range of energy resources, its power sector remains severely underdeveloped in all countries with the exception of South Africa. According to the International Energy Agency, Sub-Saharan Africa has the lowest electrification of any major world region. Although Africa is home to 14 percent of the world's population it only generates and consumes about 3.1 percent of the world's electricity. The low electricity consumption levels in Africa are due to economic under-development and low electricity access rates. The performance of the power sector is also characterized by poor security and reliability, high distribution losses, negative financial rates of return and poor cash collection. Regulatory agencies are weak and have not succeeded in making the power sector sufficiently attractive to get adequate investment resources from the private sector. Although droughts, declining terms of trade and heavy debt service burdens are contributory factors to the security and reliability problems in the energy sector, these are all seen as symptoms of weaknesses in planning, regulation and institutions.[72]

One of the major reasons for the low power consumption in Africa is the low electrification rate, which means that a large number of the African population does not have access to electricity. In Sub-Saharan Africa access levels are significantly low in the rural areas. Some four out of five people in rural areas in Sub-Saharan Africa live without electricity. The cost of extending the electric grid to remote and low-density rural areas is prohibitive, amounting to seven times the cost of providing electricity in an urban area.[73] The population that has access to electricity suffers from poor supply quality with frequent power supply interruptions. The bulk of the electricity supply is unreliable and subject to power rationing or unscheduled cuts. The power interruptions result in significant economic losses. In a World Bank survey of 55 countries, 67 percent of the firms cited electricity as a business constraint. Kenya, for example, is estimated to lose 9 percent of its annual output to power outages.[74] The losses include the cost incurred by companies in purchasing and running standby generating facilities.

Generally in Sub-Saharan Africa, the obstacles, constraints and challenges in the energy sector include lack of appropriate development strategies to facilitate, harmonize and maximize the energy potential in the region with other sectors of local economies; lack of capacity and finance; barriers to efficient measures to deliver energy; ensuring access to equitable, affordable and modern energy services; addressing the role of energy access in fostering economic and social development and supporting the micro-, small- and medium-sized enterprises.

Other challenges include ensuring that the delivery of energy services meets the needs of the people, including through the use of a variety of technologies and fuels tailored to local conditions, rather than merely aiming to increase energy supplies; increasing the access of rural and remote areas to energy supplies, including off grid systems; implementing policies, strategies, legal and regulatory frameworks to address the energy crisis in the region; addressing the linkages between energy and health; addressing the role of poverty reduction strategy and national sustainable development strategy in national energy planning; ensuring decentralized decision-making processes for energy investments and projects; and promoting participation by local governments, private initiatives, regional, communal, and community-based organizations.

The Problems and Challenges of ICT and Entrepreneurship

In the context of Sub-Saharan Africa, there are two areas of interest in terms of the challenges of information and communications technology (ICT) for the development of entrepreneurship. One is the problem of access to ICT and the other is how to transform that access into productive use. Although Sub-Saharan Africa has lagged behind in terms of access to ICT in what is popularly known as the global digital divide, recent developments in this area have seen Africa experiencing a significant growth in ICT investment. However, many observers have pointed out that the boom in ICT investment and connectivity has not been adequately transformed into productive use.

Digital divide, as we pointed out in chapter three, is a term that is often used in describing disparities in access to, and usage of, the telephone, personal computers and the Internet across demographic groups, within the same country, or between countries. As pointed out by the United Nations, the presence of a digital divide, particularly between rural communities and urban centers in Sub-Saharan Africa, directly affects the ability of small- and medium-sized enterprises to reach and compete in the larger domestic and even global markets. Compared to other regions, there is inadequate access to ICT in Sub-Saharan Africa.

There are a number of reasons for the poor access to ICT in Sub-Saharan Africa. For example, the prevalence of obsolete systems, irregular electricity and a stultifying lack of local content are partly responsible for the poor access. In addition to these problems is the burden of illiteracy in Sub-Saharan Africa, which has made access and use of ICT particularly difficult.

Experience in the region indicates that availability of information and communication technology has not been adequately transformed to productive usage. One of the reasons is the absence of enabling environment necessary for information technology to function effectively. In some cases, many potential users of ICT do not benefit from the imported information technology hardware precisely because authorities failed to create the enabling environment for the use of such technologies such as constant supply of electricity.

The problems and challenges of ICT in entrepreneurial development in Sub-Saharan Africa are as follows:

(i) The tendency to view ICT technology as a solution unto itself.
(ii) Over-hyping the power of the Internet and the tendency to encourage developing countries to invest in fancy equipment they do not really need.
(iii) The erroneous view that a new technology brought into a society not hitherto accustomed to its use can automatically jumpstart entrepreneurial initiative.
(iv) Lack of flexibility and adaptation of imported technology to fit local needs and conditions.
(v) Rural-urban migration, population explosion in urban cities and problems of unsustainable growth in African urban settings.
(vi) A disconnect and discrepancy between what Africans really needed and what technology planners and donor organizations are willing to provide.
(vii) The use of ICT for unproductive social activities rather than productive reasons.
(viii) Lack of active collaboration between the public and private sectors in the development of ICT for economic growth.
(ix) Over-emphasizing the role of information technology without developing the human resources needed to transform the availability of such technologies into economic use or for promoting entrepreneurship.
(x) The tendency to ignore the social, institutional and other supportive organizational factors necessary to transform access to productive usage.

Entrepreneurial Education and Skills Development

Setting up a business enterprise and subsequently operating it requires a whole range of knowledge and expertise in many areas such as knowledge of requisite business methods and technical expertise. Some of these knowledge and expertise are supplied by the experience a business owner gains from the market or industry, while other forms of knowledge are provided through formal educational system and apprentice training. Thus, in any given context, knowledge, skills and expertise acquired through the educational sector or apprentice play an important role in entrepreneurial development. Education in this context includes knowledge acquired from primary, secondary, university, vocational and other forms of skills training capable of promoting the development of entrepreneurship. Studies and expert commentaries on entrepreneurship and economic development in Sub-Saharan Africa have shown that the environment in which business owners operates lacks access to variety of knowledge and skills necessary for the development of entrepreneurship. In this section, we examine the educational environment and how it impedes the development of entrepreneurship.

Entrepreneurial education, in addition to the personality characteristics of the entrepreneurs, is a prerequisite in every successful entrepreneurial venture. While many of the personality characteristics are generally thought to be inborn, researchers have also attempted to identify the skills and abilities that are necessary for successful entrepreneurship. Although some abilities may, indeed, be innate or learned from experience, many attributes such as skills in product/service design, business skills, knowledge of the industry, leadership skills, administrative skills, skills in financial management, skills and ability to acquire operating resources and technical skills can be acquired through education and training. Thus, the critical importance of designing appropriate education systems to promote entrepreneurship and to prepare school leavers for self-employment has been stressed in several studies examining the relationship between entrepreneurial development and education. Specifically, the importance of technical and vocational entrepreneurial training (TVET) is seen as critical in preparing prospective business owners for the world of entrepreneurship.[75]

Weaknesses in the Formal and Informal Educational System

For many countries in Sub-Saharan Africa, the problem of entrepreneurial education is seen as major constraints inhibiting the development of entrepreneurship. Low literacy rates and low levels of secondary and tertiary school enrolment, coupled with insufficient government spending on education, mean that would-be African entrepreneurs face serious challenges when it comes to the acquisition of skills necessary for entrepreneurial undertaking. While the growth of the informal sector in Sub-Saharan Africa is fueled by unskilled labor and by lack of proper incentives and infrastructure, its transformation necessarily demands a skilled labor force, which the current environment is unable to provide.

One of the weaknesses in the formal education system is an ill-conceived educational curriculum that is irrelevant to the needs of the region's economic development. Most observers point out that until recently, management and entrepreneurial training in Sub-Saharan Africa was virtually the same as bookkeeping and feasibility studies all geared toward one thing, which is how to manage the books. Some researchers have also indicated that most of the training in Sub-Saharan Africa tends to be theoretical, with dilapidated facilities, outdated training equipment and materials.[76] In addition, business courses have been short on the use of modern training methodologies. A second related weakness is the lack of adequate educational infrastructures, textbooks, research materials and the absence of collaboration between institutions of higher learning and the business community. The consequence is that there is disconnect between the knowledge gained from institutions of higher learning and the need of the business community and aspiring entrepreneurs.

In Sub-Saharan Africa, informal sector business owners and employees often lack basic economic and management skills. Informal business owners also have little access to information on prices, or adequate skills to effectively market their products and hence suffer from poor profitability. The main training system operating in the informal economy is traditional apprenticeship, which is self-financing, self-regulating, and cost-effective. Traditional apprenticeship training, which is prevalent in Sub-Saharan Africa perpetuates traditional technologies and lacks standards and quality assurance. The low educational levels in many Sub-Sahara African countries seriously limit the results of apprenticeship training, both in the transfer and the application of knowledge and skills. In several countries in Sub-Saharan Africa, especially in West Africa, efforts to train entrepreneurs are hampered by low level of education of masters and apprentices and linkages between training and other support activities.

Infrastructural Constraints and Entrepreneurial Development

The discussion so far reveals that Sub-Saharan Africa's demand for infrastructure across sectors is hardly met for the majority of people, with its worst sectoral performance being in access to electricity. In addition to the problem of electricity supply and transportation, many firms are also faced with the supply of water. Access and affordability of basic infrastructure such as security, education, electricity, water and transport seem to be the major constraints for entrepreneurial development. Even where such access exists, supply is unreliable and the quality of services remains poor. Generally, access to infrastructure services favors the rich and is more unequal in Sub-Saharan Africa than in any other part of the world. In some cases, infrastructure projects tend to perpetuate historical inequities.[77]

Analyses of manufacturing activities and infrastructure services show how in many Sub-Sahara African countries, the business owners' access to infrastructure is limited, and cite numerous examples of self-provided infrastructure, e.g. constructing access roads to factory sites, self-provided energy supply, security, purchasing water from vendors, as a response to the lack of access to publicly provided infrastructure. Thus, a host of factors explain why existing infrastructure interventions fail to promote entrepreneurship and serve the local manufacturing sector and other forms of production activities in Sub-Saharan Africa:

(i) The inadequacy of provision in relation to the huge scale of need.
(ii) The relatively high standards adopted, which means either that the poor cannot afford what is offered, or else that a substantial subsidy is required which the government cannot afford.
(iii) Any subsidy element is likely to accrue either to large-scale manufacturing firms and other large-scale enterprises, or to the public officials who administer infrastructure services.
(iv) Failure to address the fundamental obstacles, which the small-scale enterprises face in gaining access to land and basic infrastructure.

(v) Inappropriate forms of infrastructure and services, together with inadequate resources for operation and maintenance, which means that services do not effectively reach those who need them, or fall into disrepair and disuse.

(vi) The adoption of policies which discriminate against the poor or impede them from improving their situation, such as regulatory standards which are unaffordable by the micro- and small-scale enterprises, and harassment of informal sector providers.

It has been indicated that in Sub-Saharan Africa, the cost of infrastructure borne by business owners increase their total costs by about 50 percent. Undoubtedly, the most serious obstacles to the development of entrepreneurship in Sub-Saharan Africa seems to be the transaction costs associated with infrastructural provision or lack of it. In the case of energy supply, a number of problems have limited the ability of the energy sector in Sub-Saharan Africa to drive economic growth and the development of entrepreneurship. These problems, which include high system losses in transmission and distribution, unsustainable tariffs, poor technical and financial performance, low level of private investment and failure to supply rural areas must be addressed in a systematic way. For example, governments in Sub-Saharan Africa have been able to attract private sector investment in the area of energy supply. The International Finance Corporation (IFC) estimated that foreign direct investment (FDI) in the power sector in Sub-Saharan Africa was only 6 percent of all infrastructure FDI inflows into the region between 1990 and 1998. In comparison, telecommunications accounted for 89 percent of all FDI inflows in this period. Between 1990 and 1999, private investment in electricity in Sub-Saharan Africa was $2.9 billion, representing less than 2 percent of all private electricity projects in developing countries.

The point made earlier about the consequence of this situation is worth reiterating: When a prospective entrepreneur has to add the costs of providing his or her own electricity supply, construct roads, provide pipe borne water, and his or her own security, the overhead cost is, understandably too high. For the consumer, the exorbitant price charged by the producer is beyond his or her reach. Not surprisingly, imported goods are cheaper to purchase in Sub-Saharan Africa than locally produced ones. As pointed out earlier, the spirit of entrepreneurship hardly thrives in an import-dependent economy.

In the case of Sub-Saharan Africa, the cost of providing infrastructure, and/or the lack of it, has resulted in the death of many local industries and the spirit of entrepreneurship. For example, in a discussion of how various structural adjustment policies in Nigeria skewed infrastructural development (education, energy, etc), John Ogbor shows how such ill-conceived policies unduly gave concession to trade over manufacturing and in the process, both traditionally recognized manufacturing powerhouses in Nigeria (e.g., BATA, John Holt and UACN) and small businesses diversified into the import sector.[78] Far from stimulating domestic industrial production through entrepreneurship, lack of infrastructure helps in drawing merchant-traders to the nexus of economic activities. In such a process, virtually any response to entrepreneurial initiatives, at the very least, is ambivalent.

THE INFORMAL SECTOR

The informal sector has acquired great significance over the years as a source of employment and a breeding ground for entrepreneurial activities. For a number of people in the developing countries, especially women in both rural and urban areas, the informal sector has come to constitute the major source of livelihoods. Consequently, no discussion of economic development and entrepreneurship is complete without an examination of the role of the informal sector in the context of developing countries' economy.[79] The growing importance of the informal sector in the developing economies is underscored in a report by the International Labour Organization (ILO), which stated that the informal sector employs, on average, 78 percent of the total economically active population outside farming.[80]

The informal sector is the portion of a country's economy that lies outside of any formal regulatory environment. Informal sector economic activities such as production, distribution, services, etc., are not regulated by labor or taxation laws and are rarely reflected in official statistics on economic activity (for example, gross domestic product, GDP). Economic activities in the informal sector may be invisible to authorities, unregulated (because they cannot be regulated by official policy), parallel (because they exist side-by-side with official activities), unlawful (because they are not under the purview of the law), non-structured, backyard, under ground, subterranean or residual. For example, the artisan who engages in all sorts of jobs by the roadside, the trader who hawks various wares on the street, the subsistence farmer, the motor-bike rider, the operator of unregistered commercial transportation vehicles, the market woman, the trader who buys and sells foreign exchange in the parallel market, the local water bottler, and others whose activities are not in any way reflected in the official records all constitute what is known as informal sector economic activity in so far as such activities are unregulated. They do not pay tax; save the extortions from local council official.

The informal sector as a form of economic system depends on the support it gains from the institutional environment for its survival. As an institution, it is a subsystem in a society's economy and reflects the norms and values prevalent in its environment. For example, in societies where the application of the rule of law is weaken by underlying political practices, parallel, "black", underground or unofficial markets coexist with formal or official markets such as the foreign exchange market in many African countries. Thus, many observers suggest that the informal sector can be found in the inefficiency of the law. The reason is that these activities are informal because of the cost of legality.[81]

Unlike the formal sector, which is made up of the public and organized private sector, the contribution of the informal sector has no bearing to nor is it reflected in the calculation of a country's gross domestic product, GDP. And, unlike the formal sector, the informal sector encompasses activities to which the state has no means of access in terms of regulation and making them conform to existing laws of economic exchange.

Enrique Ghersi points out that "from an economic point of view, the most important characteristics of informal activities is that those directly involved in them as well as society in general benefit more if the law is violated than if it is followed".[82] In the case of Sub-Saharan Africa, the relationship between the growth of the informal sector and the illegality of the socioeconomic environment under which it occurs cannot be overemphasized. In fact, it is safe to say that informal sector thrives in an environment of illegality. It is a product and beneficiary of illegal economic activities in an environment that condones such practices.

In Sub-Saharan Africa, as in most developing regions, the informal sector may be classified under three broad categories or sub-sectors: (i) productive, (ii) service, (iii) financial, and (iv) associations.

The Informal Productive Sub-Sector: This sub-sector consists of economic activities involving the production of tangible goods. They include agricultural production (such as farming, animal husbandry, and fishery), mining and quarrying, small-scale manufacturing, building and construction. For example, the informal productive sub-sector is seen especially in food production such as, local cassava and yam production. The traditional livestock sub-sector, which caters for both urban and rural meat, milk and other dairy-related products, including poultry farming belong to food production. Other artisan-related activities such as woodwork, furniture making, garment making, welding and iron works, including housing construction, among others fall under the informal productive sub-sector.

The Informal Service Sub-Sector: This sub-sector includes repairs and maintenance, informal education services, counseling services as well as labor for menial work. Repairs and maintenance services include tailoring, vehicle repairs and maintenance, carpentry and servicing of various household and commercial tools. Informal health services, especially in the rural areas, include traditional birth attendants, herbalists and other traditional medical practitioners. There are also traditional spiritualists who offer counseling services. The informal urban transportation system is another example of the informal service sub-sector. Examples here include moped taxing (okada in Nigeria), commercial buses and mini-buses for both urban and rural transportation. These services are rendered for fees but are not regulated in the official economy. In many parts of Sub-Saharan Africa, informal sector activities have also been extended into Information and Communication Technology (ICT) sector (e.g., computer repair and cyber cafes).

The Informal Financial Sub-Sector: The activities of this sub-sector are mostly performed under voluntary associations among contributors. In most cases, these activities are underground, unofficial, irregular, informal, shadowy, and parallel. Example is the parallel foreign exchange markets found in many cities of Sub-Saharan Africa. Others include informal financial associations called "esusu" in Nigeria. In the context of "esusu", for example, groups within the associations operate with or without written laws guiding the activities. In some cases members are made to undertake oath of allegiance and in others, participation in an activity is based on mutual trust among members. The general practice is that such financial associations contribute a fixed amount periodically and give all or part of the accumulated funds to one or more member(s) in rotation until all members have benefited from the pool.

The Informal Sector Associations (ISA): In many parts of Sub-Saharan Africa, there are organizations that are set up through voluntary efforts to cater for the interests of their members. Thus, in urban Sub-Saharan Africa, there are associations of landlords, operators of transportation vehicles, market women and other various artisan groups. In recent years, these informal associations have become powerful interest groups in the socio-political environment of developing countries. Apart from the political influence, which such associations exert, they are also known to contribute to apprenticeship training and other forms of skill development.

Main Features of the Informal Sector

Although the informal sector is often associated with the economies of the developing countries – where over 78 percent of the labor force earns its living, nearly all economic systems contain an element of informal behavior in some degree.[83] As Edgar Feige has pointed out, informal sector economic activity is a dynamic process that includes many aspects of economic and social theory including exchange, regulation, and enforcement. For this reason, it is difficult to define and measure in terms of its scope and economic consequences. To further confound attempts to define this process, informal economic activity is temporal in nature. Regulations (and degrees of enforcement) change frequently, sometimes daily, and any instance of economic activity can shift between categories of formal and informal with even minor changes in policy.[84] For example, prior to 1986, the financial sector in Nigeria was fairly regulated. However, with the introduction of structural adjustment programs and the accompanying policy of deregulation and trade liberalization, the sector became more informal to the extent that quazi financial institutions and parallel foreign exchange markets grew side by side with the official markets. Thus, given the complexity of the phenomenon of informal sector practices, the simplest definition of informal activity might be: any exchange of goods or services involving economic value in which the act is not recorded in the official description of economic activities and outside of official regulatory agencies of similar acts.

The informal sector is not only a place for employment or where people make a living. Rather, it is a place where traditions facilitate economic development. The enduring characteristic of the informal sector is its strong socio-cultural roots where the informal sector is also reflected in the origin and form of traditional apprenticeship training in the Sub-Sahara African region. More than elsewhere, parents arrange for their children to be an apprentice – not only to acquire skills but also for wider training in life skills and even morals.[85]

The main features of informal economic units include: ease of entry; small scale of the activity; self-employment, with a high proportion of family workers and apprentices; little capital and equipment; labor intensive technologies; low skills; low level of organization with no access to organized markets, to formal credit, to education and training or services and amenities; cheap provision of goods and services; and low productivity and growth potentials. Thus, Enrique Ghersi argues that the informal sector, although illegal, is not criminal and takes place in the absence of legal protection and guarantees.[86]

As far as the existence of the informal sector is concerned, opinions differ as to how it should be interpreted in terms of its contribution to economic growth. In the context of developing economies, many observers see the phenomenon of the informal sector in positive terms and it is described as an important source of employment and income for the neglected poor in both urban and rural areas.[87] In a region, such as Sub-Saharan Africa, where the governments and other organizations in the organized sector cannot provide employment to its citizens, the informal sector has been seen as the means for basic economic activities and for earning a living. In many developing countries, economic activities in the informal sector are seen as the incubator for local entrepreneurial ventures. Similarly, the informal sector has been seen as an avenue where citizens engage in economic activities that were denied them by prevailing economic and political circumstances such as the introduction of structural adjustment programs.[88] Lately, many non-governmental organizations such as the International Labour Organization (ILO), the World Bank and the International Monetary Fund (IMF) have seen the presence of the informal sector as areas where skills are developed through local apprenticeship. More importantly, the large number of regulations and bureaucratic procedures from the different institutions and levels of government in developing countries are seen as responsible for the growth of informal sector activities in the developing countries.[89]

In spite of the above contributions to the growth of developing countries' economies, the informal sector has been seen in more negative terms especially by planners and government authorities who see it as an anomaly, a source of disorder, and an obstacle to the development of a modern economy. Many observers in this group see the informal sector as the source of underdevelopment in the poor countries such as the growth in urban slums, health hazards, and growth in criminality, insecurity, bribery and corruption and other forms of social vices and exploitation. The critics of the informal sector argue for a form of formalization policies as the path towards sustainable development. Critics also see the rise of the informal sector as the reasons behind evasion of taxes that could have increased sources of government revenue. Furthermore, the growth of the informal sector has been seen as enhancing low quality standards in the production and delivery of goods and services.[90]

From the perspective of economic development policies, the issues become what to do with the informal sector and its relationship with entrepreneurial development. For example, if the informal sector thrives and provides a means of economic activities for the majority of the population because of its informality, and because rules and regulations are not vigorously enforced in the formal sector, does it make sense to try to formalize and integrate it into the formal economy with laws, codes, and standards that could disrupt its activities and growth? On the other hand, what about the health hazards, security, child abuse, sexual exploitation and other basic rights and safety of the vulnerable groups that usually consists the bulk of the labor force in the informal sector? In short, for policy makers, what to do with the informal sector poses a set of difficulties.

The Role of the Informal Sector in Developing Countries' Economies

The informal sector plays the following important roles in the growth and development of the economies of Sub-Saharan African countries:

(i) Informal sector activities are an important and growing source of employment in Sub-Saharan Africa. The informal sector provides productive outlets for a large number of people who prefer or have to be self-employed. This sector therefore contributes to the region's economy in terms of output and employment. In the informal sector, jobs are constantly been created at relatively low capital costs.

(ii) The informal sector stimulates and enhances innovation and adaptation. It has also provided a breeding ground for innovative, sustainable practices that use indigenous technology. For example, in most parts of Sub-Saharan Africa, old tires are recycled as shoes and toy cars are made from scavenged tins.

(iii) The informal sector acts as ancillaries and suppliers to large-scale enterprises. It also improves forward and backward linkages between economically, socially and geographically diverse sectors.

(iv) The informal sector helps to alleviate the negative consequences of structural adjustment programs.

(v) The informal sector provides informal education through apprenticeship training. Especially in Sub-Saharan Africa, parents arrange for their children to be an apprentice – not only to acquire skills but also for wider training in life skills, ethics and morality.

The Informal Sector and the Development of Entrepreneurship

In spite of the above important socio-economic roles played by the informal sector in the economies of developing countries, policy-makers have consistently ignored its economic efficacy. On the one hand, existing social attitudes tend to look down upon informal sector activities; on the other hand, these attitudes seem to be buttressed by an ambivalent public policy. The result is a policy framework that is largely ambiguous in its support for informal sector activities. This is clearly demonstrated by (a) development policies that favor and promote large enterprises to the detriment of small ones and (b) official tolerance of, or inaction in regard to, social and legal norms, particularly of exploitation, discrimination and even violence against certain vulnerable groups involved in informal sector activities (e.g., women and children). The absence of a policy-enabling environment consequently contributes to and accentuates the formidable problems that business owners in informal sector enterprises are usually confronted:

(i) Lack of Capital: Operators of the informal sector lacks the necessary capital to have their business running and be competitive. This is especially true in terms of the availability of working capital for start-ups and the difficulties in gaining access to credit and finance. Another problem here is that the owners of businesses tend to overrate the beneficial effect of capital and underestimate the risks of taking loans larger than their capacity to repay.

(ii) Poor management and technical skills: Informal sector business owners possess limited management and modest technical skills, which constraints firm productivity and product quality. This problem is compounded with the difficulties in obtaining relevant training.

(iii) Inadequate technology: Inadequate technology is usually stated as an access issue, but it is also an "internal" problem in that some enterprises could have access to improved technology available in the market if they had higher literacy and technical skills and stronger business planning and investment skills. But more importantly, difficulties of access to machinery, facilities and utilities can also be traced to inadequate trade and development policies on the part of governments in Sub-Saharan Africa region.

(iv) Disadvantageous market structures: Informal sector enterprises experience this problem as too much competition in low income markets, low demand for their products and services, lack of access to physical markets where larger and higher income groups shop, difficulty in procuring inputs, low prices provided by traders, etc. As a result, informal sector businesses suffer from diseconomies of scale. While market structures (which are complex) are primarily an access issue, forces external to the firm often play a key role in limiting their market access.

(v) Inadequate infrastructures: Low "access" to services such as work sites, water and electricity, roads and communications limits productivity and access to product markets. This also includes difficulties in obtaining raw materials.

(vi) Government policies, regulation or harassment: Government is one of the most significant external forces that affect the performance of informal sector businesses. As a result of government ambiguous and inefficient policies, the informal sector has not been transformed and grafted into the organized formal economic system capable of producing entrepreneurial ventures in the developing countries.

In addition to the above problems, the unregulated informal sector has been seen as the avenue for the use of child labor and the creation of hazardous working environment. According to the International Labour Organization, such an environment is characterized by working at too young an age; working for hours that are too long; working under strain; working on the street, working for inadequate pay and being subject to intimidation. On the basis of these prevailing conditions, the International Labour Organization points out, "Most children work in the informal sector, without legal or regulatory protection."[91]

The Informal Sector: Institutionalization, Change and Continuity

From the institutional perspective, it is possible to understand why the informal sector of the economy persists in spite of introduction of formal economic policies and programs. In the context of entrepreneurial innovation and economic development, one may readily see that the success of any entrepreneurial initiative or economic development policy may be determined by the degree to which significant features of the informal sector are successfully displaced without creating undue and negative consequences for the survival of local enterprises. Regrettably, in a context where the actions of the government, interest groups, the public, regulatory bodies and societal norms, values and expectations coalesced to produce an enduring system of informal economic behavior, to change such a system demands massive re-orientation.

People seldom seem able or willing to change established ways of behaving as rapidly as their societies can absorb new institutional forms. Particularly in highly stratified societies as found in Sub-Saharan Africa, a well-entrenched group may profit indefinitely from a tendency of people to old economic practices and attitudes. Most African countries did not design their new economic development systems to fit internal economic and institutional exigencies. They often graft onto their societies economic forms initially designed to cope with problems and conditions, which may not be those of African societies. This situation seems bound to complicate and proliferate the possibilities in the outcome of various economic innovations. At the very least, one possibility in such a situation is that economic innovations, which are alien to the institutional environment may be accepted without a corresponding commitment to the values originally associated with them. Secondly, continuity in economic traditions in the face of innovations may be possible simply because the existence of one helps to further the existence (or the interest) of the other. For example, it has been indicated that economic innovations introduced into Sub-Saharan Africa in the early 1980s such as the programs of structural adjustment helped in intensifying and reinforcing the conditions for the growth of informal sector economic activities, especially in the growth of the parallel foreign exchange market.[92] Secondly, the growth of the informal sector has also been seen as a result of imbalances and distortions prevailing in the formal sector of developing economies. For example, Hart points out that price inflation, inadequate wages, and an increasing surplus to the requirements of the urban labor market have led to a high degree of informality in the income-generating activities of Sub-Saharan Africa.[93] Third, the rise of the informal sector as the means of economic activity in Sub-Saharan Africa has also been seen as the consequences of failure in economic planning in the region. According to Haan and Serriere (2002), inappropriate post-independence economic policies, inspired by different forms of in-ward looking development policies, unfavorable pattern of world trade, bad weather conditions, political and social crises seriously undermined any serious effort towards a sustained economic development.[94] The adoption of structural adjustment program also led to massive layoffs of the work force from government agencies and private sector. As a result, most people in Sub-Saharan Africa were drawn or pushed to the informal sector, which includes almost all economic activities that are unregulated. The continued existence and growth of the informal sector can thus be seen as a response to conditions, institutionalized or otherwise, prevailing in society.

In words, continuity in economic traditions (as in the informal sector activities) may also be fostered by the very situation of active coexistence of indigenous and innovative economic practices. In many instances of economic innovations in a society, the multiplicities of societal demands are seldom adequately satisfied. In such a situation, there is a tendency for persons in strategic positions to take steps designed to offset or minimize the impact of economic innovations. This significantly explains the active and parallel existence between the formal and informal sectors of developing countries' economies.

CHAPTER SUMMARY

Culture denotes the historically transmitted patterns of meanings embodied in symbols, a system of inherited conceptions expressed in symbolic forms by means of which men communicate, perpetuate, and develop their knowledge about and attitudes toward life.

Cultural values such as individualism, power distance, uncertainty avoidance and long-term orientation are significantly related to traits such as internal locus of control, achievement motivation, independence, risk taking and innovativeness, which are associated with entrepreneurship, suggesting a complex interaction between entrepreneurship and cultural values.

There is strong evidence that self-reported reasons for starting a business vary systematically with variations in culture along dimensions of individualism, power-distance, masculinity and low uncertainty avoidance.

The first implication in terms of cultural values is that in the context of entrepreneurship, theories of motivation are culture bound in that different cultures emphasize different motivational needs for entrepreneurship.

The second implication is that entrepreneurial development in Sub-Saharan Africa is hampered by socio-cultural value systems.

The third implication is that national culture is likely to influence national or regional rates of entrepreneurship by creating a larger supply of potential entrepreneurs.

The fourth implication is that a combination of factors, mostly socio-cultural and institutional, have combined to produce in the African society, a type of an environment with a set of entrepreneurs or business owners who favor such areas that (1) produce quick financial results; (2) need minimum risk-undertaking; (3) require little or no innovative efforts; and (4) afford favoritism from the state through reciprocation of favors and gifts in form of state contracts.

The fifth implication is that, in the context of Sub-Saharan Africa, entrepreneurship is inhibited by gendered socio-cultural values and practices.

A major stumbling block for many potential entrepreneurs in Sub-Saharan Africa is lack of access to credit or funds necessary to start a business and lack of finance to run the business once it has been established.

Developments in the formal financial sector in Sub-Saharan Africa can be examined under two periods: (i) a period in which governments exerted strict control on the financial market and (ii) a period of liberalization and deregulation of the financial market under a structural adjustment.

Small scale enterprise financing through the formal financial and banking system is difficult because of a weak institutional, financial, socio-cultural, legal environment. The inability to provide longer-term finance in Sub-Saharan Africa for enterprise growth has meant that African economies have remained commerce- and trade-driven and not production-driven.

Informal financial transactions specialize in either lending or savings mobilization. Informal credit sources are popular as a result of collateral free lending, proximity, timely delivery, and flexibility in loan transactions.

The informal credit that micro- and small-sized firms have at their disposal is expensive, inadequate and short-term. The short-term nature of informal credit makes it impossible for long-term investments.

Problem confronting the finance and credit sectors in Sub-Saharan Africa include: undercapitalization of the banking system; a cash-based economies and weak financial sectors; lack of accessibility to rural areas; expensive and unreliable electricity and telecommunications, which limit the reach of African banks as credit providers; legal and taxation systems which are hard to deal with and property rights that are not always recognized; lack of compliance and unpredictable regulatory environment; the absence of the rule of law; absence of systems to track credit repayment histories of borrowers and blacklist bad debtors.

The political environment consists of the political culture and institutions of governance in a society.

Political culture is the set of attitudes, beliefs and sentiments which give order and meaning to a political process and which provide the underlying assumptions and rules that govern behavior in a political system. It encompasses both the political ideals and the operating norms of a polity.

Political risk is the chance that political decisions, events, or conditions in a country will negatively affect the profitability or sustainability of all investment. It is the likelihood that political actions will affect the business environment in ways that lead investors and owners to lose some or all of the value of their investment or be forced to accept a lower than projected rate of return.

The three sources of threat against indigenous businesses are (i) the existing politico-legal system, (ii) the old colonial monopolies, and (iii) the local socio-cultural system.

The consequences of the political culture on indigenous entrepreneurship are (i) conversion of indigenous enterprises into precarious businesses operating in the underground of the informal sector, (ii) non dynamic behavior of nationals considering the establishment of enterprises, (iii) increased number of bankrupt or abandoned indigenous enterprises, (iv) large number of indigenous enterprises that never survive their founders, and (v) scarcity of institutions for the supervision, financing and promotion of enterprises- small and medium – established and owned by natives. The policies of indigenization and nationalization and the prevailing political culture, attitudes and reflexes worked against non-indigenous entrepreneurship.

Cumbersome entry procedures and regulations are associated with more corruption in Sub-Saharan Africa, inferior quality of products, unsafe working conditions, growth of the informal sector and increase consumer prices and fuel corruption.

Bureaucratic corruption allows inefficient producers to remain in business, encourages governments to pursue perverse economic policies, provides opportunities to bureaucrats and politicians to enrich themselves through extorting bribes from those seeking government favors, distorts economic incentives, discourages entrepreneurship, slows economic growth, hinders the proper functioning of the market system and discourages innovation.

The reasons why existing infrastructure interventions fail to promote entrepreneurship and serve the local manufacturing sector in Sub-Saharan Africa are: (i) the inadequacy of provision in relation to the huge scale of need, (ii) the relatively high standards adopted, which means either that the poor cannot afford what is offered, or else that a substantial subsidy is required which the government cannot afford, (iii) any subsidy element is likely to accrue either to large-scale manufacturing firms and other large-scale enterprises, or to the public officials who administer infrastructure services, (iv) failure to address the fundamental obstacles which the small-scale enterprises face in gaining access to land and basic infrastructure, (v) inappropriate forms of infrastructure and services, together with inadequate resources for operation and maintenance, which means that services do not effectively reach those who need them, or fall into disrepair and disuse, and (vi) the adoption of policies which discriminate against the poor or impede them from improving their situation, such as regulatory standards which are unaffordable by the micro- and small-scale enterprises, and harassment of informal sector providers.

The informal sector is the portion of a country's economy that lies outside of any formal regulatory environment

The role of the informal sector includes (i) source of employment, (ii) serves as ancillaries and suppliers to large-scale enterprises, (iii) helps to alleviate the negative consequences of structural adjustment programs, and (iv) provides informal education through apprenticeship training.

Problems confronting entrepreneurs in the informal sector enterprises are lack of capital, poor management and technical skills, inadequate technology, disadvantageous market structures, inadequate infrastructures, government policies, regulation or harassment, the use of child labor and hazardous working environment.

CHAPTER DISCUSSION QUESTIONS

1. What is culture? Why is it necessary to understand entrepreneurship within the context of national cultures? What is the relationship between culture and entrepreneurship?

2. What are the frequently studied dimensions of culture in the context of entrepreneurship? Explain the relationship between the value dimensions of uncertainty avoidance and time orientation to the development of entrepreneurship.

3. In what ways have gendered practices and beliefs affected the development of female entrepreneurs in Sub-Saharan Africa?

4. In the context of Sub-Saharan Africa, the prevalence of short-term thinking means that there is less of a prevailing sense of urgency and more acceptance of the status quo. Examine this statement in terms of how it is related to entrepreneurial conditions such as innovation, risk-taking, creativity, etc. In your opinion, what are the cultural obstacles to innovation in the context of entrepreneurship in Sub-Saharan Africa? Be sure to include a discussion of the concept of imitation.

5. In your opinion, what led to the failure of reforms in the financial system under structural adjustment program and what are the effects of this failure in terms of enterprise financing and entrepreneurial development?

6. What are the main features of an informal financial sector? What are the reasons behind the popularity of informal credit sources in Sub-Saharan Africa?

7. In the context of Sub-Saharan Africa, why do you think that entrepreneurship can also be developed through partnership or cooperation between the public sector, international organizations, and private firms in the areas of microfinancing?

8. What do you understand by the term, "political risk"? Give examples of political risks in Sub-Saharan Africa and how they affect the development of entrepreneurship.

9. Discuss some of the threats against indigenous entrepreneurship in Sub-Saharan Africa. Do research and provide examples of how the political system or culture in a country of your choice has negatively worked against indigenous entrepreneurs.

10. With specific examples, discuss how the regulatory environment in Sub-Saharan Africa stifles the development of entrepreneurship.

11. What are the causes and consequences of bureaucratic corruption on the development of entrepreneurship in Sub-Saharan Africa?

12. Discuss the relationships between infrastructure, entrepreneurship and economic development.

13. What are the problems and challenges of the ICT sector in economic and entrepreneurial development in Sub-Saharan Africa?

14. Discuss some of the weaknesses in the formal educational system in Sub-Saharan Africa. How do these weaknesses affect entrepreneurial development in the region?

15. Discuss the causes of the informal sector economy in Sub-Saharan Africa. In your opinion, should the informal sector be banned or reformed to accommodate the needs of its economic participants?

CASE 4: THE NIGER DELTA, POLITICS OF OIL AND UNDERDEVELOPMENT [95]

Brief Overview

If corruption, the politics of clientage and mismanagement are the major features of Nigeria's economic development, the country's oil-rich south vividly illustrates the consequences of such economic and sociopolitical culture, which is the nightmarish result of four decades of corruption and bad governance. The Niger Delta, a region of mangrove swamps and creeks in Nigeria's south, is crisscrossed by thousands of miles of oil pipelines. Oil spills, which are the result of neglect by oil companies and vandalism by militants, have caused significant environmental and economic damage in the region. The area is further scarred by "gas flaring," the burning of unwanted natural gas byproduct from oil drilling, which causes acid rain and air pollution, taking a massive ecological toll in the region. The Niger Delta crisis, which grew out of this economic and environmental neglect, has thrown the area into an abyss of underdevelopment economically.

The Niger Delta extends over an area of about 70,000sqkm, making it Africa's largest delta. It account for 7.5 percent of Nigeria land mass. About one third of this area is made up of wetland and it contains the largest mangrove forest in the world (5, 400-6000sqkm), and a number of distinct ecological zones. The region traverses nine out of 36 states that make up the federal republic of Nigeria in Africa. The estimated population of the region is about 20 million comprising over forty different ethnic groups speaking 250 different dialects across about 3000 communities. The predominant occupations of the local inhabitant in the area are mainly farming and fishing. Oil was discovered 40 years ago in the Niger Delta with the major operators comprising of Shell and Chevron-Texaco.

Oil from the Niger Delta accounts for 95 percent of Nigeria's foreign exchange earnings, but the region's poverty, economic underdevelopment, and physical devastation have been the source of political unrest that has undermined this country's economic productivity. Pervasive feelings of exploitation among Delta residents have spawned increasingly aggressive militant groups with the ability to cripple the operations of oil companies. A common theme in describing the crisis is that decades of official neglect has made the residents of the Niger Delta and various militants groups to "fight" in their attempts to gain "resource control" or a fair share of the country's oil revenues. In this struggle to gain access to the oil resources, the actions of the various militant groups have received intense global attention. Since the militant groups are the pivotal organizations through which the crisis is made manifest, tracing its growth and activities will provide insight into the dynamics of the crisis.

The Militant Groups

The first Delta insurgent group to receive international attention was the Movement for the Survival of the Ogoni People (MOSOP). Led by Ken Saro-Wiwa, the group launched a nonviolent campaign in 1990 against the government and Royal Dutch/Shell to protest environmental degradation and the area's economic neglect. The group's efforts led Shell to cease production in Ogoni in 1993. Saro-Wiwa and eight other MOSOP members, the "Ogoni Nine," were executed by the military regime in 1995. Later, militant groups, which are primarily composed of young men dissatisfied at their inability to find jobs, began to proliferate in mid 1990s.

These groups, such as the Ijaw Youth Council and the Niger Delta Vigilantes, were organized at the village or clan level. Their attacks were designed to extort short-term funds or municipal development projects from multinational oil companies. In recent years, the militant groups have become more sophisticated and increasingly share a common goal of "resource control," a share of the oil revenues their region produces. In 2004, the Niger Delta People's Volunteer Force (NDPVF), an Ijaw militant group led by Alhaji Mujahid Dokubo-Asari, threatened "all-out war" against the Nigerian government. The then Nigerian President, Olusegun Obasanjo, offered Asari and another militant leader amnesty and payments in exchange for their groups' weapons. In 2005, nearly a year after this deal, Asari was arrested, charged with treason, and put in prison, where he remains until his release in the summer of 2007.

The most prominent of these militant groups is the Movement for the Emancipation of the Niger Delta, or MEND. A group with a core leadership that affiliates itself with other militant groups on a case-by-case basis, MEND has adeptly leveraged media attention to publicize its demands. The group's attacks on oil pipelines and kidnappings of foreign oil worker have reduced oil output in the Delta by more than 25 percent or roughly eight hundred thousand barrels per day, according to Nigerian oil officials. MEND increasingly serves as an umbrella organization for a loose affiliation of rebel groups in the Delta.

One of the weapons in the hands of the militants and its source of finance is hostage taking and negotiations, which can involve ransom money. For example, there are several instances of oil companies paying companies owned by militant leaders to provide "security" to oil installations.

The other major source of income for the criminally inclined militant groups is oil bunkering; a complicated process of tapping an oil pipeline and filling plastic cans with crude oil. The oil is then sold to locals or transported to barges offshore for transport to a neighboring country. Oil theft, also known as "oil bunkering", has accelerated the conflict and provided militant and criminal groups with funds to purchase arms. Since a government crackdown on oil theft began in mid-2005, piracy and kidnappings have been on the rise. Oil facilities and workers are difficult to defend, nowhere more so than in the Niger Delta's tangle of swamps and rivers.

The most potent weapon in the militants' arsenal is the growing anger among the region's twenty million inhabitants. In more than eight years of civilian rule, functionaries at the local, state and federal levels are perceived to have failed to deliver tangible economic benefits for impoverished residents. Militant groups have largely ignored the incremental administrative reforms begun since 2003 and have succeeded in drawing upon anger against a pervasively corrupt system of governance inherited from the military era. Militant groups have managed to win sufficiently broad popular support to operate openly in many communities and have not been weakened by the imprisonment since September 2005 of publicity-seeking warlord Alhaji Dokubo-Asari.

Another source of funding are the discreet payments oil companies make to militant leaders in return for "surveillance" and protection of pipelines and other infrastructure.

This practice, frequently cloaked as community development, has fueled conflict through competition for contracts and by providing income to groups with violent agendas. Oil companies also pay allowances, perks – and sometimes salaries – to "supernumerary police", as well as regular duty police and soldiers deployed to protect oil installations. Security forces consider these plum postings and are alleged to use excessive force to protect company facilities and their jobs.

Implicit support for the activities of the militant groups seems to come from the local communities. Community groups in the Niger Delta complain they have few incentives to protect oil infrastructure from militant and criminal groups. For impoverished locals, government officials and even oil company staff, oil theft offers significant rewards. Environmental claims are increasingly incorporated into the rhetoric of insurgency. Locals have long complained that spilled oil from deteriorating decades-old pipelines has devastated fishing. Whereas many residents used to work as fishermen, oil installations and spills have decimated the fish population and now must import frozen fish.

The militants, like the Niger Delta's population at large, object to the environmental degradation and underdevelopment of the region and the lack of benefits the community has received from its extensive oil resources. While there is a revenue-sharing plan in which the federal government distributes roughly half of the country's oil revenues among state governors, these funds do not trickle down to the roughly 20 million residents of the Delta. In 2003, some 70 percent of oil revenues was stolen or wasted, according to an estimate by the head of Nigeria's anticorruption agency.

The Politics of Resource Control and the Dynamics of the Crisis

It is impossible to understand the dynamics of the crisis without examining its political context at the national level. For instance, one critical issue closely related to the Niger Delta crisis is the access to and control over Delta oil and the economy in general, including the intense competition for political office. For politicians and their communities, control of federal office opens the high road to resources that can be diverted from public to private or community control. Competition is naturally intense for federal political offices and has historically turned violent in each of Nigeria's previous elections. Federal control over oil and much of the rest of the economy tends to "federalize" many economic problems, particularly in the Delta, and stimulates intense efforts to gain and hold office throughout Nigeria.

According to the International Crisis Group, removing the incentives for violence will require granting a degree of resource control to local communities. Engaging Delta groups in sustained, transparent dialogue also remains critical to finding a solution to the militant struggle. Equally important, credible development efforts must be supported and stiff penalties for corruption imposed upon those who embezzle and squander funds. Observers are of the opinion that resolving the Niger Delta crisis will require far greater commitment on the part of the federal government and corporate stakeholders in ensuring the oil industry operates fairly and transparently in the region, with visible benefits to the local population. Without serious and sustainable reforms, all parties stand to lose.

The complexity of issues and number of stakeholders involved exacerbate the crisis as well. The Delta, in part because of its riverine and swamp topography, has historically been politically extremely fragmented, and subject to frequent and at times violent disputes over land and fishing rights, as well as over traditional leaders' political jurisdictions. All of these lead to cycles of "revenge violence." As more powerful weapons became available in the Delta in the mid- and late-1990s, disputes became more violent. Youth gangs became more powerful who were willing and able to protect their villages and elders. As democratic competition returned in 1998–1999, some of these same youths took up a new line of activity, paid disruption of campaign events, and/or provided candidates protection from such unwanted attentions. Finally, traditional leaders lost much credibility and respect as they have been corrupted by payments from the military government and the oil companies. The militants see the local politicians or elders as betrayers of the legitimate fight for resource control.

In particular, on the part of the Federal Government of Nigeria, there has been lack of a credible, sustained dialogue on control of resources with Niger Delta civil society groups, including militants, activist leaders, religious leaders, women and youth. Furthermore, the persistence of the crisis has been blamed on inappropriate derivation formula of mineral resources, including oil and gas, to all Nigerian states. The persistence of an ill conceived "Land Use Act" which fails to include the opportunity for communities to seek compensation for land through legal means and failed to allow a more transparent adjudication process of potential land seizures has also been seen as fuelling the crisis. Absence of credible offer of a substantial ownership stake by the local residents in the government and transnational oil company joint ventures that control production has been seen as a political factor. Finally, the continuity of the crisis has also been blamed on a lack of commitment on the part of federal and state governments to implement poverty reduction strategies and in making budget details publicly available and responding to queries about specific spending patterns and projects.

The General Ibrahim Babangida's regime established the Oil and Mineral Producing Areas Development Commission, OMPADEC in the early 1990s. The Olusegun Obasanjo administration came up with the Niger Delta Development Commission, NDDC. These commissions and quazi-ministerial bodies were set up to cater for the development needs of the Delta region but they fell short of what is needed for the social and economic transformation that are needed to heal the wounds of decades of neglect and exploitation. Rather than addressing the roots of the crisis, the overwhelming Federal Government interest in development authorities has been in maintaining control and ensuring that any authority forms part of a centralized chain of political and economic patronage. In particular, the development commissions that have been established over the years have only served as avenues for compensating loyal party men and cronies. Little wonder they have become havens of corruption and looting. Ibrahim Babangida's OMPADEC was notorious for looting and award of bogus contracts for white elephant projects. Olusegun Obasanjo's NDDC also got entangled in corruption, which of course was the order of the day in Nigeria. Consequently, observers agree that the creation of development commissions to dish out tokens of handouts to communities in the name of development projects is no solution to the festering problem of the Niger Delta. The long period of military rule in Nigeria contributed to bad governance and corruption; and the burden for the provision of government services fell to oil and gas companies, which were ill equipped to supply water and electricity and maintain road networks. Generally, the eight-year-civilian administration of Olusegun Obasanjo, which ended in 2007 failed to produce a recognizable solution to the crisis.

On May 29, 2007, the new government of President Umaru Yar'Adua vowed to bring to an end the crisis in the Niger Delta. In his inaugural address, the new President had said, "The crisis in the Niger Delta commands our urgent attention. I will use every resource available to me, with your help, to address this crisis in a spirit of fairness, justice and cooperation." As at May 29, 2008, one year on, little or nothing has been done to change the status quo. While the President has at various fora, spoken of his administration's commitment to resolving the region's lingering crisis, no tangible effort has been made beyond rhetoric. Currently, the governors of the nine states, federal lawmakers, state lawmakers, opinion leaders and civil society groups in the region have tried to no avail to get Yar'Adua to release about N327bn (US$2.7 billion) funds belonging to the Niger Delta Development Commission. The Secretary to the Government of the Federation, Ambassador, Babagana Kingibe, had asked the people to go to court and challenge the government for withholding the funds. The government literally said the it was not willing to budge on the matter.

In the midst of the government withholding of the funds, MEND has continued to threaten more acts of sabotage against the nation's oil industry, while also accusing the government of"insincerity." "We will continue our campaign of sabotage on the oil industry as long as the government is insincere in the handling of the Niger Delta crisis," MEND spokesman, Jomo Gbomo said. Between February and April of 2008, the group has attacked major oil platforms in Rivers, Bayelsa and Delta States leading to a drastic reduction on production especially by Shell Petroleum Development Company, a major player in the country's oil sector. The ripple effect of which is constantly felt in the escalating global price of oil. Meanwhile, the government that has vowed to resolve the region's crisis "in a spirit of fairness, justice and cooperation" has now voted over N250bn (over US$2 billion) for security while less than N43bn (US$358 million) was voted for development of the nine states of the region.

With many failed attempts in the past, and so many plans to reverse the status quo always in the pipeline, it is hardly surprising that the *Punch Newspapers* suggests that the Niger Delta "remains the albatross of the Yar'Adua administration" one year after its administration vowed to resolve the crisis.

The Economic and Business Fallout of the Niger Delta Crisis

In the Niger Delta, the center of oil production, 72 percent of households live below the poverty line. In spite of decades of oil exploration, the people of the Niger Delta continue to be economically impoverished in an evolving prosperous global economy. Perhaps this condition begins to make more sense when it is acknowledged that 10 percent of the country controls over 80 percent of the country's source of revenue. Although the people of the Niger Delta have tried reformative ideas to alleviate the situation such as demanding compensation through institutional and financial agreements for oil producing communities and implementing laws regarding more efficient means of resource control, just compensation and resource efficiency have been far from being realized. Thus, economic, cultural and environmental degradation persist despite countless decades of peaceful protest and reform attempts. The frustrations emanating from the lack of attention given to environmental degradation and perpetual exploitation by the oil industry has led to a hardened resentment of the corporate world.

Not since 1958, after the discovery of crude oil in a little village in the region called Oloibiri has there been genuine effort to provide sustainable livelihood for the local populace. Over the years, owing to persistent gas-flaring, oil-spillage and production activities, the ecology, marine life and environmental conditions have worsened. The problem of poverty in those regions have been a deep-seated issue, and exacerbated by prolonged economic stagnation in Nigeria over the last 40 years. What makes the situation particularly pathetic is the egregious mismanagement of funds by politicians and soldiers and flaunting of ill-gotten wealth in midst of abject poverty. That was not helped by the flagrant disregard of native communities by oil producing companies with the connivance of government officials over the last 40 years. Meanwhile the bulk of resources yielding 85 percent of government revenue and over 90 percent of export earning are derived from those communities with little or no concern for living conditions and the environmental impact in a very harsh terrain.

The political dimension of the crisis has also led to disruptions in the economic and business activities of the local areas, especially in the cities of Port Harcourt and Warri in the Niger Delta. In each riot came destruction of businesses owned and operated by locals as politicians used the criminally minded militants as tools for the destruction of business properties owned by political opponents. In addition, any retaliatory actions by the federal government to incidences of militants' kidnapping have witnessed the closure or destruction of local businesses by men of the military or the local police force.

The full effect of the economic consequences of the Niger Delta crisis can be appreciated with the realization that as at August 2007, Nigeria was loosing 600,000 barrels of oil daily owing to the crisis, which has led to the closure of 25 percent of the oil fields in the country. In the year 2006 alone, Nigeria lost about $4.5 billion in revenue as a result of the shutdowns. Although Nigeria is one of the world's leading oil producers, it ranks 151st out of 177 of the world's poorest countries in 2006, according to the United Nations Development Program (UNDP).

Government Initiatives and Conflicting Signals

On July 30, 2008, the government announced plans to set up an International Oil and Gas Trade Fair Center in Port Harcourt, Rivers State. That is, apart from oil and gas industrial clusters in some South-South states the government has promised that. One of such, the government said, is indeed ready for establishment in Eleme, Rivers State.

The federal Minister of Commerce and Industry, Mr. Charles Ugwuh, who disclosed these to reporters in Abuja on July 30, 2008 said over $25 billion investment was also waiting in the wings when peace returns to the troubled region. According to him, so many investors have indicated interest and got approval from government to make huge investments in the region, but the elusive peace in the area has kept them away. He assured that the International Oil and Gas Trade Fair Center would impact positively on the population as well as expose the abundant economic, natural and human resources within the zone to the global economy.

The minister, who inaugurated a steering committee on the establishment of the International Oil and Gas Trade Fair Center, stressed that government had not been insensitive to the plight of the stakeholders in the oil and gas industry."
According to him: "Indeed, if anything at all, the petroleum sector has continued to be on the front-burner of government's economic reform agenda. This is once more being attested to today by the inauguration of this committee, among other measures already taken." He stressed that his ministry was working hard with the organized private sector, foreign private/portfolio investors, development partners and other stakeholders to facilitate the building of more free trade zones, industrial parks, industrial clusters, free enterprise zones and business incubators in the Niger Delta and other zones of the country. He called for peace from the people of the Niger Delta, noting that the region was missing out on so many investment opportunities.

However, the same day, while one of the leaders of the militants, Alhaji Mujahid Dokubo-Asari was preaching peace and campaigning for foreign investors to return to the region, government security agents swooped on his home in Abuja. As the minister was addressing the press conference, security agents of the government invaded the Abuja home of Dokubo-Asari and laid siege to the property. The raid came on a day Dokubo-Asari was delivering a speech on peace at the International Conference Center, Abuja, for the return of investors who have deserted the region.

The news of the raid was broken to the militant leader at the function which was organized by him for the celebration of the 2008 Major Isaac Adaka Boro's symposium with the theme: "The Niger Delta: An investment paradise." The symposium, according to him, is part of genuine efforts to engage stakeholders on sustainable way of charting a new way to the return of peace and economic activities in the Niger Delta.

According to the federal government, the raid was provoked by a speculation that Dokubo-Asari was in possession of a cache of ammunition at his Abuja home, following recent public pronouncement by him. Reacting to the development, aides of the militant leader defended their leader but accused the Federal Government of just trying to implicate him because of his stance on the Niger Delta question. They warned that they had already intimated their supporters in the creeks for prompt action should Abuja frame-up their leader.

Government's Accusation of the Oil Companies

In recent years, the federal government of Nigeria has resorted to blaming the multinational oil companies even though it has done nothing concrete to alleviate the people's suffering and anger, other than shifting blames. Recently, the government was quoted as saying the multi-national oil corporations are responsible for the Niger Delta crisis. In a more unusual way, the Government is expecting the oil companies to undertake development programs that fall under its jurisdiction. In more general terms, the federal government of Nigeria accused the oil companies for not doing enough for the local economy. One area in which this accusation is directed is employing locals rather than expatriates. In fact, the government has gone as far as suggesting to the Nigerian

Labor Union to direct its anger and frustration at the multinational oil corporations for failing to employ significant numbers of the local population. Speaking to journalist on July 31, 2008, through the Minister of Labor, Dr. Hassan Lawal, President Umaru Yar'Adua identified failures of the oil companies to engender community development over a long period as a major contributory factor to the crisis in the Niger Delta. The Minister of Labor questioned the role of multinational oil companies:

"What is the number of industries that have so far been established by these so-called multi-national oil giants? If you go to the Niger Delta, poverty confronts one in the face, when in actual fact, the people of the Niger Delta should have no business with poverty if the oil companies that are operating in the area live up to the expectation of providing even cottage industries everywhere. It is these neglects in all areas of human endeavors that are chiefly responsible for the instability that we now confront in the area."

The President noted that Nigerians, especially those in the oil and gas industry, have a misunderstanding of what constitute the local content in the oil industry. According to him, most people in the oil industry do not understand what constitute local content. Local content, according to him, means the number of jobs that are created for the people. "In countries such as Kuwait, Saudi Arabia and other oil-producing countries, they often ask what number of jobs is available for their people. But here in Nigeria, they just come and offer any kind of jobs to our people. While the oil companies get jobs for their country people, our people remain jobless."

He also charged the leadership of the Petroleum and Natural Senior Staff Association of Nigeria (PENGASSAN) not to measure their achievements in office strictly in terms of number of strikes they are able to embark upon but rather in terms of how they have negotiated on behalf of their members that result in the improvement of the living standard. He berated the labor leaders for not rising against oil companies to resist imposition of expatriate workers but instead resort to threatening the Federal Government with strike.

The Multinational Oil Corporations

Over the years, multinational oil corporations, especially, Shell, have received increased attention both locally and globally. To understand the reason for this attention, it is appropriate to examine the pattern of economic activities of the MNCs and their social responsibility initiatives vis-à-vis the socio-economic conditions of the Niger Delta derived from oil exploration. The history of MNCs' corporate social responsibility and stakeholder management in Nigeria has followed four distinct strategies: obstructionist, defensive, accommodative and proactive strategies.

In the beginning, many of the oil multinational corporations conspicuously avoided social responsibility and their presence in the Niger Delta and Nigeria in general reflected mainly economic priorities – they even attempted in several instances to fight and obstruct social justice and demands. This obstructionist approach was synonymous to a colonial mentality of extracting mineral and raw materials from the colonies without any commitment to development except in areas the facilitate transportation of oil to the ports. During this period, economic activities were decimated as fishing ponds were covered with dark oil and farms burnt as a result of spillage from oil wells and oil pipelines that exploded in the middle of villages.

In the seventies and mid-eighties, the oil companies adopted a defensive strategy whereby they seek to protect their interests by doing the minimum legally necessary to satisfy expectations. Their corporate behavior conforms to the demands of the military dictators who were even using state apparatus and military might to defend themselves against legitimate demands from other stakeholders, especially the local communities. The actions of many of the oil corporations were in response to global competitive market pressure. Whenever they were criticized of any wrongdoings (such as environmental pollution, discriminatory labor and employment practices, etc), the MNCs denied such claims. At a minimum, they began to pay "compensation" to the damages done to local farms in response to legal actions brought against them.

Beginning from the mid-eighties to the late nineties, the oil company's responses to stakeholder issues and social responsibility demands were, at best, accommodative, by doing the minimum ethically required. They accept social responsibilities in so far as it is beneficial to corporate image and profit-seeking motive. They try to satisfy economic, legal, and ethical criteria of performing in a poorly regulated and corrupt society. In fact, it is possible to say that their corporate behavior during this period was (and still) congruent with society's prevailing norms, values, and expectation. Existing in a society that derives economic activities on the basis of clientage, bribery and corruption, the oil companies responded by cultivating the friendship of those in power- powerful politicians, military dictators, traditional rulers and local opinion leaders, without any social responsibility strategy and initiative that was beneficial to the masses. Whatever "compensation" paid by the oil corporations to the "local communities", it was "shared" among the power brokers and local chieftains to the detriment of the locals whose farms and other means of livelihoods have been destroyed. It is thus to this group that the militants turned to for support in their fight for "resource-control." Typically, the multinational oil corporations began to willingly "accommodate" with cleanup activities when oil spill occurs, but remain quite slow or uncommitted in taking actions to prevent spills in the first place.

In recent years, however, the multinational oil corporations, with Shell at the forefront, have re-examined their roles and become more proactive in their responsibility to the various stakeholder groups, especially the local community. In the economic, education, and social areas, some of the corporations have taken leadership role in developmental initiatives taking on discretionary performance in areas that demand both financial and technological assistance. In short, what is being done is taking preventive actions to avoid adverse social impacts in areas that have nothing to do with their core businesses, such as funding educational initiatives at universities and providing seed money to prospective businesspersons. Significantly, some of these organizations are taking the lead in identifying and responding to emerging social, economic, and technological issues.

We will illustrate the relationship between the multinational oil cooperation and the Niger Delta crisis with the experience of Shell for the reason below.

Shell Petroleum Development Company is a company of Shell Nigeria, and according to its website "the largest oil and gas company in Nigeria." It is the operator of a joint venture involving: Nigerian National Petroleum Corporation (NNPC), 55 per cent, Shell 30 percent, Elf Petroleum Nigeria Limited (EPNL, a subsidiary of Total), 10 percent, and Agip Oil Nigeria, 5 percent. Its mission is "to be the operator of first choice in Nigeria through its commitment to strong economic performance and to every aspect of sustainable development." Currently, it produces 43 percent of the nation's oil and has more than 4,500 in staff. Below, we examine three areas that Shell has proactively committed itself.

Provision of Microfinance to Local Business Owners:
Shell has been involved in the promotion of local entrepreneurship through its microfinance program geared towards helping disadvantaged locals seeking financing opportunities for local businesses. In one of those programs, the company gave out US$2.3 million in August of 2007 to 48 communities within Nigeria. The loan is part of SPDC's micro-credit and business development program aimed at "enabling entrepreneurs to take advantage of the economic opportunities in their locality." Benefiting communities included in the loan are from Edo, Delta and Bayelsa States. Mr. Ubaka Emelumadu, Community Affairs Director, Shell disclosed that the amount will be disbursed to 5,780 beneficiaries in the company's western area of operations. The beneficiaries are expected to invest the fund in the businesses they have indicated interest in and have been trained for. Mr. Emelumadu further noted that in batch one which had been disbursed in June of 2007, Shell gave out N270 million (US$ 2.1 million) as micro-credit loans to 5,297 persons drawn from 45 host communities, bringing up the total loans dispersed thus far to around US$ 4.4 million.

US$1 billion Contracts to Nigerian Indigenous Contractors: The Shell Petroleum Development Company of Nigeria awarded contracts worth $1bn to indigenous contractors in 2007 as part of its Nigerian Content Development initiative. The SPDC's General Manager, Mr. Mutiu Sumonu, made this known while introducing Mr. Simbi Wabote, as the new General Manager, NCD to newsmen in Port Harcourt, Rivers State. According to Shell Petroleum Development Company of Nigeria, the NCD provided the platform for the promotion of internal contracting environment, which encouraged more Nigerians to execute contracts within the oil and gas industry.

To show SPDC's sincerity of purpose, the corporation created a separate department within its organization structure to drive the implementation of policies associated with growing Nigerian content. He said the firm had been involved in activities aimed at developing indigenous capacity in the oil and gas sector even before the National Assembly initiated the local content bill. From the position of SPDC, its approach to indigenous content went beyond the narrow confines of awarding contract to indigenous firms but also embraced capacity building and skills acquisition by Nigerians. SPDC's general manager said, "It is really about developing capacity and technology as well as generating wealth for Nigerians. It is helping the manufacturing industry in Nigeria to start playing key roles in the oil and gas industry. We believe firmly in involving more and more Nigerians in the oil and gas business especially at the level of project execution and that is why we have created a separate department to encourage Nigerian content development." He also said, "Last year, we created a Community Content Department to work with our host communities on how Niger Delta indigenes can contribute to and benefit from our supply chain processes."

Employing More Nigerians:
Shell has also been involved in creating employment opportunities for many Nigerians even as the Federal government accuses the oil corporations for not doing enough in employing local labor. Managing Director of Shell Petroleum Development Company (SPDC), Mr. Mutiu Sumonu, stated that the success of the Nigerian Content Development policy of the company is evident in the fact that 95 percent of its workforce is Nigerians. He said this translates into technological transfer. He stated that it would not be healthy to have 100 percent Nigerian work force in Shell as some Nigerians are working in other countries under the organization, adding that there were about 300 expatriates in Shell Nigeria while there are over 280 Nigerians working for the company in other countries. He noted that if some Nigerians are working for Shell abroad, there should also be other nationals working in Nigeria since the company is an international conglomerate.

Sumonu, who addressed newsmen on August 11, 2008 lamented that people have a narrow view of local content, pointing out that it is not all about giving contract to local firms. He said that the essence of empowering even the local contractors was to create employment and opportunities which will have a trickle down effect since the company has limited number of chances in terms of employment. According to him, to compensate for the limited employment opportunities, Shell is empowering local and community firms that stand better chances of offering employment to the people.

"Nigerian content goes far beyond contracts. It is about developing capacity, transferring technology and generating wealth for the country. The scope is so wide. Part of it is to help the manufacturing sector to play key role in the oil and gas sector. ... They complain that we are not employing people but our staff strength is about 4,000, so how many people can we take? We are aiming at enhancing Nigeria's industrial base. We can by our actions and policies, multiply employment opportunities. We are in it and we genuinely believe in it as it can engender lasting industrial growth," he explained.

Empowering Indigenes of Host Communities:
In addition to providing employment opportunity and awarding contracts to the indigenes and entrepreneurs, Shell has also been involved in empowering the indigenes through skills development and capacity building through various programs. One of such programs is skills development program for employees of the corporations' contracting companies. Seen by many as one of its kind in Nigeria, the program is seen as an approach that is economically and technologically beneficial to local entrepreneurs and businesses.

Jimmy Abatu, one of the 28 other beneficiaries of the training program sponsored by the Anglo-Dutch oil giant, said that "The training was like the first of its kind and there were irregularities, which I believe would be corrected when the next set of people come in; but on the whole, it was okay. I learnt so much from the whole thing."

Henry Chukwunyere of Fidel Limited shared the same feeling. To him, the training was an eye opener. He said the training exposed him to how to maintain safety regulations in the office and work area. Chukwunyere, like other graduates, were effusive in praise for SPDC's gesture in footing the bills for the three months program.

"On the whole, I say thank you SPDC for giving us this privilege to attend this training and I pray God should continue to give them the wisdom and understanding to extend it to other areas,'" he said. The other areas, according to him, are electrical, carpentry, architecture and welding. Besides, he believes that for them to catch up with modern trend in engineering, knowledge of auto card drawing should be included in the curriculum.

The beneficiaries commended SPDC for the initiative in identifying with the needs of their contractors in Rivers and Delta states, as the knowledge acquired would go a long way to improve their performances at work. They called on the oil firm to address some of the problems encountered during the program, which include improvement in welfare package and elongation of course duration. They also commended Petroleum Training Institute (PTI), describing it as the ideal place for training and molding capable and proficient hands for the oil, gas and allied sector not only in Nigeria but the continent.

The Chief Coordinator, PTI Consultancy Service, A. J. Orukele, underscored the import of the program, saying that it was designed to enhance workers' performance in the areas of their operations with their respective companies. He pointed out that training was key to organizational survival as it does not only impact the current trend obtainable in the industry, but also brings the workers closer to the achievement of the organizational goals and objectives. While thanking SPDC for reposing confidence in the institute to train the workforce trainees, he enjoined the management of the various upstream sector of the oil and gas industry to utilize the abundant opportunities available in the school to train their workers.

The training program, according to SPDC, was in furtherance of its Niger Delta content initiative and that the seven companies were picked after consultation with its engineering department. The workforce-training program is aimed at enhancing the capacity and capability of these contractors engaged in flow line and dredging activities for the oil firm.

A statement by SPDC stated that in November 2007, a gap analysis workshop was conducted to identify weaknesses and areas required to enhance contractors' performance, adding that a follow-up Vendor Development Program was also conducted to train the chairmen/chief executive officers, supervisors and health safety and environment officers in health safety environmental management, quality management system, and general contracting. In addition, a contract agreement was reportedly signed between SPDC and PTI in March of 2008 to train electrical and mechanical workforce of the Niger Delta flow line and dredging companies for three months. The central part of the SPDC Niger Delta Content Initiative is to deliver sustainable growth in the oil-rich region through communities' ability to supply services and materials to oil and gas industry. Furthermore, it is meant to assist the growth of existing contractors and develop new ones in the region. The initiative would also ensure the development of "pipeline" of opportunities for contractors and enable them participate in the opportunities through training and capacity building.

Loss of Foreign Investment and Entrepreneurial Development

Militant insurgency in the Niger Delta has taken a heavy toll on the economy. Not only is oil production on the decline, workers, particularly expatriates have had to abandon oil locations; while others including Nigerians who remain on the job do so at great peril to their lives. The country is losing so much on this account both in terms of revenue and image. Angola, for the first time since 1978, has overtaken Nigeria in crude oil production. In the month of April, 2008, Angola pumped 1.873 million barrels per day, 55,000 bpd more than Nigeria whose production has plummeted by 1.36 million bpd, or more than 40 percent of its installed capacity in recent months. This grave situation is directly linked to the violence perpetrated by militant groups in the Niger Delta. The continuous flaring of gas in the Niger Delta, for example, is a thorny issue, and the absence of a clear program to keep the teeming youths gainfully engaged remains a major cog in the wheel as far as economic development is concerned.

Economically, the crisis has made sure that the region is starved of any inflow of foreign direct investment. This is especially so because some of the casualties of the Niger Delta crisis are the multinational oil corporations. For example, in early 2006, US-based oil-service and pipeline construction company Wilbros announced its withdrawal from Nigeria after so many decades of operating in the region. Even well known multinational corporations such as construction giant like Julius Berger had threatened to pullout from the region. Every now and then major producers withdraw their staff from hotspots. Travel advisory by the US, British and other European governments have warned their citizens to stay clear of the region - personnel that are critical to the vitality of the oil industry.

The import of this crisis is grave considering the fact that the oil and gas industry is very capital-intensive and Nigeria's situation is especially precarious because large multinational producers who are accountable to foreign management and foreign shareholders dominate the sector. Expectedly, when the pressure in the region hits boiling point, the question of continued stay or operation in Nigeria becomes an issue for owners of these multinational corporations. That the crisis in the region has led to disruptions in the operations of multinational oil corporations is an understatement. Indeed, with each disruption comes loss of direct and indirect contributions to economic development associated with investments flowing from the presence of the oil and gas multinational corporations.

In classical economics, direct private foreign investment might involve the attraction or creation of factors of production. Initially, the oil and gas industry established with foreign investment attracts foreign capital, innovation, entrepreneurship, technology and management skills. The creation of factors implies that in the process of its operation the oil and gas industry might contribute certain types of factors to the local or domestic economy, particularly foreign exchange, investment resources, training of skilled labor and management and the development of local entrepreneurship. As in the oil and gas industry, if the foreign investment occurs in an export industry (crude oil) or import substitution industry (refined gasoline) that creates a net saving of foreign exchange, then the industry will be a provider of this potentially important factor to other domestic sectors. In addition, the foreign capital inflow automatically translates into available investment resources for the domestic economy. Skilled laborers (including entrepreneurs and managers) might be trained in the new industry and then choose to move to other domestic industries.

In classical economic theory, private foreign investment in the oil and gas industry can also result in indirect gain for the Nigerian economy if the operation of the industry that it creates increases the profitability of other domestic industries through inter-sectoral relationships or linkages. Linkage effects are the economic benefits or costs resulting from relationships with another industry. Investment linkages require that the oil and gas industry use inputs supplied by backward-linked domestic industries, or that its outputs be used as intermediate inputs by forward-linked local industries. Backward linkages concern inputs demanded by the new industry. New industries may be established to supply inputs into the oil and gas industry. Furthermore, certain industries already established (e.g., electricity, transport) can expand output to meet the demand of the new industry and might thereby enjoy (additional) economies of scale. In fact, for all intent and purposes, the oil and gas industry in Nigeria could have been a source for entrepreneurial development and the creation and growth of local industries.

Unfortunately, the reverse has been the case. Rather than stimulating local entrepreneurship through its linkage effects, the oil and gas industry created underdevelopment both economically and ecologically in the Niger Delta. Whatever new industry that came into being as a result of the oil and gas industry, has been the growth of criminally-induced industries: oil bunkering and official corruption. One of the consequences of these crises is the continued disruptions of oil production and the smooth working of the oil and gas industry. As a result of these disruptions, the linkage effects and the associated secondary/supplier industries that normally accompany the gas and oil industry have not been realized. For example, in spite of its position as the world's sixth largest exporter of crude oil, and in spite of its huge investments in refinery for the past forty years, Nigeria still imports all of its gas and fuel needs.

Case Discussion Questions

1. Identify the nature of the Niger Delta crisis and the root of the conflict in this case.

2. In what ways does politics affected economic development in the Niger Delta? Who bears the blame?

3. In your opinion, how could the oil and gas industry help in the development of local industries and entrepreneurship through a linkage effect?

4. What recommendations would you give to the Nigerian authorities in terms of how they can use the oil and gas industry in the development of local industries and entrepreneurship?

Chapter 5

THE ORGANIZATIONAL AND MANAGEMENT CONTEXT

The test of sound management rests on its ability to manage and turn environmental constraints into resources through astute management and organizational skills and capabilities.

CHAPTER LEARNING OBJECTIVES
After studying this chapter, you should be able to:

1. Understand why it is necessary to examine entrepreneurship from a management and organizational perspective.

2. Understand the management processes and functions as they apply to entrepreneurship.

3. Understand the various management and organizational constraints facing small businesses in Sub-Saharan Africa.

4. Understand why business owners in Sub-Saharan Africa often neglect strategic planning.

5. Understand the relationship between leadership styles, authority relations and employee motivation in small businesses in Africa.

6. Understand the problems of unethical business practices on small business management in Sub-Saharan Africa.

7. Understand the marketing and financial management problems confronting the management of small firms in Sub-Saharan Africa

INTRODUCTION: ENTREPRENEURSHIP AND MANAGEMENT

To be an entrepreneur is to decide to do something; it means to prepare a project and embark on its implementation. Entrepreneurship therefore involves a conscious content, a precise commitment and a definite practice. It involves a project, a framework for its implementation and a recurrent activity geared to the materialization of the project. Thus, entrepreneurship, organization and management are related. Without distinction, entrepreneurs perform the following functions: imagine or create from nothing some unprecedented realities (opportunities, objects, procedures, relations, modes) and endeavor to disseminate these innovations within a new, stabilized framework, namely the enterprise. Technical know-how transforms the entrepreneur into a manager by putting the project into the process of its daily implementation. Implementation does not occur in a vacuum. It occurs in an entity that we call an organization. In other words, entrepreneurship involves the planning, organizing, leading and controlling of activities.

Entrepreneurship and management are constituent dimensions of the human being. This chapter describes the relationship between managerial and organizational capabilities as they relate to entrepreneurship. Essentially, the managerial and organizational perspective proposes that a firm's ability to grow is directly related to its ability to add managerial capacity to administer the growth. The lack of managerial capacity on the part of the African entrepreneur has been noted as one of the main reasons why the continent is lacking behind in global competitiveness. According to the managerial and organizational perspective, environmental constraints can be managed and turned to resources through astute management and organizational skills and capabilities.

In an examination of the typical African entrepreneur, Basil Enwegbara argues that most African entrepreneurs lacked the understanding of what it would take to be successful entrepreneurs, lacking the necessary technical and management skills and the independence and confidence. They lacked consistent personal ambition and willingness to delegate authority for fear of sharing ownership, and failed to form partnerships to pool finance and managerial skills. Furthermore, the author argues that if the desire to financially support others is a valid impetus for establishing businesses, African entrepreneurs exaggerated it, as they used it for employing immediate family members and more distant kinsmen. This kind of personal preference for a paternalistic labor system brought severe problems, such as lack of cooperation, pilfering, and low productivity. Another element of African business philosophy that contributed to the failure of indigenous capitalism is the tendency to hand over the business to a son or a family member – even when the training, experience, and passion required were lacking.

According to Basil Enwegbara, the tendency for entrepreneurs to use business profits for luxury purchases – whether for fancy housing, cars, or expensive public donations to demonstrate wealth – caused not only financial problems related to the financing of day-to-day operations but also early collapses and exits from business. Capital shortages, low rates of return to investment, and poor capital accumulation served as a major barrier to the advancement of business. In addition, other obstructive tendencies associated with corruption, governmental hostility and indifference, and endless regulations and bureaucracy at all levels of government also limited the emergence of a strong African capitalist class.[1]

Thus Basil Enwegbara has argued that if African entrepreneurs are to have any hope of carving out a leading place in African economy, they must surmount three main hurdles. First, they must utilize higher levels of technology with proper training and specialization. Second, they must obtain greater degrees of organizational competence, and delegate authority and establish more impersonal systems of control. Third, they must establish wide-ranging market outlets based on an elaborate sales network and distribution system.

The research on entrepreneurship in general and its African variant in particular, has identified a number of external factors or constraints accounting for the success or failure of entrepreneurship. The external environment includes a number of factors such as local and national politics, the quality of public administration, society and culture. It also includes the financial and economic environment, market, technology, the physical environment, the regional and global economy and society and the prevailing industrial relations system. These external factors, many researchers have argued, present opportunities and threats which the individual entrepreneur must respond. The ability to transform these externalities into entrepreneurial resources depends on the entrepreneur's idiosyncrasies, namely individual attributes and skills and capabilities. Drawing on the experiences of recent political and macro-economic reforms in many parts of the globe, especially in India, it would appear that an enabling environment for entrepreneurial development is necessary, but not sufficient by itself, to sustain changes in entrepreneurial behavior and firm performance. The missing link here seems to be the competencies developed and acquired by the individual entrepreneur.

The relationship between education and skills training and entrepreneurial success leads us to examine the organizational and management context of entrepreneurship. In the context of Sub-Saharan Africa, studies have concluded that entrepreneurs who were good at organizing and presenting ideas in a sensible and logical way were more likely to be successful than those with poor organization of knowledge. Researchers such as Harrison and Friedrich found that the entrepreneurs with low education and little experience in their line of business, or those who lacked basic skills in bookkeeping and accounting were less successful.[2] Harper and Soon, drawing on various small enterprise case studies in developing countries concluded, "The skill and initiative of the individual entrepreneur are by far the most important determinants of success or failure."[3] Other researchers have indicated that African entrepreneurs were helped by university education, previous work experience, managerial, organizational, marketing, financial, and networking skills.[4]

The ability to manage a new venture and to organize the requisite resources for success is a key *entrepreneurial competence*. Competencies are the total sum of the entrepreneur's requisite attributes: attitudes, values, beliefs, knowledge, skills, abilities, personality, wisdom, expertise (social, technical, organizational, managerial), mindset, and behavioral tendencies needed for successful and sustaining entrepreneurship.[5] In the context of entrepreneurial undertaking, managerial capabilities determine strategy, formulate plans, design appropriate organizational arrangements, coordinate workflow through the value chain, and monitor firm performance. Productivity and the capacity to innovate, to introduce new technology, and to manage strategically are related to owner entrepreneurial competencies. Thus, management and organizational skills are a key entrepreneurial competence that is acquired and crucial for the success of an entrepreneurial firm. As pointed out by Moses Kiggundu, these competencies may relate to ability to access critical resources or contacts, internal management of the business, or external strategic management and networking, dealing with potential business threats or opportunities.[6] Although entrepreneurial competencies vary across time, place and stages of entrepreneurial development, they are nevertheless universally applicable within the context of entrepreneurial success. In fact, the term, entrepreneur, and its success factors (such as managerial capabilities) have been universalized.

As has been pointed out by a number of studies, one of the primary causes of business failure in Sub-Saharan Africa is the inability of business owners to properly manage the business from start to growth. Sometimes, the owner or manager of the small business does not have the knowledge or skill sets needed to operate it successfully. Sometimes, he or she lacks the leadership ability, sound judgment, and knowledge necessary to make the business work. Consequently, the transition from the entrepreneurial stage to the growth one is often very difficult. It is worth emphasizing here that what kills companies has less to do with insufficient money, talent, or information than with something more basic: a shortage of good judgment and understanding at the very top.

In a study on the determinants of small business growth constraints in a Sub-Saharan African economy by John Okpara and Pamela Wynn it was observed that 96 percent of those surveyed listed lack of managerial experience as a major problem. Other problems mentioned were: inadequate bookkeeping (94 percent of the respondents), lack of training (91 percent), poor location (90 percent) and withdrawing too much cash for personal use (81 percent).[7] These are all manifestations of weak or lack of managerial capabilities. In this chapter we will examine some of these management and organizational problems as they affect the success or profitability of small businesses in Sub-Saharan Africa.

For ease of presentation, the discussion in this chapter will be based upon a framework developed in earlier studies, which classifies the managerial and organizational context into three types of decisions and practices.[8] This framework categorized small-business problems as strategic, administrative and operating problems. Strategic problems involve the ability of small-business owners to develop appropriate strategic plans, strategies and tactics that match their product or service with the demands of the external environment in order to remain competitive. Administrative problems focus on the organizational structure, leadership of the enterprise and its ability to obtain and develop necessary resources (personnel, finance, management, etc) and ethical and social responsibility issues. As will be shortly discussed, the problem of succession and entrepreneurial leadership is particularly an inhibiting factor in terms of entrepreneurial development. Administrative problems also include personnel, finance, and management issues. Operating problems deal with allocating resources in an efficient manner and are more common in the functional areas of a business including marketing, pricing, inventory and location decisions and practices.

PLANNING FOR THE ENTERPRISE

Aversion to planning for the business has been seen as one of the foremost reasons for the high mortality rate among small businesses in Sub-Saharan Africa. Planning for the business, in general, is good for the firm. However, in the context of this book, we are referring to strategic planning at the firm's level. **Strategic planning**, in this context, is a management approach concerned with the long-term mission and objectives of a firm, the resources used in achieving those objectives, and the policies and guidelines that govern the acquisition, use, and disposition of those resources. Strategic planning at the firm level must also take into account the **Opportunities** available to the firm, and an assessment of its ability to exploit those opportunities with a view to gaining a distinct competitive advantage.

Too many small business owners and managers neglect the process of strategic planning because they think that it is something that only benefits large corporations. Common comments from small business owners include "we don't have the time to do strategic planning" or "strategic planning is an academic exercise." Failure to plan, however, usually results in failure to survive and to confront competitors. Without a clearly defined strategy, a business has no sustainable basis for creating and maintaining a competitive edge in the marketplace. Refusal or inability to develop business plan can only go well in an informal economic setting where most of business activities are undertaken as survivalist-strategies. In more formal economic context, planning strategically for the business is the recipe for competitive success.

Building a strategic plan forces an entrepreneur to assess realistically the viability or potential of a proposed business venture. Is the service or product that is offered something customers are willing and able to purchase? Who are the target customers? How will the business attract and keep those customers? What is the firm's basis for serving customers' needs better than existing companies? How will the business gain a sustainable edge over its rivals? How can the strengths of the firm be converted into a competitive advantage? How can the weaknesses of the firm be managed? How can the firm capitalize on opportunities and deal with threats in its environment? These are all relevant questions to which the average African business owner has no time to answer.

There are several reasons why business owners in Sub-Saharan Africa fail to develop strategic plans or engage in planning in general. The first reason relates to the cultural belief systems and practices, which see planning as an attempt to control external forces. In chapter four, it was noted that most cultures in Sub-Saharan Africa tend to avoid uncertainty and ambiguity. In such cultures, each day is accepted as it comes and people are not likely to show risk-taking and other future-directed activities that are commonly associated with entrepreneurial behavior such as planning and the development of business plans. Because fatalistic viewpoint prevails in many societies in Africa, "determinism," has become a part of the cultural fabric. Individuals influenced by this viewpoint believe that they cannot control their destiny, that God or some supernatural forces have predetermined their existence and willed what they are to do during their lives.

Such cultures, as was discussed earlier, are dominated by beliefs that are antithetical to planning for the future. Rational planning is either seen as foolish or dangerous because the correct approach is to live in existing systems, react in terms of one's experience, and not to try to change them by means of some scientific or rational means. As Weber pointed out, a rational economic ethos would not develop in such cultures owing to their belief in fatalism, excessive ritualism and reliance on supernatural. Planning and implementing entrepreneurial activities in these cultures is therefore difficult.

A second reason has already been mentioned, which is the belief that planning or strategic management is an exercise for large firms. This belief is the result of inadequacy of knowledge in the planning process. Not until recently, management education in most African countries was devoid of strategic management. In one study, Per Trulsson concludes that entrepreneurship in Tanzania is largely a matter of "muddling through" not with predefined decision rules such as equating marginal cost and revenue, but with "successive limited comparisons," which is an ad hoc response to things as they materialize.[9] In fact, it is possible to suggest that lack of planning has given rise to the *culture of imitation* (as opposed to the culture of innovation), which is so prevalent in the typical African business environment.

In one study detailing the causes of business failure in Uganda, the researcher reported that 17 percent of respondents listed lack of planning as a cause of businesses failure during their startup phases. In addition, less than a third prepare a formal business plan prior to starting up and 37 percent do not plan at all. The survey found that most businesses just start without plans. Small business owners end up with no set goals or targets to meet. The study also revealed that the cost for preparation of a simple business plan ranges from USD100-200. Small business owners looking for start up capital cannot manage this amount.[10]

ORGANIZATIONAL CHALLENGE AND MANAGING GROWTH

In Sub-Saharan Africa, there is no shortage of entrepreneurs or people willing to take risks to start business activities either in the informal or formal sectors. In either case, most of these business ventures are very small one-person operations mostly in the easy-to-enter trading and service sector, which is also the least profitable and requires minimum risk. In particular, these types of businesses constitute the informal sector and they provide only a limited range of services or products, and do not innovate either by way of new products and services or markets. The more the macroeconomic conditions worsen, the more of these micro enterprises open up because they are predominantly a push type. The basic problem confronting these businesses whether in the formal or informal sector is the inability to manage leadership and management succession and growth and the inability to manage the transition from small to medium or from informal business entity to a formal one.

In any organizational setting, there is always the need for succession. First, a "succession event" is the process of filling the vacancy of a top managerial or leadership position with a manager new to that position. Thus, managerial succession is the implementation of a new manager into the organizational structure. With change in the incumbency of a leadership position comes a new challenge of how to fill that role and position. Effective managerial and leadership succession means having a plan and making plans to create positive and coordinated flows of leadership across many years in the organization.

Every business organization must experience a leadership or managerial succession, the process by which key officials, especially the top managers, are replaced by others. Leaders and owners of businesses, like all human beings, are mortal. Therefore, it is imperative for any organization's long-term stability, survival and growth, to always look beyond the incumbent leader and develop strategies and create conditions for a smooth succession. One of the greatest challenges facing businesses in Sub-Saharan Africa today is the crisis of succession, that is, uncertainty about the future of the organization beyond the founder.[11]

Many studies indicate that African enterprises have very often died with their founders. Although this problem is not peculiar to African businesses, history is replete with business failures resulting from poor succession policies in Sub-Saharan Africa. In a recent study in Nigeria, one researcher found that although many of the founders of the businesses she studied had reached an age where the question of succession arises; many of them still did not have clear succession plans.[12] A study of Zimbabwean indigenous small-scale businesses indicated that succession had not yet become a serious issue for the business owners. Six out of the 10 businesses studied did not have a clear succession plan. While all the owners of the business knew the individuals whom they wanted to take over their businesses, only three of the business-owners had actually appointed those people to positions that would enable them to exercise a substantial amount of authority and responsibility to prepare them to take over in the event of a sudden death or incapacitation of the founder.[13] In a longitudinal study of the high rate of business mortality of small firms in Nigeria, Moribo and Kilby found that most of the closures were succession-related, occurring in the mature age of firms.[14]

The problem of the continuity of the business after the founder is thus very prevalent in Sub-Saharan Africa. The various explanations that have been given to account for this phenomenon are characterized by a dichotomy between a focus on the successor on the one hand, and a focus on the founder on the other. Those who focus on the successor have argued that businesses fail after the founder because the successor usually lacks the personality characteristics or other requisite skills of the founder. Those who focus on the founder have argued that the reasons why many businesses fail relate the founder's inability to plan for succession.[15]

Succession and the Problem of Entrepreneurial Leadership

Many organizations owe their existence to the individual efforts of entrepreneurs. New organizations are formed as entrepreneurs devote time and effort and assume personal financial, psychological, and social risks to introduce innovations. The formation and the survival of an organization during its formative stages might depend on the individual efforts and personality of its founder. As rightly pointed out by one researcher, the problem with entrepreneurial leadership, however, is that it is personalized. Entrepreneurs are visionaries who value the autonomy to make decisions as they see fit and to take personal responsibility for those decisions in order to realize their visions. As a result, entrepreneurial leaders tend to maximize control and shun delegation of authority and responsibility, preferring instead to directly carry out or to supervise most of the day-to-day operations of their organizations themselves.[16] Although this type of management allows entrepreneurs to offer personalized service or attention to their clients thus giving them a competitive advantage over large enterprises, it nevertheless skews delegation of authority and responsibility. Most seriously, this type of management does not provide room for planning for succession.

Another aspect that is intimately related to succession is the absence of delegation and sharing of responsibilities. As we know it, delegation is related to the expansion of the business. As the business expands, there is more division of labor and the entrepreneur has to be aware of the extent of the growth of the business so that division of labor, allocation of duties and responsibilities and delegation can be properly planned. However, the archetypal entrepreneur is the embodiment of the business with his or her own personal welfare being closely intertwined with that of the enterprise. This close identification of the business with its owner prevents the development of businesses into corporate identities with interests, which are distinct from those of their owners. The lack of separation between the individual owner's and organizational interests prevents the formation of shared responsibilities with others.[17] The refusal to accept shared responsibility is perhaps rooted in the lack of trust and a general suspicion that the other partner may be involved in secret "deals" with other persons or organizations at the expense of the company. The unwillingness to delegate authority for fear of sharing ownership and failure to form partnerships to pool finance and managerial skills are critical failure factors among African entrepreneurs.

Age of the Founder

The lack of attention to succession in indigenous African businesses has in some cases been attributed to the age of the founders. As reported by one researcher, young, first generation business owners are still too preoccupied with establishing and consolidating their businesses to think about succession. In the Zimbabwean study referred to above, 6 of the businesses studied (out of a total number of 10) did not have succession plans.[18] Wilier's study of indigenous firms in Nigeria found that in some instances, children were given the title of director at an early stage, even while still at school, but in 10 out of 13 cases, the potential successor did not act even as a mere assistant to the director. Sometimes, the African entrepreneur refuses to accept his or her mortality. When he or she does, however, the issue of succession is left for fate to decide.[19] In the study conducted by France Maphosa, one business owner responded to the issue of succession thus: "…Well if God decides to take me early then that would be unfortunate. But you cannot always be thinking about death and accidents, otherwise you cannot do anything".[20]

Lack of preparation and grooming potential successors following the age of the founder is a typical problem. In some businesses, the owners indicated that they preferred their spouses or children to take over their businesses without preparing these for succession. As pointed out by Tom Forrest, the problem with the choice of spouses and children as successors is that most of these would-be successors often come too late into the business, and in some cases, after the death of the incumbent owner/manager.[21] In many instances, although spouses, especially wives of businessmen, may be registered as partners, they often assume little or no authority or responsibility to meaningfully prepare them for succession. In cases were children are selected as successors, some of them would still be very young. This makes the future of the business very precarious in the event of the sudden death of its founder.

Self-employment and Prestige

Another reason for unsuccessful successions in indigenous African businesses identified by a researcher, Volker Wild, is the low prestige accorded a career in business by second generations compared to professions such as medicine and law. As an important status symbol, the acquisition of formal education has always been the pursuit of many children of business owners as well as their parents. The dream of many second generation-educated children is to gain employment in the more prestigious professions such as banking, multinational corporations or in the civil service.[22] Secondly, the colonial legacy of the prestige accorded to membership in the political class or employment in the civil service still holds sway today in many parts of Sub-Saharan Africa. In the African context, many people go into business because success in business activities is recognized as the gateway to the political class. In other words, most Africans who moved into the private sector did so with some sense of reluctance, and wanted to join the political class as soon as they could. The consequence of this is that as soon as these entrepreneurs entered into politics, sooner than later, their businesses, like their political fate, become victims of the political culture – victimization, closure and early death.

Traditional Practices

Traditional practices that interfere with smooth succession in small- and medium-scale African firms include those associated with polygamy and inheritance. At the death of a polygamous businessman the tendency is towards the subdivision of the business assets among the many wives and children as well as other relatives. Even in monogamous families the subdivision of the business assets among numerous relatives has often been inevitable. In many instances, tradition refuses the widow from inheriting a business left behind by a deceased husband. In one study, it was reported that at the death of a businessman the relatives fell on the legacy and divided it against themselves and left the widow penniless.[23]

Tradition may influence the selection of the heir even if he or she is unsuitable for the position. The strength of the relations between the founder of a business and his or her relatives determines the latter's influence on the selection of the successor to the founder. This is especially true in cases where the founder has received assistance from relatives especially initial capital to help set up the business. In the study by France Maphosa, it is reported that the receipt of financial assistance from relatives is likely to complicate the succession process. This results from the numerous demands on the organization by relatives who might feel that they have a stake in the business because of the assistance they gave. These demands might include the appointment of a relative a successor even though he or she might not be the best qualified for the job.[24] The high failure rate among businesses in Sub-Saharan Africa is also due to the inability of owner-managers to properly provide a will specifying how business assets are to be shared among family members at the death of the owners. Monibo Sam provides an account of how many Nigerian family-owned firms had to close because when the owners died, the siblings, from polygamous families, could not agree among themselves on how to settle the estate without dissolving the businesses.[25]

The mechanism and process of inter-generational transfer of wealth in many Sub-Saharan Africa cultures are also detrimental for an effective succession. First-male children (or those born by the first wife) as heirs, are given ownership control and management of an enterprise without having both the ability and the inclination to go into business and the type of business he or she is called upon to take over. In some studies there is ample evidence to suggest that the selection of some successors was influenced by traditional and sentimental factors. Older male children were the most preferred would-be successors. This is in line with some traditional African customs where, for instance, "the oldest son — provided he was of age — would, as the future head of the family, inherit the father's fortune."[26]

Delegation and Succession

As pointed out previously, effective delegation is a necessary condition for a smooth succession. This is because delegating some of the owner/manager's authority and responsibilities to the possible successor prepares the latter and the subordinates for the eventual takeover. In large organizations, the succession process is generally routinized through the use of rules regulating retirement, rotation, and promotion of officials. In large organizations the succession event is less likely to be disruptive as there are laid-down principles and guidelines that guide the selection process. In such organizations, delegation of authority, duties and responsibilities becomes an indispensable condition for a smooth succession. Even in the event of a sudden death or incapacitation of an incumbent manager, an organization, which has been encouraging delegation of power and responsibilities, is less likely to experience serious instability during succession than one, which does not.

One of the characteristics of African small businesses is that they are generally small and are run for the most part as informal structures without rules and regulations. Where there are rules, they tend be built around the personality of the owner/manager. These characteristics, coupled with the autocratic leadership characteristic of the owners, are likely to render the succession process in the organizations unpredictable and more likely to be disruptive.

Extended Family Demands and Inefficient Organizational Arrangements

Although there are many entrepreneurial activities and firms in Africa, most of these are very small in size and have remained small, which makes them vulnerable. Failure rates are quite high, especially in the first two to five years.[27] As pointed out in the preceding discussion, the high mortality rates among African start-ups are due to the problems of management and lack of organizing skills. Inability to understand and apply sound management skills makes the business suffers partly as a result of neglect and other extra extended social obligations. In particular, the demand of the phenomenon of extended family relations, which is embedded in the African society, places considerable social and economic costs on businesses owned by Africans. Samuel Buame provides an excellent example of the interplay between entrepreneurial practices and institutionalized obligations to relations about a Ghanaian entrepreneur. According to the researcher, a Ghanaian entrepreneur had to relocate his business away from his hometown at great expense in order to protect his business interest because; as he puts it "it is your closest people who seek your downfall through superstitious means."[28]

In addition to managerial competencies of the entrepreneur, entrepreneurship requires effective and dynamic organizational arrangements in order to remain successful. Such arrangements are needed for mobilizing, organizing, utilizing, protecting and developing resources, keeping in place strategic plans and sustaining beneficial networks. Thus, several studies have pointed out that African entrepreneurs experience serious difficulties in developing and sustaining effective organizational arrangements, especially as the business moves from the informal to the formal; when it faces external threats such as new technology and fluctuations in the political or macroeconomic environment; during succession or when facing regional or global competition. These constraints constitute a serious obstacle to entrepreneurial development and the implementation of strategies or any actions needed for survival, growth and competitiveness.[29] It is precisely as a result of these reasons that the graduation rate from micro- to more complex modern entrepreneurial- and medium-sized enterprises is lower in Africa than elsewhere.

The Challenge of Managing Growth and Complexity

Expansion usually requires major changes in organizational structure and culture, business practices such as inventory and financial control procedures, personnel assignments, and other areas. But the most important change occurs in managerial expertise. As the business increases in size and complexity, problems increase in magnitude, and the entrepreneur must learn to deal with them. Sometimes entrepreneurs encourage rapid growth, only to have the business outstrip their ability to manage it. The transition from the entrepreneurial phase is always faced with numerous organizational problems to the extent that the entrepreneurial culture must give way to a different culture that can sustain the growth of the firm. The process of this transition usually requires a radically different style of management than the one associated with entrepreneurial style. The reason is that the very abilities that make an entrepreneur successful often lead to managerial ineffectiveness. Growth requires entrepreneurs to delegate authority and to relinquish hands-on control of daily operations - something many business owners simply cannot do or unwilling to do. Growth pushes them into areas where they are not capable, yet they continue to make decisions rather than involve others.

One major feature of the African entrepreneur is the tendency to branch out into other businesses without first putting an existing one in a strong competitive position. The conventional practice by many African business owners in which unrelated business lines are set up without a focus on strategic competencies has led to inability to identify and concentrate on the growth of profitable businesses. But by shutting out the benefits of growth through concentration, they in fact ended up with total assets of a lower net value than might otherwise have attained.

THE CHALLENGE OF HUMAN RESOURCE MANAGEMENT

Human resources are very important for enterprise growth and this becomes increasingly important the larger the organization becomes in size. A good manager will pick the right people, ensure that the staff gets the right incentives, and maintain adequate controls. He or she will also make sure that complacency in work performance does not spread throughout the organization. In the context of Sub-Saharan Africa, many business owners face human resources problem as a result of several reasons such as the practice of hiring friends and relatives, lack of employee training and lack of motivational incentives.

Employing Friends and Relatives

Employing members of the "extended family" is a fundamental aspect of the labor market in Sub-Saharan Africa. In fact, there appears a lot of ambiguities on the part of the Africa business owner in terms of his or her approach to human resource and financial management. One researcher, Per Trulsson, provides an excellent example of this ambiguity and inconsistency about the entrepreneurs in his study. In one case, there was a business owner who purchased laborsaving technologies while at the same time employing a large number of his family members who were not needed. In a second case, there was a businessman who was a producer of plastic containers. According to Per Trulsson, this man was using his business profits paying for the education of 35 children belonging to his family.[30] Significantly, the profit motive expressed by many African entrepreneurs is subjected to a host of other priorities that have no bearing on the survival of the business enterprise.

Studies have indicated that some owners/managers employ family members simply because of kinship relations. In some cases, these have turned out to be undisciplined and ineffectual, a factor that has led to eventual and sometimes rapid failure of businesses.[31] As has been pointed out, this kind of personal preference for a paternalistic labor system brought severe problems, such as lack of cooperation, pilfering, and low productivity.

Lack of Training

Many studies have also indicated that majority of African small business owners see their employees as inputs rather than as human resources. As a result, most employees are not trained except the traditional form of apprenticeship training in which the knowledge of the employee is limited to what the owner/manager can possibly offer from past experiences. It should be noted that although such traditional apprenticeship training has its advantages in the informal sector, it perpetuates traditional technologies and lacks standards and quality assurance. Second, traditional apprenticeship training lacks the knowledge base necessary to produce innovative products and services. Seeing the value of having a well-trained and committed staff, successful enterprises are generally more prone to invest in the development of employee skills. However, many small-scale enterprises do not only fail to provide employees with on-the-job training, they also fail to send their employees for training outside of the company.

LEADERSHIP, AUTHORITY RELATIONS AND THE CHALLENGE OF EMPLOYEE MOTIVATION

Studies that have examined leadership, authority relations, and employee motivation in the context of Sub-Saharan Africa have for the most part anchored their analyses on the relationship between culture and leadership behavior or styles. According to this research and literature, African culture has high power distance (the degree of inequality among people which the population of a country considers as normal); values collectivism, avoids uncertainty, and a strong humane orientation. It should be noted that in spite of the pluralistic cultures and ethnic orientations, there is tendency among researchers in this tradition to homogenize Africa, while overlooking the diversity of cultures within countries and across the continent. However, among those researchers that have contextualized their studies, a common theme regarding African organizational leadership and its motivational basis emerges. Significantly, the picture of the African organizational leadership is that of leadership and authority relations in which the criteria for role recruitment and allocation are ascriptive rather than achievement oriented; quality for official and organizational relations are diffuse, paternalistic and based on personal loyalty as against specific functions and impersonal loyalty; criteria for organizational membership and participation are particularistic rather than universalistic; and the criteria for distribution of reward are based on privilege and status rather than performance, skills, and contribution to objective goals. Essentially, the type of organizational leadership and managers that emerge from such a context exhibit the qualities commonly associated with the benevolent autocrat, the paternalistic authority figure and the authoritarian manager.[32]

In terms of cultural relativity, some have argued that African management thought is characterized by a strong belief in the individual's relation to nature and supernatural beings and connections between the individual and ancestors.[33] On this basis, some have proceeded with the argument that the continuity from the material to the spiritual is the universal basis of African management thought.[34] Attributes of managers and business owners operating within this system would be expected to reflect societal practices and expectations. With a control orientation, refusal to delegate authority, reliance on traditional wisdom, and a self-perpetuating inputs orientation, Terrence Jackson argues that managers who fit in well could be expected to be motivated by control features of their jobs and economic security.[35] While little research has been undertaken on management motivation in Africa, the few studies that have examined leadership and authority relations in the continent do provide preliminary insights into the motivational basis of organizational members in the area.

The direction of employee commitment to the goals of the organization and the motivational basis can thus be derived from the above discussion. For example, an indication of a commitment to a business objective involves the extent of an employee's personal loyalty to the superior, owner or manager. Now, since rewards are tied to privilege and status, the motivational basis is that of kinship connection rather than on performance and on achievement. This may reflect an ethical disregard for wider stakeholders and a pursuit of company objectives only insofar as they meet personal goals and objectives.[36] The identification with personal figure in place of the objective goals of the organization leads to a situation where the dynamics promoting a sense of organizational citizenship is weak.

The consequences of a weak organizational citizenship among African employees are manifested in lack of commitment to the achievement of organizational goals, apathy, graft, bribery and corruption, pilfering, theft, misappropriation of fund, low morale and high employee turnover. As a consequence, practices that are antithetical to the productivity of firms such as employee alienation are widely recognized and conspicuous within the administration of organizations in Africa.[37] Thus, it is possible to suggest that motivation and organizational commitment may be tied to what individuals get not directly connected with the performance of the job, but with their identification with the authority figure. There is also evidence, from the discussion above, of family influence in organizations, and commitment or motivation of workers may well be directed to these family connections. Thus, the absence of organizational citizenship, (the extent to which an individual's voluntary support and behavior contributes to the organization's success) among many employees is related to non-identification with the goals/objectives of the organization.[38]

In a study that investigates the effects of societal culture on group organizational citizenship behavior (GOCB), and the moderating role of culture on the relationship between directive and supportive leadership and GOCB, Martin Euwema finds out that individualism and power distance affect the degree to which members are organizationally committed. Directive leadership had a negative relation, and supportive leadership a positive relation with group organizational citizenship behavior. According to this researcher, culture moderated this relationship: Directive leadership was more negatively, and supportive behavior less positively, related to GOCB in individualistic compared to collectivistic societies.[39]

Reward systems that are based on paternalistic, authoritarian and benevolent organizational and leadership practices (family-ties, friendship, gifts or even bribery) may be discriminatory as a result of preferences given to in-group or family members. Such a system is also capable of breeding alienation among employees. Similarly, this may lead to organizational and management decisions based on relationships rather than the application of universal rules, and may therefore be regarded as discriminatory. In such a situation, too, promotion is by ascription (who you are rather than what you have achieved).[40] A reflection also of the **Theory X** nature of management and general distrust of human nature, as well as a lack of organizational democracy may be revealed in policies geared toward "employee motivation" or management policies aimed at duties of workers rather than of rights.[41]

Not surprising, the working relationship between managers/owners in such organizational and management situations may be revealed in employee alienation. Poor motivation, risk aversion and unwillingness to take independent action; close supervision of subordinates with little delegation; operations often inefficient and high cost with low productivity, over-staffing, under-utilizations, poor pay and poor morale indicated by high turnover and absenteeism, are all features of such organizations.[42]

Some researchers have argued that the autocratic authority relations prevailing in organizations in many African countries may well reflect also a mistrust of human nature, and a belief in the undisciplined nature of African workers to industrial life. Others have also pointed out that because action is focused on the short term, success orientation may be moralistic rather than pragmatic. This may reflect a lack of achievement orientation and a status orientation as a management principle. Since a passive-reactive orientation is assumed in this context, an authority and leadership relation based on a **Theory X** conception dominates the attitudes of owners and employees.[43]

Generally speaking, the system of management and leadership styles that are peculiar to Africa seem to reflect a **Theory X** style of management (from McGregor) which generally mistrusts human nature with a need to impose controls on workers, allowing little worker initiative, and rewarding a narrow set of skills simply by financial means. To be sure, **Theory X** Management assumes that employees are inherently lazy and will avoid work if they can. Because of this, workers need to be closely supervised and comprehensive systems of controls developed. A hierarchical structure is needed with narrow span of control at each level. According to this theory, employees will show little ambition without an enticing incentive program and will avoid responsibility whenever they can. Managers that subscribe to **Theory X** tend to take a rather pessimistic view of their employees. A **Theory X** manager believes that his or her employees do not really want to work, that they would rather avoid responsibility and that it is the manager's job to structure the work and energize the employee. The result of this line of thought is that **Theory X** managers naturally adopt a more authoritarian style based on the threat of punishment. On the other hand, **Theory Y** Management assumes employees *may be* ambitious, self-motivated, anxious to accept greater responsibility, and exercise self-control, self-direction, autonomy and empowerment. It is believed that if given the chance employees have the desire to be creative and forward thinking in the workplace. There is a chance for greater productivity by giving employees the freedom to perform at the best of their abilities without being bogged down by rules. A **Theory Y** manager believes that, given the right conditions, most people will want to do well at work and that there is a pool of unused creativity in the workforce.

The prevalence of **Theory X** Management in African organizations as the basis for motivational practices and as a system of management control is widely accepted in the existing literature. For many of these studies, management and leadership practice in many instances privileges authoritarian management styles with reliance on the hierarchy, use of rank, low egalitarianism, and a lack of openness in communication and information giving.[44]

Thus, the problem of authority relations and motivation among small-scale enterprises in Sub-Saharan Africa is often manifested in the unwillingness of supervisors or superiors to delegate to subordinates. Owners tend to manage these businesses themselves as a measure of either reducing operational costs or inability to trust subordinates to run the affairs of the enterprise. One particular study conducted in Uganda provided the example of a businessperson who locks the shop for a full day whenever he goes shopping in Kampala. He does this once every week, a total of four days a month. One result of this is loss of customer loyalty.[45]

BUSINESS ETHICS AND SOCIAL RESPONSIBILITY

One of the most frequently forgotten causes of business failure in Sub-Saharan Africa in the literature is the devastating effect of unethical business practices on the part of business owners. Most often, researchers focus their studies and analyses on the negative impact of bribery and corruption at the official level (such as official bribery and corruption) without considering how unethical business practices, lack of social responsibility and inability to manage stakeholders from the enterprise level negatively affect the survival of enterprises owned by Africans. In fact, very few studies have suggested that lacking a sense of citizenship and social responsible obligations, the typical Africa businessman perpetuates and reinforces the dynamics of illegality in his or her business relationship with the firm's various stakeholders. Because many African business owners do not understand nor appreciate the value of a stakeholder analysis, people do not adequately understand the impact of their business practices on society at large. On a more serious note, most business owners do not understand how unethical business practices and lack of social responsibility negatively impact on the long-term survivability and profitability of the firm.

It is unfortunate that the extant literature on business enterprise within the context of Sub-Saharan Africa rarely touches upon the important subject of stakeholder analysis. In Africa, particularly in Nigeria, there are abundant examples of businesses that have failed not because they were not founded on solid financial ground (profitable), but because their owners were arrested for corrupt practices or politically victimized as a result of their relationship between corrupt government officials and business dealings with their stakeholder bordering on illegality. In the context of Sub-Saharan Africa, unethical business conduct is manifested in various forms such as in deceptive marketing practices and deceptive packaging, including the practice of offering fake products to unsuspecting customers.

One thing that is increasingly rare among African business owners is the practice of "giving back to the community." In many developed countries, philanthropic endeavors have been associated with promoting good corporate image among business owners. This is not to deny the altruistic motives of the givers. With the exceptions of very few entrepreneurs, the typical African business owner does not embark on goodwill efforts that promote the image of a business, except to engage in excessive display of wealth. In the typical African business culture, business success is measured in terms of acquisition of societal and traditional titles and perks that have nothing to do with the growth of the business. At the extreme, wealth acquired through illegal means is used to further perpetuate illegal economic activities on a grander scale. The conventional practice whereby business owners use business profits for luxury purchases – whether for fancy housing, cars or extra wives and concubines to demonstrate wealth – caused not only financial problems related to the financing of day-to-day operations but also early collapses and exits from business.

As pointed out by a number of studies, illicit, improper, or illegal business conduct that are used to criminalize entrepreneurial activities undermines the trust and confidence of business owners which is also required in order to secure customers' patronage.[46] As an example, it is not difficult to see the dilemma of the African entrepreneur who intends to do business within or outside of Africa as a result of the fraudulent practices of money extortions by Nigerian conmen: the phenomenon commonly referred to as "419." Many studies have also shown that the pervasiveness of corruption and unethical business practices in Sub-Saharan Africa has a great cost to entrepreneurs, the economy, public administration, and society.

CASE IN POINT: NIGERIAN ADVANCED FEE FRAUD, AKA 4-1-9.[47]

The Nigerian Advance Fee Scheme (also known internationally as "4-1-9" fraud after the section of the Nigerian penal code which addresses fraud schemes) is generally targeted at small and medium sized businesses, as well as charities. This global scam involves the receipt of an unsolicited letter purporting to come from someone who claims to work for the Nigerian Central Bank or from the Nigerian government. (The Central Bank of Nigeria denies all connection to those who promote this scheme.) In the letter, a Nigerian claiming to be a senior civil servant will inform the recipient that he is seeking a reputable foreign company into whose account he can deposit funds ranging from $10-$60 million which the Nigerian government overpaid on some procurement contract.

The goal of the scam artist is to delude the victim into thinking that he or she has been singled out to participate in a very lucrative (although questionable) arrangement. The intended victim is reassured of the authenticity of the arrangement by forged or false documents bearing apparently official Nigerian government letterhead, seals, as well as false letters of credit, payment schedules and bank drafts. The scam artist may even establish the credibility of his contacts, and thereby his influence, by arranging a meeting between the victim and "government officials" in real or fake government offices. Once the victim becomes confident of the potential success of the deal, something goes wrong. The victim is then pressured or threatened to provide one or more large sums of money to save the venture. For example, an official will demand an up-front bribe or an unforeseen tax or fee to the Nigerian government will have to be paid before the money can be transferred. Each fee paid is described as the very last fee required. The scheme may be stretched out over many months.

Institutionalization of Illegality

The institutionalization of illegality among businessmen is also detrimental to the development of a viable entrepreneurial culture. In a study of the Nigerian illegal cross-border trade, Fadahunsi and Rosa point out that that illegal practices are so widespread that they are a norm, an almost parallel economy with its own traditions and values. Furthermore, the "entrepreneurial advantages" of trading in illegal goods and evading duties appear overwhelming, as bribery of officials is widely accepted, which reduces risk of law enforcement to negligible levels, and most traders do not view illegal trading as immoral. In addition, traders need to bribe to trade any goods, legal as well as illegal. Consequently, bribery becomes a part of a system of harassment by officials that pervades all aspects of the trade. In this climate, there are no special advantages in targeting illegal goods to trade in. As the distinction between what is legal and illegal becomes blurred and irrelevant, even those with the best of motives are pushed or pulled into illegality. As pointed out by the researchers, traders target any goods irrespective of their legal status if potential profit margins are high. Similarly, most entrepreneurial energy is devoted to creatively circumvent the harassment of corrupt officials, in addition to exploiting illegal business opportunities.[48] Thus, the illegality of the trade is of some benefit in that it has created hundreds of associated jobs and businesses, which enable traders to operate more securely and efficiently in the climate of corruption, harassment, and uncertainty. In spite of the "benefits" of institutionalized illegal trading, illegality is more harmful than beneficial for economic development. Second, illegal practices are more tolerant of the informal economic sector and inhibit the transformation of an economic system into a more formal one capable of competing in a more formal and global context.

In general, the issue of business ethics and social responsibility is crucial to the emergence of a modern entrepreneurial class of business owners in the context of Sub-Saharan Africa. As acutely pointed out by Kiggundu, questions of corporate strategic management, accountability, transparency, responsibility to stakeholders (especially creditors and shareholders), social responsibility, and compliance with incorporation regulations such as disclosure rules remain problematic among the emerging African entrepreneurial class.[49] Many organizations, including NOGs and especially the World Bank have recognized the need for African businesses to operate in a more ethical and social responsibility environment, and among other things, have established mechanisms for improving the ethical business climate by promoting entrepreneurial accountability, transparency, responsibility and fairness.[50]

Coupled with bribery and corruption, the unethical business environment in most parts of Sub-Saharan Africa allows inefficient producers to remain in business and encourages governments to pursue perverse economic policies. Unethical business practices, bribery and corruption provide opportunities to civil servants and politicians to enrich themselves through extorting bribes from those seeking government favors. Consequently, unethical business practices and corruption distort economic incentives, discourages entrepreneurship, and slows economic growth.

WEAK CORPORATE GOVERNANCE AND POOR INVESTMENT OPPORTUNITY

Corporate governance is one of the key elements in improving economic efficiency and growth as well as enhancing investor confidence in any economy. In the case of Sub-Saharan Africa, it is widely recognized that massive institutionalized graft and corruption arising from weak corporate governance mechanism has retarded the region's economic, corporate and entrepreneurial development. In particular, weak corporate governance environments in Sub-Saharan Africa have yielded poor investment opportunities in the sub-continent. In many parts of Sub-Saharan Africa, with the notable exception of South Africa and Botswana, there is a lack of concrete achievable strategies for improving transparency, accountability and consequently investor confidence for the region has been on the decrease. Many business owners in the region, in active collaboration with state officials, are culpable for the tremendous capital flight from Africa as a result of weak corporate governance mechanism. First, what is corporate governance and why is it important for economic and entrepreneurial development?

Corporate governance is the system by which companies are directed and controlled, including the roles of the board of directors, management, shareholders, and other stakeholders. Corporate governance, according to the Organization for Economic Cooperation and Development (OECD) involves a set of relationships between a company's management, its board, its shareholders and other stakeholders. Corporate governance also provides the structure through which the objectives of the company are set, and the means of attaining those objectives and monitoring performance are determined. Good corporate governance should provide proper incentives for the board and management to pursue objectives that are in the interests of the company and its shareholders and should facilitate effective monitoring. The presence of an effective corporate governance system, within an individual company and across an economy as a whole, helps to provide a degree of confidence that is necessary for the proper functioning of a market economy. As a result, the cost of capital is lower and firms are encouraged to use resources more efficiently, thereby underpinning growth.[51]

In a narrower perspective, some authors see corporate governance as dealing "with the way in which suppliers of finance to corporations assure themselves of getting a return on their investment."[52] According to James D. Wolfensohn (former president of the World Bank), "Corporate Governance is about promoting corporate fairness, transparency and accountability."[53]

In any case, corporate governance deals with a set of procedures, mechanisms or principles to be followed for the good of shareholders, employees, customers, bankers and indeed for the reputation and standing of a nation and its economy. It is a relationship between a company's management and the company's shareholders, as well as a relationship between company's conduct and society. According to Charles Okeahalam and Oludele Akinboade, corporate governance is concerned with creating a balance between economic and social goals and between individual and communal goals while encouraging efficient use of resources, accountability in the use of power and stewardship and aligning the interests of individuals, corporations and society. It also encompasses the establishment of an appropriate legal, economic and institutional environment that allows companies to thrive as institutions for advancing long-term shareholder value and maximum human-centered development while remaining conscious of their other responsibilities to stakeholders, the environment and the society in general.[54]

The point of corporate governance is to ensure that management and majority shareholders at companies behave in a manner that balances the profit motive with the interests of minority shareholders and other stakeholders. Significantly, entrepreneurs and owners of businesses recognize the value of following good corporate governance principles, understanding that it can help companies to attract funding from domestic and international investors – indeed, most serious investors insist on it. There is strong evidence companies with good corporate governance are more likely to be profitable and sustainable than ones without it. Concern for shareholders, employees, the broader community and the environment improve profitability rather than damage it.

As appropriately pointed out by Charles Okeahalam and Oludele Akinboade, Africa is traditionally viewed as a high-risk continent by international investors. It is often believed that African economies are characterized by macro-economic instability, trade restrictions, weak institutional environment regarding property rights and the judicial system, and high state regulation of economic activities. In effect, countries that fail to establish acceptable standards of transparency and governance, within the bounds of good laws and an efficient criminal justice system, will lose the trust and support of their citizens and the international community. Such countries will find it increasingly difficult to attract trade and foreign investment. Foreign investors will comfortably assess political risk, business risk, market risk and currency risk but they will shy away from the risks of lawlessness and the corruption that too often results from poor governance.[55]

In this era of globalization, many commentators have seen Africa as rife with risk and opportunity for international investors. On the one hand, countries throughout the continent offer explosive economic growth and the potential for high returns. On the other, impenetrable legislation in many countries, coupled with poor corporate governance has spelled disaster for so many investors who are less knowledgeable about the prevailing business environment. As pointed out by Ayisi Makatiani, CEO of the African Management Services Company, African businesses, particularly SMEs, have not always understood the value of corporate governance, since adopting best practices can seem expensive and complicated for small businesses in a growth phase. A lack of confidence in corporate governance standards and legal frameworks in many African countries is a major reason that there is a mere trickle rather than a flood of foreign investment into the continent's private sector.[56]

According to Makatiani, many African businesses are family-owned and operated. These enterprises are managed along informal lines rather than operated in adherence to corporate governance best practices. These businesses are not run transparently, and the interests of management and/or majority shareholders are sometimes put above those of minority shareholders and other stakeholders such as employees, consumers, the general public and creditors. Particularly in some African countries, a combination of poor records, weak property rights and protections might mean that ownership of a certain piece of land could be disputed by several people in a long legal process that ends with someone who has just paid thousands of dollars for the property losing out. That could mean a costly financial investigation before an investor feels comfortable putting money on the table.[57]

In the context of Sub-Saharan Africa, several elements associated with good corporate governance are simply weak or absent. These corporate governance elements include internal and external audits, risk management, succession planning, minority shareholder rights, disclosure of information to analysts and shareholders, as well as compliance with legislation, stock exchange regulations and industry regulatory frameworks, and so on. Other important issues in corporate governance such as ethical business conduct, health and environmental standards and non-discriminatory hiring policies are questionable in many parts of Africa. While many countries and organizations in Sub-Saharan Africa are doing a great deal to win trust from potential investors, some African governments need to tackle some basic gaps in the detail and enforcement of their legal frameworks. For example, property rights in many African countries remain weak.

In developing and enforcing corporate governance principles, the African situation is peculiar and difficult precisely because African economies are very much transition economies. Some of the peculiarities include: the existence of a large number of state-owned enterprises, the culture of corruption or the pursuit of easy wealth, the weak nature of businesses environment, and low financial intermediation, among others.[58]

Corruption has been seen as one of the reasons behind weak corporate governance in Africa. A KPMG survey of more than 400 Chief Executive Officers (CEOs) and chief financial officers, released in June 2002, strongly suggested that fraud and corruption in business are on the rise in East Africa. Fraud was considered a major problem by 61 percent of respondents and 88 percent said their companies had suffered from fraud during the previous year. Weak internal controls and corporate governance were seen as a key factor.[59]

One prerequisite for a strong and effective system of corporate governance is the presence of effective financial system in a nation. For example, effective financial systems provide financial intermediaries that channel saving into long-term assets that are more productive than short-term assets. The financial system facilitates portfolio diversification for savers and investors. As a nation's financial system develops, more choices are offered to investors, allowing them to allocate resources in more productive activities. Furthermore, a nation's financial system collects, processes and evaluates information about investment projects more effectively and less expensively than individual investors because of the economies of scale. As a result, the overall cost of investment declines, which stimulates economic growth. In most developed countries, capital markets and/or stock exchanges perform these financial functions and intermediation. A corollary to this argument is that low financial development or distortions in the financial system increase the cost of investment and thus retard economic growth. Most importantly, in the context of this discussion, an efficient financial system such as a strong and effective capital market and/or stock exchange begets an environment of strong corporate governance. Stock exchanges and commercial/industrial associations have an important role to play in encouraging businesses to adopt sound corporate governance and persuading governments to put the right frameworks in place to create a climate of confidence and certainty for investors.[60]

Many organizations acting as custodians of corporate governance in Sub-Saharan Africa such as chambers of commerce, stock exchanges, bankers' institutes, accounting associations are still in their infancy. In many African economies, the financial systems are poorly developed and unsophisticated, and there are fewer investment opportunities, implying a higher probability that resources are wasted on unproductive uses. Most African capital markets are still tiny, illiquid and fledgling, which makes external monitoring more costly and prone to error. The average number of listed companies on Sub-Saharan African stock markets excluding South Africa is 39 compared with 113, with the inclusion of Egypt and South Africa. Market capitalization as a percentage of GDP is as low as 1.4 in Uganda. The Johannesburg Securities Exchange in South Africa has about 90 percent of the combined market capitalization of the entire continent. Excluding South Africa and Zimbabwe the average market capitalization is about 27 percent of GDP. This is in contrast with other emerging markets like Malaysia with a capitalization ratio of about 161 percent.[61] Indeed, the Nigerian Stock Exchange (NSE), ranked second among Sub-Saharan exchanges in 2006, had a market capitalization of approximately N4 trillion or $31.5 billion (equivalent to 6.1 percent of gross domestic product) with about 282 enrolled companies.[62] The consequence of a poorly developed and inefficient capital market as in the case of Sub-Saharan Africa implies that African economies are still bereft of poor corporate governance. With poor corporate governance, African entrepreneurs in need of investment capital are at disadvantageous position.

MARKETING CHALLENGES

Enterprises that grow do so because they are good at finding their market niche and understanding market demands. Most enterprises start by targeting the home market and as the home market becomes saturated, they look to expand their markets geographically or by targeting new untapped customer groups. There are several reasons why businesses do not grow and one of them is the inability to identify market and demand trends. A second related reason is the inability to master the fundamentals of marketing. In one study on African entrepreneurship, the researcher provides several examples of enterprises that, at least for a period of time, stopped growing because they did not keep up with market developments. Other issues identified include the inability to adequately identify their market niches and how to exploit them. Many small businesses in the region are known to lack information on a number of issues, such as market, technology and suppliers. In addition, most business owners fail to appreciate the importance of putting the customer first and what that implies for their operations.[63]

Another related marketing problem is that of poor market research and poor marketing effort. In many Sub-Sahara African countries, there is a pervasive belief that a good product or service automatically sells itself. Consequently, most small business owners are often unwilling to invest in marketing their products or services through promotion and advertisement. In addition, there is the problem related to the inability to perform adequate market research before plunging into the business. Many small business owners are unable to define their target market, the special needs of their prospective customers or the attractiveness of the market overtime. Building a growing base of customers requires a sustained, creative marketing effort. Keeping customers coming back requires providing them with value, quality, service, and timely deliveries. The inherent motive among African small business owners to acquire financial wealth with a minimum of efforts propels them into engaging in sharp and dubious practices by selling fake products to their customers.

A number of studies have reported that lack of sales is a major predicament during the inception of small businesses in Sub-Saharan Africa. This is because most of these businesses lack the competence of challenging already established businesses. In a study of small business failures in Uganda, Charles Tushabomwe-Kazooba reports that Ugandan small businesses usually lack a public image and business owners start enterprises without careful regard to the location of the business; thus less sales and less profits and this delays growth. Furthermore, the owners and managers of these small-scale enterprises do not undertake any form of market study in order to test the acceptability of the quality of goods and/or serves offered to customers. In addition, most of the small business owners or managers do not understand the scope and use of marketing knowledge and most of them are not always present in the business to attend to customers and answer their queries.[64]

In the study, it is also reported that the problem of pricing was prominent among the startup reasons of small-scale business failure. Owners lack the capacity to ascertain best prices and they tended to operate at high prices in relation to already existing businesses. This tends to drive away most customers to their competitors who are already in the business and maneuver at lower costs. Among the business owners, faulty products were also identified as an additional startup problem. Since most new business owners are not experienced in the sector, they are not normally familiar with the condition of the products they purchase. Consequently, products, which do not suit the tastes of the customers, remain in stores thus tying up working capital.[65]

In a survey of management issues confronting business owners in South Africa, Louise van Scheers and Simon Radipere wanted to know whether market-related issues have impact on the respondents' businesses. Most of the respondents in the study believed that a lack of knowledge of market related issues could have a negative impact on their businesses. A lack of knowledge about competitors seems to have the largest impact on the success of small businesses. About 88 percent believe that low product demand can have an impact on the success of a business. Respondents also believe that ineffective marketing and a poor locality (84 and 85 percent respectively) can have a negative impact on the success of their business.[66]

In a study of small-scale manufacturing in Kenya, some researchers provided evidence that in the area of business management, the most noteworthy factor was the absence of an aggressive marketing strategy. Moreover, among the businesses surveyed, only few of them employed one or two components of the marketing mix of product, place, price, and promotion. In most cases, the businesses produced products, which were copies of others in the industry.[67]

THE CHALLENGES OF FINANCIAL MANAGEMENT

One major constraint facing small business owners in Sub-Saharan Africa is the problem of how to secure the necessary capital for start-up and to finance the growth and/or expansion of the business. Ideally, expansion is financed by the profit the company generates (retained earnings) or by capital contributions from the owners. This continuous reinvesting of profits is necessary to insure continuous growth of a business, and in turn, the continuous increasing profits which follows. The other option is that many businesses wind up borrowing at least a portion of the capital investment from the financial markets. However, as we examined in chapter four, the nature of the financial markets in Sub-Saharan Africa makes the last option impossible. In the context of Sub-Saharan Africa, many small business owners who start small often end small if they are lucky. One of the reasons is that many small business owners do not invest in growth precisely because the styles of leadership and ownership attitude they bring into their firms do not encourage the use of profits for investment.

As we also noted in this chapter and the preceding one, there is a prevailing attitude and cultural practices whereby profits are used for prodigious expenses that have no bearing with the business. The typical African business owner rarely has plans for reinvesting profits to help the company grow, either by buying equipment, building facilities, or funding new hires etc. Thus, it is not uncommon that many businesses run out of cash just when the cash becomes essential to facilitate business growth and then die down to fierce competition later on.

Another conspicuous reason behind the high rates of failure among African businesses is that most African business owners lack the requisite conditions needed to secure credit facilities. As we noted in chapter four, one of the constraints facing the Africa entrepreneur is the inability to gain access to finance. Whereas the literature and research have indicated the inability to access finance as a significant constraint, many studies have concluded that enterprise owners and managers seem to underestimate the importance of financial management. In a study on African entrepreneurs, Per Trulsson pointed out that although entrepreneurs did not raise the importance of financial management as a constraint, many of the financial problems raised by them would not best be addressed by additional capital resources, but by better financial management. In many cases, cash-flow problems are quite common. In addition, there are several financial leakages as a consequence of poor credit management, theft/fraud and not using resources efficiently enough.[68] In general, the financial management problems boils down to a lack of systematic use of record-keeping and being able to monitor and interpret these records so that the appropriate action may be taken. This problem is compounded by what appears to be a relatively poor understanding of the macroeconomic context among the majority of business leaders. For example, the mechanisms behind interest and exchange rate fluctuations are quite often poorly understood. For most business owners, it is preferable to source foreign exchange from the unofficial parallel market than from the banks. This is likely to have an impact on their ability to plan for the future.

Cash flow problems also result from the inability to separate business accounts from personal ones. In one study, a researcher points out that during the early stages of some business start-ups, owners were unable to separate their business and family/domestic situations. Business funds were put to personal use and thus used in settling domestic issues. This has a negative impact on profitability and sustainability.[69] Thus, as one observer astutely pointed out, if the desire to financially support others is a valid impetus for establishing businesses, African entrepreneurs exaggerated it, as they used it for employing immediate family members and more distant kinsmen.[70]

In a study of entrepreneurial firms in West Africa, Enyinna Chuta argued that in spite of their contribution to employment and value-added of the economies of West African countries, often the right motivations are lacking, problems are ill-defined and record keeping as a major tool of information gathering and analysis is not practiced.[71] Inadequate recordkeeping is also a major cause of business failure. In most cases this is not only due to the low priority attached to it by new business owners, but also to the lack of basic business management and accounting skills. In one study, it was reported that "Most business owners end up losing track of their daily transactions and cannot account for their expenses and profits at the end of the month."[72] In any business context, good recordkeeping provides a small business with accurate information on which to base decisions, such as projecting sales and purchases, determining break-even points, and making a wide range of other financial analyses. In the context of Sub-Saharan African, inefficient skills and lack of knowledge in record- and bookkeeping results in financial mismanagement, thereby accelerating the high mortality rate among African small businesses.

It is generally regarded that liquidity is a major problem because of bureaucratic delays, frequent changes in government policy, lack of access to credit, etc. According to one researcher, however, the biggest obstacle to saving appears to be family obligations and lack of financial planning, which discourages foresight and accumulation for future consumption. According to Per Trulsson, some entrepreneurs "think of the company primarily as a unit for short term subsistence rather than long term wealth accumulation."[73]

The inability for African business owners to secure necessary financing from the banking and other financial institutions in the region has been documented in the extant literature. There are many factors that have discouraged banks and other lending institutions from lending to SMEs in Africa. Among them are poorly compiled records and accounts; low levels of technical and management skills; outdated technologies; lack of professionalism and networking; lack of collateral; lack of market outlets due to poor quality and non-standardized products; poor linkages and limited knowledge of business opportunities.

In particular, lack of adequate knowledge in financial planning, budgeting and control is seen as a major management problems leading to business failure in Sub-Saharan Africa. The business practice in many developing countries provides instances where small business owners cannot differentiate between profits and working capital. Business success requires having sufficient amount of capital on hand during the start-up phase. Undercapitalization is a common cause of business failure because companies run out of capital before they are able to generate positive cash flow. Many small business owners also make the mistake of beginning their businesses by being overly optimistic and often misjudge the financial requirements of going into business. Stories also abound about small business owners who would rather purchase flashing cars than invest their profits for the growth of their businesses. Most importantly, there is a pervasive practice in which business owners are unable to separate working capital from personal expenses.

In addition to the above problem is that of the implementation of proper cash management techniques, as many business owners seem to succumb to the notion that profit is what matters most in a new venture. But profit only becomes important in the long run when it is adequately used to finance the business and keeps it running. Maintaining adequate cash flow to pay bills on time is a constant challenge for entrepreneurs, especially those in the turbulent start-up phase, or for established companies experiencing rapid growth. Poor credit policies, sloppy debt collection practices, and undisciplined spending habits are common factors in many business bankruptcies.

POOR LOCATIONAL DECISIONS

Location is an important determinant of the success of any business. In the developing countries, due partly to the absence of infrastructure, small business owners are forced to locate their businesses in areas that are not only accessible to customers but disruptive to the general functioning of society. In many parts of Sub-Saharan Africa, it is not out of place to see a medical practitioner with a clinic in an area that is inaccessible to ambulances.

Choosing the right location is critical to the success of any business. Whereas a good location may enable a struggling business to ultimately survive and thrive, a bad location could spell disaster to even the best-managed enterprise. A decision concerning location must consider where the customers are, future development of the area, infrastructure, traffic, accessibility, parking, reputation of the area, location of competitors and, in the case of developing countries, interference from the authorities. Too often, business locations are selected without proper study, investigation, and planning in terms of where they are going to be located. Some beginning owners choose a particular location just because they noticed a vacant building. But the location question is much too critical to leave to chance. Especially for retailers, the livelihood of the business is heavily influenced by choice of location.

In Sub-Saharan Africa, the problem of location is more pronounced, as many business owners in the region tend to hawk their wares, workshops, and other services along busy roads and streets in densely populated urban areas. The result of poor locational choices has been government dismantling of what they consider as illegal structures. In Zimbabwe, for example, a government-sponsored urban clearance campaign known as "Operation Murambatsvina", which is a clean-up operation intended to rid the capital, Harare, of illegal structures and crime, has led to the demise of many of the country's small businesses. In his defense of the demolition, President Robert Mugabe insists, "The current chaotic state of affairs, where SMEs (small businesses) operated outside the regulatory framework and undesignated and crime ridden areas, could not be countenanced for much longer". Although the weaknesses of government planning controls and the haphazard developments associated with the informal sector may be blamed for the locational problems confronting business owners in Africa, we must not loose sight of the problems that locating a business on the wrong site has caused for the individual business owners. In particular, such demolitions have resulted in the massive displacement of hundreds of thousands of businesses from entire communities, with a spiraling effect on employment. In the aftermath of such demolitions, not many ventures remain in business. Some of the demolitions, as in Lagos and Port Harcourt in Nigeria, were accompanied by violence perpetrated by officials and bandits.

In addition to these problems majority of small enterprises are based in residential premises, including manufacturing enterprises. Many of these businesses operate from sub-standard premises that are too small, badly located or not provided with the necessary infrastructure, transport and communication services.

CHAPTER SUMMARY

Entrepreneurship involves the four functions of management: planning, organizing, leading and controlling of activities.

The managerial and organizational perspective implies that environmental constraints can be managed and turned to resources through astute management and organizational skills and capabilities.

Managerial and organizational competencies are the total sum of the entrepreneur's requisite attributes: attitudes, values, beliefs, knowledge, skills, abilities, personality, wisdom, expertise (social, technical, organizational, managerial), mindset, and behavioral tendencies needed for successful and sustaining entrepreneurship.

The management and organizational challenges can be grouped into strategic, administrative and operating problems.

Inability to plan strategically and to develop business plans is one of the major causes of business failures in Sub-Saharan Africa.

The reasons why business owners in Sub-Saharan Africa fail to develop strategic plans or engage in planning are: the cultural belief systems and lack of knowledge of strategic management and its benefits.

One of the greatest challenges facing businesses in Sub-Saharan Africa is the crisis of succession, that is, uncertainty about the future of the organization beyond the founder. The problem of succession either comes from the successor's lack of the abilities needed to run the business or the founder failed to plan for succession.

Succession problems are manifested in the nature of the entrepreneurial leadership, age of the founder, the prestige accorded to employment in the civil services, multinational corporations, occupations in certain fields and the prestige accorded to acquisition of higher education, traditional practices, lack of delegation and shared responsibilities,

Other challenges of organization and management include demands from extended family and inefficient organizational arrangements, the challenge of managing growth and complexity,

The challenge and problems of human resource management include the conventional practice of recruiting relatives and friends, lack of training and employee development and employing paternalistic motivational practices.

African organizational leadership exhibits the qualities commonly associated with the benevolent autocrat, the paternalistic authority figure and the authoritarian manager.

The consequences of a weak organizational citizenship among African employees are: lack of commitment to the achievement of organizational goals, apathy, graft, bribery and corruption, pilfering, theft, misappropriation, low morale and high employee turnover.

Reward systems that are based on paternalistic, authoritarian and benevolent organizational and leadership practices (family-ties, friendship, gifts or even bribery) may be discriminatory as a result of preferences given to in-group or family members.

An organizational system that is discriminatory breeds alienation among employees.

The working relationship between business owners and employees in an autocratic situation breeds employee alienation, poor motivation, risk aversion, unwillingness to take independent action, close supervision of subordinates with little delegation, inefficient operation, high cost with low productivity, over-staffing, under-utilizations, poor pay, high turnover and absenteeism.

In general, many African business owners do not understand nor appreciate the value of a stakeholder analysis. As a result, they do not adequately understand how the impact of their business practices is felt in society.

In the context of Sub-Saharan Africa, unethical business conduct manifest itself in various forms such as deceptive marketing practices, deceptive packaging and offering fake products.

The institutionalization of illegal economic activities is more harmful than beneficial for entrepreneurial development and economic growth.

Because illegal practices are more tolerant of the informal economic sector, they inhibit the transformation of an economic system into a more formal one capable of competing in a global context.

A lack of confidence in corporate governance standards and legal frameworks in many African countries is a major reason why foreign investment in the region is meager. A strong and effective system of corporate governance results from an effective financial system in a nation. The consequence of a poorly developed and inefficient capital market as in the case of Sub-Saharan Africa implies that African economies are still bereft of poor corporate governance. With poor corporate governance, African entrepreneurs in need of investment capital are at disadvantageous position.

From a marketing perspective, there are several reasons why businesses fail. These include: the inability to identify market and demand trends, the inability to master the fundamentals of marketing, the inability to adequately identify market niches and how to exploit them, lack information on a number of issues, such as market, technology and supplier, failure to appreciate the importance of putting the customer first and what that implies for the operation of the business, and unwillingness to invest in promotion and advertisement.

From the perspective of financial management, the problems confronting the African business owners, in addition to lack of access to credit include: cash-flow problems, poor credit management, theft and fraud, lack of systematic use of record-keeping, inability to monitor and interpret financial records for sound decisions, poor understanding of the macroeconomic context, the inability to separate business accounts from personal ones, lack of adequate knowledge in financial planning, budgeting and control, undercapitalization, being overly optimistic and misjudging the financial requirements of going into business, poor credit policies, sloppy debt collection practices and undisciplined spending habit.

The problem of location is more pronounced in Sub-Saharan Africa as a result of uneven development, absence of infrastructure, and the habits of hawking wares and locating stores and workshops along busy roads in urban areas.

CHAPTER DISCUSSION QUESTIONS

1. From a management and organizational context, what are the main features of the African entrepreneur as discussed in this chapter?

2. In your opinion, why do you think it is necessary to examine entrepreneurship from a management and organizational context?

3. Explain why business owners in Sub-Saharan Africa often neglect the need and process of strategic planning?

4. Why is succession a problem among African small business owners?

5. It is often stated that the different cultures in Sub-Saharan Africa have produced a type of leadership style that is antithetical to the demand of managing and leading entrepreneurial and small firms in the region. From the discussion in this chapter, what are the cultural features of African leadership style and authority relations? How are these features manifested in organizational leadership and management practices? What type of motivational problems can one deduce from the leadership and management styles of African business owners and managers?

6. From a marketing point of view, what are the major reasons why small businesses fail in Sub-Saharan Africa?

7. From the perspective of financial management what are the problems confronting the typical African business owners?

CASE STUDY 5: NOLLYWOOD AND THE CHALLENGES OF ENTREPRENEURS AND ENTREPRENEURSHIP[74]

Nollywood is the name given to the Nigerian video movie industry. The term is of uncertain origin, but was derived from Hollywood in the same manner as Bollywood (the Indian movie industry). Nollywood has no studios in the Hollywood sense. Many of the known producers have offices in Surulere, Lagos. Idumota market on Lagos Island, Onitsha in Anambra State, and Aba in Abia State are the primary distribution centers. The video movies are shot in locations all over Nigeria with distinct regional characteristics between northern movies primarily in the Hausa language, the Yoruba movies produced in the west, the Igbo movies shot in the East and the popular English-language productions shot in Lagos and the southeast.

As the third largest movie industry in the world, Nollywood brings into the Nigerian economy over $250 million a year and superseded only by the American and India movie industries, known respectively as Hollywood and Bollywood. Many observers have come to see the importance of the Nigerian movie industry in terms of its contribution to the nation's economic development. The Nigerian government has come to recognize the growing importance of the movie industry as a necessary vehicle for socio-economic development.

The emergence of Nollywood as an important industry started by accident in 1992, when Kenneth Nnebue, a Nigerian trader based in Onitsha, was trying to sell a large stock of blank videocassettes he had bought from Taiwan. He decided that they would sell better with something recorded on them, so he shot a film called "Living in Bondage" about a man who achieves power and wealth by killing his wife in a ritualistic murder, only to repent later when she haunts him. The film sold more than 750,000 copies, and prompted legions of imitators. Nollywood now makes over 2,000 low-budget films a year, about two-thirds of them in English. That is more than either Hollywood or India's Bollywood.

Nollywood movies are aired quite often both on state and private stations in Nigeria. Nigerians rich enough to afford digital satellite television services also have access to Nollywood movies aired for hours on end on a station called Africa Magic, a part of South Africa's MNet Movies station. Most Nollywood movies are shot in English, once in a while intermixed with a bit of Pidgin English – a language widely spoken in Nigeria, which borrows from the vocabulary of English and local languages, but mainly utilizing the grammatical structures found in the latter like Yoruba, Efik, Urhobo, Hausa and Igbo. The films cost anywhere between $15,000 and $100,000 to make, and the money comes directly from the market. Producers, or "marketers", as they are known, use some of the profits from one film to pay for the next. Banks do not lend to Nollywood, as there are no statistics from which they could estimate likely returns.

Nollywood movies have achieved the difficult feat of outselling Hollywood films in Nigeria and in many other African countries. Currently, some 300 producers churn out movies at an astonishing rate—somewhere between 2,000 and 2,500 a year. Nigerian directors adopt new technologies as soon as they become affordable. Bulky videotape cameras gave way to their digital descendents, which are now being replaced by HD cameras. Editing, music, and other post-production work are done with common computer-based systems. The films go straight to DVD and VCD disks. Thirty new titles are delivered to Nigerian shops and market stalls every week, where an average film sells 50,000 copies. A hit may sell several hundred thousand. Discs sell for two dollars each, making them affordable for most Nigerians and providing astounding returns for the producers.

In just 13 years, Nollywood has grown from nothing into a US$250 million-a-year industry that employs thousands of people. The Nollywood phenomenon was made possible by two main factors: Nigerian brand of entrepreneurship and digital technology. Nollywood producers and directors know they have identified an opportunity and struck a lucrative and long-neglected market—movies that offer audiences characters they can identify with and stories that relate to their everyday lives with very little cost. Specifically, the allure of Nollywood movies is that they have themes that deal with the moral and existential dilemma confronting modern Africa.

INDUSTRY HISTORICAL BACKGROUND AND GROWTH

Historically, modern movie making in Nigeria commenced in the early seventies. Ola Balogun, Late Herbert Ogunde, Jab Adu, Eddy Ugbomah, Late Ade Love, Adebayo Salami, Moses Adejumo (Alias Baba Sala) and a host of others are known as the pioneers of Nigerian filmmaking. These early seventies' filmmakers shot their movies on celluloid, which was introduced to Nigeria during the fifties by the British colonialists. The use of celluloid posed some problems and challenges in the early years of movie making, as the necessary facilities meant to facilitate its use were not readily available. In addition, the color laboratory to process films and much-needed professionals and technical help involved were not available. Although, the federal film unit and color laboratory were built in the late seventies, these did not offer much assistance as filmmakers still traveled abroad to process their films. In essence, every film producer was making film under unfavorable conditions.

To compound the problem, the number of cinema houses to present the films to the public was inadequate. The few available cinema houses were owned by expatriate Lebanese and Indian businessmen and merchant traders. During this period (1960s and 1970s), the Nigerian movie industry was dominated by foreign imported productions. Soon vast acres of the urban surroundings became flooded with wall posters of alien culture in the form of American, Indian, Chinese, and Japanese films. The Nigerian youth, as it were, caught on to the Kung-fu and Karate culture. Nigerians began to know more about Bruce Lee, James Bond, and the travails of the American Indians than they did about local productions featuring local themes.

The lack of support suffered by the early filmmakers may have stemmed from the general belief then that stage and movies practice is a past time reserved only for loafers or unemployed members of the community. In spite of these conditions, some indigenous producers through self-effort thrived in the vocation and were able to stimulate interest in filmmaking. Some significant successes were recorded after independence when for about ten years after the Nigeria civil war, Nigerian literature and theater got introduced to motion picture. This early example of Nigerian art on celluloid using the best of Western film techniques, was a breath of fresh air even if it was a low technology, low budget experiment unable to impress the market against the dominance of imports which though exotic did little to promote Nigerian art.

Some observers have suggested that the infant film market in the 70s was destroyed as a result of the oil boom together with other sectors of the economy. For example, the Indigenization Decree of 1972, which sought to transfer ownership of about 300 cinema houses in the country from their foreign proprietors to Nigerians, did little to help matters. Though this transfer resulted in the eruption of the latent ingenuity of Nigerian playwrights, screenwriters, poets, and film producers, the gradual dip in the value of the local currency (the Naira), combined with lack of finance, marketing support, quality studio and production equipment as well as inexperience on the part of practitioners, contributed to the demise of the industry or hampered the growth of the local entrepreneurs in the form of producers.

Hampered by the lack of quality studio and production equipment, the 1980s ushered in an innovative idea when local producers decided to produce television dramas reflecting popular but cheaper to-make socio-cultural themes. The late 1970s and 80s saw a rich mixture of Nigerian television being developed as oil prices spiked and Nigerians used their new-found wealth to buy consumer electronics. This coincided with the invention of video in 1976. Having a VCR became a status symbol for Nigerians and they were purchased in large numbers. Consequently, in the 1980s, the TV serialization of Chinua Achebe's "Things Fall Apart" became hugely successful. This period also witnessed the rise of popular television dramas on local programming. Hits such as the "Adio Family", "Village Headmaster", "Cock Crow at Dawn", "The Masquerade", "Mirror in the Sun" appeared on national television. It is possible that these early productions were indeed instrumental to the revival of the local film industry and hence the birth of the home video culture in Nigeria.

Many have pointed out that the austerity measures of the early eighties and the Structural Adjustment Program introduced in 1986 helped to promote indigenous film production. Specifically, the Nigerian economy took a downturn in 1979 and the IMF's

Structural Adjustment Program recommended that the government withdraw funding of the national television agency and privatize the body. Furthermore, the depreciation of the local currency and the scarcity of foreign exchange made the importation of foreign films extremely expensive and difficult. Consequently, the entertainment industry was one of the worst victims and had to move inward for survival and the few cinema houses existing had to close shop. This accelerated the birth of home video entertainment and, by implication, local production.

In the early 90s, after the DVD was invented, suppliers on the Nigerian market dumped "old-technology" VHS tapes and people started recognizing the potential for local content on video. It was at this time that "Living in Bondage" was produced in the style that has come to characterize the current Nigerian film market. In 30 days, the film had sold over 200,000 copies. On the back of the success of "Living in Bondage", entrepreneurial electronics merchants began financing local films and the demand for local content grew exponentially. Thus, Nigerian producers, directors and actors, frustrated by the lack of market for their products, began to go straight to the people in the early 1990s by shooting on video (later with digital cameras) and selling their movies, cassette by cassette, in open-air stalls and markets.

Today, the $4billion industry has perfected the workflow of films from concept to finished product. Movies are currently distributed at four major markets in Nigeria's major cities but there are plans to increase the footprint of electronically-linked distribution centers so that the movie industry's army of retailers can easily get access to additional copies.

The Nigerian movie industry has three distinctive roles and economic relevance. Firstly, it serves as a source of earning foreign exchange thus fitting into the federal government's economic objective of diversification from oil dependence. Secondly, it is a source of employment for Nigerians. Thirdly, it is a veritable avenue for projecting and promoting Nigeria's rich and diversified cultures.

Nigeria is the main market for Nollywood films and the home market is large by any standard. One eight of the world's black people are Nigerian and one seventh of African population is Nigerian. Moreover, the industry is completely owned, managed and controlled by Nigerians. Thus, the Nigerian film industry is seen as an international medium that expresses African ideas in a way that Africans can relate to, cutting across all backgrounds. As far as production and consumption is concerned, Nollywood is a Nigerian thing.

Outside of Sub-Saharan Africa, the demand for Nollywood films is growing. Already, Nollywood films have had huge success with the South African satellite broadcasting company, Multichoice's "Africa Magic" channel which carries almost all Nigerian films and television programs. Thus, Nollywood's appeal has reached far beyond Nigeria: its films are watched all over Africa, and beyond. In addition to South Africa's MultiChoice, other television channels outside Africa are now devoted to Nigerian films. For example, Zenithfilms, a British company, which distributes Nigerian programming to airlines, has launched a new channel, called Nollywood Movies, on BSkyB, a British pay-television operator controlled by Rupert Murdoch. An American cable television, Comcast, is also launching a channel devoted to Nollywood movies in April of 2008.

Especially, for African immigrants in Europe and North America, Nollywood movies remind people of everyday life back home. Similarly, the movies are gaining popularity among the America's fast-growing African immigrant population, offering their very Americanized children a glimpse of African life, particularly the clash of modernity and traditionalism and the battle between fundamentalist Christian, Islamic and tribal religions that is sweeping Africa. The consensus opinion among industry observers and players is that of an optimistic growth scenario now and in the future. With the number of television sets and access to VCD and VCR players growing by about 44 percent every year, the industry is expected to grow in the future.

CONSTRAINTS AND CHALLENGES

The Nigerian movie industry is faced with a number of challenges and constraints such as the impact of the informal environment, in which it is embedded, labor disputes among producers and actors, piracy, poor quality, financing, marketing, promotion, advertising and distribution, and lack of skills and professionalism among the producers and marketers.

The Pervasive Effects of an Informal Environment
Unlike Hollywood, the Nigerian movie industry is chronically hampered by the features commonly associated with a subterranean economy reflecting the characteristics of a growing informal sector in an unregulated developing economy. It should be noted, however, that this unregulated aspect is both the appeal and a problem for the industry. Paul Salopek provides a poetic description of the interplay between informal forces and the growth of the industry:

"Here (Lagos), hundred of film distributors have set up shop in cramped offices and mom-and-pop storefronts. Exhaust-grimed banners advertising the latest films hang in the sweaty air above the vast Idumota street market, where truckloads of new video releases are snapped up by hordes of cinema fans every weekend. And dented vans marked "Movie Crew" can be spotted trolling the city for shooting locations. The usual protocol: knock on somebody's door and ask to shoot scenes in their living room. ... 'We pay nothing to shoot in private homes,' Williams explained. 'Nigerians are just happy to see their houses featured in a movie.'"

The global movie industry is valued at over $200 billion US dollars. But in spite of its volume of production and rating, the Nigerian film industry's share of the global market is a paltry five percent of the pool. The principal reason as aptly documented by the Nigerian Film Corporation, is that the sector is under invested as the financial institutions and investors, in Nigeria, ironically, are unaware of the huge potential that abound in the sector. In addition, the distribution/exhibition part of the industry is evidently unstructured and ineffective. Indeed, some policies and laws regulating the sector call for review to synchronize with the reforms permeating other sectors of the Nigerian economy since 1999. One of the consequences of this lack of regulation is the growth of piracy in the industry, which has become even more monstrous and taking its toll on profitability.

Labor Disputes
Another major problem confronting the industry is the relationship between producers, marketers and artistes, which has created labor dispute among its stakeholders. For example, in October of 2004, the Association of Movie Marketers in Nigeria suspended top rated movie stars and movie directors on the basis of what the marketers saw as "unethical behaviors, high fees and indiscipline." Some of the artistes were accused of not showing up on location after collecting money from producers. As a result of this action, some Nigerians lost interest in watching Nigerian movies because of the absence of what they considered their "screen idols". This has also negatively affected the growth of the young industry for some time.

In addition to actors-marketers disputes, labor disputes have also extended to the relationship between actors and producers. This is aptly captured in Paul Salopek's description of the shooting of "The Last Sacrifice":

"Plagued by technical glitches, filming had dragged into its third week – an eternity by Nigerian standards. The unpaid cast and crew were holding the executive producer for ransom in his stuffy hotel room. (Grips and makeup artists hunched sullenly on the bed while their hostage, holed up in the toilet, begged for extra funds on his cell phone.) And now one of movie's megastar, a 3-foot-tall actor stage-named Pawpaw, had abandoned the set. He was last seen commandeering a visitor's car. Apparently, he went to look for a gold neck chain lost at a fast-food restaurant. 'I've got one scene left to shoot, and then this happens,' said Chike Bryan the haggard director, sighing and rubbing his fatigued-reddened eyes. 'That's show business, right?'" (Paul Salopek, Chicago Tribune, November 27, 2005). The inability to manage human resources in the industry coupled with unethical business practices by both producers and actors are major constraints facing the industry. In addition, the seemingly intractable differences and constant conflicts and bickering among the various associations within the movie sector is an obstacle to the proper harnessing of potentials of the industry.

Lack of Skill and Professionalism
Lack of professionalism is also seen as one of the reasons why there are conflicts among industry participants. In particular, the seemingly intractable differences and constant conflicts and bickering among the various associations within the movie sector do not augur well for the proper harnessing of potentials of the industry. Lack of professionalism is also responsible for the activities of quacks and charlatans who have invaded the industry. The lack of honesty of purpose and sincerity in operation is also a major cause for frequent crisis among stakeholders. It is also observed that the potentials of the marketing and distribution prospects of the sector are being undermined by the reluctance of practitioners to stretch their dreams beyond the traditional means of distribution.

In Nigeria, many of the "producers" lack the necessary credentials. In fact, any popular actor is a prospective producer. For this reason, there has been a massive exhibition of ignorance in the field of management by these would-be producers because of inadequate training. Many observers have pointed out that quite a number of the existing producers in the Nigerian movie industry are unskilled and unprofessional and lack the basic training in the ethics of theater and filmmaking. The focal point for many of them is on profit making in the shortest possible time. The result is that Nollywood has movies with poor finishing in spite of an obviously good storyline.

The Impact of Piracy
Nigerian filmmakers estimate losses of as much as US$20 million annually to piracy and to inexpensive duplication and exploitation of their works. According to the Nigeria Copyright Commission (NCC) and the National Film and Video Censors Board (NFVLB), the Nigerian movie industry loses over N105 million (over US$800,000) to piracy yearly.

This kind of revenue loss stifles innovation, frustrates creativity, and above all, denies local entrepreneurs, producers, artistes, and writers the revenue needed to meet international standards. With 600 million Africans increasingly engaged in the digital revolution, access to DVD burners, as well as greater cable access throughout the continent, industry analysts are of the opinion that piracy will escalate in the future if the government is unable to fight it.

Although international pirating of films is rampant, the experience of Nollywood has put the industry in an extremely dire situation. Intellectual property law experts noted that the pirating of Nigerian films would probably continue, in part because the filmmakers cannot afford legal costs of fighting it. The basic Nollywood formula is that cheaply made films are rushed straight to videotapes and DVDs – then often pirated endlessly. Producers and directors do not see much of the money their films make, which causes much hand wringing and calls for more secure distribution channels. Pedro Agbonife Obaseki, a Nigerian filmmaker who is president of the Filmmakers Consortium of Nigeria, expressed outrage at the pirating. "For all the films sold in the Bronx or Washington, not a dime comes to the Nigerian filmmaker, not a dime," he said.

Problem of Poor Quality
One of the challenges facing Nollywood is the quality of its movies. Some observers have pointed out "quantity has long trumped quality." Unlike Hollywood and Bollywood, Nollywood has no state-of-the art studios. Shooting at the homes of individuals is not uncommon. Movies are often shot openly in the cities (predominantly in Lagos). Industry observers assert that the brand value of Nollywood has not become a major force in competing with films from Hollywood and India. There are a number of factors for this: public perception in terms of being produced in Africa is one (country of origin). Second, in the context of quality, Nigerian movies are seen as sub-par compared to Hollywood. Third, Nollywood directors, producers and writers are in for making quick money and quantity has truncated quality. Critics complain that lack of professionalism in the industry has contributed to these problems.

Thanks to the home-video industry's penchant for duplication, the Nigerian movie industry is internationally recognized for its quantity but not for quality. The spectacle of unprecedented international media attention lately received by the movie industry seems focused on sheer volume and the unfathomable speed with which the videos are churned out. Buried inside all the attention is the disturbing snicker and innuendos on the very poor quality and standards of these productions.

Problem in Funding and Financing

Movie making is seriously capital intensive. In any context, growth in an industry depends on the role of banks and other financial institutions and intermediaries. In the Nigerian situation, lack of fund and access to finances has seriously contributed not only to underdevelopment of the industry, but more particularly to the low quality of its products. Here is a situation where merchant traders doubled as executive producers and venture capitalists – a dual role that promotes short-sightedness in terms of regenerating the industry with new ideas and new practitioners and breaking new markets in the global economy. As a consequence, aspiring moviemakers have no structure to provide a financial springboard for them to work. Movie financing is largely sought and obtained from informal or personal sources. The financial institutions and banking organizations are yet to come to terms with the industry as a viable investment target. Movie producers are thus under the mercy of merchant-traders who serve as venture capitalists in an economically unregulated environment. Since the primary aim of these investors is to recoup their investment at the shortest interval, quality and standards have been seriously compromised.

The Nigerian financial market has admittedly shunned Nollywood in many ways. As financial intermediaries and institutions, there is a lot the banks can do in the development and competitiveness of the movie industry in Nigeria. For example, the banks can easily provide credit in the form of loans to the industry, provide financial advisory services, and serve the industry's domestic and international money transfer need.

Tayo Aderinokun, the managing director of Nigeria's Guaranty Trust Bank pointed to the need for partnership between Nigerian banks and the film industry. He noted that as financial intermediaries in the economy, banks have a key role to play in the development of the industry. Although banks are willing to provide financial services for Nollywood, the nature of the industry as a product of an informal sector, makes such willingness impossible. Aderinokun stressed that banks, like any other financial institutions, are interested in helping to build successful businesses out of ideas and if the film industry should open itself up to the same evaluation and analysis that banks subject all their borrowers to, banks would really want to lend to them.

To be subject for financial help from the banking industry, however, there are certain preconditions as in any other industry. For instance, financial institutions would like to know: (i) the economic worth of the film industry; (ii) how much it costs to produce a good movie; (iii) the annual turnover of an average movie produced; (iv) if firms in the movie industry have collateral to pledge for credit; (v) if companies in the film industry have audited accounts, and (vi) if companies in the film industry have formal structures.

Undoubtedly, it is an illusion to look to the banking sectors to finance Nollywood production in its present state. Bankers usually do not start a banking relationship until after conducting due diligence on the institution of their interest. This usually involves an assessment of need and an analysis of the credit risks involved. Banks, like any other financial institution, want to be able to determine, to a large extent, the viability of the project they finance. So far, Nollywood, being a product of the informal sector, lacks the structure to provide the conditions for financial assistance from the banks.

Distribution Problems

Another major problem facing the Nigerian movie industry is that of poor distribution system. As noted earlier, Nollywood today sells its wares in three major cities. These are Lagos (Idumota), Onitsha and Aba. The peculiar problems this concentration structure occasioned is readily apparent - problem of access and recourse to piracy. Essentially, as a result of poor distribution channels, revenue from films sold in the rest of Nigeria and in international markets mostly goes to pirates. About half of the industry's revenue is lost because of its poor distribution network. Currently, traders and non-professionals dominate the informal distribution structures while exhibition theaters are practically non-existent. Although lack of exhibition theaters is not really a problem because quite a lot of movies made in developed countries do now go straight to DVD and video, movie theaters will check the activities of pirates. The issue of distribution is also important because it facilitates the provision of credible data on the structure of the industry. Presently, no one seems to have any hard numbers on how many videos are actually produced. The industry does not know how many are actually sold because the appearance of video clubs renting home video beclouds estimation. Without credible statistics and numbers, it is impossible for serious investment to come into the industry.

Marketing, Promotion and Advertising

The Nigerian movie industry as it is today operates under the old concept of attempting to produce a good product and placing less emphasis on the marketing strategy. The existing marketing and distribution structure in the Nigerian movie industry can be said to be inadequate and skewed in favor of piracy. Since the producers operate on very frugal budgets, their main target is to produce only a limited number of movies, which can yield the desired profit margins. For example, the usual target is first to produce about 10,000 units of cassettes or VCDs to release the movie into the market. Thereafter production follows in batches. In most cases the initial production is as high as 30,000 – 50,000 units depending on the producers' expectations for the success of the movie. In a market that has approximately 8 million potential viewers, this creates a serious demand gap. Consequently, the pirates enjoy the privilege of filling this demand gap with fake reproduction of the movie, such that the pirates make huge profit while the sponsor or executive goes home with marginal profits.

In Nollywood, moviemakers employ various advertising media. The most commonly used media are television and posters. Thus, the industry is inextricably linked with the printing and media sub sectors. Television adverts generally follow the same pattern and are generally repetitious. The adverts are sometimes monotonous and project a lack of imagination. In some cases, movies that are in the making are advertised in completed productions to stimulate the demand when they are eventually released.

Posters however, appear to be the dominant form of advert. They are less expensive and can be viewed at all hours of the day. They are usually quite colorful and attempt to convey the message of the movie to the viewers. The other methods of advertising include radio jingles and newspaper or magazines. Nigerian moviemakers are yet to adopt the

Internet as a veritable form of advertising. The few Internet adverts are usually done by retailing and rental companies abroad who specialize in Nigerian movies.

Case Discussion Questions

1. It has been stated that the production and release of "Living in Bondage" by Kenneth Nnebue was the precursor to the emergence of Nollywood as an industry. From the materials in this book, put the role of "Living in Bondage" and its producer, Kenneth Nnebue in the context of entrepreneurship. Please, pay particular attention to entrepreneurial issues such as (a) conditions driving entrepreneurship and (b) the concept of innovation in entrepreneurship.

2. With reference to Nollywood as an emerging industry and using examples from other emerging industries in Sub-Saharan Africa (such as the fast food industry, the ICT industry, etc), what are the factors driving entrepreneurship in the context of a developing country? What are the problems faced by aspiring entrepreneurs? In particular, what are the management and organizational constraints and challenges confronting Nollywood producers? What suggestions can you offer?

3. It has been stated that government cannot mandate competitiveness in an industry. However, for creativity and innovation to occur in an economy, governments are expected to be a catalyst by creating the enabling environment for entrepreneurial activities such as innovation and creativity. With particular references to the problems and challenges in the Nigerian movie industry, what roles, in your view should the government play?

PART II: STRATEGIC MANAGEMENT & ENTREPRENEURSHIP

Chapter 6:   Principles of Strategic Management and Entrepreneurship

Chapter 7:   Business Description, Vision, Mission and Objectives

Chapter 8:   Industry and Competitive Analysis

Chapter 9:   Strategy Formulation for Entrepreneurial Firms

Chapter 6

PRINCIPLES OF STRATEGIC MANAGEMENT AND ENTREPRENEURSHIP

"Nothing focuses the mind better than constant sight of a competitor who wants to wipe you off the map" (Wayne Calloway).

CHAPTER LEARNING OBJECTIVES
After studying this chapter, you should be able to:

1. Understand the meaning of strategy and a business environment.

2. Understand the meaning and importance of the concept of strategic group.

3. Understand the different levels of strategies and how they apply to the entrepreneurial firm.

4. Understand the importance of strategic management to the success of small businesses and entrepreneurial firms.

5. Explain why and how a small business must create a competitive advantage in the market.

6. Understand the basis of a firm's competitive advantage and its strategy.

7. Develop a strategic plan for a business using the eight steps in the strategic management process.

INTRODUCTION: STRATEGY AND ENTREPRENEURSHIP

This book is about the entrepreneurial task of formulating and implementing a firm's strategy in order to achieve *competitive advantage* and to be profitable in the long-run. The position maintained in this book is that success in a business venture depends on the ability to think and manage a business following a strategic management process. As pointed out in chapter one, an entrepreneur is the ultimate strategist: He or she tracks industry and competitive trends, searches for opportunities, develops forecasting models and scenario analyses, evaluates business performance, spots emerging market opportunities, identifies business threats, and develops creative action plans. Understanding and applying the concepts of strategic management process is the corner stone for the success of all business – large and small, public and private, profit and nonprofit organizations. The success stories of the world's entrepreneurs point to one particular point: They have (or had) a strategy (or a plan of action) put in place. As an entrepreneur or an operator of a small business, the success of your firm depends on certain plans of actions and how you or your management is able to implement these plans – this is the essence of strategic management. Let us understand the basis upon which this chapter is to be presented: *a firm's strategy is the game plan it hopes to use in order to stake out a market position, conduct its operations, attract and please customers, compete successfully and achieve targeted business objectives*.[1] In other words, the strategy of a firm is based on the idea that winning a durable competitive edge over rivals hinges more on building competitively valuable expertise and capabilities that rivals cannot easily copy.

Today, most of the world is living in a free market system in which goods and services are provided to the public for the purpose of earning profits and most business owners must compete against other business owners in order to be profitable overtime. In the context of entrepreneurship, the success of a small business venture depends on having a niche and most importantly, designing appropriate strategies that serve the niche on a timely basis. In short, the firm must have in place a working strategy. Specifically for the small business firm, ultimate success is hinged on two things: (i) focusing on a narrow market niche and gaining a competitive advantage by doing a better job than rivals and by serving the special needs and tastes of a particular buyer segment; and (ii) out-competing rivals based on such differentiating features such as providing good value for the money and better service.

Firms, whether small, medium or large, must compete with each other to gain access to customers. Yet, not all firms will necessarily compete with one another in the same way. Each firm is likely to devise its own strategy to deal with its competitive rivals, to serve its particular base of customers, and to act upon the changes that impact the way it operates. Each firm's strategy needs it to develop a **competitive advantage** that enables it to compete effectively. The reason for having a strategy is for the firm to achieve a competitive advantage. In the broadest sense, competitive advantage is what allows a firm to gain an edge over its rivals. Competitive advantage enables a firm to generate successful performance over an extended period of time. Throughout remaining part of this book, which focuses on the concepts of strategy and competitive advantage, you will learn how firms from variety of different industries, settings, and situations develop strategies to achieve competitive advantage. Activities undertaken to achieve this end form the basis of the strategic management process.

A **strategy** refers to the ideas, plans, and support systems that firms employ to compete successfully against their rivals. Strategy is designed to help firms achieve competitive advantage. One of the reasons we say that the entrepreneur is an utmost strategist is because in entrepreneurship, one must follow some logical steps in the process of developing and running a business towards profitability. The challenge is for business owners and managers to keep their strategies closely matched to such *outside drivers* such as changing buyer preferences, the latest actions of rivals, new technological capabilities, the emergence of attractive market opportunities, and newly appearing business conditions.

Competitive rivalry characterizes economic activity in most parts of the world where market forces determine the conduct of business and where the mechanisms of a free market system are upheld as a necessity for economic growth. Much organized activity outside the realm of business and commerce is also highly competitive. As stated in chapter one, nonprofit organizations such as colleges, churches, and charities, for example, generally face numerous rivals eagerly seeking the same students, parishioners, and contributors. Because competitive rivalry is such a pervasive aspect of so many different kinds of activities, the concepts developed in this book will be useful to managers and administrators operating in a wide range of settings. How to deal with competitive rivalry from a strategic management perspective is one of the primary questions addressed in this book. Crafting a good strategy also calls for good entrepreneurship. As pointed out by Thompson, Strickland and Gamble, "Masterful strategies come partly (maybe mostly) by doing things differently from competitors where it counts; out-innovating them, being more efficient, being more imaginative, adapting faster, rather than running with the herd. Good strategy making is therefore inseparable from good business entrepreneurship. One cannot exist without the other."[2]

From the perspective of entrepreneurship, crafting, implementing, and executing a strategy are top-priority entrepreneurial and managerial tasks for one very crucial reason. An entrepreneur or the manager of a business must shape the direction or competitiveness of its firm or business before unforeseen forces work against its profitability. Thus, there is a compelling need for managers and entrepreneurs to *proactively* shape how the company's business will be conducted. It is the responsibility of management and business owners to exert strategic leadership and commit the enterprise to going about its business in a well-defined path of actions. Without a strategy, entrepreneurs and managers of businesses have no prescription for doing business, no road map to competitive advantage, no game plan for pleasing customers or achieving good performance. Lack of a consciously shaped strategy is a recipe for organizational drift, competitive mediocrity and lackluster results.

This chapter will show how strategy can help a firm deal with competition in an industry. We will examine the concept of strategy and introduce the notion of competencies such as core competencies and distinctive competencies. We will then examine the basic ingredients that make up the strategic management process and show how it is applicable to the entrepreneurial firm and small businesses.[3] The chapter argues and indicates that strategic management is as important to the small and medium-sized enterprise as it is to a large corporation. In other sections, the chapter identifies the various responsibilities of entrepreneurs and small business owners in the strategic management process along the lines of turning core competencies into competitive advantages. To understand and appreciate the importance of strategic management in the context of small businesses, it is necessary that we understand the concept of a business environment and why it is sometimes construed as a battlefield. We will follow this through an examination of the concepts of competitive advantage and a firm's core competence. Later, we will examine how these two concepts form the basis of a firm's strategy.

THE BUSINESS ENVIRONMENT AS A BATTLEFIELD

From the perspective of strategic management, a **business environment** refers to the environmental setting in which a competitive engagement with an adversary (that is, the competitor) takes place. In the context of strategic management, an adversary is the business competitor. A business environment is thus like a military terrain. In the military realm, a terrain (environment) may be a plain, a forest, a marsh, or the mountains. The characteristics of these settings influence which type of troops or deployments can be used effectively. In the world of business, competitors do not confront each other directly on a battlefield as armies do. Rather, they compete with each other in an industry environment or business environment with their products or services. As an entrepreneur or a potential one, you will attempt to target a market segment and attempt to win customers. It is customers who determine, each time they make a purchase, which competitors "win" and which ones "loose". The industry or business environment thus constitutes the ultimate *terrain* on which business competition takes place. Thus, a market is a competitive battlefield where it is customary and expected that rival sellers will employ whatever resources and weapons they have in their arsenal to improve their market positions and performance.

The fundamental premise of strategy is that an adversary can defeat a rival – even a larger, more powerful one – if it can maneuver a battle or engagement onto terrain favorable to its own capabilities. In a free-market economy, there are large business organizations and there are small business firms fighting to gain access to the same customer groups in their industry. Competition is seen here as the battle to win customers from your competitors and maintain them. The essence of a strategy is that a business exists in an environment and this environment consists of factors that can help or impede its ability to compete and be successful. Whether or not a business is for profit or nonprofit, it is not immune from forces in the environment. Because these environmental forces are both numerous and powerful (e.g., sociopolitical forces, economic forces, technological forces, and regulatory forces), the entrepreneur must continually monitor them and use them to his or her competitive advantage. Whether or not a business entails importation of goods, provision of financial services, manufacturing goods, building houses, operating a church or hawking groceries along the street, it exists in an environment. As pointed out above, this environment is known, in strategic terms, as the *terrain* of the business. The business environment, also known as industry or market environment is the place where the success of your strategies or tactics is determined. In the military world, this is known as the battlefield where the tactics of enemies are evaluated and appropriate responses made to successfully attack the "enemy" (namely, your existing or potential competitors).

The Business Environment and the Concept of Strategic Group

Because most industries contain numerous customers displaying different needs, firms generally have many different possible terrains from which to choose. Consider the restaurant industry or business environment, for example. It contains a number of different groups of customers: those wanting low-cost meals, people desiring gourmet hamburgers, individuals preferring ethnic menus or continental dishes, customers who prefer fast-food, and those who prefer health-conscious menus. The terrain of the restaurant business thus constitutes different groups or segments upon which rivals compete. Furthermore, each of these groups can be further divided into smaller subgroups of customers with even more specific needs and characteristics. For example, ethnic food runs the entire range from Chinese to French to Mexican to Yoruba, Ibo, etc. Each of these individual segments has somewhat different competitive characteristics that define the *sub terrain*. As an entrepreneur, you should be able to identify those little groups that constitute your target market. In strategic management, we call these "strategic groups."

A *strategic group* consists of those rival firms with similar competitive approaches and positions in the market, adopting similar strategies, and tends to be affected by, and respond to competitive actions and external events in similar ways. To be competitive in the business environment, one thing to look for is whether the nature of the "terrain" favors some strategic groups and hurt others. Knowing the competitive strategies of those in your strategic group enables you to plan your offensive or defensive moves. Most importantly, your success in the business battlefield depends on your competitive advantage over your enemies. Similarly, your competitive advantage lies in your resources and how you are able to organize and mobilize them. Firms in the same strategic group "pursue similar strategies with similar resources."[4] Companies in the same strategic group can resemble one another in any several ways: They may have comparable product line breadth, be vertically integrated to much the same degree, offer buyers similar services and technical assistance, use essentially the same product attributes to appeal to similar types of buyers, emphasize the same distribution channels, depend on identical technological approaches, and/or sell in the same price/quality range. Surely, these characteristics represent the media industry in Nigeria or in most other countries. Thus, an industry such as the newspaper industry contains a number of strategic groups. In Nigeria, for example, there are the national upscale newspapers (e.g., the Guardian, Thisday, Punch, etc), the regional newspapers (e.g., Tribune, Champion, The Tide, etc), the tabloids (e.g., The Daily Sun, National Mirror), business dailies (BusinessDay, Financial Standard). A strategic group exists when all sellers pursue essentially identical strategies and have comparable market positions.

Thus an industry such as the newspaper industry contains more than one strategic group when newspaper companies appeal to different market segments. At the other extreme, there are as many strategic groups as there are competitors when each rival pursues a distinct competitive approach and occupies a substantially different competitive position in the marketplace.

Categorizing firms in any one industry into a set of strategic groups is very useful as a way of better understanding the nature of the competition in that market or business environment. The concept of strategic groups has a number of implications for identifying threats and opportunities within a chosen industry. First, a company's closest competitors are those in its strategic group – not those in other strategic groups. Since all the companies in a strategic group are pursuing similar strategies, consumers tend to view the products of such enterprise as direct substitute for each other. Thus, a major threat to a firm's profitability can come from within its own strategic group.[5]

FIRM'S COMPETITIVE ADVANTAGE AND ITS STRATEGY

As pointed out in the introductory section of this chapter, the goal of developing a strategic plan is to create for the small company a competitive advantage. A **competitive advantage** is the aggregation of factors that sets a business firm apart from its competitors and gives it a unique position in the market superior to its competition. From a strategic management perspective, the key to business success is to develop a unique competitive advantage: one that creates value for the customers and is difficult for competitors to duplicate. For example when Zenith International Bank was established in Nigeria in 1990, it set itself apart from other banks through its unique customers services. In the late seventies, Societe Generale Bank of Nigeria was able to distinguish itself from other banks through its unique computerized banking system.

A company can compete successfully when it has a competitive advantage. A company has a competitive advantage when it has an edge over rival firms in attracting customers and defending against competitive moves from rivals. Building a competitive advantage alone is not enough: the key to success is building a *sustainable* competitive advantage. Sustainable competitive advantage is about how a firm builds long lasting strategies to sustain its competitiveness in the market place. A sustainable competitive advantage is also about the firm's ability to insulate the business as much as possible from the actions of rivals and other threatening competitive developments. To be sustainable, a firm's competitive advantage must pass through two important tests: durability and imitability.[6]

The **durability** of a sustainable advantage is the rate at which a firm's underlying resources and capabilities depreciate or become obsolete. New technology can make a company's competitive advantage or distinctive competence obsolete or irrelevant. **Imitability** is the rate at which a firm's underlying resources and capabilities can be duplicated by others. To the extent that a firm's distinctive competency gives it competitive advantage in the marketplace, competitors will do what they can to learn and imitate that set of skills and capabilities. Competitors' efforts may range from "reverse engineering" (taking apart a competitor's product in order to find out how it works), to hiring employees from the competitor, to outright patent infringement. A firm's competitive advantage or core competence can be easily imitated to the extent that it is transparent, transferable, and replicable.[7] Transparency is the speed with which other firms can understand the relationship of resources and capabilities supporting a successful firm's strategy. Transferability is the ability of competitors to gather the resources and capabilities necessary to support a competitive challenge. Replicability is the ability of competitors to use duplicated resources and capabilities to imitate the other firm's success.

We can say that a firm's strategy concerns *how*: how to grow the business, how to satisfy customers, how to outperform rivals, how to respond to changing market conditions, how to manage each functional piece of the business and develop needed organizational capabilities, how to achieve strategic and financial objectives. The *"hows"* of strategy tend to be company-specific, customized to a company's own situation and performance objectives. Remember that most successful firms do not copy the strategies of their rivals. They develop their own strategies based on their own unique core competencies and the requirements of their environments.

There are three areas for developing and implementing a business competitive strategy that yields sustainable competitive advantage: (i) a company has to decide on the attributes of the product or service it is offering to win a competitive edge, such as lower costs and prices, a better product, a wider product line, superior customer service, emphasis on a particular market niche; (ii) a company has to develop skills, expertise, and competitive capabilities that set the company apart from rivals; and (iii) the company must try to insulate the business as much as possible from the effects of competition.

What a firm has at its disposal to compete or to fight its adversaries (competitors) can be termed as the firm's **distinctive competence** – the aspect(s) of business that the firm performs better than its competitors. From a strategy perspective, you have no business going into one without having a distinctive competence or competencies. Thus, a firm may have several areas of activity or skill that lead to competitive advantage. Competitors in the restaurant industry, for example, use a variety of methods for building competitive advantage, including warm and friendly service and gourmet hamburger recipes (*Mr. Biggs*). In the newspaper industry, high quality and a select customer group may be a chosen strategy (*The Guardian* Newspapers of Nigeria), consistent quality and low-cost operation (*The Punch* Newspapers of Nigeria), and low-cost, circulation-driven (*The Daily Sun*). In general, companies may compete on the basis of identification of new market segments (*UACN*). A distinctive competence "is a basis for competitive advantage because it represents expertise or capability that rivals don't have and cannot readily match."[8]

A **distinctive competence** is a unique strength that allows a company to achieve superior efficiency, quality, innovation, or customer responsiveness and thereby create superior value and attain a competitive advantage. A firm with a distinctive competence can differentiate its products or services from the ones provided by the competitors in order to achieve substantially lower costs than its rivals. Consequently, a distinctive competence creates more value than its rivals and will earn a profit rate substantially above the industry average. The distinctive competencies of a firm arise from two complementary sources: its **resources** and **capabilities.**[9]

The resources at the disposal of the firm can be grouped under two broad categories: *tangible* and *intangible resources*. Tangible resources include such things as land, buildings, plant, equipment, human, finance, technological, organizational, etc. Intangible resources include such things as the firm's brand name, reputation, patents, and technological or marketing know-how. To give rise to a distinctive competence, a company's resource must be both *unique* and *valuable*.[10] A unique resource is one that no other company has and that is why it is distinctive. For example, Zenith International Bank of Nigeria was able to compete on the basis of distinctive competence: the ability to offer banking services through its application of the most recent developments in IT industry. Zenith International Bank was founded in 1990 at a time when the Nigerian banking and financial industry was struggling for survival. With the bank's customized services, its superior service qualities, and its focus on high-income earners, it was able to create a niche for itself. What Zenith International Bank has developed over the years became its resource capability because it is a resource that in some way helped the bank to create strong demand for its product and services.

Capabilities refer to a company's skills at coordinating its resources and putting them to productive use. As an entrepreneur or the owner of a small venture, these skills reside inside your firm's organization; that is, in the way your company makes decisions and manages its internal processes in order to achieve its objectives. For example, if you are good at designing furniture, your ability to design is a resource that you have possessed. To put this resource for productivity sake is your capability. Second, if you have a lot of money, one can say that you have financial resources. The ability to use the financial resources for productive purposes is your capability. Most successful entrepreneurs are those who are able to transform their resources into capabilities. More generally, a company's capabilities are the product of its organizational structure and control systems. They specify how and where decisions are made within the company, the kind of behaviors the company rewards, and the company's cultural norms and values.

The distinction between resources and capabilities is critical to understanding what generates a distinctive competence. As pointed out earlier, a firm may have some unique and valuable resources, but unless it has the capability to use those resources effectively, it may not be able to create or sustain a distinctive competence. In the context of entrepreneurship, the distinctive competencies of small business usually fall into three areas: the ability to identify new niches in established markets, the ability to identify new markets, and the ability to move quickly to take advantage of new opportunities.

Identifying Niches in Established Markets

An established market is one in which several large firms compete according to relatively well-defined criteria. For example, throughout the 1970s and eighties in Nigeria the big three banks (First Bank of Nigeria, Union Bank and United Bank for Africa) competed according to three product criteria: current account, saving deposits, and loans. Over the years the banking services and quality of services delivered by these firms continued to improve.

However, as soon as deregulation, coupled with IT affected the banking sector, the dynamics or factors shaping the industry changed. For the banks, user friendliness, electronic banking services, ATMs, was to be the basis of competition. The new generation banks targeted every bankable individual, develop new products and took banking to a different level by adding new services that were only possible in Europe. The major entrepreneurial act of the new banks was not to invent a new banking services based on loan, current and savings account deposits), but to recognize a new kind of services, developed new ways to satisfy the customer and new ways to compete in the banking industry.

The approach of the new generation banks to competition was to identify a new niche in an established market. As pointed out in chapter two, a niche is simply a segment of a market that is not currently been served or exploited. In general, entrepreneurial ventures are better at discovering these niches than are larger organizations. Large organizations usually have so many resources committed to older, established business practices that they may be unaware of new opportunities. Entrepreneurs can see these opportunities and move quickly to take advantage of them.

Identifying New Markets

Entrepreneurs also succeed because they were able to identify whole new markets. Discovery can happen in at least two ways. First, an entrepreneur can transfer a product or service that is well established in one geographic market to a second market. Second, entrepreneurs can sometimes create entire industries. For example, Dr. Abiola Odeyemi the founder of AB Bumps Specialist Centre in Lagos, Nigeria discovered a new market for people suffering from various skin ailments, bumps, kelloids, unhealed sores and other skin related problems. His products and healing services were highly established in the market he created in Nigeria. Secondly, Dr. Odeyemi has also created a market for his products and service in another geographical market, London, England. He opened an office and a center in London. He says, "Currently plans are on to open offices in the USA, Germany, Jamaica and Ghana."[11] Another example is that of *Mr. Biggs*. After pioneering the fast food industry in Nigeria, the firm has now transferred it products and service to Ghana, creating a new geographic market. Again, because entrepreneurs are not encumbered with a history of doing business in a particular way, they are usually better at discovering new markets than are larger, more mature organizations.

New Opportunities and First-Mover Advantages

A first-mover advantage is any advantage that comes to a firm because it exploits an opportunity before any other firm does. Sometimes large firms discover niches within exiting markets or new markets at just about the same time as small companies to take advantage of these opportunities. At other times, however, smaller firms respond to new opportunities than large corporations. One of the reasons for this is that many large organizations make decisions slowly because each of their many layers of hierarchy has to approve an action before it can be implemented. Also, large organizations may sometimes put a great deal of their assets at risk when they take advantage of new opportunities. Because entrepreneurial firms are more agile and free from bureaucratic bottlenecks, they are known to be more innovative and dynamic – responding quicker to market forces and opportunities. On other occasions, large organizations may take advantage of their size and resources in responding to new opportunities, especially when such opportunities demand large-scale investments. *Mr. Biggs*, for example, became a pioneer in the Nigerian fast-food industry thanks to the backing it received from its parent company, *UACN* and its knowledge of the food industry from its operation of *Kingsway* snacks in the early eighties. The firm's competitiveness is based in part by the experience it has accumulated in the industry.

In a sum, for a company to have a distinctive competence, it must at a minimum have either (i) a unique and valuable resource and the capabilities (skills) necessary to exploit that resource or (ii) a unique capability to manage common resources. A company's distinctive competence is strongest when it possesses both unique and valuable resources and unique capabilities to manage those resources. The possession of unique and valuable resources and the unique capabilities to manage the resources is the root of a firm's competitive advantage.[12]

Core Competence and Competitive Advantage

One of the most valuable resources a company has is the ability to perform a competitively relevant activity very well. We call these valuable resources the company's **core competence** – a competitively important internal activity that a company performs better than other competitively important internal activities. In the long run, a company gains a sustainable competitive advantage through its ability to develop a set of core competencies that enables it to serve its selected target customers better than its rivals and maintaining it. **Core competencies** are unique set of capabilities that a company develops in key areas, such as superior quality, customer service, innovation, team building, flexibility, responsiveness, product design, low cost manufacturing, proprietary technology, superior distribution, etc.

What distinguishes a core competence from a competence is that a core competence is central to a company's competitiveness and profitability rather than peripheral. Thus whether a company's core competence represents a *distinctive* competence depends on how good the competence is relative to what competitors are capable of. The question to answer here is that, is it a competitively superior competence or just an internal competence? Core competencies become the nerve center of a company's competitive advantage and are usually quite enduring over time. Markets, customers, and competitors may change, but a company's core competencies are more durable, forming the building blocks for everything a firm does. To be effective, these competencies should be difficult for competitors to duplicate, and they must provide customers with an important perceived benefit. Small companies' core competencies often have to do with the advantages of their size. For example, agility, speed, closeness to their customers, superior services, absence of bureaucratic bottleneck, and ability to innovate are some core competencies with which small firms can compete with bigger ones. In short, their smallness is an advantage, allowing them to do things that their larger rivals cannot. The key to success is building these core competencies (or identifying the ones a company already has) and then concentrating them on providing superior service and value for its customers.

We noted in chapters four and five that one of the problems facing entrepreneurial development in developing nations is the culture of imitation. This culture of imitation inhibits innovation and without innovation, there is no way a firm can compete successfully with its rivals in the long-run. It should be recognized that no business could be everything to everyone. In fact, one of the biggest pitfalls many entrepreneurs stumble into is failing to differentiate their businesses from the crowd of competitors. Developing core competencies does not necessarily require a company to spend a great deal of money. It does, however, require an entrepreneur to use creativity, imagination, and vision to identify those things that it does best and that are most important to its target customers. The environment in which businesses operate provides numerous opportunities that can provide the basis upon which an entrepreneur can develop core competencies for the firm.

The essence of strategy is to match strengths, core competence and distinctive competence with the environment or the terrain in such a way that one's own business enjoys a competitive advantage over rivals competing on the same terrain. In the military world, the strategic imperative for commanders is to select a battlefield favorable to their force's particular strengths and unfavorable to the adversary. In management, we call these particular strengths a firm's core competencies. The thrust of strategic management is that, as an entrepreneur or the manager of a business, your success depends on how well you are able to monitor the environment and act upon it in order to compete successfully with the competitors. In the following section, we will gain an understanding of how this task of environmental monitoring and fighting the enemy in the battlefield of customers is achieved through examination of the process of strategic management.

STRATEGY MANAGEMENT AS A PROCESS

Designing and implementing a firm's strategic actions is a process that must be done stepwise whereby owners and managers of businesses choose a set of strategies and action plans in order to be competitive in a particular business or market. In general, the strategic management process consists of two major stages: *the strategy formulation stage* and *the strategy implementation stage*.

In the strategy formulation stage, the process consists of analyzing the current situation of the firm, selecting strategies that seem to best fit the needs of the firm, and making plans to pursue those strategies. In the discussion of strategic management process, the task of analyzing a firm's external and internal environment and then selecting an appropriate strategy is normally referred to as the planning stage. During this stage, you are designing a plan of action. On the other hand, strategy implementation is putting your plans into action. Once strategies are created, they must be acted upon successfully to achieve the desired results. As an entrepreneurial task, the strategy implementation stage thus consists of a process by which strategies and policies are put into action through the development of programs, budgets, and procedures. Implementing or executing your business plan of action involves putting into place the evaluation mechanisms for the implemented strategies.

These two broad stages (strategy formulation and strategy implementation) can be grouped into six main steps or phases as illustrated in Figure 6-1 below. The six steps are:

(i) Defining the firm's business, developing the firm's vision and mission statement, setting the firm's objectives and goals. The strategic management process begins with a careful review and clarification of organization's product or service, its vision, mission, values and objectives. This sets the stage for critically assessing the organization's resources and capabilities as well as competitive opportunities and threats in the external environment.

(ii) Analyzing the firm's internal operating environment to identify its strengths and weaknesses. Given an understanding of the mission, values, and objectives, the strategic management process next analyzes organizational resources and capabilities. A major goal is to identify core competencies in the form of special strengths that the organization has or does exceptionally well in comparison with competitors. The owners or managers must also identify and gain a realistic understanding of the firm's weaknesses or resource deficiencies.

(ii) Analyzing the firm's external competitive environment to identify opportunities and threats. After an understanding of the strengths and weaknesses, the next stage is an analysis of opportunities and threats in the external environment. They can be found among macroenvironmental factors such as technology, government, social structures, population demographics, the global economy, and the natural environment. They can also include developments in the industry environment (*microenvironment*) of resource suppliers, competitors, and customers.

(iii) Generating, evaluating and selecting strategies that build on the firm's strengths and correct its weaknesses in order to take advantage of external opportunities and counter external threats. A number of strategies have been identified in the literature, including Porter's Competitive strategies (differentiation, cost leadership, focused differentiation and focused cost differentiation. The major question here is how a firm can best compete for customers in an industry

(iv) Implementing and executing the strategies. No strategy, no matter how well formulated, can achieve long-term success if it is not properly implemented. This includes the willingness to exercise control and make modifications to meet the needs of changing conditions.

(v) Evaluating the strategies and measuring success. The owner and/or management of the firm must put in place necessary systems and procedures for tracking and measuring performance.

Figure 6-1:
The Strategic Management Process

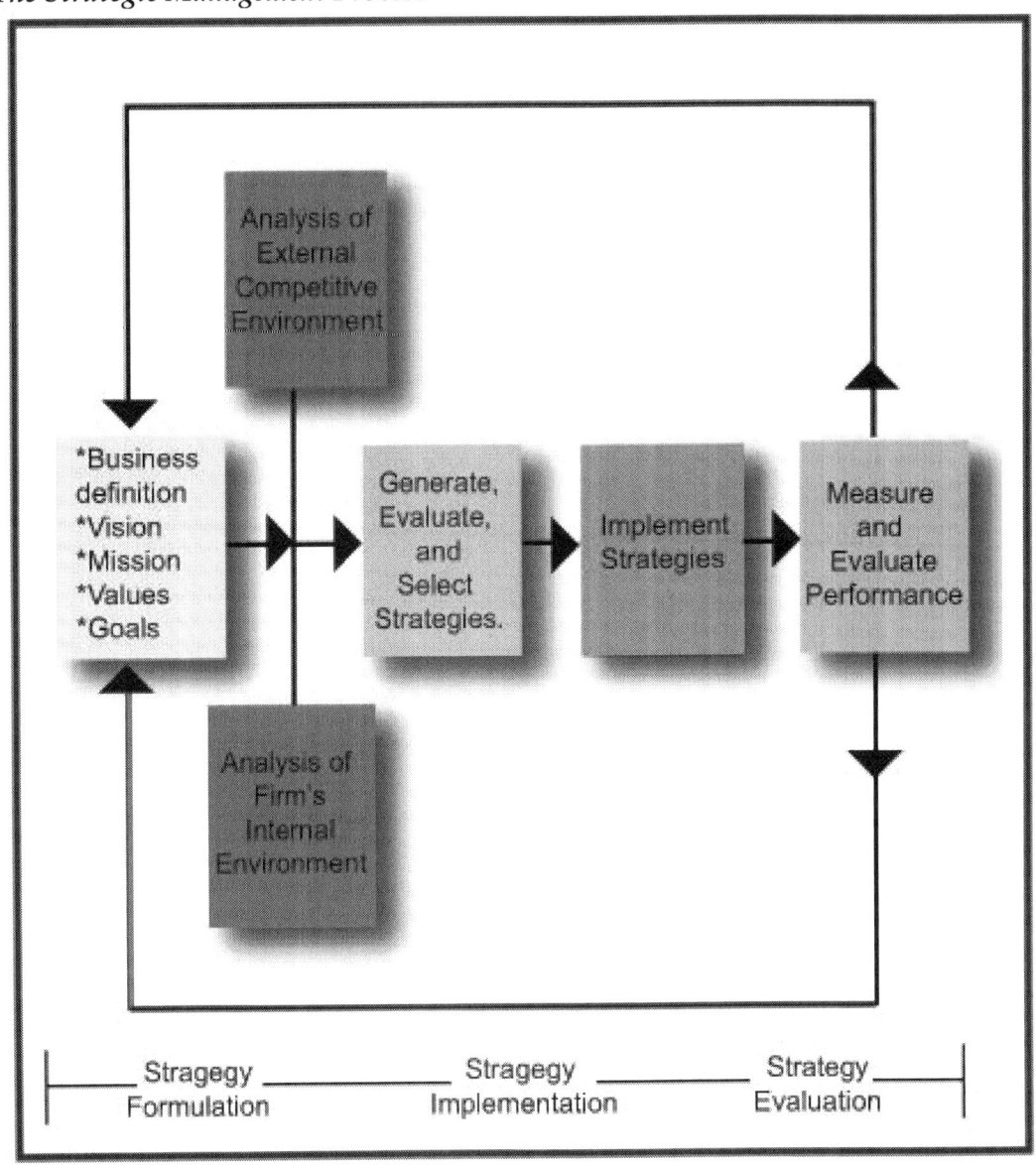

In general, we say that strategic management is a process because it involves logical steps that must be taken by the strategist in order to achieve the firm's mission, goals and objectives. It is impossible to skip one aspect of the process and hope to achieve a competitive advantage. Strategy formulation and implementation follow a well-designed step-by-step approach. Strategic management is a process because it is an ongoing, never-ending set of actions, not a start-stop event that, once done, can be safely put aside for a while. As an entrepreneur or a business owner, you have an ever-present responsibility for detecting when new developments require a strategic response and when they don't. Your job is to track progress, spot problems and issues early, monitor the winds of market and customer change, and initiate adjustments as needed. This is why the task of evaluating performance and initiating corrective adjustments is both the end and the beginning of the strategic management cycle. Figure 6-1 as shown above is generic in the sense that it is applicable to all types of businesses, whether large or small.

LEVELS OF STRATEGIES

As a business owner or an entrepreneur, there are several levels of strategies to work from. Usually, four types of strategies can be identified depending on the size and complexity of the company.[13] In large enterprises, decisions about what business approaches to take and what new moves to initiate involve senior executives in the corporate office, heads of business units and product divisions, the heads of major functional areas within a business or division (manufacturing, marketing, and sales, finance, human resources, and the like). In diversified enterprises, strategies are initiated at four distinct organization levels. There is a strategy for the company and all of its businesses as a whole (*corporate strategy*), There is a strategy for each separate business units the company has diversified into (*business strategy*), and then there is a strategy for each specific functional unit within a business (*functional strategy*). For example, some business units usually have a production strategy, a marketing strategy, human resources strategy, a finance strategy, and so on. We call these functional strategies. And, finally, there are still narrower strategies for basic operating units – plants, sales districts and regions, and departments within functional areas (*operating strategy*). In most entrepreneurial firms existing as single-business entities, there are only three levels of strategy making (business strategy, functional strategy, and operating strategy) unless diversification into other businesses becomes an active consideration.

Corporate Level Strategies

Corporate strategy consists of the kind of initiatives the company uses to establish business positions in different industries, the approaches corporate executives pursue to boost the combined performance of the set of businesses the company has diversified into, and the means of capturing cross-business synergies and turning them into competitive advantage. A corporate strategy is more applicable to diversified, multi-business companies where the strategies of several different businesses have to be managed from the corporate office.[14] Example is the diversification strategies adopted by the Dangote Group, Ibru Group or the Michael Adenuga Group in Nigeria. Specifically, the Dangote Group, the company exists in a wide range of industries some of which are not complimentary. In other words, the Dangote Group adopts a strategy of both related- and unrelated corporate diversification approach, as it exists broadly in many industries.

Notable amongst the businesses within the corporation are: Dangote Industries, Dangote Agro Sacks, Nigerian Textile Mills, Dangote Textile Mills, Dangote Ginnery, Dangote Cement and Sugar Refinery. Its strategic business units cover areas such as transportation and haulage, salt, flour and real estate.

When a company diversified into businesses with related technologies, similar operating characteristics, common distribution channels or customers, or some other synergistic factors, it gains competitive advantage potential not open to a company that diversifies into totally unrelated businesses. Example of this is Tourist Company of Nigeria with different, but related types of businesses in the hospitality industry: hotels, restaurants and tourism.

Corporate strategy is crafted at the highest levels of management in line with the demands placed on it by its board of directors. Senior corporate executives normally have lead responsibility for devising corporate strategy and for choosing among whatever recommended actions bubble up from lower-level managers. Heads of key business units may also be influential, especially in strategic decisions affecting the businesses they head. Major strategic decisions are usually reviewed and approved by the company's board of directors.

Business Level Strategies

The term business strategy (or business-level strategy) refers to the managerial or entrepreneurial game plan for a single business. Basically, your business strategy is mirrored in the pattern of approaches and moves crafted by you to produce successful performance in your own specific line of business. The central thrust of business strategy (and mostly applicable to the entrepreneur) is *how* to build and strengthen the long-term competitive position of your firm in the marketplace. A business strategy is concerned principally with (i) forming responses to changes under way in the industry, the economy at large, the regulatory and political arena, and other relevant areas; (ii) crafting competitive moves and market approaches that can lead to sustainable competitive advantage; (iii) building competitively valuable competencies and capabilities; (iv) uniting the strategic initiatives of functional departments; and (v) addressing specific strategic issues facing the company's business.

Many entrepreneurial conglomerates in Nigeria have distinctive strategic business units (SBUs) that are organized and managed in ways that enhance their competition within the particular business or market. For example, the Michael Adenuga Group (MA) consists of some independent business strategic business units standing on their own: Globacom, a telecommunication business unit, Conoil, a downstream oil operations business unit, Consolidated Oil, an oil exploration and exploitation business, Equitorial Trust Bank, in addition to stakes and interests in construction and real estate firms. Now, as a business unit, Globacom as a strategic business unit has its own competitive strategies, as it must compete with similar businesses in the Nigerian telecommunication market (or industry) such as MTN, Econet and MITEL.

As an entrepreneur, your business strategy involves initiating whatever actions and responses you deem prudent in light of competitive forces, economic trends, technological developments, buyer needs and demographics, new legislation and regulatory requirements, and other such broad external factors. The most successful business strategies typically aim at building uniquely strong or distinctive competencies in one or more areas crucial to strategic success and then using them as a basis for winning a competitive edge over rivals. Whether one is a manager of a business unit or an entrepreneur managing a firm, the responsibility for business strategy falls in the lap of whoever is in charge of the business. As an entrepreneur, you are accountable for the strategy and the results it produces. A good strategy is well-matched to a company's external and internal situation; as the company's situation changes in significant ways, then adjustments in strategy typically are needed. Some changes in a company's external and internal environment require little or no response, while others call for significant strategy alterations. For example, conventional retailers are rushing to establish their own Internet sales capabilities to defend against competition from thousands of enterprise Internet retailers.

A firm's business strategy for competing is typically both offensive and defensive. Some actions are aggressive and amount to direct challenges to competitors' market positions (the route most entrepreneurial firms normally take). Other firms aim at countering competitive pressures and actions of rivals (this is the preferred route for large, well established companies). Three of the most frequently used competitive approaches are (i) striving to be the industry's low-cost provider; (ii) pursuing such differentiation features as higher quality, added performance, better service, more attractive styling, technological superiority, or unusually good value; and (iii) focusing on a narrow market niche and doing a better job than rivals of serving the special needs and tastes of its buyers.

As the owner of a business, you are the chief strategist for the business and you have at least two other responsibilities. The first is seeing that supporting strategies in each of the major functional areas of your business are well conceived and consistent with each other. For instance, you should be able to know that the people you intend to employ (the function of the Human Resource Department) match those that the Marketing Department wants. The people needed by the marketing department should have the qualifications needed not only to sell the company's products or services but also its image. The second is getting major strategic moves in accordance with developments in the particular industry in which your business operates. That is, as an entrepreneur, you must craft your strategies in accordance with what is happening in the industry.

Functional Level Strategy

The third level of strategy-making in an organization is in the functional level. The most common approach to strategic decision-making, especially among entrepreneurial firms, is by function. The term functional strategy refers to the managerial game plan for a particular functional activity, business process, or key department within a business. As a firm, a functional unit groups together those jobs involving the same or similar activities. For example, the marketing activities of a firm are performed by those with the requisite marketing expertise and are grouped under the marketing unit or department. In a similar manner, those who have competency in finances and accounting perform the financial and accounting activities of the firm. A company's marketing strategy, for example, represents the firm's game plan for running the marketing part of the business. To manage a company, marketing experts are hired to run the marketing function. A firm's new product development strategy represents the managerial game plan for keeping the company's product lineup fresh and in tune with what buyers are looking for. As a business owner, your company needs a functional strategy for every major activity performed in the organizational unit.

Like business strategy, functional strategy must support the company's overall business strategy and competitive approach. A related role is to create a strategic road map for achieving the functional areas' objectives and mission. No matter how big or small your business is it needs a functional strategy. For example, your functional strategy in the finance area consists of how financial activities will be managed in supporting your business strategy and achieving the finance department's objectives and mission.

Operating Level Strategies

An operating strategy deals with the strategic initiatives and approaches for managing key operating units such as procurement in the production department, advertising in the marketing department, payroll in the human resources department, debt collection in the accounting department. Operating strategy is also concerned with handling daily operating tasks with strategic significance (advertising campaigns, materials purchasing, inventory control, maintenance, shipping, etc). An advertising unit manager or supervisor within the marketing department needs a strategy for accomplishing the unit's objectives, carrying out the unit's part of the marketing department's overall marketing game plan, and dealing with any strategy-related problems that exist within the advertising game plan in relationship with accomplishing the marketing objective of the company. As an entrepreneur, your district sales manager (working under a marketing manager) needs a sales strategy customized to the district's particular situation and sales objectives. The sales objectives are expected to be in line with the objectives of the marketing functional department. The objectives of the marketing department are also expected to be in line with the objectives of your overall business.

Although operating strategy is at the bottom of the strategy-making pyramid, its importance should not be downplayed. Operating-level strategies provide valuable support to the other higher-level strategies. Consider the case of Bhojsons and Co. a departmental store in Lagos, Nigeria whose business strategy is to compete with other departmental stores in Lagos. As a chain store, Bhojsons supplies furniture, household appliances, textiles, clothing, photographic equipment and optical equipment. In clothing and apparel, Bhojsons carries different lines of products and one of those lines is the shoe department. Within this department, there are several lines: such as children lines, ladies lines, and men lines. The shoe department is under the control of a shoe department manager. The men's line is under the supervision of a line supervisor. The line supervisor is in constant interaction with the buyers or customers. He or she knows what the customers' needs and utilities are. The supervisor is in a position to devise strategic plan for this particular unit. However, the plan must meet the objective and strategies of the shoe division (as a functional division). The strategies of the shoe division must meet the strategic objective of the whole store. Finally, the strategic objective of the whole store must be in line with that of the strategic options available to Bhojsons in order to compete with other stores in the same industry.

Another instance of the importance of operating strategy occurs in manufacturing companies. A major plant that fails in its strategy to achieve production volume, unit cost, and quality targets can undercut the achievement of company sales and profit objectives and wreak havoc with the whole company's strategic efforts to build a quality image with customers.

CASE IN POINT: EXAMINING LEVELS OF STRATEGY-MAKING AT A DIVERSIFIED COMPANY: UACN.

The United African Company, Nigeria Limited, is the foremost diversified company in Nigeria. Known presently as UAC of Nigeria Plc (UACN), the company was first incorporated in Lagos, Nigeria under the name Nigerian Motors Ltd on April 22nd, 1931 as a wholly owned subsidiary of the United Africa Company Ltd. The name was changed to UAC of Nigeria Limited on March 1st, 1973 in response to the indigenization decree of the Federal Government of Nigeria. UACN has an active foreign investor, Actis Capital, which owns 20 percent of the company's equity and has a representative on the Board. Today UACN has become a food-focused conglomerate with leading brands such as Mr. Biggs, Gala, Grand Oils, Supreme Ice cream, Swan spring water and Gossy spring water. The company's brand portfolio also includes franchised international food brands such as Nando's, Creamy Inn, Chicken Inn, Pizza Inn and Dial-A-Delivery among others.

UACN distributes its products and services throughout the country. The company also operates in the manufacturing, logistics, automobile and real estate sectors of the economy. The businesses of UACN are as follows: UAC Restaurants, UAC Foods, UAC Franchising, UAC Dairies, Grand Cereals & Oil Mills Ltd., Swan Spring waters Nigeria Ltd., Gossy Warm Spring Waters Nigeria Ltd., MDS Logistics, UACN Property Development Company Plc, Chemical & Allied Products Plc, General Motors Nigeria Limited, UNICO CPFA Limited (closed pension fund) and UAC Registrars Ltd.[15]

The Nigerian economy is made of several industries or sectors. An industry consists of number of sellers or firms providing similar services or products. In Nigeria, for example, there is the restaurant industry or market, the transportation industry, the food processing and distribution industry, the entertainment industry, the brewery industry, the oil and gas industry, etc. Each of these industries has characteristics that differentiate it from other types of industries.

As one of the most diversified corporations in Sub-Saharan Africa, UACN has operations in diverse industries or business areas such as manufacturing, merchandising, warehousing, services, technical operations, food processing and distribution and agro-related businesses. Each of these businesses is organized as separate entities and profit centers or strategic business units (SBUs). Some of these business units are publicly held and quoted in the Lagos Stock Exchange. UACN is well diversified into different lines of business and possesses the ability to utilize the synergies available across the different business lines. This improves efficiencies and leads to economies of scale with the resultant decline in costs.

The corporate strategy of UACN concerns how this heavily diversified company intends to establish business positions in different industries and the actions and approaches employed to improve the performance of the group of businesses UACN has diversified into. Thus, a key piece of UACN's corporate strategy is how many and what kinds of businesses or industries the company should be in- - specifically, what industries or markets to enter and whether to enter the industry by starting a new business, acquiring another company, or a troubled company (with turnaround potential), or forming an alliance with another company. In the case of the automobile or transportation industry, UACN formed a strategic alliance with General Motors to sell and service Chevrolet cars, Buick and other brand of cars produced by General Motors such as Bedford. Thus UAC General Motors competes with SCOA Motors and other businesses in the Nigerian auto industry.

For UACN, its corporate strategy is set at its headquarters located in Niger House, Lagos as the strategy is to initiate actions to boost the combined performance of the businesses the corporation as a whole has diversified into. As positions are created in the chosen industries, UACN's corporate strategy making concentrates on ways to strengthen the long-term competitive positions and profitability of all the business areas it has invested in. If a particular business is not doing well (e.g., UAC Foods), the parent company (UACN) can help it to be more successful by financing additional capacity and efficiency improvement, by supplying missing skills and managerial know-how, by acquiring another food company in the same industry and merging the two operations into a stronger business, or by acquiring new businesses that strongly complement existing businesses.

STRATEGIC BUSINESS UNITS WITHIN UACN

UACN is well diversified into different lines of business and possesses the ability to utilize the synergies available across the different business lines. As a corporation, UACN has several business units. Presently, UACN has the following business units: UAC Restaurants, UAC Foods, UAC Franchising, UAC Dairies, GCOM, SWAN, WSWNL, MDS, UPDC, CAPL, GMNL, UNICO, and UAC Registrars. Below is a brief mention of the areas:

UAC Restaurants is the result of the merger of the two restaurant businesses of UACN - Mr. Bigg's & Menu Masters Divisions.

UAC Foods is Nigeria's leading manufacturer and marketer of tasty and nourishing convenience foods.

UAC Franchising is the brand house responsible for all the Quick Service Restaurant brands under the UAC stable. The division is in charge of marketing, sub-franchising, brand standards, brand performance analysis, menu engineering, projects, point of sales and new entry strategies for the various brands under its care.

UAC DAIRIES is the business unit positioned to play a greater role in the broader dairy segments. UAC Dairies is the producer of Supreme Ice Cream, the leading brand of ice cream in Nigeria.

GCOML, Grand Cereals & Oil Mills Limited is engaged in the production and marketing of leading brands including Grand Pure Groundnut Oil, Grand Pure Soya Oil, Gold Medal Deodorized Groundnut Oil and Desire Natural Palm Oil; Richfil Cereal Meal, Mealia Cereal Meal and Vital Feed range of feeds, Premix and concentrates.

Spring Waters Nigeria Limited is the producer of SWAN Natural Spring Water, the pioneer brand of bottled water in Nigeria and the West African sub-region.

Warm Spring Waters Nigeria Limited (WSWNL) is engaged in the bottling and sale of GOSSY brand of spring water.

MDS Logistics is the leading integrated supply chain solutions company in Nigeria, with service offerings broadly categorized into warehousing, haulage and secondary distribution.

Chemical and Allied Products Plc (CAPL), previously called ICI Nigeria Limited, is the West African technological licensee of ICI for the production and marketing of Dulux – The World's No 1 Paint.

UACN Property Development Company Plc (UPDC) is a composite real estate company with the mission of providing solutions in the area of property development and management.

GM Nigeria Limited (GMNL), a foremost automobile company, markets the popular Isuzu Pickups Van. GMNL also markets the Isuzu NPR Medium Commercial and FTR heavy commercial trucks (assembled from CKD kits).

UNICO CPFA Limited is a Closed Pension Fund Administrator. Formally known as UNICO Pension Trust Limited, it was founded in January 1958. Following the implementation of the new pension reform, the Company was registered as a Closed Pension Fund Administrator in 2006.

Registrars Limited is a capital market registrar's outfit with a proven track record. Established in 1978 as a department of UAC of Nigeria Plc, it was incorporated as a limited liability company in 2005 in compliance with the directives of the Securities and Exchange Commission (SEC).

As a result of this diversification, there is constant improvement of efficiencies, which leads to economies of scale with the resultant decline in costs. Furthermore, the renewed focus on the food business due to favorable trends in the market (under-penetrated market, economic growth and a growing middle class) has enabled UACN to claim more of the available market share especially in underserved markets. In addition, UACN is embarking on an innovative retail format by mobilizing its food court concept to enhance speed to market through a bundled menu approach; this has also enabled the corporation to offer more of their restaurant/franchise offerings at one location. E.g. a Creamy Inn,

Village Kitchen and Pizza Inn all at one location. Most importantly, numerous internal synergies between subsidiaries and associated companies have enabled UACN to do a lot more with less; this leads to lower production costs and more ability to increase volumes.[16]

In a diversified company, strategic questions faced by corporate-level managers would include (i) how to make moves to establish positions in different businesses and achieve corporate objectives through diversification, (ii) how to initiate actions to boost the combined performance of the businesses the firm has diversified into, (iii) how to pursue ways to capture valuable cross-business strategic fits and turn them into competitive advantage, (iv) how to establish investment priorities and steer corporate resources into the most attractive business units.

STRATEGIC MANAGEMENT PROCESS AND ENTREPRENEURIAL VENTURES

We have noted that an entrepreneur, like a corporate manager, is the ultimate strategist. However, unlike the corporate manager, the entrepreneur or the small business owner makes all the strategic as well as operational decisions. The last three levels of strategy – business, functional and operational – are the concerns of the founder and owner of the business. Entrepreneurs are strategic planners without realizing it.

In performing the entrepreneurial function as a strategist, the owner of a venture is expected to follow some steps in managing the firm such as having a basic business idea that has not yet been successfully tried, a definition of the business on the basis of identification of customers' needs, identification of the customer groups, and how the customers' needs will be satisfied. The vision and mission of the firm or that of the entrepreneur follow this. After the mission and vision statement, the entrepreneur now states the objectives and goals of the firm. These could be the strategic objectives, namely, how to compete successfully in the market place and financial objectives, that is, how much is to be realized financially in order to keep the business running and compensate those who have invested in the business. The next stage for the entrepreneur is that of performing the task of external analysis - trying to understand the industry and the nature of competition within it. This is followed by an internal assessment, that is, understanding ones' own capabilities and weaknesses. In the light of this external and internal analysis, the next stage for the entrepreneur is that of crafting the strategies the firm intends to use in pursuing and achieving the stated goals and objectives of the firm. Finally, the entrepreneur must put in place necessary evaluation and control mechanisms to see if the firm's stated objectives and goals have been achieved.

In general an ideal model for a strategic management approach for the entrepreneurial firms should follow basic eight steps described below. These will be discussed in detail in this book:

1. **Develop a Basic Business Idea:** A business idea comes from a conception of *what* you intend to offer, *why* you want to offer it and *how* you are going to offer it. It consists of a product or a service that you intend to offer to existing or prospective customers. Most importantly, the product or service must have a target market or markets. As discussed in chapter one, the idea can be developed from your own experience or generated in a moment of creative thinking. An idea can also be generated through extensive market research.

2. **Develop a Clear Vision and translate it into a Meaningful Mission Statement:** A vision is the result of an entrepreneur's dream of something that does not exist yet and the ability to paint compelling picture of that dream for everyone to see. An entrepreneur's vision sets the stage for the mission statement of the firm. Whereas a mission is what the firm does and what it stands for, a vision is where the firm wants to be in the long run. The mission stands for the values espoused by the founder or founders of the firm. The vision statement tells the public where the firm intends to be in the future.

3. **Set Objectives and/or Goals for the Firm**: As we shall see in the next chapter, objectives and goals are the ultimate and concrete aspects of your business. You have to achieve your objectives in order to realize your mission and vision. As an entrepreneur, what your firm aims at achieving is your goal and what your firm intends to do by reaching that goal is its objective. In strategic management, a firm must strive to achieve two sets of objectives: strategic objectives and financial objectives. Strategic objectives represent the firm's achievement in competition, such as increased market share, product or service quality and good reputation, among others. On the other hand, financial objectives are stated in monetary terms such as annual return on investment, growth in earnings, etc. All these objectives have one thing in common: leading you to achieve the goal of the firm.

4. **Scan and Assess the External Environment**: Environmental scanning is done in order to locate factors in the societal, economic, business and technological environment to understand opportunities and threats. The scanning should focus on market potential and resource accessibility. Environmental scanning also includes efforts to understand the nature of competition within the particular industry one wants to enter. In the process of scanning and assessing the external environment, the entrepreneur should be able to recognize the key success factors in that industry. Every business is characterized by controllable factors or variables that determine the relative success of market participants. Identifying and applying these variables is how a small business gains a competitive advantage. Key success factors are factors that determine a company's ability to compete successfully in an industry. If, for instance, you intend to go into the restaurant business, it is important that you understand the factors that make restaurant owners successful.

    Environmental scanning and assessment also allows you to get a picture of how intense is the competition. As pointed out in this chapter, business is like any battlefield. If an entrepreneur wants to win the war, he or she must know what the firm is up against. Sizing up the competition gives you, as a business owner, a more realistic view of the market and your company's position in it. As an entrepreneur, you are required to understand what your competitors have or do not have in terms of their competitiveness in the market.

5. **Assess the Internal Factors**: Internal factors relevant to the success of the business must also be assessed. The entrepreneur should objectively consider personal assets, areas of expertise, capabilities, and experience, all in terms of the organizational needs of the new venture. At this stage, the entrepreneur is required to know his or her strengths such as a skill, valuable assets, or any of those things that the firm can do exceedingly well and those things that it is not good at compared to competitors' capabilities and weaknesses.

6. **Formulate Strategic Options and Select the Appropriate Strategies:** At this point in the strategic management process, entrepreneur should have a clear picture of what the business does best and what its competitive advantages are. The entrepreneur should also at this point understand the weaknesses and limitations of the firm as well as those of its competitors. On the basis of this knowledge, he or she is now in a position to evaluate the strategic options and then prepare a game plan designed to achieve the stated mission, goals, and objectives. The questions to be asked here are: What should I do now to enter the market or industry? How do I compete with those already there? How do I take customers from the existing providers of products or services? Answers to these questions provide you with a strategic option and the appropriate strategy to formulate.

7. **Generate a Business Plan:** From the point of view of entrepreneurship, a business plan is your game plan in the sense that it specifies how your ideas will be transformed into reality. In addition to the six points discussed above, a business plan helps you to put your business ideas to the test, shows you what you are up against, specifies what you need to start your business, know how much it will cost you to run your business, tells people who you are and where you are heading. The content of a business plan should include the firm's marketing strategies and approaches, sources and uses of finances, including projected performance results, the location of the firm, the legal form the business will take, the staff and management of the firm, and how the entrepreneur or the owners of the business intend to manage organizational growth and transition. The nature of a business plan, its uses and strategies for designing a winning one are discussed in detail in chapter fifteen.

8. **Implement and Evaluate the Business Plan:** A business plan, like a strategic plan, consists of ideas and plans. A business plan is nothing until it is put into practice. As stated earlier, this can be done through the use of action plans, programs and procedures. Evaluation is done through comparison of actual performance against projected performance results. To the extent that actual results are less than or

much greater than the anticipated results, the entrepreneur needs to reconsider the firm's current business idea, mission, objectives, strategies, policies, and programs, and possibly makes changes to the original business plan. This is why we call strategic management as a process; it has no end, as it must be continually revised to see where things have gone right or wrong.

CONDITIONS FOR A WINNING STRATEGY

As an entrepreneur how do you know that the strategy you've crafted is a winning one? According to Arthur Thompson, A. Strickland and John Gamble, three questions can be used to test the merits of one strategy versus another and distinguish a winning strategy from a flawed strategy[17]:

1. *How well does the strategy fit the company's situation?* To qualify as a winner, a strategy has to be well matched to industry and competitive conditions, a company's best market opportunities, and other aspects of the company's external environment. At the same time, the strategy has to be tailored to the company's resource strengths and weaknesses, competencies, and competitive capabilities. Unless a strategy exhibits tight fit with both the external and internal aspects of a company's overall situation, it is likely to produce less than the best possible business results.

2. *Is the strategy helping the company achieve a sustainable competitive advantage?* Winning strategies enable a company to achieve a competitive advantage that is durable. The bigger and more durable the competitive edge that a strategy helps build, the more powerful and appealing it is.

3. *Is the strategy resulting in better company performance?* A good strategy boosts company performance. Two kinds of performance improvements tell the most about the caliber of a company's strategy: (a) gains in profitability and financial strength, and (b) gains in the company's competitive strength and market standing.

In short, a winning strategy must fit the company's external and internal situation, build sustainable competitive advantage, and improve company performance. Once a company commits to a particular strategy and enough time elapses to assess how well it fits the situation and whether it is actually delivering competitive advantage and better performance, then one can determine what grade to assign that strategy. Strategies that come up short on one or more of the above questions are plainly less appealing than strategies that pass all three test questions with flying colors.

Entrepreneurs and managers can also use the same questions to pick and choose among alternative strategic actions. A company evaluating which of several strategic options to employ can evaluate how well each option measures up against each of the three questions. The strategic option with the highest prospective passing scores on all three questions can be regarded as the best or most attractive alternative.

Other criteria for judging the merits of a particular strategy include internal consistency and unity among all the pieces of strategy, the degree of risk the strategy poses as compared to alternative strategies, and the degree to which it is flexible and adaptable to changing circumstances. These criteria are relevant and merit consideration, but they seldom override the importance of the three test questions posed above.

CHAPTER SUMMARY

A business environment refers to the environmental setting in which a competitive engagement with an adversary (a competitor) takes place. A business environment is like a military terrain.

A strategic group consists of those rival firms with similar competitive approaches and positions in the market. Firms in the same strategic group pursue similar strategies with similar resources.

A company's strategy is the game plan management is using to stake out a market position, conduct its operations, attract and please customers, compete successfully and achieve organizational objectives. Each firm is likely to devise its own strategy to deal with its competitive rivals, to serve its particular base of customers, and to act upon the changes that impact the way it operates.

A company has competitive advantage whenever it has an edge over rivals in attracting customers and defending against competitive forces. The reason for having a strategy is for the firm to achieve a competitive advantage.

Crafting strategy is an exercise in entrepreneurship because the entrepreneur must follow some logical steps in the process of developing his or her own business.

A competitive advantage is the aggregation of factors that sets a business firm apart from its competitors and gives it a unique position in the market superior to its competition. The key to business success is to develop a unique competitive advantage: one that creates value for the customer. Sustainable competitive advantage is about how a firm builds its own strategies and competitive advantage and maintains them over a long period of time.

The resources of a firm can be grouped under two broad categories: tangible and intangible resources. Tangible resources include such things as land, buildings, plant, equipment, human, finance, technological, organizational, etc. Intangible resources include such things as the firm's brand name, reputation, patents, and technological or marketing know-how.

Capabilities refer to a company's skills at coordinating its resources and putting them to productive use. Most successful entrepreneurs are able to continually transform their resources into capabilities.

A distinctive competence is a unique strength that allows a company to achieve superior efficiency, quality, innovation, or customer responsiveness and thereby create superior value and attain a competitive advantage.

A small business can gain a distinctive competence from three areas: (i) its ability to identify new niches in established markets, (ii) the ability to identify new markets, and (iii) the ability to take advantage of new opportunities.

A first-mover advantage is any advantage that comes to a firm because it exploits an opportunity before any other firm does.

A core competence is a unique set of capabilities that a company develops in key areas, such as superior quality, customer service, innovation, team building, flexibility, responsiveness, product design, low cost manufacturing, proprietary technology, superior distribution, etc. In other words, a core competence is a competitively important internal activity that a company performs better than other competitively important internal activities.

Developing core competencies require an entrepreneur to use creativity, imagination, and vision to identify those things that the company does best and that are most important to its target customers.

The strategic management process consists of two major stages: (i) the strategy formulation stage and (ii) the strategy implementation stage. The strategy formulation stage consists of analyzing the current situation of the firm, selecting strategies that fit the needs of the firm, and making plans to pursue those strategies. The strategy implementation stage is a process by which policies, procedures, programs and budgets are put in place to achieve the strategic objectives.

There are four types or levels of strategies: (i) corporate strategy, (ii) business strategy, (iii) functional strategy, and (iv) operational strategy. Most entrepreneurial firms have only the business, functional and operational types or levels of strategies.

The eight steps in the strategic management process for entrepreneurial ventures are: (i) developing a basic business idea, (ii) developing a clear vision and mission statements, (iii) setting objectives and goals for the firm, (iv) scanning and assessing the external environment, (v) assessing internal factors, (vi) formulating and selecting appropriate strategies, (vii) generating a business plan and (viii) implementing and evaluating the business plan.

A winning strategy must fit the company's external and internal situation, build sustainable competitive advantage, and improve company performance.

CHAPTER DISCUSSION QUESTIONS

1. What is a business environment? Why a business environment is often described as a battlefield?

2. What do you understand by the concept "competitive advantage?" Give examples of firms' competitive advantages with which you are familiar.

3. What is firm's distinctive competence?

4. What are the two complimentary sources for a firm's distinctive competence?

5. What is a firm's core competency? Provide examples of core competencies of firms that you know.

6. What is a business strategy?

7. What are the two major reasons why managers and entrepreneurs devise company strategies?

8. What is a business environment?

9. Why is a strategy important to your business and its competitiveness?

10. What are the eight steps involved in developing an ideal strategic management plan for an entrepreneurial venture?

CASE STUDY 6: ENTREPRENEURIAL STRATEGIES IN A DEVELOPING ECONOMY: ALIKO DANGOTE AND THE DANGOTE GROUP[18]

"I can remember when I was in primary school, I would go and buy cartons of sweets and I would start selling them just to make money. I was so much interested in business. Even at that time, I was very used to buying and selling. It is in my mind all through. I did that on a part-time basis. I usually bought packets of sweets and gave some people to sell for me. I would join them whenever I closed from school. I would collect my profit and give them something out of it. And we continued like that" (Aliko Dangote, World's richest Black person).

Aliko Dangote, President and Chief Executive Officer of Dangote Group of Companies is a case study of African private entrepreneurship that has emerged from trading and branched into diversified unrelated business units – a phenomenon commonly associated among Africa's brand of successful entrepreneurs. The story of Aliko Dangote and the Dangote Group illustrates entrepreneurial strategies suitable in the context of a developing economy. Most significantly, it illustrates not only the existence of business opportunities, but also the type of strategies applicable in such an environment.

Aliko Dangote, with his Dangote Group of companies, runs about 13 companies with interests in oil, banking, agriculture, manufacturing, textile and transportation spread across the Sub-Saharan region. As at 2008, he listed two of these companies on the Nigerian Stock Exchange and analysts put his stakes in these two alone as being more than $4 billion. His cement business is also listed on the London Stock Exchange and the Johannesburg Stock Market. His on-going projects are said to be about $10 billion and this include the world's biggest sugar refinery, a 300,000 barrels a day oil refinery and a 5,000 megawatt power project. Already, he owns one of Africa's biggest cement plants, the $800 million cement plant, including three other cement plants and a joint ownership of a cement plant in South Africa; co-owns a charter airline; several dollar-denominated luxury high rises; and the most viable of Nigerian textile and flour mills. According to the 2008 Forbes International Billionaire List, Aliko Dangote, with a net worth of $3.3 billion is the richest black person in the world.

From the Beginning

His unlikely run to the top of the Nigerian business sector started at the age of 20 in 1977 when he got a loan of N500,000 from his maternal grandfather, the patriarch of a very successful trading family, the Dantatas. That loan was what he parlayed into enormous wealth. His father, a notable but less-business inclined politician, left him two buildings. "I did not really inherit anything apart from, maybe, two buildings. I had three (Benz) 911 (10 tonner trucks) which my grandfather bought for me and they were working and he was keeping the money for me at that time. So by the time I came out, I had about N127,000 or so. And then my grandfather also gave me a letter to collect N500,000 as loan to be paid back in two years but there was no interest," he told The Guardian, Nigeria's foremost newspaper.

Before then he had worked for his uncle. In fact, in his word, he 'squatted' in the latter's office when he started with two staff: a manager and a secretary. "I started with the business of cement, which was giving us a lot of money because at that time Nigeria was making so much money and we were doing a lot of constructions. On a vehicle which I normally get from my uncle, I was making about Nl,350 to Nl,400 and everyday I had an allocation of about 3-4 trucks including Saturdays and Sundays.

"Later I realized that I was making a lot of money though then I didn't have a lot of ideas of what to do. It was only cement business that I knew and I stuck to it up till 1980 when I started knowing Lagos, becoming a Lagosian, understanding where to go and finding people to buy import licenses from. Within three months I paid my grandfather back because I had no further need of his money," he said. Dangote would always credit his move to Lagos in the 1980s as one of his biggest breakthroughs. Kano, his family operating base and business headquarters though one of West Africa's biggest trading hubs, lacks Lagos' many opportunities. He was afraid that his family wouldn't want him to come to Lagos. They felt Lagos' fast-paced life could corrupt him. "In fact, when I told my grandfather that I will like to be given the opportunity to come to Lagos, I just tried him because I thought the answer was going to be no but he allowed me to go," he said. And again he felt he should leave the family business and strike out on his own. "Working with family, you hardly succeed because you have other children. You know, it is difficult when you come from a large family," he said.

Dangote's greatest fear when he started business was that of failure. "I had that fear of being totally on my own because if there is a failure it will show immediately but if you are with somebody and there's a little failure, you'd still have a cover up because they'll be looking at that bigger signboards," he said. Fortunately for him, shortly after his arrival in Lagos and after he had made good money in the cement business, the military came and clamped all the leading businessmen into jail after accusing them of working with corrupt politicians. It was an opportunity of a lifetime for Dangote to take over the market left by this huge vacuum. He seized it with both hands. He cornered the sugar market and also made massive inroads into the importation of rice.

But he has also made mistakes. His biggest was his initial foray into banking, where a bank that he invested in heavily went bankrupt. But before it did, he had pulled out and cut his losses saying that he felt he should only operate a business that he understood. He said one of the reasons for the fast growth of his businesses is its prudence and wise investment decisions, the biggest of which is decision to always plough his profits back into Nigeria. "The difference between our company and others is that we always invest. We don't go on buying this one, or that one, spending money the normal (way) Nigerians kill business. We always try to re-invest whatever we make in the business not to take the money and keep it in an offshore account. (It is) not that we don't have money abroad. We have but not the majority of our money. We try as much as possible to invest our money here," he said.

But his biggest break was his shift from the importation business to manufacturing. That shift was inspired during a trip to Brazil in the late eighties. "The first company I visited was a company called Arisco, a company that produces 503 different items. I was impressed when I went to one of their factories. They had over 4,000 workers. Even though in Nigeria at that time we were not in manufacturing, the only manufacturing company we had at that time was textiles.

"Going to Brazil I thought that we were at the same level with Brazil because I used to hear of Brazil as a debtor nation owing so much money. But when I went there, I saw massive industrialization, it was unbelievable. I started thinking that how come they have these things in Brazil and we don't have it in Nigeria. So with that now, when I came back I said okay, fine, I want to venture into industry," he said.

But he said he realized that the safest way of venturing into industry was to avoid a situation where both manufacturing and the marketing side of business will compete for his attention at the same time.

"So, the easiest for me to do is to now pick the same item that I am now trading in and do a backward integration, which will be much easier and faster for me. So we started with sugar refinery. Then when we met again we said what about spaghetti we are doing (importing) about 360 containers every year, we should go and do spaghetti. So, we jumped into spaghetti. Polypropylene bagging, because we didn't want somebody to hold us to ransom in terms of bagging. Believe me, each and everyone item that we've gone into has been a blessing because there's not a single one that we are not making good money out of today. I realize that it is much better than trading, even though industries too have their own headaches (in terms of margin). If you have good margin like we have, you won't have any problems," he said.

Growth and Expansion

The growth and transformation years of the company spanned a period of five years, which is from 1997 to 2002. To start with, the company had a vision to be a world-class enterprise that is passionate about the living standards of the general populace and high returns to stakeholders and the mission to touch the lives of people by providing their basic needs. Thus, in 1997, Dangote Group reviewed its business vis-à-vis the opportunities and threats in the environment with a view to determining the strategic options for sustaining its market leadership in trading commodities such as sugar, rice, flour, salt, pasta, textiles, etc.

The outcome of that review was a decision by the group to transform itself from the leading commodity trader in the country to the leading manufacturer of essential needs of food, shelter and clothing. This was to be achieved by embarking upon an import substitution strategy along the group's traditional line of trading activities. And at that time, the company was already importing salt, sugar, flour, rice, and more. Management then decided to set up manufacturing companies in Nigeria to make and sell the products locally. Towards this end, Dangote Industries Limited (DIL), the group's brand name, was incorporated as the vehicle for executing the group's import substitution strategy in the following products: salt processing, sugar refining, flour milling, bulk cement terminals and pasta production.

Dangote made his name in commodity trading especially sugar importation into Nigeria, which he controls over 70 percent today. Given the heavy demand by Nigeria's soft drink industry, breweries and confectionery industries for sugar, he makes a huge success by doing volume business (economy of scale) and gaining advantages to undercut competitors. Dispelling rumors of his cornering the market with the connivance of government support, he says it is an open market but because of his enormous investment in the business and his transport haulage business, he was able to distribute his sugar faster, cheaper and at a uniform prize nationwide, which the competition cannot match. Dangote is reputed to have good investments even in foreign-based sugar refineries that supply him.

His business interest spans the export and import businesses. He exports cashew nuts, cotton, cocoa, millet and textile. His extensive network enables him to source these commodities not only in Nigeria but the entire west coast of Africa where he has become a visible player. Dangote also imports and sells rice, vegetable oil, and cement. He employs similar strategies in the distribution of these commodities as in the sugar business. In December 1996, Dangote says, in response to a mandate from government, he imported and sold so much rice that the local market crashed by almost 80 percent. In the 1980s, Dangote decided to move from being just a successful commodity dealer to a more rounded entrepreneur with solid investments in finance and manufacturing. Dangote's entrepreneurial strategy lay in the acquisition of and buying into existing companies.

In the manufacturing sector, he started out with Dangote General Textile Product, which he acquired from its former owners thereby establishing control over the source of his trade. In 1993, he acquired controlling shares in the Lagos-based Nigerian Textile Mills and invested enormous resources in re-capitalizing, refurbishing its machinery and restructuring its management. And within a few years, he turned it from a loss maker back to its days of good profits. Looking beyond just making and exporting textile materials, the Dangote Group began to explore opportunities to manufacture jeans materials for the export market.

His venture into the sugar market is also a story of success in entrepreneurship. When the company started the sugar refinery in Apapa, Lagos, it was producing about 600 thousand metric tonnes annually. As a result of several expansions, it outgrew that capacity to about 1.35 million metric tonnes annually. Today, the Dangote Sugar Refinery is the second largest sugar refinery in the world and the most capitalized company on the Nigeria Stock Exchange, valued at over $3 billion with Aliko Dangote's equity at $2 billion in 2007. The sugar company is a market leader in sugar importation (to the tune of 400,000 metric tones or 70 percent of Nigeria's total requirements). Dangote also bought 40 percent shares of the Nigerian Salt Company to broaden his investment portfolio.

The Dangote Group, originally a small trading firm founded in 1977, is now a multi-billion dollar conglomerate with operations across Africa. The Group's manufacturing interest did not end in textiles and sugar, but also in cement, making it one of Africa's largest industrial group, including Africa's largest cement production plant. The Dangote Group's transformation from being an importer of cement to a manufacturer has largely been driven by the vision of Aliko Dangote to create an industrial conglomerate in Nigeria substituting the massive cement imports with locally produced product. This aligns fully with the industrialization policy of Nigeria's federal government.

In the flourmill business unit, the group has four mills. It started with one in Apapa, Lagos, which had the capacity to produce about 500 thousand metric tones annually. With expansion, the group now has other mills in Kano, Calabar and Ilorin. Presently, it has four thousand tonnes milling capacity per day and 1.35 million metric tonnes annually.

The Group has three salt manufacturing plants with 10 million tonnes annually, which has doubled to 20 million tonnes now. The company has also built some special mills in that area that would focus only on the production of Semolina, which they use for the pasta. Presently, the company uses part of the capacity in the Lagos Flour Mills to provide the raw materials for the pasta. In haulage, the group has a fleet of over 2000 trucks. In real estate, it boasts of four blocks consisting of 72 luxury apartments in prime areas of Lagos (Ikoyi and Victoria Island), the British High Commission Consular office in Abuja and 40 houses in Kano.

Significantly, the group's strategy is to progressively substitute its market share – previously sourced entirely from imports – with domestic production. In the month of April 2008, the Dangote Group acquired a 45 percent stake in South Africa's Sephaku Cement for 3 billion rand (about US$378 million or N44.75 billion). According to the agreement, the cash from the strategic partnership would help finance the building of a 2.2 million tonnes per year cement plant in South Africa that is expected to start production by mid 2010. The deal is the latest move by the group, which intended to expand its cement interests among countries in Sub-Saharan Africa. The Dangote group has previously signed contracts worth $1.2 billion in February of 2008 with China's Sinoma International to built cement plants in the Democratic Republic of Congo, Equatorial Guinea, Ethiopia, Tanzania, Senegal and Zambia. Sinoma and Dangote also signed another contract in February of 2008 worth $1.6 billion to build six cement production lines in Nigeria. The group commissioned two cement plants in May of 2007 in central Nigeria with a combined capacity of 8 million tonnes a year, after it first bought control of the Benue Cement Company. Dangote Cement plans to list on the Nigerian stock exchange through an IPO, and is also targeting a GDR listing on the London Stock Exchange.

In 2007, Dangote purchased the majority shares in Port Harcourt and Kaduna petroleum refineries with plans to build a 300,000 bpd refinery in Lagos. The refineries were later seized by the new administration of President Umaru Yar'adua, who believed that the refineries were one of the most important assets of the nation and it is unwise to sell them to private sector.

The Dangote Group generated revenue in excess of $1.255 billion in 2005. The group is one of the foremost-diversified business conglomerates in Sub-Saharan Africa and has about 11,000 people in its employment. With an estimated current net worth of around US$3.3 billion, Aliko Dangote is ranked by Forbes Magazine as the 334th richest man in the world as of March 5, 2008, making him the richest African person. Dangote Group is currently the largest industrial conglomerate in West Africa and one of the largest in Africa.

The core business philosophy of the Dangote Group is to provide their customers with a high level of customer care and service. The group is continually investing in qualified staff and IT network that will ensure that these high levels of service is carried through into a market place that is becoming more sophisticated. The Dangote Group has four regional offices located in strategic locations throughout Nigeria. Each of these offices has regional autonomy and responsibility for specific targets. By having these regional offices the Dangote Group ensures easy and frequent communication with all their customers, which again allows for superior customer care.

Entrepreneurial Strategies in a Developing Economy

The key success factors contributing to the growth of Dangote Group remain the entrepreneurial drive to identify and exploit opportunities such as market discontinuities and untapped demand well ahead of competition, a synergistic effect from its various businesses, prudent cash management strategy of reinvesting funds in massive production capacity, utilizing state-of-the-art plants and technology. The group also believes in developing strong asset base and brand equity to alter the competitive forces in the industry to the group's advantage.

The Dangote group understands the inherent constraints of operating in a developing economy, and has structured its business around an extended value chain – thereby ensuring the care and service that the Dangote Group has become known for. Although the group's primary activities are manufacturing, imports packaging and nationwide distribution, it has made sure that there is a synergistic effect between the various business units. Also, another strategy adopted by the group is that of in-ward looking. Thus, in line with the Nigerian Governments' stated objective of driving economic growth, importation of raw material will gradually be replaced by the manufacturing or cultivating of these materials within Nigeria. Some of the Dangote products are also exported to other countries in West Africa such as Benin and Ghana. Although currently a small contributor to the overall business, exports are expected to show growth of between 15 – 20 percent over the next 5 years.

A number of factors contributed to the current success of the group. One, as a marketer, Dangote believes in earning low profit in exchange for huge volume sales. This strategy gave it a competitive edge in the market. And with its pricing, consumers perceive its products' pricing as pocket friendly. Two, as a believer in backward integration moving from mere trading to real manufacturing, Dangote has been able to throw its competitors who were still entrenched in mere imports into disarray. Three, Dangote believes in aggressive marketing strategy, deploying the legion of trucks in its fleet on the road; its products are available in the nooks and crannies of the country. Four, it also employs a mixed grill of advertising, public relations, promotions and other relevant strategy in the marketing mix to sell its products. Beyond these however, over the years Dangote has operated as a socially responsible citizens by contributing huge chunk of funds to philanthropy and sundry other positive causes by its spheres of operation. In the Dangote Group, as in most Africa's conglomerates, corporate diversification has led to improved efficiencies, which leads to economies of scale with the resultant decline in costs.

Dangote Group is currently the largest industrial conglomerate in West Africa and one of the largest in Africa. It generated revenue in excess of $1.255 billion in 2005. The group is one of the foremost diversified business conglomerates in sub-Saharan Africa. With a hard-earned reputation for excellent business practices and product quality, it has about 11,000 people in its employment.

Case Discussion Questions

1. With the experience of Aliko Dangote and the Dangote group, what are the opportunities and threats facing entrepreneurs in a developing economy such as Nigeria?

2. Examine the strategies used by the Dangote Group in Nigeria. Describe these strategies and how appropriate they are in a developing economy.

3. Is Aliko Dangote an entrepreneur? Please support your position with materials discussed in chapter one and two of this book.

4. What lesson can other African business owners learn from the experience of Aliko Dangote and the Dangote Group?

Chapter 7

BUSINESS DEFINITION, VISION, MISSION, VALUES & OBJECTIVES

"Where there is no vision, the people perish" (The Book of Proverbs 29:18)

CHAPTER LEARNING OBJECTIVES
After studying this chapter, you should be able to:

1. Understand the meaning of a business and how to define one.

2. Examine and understand the key components of a business.

3. State the vision of the firm.

4. Craft the mission of the business.

5. Understand the components of a mission statement and the importance of a clear mission statement.

6. Understand the importance of value statement for the entrepreneurial firm.

7. Differentiate between firm's objectives and goals.

8. Differentiate between a firm's strategic and financial objectives.

INTRODUCTION: THE IMPORTANCE OF VISION, MISSION, VALUES AND OBJECTIVES

This chapter focuses on the concepts and tools needed to evaluate and write business definition, vision, mission and value statements, including how to establish and differentiate between a firm's goals and its objectives. A practical framework for developing mission statements is provided. Actual vision, mission and values statements from large and small organizations and for-profit and nonprofit organizations are presented and critically examined. The process of creating a vision and mission is discussed.

As we shall see in this chapter, the first step in the entrepreneurial process is defining the business. First, a business is not defined by its name, statuses, or articles of incorporation. Rather, it is defined by what it offers, to whom it is offered, and how it is offered. These three things are based on the mission of the firm. In general, a business definition helps keep the business focused.[1] Once you have adequately defined the business (at least a good draft), you can begin to focus on the market specifically. A business definition also assists in setting goals or objectives. If the market segment is adequately defined then it becomes reasonable to ask how large it is. You could further ask what the competition is like (those with similar definitions, even if they don't know it.) You could pose the question as to what degree of market penetration you might experience. You might also realize how your company differs from that of your competitor and what you can do better. The definition then helps in setting an appropriate goal.

In a similar manner, a firm needs a vision as well as a mission. A vision of a firm focuses, directs, motivates, unifies, and even excites a business into superior performance. The job of a strategist is to identify and project a clear vision and mission. The importance of a vision is underscored in the Book of Proverbs where it reminds us that, "where there is no vision, the people perish."

The successful entrepreneurs whose history we examined in chapter two are those who came up with clear vision and mission statements. They are those who translated the vision into mission statements. The objectives and goals of their businesses were guided toward success through the successful translation of their mission statements into workable, achievable and measurable goals. We also noted in chapter two that starting a business rests on a set of beliefs and that the organization can offer some product or service to some customers, in some geographic area, using some type of technology, at a profitable price.

The importance of mission and value statements for the entrepreneurial firm cannot be over-stated. First, passion sells! No matter what business you are in, or what you are selling, people want to buy passion and enthusiasm. Many lack it in their own lives and they are drawn to passion and enthusiasm like moths to a flame. To exude passion and enthusiasm day in and day out in your business, your business must align with your personal values and mission. Face it, if you don't enjoy going that extra mile for customers, for example, you are not going to get far with a business that requires a lot of customer hand holding. And that is okay. There are many businesses in which you can thrive that don't rely on extensive customer service, but you need to be brutally honest with yourself about whether you are passionate about what your business is offering. Nobody is going to be fooled if you're not walking your talk. Your mission and value statements help you walk your business talk.

Second, defining a core mission for your business which is aligned with your personal values (and therefore, you) will allow you to craft a business brand or reputation for which your business will become known. This mission/brand will become your compass as your business grows. Every opportunity and challenge will be measured against this core mission/brand. If a given opportunity or challenge runs contrary to your business' core mission, then either the opportunity or challenge should be abandoned, or consideration must be given to whether the stated mission needs to be refined.

Third, being crystal clear on your values and mission and articulating the same in a brand message will allow you and your business to attract exactly those customers who want what you are offering. The common thread running throughout each of the foregoing points is consistency! To attract the ideal customers, you need to build your brand. To build your brand, you need consistent behavior. To be consistent, you need to align your walk and your talk. To align your walk and talk, you need to understand what they are. In short, knowing who you are and what you stand for, and consistently employing this message, easily translates into a marketing message that will let the world understand – at a glance – what your business is offering and that you are offering it with passion and enthusiasm.

WHAT IS A BUSINESS?

A **business** can be defined in terms of what a firm offers such as products or services, the needs of the customers, the geographical areas the firm intends to cover, and type of technologies the firm will employ in order to deliver its goods or services. A business definition explains the nature of the industry in which an entrepreneur intends to operate. Those who provide food to customers operate in the restaurant business; those who operate nursery schools, secondary schools and universities are in the education business. An entrepreneur should first and foremost define the area in which business is to be undertaken. As we shall note in the next section, the definition of a business is connected to a firm's mission statement. In fact, without adequate definition of a firm's business, there is no basis for mission statement. It is not easy to come up with a business definition; one must have adequate knowledge of the industry and what one wants to achieve before a business definition can be offered. For example, how can one distinguish a beauty salon business from a fashion business? What are the differences between information business and data-processing business? What are the differences between a consulting business and an education business? From a strategic management point of view, the first step in knowing your business is to know "what, who and how" of the business.[2]

CASE IN POINT: THE VISION AND MISSION OF DAAR COMMUNICATIONS

DAAR Communications is a private communication company based in Lagos, Nigeria's former capital and the economic nerve center of the West African sub-region. DAAR Communications, which was incorporated in Nigeria in August 1988 boasts of a successful background in the closely related fields of TV and radio broadcasting, printing and publishing. DAAR launched its broadcast services in 1994 with the promotion of Nigeria's first private independent radio station Raypower 100.5 FM. A second channel Raypower 2 106.5 FM commenced formal operation in April 1999. Before then, DAAR Communications had launched a 24-hour global television service with the call sign Africa Independent Television (AIT) with thematic philosophy that is geared towards the promotion of African values and traditions of black people across the world. The owners of DAAR Communications know what business areas they are into (**what they are offering**), they know what direction they want to take the company (**vision**) and they know what they are doing in the industry (**mission**).

In the last quarter of 1999 DAAR Communications launched into the information super highway with the commencement of the DAAR broadband Internet Services with capacity for voice, internet access, video conferencing, data, telephony and other multi-media capabilities. DAAR Internet Service completes the circle of DAAR's communications convergence strategy. DAAR Communications with a staff of about 600 people in Africa, Europe and the United States is worth about 3.5 billion Nigerian Naira (about US$30 million as at 1999).

In line with the global trend of the new information age which has achieved a convergence of broadcasting and telecommunication, DAAR Communications strategy was to fully install and integrate equipment using the latest international satellite gateway system capable of handling voice, data and video telecommunications to virtually every country in the world. Technological innovations in digital and fiber optic networks and other areas of communication and broadcasting transmission was seen by DAAR Communications as the drivers redefining the total nature and system of communication in the age of information and communication technology. DAAR Communications sees the synergy of voice, data, and video is an area of intense technological revision.

In appreciation of the fact that the synergistic combination of computer, telephone, fiber-optic, and video will open a new chapter in revenue generation across multi-industry frontiers in the twenty first century, DAAR Communications Limited has properly positioned itself by installing equipment and facilities capable of handling voice, data and video telecommunications globally.

From the above case-in-point, it is apparent that DAAR Communications Limited has unambiguously defined its core business areas, which is the communication business sector. Its subsequent expansion and growth has been tailored to meet the needs of customers in the communication industry such as radio broadcasting, television broadcasting, Internet services, video conferencing and other multimedia services. This business definition is borne out of emerging global trends and developments in the information age and the convergence of broadcasting and telecommunication.

To arrive at a strategically revealing business definition, the following three elements need to be incorporated:

   i. Customer needs, or *what* is being satisfied.
   ii. Customer groups, or *who* is being satisfied.
   iii. Distinctive competencies or the technologies used and functions performed, or *how* customers' needs are being satisfied.

Customer Needs: Defining a business in terms of what to satisfy, who to satisfy, and how the firm will go about producing the satisfaction gives a comprehensive definition of what a firm does and what business it is in. Just knowing what products or services a firm provides is never enough. Products or services *per se* are not important to customers; a product or service becomes a business when it satisfies a need or want. Without a need or want there is no business. Customer needs are desires, wants, or cravings that can be satisfied by means of the characteristics of a product or service. For example, a person's craving for fast food can be satisfied by a hamburger, carton of ice cream, a bowl of pepper soup, or a piece of meat pie. One way to know how you can satisfy the needs of your customers is through product differentiation. *Product differentiation* is the process of creating a competitive advantage by designing products or services capable of satisfying the needs of customers.

All firms must differentiate their products or services to a certain degree in order to attract and satisfy some minimal level of need. However, some firms differentiate their products or services to a much greater degree than others, and this difference can give them a competitive edge. Some firms offer the customer a low-priced product or service without engaging in much product differentiation. Others seek to create something unique about their product or service so that they satisfy customers' needs in ways that other product or services cannot. As we pointed out in chapter six, the uniqueness of a product or service may relate to the physical characteristics of the product, such as quality or reliability, or it may lie in the product's or service's appeal to customers' psychological needs, such as the need for prestige or status. Thus a Japanese car may be differentiated by its reputation for reliability, and a Corvette or a Porsche may be differentiated by its ability to satisfy customers' needs for status. In a similar manner, a "gala pie" may be distinguished from a hamburger on the basis of how it satisfies not the customer's hunger for food, but the reputation attached to what is being eaten.

Customer groups: The knowledge of the customer groups is relevant because they indicate the market to be served, the geographic domain to be covered and the type of buyers or users the firm is going after. One way to achieve this is through *market segmentation*, pointing out to the way a firm decides to cater for a particular group of customers with distinctive attributes based on important differences in their needs or preferences, in order to gain competitive advantage. Many firms adopt three alternative strategies toward market segmentation.[3] First, a firm can choose not to recognize that different groups of customers have different needs and instead adopt the approach of serving the average customers. Second, an entrepreneur can chose to segment its market into different constituencies and develop a product or service to suit the needs of each. For example, a beauty salon located in the business and commercial district of Ikeja, Lagos, segmented its market into three different constituencies or groups -- ladies, gentlemen, and children. A law firm located in the same area has three groups of customers (family practice, criminal practice and commercial services). Third, a firm can choose to recognize that the market is segmented but concentrate on servicing only one market segment, or *niche*, such as when an entrepreneur with a law firm decides to concentrate his or her efforts only on family practices.

Why would a company want to make complex product/market choices and create a different product tailored to each market segment rather than create a single product or service for the whole market? The answer is that the decision to provide many products or services for many market niches allow a company to satisfy customers' needs better. As a result, customers' demand for the company's products rises and generates more revenue than would be the case if the company offered just one product for the whole market.[4] Sometimes, however, the nature of the product or the nature of the industry (such as the bottled-water industry) does not allow much differentiation and market segmentation. These industries afford little opportunity for obtaining a competitive advantage through product differentiation and market segmentation because there is little opportunity for serving customers' needs and customer groups in different ways (to the customer, a bottled-water is a bottled-water). Instead, price is the main criterion by which customers evaluate the product, and the competitive advantage lies with the company that has superior efficiency and can provide the lowest-priced product.

Technology, Functions and Distinctive Competencies: Technology and functions performed are important because they indicate *how* the firm will satisfy the customers' needs and how much of the industry's production and distribution chain its activities will span. For instance, a firm's business can be *fully integrated*, extending across the entire range of industry activities that must be performed to get a product or service in the hands of end users. On the other hand, a firm may stake out partially integrated positions, participating only in selected stages of the industry. *How* to satisfy customer needs and wants answers the crucial question: What is the firm's *distinctive competence*? As noted in chapter six, there are four ways firms can achieve a competitive advantage through their distinctive competencies: (i) superior efficiency, (ii) quality, (iii) innovation and (iv) responsiveness to customers' needs. These four issues form the basis of a firm's *technology*; the functions perform by the services or products and the firm's distinctive competence.

Trying to identify needs served, target market, and functions performed in a single, snappy sentence is a challenge, and many firms' business definitions fail to illuminate all three bases explicitly. The business definition of some firms are thus better than others in terms of how they cut to the base of what the enterprise is really about and the strategic position it is trying to stake out.

Examples of Business Definitions

The following examples of business definitions indicate that a firm must state to the public and its stakeholders the nature of its business. I suggest that the reader do some research on other companies, both large and small to get more knowledge about how other companies defined their businesses. Remember that one of the reasons for defining your business in clear terms is to declare your strategic intent, which gives a sense of direction and purpose to those within your firm and helps drive strategic decision-making and resource allocation. The following examples illustrate the business definitions of some companies.

Punch (Nigeria) Limited
PUNCH (Nigeria) Limited was registered on August 8, 1970 under the Companies Act of 1968 to engage in the business of publishing newspapers, magazines and other periodicals of public interest. It was designed to perform the tripartite functions of the popular mass media: informing, educating and entertaining Nigerians and the world at large.

Daar Communications Limited (Nigeria)
We are in the business of communications.

Avis-Rent-a-Car
Our business is renting cars.

Eastman Kodak
We are in the picture business.

The above examples tell us exactly what businesses the companies are in. As pointed out above, the business definition of a firm must clearly state what product or service the firm intends to offer.

THE VISION OF A FIRM

Most often the vision of an organization (where the organization wants to be) originates from the purpose or dream of its founder or founders. The founder of DAAR Communications had a vision or a dream of what he intended to give to society and what he expected from society. It was this vision that he translated to the company's mission and its goals or objectives and applied to other business units of the corporation as it expands. One of the key tasks of an entrepreneur is to give the firm a sense of direction. Successful entrepreneurs seem to have a vision of where the firm should go, based on their own dreams. Moreover, they are successful at communicating this vision to others within and outside the firm in terms that can energize people.

The vision of a firm is what the organization (or the firm) is trying to achieve over the long term as formally declared in dreams or purposes of their owners (the owners can be the government, group of individuals or an individual). In practice, the terms *vision* and *mission* are often used interchangeably, and some firms or management writers tend to use the term *purpose* instead of vision.

Like the definition of the business, the vision statement articulates the company's *strategic intent*. The vision of a business is what a firm or the owners of the firm want to accomplish in the future. In other words, a vision of a business is future-directed. Some firms develop both a mission and a vision statement. In most cases, a vision statement can replace a mission statement and vice versa. However, as we shall note in a following section, there is a huge difference between a vision and a mission. The mission statement answers the question: "What are we providing now and for what purpose?" On the other hand, the vision statement answers the question "What do we want to become?" In any case, a clear vision provides the foundation for developing a comprehensive mission and the vision statement should be established first and foremost. The vision statement should be short and preferably one sentence.

For our purpose here, we will try to clarify the difference between a vision statement and a *value statement* of a firm. Although some organizations use their vision statements to describe the values of their organizations, they nevertheless show what the firm is doing now, what it intends to become in the future, and *how* it intends to get there. The *values* of a firm state how the owner or managers of the business intend to conduct themselves, how they intend to do business, and what kind of organization they want to build. Their values are their philosophies or what they stand for, their belief systems.

Examples of Firms' Vision Statements

The following examples provide what some companies' vision statements are all about. As usual, it is important to do your own research and get more insight into other companies' vision statements.

UACN (Nigeria)
To be Number One in our chosen markets, providing exceptional value to our customers.

Cape Winelands District and Municipality (South Africa)
To provide a safe, prosperous and united Boland where all of its people enjoy high standards of living.

McDonald's (USA)
McDonald's vision is to dominate the global foodservice industry. Global dominance means setting the performance standard for customer satisfaction while increasing market share and profitability through Convenience, Value, and Execution Strategies.

First Bank of Nigeria, Plc.
Be the Clear Leader and Nigeria's Bank of Choice.

Central Bank of Nigeria
To be one of the most efficient and effective world's central banks in promoting and

sustaining economic development.

Breed Valley Municipality (South Africa))
The challenge of our municipality is to attract investors and simultaneously create employment to sustain local livelihood, and moreover integrate disadvantaged entrepreneurs into the mainstream economy. In the Valley of Hope we plan, work and grow in unity!"

MTN (South Africa and Nigeria)
To become the leading telecommunications operator on the African continent. To improve telecommunications infrastructures and access throughout the countries in which we operate. Becoming a good corporate citizen and becoming a major player in the Nigerian economy.

First Atlantic Bank (Nigeria)
To be the clear leader in our chosen markets and the benchmark for customer service worldwide.

Zenith International Bank (Nigeria)
To become the leading Nigerian, technology-driven, global financial institution, providing distinctively unique range of financial services.

Mr. Bigg's (Nigeria)
Mr. Bigg's will be the preferred Quick Service Restaurant experience in West Africa, meeting customers' needs of value, convenience, quality, taste, and fast, friendly service.

Oceanic Bank (Nigeria)
Think Banking ... Think Oceanic.

The Promise (a restaurant owned by Integrated Catering Company)
To be at the zenith of the food industry in Nigeria and beyond.

Now, the First Bank of Nigeria might not be the clear leader and Nigeria's bank of choice. However, their vision (or dream) is to be one. In the same vein, the Central Bank of Nigeria is not the most efficient and effective central banks in the world in promoting and sustaining economic development. However, their dream is to become one. Therefore, you can see that a vision is a dream of where you want to be in the future. Not where you are presently.

The vision of your firm must be communicated to its external and internal stakeholders. Not only do external constituents, customers and investors have a need to believe that you and your management knows where you are trying to take the company and understand what changes lie ahead both externally and internally, but unless and until your frontline employees understand why the strategic course that you and your management have charted is reasonable and beneficial, they are unlikely to rally behind your managerial efforts to get the business moving into the direction you intended.

THE MISSION OF A FIRM

In the beginning, a new business is simply a collection of ideas. Starting a new business rests on a set of beliefs that the new venture can offer some product or service, to some customers, in some geographic area, using some type of technology, at a profitable price. That is what we termed as a business definition. At the same time, the founder of the business has a dream of where he or she intends to go in the future and we call this the vision of the founder. In strategic management, this vision must be translated into a mission statement. Whereas a vision describes what the firm intends to achieve based on some altruistic beliefs of its founders and management, a mission statement is about translating this vision in terms of how the firm intends to achieve the stated vision of its founders. Unlike a vision statement, a mission statement is not a dream: It describes what the firm is presently doing, not that of its founders. Unlike a vision that says what "we want to be in the future", a mission statement is about what "we intend to be now."

A new business owner typically believes that the management philosophy of the new enterprise will result in a favorable public image and that this concept of the business can be communicated to, and will be adopted by, important constituencies. When the set of beliefs about a business at its inception are put into writing, the resulting document mirrors the same basic ideas that compose a mission statement. As a business grows, owners or management may find it necessary to revise the founding set of beliefs, the vision of its founders to accommodate the realities facing the organization. However, the original vision or ideas of the founders usually are reflected in the revised statement of mission.

The mission statements of many organizations can often be found in the front pages of annual reports of most established organizations. Mission statements are often displayed throughout a firm's premises, and they are distributed with company information sent to constituencies or stakeholders. The mission statement is a part of numerous internal reports, such as business plans, loan requests, supplier agreements, labor relations contracts, and customer service agreements. Particularly for an entrepreneurial firm, a mission statement is all the more crucial in a business plan because it is the first thing your prospective investors would judge in granting you financial assistance. It not only tells your banks what kind of person you are, but more importantly, what kind of business you intend to run.

A firm's **mission** is the purpose or reason for its existence. It tells what the firm is providing to society, either a service like housecleaning, hairdressing, information service, consulting or a product such as an automobile. When an entrepreneur is confronted with the question: "What is our mission?" The entrepreneur is asked the same question: "Why are you in business?" A well-conceived mission statement defines the fundamental, unique purpose that sets a company apart from other firms and identifies the scope of the company's operations in terms of products or services offered and markets served. It may also include the firm's philosophy about how it does business and treats its employees. Unlike a vision, the mission describes what the firm is doing now. The mission statement promotes a sense of shared expectations in employees and communicates a public image to important stakeholder groups in the firm's environment.[5]

The Nature of Mission Statements

Missions chart a firm's future: An entrepreneurial vision is inherently more future-oriented than the oft-used terms *business purpose* or *mission statement*. The statements of a mission, on the other hand, tend to deal more with the present ("what is our business and why we are in it") than with the firm's aspirations and long-term direction (where are we headed, what new things we intend to pursue). A here-and-now-oriented mission statement highlighting the boundaries of the company's current business is a logical vantage point from which to look down the road, decide what the firm's future business makeup and customer focus need to be, and chart a strategic path for the company. For example, MTN was able to chart its future through its mission statement: "To be the acknowledged pre-eminent telecommunications company in Nigeria."

Missions are Firm-Specific, Not Generic: The mission statement of entrepreneurs or business owners ought to be highly personalized and unique to the firm for which they were developed; a mission statement cannot be copied from that of a competitor. *The whole idea behind developing a strategic mission is to set a firm apart from others in its industry and give it its own special identity, business emphasis, and path for development.* Generically worded statements, couched in everything-and-everybody language that could apply just as well to many companies and lines of business, are not entrepreneurially or strategically useful. The reason is that such mission statements paint no mental picture of where the company is destined and offer no guidance to owners and managers in deciding which business activities to pursue and not to pursue and what strategies make the best sense. Nor do they communicate useful information about the firm's long-term direction and future business makeup to employees and investors. Ambiguous or vaguely worded mission statements may have some public relations value, but they don't help business owners manage their firms strategically. *The best mission statements are worded in a manner that not only clarifies the direction in which a firm needs to move, but more importantly describes how the firm is different from others in the provision of its goods or services.*

The Mission Is Not to Make a Profit: Sometimes firms state their business purpose or mission in terms of making a profit. This is misguided because profit is more correctly an *objective* and a *result* of what the company does. The desire to make a profit says nothing about the business arena in which profits are to be sought. Missions or visions based on making a profit are incapable of distinguishing one type of profit-seeking enterprise from another - the business and long-term direction of Zenith International Bank are plainly different from the business and long-term direction of Mr. Bigg's, even though both endeavor to earn a profit. A firm that says its mission is to make a profit begs the question "What will we do to make a profit?" To understand a company's business and future directions, we must know the owner's answer to "make a profit doing what and for whom". For instance, *The Daily Sun* of Nigeria did not state in its mission statement about making money. However, the publishers send the message that every stakeholder will gain from its operations: "To practice journalism in the classical tabloid newspaper tradition of presenting the news and features in an exciting style, with impact, objectivity and appeal that generate returns to all stakeholders: the society, the investors and the practitioners."

A Mission is a Declaration of Attitude: A mission statement is a declaration of attitude and outlook more than a statement of specific details. It is an organization's self-concept. It is usually broad in scope for two reasons: First, a good mission statement allows for the generation and consideration of a range of feasible alternative objectives and strategies without stifling entrepreneurial and management creativity. Excess specificity would limit the potential of creative growth for the organization. Second, a mission statement needs to be broad to effectively reconcile differences among organization's diverse stakeholders, the individuals and groups of persons who have a special stake or claim on the company. Reaching the fine balance between specificity and generality in the formulation of a mission statement is difficult to achieve, but is worth the effort. George Steiner offers the following insight on the need for a mission statement to be broad in scope:

> "Most business statements of missions are expressed at high levels of abstractions. Vagueness nevertheless has its virtues. Mission statements are not designed to express concrete ends, but rather to provide motivation, general direction, and image, a tone, and a philosophy to guide the enterprise. An excess of detail could prove counterproductive since concrete specification could be the base for rallying opposition. Precision might stifle creativity in the formulation of an acceptable mission or purpose. Once an aim is cast in concrete, it creates rigidity in an organization and resists change. Vagueness leaves room for other managers to fill in the details, perhaps even to modify general patterns. Vagueness permits more flexibility in adapting to changing environments and internal operations. It facilitates flexibility in implementation."[6]

An effective mission statement arouses positive attitude, feelings and emotions about an organization; it is inspiring in the sense that it motivates readers to action. An effective mission statement generates the impression that a firm has direction and is worthy of time, support, and investment. The creed or mission of *The Guardian* newspaper in Nigeria is to practice journalism, which is based on a "conscience (that is) nurtured by truth." The implication of this creed/mission statement is that *The Guardian* must strive to abhor all forms sensationalism in its reporting. The relationship of the newspaper and that of its stakeholder groups, and especially its readers, is based, therefore, upon this mission statement.

A Mission must be Customer Oriented: A good mission statement reflects the anticipations of customers. Rather than developing a product and then trying to find a market, the operating philosophy of a firm should be to identify customers' needs and then provide a product or service to fulfill those needs. Good mission statements identify the *utility* of a firm's products or services to its customers. That is why Mr. Bigg's mission statement focuses on "the most convenient quick service eating experience offering affordable high quality meals and great fun for individuals and families". And that is why Daar Communications' mission statement focuses on voice, data and video telecommunications rather than broadcasting. That is why it is often suggested that mission statements should adopt a *consumer-oriented approach*, rather than a *product-oriented approach*. According to Derek Abell, a product-oriented mission statement focuses just on the products sold and the markets served. Such an approach obscures the company's function, which is to satisfy consumer or customer needs.[7] A mission statement should focus on the *utility*, that is, what a product or service does for the customer. To achieve such a customer-oriented perspective, the following utility statements are relevant in developing a mission statement.

> ➢ "Do not offer me things. Offer me what I can get from these things."
> ➢ "Do not offer me clothes. Offer me attractive looks."
> ➢ "Do not offer me shoes. Offer me comfort for my feet and the pleasure of walking."
> ➢ "Do not offer me a house. Offer me security, comfort, and a place that is clean and happy."
> ➢ "Do not offer me a house. Offer me a home."
> ➢ "Do not offer me books. Offer me hours of pleasure and the benefit of knowledge."
> ➢ "Do not offer me records. Offer me leisure and the sound of music."
> ➢ "Do not offer me furniture. Offer me comfort and the quietness of a cozy place."
> ➢ "Do not offer me things. Offer me ideas, emotions, ambience, feelings, and benefits."
> ➢ "Please, do not offer me things. Offer me what I can get from those things."

A major reason for developing a business mission is to attract customers who give meaning to a firm. Referring to the importance of the *utility* of a product or service, Peter Drucker suggests that:

> The customer determines what a business is… What a business thinks it produces is not of first importance, especially not to the future of the business and to its success. What the customer thinks he/she is buying, what he/she considers value, is decisive – it determines what a business is, what it produces, and whether it will prosper. And what the customer buys and considers value is never a product. It is always utility, meaning what a product or service does for him. The customer is the foundation of a business and keeps it in existence.[8]

Many business firms and organizations pay a good attention to what they have to offer to their customers not in terms of the actual products or services, but in terms of what customers get from using the products or services. A good example is provided by *Pfizer, Inc.*, a research-based global health care company:

"Our principal mission is to apply scientific knowledge to help people around the world enjoy longer, healthier and more productive lives. The company has four business segments: health care, consumer health care, food science and animal health. We manufacture in 39 countries, and our products are available worldwide".

Zenith International Bank of Nigeria states its mission statement as follows:
"To offer a unique range of financial services that underscore our corporate commitment to customer enthusiasm and value creation for stakeholders."

MTN in Nigeria, for example, declares that the firm is the "Network of Choice", and you might ask, "Network of choice for what?" Prior to its existence, Nigerians had no choice in terms of communication as everyone was made to rely on the monopoly exercised by Nigerian Telecommunications Limited (NITEL). Their coming to being provides a choice for Nigerians in the area of communications.

Notice that in the above examples, the companies stated the reasons why the products or services are provided and not the products or services that are provided. The rule is that a good business statement reflects the anticipations of customers. Rather than developing a product and then trying to find a market, the basic idea is to identify customers' needs and then provide a product or service to fulfill those needs.

CASE IN POINT: THE DAILY SUN'S MISSION STATEMENT

"To practise journalism in the classical tabloid newspaper tradition of presenting the news and features in an exciting style, with impact, objectivity and appeal that generate returns to all stakeholders: the society, the investors and the practitioners".

We pursue our mission by striving to achieve the following:

* To be the highest circulating newspaper in Nigeria and Africa, which delivers superior reader satisfaction

* To be the undisputed leader in newspaper sales and a dominant media content provider in Nigeria and Africa

* To create business processes and systems that are driven by the brightest and best people around

* To use the best available technology systems to provide rich content on different media platforms

Thus, a good mission statement describes a firm's purpose, customers, products or services, markets, philosophy, and basic technology. In the case of the Daily Sun, the firm goes further to indicate how it intends to achieve its mission. A good mission statement should be able to meet the following criteria:

i. Define what the firm is and what the firm aspires to be.
ii. Be limited enough to exclude some ventures and broad enough to allow for creative growth.
iii. Distinguish a given organization from all others.
iv. Serve as a framework for evaluating both current and prospective activities, and
v. Be stated in terms sufficiently clear to be widely understood throughout the firm.

Why is the Mission especially important for small businesses?

According to Charles N. Toftoy & Joydeep Chatterjee of the School of Business & Public Management at the George Washington University,[9] a small business is like a little baby – it doesn't have sufficient immunity towards diseases and hence needs to be protected from mishandling. Therefore a small business cannot afford to run without a clearly defined mission. Such misguided functioning may lead to the ultimate failure of the venture. Writing a mission statement is the first strategic decision a small business needs to take.

As we pointed out in chapter five, too many entrepreneurs dismiss the importance of creating a strategic plan for their ventures. The overarching attitude is that they can have their company up and running by the time they finish writing a strategic plan, while a few others are blinded by the idea that their companies are too small for a strategic plan, thereby making the tacit, though flawed assumption, that strategic plans are only for big companies! Therefore, the small business owner does not do the mission statement, which forms the foundation of the strategic plan. From the perspective of this book, such excuses are unfounded and reveal a lack of strategic thought. The subsequent time lost in misguided ventures by the company in the future, will more than offset the time gained by not writing the strategic plan. Another major reason for developing a mission statement is to attract customers who give meaning to an organization.

Entrepreneurs starting a small business are generally too preoccupied in the operations and marketing aspects to devote adequate time to formulating a mission statement. They have too many pressing demands on their time, and hence they are easily led into the traps: – "I don't have the time and need for a mission statement, I know it all, I know best, what my business is and what is best for my firm." A well-formulated mission statement will help them to focus on the tasks and activities that are most important to the business, thereby helping him/her to escape the traps and conduct operations smoothly and effectively.

A small business owner without a mission is like a traveler without a destination, he or she has no way of knowing if he or she is making any progress! Without a concrete statement of organizational mission, the values and beliefs of a small business must be interpreted from the actions and decisions of individual managers. This situation makes it difficult to set clear goals and strategies. Therefore, the owner or the founder of the small business must articulate such a statement of goals and business philosophy. This mission is then maintained through generations of succeeding management long after the founder has left.

Even though the business changes its products, customers, market, technology and service method, its basic beliefs and philosophy is still maintained in its modified mission statement. An effective mission statement arouses positive feelings and emotions about an organization; it inspires employees to put in their best effort for the overall success of their business. A small business has limited resources and a good mission statement generates the healthy feeling that the business is successful and progressing in the right direction. This feeling ensures the employees that their time, effort and energy are worthwhile for supporting the small business. The mission statement is futuristic in nature and speaks of the direction a business is headed. Such a statement develops a heightened sense of purpose in the small business when the employees, managers, owners develop and communicate their mission effectively. This is a recipe for success.

A well-designed mission helps in formulating, evaluating and implementing business strategy. In spite of this, developing and communicating a clear mission statement is one of the most neglected tasks in a small business. In absence of this mission, a small firm is vulnerable to a very serious blunder of taking short-term decisions that are counter productive to its long-term interests. Profit over the long-term is one of the clearest indications of a firm's ability to satisfy the principal claims of all stakeholders. A small business might be misguided into overlooking the concerns of its clients, suppliers, creditors, government regulators, tax collectors, ecologists: such a policy may bring in short term gains, but is likely to reap serious long term losses. The statement of company's mission or creed statement, as it is sometimes referred, helps avoid such strategic errors.

The principal value of the company mission is derived from its illustration of the ultimate aims of the company and its corporate culture. It provides managers with a unity of purpose and direction that transcends individual, parochial and ephemeral needs. It promotes a sense of shared expectations among all levels and generations of employees, consolidates values over time and across individuals and interest groups. It projects a sense of goodness and desire that can be identified and understood by outsiders. The mission promises a company's commitment towards responsible action, which goes hand in hand with its necessity to preserve and protect the claims of its insiders for sustained survival and prosperity.

Tips for Small Business Owners for a Mission Statement

- Every small business should have a mission statement.
- The mission statement should consider all stakeholders of the firm.
- A mission statement should always be in writing.
- The mission statement should be participatively formulated by including representatives from all levels of employees.
- The mission statement should be accessible and known to all employees and stakeholders.
- The mission should be clear, concise, inspirational and easy to remember.
- The mission must be used and implemented.
- The mission should be reviewed annually.
- The mission statement should be included as a part of the annual report, company newsletters, and any other brochures viewed by the employees.
- A mission must be realistic – every word should portray the truth and images of the company that are attainable.

The Mission Statement provides the glue that holds the small business together over time.

Components of a Mission Statement

There is no one best mission statement for a particular firm, so good judgment is required in evaluating mission statements. Mission statements can and do vary in length, content, format, and specificity. Most practitioners and academicians of strategic management consider an effective mission statement to exhibit one or more of nine characteristics or components. Since a mission statement is often the most visible and public part of the organization's strategic management process, it is important that it includes all or some of the essential components stated below. These components and the corresponding questions that a mission statement should answer offer a possible direction where your firm should follow.

1. *Customer*: Who are the firm's customers?

2. *The utility*: What are the firm's major products or services? What benefits do the product or service offered to the customer: What does the firm's major products or services provide?

3. *Markets*: Geographically, where does the firm compete?

4. *Technology*: How customer needs are satisfied. Is technology a primary concern of the firm? Is the firm's technology current?

5. *Concern for survival, growth, and profitability*: Is the firm committed to growth and financial soundness? Why would investors put their money in the business?

6. *Philosophy:* What are the basic beliefs, values, aspirations, and philosophical priorities of the firm?

7. *Self-concept or Distinctive competence*: What is the basis for the firm's competitive advantage? What is the expertise or capability that rivals don't have or cannot readily match?

8. *Concern for public image*: Is the firm responsive to social, community, and environmental concerns?

9. *Concern for employees*: Are employees considered valuable asset to the firm?

Examples of the Nine Components of a Mission Statement

Customers

"Mr. Bigg's will be the most convenient quick service eating experience offering affordable high quality meals and great fun for individuals and families. Mr. Bigg's will be a great place to work for and be at" (*Mr. Bigg's*).

"We believe our first responsibility is to the doctors, nurses, and patients, to mothers and all others who use our products and services"(*Johnson &Johnson*).

"The mission of Wash-n-Go Self-service car wash is to provide a quick, convenient, and thorough car wash that will satisfy even the most busy and particular customer" (*Wash-n-Go-Self-Service*).

"Our customers are national and local health care providers who share our goal of enhancing the patients' quality of life. In each community, our customers consider us a partner in providing the best possible care. Our reputation is based on our responsiveness, high standards, and effective systems of quality assurance. Our relationship is open and productive" (*NovaCare*).

Products' or Service Utility

"When you connect to MTN, we want you to have great experience" *(MTN*, Nigeria).

"Remain True to Our Name by Providing the Best Financial Services Possible" (*First Bank of Nigeria, Plc.*)

"Our business is renting cars. Our mission is total customer satisfaction" (*Avis Rent-a-Car*).

"NovaCare is a health care company specializing in providing patient rehabilitation services on a contract basis to nursing homes" (*NovaCare*).

"To give our country a unique Sunday paper which combines the best in serious and popular journalism" (*Sunday Punch*, Nigeria).

"To continue to invest in the best people, technology and environment, to underscore our commitment to achieving customer enthusiasm" (*Zenith Bank, Nigeria*).

Markets

"To be the acknowledged pre-eminent telecommunications company in Nigeria
We want the calls you make on our network to be of the best quality in Nigeria.

We want our network to cover the broadest areas of Nigeria and we want to continue to enhance the convenience and value you derive from using our network" *(MTN, Nigeria)*.

Technology

"We resolve to provide at all times, exotic cuisine of very high standard and extensive varieties, with service approach that is highly professional, imaginative and innovative" (*TP, The Promise Restaurant*, Port-Harcourt, Nigeria).

"To provide excellent and comprehensive service to all our customers in a friendly environment using qualified and experienced personnel with appropriate technology" (*Oceanic Bank*, Plc, Nigeria).

"Our mission is to provide any customer a means of moving people and things up, down, and sideways over short distances with higher reliability than any similar enterprise in the world" (*Otis Elevator*).

"We apply our clinical expertise to benefit our patients through creative and progressive techniques. Our ethical and performance standards require us to expend every effort to achieve the best possible results" (*NovaCare*).

Survival, growth and profitability

"To delight our customers through the innovative use of technology and people, thereby creating wealth for our stakeholders" *(First Atlantic Bank, Plc)*.

Philosophy

"To promote and defend the values of democracy and free enterprise and to foster the principles of equal opportunities for all" (*Punch, Nigeria*).

"We believe human development to be the worthiest of the goals of civilization and independence to be the superior conditions for nurturing growth in the capabilities of people" (*Sun Company*).

"It's all part of the Mary Kay philosophy – a philosophy based on the golden rule. A spirit of sharing and caring where people give cheerfully of their time, knowledge and experience" (*Mary Kay Cosmetics*).

"NovaCare is people oriented committed to making a difference ... enhancing the future of all patients ... breaking new grounds in our professions ... achieving excellence ... advancing human capability ... changing the world in which we live" (*NovaCare*).

"The mission of the Red Cross is to improve the quality of human life; to enhance self-reliance and concern for others; and to help people avoid, prepare for, and cope with emergencies" (*American Red Cross*).

Distinctive Competence

"To experience the thrill of adding value to lives and businesses by being a *superior convenience provider*" (UACN).

"To provide excellent and comprehensive service to all our customers in a friendly environment using *qualified and experienced personnel with appropriate technology*" (Oceanic Bank).

Concern for Public Image

"We aim to achieve commercial success by meeting our customers' needs through the provision of high quality, good value products with exceptional service and relevant information, which enables customers to make informed and responsible choices" (*The Body Shop*).

"To share the world's obligation for the protection of the environment" (*Dow Chemical*).

Concern for Employees

"Our people are our asset. We are committed to the personal, professional, and career development of each individual employee. We are proud of what we do and dedicated to our Company. We foster teamwork and create an environment conducive to productive communication among all disciplines" (*NovaCare*).

"We are responsible to our employees, the men and women who work with us throughout the world. Everyone must be considered as an individual. We must respect their dignity and recognize their merit. They must have a sense of security in their jobs. Compensation must be fair and adequate, and working conditions clean, orderly and safe. We must be mindful of ways to help our employees fulfill their family responsibilities. Employees must feel free to make suggestions and complaints. There must be equal opportunity for employment, development and advancement for those qualified. We must provide competent management, and their concerns must be just and ethical" (Johnson & Johnson).

To reiterate, there is a fundamental difference between your firm's vision and its mission statements. Specifically, your company's strategic vision is what it says about "the direction we are headed and what our future products/market/customer/technology focus will be." In contrast, your mission statement provides a brief overview of your company's present business purpose and raison d'etre, and sometimes its geographic coverage or standing as a market leader.

A FIRM'S VALUES STATEMENT

It is essential that we distinguish a firm's mission statement from its values statement. Whereas a firm's mission tells the public the type of service and products offered, the value statement of a firm tells the public its creed statement, a statement of purpose, the firm's guiding belief systems, a statement of philosophy, and a statement of business principles. All firms have a reason for being and the guiding principles with which they hope to conduct their business activities even if their owners have not consciously transformed these into writing.

Usually, the values of a firm or its philosophy come from the deep concerns or beliefs of the founder(s). Most entrepreneurs are driven by deep philosophical underpinnings and convictions that they take to bear upon their businesses. In many instances, the values of an organization reflect the travails and life stories of their founders.

An organization's values are the operating philosophies or principles that guide an organization's internal conduct as well as its relationship with the external world. Core values are usually summarized in the mission statement or in the statement of core values. It is important that your firm have a well-developed value statement that guide the behavior and actions of everyone who is associated with your business – employees, customers, vendors, etc. Each firm's approach will depend on the context in which it is operating and its unique characteristics. Most importantly, such a statement should reflect the beliefs and philosophy of the founder/entrepreneur.

The Importance of Value Statements

In an organization with well-integrated and shared values, the following benefits are possible:

i. Statement of values encourage a productive work environment, with fewer complaints, grievances or disrespectful behavior,
ii. Statement of values create greater organizational commitment, leading to closer cooperation in the workplace and enhanced corporate citizenship,
iii. Statement of values increase organizational effectiveness as a result of improved morale, cooperation, job satisfaction, retention and recruitment,
iv. Statement of values reduce ethical risk as a result of a proactive approach to ethics rather than reactive crisis management,
v. A value statement communicates to stakeholders the organization's values and its expectations of high ethical standards,
vi. A statement helps to align organizational, professional and personal values, encouraging individuals to identify with organizational goals and values. It provides a common framework to guide teams and organizational processes,
vii. A statement communicates the organization's commitment to employees, and helps to promote positive and productive behavior in the workplace,

viii. A statement raises employee awareness of the importance of shared values. It provides supportive guidance, encouraging reflection and good judgment in solving ethical problems.

Examples of Firm's Core Values

Zenith Bank (Nigeria)
Customer satisfaction, sustainable stakeholder value creation, professionalism and good corporate governance underline and mould the corporate and business strategy of the Bank.

UACN (Shared values)
Customer Focus
Respect for the Individual
Integrity
Team Spirit
Innovation
Openness & Communication

Oceanic Bank
T -Transparency
E -Equal Opportunity
A -Accountability
M -Merit

Mr. Bigg's
Our promise to Mr. Bigg's customers is as follows:
Quality - Snacks, meals, ice cream & drinks
Service - That is prompt and efficient
Clean - Hygienic surroundings
Value - For money
Friendly - Courteous and enthusiastic staff
Consistent - Emphasis on putting the customer first

The purpose of the strategy is to position Mr. Bigg's to achieve its mission of offering a world-class QSR experience as well as lead the business in the West African region.

Values are needed to guide the company's pursuit of its vision, mission, strategy and ways of operating. Remember that values are the beliefs, traits, and ways of doing things that management has determined should guide the pursuit of its vision and strategy, the conduct of company's operations, and the behavior of company personnel.

UNDERSTANDING A FIRM'S OBJECTIVES AND GOALS

A firm's objectives represent its commitment to achieving specific performance targets and result within a specific time frame. Setting objectives converts a firm's vision and mission into specific performance targets. Goals are the things a firm intends to achieve and objectives are the steps the firm must take to achieve the goals. Objectives are a call for action and for results. Specifically, goals establish and tell you where you intend to go. In the game of soccer, we call this "the goal" – the ultimate destination of the ball is the goal post. As in the world of business, your business goal is really what you intend to achieve running the business.

Well-chosen goals point a new business in the right direction and keep almost any company on the right track. We should understand that the goals a firm sets for its self inspire and motivate the business team and push everyone to go that extra mile. Unless a firm's long-term direction and business mission is translated into specific performance targets and the owner is pressured to show progress in reaching these targets, the vision and mission statements are likely to end up as nice words, window dressing, and unrealized dreams of accomplishment.[11] In other words, goals are the results of your firm's activities. They are your firm's performance targets, the results and outcomes it wants to achieve and they function as yardstick for tracking your firm's performance and progress.

While goals tell you *where* you want to go (such as achieving a larger market share, improving quality standard or achieving increased earning for share holders), objectives tell you exactly *how* and *when* you get there. Thus, *objectives* are the specific steps you and your company need to take in order to reach each of your goals. Objectives specify precisely what must be done, and when. While goals are typically described in words, objectives often have numbers and specific dates attached to them.

Objectives are often goal related. At times they are quantitatively expressed as in financial objectives or other performance objectives such as production cycle time goals, process, product or service quality standard goals, goals for the reduction of waste or other process efficiency measures. The key to understanding the term objective in the context of strategic management is to think of an objective as a "continuous improvement activity"; one about which we will want answer the question "How are we doing in this activity over the long run?" rather than "Has it been reached?" Here we can see that we really never "achieve" or "attain" our objectives, but rather improve or maintain our objective performance over time until the goal is achieved. What we are really interested in, with regards to our objectives, are the associated performance trends in relation to our stated performance targets (or goals) of these continuous improvement activities and how the performance of one objective impacts other objectives until the goal is reached.

Thus, the achievement of your firm's objectives and goals should result in the fulfillment of your firm's mission and vision. From a strategic management point of view, for objectives to function as yardsticks of a firm's performance, they must be stated in quantifiable or measurable terms and they must contain a deadline for achievement. Objectives have to spell out *how much* of *what* kind of performance by *when*.[12]

In stating the objectives or goals of a firm, a business owner must therefore be cautious in differentiating the goals of the firms from its objectives. In order to do that, one must be cautious in using such general statements as: "Our goal is to maximize profits", "Our objective is to reduce costs," "Our objective is to become more efficient", or "Our objective is to increase sales". These are examples of vague goals; they are not objectives because they fail to specify how much or when to get there! As Bill Hewlett, cofounder of Hewlett-Packard, once observed, "You cannot manage what you cannot measure … And what gets measured gets done."[13] It is important to note that the objectives of your firm are in line with its goals. Secondly, an entrepreneur should make sure that his or her objectives are focused and measurable. Finally, a time frame for achieving each objective must be set.

There are two kinds of objectives an entrepreneur must set, at least from the perspective of strategic management. These are: (i) financial objective and (ii) strategic objective reflecting the two types of key result areas in any firm.

Financial Objective is about achieving acceptable financial performance, and *Strategic Objective* is about achieving acceptable strategic or competitive position, which is essential to sustaining and improving the company's long-term market position and competitiveness. Financial performance depends on strategic performance. For example, without sustainable competitive position it is difficult for a firm to be financially profitable overtime. The idea is that as an entrepreneur, you cannot make money (financial goals/objectives) without knowing *how* you will make the money (strategic objectives and goal). Remember that strategic objectives refer to the long-term goals of an organization which are stated in concrete terms and their progress is determined by measuring results. Whereas financial objectives refer to the goals that are related to the returns on investment that a firm will try to accomplish during the period covered by its financial plan.

Examples of financial objectives include:

- Growth in revenue by percentage
- Growth in earnings by percentage
- Higher dividends by percentage
- Wider profit margins in percentage
- Higher returns on invested capital by percentage
- Bigger cash flows by percentage
- Rising stock price

Examples of strategic objectives include:

- A bigger market share
- Higher product quality than rivals
- Lower costs relative to competitors
- Broader or more attractive product line than rivals
- A stronger reputation with customers than rivals

- Superior customer service
- Wider geographic coverage than rivals

Deciding on Financial and Strategic Objectives

From the point of view of strategic management and entrepreneurship, it is important to stress the differences and relationships between strategic and financial objectives. In several instances, most small business owners fail to differentiate between the two and therefore erroneously place more priority on financial objectives than strategic ones. Although financial objectives are crucial for the survival of the business, it has been shown that strategic objectives should receive more priority than financial ones. Granted, there a number of reasons why many owners of business prioritize financial objectives over strategic ones. The pressures on owners and managers to opt for better short-term financial performance and to sacrifice or cut back on strategic initiatives aimed at building a stronger competitive position become especially pronounced for several reasons:

- When a firm is struggling financially,
- When the owner or owners are struggling financially,
- When the resource commitments for strategically beneficial moves will materially detract from the bottom line for some time, and
- When the proposed strategic moves are risky and have an uncertain competitive or bottom-line payoff.

Previous research has shown that for a small business owner just starting from the scratch, the urge to prioritize financial gains or profits over competitive strategic initiatives is very seductive indeed. This is especially so when the underlying motive for going into business is financial. However, opening and running a business provides no guarantee that an entrepreneur will earn enough money to survive. Because the entrepreneur must survive financially, the pressure to opt for financial profits in place of strategic ones can be understandable. In an environment where members of an extended family depend on a business owner for financial and other economic necessities, it is common to hear owners of business saying that the pressure to feed the family outweighs the need to "invest the money in promotional activities." Then, there is this expectation to act and behave as a business owner in a culture that celebrates profligacy and the pressure to show that "one has made it" by being ones' own boss, the opportunity to create ones' own destiny, and the opportunity to reap unlimited profits. These are financial objectives that sometimes distract the entrepreneur from pursing more strategic objectives.

Many small business owners and entrepreneurs feel compelled to show that they have made the right decision in establishing their own businesses to their friends, family members and social surroundings. In several cases, this entrepreneurial ego is manifested in pursuing material things that have no bearing on the survival or competitiveness of the firm. The pressures on entrepreneurs and small business owners to opt for better short-term financial performance and to sacrifice long-term strategic objectives are thus overwhelming. From a strategic management point of view, there are dangers when entrepreneurs succumb repeatedly to the lure of immediate gains in profitability when what the business really needed is paring or forging strategic moves that would build long-term competitive advantage.

CHAPTER SUMMARY

A business can be defined in terms of what the start-up firm can offer such as products or services, the needs of the customers, the geographical areas the firm intends to cover, and the type of technologies the firm will employ in order to deliver the goods and services. A business definition explains the nature of the industry in which an entrepreneur intends to operate the business.

A business definition should at least encompass one of the three basic elements: customer needs, customer groups and technology or function of the product or service.

The vision of a firm is what the company is trying to achieve over the long term as formally declared in the dreams or purposes of their owners. The vision statement of a firm answers the question: "What do we want to become?"

A firm's mission is the purpose or reason for its existence. It tells what the firm is providing to the customer or society. A mission describes what the firm is doing right now. The mission of a firm grows from the vision of the firm.

A mission statement should be able to chart the future of the firm, specific, formulated in non-profit terms, a declaration of the firm's attitude, and must be customer-oriented.

The reasons why companies develop mission statement are to ensure unanimity of purpose within the firm, provide a basis for allocating the firm's resources, and establish an atmosphere or mood for the employees of the company, to facilitate the translation of company objectives into work structure.

An organization's values are the operating philosophies or principles that guide an organization's internal conduct as well as its relationship with the external world.

The objective of a firm is the commitment of the owners or management to achieve specific performance targets and results within a specific time frame. Objectives are the results of a firm's activities.

There is a difference between the goal of a firm and the objective of a firm. Goals are set because they tell you where you want to be. Objectives are the results and outcomes of your goals. While goals tell you where you want to go, objectives tell you exactly how you get there.

There are two types of objectives for a firm. The first one is the firm's strategic objective and the second is financial objective. Financial objective is about how the firm achieves an acceptable performance in monetary terms. Strategic objective is about how the firm achieves acceptable strategic or competitive position.

Reasons why entrepreneurs attach more importance to financial objectives than strategic ones include: (i) the firm is struggling financially, (ii) the owner has financial difficulties, (iii) when owners or management are more concerned with the bottom line, and (iv) when the proposed strategic moves are risky.

CHAPTER DISCUSSION QUESTIONS

1. What is a business? Explain what customer needs, customer groups, and technology mean as they apply to an entrepreneur's ability to understand the business he or she wants to get into.

2. As an entrepreneur, what does the vision and mission statements of a firm stand for? What are the major differences between a vision and a mission statement?

3. What are the criteria upon which one should judge a good mission statement? What are the components of a mission statement?

4. Do local beauty salons need to have written mission statements? Why or why not?

5. According to this chapter, what are the major differences between the goal of a firm and its objectives? What are the two kinds of objectives that an entrepreneur must set? What issues must you take into consideration when deciding between the two kinds of objectives? Provide examples to support your opinion.

6. If you are in a college, what is your college or university's self-concept? How would you state that in a mission statement? If you are employed, what is the mission statement of your organization? Using the nine components for a mission statement discussed in the chapter, evaluate how comprehensive is the university's or organization's mission statement.

CASE STUDY 7: AYODELE SLIMMER'S CLUB: NATURE'S WAY TO SLIMMING[14]

Between 2001 and 2002, a new industry came into being in Nigeria: the herbal health care business. Its popularity can perhaps be adduced to two factors: (i) the rising cost of imported drugs to the Nigerian market and (ii) the popularity of "natural products" as alternative to scientifically manufactured and organic products in Europe and the United States of America. There are varieties of this brand in Nigeria such as YEM - KEM INT'L, whose mission is "wonderful and miraculous herbal formula for all deadly diseases", Owoyemi Natural Cure Centre, which proclaims to "have developed various herbal products to all form of diseases such as: staphylococcus, syphilis, E-coli, Herpes Virus and Cadidiasis, etc." There are other outfits whose mission is to cure all types of diseases, including aids, heart pain, sexual problems, and general health-care services such s weight watching, using herbs rather than going to the gym.

Ayodele Slimmer's Club was established by Mr. Isaac Ayodele, to provide slimming weight watching and other health-care related services using herbs without any harmful or negative side effects. The company says it "takes you through a systematic programme."

According to the founder and CEO, Isaac Ayodele, the company grew out of his passion for the herbs and as a hobby. "Initially, it was a hobby I engaged in, using herbs which I got through my grandparents who were into herbs. My grandmother came to the rescue of people through herbs whenever they were sick. Sometime after I had left school, I started to treat people who had problems with obesity. They went away and told people about it. Then more and more people started coming until it became a business." According to the owner, "We are interested in making people stay slim and the approach is natural. We equally want it to be safe. People usually want a specific figure they want to look like. Some even come with photographs of people they want to be. Some come with their friends they want to look like. Others describe how they want their hips to look like, their tummy, their upper arms and their general body. We treat people beyond slimming."

According to Isaac Ayodele, the company he founded "was able to heal those who had arthritis. Rheumatism cases were solved. People with high blood pressure had normal blood pressure. Many of them who had stress got rid of it. Many homes were united. Many broken families were brought together. People felt better in their minds. Places people could not go, they were able to go. They also had their self-confidence restored. We tell our clients that we have failed if we make you look like a broomstick and your health does not improve. We are interested in the totality of your living a fulfilled life."

Mr. Isaac Ayodele explained how his firm gets rid people of problems they never thought of initially. "As I grew up, I developed my own herbal approach that is devoid of side effects. I used to be 90 kilogram. But I came down to 70 kilogram, which I have since maintained. I conducted research into the use of fruits and vegetables. We employ our own concept of hydrotherapy. You can do a lot with water. It can cure obesity. Water can be used to cure headache. Most of the time when people have headaches, it is because they are getting dehydrated. And if you take enough water at the time, you will realize that you have a relief. Some people have problems of indigestion. This could be related to inadequate water. Fruits are very good; pawpaw for example is good for the digestive system. Pineapple is good for appetite suppression. Apples contain a lot of fiber, which is good for losing weight. Vegetables solve the problem of indigestion and reactivate your hormones for growth. There are a lot of medicinal advantages in water, fruits and vegetables, which we ignore. With my study of psychology, I discovered that there is a correlation between the mind and the body. It is the mind that controls the body. There is also a correlation between the spirit and the body. What you do not see are the things which control what you can see."

The owner of the business explains how he is able to help with the above health problems: "A lot goes into weight management. You cannot pin it to a particular thing. Somebody came to me recently. I met her two months before then. She is a lawyer, has money and is comfortable. But she had not been able to practice her legal profession, because she could not afford to go out. She was massively big. She told me she could not remember the day she laughed last. I asked her to estimate. She told me it had been at least 18 years. In other words, she is very hostile to the world and could not wear clothes of her choice. After two months, when she came back, she was full of life. She has been able to go places. This lady had wired her jaw at least five times. Each time she did that, she lost about 10 kilogram. But as soon as she removed them, she goes back to her former size. She was on the verge of packing it up, when she came. And since then, she has realized that there is more to life."

Mr. Isaac Ayodele also explained the emergence of the industry in which he has his business: "In the Western world today, they are combating obesity by changing their foods, especially with the outbreak of foot and mouth disease, which is killing them. Artificial foods do a lot of harm to health. Go to Allen Avenue, fast foods everywhere. We have imbibed a sedentary lifestyle and poor eating habits. Culturally, the person with a potbelly is seen as a symbol of affluence, they say, it is evidence of good living. Big tummy is big trouble. Many men are no longer virile due to their big tummies."

In addition to the slimming outfit, the company also operates its own restaurant where the menu reflects the philosophy and mission of the firm. Called "the Health Kitchen", the owner explained that the idea behind the restaurant is to help curtail the spread of the culture of fast food-eating habit. He pointed to "the problem of processed food in our country and other parts of Africa, which is spreading like a wildfire." According to him, "very soon, people will begin to depend on these fast foods. A diabetic for instance, cannot eat everything. He cannot go to any of these fast foods (restaurants) to eat. Where do you expect him to go and eat? We must have health kitchens where the diabetic can eat. He can eat here. We have plantain flour, which he can eat with plenty of vegetables."

Case Discussion Questions

1. What are the sources of Isaac Ayodele's business idea and innovation?

2. What business is Ayodele Slimmer's Club in? Using the three criteria of business definition examined in this chapter, define this business.

3. Do you think that the business concept of Ayodele Slimmer's Club a sound one? Why or why not? Give reasons to support your position.

4. From the materials discussed in this chapter, write a vision statement for Ayodele Slimmer's Club. Write a mission statement for Ayodele Slimmer's Club using the nine components of a mission statement discussed in this chapter as a guide. You are Mr. Isaac Ayodele; write a value statement for the firm.

5. What industry poses the greatest threat to Ayodele Slimmer's Club? Explain.

Chapter 8

INDUSTRY AND COMPETITIVE ANALYSIS

"I don't believe in luck. I think luck is preparation meeting opportunity" (Oprah Winfrey, founder and owner of Harpo, Inc.).

"If everyone is thinking alike, then somebody isn't thinking" (George Patton).

CHAPTER LEARNING OBJECTIVES
After studying this chapter, you should be able to:

1. Understand the life cycle of an industry and how to design appropriate competitive strategies in relation to the stage the industry finds itself.

2. Analyze and understand the structure of an industry and the competitive forces shaping it.

3. Analyze and understanding the forces that shape an industry.

4. Analyze and understand the key success factors in an industry. That is, what an entrepreneur must do to be competitive in the chosen industry.

4. Analyze and understand the strengths and weaknesses of a firm relative to those of its competitors.

5. Analyze and understand the opportunities and threats available in an industry.

6. Apply the above ideas in creating a successful business plan.

INTRODUCTION: THE POWER OF INDUSTRY KNOWLEDGE

Every industry passes through various phases in what is called an industry life cycle. In each phase of the cycle, successful firms design appropriate competitive strategies to cope with the challenges of change. No industry ever remains static; from its evolution, growth, and maturity, several forces are at play that shape the way organizations design competitive strategies in the industry. For example, the banking industry in Sub-Saharan Africa has gone through significant phases in its life cycle. Specifically, the banking industry in Nigeria has passed through a number of phases – from its inception in the colonial era, through its growth, following the indigenization decree and the structural adjustment era, to maturity, which led to its consolidation between 2004 and 2006. Individual banks in each of these eras had to design appropriate strategies in order to survive the intense and increased competition brought about by these changes.[1] Change and dynamism are the key words in most industries. Sometimes changes come from within the industry itself. In a well-developed economy, change in an industry is internally generated through market and competitive forces. In developing economies, change is most often initiated by forces external to the industry (political change or change in political systems/ideology, macro-economic forces, government regulation, etc). In any case (whether internally or externally generated), change must be met with appropriate competitive strategies.

Changes can also come from the forces of globalization, as we discussed in chapters one and two. In every change come opportunities and threats. Surely, the consolidation phase of the Nigerian banking industry brought opportunities, threats and challenges. To respond appropriately and effectively to any change (threat or opportunity), the firm must have the resources, capabilities and competencies (the strengths) to overcome its resource deficiencies (its weaknesses). For the entrepreneur, the business environment will be hostile to you because it is constantly changing and you must be alert to the changes, adapt to them or bring about change in the environment. In fact, successful entrepreneurs do not only react to changes in an industry environment, they initiate them through innovative practices. Then there are competitors who are probably providing better services or selling their business ideas better than you. The most important thing to consider is that your success in getting customers to buy your product or service depends on your knowledge of the industry. You cannot design and implement any competitive strategy without having a solid knowledge of the industry and especially the dynamics or forces at work in the industry.

Formulating and implementing an appropriate strategy for a small business, as in large corporations, is an analysis-driven exercise, not a task where entrepreneurs or owners/managers can get by with opinions and good instincts. Decisions about what strategy to pursue need to flow directly from solid analysis of a firm's external environment and internal situation. In strategic management, the two biggest considerations are (i) industry and competitive conditions of your firm, that is, the "external environment" of the firm, and (ii) the competitive capabilities, resources, internal strengths and weaknesses, and market position of your firm relative to competitors.

The rationale behind industry and competitive analysis is that a firm cannot begin to think about entering an industry without the knowledge of the forces shaping that industry. An entrepreneur cannot design its competitive and market strategies without knowing the kind of strategies other firms or entrepreneurs are using in the market. An entrepreneur cannot go into a business without knowing the key factors that will determine success or failure in the particular industry he or she wants to enter. Let us begin this discussion with the definition of an industry.

An **industry** can be defined as a group of companies offering products or services that are close substitutes for each other. Close substitutes are products or services that satisfy the same basic consumer needs.[2] This definition means that an industry is a group of firms whose products or services have so many of the same attributes that they compete for the same buyers.[3] Industries differ widely in their economic characteristics, competitive situations, and future profit prospects. The economic and competitive character of car-rental industry bears little resemblance to that of discount retailing. The economic and competitive traits of the fast-food business have little in common with an industry that provides Internet-related products. The fashion business is shaped by industry and competitive conditions radically different from those in the transportation industry. In the same manner, the soft drinks industry is different from the financial industry.

Entrepreneurial firms have gone out of business because of their failure to adapt to environmental change or, even worse, by failing to create change as conditions change in their industries. A firm can create a change in its industry environment simply by developing and implementing competitive strategies. However, it must be understood that change cannot be created if one does not understand the forces driving change in the industry environment. To be successful overtime, a firm needs to be in tune with its external environment. There must be a strategic-fit between what the environment wants and what the firm has to offer, as well as between what the firm needs and what the environment can provide. Today, we are living in an era of *environmental uncertainty*, that is, our business world is a complex one and change is constant. These complexity and dynamic changes affect the way we do business. In the context of the present global economy, it is safe to assert that same old saying: "No one can predict the future!" As more and more markets become global, including the high rate and effects of technological changes, the number of factors that an entrepreneur must take into consideration before launching a business venture is becoming more complex. With new technologies being discovered overtime, markets change and products or services must change with them. In other words, knowing your industry is an important key factor in order to compete successfully.

The purpose of this chapter is for you to understand that the competitive success of your firm depends on two important factors: You either shape the firm's strategy to fit the industry environment or you should be able to reshape the industry environment to your firm's advantage through a chosen strategy. Consistent with our strategic management approach, this chapter considers the influence of the industry environment in which a firm wishes to compete. First, the chapter introduces us to the concept of industry life cycle. Here, the purpose is to gain an understanding of an industry in terms of its age before a business is launched. Second, we discuss a number of models that can assist the entrepreneur in analyzing and understanding industry environment (in strategic management, we called this: the five-forces model). Third, the chapter discusses how an entrepreneur can identify and know the key success factors in an industry to be better prepared for the competitive challenge with which he or she will be confronted; it shows the entrepreneur how to know what it takes to succeed in an industry or market. Fourth, this chapter provides us with a framework for identifying environmental opportunities and threats. *Opportunities* arise when a firm can take advantage of conditions in its external environment to formulate and implement strategies to gain competitive advantage and to earn higher profits. *Threats* arise when conditions in the external environment endanger the profitability or competitive advantage of the firm. This model also helps us understand our or the firm's strengths and weaknesses. The *strengths* of a firm are those things that the business is good at doing compared to its competitors. The strengths can become the distinctive competencies if they really differentiate the business from its competitors'. The *weaknesses* of the firm are those things that hinder it from being competitive. Let us start with the idea of the life cycle of an industry and see how we can apply it in our effort to understand the competition that exists in an industry one wishes to enter and what competitive strategies one will adopt.

UNDERSTANDING THE LIFE CYCLE OF AN INDUSTRY

Let us assume that you brought an ailing person to a General Hospital somewhere close to you and you asked for a doctor to examine the patient. I bet before the doctor makes his or her decision concerning the type of medication to recommend and apply, the first question would probably be about the age of the patient. Knowing the age of the patient helps the doctor perform appropriate diagnosis. In the same manner, knowing the age of your industry allows you to diagnose the prospect and problems within that particular industry.

Thus, an industry or a market goes through a life cycle, just like people. An industry is born, grows, matures and reaches difficult times. Finally, it dies or it is reborn by some new technology or some other forces that give it a new life. Thus, most industries, overtime, evolve through a series of stages from growth, maturity to eventual decline.

Firms in a single industry are forever bound by the type of product or service that they provide, and they are constantly competing with one another for market share, consumer acceptance, as well as technological leadership in their particular sub-sector. These competitive and consumer forces shape an industry's firms and determine the status of the industry as a whole. These forces have followed roughly the same patterns over time, providing a very clean model for an industry, the various stages of growth (and decline) experienced by its firms. Here we take a look at these stages and how they determine what kind of strategies these companies require. Thus, the industry life cycle model is useful for explaining and predicting trends about the forces driving an industry and how to respond strategically to each state or stage of the developmental process: birth, growth, maturity and declining process. The stages in the life cycle of an industry are described below.

Birth and Emerging Industries

All companies have to start their business somewhere, and it takes only a single company or small group of companies to jumpstart an entire industry. Looking back in time, we see that it was not even a company but an individual by the name of Alexander Graham Bell who, with the invention of the telephone, started the entire industry of telecommunications. Arguable in Nigeria, it took the ingenuity of two individuals (Chris Obi Rapu and Okey Ogunjior: directors of "Living in Bondage") to jump-start the Nigerian movie (Nollywood) industry in its present vibrant form. It was Mr. Bigg's, the fast-food business unit of UACN that pioneered the emerging Nigerian fast-food industry.

A new industry emerges perhaps as a result of the discovery of a new technology (new ways of doing things) or changes in the demographics of a society. In many developing countries, the fast food industry is an excellent example of how changes in the demographics affect the arrival of a new industry and the demise of existing ones. The evolution of the fast food industry in many countries came into being as a result of the changing working and family conditions as well as other social cultural developments in societies. Consequently, the traditional food restaurant is gradually fading and is been replaced by fast food restaurants. The same can also be said about the communications industry. The arrival of mobile telephone system has seen the demise of the traditional line-telephone system in many developing countries such as Ghana, Nigeria, Kenya, Brazil and Bangladesh.

When an industry is new, people patronize it. Here, people often buy the product or service regardless of price because it fulfills a unique need. When the industry is at its birth stage, we have very few sellers who have initially introduced the product or technology. The technology has not yet been diffused in the industry. Consequently, competition is not strong. Those who introduced the product are experiencing market domination, and they control a monopolistic position in that industry.

Firms involved in establishing emerging industries are generally participating in perilous business, as their primary concerns are raising sufficient funds to engage in early-stage research and development. In their developmental stages, which may last months or even years, these companies are likely operating on a shoestring budget, while at the same time presenting to the world a product or service that is yet to be accepted. These pioneering companies might face bankruptcy, development failure and poor consumer acceptance. Firms in emerging industries typically make use of innovative strategies, new product development and aggressive marketing in order to make their products or services acceptable.

Growth Industries

The initial firms in the new industry go through a lot of experimentation and changes as they adapt to customer expectations during the time that they have the technological know-how and proprietary rights that exclude others from competing. This is what we called a fragmented industry, because no firm has large market share and each firm serves only a small piece of the total market in competition with others. Over time, as the industry grows and more firms enter, you begin to see intense product and service differentiation through product development, promotion and advertisement. Less uncertainty is evident because standards have been established and proprietary rights have become less exclusive. Most importantly, the initial technology is now available to almost everyone interested in entering the industry. Do not be surprise that during this stage, existing firms are confronted with the presence of imitation products. The industry becomes very competitive.

Firms in industries that are benefiting from rapid growth have sales and earnings that are expanding at a faster rate than firms in other industries. As such, these companies should display an above average rate of earnings on invested capital for an extended period of time, probably years. Prospects for rapid growth companies should also appear bright for continued sales and earnings growth in ensuing years.

During this period of rapid growth, companies will eventually begin to lower prices in response to competitive pressures and the decline of costs of production, which is often referred to as economies of scale. But costs decrease at a higher rate than prices, so companies entrenched in growth industries often experience growth in profits as their product or service becomes fully accepted in the marketplace. The consumer electronics industry, for example, is characterized by much research and development, followed by significant economies of scale in production. Prices in home electronics inevitably fall, but the costs of production fall faster, thereby ensuring increasing profitability.

Mature Industries and Shakeout

Once an industry has exhausted its period of rapid growth in revenues and earnings, it moves into maturity. Growth in the companies in mature industries closely resembles the overall rate of growth of the economy (the GDP). Earnings and cash flow are still likely positive for these companies, but their products and services have become less distinguishable from those of their competitors. Price competition becomes more vicious, taking profit margins along with it, and companies begin to explore other areas for products or services with potentially higher margins. Some of our economy's most closely watched industries, such as insurance, textile and banking can be categorized as mature industries. A growing local industry can suddenly become matured when confronted with stiff competition from imported foreign products and services as in the case of the Nigerian textile industry. Stiff competition can also come from industries that provide substitute products.

At the most intense point of competition, there is a shakeout, and those firms that are unable to successfully compete leave. At this stage, firms use the experience curve and economies of scale to reduce costs faster than the competition or new entrants. Companies also integrate to reduce costs even further by acquiring their suppliers and distributors. During this stage, those firms that cannot compete as a result of inadequate competitive strategies are shaken out. The industry has thus reached a stage in which the survival of the fittest exists. At this point, in order to survive larger firms either acquire their smaller rival ones or introduce new products and services. In order to survive firms come up with innovative ideas but within a short period of time the competitors have imitated or improved on those new ideas.

By the time an industry enters maturity, products or services tend to become more like commodities. This is the case in the Nigerian banking industry, which has become so matured that the only way to compete is through consolidation and mergers and/or seeking new geographic markets across borders. In so far as the competition increases, the industry becomes a *consolidated industry* - dominated by a few large firms, each of which struggles to differentiate its products further from the competition. Another strategy is to look for new geographic markets or new uses for existing customers. As buyers become more sophisticated over time, purchasing decisions are based on better information. One consequence of this consolidation is the merger frenzy within the banking industry in Nigeria in the period between 2003 and 2006. Price and service become a dominant concern, given a minimum level of quality and features.

One example of this trend is the videocassette recorder industry. By the 1990s, VCRs had reached the point where there were few major differences among the available brands and consumers realized that because slight improvements cost significantly more money, it made little sense to pay more than the minimum for a VCR. In a matured market, you either merge or come up with a new service or product in order to survive. In order to compete effectively, United Bank for Africa has to merge with Standard Trust Bank Plc (STB) in August of 2005.

Declining Industries

As an industry moves through maturity toward possible decline, its products' growth rate of sales slows and may even begin to decrease. To the extent that exit barriers are low (when it is easy to get out of the business), firms will begin converting their facilities to alternate uses. However, when the exit barrier is high problem firms may decide to sell their facilities to other firms. At this point, the industry is declining and forcing firms either to consolidate further (e.g., through retrenchment) or leave the industry (e.g., through acquisition by another company or bankruptcy). Another major reason why the industry may decline and eventually be phased out is the emergence of new substitute products. A good example, again, is the VCR. The emergence of the DVD player and recorder not only saw the decline of the VCR but also its eventual extinction. The same can be said about cassettes; the arrival of CDs saw the demise of the cassette in the music industry.

Other factors that could contribute to a declining industry are consumers decreasing their demand for the industry's product or service, technology that supplants legacy products with new and better ones, or companies in the industry failing to be competitive in pricing. Industries that exemplify all the tendencies of a declining market is the postal service and tape-cassette sub-sectors, which have experienced decreased demand - largely due to the arrival of the Internet and email and CD player. We should note that declining industries might experience periods of stable or even increasing growth from time to time, even if their overall prospects are on the way down.

Classifying industries according to their stage of growth can be extremely useful for the purposes of choosing the appropriate competitive strategy and to examine whether or not an entrepreneur should even consider entering into that industry – especially those without growth potential. Here is a graph (Figure 8-1) outlining the stages we discussed:

Figure 8-1:
The Industry Life Cycle a Model for Understanding Industry Competition

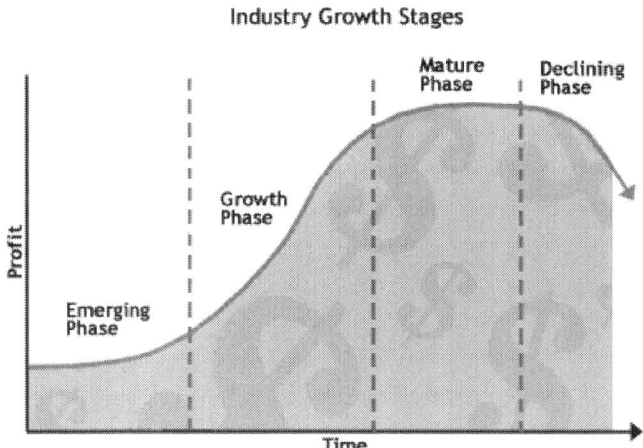

Figure 8-1: Industry Life Cycle

As pointed out earlier in this chapter, the point at which one enters the industry determines the chosen strategies of the firm and its ability to succeed. The point is that the industry life cycle, as a model, is useful for explaining and predicting trends among the forces driving the competition within an industry. Unless an entrepreneur pays attention to the stage of development in which an industry finds itself, one may end up introducing a business idea, product or service in a market where customers are looking for something different. Second, if an entrepreneur does not know what stage the industry is, it becomes difficult to choose what competitive strategies to adopt.

ANALYZING INDUSTRY STRUCTURE

Let us assume that as a prospective entrepreneur you want to start your business in the restaurant industry or sector. The rule is that you must understand the nature or **structure** of the restaurant business or industry. It means that you must know who your competitors are, how intense is the competition, what drives them and what shapes the industry. Industry and competitive analysis uses a tool kit of techniques to get a clear picture on key industry traits, the intensity of competition, the drivers of industry change, the market positions and strategies of rival companies, the keys to competitive success, and the industry's future profit outlook.[4] The tool kit provides a way of thinking strategically about the industry and drawing conclusions about whether the industry represents an attractive investment for your company's funds. It entails examining your firm's business in the context of a much wider environment. Industry and competitive analysis aims at developing, probing, and gaining insightful answers to seven key questions:

1. What are the industry's dominant economic features?
2. What competitive forces are at work in the industry and how strong are they?
3. What are the drivers of change in the industry and what impact will they have?
4. What key factors will determine competitive success or failure?
5. How attractive is the industry?

The answers to these questions build an understanding of your firm's surrounding environment and, collectively, form the basis for matching its strategy to changing industry conditions and competitive realities.

UNDERSTANDING INDUSTRY'S ECONOMIC FEATURES

An entrepreneur who wishes to go into the restaurant business must first answer a series of questions. In strategic management, the first question you should ask yourself is the dominant economic feature in the restaurant industry. Answers to this question must take into consideration the reason why the restaurant industry is a profitable one. The factors to consider in profiling an industry's economic features are:[5]

- Market size, that is, how large is the market: Is it growing or in a recession?
- Are there enough customers to buy your products or services?
- Scope of competitive rivalry (local, regional, national or global). Here, you would want to know if existing or potential competitors exist in your town, in your state or in the country at large.
- Market growth rate and where the industry is in the growth cycle (early development, rapid growth, early maturity, mature, saturated and stagnant, declining).
- The number of rivals and their relative sizes. Here, you should know the size of your competitors, both existing and potential.
- The number of buyers (customers) and their relative sizes.
- The prevalence of backward and forward integration.
- The types of distribution channels used to access buyers.
- The pace of technological changes in production process, innovation and new product introductions.
- Whether the products or services of rival firms are highly differentiated, weakly differentiated, or essentially identical.
- Whether firms can realize economies of scale in purchasing, manufacturing, transportation, marketing, or advertising. Here, you should ask your self whether size matters and whether you can compete with the existing big players in the market or industry.
- Whether strong learning and experience effects characterize certain industry activities such that unit costs decline as cumulative output (and thus the experience of "learning by doing") grows.

> Resource requirements and the ease of entry and exit. What do you need to start and run your business? What do you do to terminate your business if things do not work well as planned?

These are logical questions for which you must provide answers. An industry's economic features are important because of the implications they have for strategy.

UNDERSTANDING THE NATURE OF COMPETITION IN THE INDUSTRY

An important part of industry and competitive analysis is to delve into the industry's competitive process to discover the main sources of competitive pressure and how strong each competitive force is. This question is important because entrepreneurs cannot devise a successful strategy without understanding the industry's competitive structure. Michael Porter of the Harvard Business School has developed a framework for understanding the state of competition in an industry.[6] Termed as the *Five-Forces Model of Competition*, the model serves as a powerful tool for systematically diagnosing the competitive pressures in your market or industry and assessing how strong and important each one is. Although Michael Porter mentions only five forces (threat of new entrants, bargaining power of buyers, threat of substitute products and services, bargaining power of suppliers and rivalry among existing firms), several other authors have added a sixth force, which they termed as "other stakeholders" such as the relative power of unions and governments.[7] Not only is the model most widely used technique of competition analysis; it is also relatively easy to understand and apply. The model examines the following competitive issues in a particular industry:

1. The rivalry among existing firms in the market or industry.
2. Threats of substitute products or services. That is, the attempts of firms in other industries to win customers over to their own substitute products.
3. Threats of new entrants. That is, the potential entry of new competitors.
4. The bargaining power and leverage suppliers can exercise.
5. The bargaining power and leverage buyers of the product or service can exercise.
6. The power of other stakeholders such as the relative power of unions, social movements, governmental requirements, to determine the nature and degree of competition within an industry.

Rivalry Among Existing Firms and Sellers

According to Michael Porter, the strongest of the five competitive forces is usually the jockeying for position and buyer favor that goes on among rival firms in an industry. In some industries, rivalry is centered around price competition; sometimes resulting in prices below the level of unit costs and forcing losses on most rivals (example is automobile industry). In other industries, price competition is minimal and rivalry is focused on such factors as performance features, new product innovation, quality and durability, warranties, after-sale service, and brand image (example is the newspaper and banking industries). Competition among industry rivals heats up when one or more competitors sees an opportunity to better meet customer needs or is under pressure to improve its performance. The intensity of rivalry among competing sellers is a function of how vigorously they employ such tactics as lower prices, increased features, expanded customer services, longer warranties, special promotions, and new product introductions. Regardless of the industry, several common factors seem to influence the tempo of rivalry among competing sellers:[8]

1. Rivalry intensifies as the number of competitor's increases and as competitors become more equal in size and capability.
2. Rivalry is usually stronger when demand for the product or service is growing slowly.
3. Rivalry is more intense when industry conditions tempt competitors to use price cuts or other competitive weapons to boost unit volume.
4. Rivalry is stronger when customers' costs to switch brands are low.
5. Rivalry is stronger when one or more competitors are dissatisfied with its market position and launches moves to bolster its standing at the expense of rivals.
6. Rivalry tends to be more vigorous when it costs more to get out of a business than to stay and compete.

Two facets of competitive rivalry stand out: (i) the launch of a powerful competitive strategy by one company intensifies the pressures on the remaining companies and (ii) the character of rivalry is shaped partly by the strategies of the leading players and partly by the vigor with which industry rivals use competitive weapons to try to outmaneuver one another. In determining the competitive pressures created by rivalry among existing competitors, the entrepreneur's job is to identify the current weapons and tactics of competitive rivalry, to stay on top of which tactics are most and least successful, to understand the "rules" that industry rivals play by, and to decide whether and why rivalry is likely to increase or diminish in strength.

Threat From Substitute Products or Services

Remember that your competition comes not only from companies that deal in the same products and services that you do, but also from companies that have substitute products. These products accomplish the same function but use a different method. For example, if you want to go into the laundry business in a chosen locality and there is a new apartment development project in that area that offers laundry services, you should know that the owners of that apartment project is a prospective competitor. In a similar manner, cable news television networks are direct competitors to newspapers although they exist in totally different industries.

According to Michael Porter, the existence of substitute products in your market or industry limit's the potential returns of an industry by placing a ceiling on the prices firms in the industry can profitably charge.[9] To the extent that switching costs are low, substitutes may have a strong effect on an industry. In the transportation industry in many Sub-Sahara African countries, for example, it may be cheaper for commuters to switch to the motorbike from the traditional cab as their means of transportation. If the fare for a cab goes up, commuters will easily find a cheaper way of transportation through the motorbike. Tea can be considered a substitute for coffee. If the price of coffee goes up high enough, coffee drinkers will slowly begin switching to tea. The price of tea thus puts a price ceiling on the price of coffee.

Figure 8-2
The Five-Force Model of Competition for Understanding Forces Driving Industry Competition

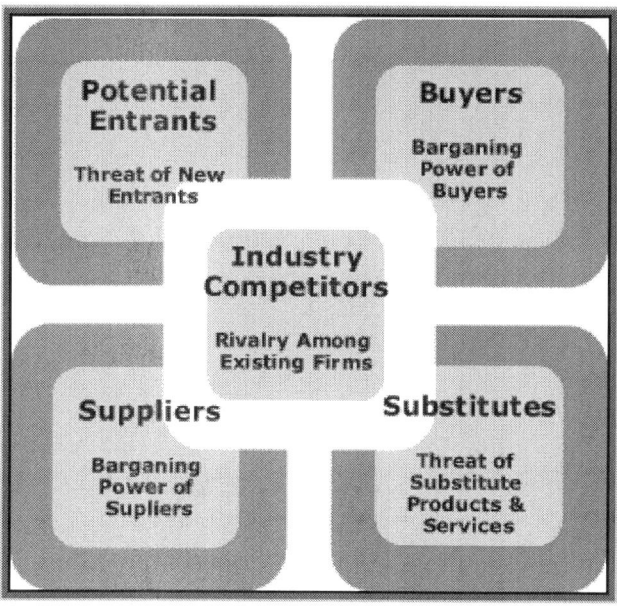

Source: Adapted from Michael E. Porter, "How Competitive Forces Shape Strategy," *Harvard Business Review* 57, No. 2 (March-April 1979), pp. 137-45 and Michael E. Porter, *Competitive Strategy: Techniques for Analyzing Industries and Competitors* (New York: The Free Press, 1980).

Another example is the case of the communication system in the developing countries. Most people want to communicate with the outside world. Prior to the late nineties every route of communication goes through the government controlled carriers such as Nigeria Telecommunications Limited (NITEL) with its "normal telephone system". But today, there is a substitute product and service offered by independent operators: the mobile phone, which is a substitute product or service to the traditional telephone system as they both perform the same function. To get the news, the newspaper is a substitute of the radio or the television. The rise of the motorbike as a means of transportation in both the urban and rural areas of Africa is a substitute to the traditional means of urban transportation, the cab.

Identifying possible substitute products or services is sometimes a difficult task. It means searching for products or services that can perform the same function, even though they have a different appearance and may not appear to be easily substitutable.

The Competitive Force of Potential Entry

New entrants to a market bring new production capacity, the desire to establish a secure place in the market. Sometimes, too, they bring substantial resources. Just how serious the competitive threat of entry is in a particular market depends on two classes of factors: *barriers to entry* and the *expected reaction of incumbent firms to new entry*. A barrier to entry exists whenever it is hard for a newcomer to break into the market and/or economic factors put a potential entrant at a disadvantaged competitive position. Below are some types of entry barriers.[10]

1. *Economies of scale:* Economies of scale deter entry because they force potential competitors either to enter on a large-scale basis (a costly and perhaps risky move for entering a market) or to accept a cost disadvantage (and lower profitability). These are product volumes that enable businesses to produce goods more inexpensively than a new business can. As an entrepreneur, you cannot compete with low costs of the established firms. To combat economies of scale, your new firm must form alliances that give it more clout.

2. *Inability to gain access to technology and specialized know-how:* Many industries require technological capability and skills not readily available to a newcomer. Key patents can effectively bar entry as can lack of technically skilled personnel and an inability to execute complicated manufacturing techniques.

3. *The existence of learning and experience curve effects:* When lower unit costs are partly or mostly a result of experience in producing the product and other learning curve benefits, new entrants face a cost disadvantage competing against firms with more know-how. For example, experience, as a resource, is especially crucial in such fields as management consultancy and training where there are already established and reputable firms in the industry. To be successful, a prospective entrepreneur must have acquired some experience in the field through working for known firms in the industry. This experience must be combined with a client base that has been built up over the years while working for the firm.

4. *Brand preferences and customer loyalty:* Buyers are often attached to established brands. High brand loyalty means that an entrepreneur or a potential entrant must build a network of distributors and dealers, and then be prepared to spend enough money on advertising and sales promotion to overcome customer loyalties and build its own clientele. Establishing brand loyalty and building customer loyalty can be a slow and costly process. In addition, if it is difficult or costly for a customer to switch to a new brand, a new entrant must persuade buyers that its brand is worth the costs. To overcome the switching-cost barrier, new entrants

may have to offer buyers a discounted price or an extra margin of quality or service. All this can mean lower profit margins for new entrants - something that increases the risk to start-up companies dependent on sizable, early profits.

5. *Resource Requirements*: The larger the total financial investment and other resource requirements needed to enter the market successfully; the more limited the pool of potential entrants. The most obvious capital requirements are associated with manufacturing plant and equipment, distribution facilities, working capital to finance inventories and customer credit, introductory advertising and sales promotion to establish a clientele, and cash reserves to cover start-up losses. Other resource barriers include access to technology, specialized expertise and know-how, and R&D requirements, labor force requirements, and customer service requirements.

6. *Access to Distribution Channels:* In the case of consumer goods, a potential entrant may face the barrier of gaining access to consumers. Wholesale distributors may be reluctant to take on a product that lacks buyer recognition. A network of retail dealers may have to start from the scratch. Retailers have to be convinced to give a new brand display space and a trial period. The more existing producers tie up distribution channels, the tougher entry will be. To overcome this barrier, potential entrepreneurs may have to "buy" distribution access by offering better margins to dealers and distributors or by giving advertising allowances and other incentives. As a consequence, a potential entrant's profits may be squeezed unless and until its product gains enough acceptances that distributors and retailers want to carry it.

7. *Governmental Regulatory Policies:* Government can limit entry into an industry through licensing requirements by restricting access to raw materials, such as oil-drilling sites in protected areas. That is why many new ventures form strategic alliances with larger companies to help support the costs along the way. In many developing countries, business regulation is seen as one of the greatest barriers to entrepreneurial development. As pointed out by the World Bank, regulation in poor countries is more cumbersome and brings about increased costs in establishing and running a business venture. Over-regulation also causes bribery and corruption in many developing countries and the inability to pay the costs associated with bribery and corruption can also deter aspiring entrepreneurs from taking the initiative.

The Bargaining Power and Leverage of Suppliers

Whatever industry one wishes to establish his or her own firm, there is always the possibility that the firm will have suppliers. Suppliers can affect an industry through their ability to raise prices or reduce the quality of purchased goods and services. Do not forget too that labor is also a source of supply, and in some industries like software, highly skilled labor is in short supply; therefore the price goes up. A supplier or supplier group is powerful if some of the following factors apply:

(i) The supplier industry is dominated by a few companies, but it sells to many consumers (e.g., the petroleum industry).
(ii) The product or service is unique and/or it has built up switching costs (e.g., word processing software).
(iii) Substitutes are not readily available (e.g., electricity).
(iv) Suppliers are able to integrate forward and are able to compete directly with their present customers (e.g., a national airline carrier might decide to go directly to those buyers of its airline tickets without depending on the services of its travel agents).

The Bargaining Power and Leverage exercisable by Buyers

Buyers affect an industry through their ability to force down prices, bargain for higher quality or more services, and play competitors against each other. A buyer or a group of buyers is powerful if some of the following factors hold true:

(i) A buyer purchases a large proportion of the seller's products or services (e.g., newsprints purchased by a major newspaper organization or publishing house).
(ii) A buyer has the potential to integrate backward by producing the product itself (e.g., a major fast-food franchise decides to produce its own bread or chicken).
(iii) Alternative suppliers are readily available because the product is standardized or undifferentiated (e.g., motorists can choose among many gas stations).
(iv) Changing suppliers costs very little (e.g., office suppliers are easy to find).
(v) The purchased product is unimportant to the final quality or price of a buyer's products or services and thus can be easily substituted without affecting the final product adversely (e.g., electric wire bought for use in lamps).

UNDERSTANDING FACTORS DRIVING INDUSTRY CHANGE

As we pointed out in the beginning of this chapter, no industry ever remains static. All industries are characterized by trends and new developments that gradually or speedily produce changes important enough to require a strategic response from participating firms. Earlier, we pointed out in this chapter that industries go through a life cycle of birth, growth, maturity, stagnation or decline. In this life cycle there are certain factors or drivers at work that shape the structure of the industry and thus, the competitive strategies of participating firms. According to A. Thompson, A. Strickland and J. Gamble, industry and competitive conditions change because forces are enticing or pressuring certain industry participants (competitors, customers, suppliers) to alter their actions in important ways.[11] The driving forces in an industry are the major underlying causes of changing industry and competitive conditions. Some driving forces originate in the macro environment (such as economic factors, technological changes, shift in societal values and life styles, change in population demographics, and legislation and regulations). The major driving forces originate in the company's more immediate industry and competitive environment.

Driving-forces analysis has three steps: (i) identifying what the driving forces are; (ii) assessing whether the drivers of change are, on the whole, acting to make the industry more or less attractive; and (iii) determining what strategy changes are needed to prepare for the impacts of the driving forces. We consider these steps below:

Identifying an Industry's Driving Forces

Many developments can affect an industry powerfully enough to qualify as driving forces. Some drivers of change are unique and specific to a particular industry situation, but most drivers of industry and competitive change fall into one of the following categories:

- *Emerging new Internet capabilities and applications*: Since the late 1990s, the Internet has woven its way into everyday business operations and the social fabric of life all across the world. The ever-growing Internet use, acceptance of Internet shopping, the emergence of high-speed Internet service, and an ever-increasing series of Internet applications and capabilities have been major drivers of change in industry after industry. Significantly, companies are increasingly using online technology (i) to collaborate closely with suppliers and streamline their supply chains and (ii) to revamp internal operations and squeeze out cost savings. Manufacturers can use their Web sites to access customers directly rather than distribute exclusively through traditional wholesale and retail channels. Although Internet-related impacts vary from industry to industry, the challenges here are to assess precisely how emerging Internet developments are altering a particular industry's landscape and factor these impacts into the strategy-making equation.

- *Increased globalization*: Competition begins to shift from primarily a regional or national focus to an international or global focus when industry members begin seeking out customers in foreign markets or when production activities begin to migrate to countries where costs are lowest. Globalization of competition really starts to take hold when one or more ambitious companies precipitate a race for worldwide market leadership by launching initiatives to expand into more and more country markets. Globalization can also be precipitated by the blossoming of consumer demand in more and more countries and by the actions of government officials in many countries to reduce trade barriers or open up once-closed markets to foreign competitors.

- *Changes in an industry long-term growth rate*: Shifts in industry growth up or down are a driving force for industry change, affecting the balance between industry supply and buyer demand, entry and exit, and the character and strength of competition. An upsurge in buyer demand triggers a race among established firms and newcomers to capture the new sales opportunities; ambitious companies with trailing market shares may see the upturn in demand as a golden opportunity to launch offensive strategies to broaden their customer base and move up several notches in the industry standing.

- *Changes in who buys the product and how they use it*: Shifts in buyer demographics and new ways of using the product can alter the state of competition by opening the way to market an industry's product through a different mix of dealers and retail outlets; prompting producers to broaden or narrow their product lines; bringing different sales and promotion approaches into play; and forcing adjustments in customer service offerings. The growing popularity of downloading music from the Internet, storing music files on PC hard drives, and burning custom discs has forced recording companies to reexamine their distribution strategies and raised questions about the future of traditional retail music stores; at the same time, it has stimulated sales of disc burners and blanc discs.

- *Product Innovation*: Competition in an industry is always affected by rivals racing to be first to introduce one new product or product enhancement after another. An ongoing stream of product innovations tends to alter the pattern of competition in any industry by attracting more first-time buyers, rejuvenating industry growth, and/or creating wider or narrower product differentiation among rival sellers. Successful new product introductions strengthen the market positions of the innovating companies, usually at the expense of companies that stick with their old products or are slow to follow with their own versions of the new product.

- *Technological change and manufacturing process innovation*: Advances in technology can dramatically alter an industry's landscape, making it possible to produce new and better products at lower cost and opening up new industry frontiers. For instance, Voice over Internet Protocol (VoIP) technology has spawned low-cost, Internet-based phone networks that are stealing large numbers of customers away from traditional telephone companies (whose higher cost technology depends on hardwired connections via overhead and underground telephone lines), especially in Sub-Saharan Africa.

- *Marketing innovation*: When firms are successful in introducing new ways to market their products, they can spark a burst of buyer interest, widen industry demand, increase product differentiation, and lower unit costs – any or all of which can alter the competitive positions of rival firms and force strategy revisions. Online marketing and online provision of services is shaking up competition in various industries including the education and knowledge industries to the extent that the traditional classroom-based educational system is gradually becoming a thing of the past.

- *Entry or exit of major firms*: The entry of one or more foreign companies into a geographic market once dominated by domestic firms nearly always shakes up competitive conditions. Likewise, when an established domestic firm from another industry attempts entry either by acquisition or by launching its own start-up venture, it usually applies its skills and resources in some innovative fashion that pushes competition in new directions. Entry by a major firm thus often produces a new ball game, not only with new key players but also with new rules for competing. Similarly, exit of a major firm changes the competitive structure by reducing the number of market leaders and causing a rush to capture exiting firm's customers.

- *Diffusion of technical know-how across companies and more countries*: As knowledge about how to perform a particular activity or execute a particular manufacturing technology spreads, the competitive advantage held by firms originally possessing this know-how erodes. Knowledge diffusion can occur through scientific journals, trade publications, on-site plant tours, word of mouth among suppliers and customers, employee migration, and Internet sources. It can also occur when those possessing technological knowledge license other to use that knowledge for a royalty fee or team up with a company interested in turning the technology into a new business venture. Quite often, technological know-how can be acquired by simply buying a company that has the wanted skills, patents, or manufacturing capabilities.

- *Changes in cost and efficiency*: Widening or shrinking differences in the costs among key competitors tend to dramatically change the state of competition. The low cost of fax and e-mail transmission has put mounting competitive pressure on the relatively inefficient, unreliable and high-cost operations of many postal service organizations in Sub-Saharan Africa.

- *Reductions in uncertainty and business risk*: An emerging industry is typically characterized by much uncertainty over potential market size, how much time and money will be needed to surmount technological problems, and what distribution channels and buyer segments to emphasize. Emerging industries tend to attract only risk-taking entrepreneurial companies. Over time, however, if the business model of industry pioneers proves profitable and market demand for the product appears durable, more conservative firms are usually enticed to enter the market. Often these later entrants are large, financial strong firms looking to invest in attractive growth industries.

- *Regulatory influences and government policy changes*: Government regulatory actions can often force significant changes in industry practices and strategic approaches. Deregulation has proved to be a potent pro-competitive force in the airline, banking, natural gas, telecommunications, and electric utility industries. Across Sub-Saharan Africa, government efforts to privatize public enterprises have changed the competitive position in many of these sectors: air transportation, education, healthcare, electricity, etc.

- *Changing societal concerns, attitudes, and lifestyles*: Emerging social issues and changing attitudes and lifestyles can be powerful instigators of industry change. For instance, growing antismoking sentiment in Europe and North America has emerged as a major driver of change in the tobacco industry; concerns about theft and safety has altered the public transportation industry in many African countries; concerns about health and obesity has dramatically altered the traditional restaurant industry in Africa. Social concerns about air and water pollution have forced industries to incorporate expenditures for controlling pollution and other environmental protection initiatives in their policies. Shifting social concerns, attitudes, and lifestyles alter the pattern of competition, usually favoring players to respond quickly and creatively with products or services targeted to the new trends and conditions.

Assessing the Impact of the Driving Forces

Simply identifying the industry driving forces is not sufficient, however. The second, and more important, step in driving-forces analysis is to determine whether the prevailing driving forces are, on the whole, acting to make the industry environment more or less attractive. Answers to the following three questions are needed here:[12]

1. Are the driving forces collectively acting to cause demand for the industry's product to increase or decrease?
2. Are the driving forces acting to make competition more or less intense?
3. Will the combined impacts of the driving forces lead to higher or lower industry profitability?

Getting a handle on the collective impact of the driving forces usually requires looking at the likely effects of each force separately, since the driving forces may not all be pushing change in the same direction. For example, two driving forces may be acting to spur demand for the industry's product or service while one driving force may be working to entail demand. Whether the net effect on industry demand is up or down hinges on which driving forces are the more powerful. Your objective here is to get a good grip on what external factors are shaping industry change and what difference these factors will make.

Developing a Strategy That Takes the Impacts of the Driving Forces into Account

The third step of driving-forces analysis – where the real payoff for strategy making comes – is for owners and/or managers to draw some conclusions about what strategy adjustments will be needed to deal with the impacts of the driving forces. According to Arthur Thompson, A. Strickland and John Gamble, the real value of doing driving-forces analysis is to gain better understanding of what strategy adjustments will be needed to cope with drivers of industry change and the impacts they are likely to have on market demand, competitive intensity, and industry profitability.[13] In short, the strategy-making challenge that flows from driving-forces analysis forces managers/owners to prepare for the industry and competitive changes being caused by the driving forces. We know that industries rarely remain static. They are constantly changing and we must understand the factors driving the change. Indeed, without understanding the forces driving industry change and the impacts these forces will have on the character of the industry environment and on the company's business over the next one to three years, owners/managers are ill-prepared to craft a strategy tightly matched to emerging conditions. Similarly, if owners/managers are uncertain about the implications of one or more driving forces, or if their views are incomplete or off the base, it is difficult for them to craft a strategy that is responsive to the driving forces and their consequences for the industry. So driving-forces analysis is not something to take lightly; it has practical value and is basic to the task of thinking strategically about where the industry is headed and how to prepare for the changes ahead.

UNDERSTANDING AN INDUSTRY'S KEY SUCCESS FACTORS

Within an industry there are certain variables that determine the success of a firm in that industry. In strategic management, these variables are called "key success factors." They are the factors the owner of a business venture or its management must understand and apply in order to be successful. **Key success factors** are those variables that can significantly affect the overall competitive positions of a firm within any particular industry. Key success factors concern the product attributes, competencies, competitive capabilities, and market achievements with the greatest direct bearing on company profitability.[14] They typically vary from industry to industry and are crucial to determining a company's ability to succeed within that industry. Key success factors are usually determined by the economic and technological characteristics of the industry and by the competitive weapons on which the firms in the industry have built their strategies.

As an entrepreneur in a particular industry, key success factors in that industry are those things that you must do and do well in order to succeed and compete in a profitable manner. Take for example a prospective entrepreneur who wants to start a hotel and hospitality business. He or she must know what is required to be competitive in that industry. Questions that must be asked should include but not limited to: Is there availability of power supply and transportation facility? Is there availability of management competency? Is the location ideal? All industries have key success factors and it is important to consider them when designing your competitive strategies. For example, if you want to go into the newspaper business, you must understand those factors that make a newspaper successful. Key success factors are the rules that shape whether a company will be financially and competitively successful.[15] The answers to three questions help identify an industry's key success factors:

(i) On what basis do customers choose between the competing brands of sellers? What product attributes is crucial?
(ii) What resources and competitive capabilities does a seller need to have to be competitively successful?
(iii) What does it take for sellers to achieve a sustainable competitive advantage?

One important condition for achieving a competitive advantage in an industry or market is the fit between an industry's key success factor and a company's strategic factors. An industry's key success factors deal with an entire industry: those things all firms in that industry must do to compete; whereas, **strategic factors** deal with a particular company: those things a firm must do differently from the existing firms in other to out compete rivals in the same market. For example, good or courteous customer service can be marketing-related key success factor in a particular industry. On the other hand, the way you provide customer service compared to those of your competitors can be your strategic factor. The most common types of an industry's key success factors are:

- Product design
- Market segmentation
- Distribution and promotion
- Pricing
- Financing
- Customer service
- Securing of key personnel
- Research and development
- Production
- Servicing
- Maintenance of quality/value
- Securing key suppliers.

UNDERSTANDING FIRM'S COMPETITIVE POSITION

As pointed out earlier in chapter six, strategy formulation and implementation is concerned with developing a company's basic business idea, its mission, objectives, strategies, and policies. However, a strategy is developed after a careful analysis of the firm's competitive position. An understanding of a firm's competitive position begins with situation analysis: the process of finding a strategic fit between external opportunities and internal strengths while working around external threats and internal weaknesses. In strategic management we call this exercise as the process of "SWOT-ing" your firm. **SWOT** is an acronym used to describe the particular **S**trengths, **W**eaknesses, **O**pportunities, and **T**hreats that are strategic factors for a specific company. SWOT analysis should not only result in the identification of your firm's **distinctive competence** - the particular capabilities and resources that your firm possesses and the superior way in which you use them – but also in the identification of opportunities that the firm is not currently able to take advantage of due to a lack of appropriate resources (weaknesses). Over the years, SWOT analysis has proven to be the most enduring analytical technique used in strategic management.[16]

SWOT analysis has the advantage of helping business owners and managers look at their businesses objectively. Being objective to oneself is usually difficult: People tend to accentuate the positive – and play down the negative. And anything but an honest assessment of your company's resources and capabilities can mean big trouble down the road. Many business owners and prospective entrepreneurs have asked this question a number of times: "Do I need to know my strengths and weaknesses before I venture into my business or do I learn about these through my experiences in the industry." This is a very good question, at least from the perspective of entrepreneurship. The rule is that without a thorough analysis and understanding of the external environment, the nature of the competition within the industry, the strengths of your rivals, etc., it is impossible for you to know your strengths and weaknesses. Consequently, you cannot go into your business venture without undertaking an analysis of your firm's resource strengths and weaknesses and its external opportunities and threats. Ignoring an understanding of these things is recipe for disaster sooner or later.

SWOT analysis is grounded on the basic principle that *strategy-making efforts must aim at producing a good fit between a company's resource capability* (as reflected by its balance of resource strengths and weaknesses) *and its external situation* (as reflected by industry and competitive conditions, the company's own market opportunities, and specific external threats to the company's profitability and market standing). Without crafting a strategy that capitalizes on your firm's resources, aims at capturing your firm's best opportunities, and neutralizes the threats to its well-being, it is difficult to stake out a competitive position in your industry. In SWOT analysis, the best strategies accomplish an organization's mission by (1) exploiting an organization's opportunities and strengths while (2) neutralizing its threats and (3) avoiding (or correcting) its weaknesses.[17]

KNOWING THE STRENGTHS AND WEAKNESSES OF YOUR FIRM

The strengths and weaknesses of your firm (or your prospective firm) can come in different forms because a particular strength that your firm possesses can be a weakness for other firms.

Company Strengths and Resource Capabilities

First, we should understand that strength is something your company is good at doing or a characteristic that gives it enhanced competitiveness. A company's strength can take any of several forms:[18]

(i) *A skill or important expertise*: low-cost manufacturing capabilities, strong e-commerce expertise, technological know-how, a proven track record, etc.

(ii) *Valuable physical assets*: state-of-the-art plants and equipment, attractive real estate locations, worldwide distribution facilities, ownership of valuable resource deposits, etc.

(iii) *Valuable human assets*: an experienced and capable workforce, talented employees in key areas, motivated and energetic employees, cutting-edge knowledge and intellectual capital, astute entrepreneurship and managerial know-how, etc.

(iv) *Valuable organizational assets*: proven quality control systems, proprietary technology, key patents, a base of loyal customers, a strong balance sheet and credit rating, a good supply chain management system, a well-functioning company intranet, and e-commerce systems for accessing and exchanging information with suppliers and key customers, etc.

(v) *Valuable intangible assets*: brand-name image, company reputation, buyer goodwill, or a motivated and energized workforce.

(vi) *Competitive Capabilities*: short development times in bringing new products to market, a strong dealer network, strong partnership with key suppliers, an R&D organization with the ability to keep the company's pipeline full of innovative new products, a high degree of organizational agility in responding to shifting new products, shifting market conditions and emerging opportunities, a cadre of highly trained customer service representatives, or state-of-art systems for doing business via the Internet.

(vii) *An achievement or attribute that puts the company in a position of market advantage*: low overall costs, market share leadership, a superior product, a wide product selection, strong name recognition, state-of-the-art e-commerce technologies and practices, or exceptional customer service.

(viii) *Alliances or cooperative ventures*; fruitful collaborative partnerships with suppliers and marketing allies that enhance the company's own image and competitiveness.

As can be seen from the list above, company strengths have diverse origins. Sometimes they relate to fairly specific skills and expertise and sometimes they flow from different resources teaming together to create a competitive capability (like continuous product innovation – which tends to result from a combination of knowledge of consumer needs, technological know-how, R&D, product design, and other types of intellectual capital.

Company Weaknesses and Resource Deficiencies

A weakness is something a company lacks or does poorly (in comparison to others) or a condition that puts it at a disadvantaged competitive position. A company's internal weaknesses can relate to:

(i) Deficiencies in competitively important skills or expertise or intellectual capital of one kind or another.
(ii) A lack of competitively important physical, organizational, or intangible assets.

(iii) Missing or weak competitive capabilities in key areas.

Internal weaknesses are thus shortcomings in a company's complement of resources.[19] The best approach we have found for getting a handle on what you do well - and where you fall short - is to look at eight key capabilities, which together make up essential elements of any business:

(i) *Research and Development (R&D):* Your ability to design and develop new products, services, or technologies. Remember that *innovation* is the essence of entrepreneurship. In order to compete successfully, you must continually search for new ideas and improve on your existing products or services.

(ii) *Operations*: Having what it takes to produce the highest quality products or services in the most efficient ways possible is important for your competitiveness.

(iii) *Sales and Marketing:* How well you get your products or services into the marketplace and into the customers' radar screens.

(iv) *Distribution and Delivery*: The ability to get your products or services reliably into customers' hands.

(v) *Customer Service*: Everything you do to satisfy customers in order to create a loyal clientele, supporting you with their purchases and their praise.

(vi) *Management:* The ability to provide leadership, direction, and a vision for the company.

(vii) *Organization*: The procedures and company structures that enable you to make the most of your staff and resources.

(viii) *Financial Condition*: Both the long-term and short-term financial health of your company.

Not all of the above capabilities are equally important to every business. A state-of-the-art distribution and delivery system may be essential to the success of one firm but not be particularly important to another. Research and development (R&D) may be crucial for a company in the high technology business such as those in the computers or biomedical fields and not very important to someone who operates a health and massage center. Although an owner/manager running a firm may have all the management responsibilities, he or she must still have to master the art of managing the various functional areas of the business.

Consider a small gourmet catering service we will now call *Island Catering Services Limited*, located in Lagos, Nigeria. The company's management team was interested in expanding the business to form a national chain of stores in four major Nigerian cities (Ibadan, Port Harcourt, Abuja, and Kaduna). They needed to act quickly, but they were not quite sure that they were up to the task. So the managers went on a retreat to seriously consider the resources and assets the company could bring to the expansion plan. To help them in their analysis, they came up with a table that lists the various capabilities required by the company to run successfully such as the one shown in Figure 8-3. The figure shows how the management team ranked the importance on how eight key capabilities are relevant to their business and then graded themselves on how well the company was doing from poor, fair, good, to excellent in each area.

Figure 8-3:
Company Strengths and Weaknesses Survey of Island Catering Services

KEY SUCCESS FACTORS	IMPORTANCE TO BUSINESS IN THE CATERING SERVICES			HOW DOES ISLAND CATERING SERVICES RATE?			
Research and Development	Low	**Medium**	High	**Poor**	Fair	Good	Excellent
Operations	Low	Medium	**High**	Poor	Fair	Good	**Excellent**
Sales and Marketing	Low	Medium	**High**	**Poor**	Fair	Good	Excellent
Distribution and Delivery	Low	Medium	**High**	Poor	Fair	Good	**Excellent**
Customer Service	Low	Medium	**High**	Poor	Fair	**Good**	Excellent
Management	Low	Medium	**High**	Poor	**Fair**	Good	Excellent
Organization	Low	Medium	**High**	Poor	**Fair**	Good	Excellent
Financial Condition	Low	Medium	**High**	Poor	**Fair**	Good	Excellent

Here is a little background on what went into the thinking of the management at *Island Catering Services Ltd.* As a gourmet catering company, research and development (R&D) would not be of much importance to its competition. However, part of their strategic plan was to establish a good Web site where customers could go to view the current selection of dishes available, create personalized menus, and schedule their own catered events. Getting up to speed on the Internet would require R&D of sorts, so they gave research and development a ranking of medium importance. They used the category of operations to describe how accurately the orders were filled and how well the meals were prepared. Management sees the importance of operation as a highly needed key success factor in the business of catering. Sales and marketing is also seen as a key success factor in the business, but they decided to rate its importance as medium. Management defined distribution and delivery as how efficiently they got the food to their customers' events and supervised set-up, serving, and clean-up and they rated it high on their scale. The catering and gourmet business requires high level of customer service. They arrived at the conclusion that a good financial condition is necessary to run the business successfully. They noted also that to be successful overtime, such a business requires a good management team with proving organizational capability. All these capabilities, of course, are very important to the catering business.

Using the information, the management team at *Island Catering Services* began to collect valuable information on the important success factors in their business, as well as their own relative strengths and weaknesses. Next, they turned to another way of organizing the same information, which offered additional insights. Figure 8-3 also shows how the company's capabilities lined up in a strengths and weaknesses grid.

A completed grid allowed the management team at *Island Catering Services* to see at a glance where the most important strengths and weaknesses fell. The news was both good and bad. On the plus side, operations, distribution and delivery ranked high in importance to the catering business – and the company received "excellent" grades in each area. That was great. Customer service also ranked high in importance, and it scored "good" rating for the company. That was still okay.

But then the red flags began to appear. While management team and the financial conditions of a company in the business were rated as "highly important," the company received only "fair" grades in these areas. And they found an even more troubling note in the area of sales and marketing which is rated "poor". The plan called for an expansion into new geographic areas, yet in its current location, the company depended on repeat business and word of mouth for new customers. So in all honesty, the management team had to grade themselves as "poor" in sales and marketing. They also saw problems with research and development and, therefore, their Internet strategy. Because no one on staff had any experience with Web site development, another "poor" grade showed up. In terms of organization, the team found out that the turnover rate at *Island Catering Services* was high and there have been numerous complaints about the company's leadership performance. Consequently, the team gave "fair" as a score to the organization's performance.

After carefully reviewing the company strengths and weaknesses grid, the managers agreed to take a time-out from their expansion plans. The goal: to work on improving several of the key business capabilities where *Island Catering Service* had scored badly.

It is important that before an entrepreneur launches his or her business, one should set some time aside to complete the company strengths and weaknesses survey, using figure 8-3 as an example. First rank the eight key capabilities based on their importance to your business. Then grade yourself in each area. Be honest! The more honest you can be about yourself and your company's strengths and weaknesses right now, the more useful this exercise will be in helping you develop a business plan that will be of real use to you in the future.

If your company is already in business, assessing these eight capabilities can be a fairly straightforward task. If you are creating a brand new business plan, however, you may have to think harder about how well equipped you are – right here, right now – to succeed in each of these areas. Your firm has essentially two ways of addressing weaknesses. First, it may need to make investments to obtain the strengths required to implement strategies that support its mission. Second, it may need to modify its mission, goals and objectives so that they can be accomplished with existing skills and capabilities.

If you are completely on your own – the boss and the entire staff of your little company (what we call owner-manager) – you may feel a bit overwhelmed with all this talk about strengths, weaknesses, and business capabilities. After all, what could research and development or operations possibly have to do with being a freelance designer, a restaurant owner, a furniture maker, an automobile workshop owner, an operator of small hotel, or an interior decorator? There are several reasons. Many of the same issues that confront big companies are just as important to a one-man business. All you have to do is think small. For example, Funke Babalola who is a computer-networking specialist decided to go out on her own after getting tired of the corporate rat-race and her long commute from her home to the office. Here is how she filled in the blanks to make sense out of those eight key business capabilities in her own words:

Research and development: This include staying current with new software and hardware technologies using online training courses and certification programs.

Operations: This is stuff like billing, accounting, and scheduling. I also need to set up an answering service to field calls when I am out and make sure I am always reachable in an emergency (she now depends entirely on her cell phone).

Sales and marketing: This includes business cards, stationary, and maybe a Web site in the future. This also includes my ability to make cold calls to prospective clients.

Distribution and delivery: This includes reliable transportation to and from clients' locations. Also, I have to make sure I have the right equipment and software in the right place at the right time.

Customer service: This is my close working relationship with local clients who have information technology needs.

Management: This includes my sense of direction and vision, plus the goals and objectives I set for myself. I also define this as my ability to be my own boss, manage my business and myself.

Organization: This includes the support services I will need, such as accounting, secretarial, and so on. Most of the time I try to network or outsource some of the services I provide; an accounting firm prepares our books and other accounting services.

Financial Condition: This means having enough cash to stay afloat until invoices start getting paid, plus having a financial cushion so that I can buy testing equipment along with other hardware and software I need.

As Funke Babalola realized, no matter what the size of your company, it is important that the business owner defines these key business capabilities in whatever way makes the most sense to him or her. All that is required is that you give each one of these factors careful consideration. Do not be afraid to blow your horn when you describe your business strengths and weaknesses, especially when you can identify important company strengths. At the same time, however, you cannot afford to ignore the weaknesses you have discovered. So, acknowledge the fact that you need to seriously address certain business capabilities and make sure your business plan of action includes a detailed strategy for turning those company weaknesses around. Identifying and evaluating what a company is really good at doing and what capabilities it has for competing is a critical component of assessing a company's situation.

UNDERSTANDING ENVIRONMENTAL OPPORTUNITIES AND THREATS

After you have seriously examined the strengths and weaknesses of your business, the next step is to take a serious look around the forces outside of your business that will ultimately shape your company's destiny. Whether those forces represent opportunities or threats depends in large part on the strengths and weaknesses your company possesses. For example, if the government places a ban on the importation of certain goods from foreign markets, this is a threat to your business if you are an importer of these goods. At the same time, this could be an opportunity for your venture if it can produce these goods locally. When, for example, the Nigerian government of Olusegun Obasanjo inaugurated a presidential committee to promote the exportation of cassava with the mandate to bring in $5 billion from export of the commodity, many cassava growers saw this as an opportunity in their environment. Opportunities and threats can come in any form and from all directions. For example, the sudden appearance of a new competitor, the emergence of a totally unique technology, changes in population and popular taste, changing trade regulations, economic growth or recession, and unforeseen fad or fashion craze can represent big opportunities or major threats to your business.

When the small gourmet catering service called *Island Catering Services* began planning to expand from a one-city outfit to a national chain, the management team put together a list of opportunities and threats that they thought they should take seriously. Figure 8-4 shows what the managers came up with.

The management team saw opportunities in the increasing number of married couples who work and have money to spend, but do not have the time to cook at home. They also saw a growing interest in healthy, organic high quality food. There is a growing sophistication of consumers who demand gourmet take-out food. There is business boom in the areas they intend to expand and the growing use of Internet technology as a delivering system is seen as an opportunity to expand the business. The threats management found out included a tight labor market, competition from local grocery stores, the growing trend in local food suppliers to office workers and street vendors and street-corner bukaterias and the growth of fast-food chains in the country. Looking over the list, the management team at *Island Catering Services* was encouraged. After all, at least their opportunities outnumbered all the threats they could think of! And given the plus-and-minus list, the managers were convinced that they could capitalize on the opportunities they saw and counter any threat they identified.

Figure 8-4:
Island Catering Services: Opportunities and Threats

POSSIBLE OPPORTUNITIES	POTENTIAL THREATS
• Increasing number of working couples who cannot or will not cook.	• Poor infrastructure such as electricity and roads.
• Growing interest in healthy, organic, high quality meal.	• Difficulty in finding reliable staff in a very tight regional labor market.
• Growing sophistication of consumers and a growing demand for "true" gourmet take-out-food.	• Indirect competition, especially from the "waiters-on-the-wheel" who will deliver from a number of local restaurants.
• Business boom in the area, creating a strong market for business catering services.	• Street bukaterias, vendors, and fast-food restaurants.
	• Growing staff canteens.
• Promise of the Internet to improve marketing and customer service.	• New hotels in the business districts

You can create your own list of opportunities and threats you see out there on the business terrain or environment. Do not forget to think about the less obvious shapes than an opportunity or threat can take and the numerous directions they can come from. If you are having a tough time coming up with specifics, try to find out about the strengths and weaknesses of your existing or potential competitors. You will not know as much about them as you know about yourself, but chances are, you know enough to know what areas they are strong in and where they have weaknesses. Their strengths represent potential threats to you. Their weaknesses represent possible opportunities.

Lining Strengths and Weaknesses Against Opportunities and Threats

How well will you be able to exploit business opportunities and sidestep potential threats? From the perspective of strategic management, it is difficult to predict an answer. However, we do know that part of the answer depends on how well your strengths and weaknesses line up against the opportunities and threats you face. And that is where a SWOT analysis comes in. As pointed out earlier, it is an easy-to-use tool that helps you undertake the planning of your business and the direction you want it to follow. A SWOT analysis allows you to bring together all the internal factors you have identified and weight them against the external forces you see. Exactly how they line up tells you something about the next steps you need to take in planning your business.

The management team of *Island Catering Services* made a number of significant decisions around their business plan as a result of a SWOT analysis. Figure 8-5 shows how they fill in the SWOT grid

Based on their SWOT analysis, *Island Catering Services* brought a consultant on board who had marketing expertise and a background in developing restaurant chains. They researched Web site development to get a sense of the resources they would need to commit if they wanted to achieve a true Internet presence. They also tighten up their management structure so that they would be prepared for the growth they were expecting. Finally, with the help of two big investors, they improved their financial condition to the point where the entire team felt comfortable signing on to the expansion effort.

So, *Island Catering Services* is about to grow bigger. While it is certainly true that they will have increased competition for catering and take-out services, demand is growing, which leaves room for several companies to prosper. What is more, the company's management is confident that by focusing their new resources on quality, consistency, and sophisticated menus, the company can compete successfully against both grocery stores and other types of restaurants. And *Island Catering Services* has increased its chances of success, because the company spent extra time upfront understanding its own strengths and weaknesses and dealing with the opportunities and threats they faced before inviting all those new guests to dinner.

The result of this lining up provides *Island Catering Services* answers to the following questions:
- What competitive capabilities need to be strengthened immediately, so as to add greater power to the company's strategy and boost sales and profitability?
- What actions should be taken to reduce the company's competitive liabilities? Which weaknesses or competitive deficiencies are in urgent need of correction?
- Which market opportunities should be top priority in future strategic initiatives?
- What should the company be doing to guard against the threats to its wellbeing?

Figure 8-5
Island Catering Services' SWOT analysis Grid

	OPPORTUNITIES	THREATS
STRENGTHS	Use superior operations and delivery system to go after increasingly sophisticated high-end-take-out catering market (EXPLOIT)	We depend on our high quality services, but it is harder to attract and keep good people. (MONITOR)
WEAKNESSES	Big growth in catered events market, but we are weak in marketing. Promise of the Internet, but we have no R & D (IMPROVE)	Our poor marketing and precarious financial conditions are dangerous, given the increased competition we face. (ELIMINATE)

The strengths, weaknesses, opportunities, and threats you feature in your SWOT grid have to be more than broad generalizations if you want your resulting analysis to be at all useful in your business plan: Each item should be detailed, specific, and supported by the facts you have at hand. Using your SWOT analysis as a guide, make sure your written plan addresses each of the following:

➢ How you intend to capitalize on your company's strengths where they match up with your business opportunities.

- How you plan to eliminate the weaknesses you have identified in areas where you face serious outside threats.

- How you plan to improve on weak areas where you may be able to take advantage of future business opportunities.

- How you intend to monitor and maintain your other strengths, so that you will be ready for threats before they appear.

As an entrepreneur or a prospective one, do not forget that your company's capabilities and the external forces you face are constantly changing. That is just the nature of business. Consequently, you must plan on revisiting your SWOT analysis on a regular basis to see how the balance of strengths, weaknesses, opportunities, and threats may have shifted or changed. That way, your business plan will be based on the way the world around you *is*, not the way it *was*. To get a complete understanding of the discussion on SWOT, we use the following list to summarize what to look for in sizing up your company's strengths, weaknesses, opportunities and threats.

CONDUCTING A SWOT ANALYSIS

Potential Resources, Strengths and Competitive Capabilities

- A powerful strategy
- Core competence in …
- A distinctive competence in …
- A product or service that is strongly differentiated from those of rivals
- Competencies and capabilities that are well matched to industry key success factors
- A strong financial condition; ample financial resources to grow the business
- Strong brand-name, image and company reputation
- An attractive customer base
- Economy of scale and/or learning/experience curve advantage over rivals
- Proprietary technology/superior technological skills/important patents
- Superior intellectual capital relative to key rivals
- Cost advantages over rivals
- Strong advertising and promotion
- Product innovation capabilities
- Proven capabilities in improving production processes
- Good supply chain management capabilities
- Better product quality relative to rivals
- Wide geographic coverage and/or strong distribution capability
- Alliances/joint ventures with other firms that provide access to valuable technology, competencies, and/or attractive geographic markets.

Potential Resource Weaknesses and Competitive Deficiencies

- No clear strategic direction
- Resources that are not well matched to industry key success factors
- No well-developed or proven core competencies
- A weak balance sheet; burdened with too much debt
- Higher overall unit costs relative to key competitors
- Weak or unproven product innovation capabilities
- A product/service with ho-hum attributes or features inferior to those of rivals
- Too narrow a product line relative to rivals
- Weak brand image or reputation
- Weaker dealer network than key rivals and/or lack of adequate distribution capability
- Behind on product quality, R&D, and/or technological know-how
- In the wrong strategic group
- Losing market share because of …
- Lack of management depth
- Inferior intellectual capability relative to leading rivals
- Sub-par profile because …
- Plagued with internal operating problems or obsolete facilities
- Behind rivals in e-commerce capabilities
- Short on financial resources to grow business and pursue promising initiatives
- Too much underutilized capacity.

Potential External Opportunities

- Openings to win market share from rivals
- Sharply rising buyer demand for the industry's product
- Serving additional customer groups or market segments
- Expanding into new geographic markets
- Expanding the firm's product line to meet a broader range of customer needs
- Using existing company skills or technological know-how to enter new product lines or new businesses
- Online sales
- Integrating forward and backward
- Falling trade barriers in attractive foreign markets
- Acquiring rival firms with attractive technological expertise or capabilities
- Entering into alliances or joint ventures to expand the firm's market coverage or boost its competitive capability
- Openings to exploit emerging new technologies
- Changes in demographics and life-style that boost demand for products or services
- Exit of major competitors
- Deregulation policies that bring about new markets and increased demands.

Potential External Threats to A Company's Future Prospects

- Increasing intensity of competition among industry rivals – may squeeze profit margin
- Slowdowns in the market growth
- Likely entry of potent new competitors
- Loss of sales to substitute products
- Growing bargaining power of customers or suppliers
- A shift in buyer needs and tastes away from the industry's product
- Adverse demographic changes that threaten to curtail demand for the industry's product
- Vulnerability to unfavorable industry driving forces
- Restrictive trade policies on the part of foreign governments
- Costly new regulatory requirements.

CHAPTER SUMMARY

An industry is a group of companies offering products or services that are close substitutes for each other. Close substitutes are products or services that satisfy the same basic consumer needs. An industry is a group of firms whose products or services have so many of the same attributes that they compete for the same buyers.

The drivers of an industry (or industry drivers) are all the relevant factors and influences outside the company's boundaries that shape the behavior or state of that industry. These drivers emanate from the economy at large, population demographics, societal values and life styles, governmental regulation, technological factors and the industry and competitive arena in which the company operates.

A firm can create a change in its industry environment by developing and implementing competitive strategies. A firm cannot change its industry environment nor craft competitive strategies without an understanding of the forces driving change.

The industry life cycle model is an explanatory model that is used for analyzing and understanding the effects of industry evolution on competitive forces. The success of a firm in understanding the forces driving change depends on the firm's understanding of the developmental stage in which the industry finds itself. Understanding these stages directs us to see an industry in evolutionary stage or the industry life cycle. The life cycle of an industry starts with its birth, growth, shakeout, maturity, and decline to the death stage. Each of these stages demands an appropriate entry and/or exit strategy.

The Five Forces Model of Competition helps us to understand the structure of an industry and the application of appropriate competitive strategies. It is an appropriate tool for understanding the competition within an industry. The model helps industry participants to understand the intensity of rivalry among existing firms, the threats from substitute products or services, the threat from potential new comers to the market, and the bargaining power of suppliers and buyers.

Industry conditions change because important forces are driving industry participants (competitors, customers, or suppliers) to alter their actions. The driving forces in an industry are the major underlying causes of changing industry and competitive conditions. Industry driving forces have the biggest influence on how the industry landscape will be altered.

Industry Key Success Factors are those things that a firm in an industry must do in order to succeed in a particular market. In order to design appropriate competitive strategies in an industry, an entrepreneur must also understand what it takes to be successful overtime within an industry.

SWOT analysis is an acronym for analyzing the strengths, weaknesses, opportunities and threats facing a company. Success in an industry demands that an entrepreneur knows the strengths, weaknesses, opportunities and threats facing the company. Strengths and weaknesses reside within the company and opportunities and threats exist in the firm's environment.

Strengths and weaknesses can be found by examining the company's R&D, operations, sales and marketing, distribution and delivery, customer service, management, organization and the financial condition of the firm.

Opportunities and threats facing the company can be found in the company's size of customer groups, its product line, its skills, availability of markets, growing demand, shift in demography, new technologies, entry of new potent competitors, new regulatory requirements, emergence of substitute products, etc.

CHAPTER DISCUSSION QUESTIONS

1. What is an industry? Provide two examples of industries that you are familiar with. Discuss why you consider them as industries.

2. What is an industry life cycle? Why do we use this term to understand an industry? Choose a particular industry you are familiar with and describe its phase in the industry life cycle.

3. What are the different five stages in an industry's life cycle? What strategies must you use in these different stages?

4. What are the two most important questions you must ask yourself when trying to understand the structure of an industry?

5. What are the components of the "Five-Forces Model of Competition" discussed in this chapter? Why do you think they are helpful in designing a firm's competitive strategies?

6. What are the most common industry driving forces?

7. What do we mean when we talk about an industry's key success factors? Chose an industry and discuss its key success factors.

8. What does the acronym "SWOT" stands for? Provide examples to illustrate your understanding of "SWOT."

CASE STUDY 8: COMPETITIVE STRATEGIES IN THE NIGERIAN FAST FOOD INDUSTRY[20]

One would have thought that Nigeria, with an estimated population of over 130 million people, and esteemed positions as Africa's largest market, the world's 6th largest oil producer and the 10th most populous nation in the world will be a sought- after market by multinational firms, especially in the restaurant and fast-food sector, but surprisingly this is not the case. For reasons, which are difficult to understand, McDonalds, Burger King, Pizza Hut, KFC, Subway and such other global fast-food giants have not yet established any form of franchise or presence in Nigeria, they are yet to start taking advantages of the immense opportunities which abound in Nigeria, especially in the fast-food sector. A sector which industry giant Folu Ayeni of Tantalizers estimate to be currently worth about N190 billion (about $760 million). However, Matanmi and Awodun (2005) cite 2001 figures which estimate the sector to be worth about N12 billion (about $10 million) with potentials to grow to about N100 billion ($400 million). Whichever estimates are used, the indicators all point to a positive and upward direction.

So why are the multinational fast-food franchise corporations such as McDonald's keeping out for now? Could it be that these multinational firms are still being deterred by their perceptions and views of Nigeria as a potential trouble spot, and therefore an unsafe country for investments? These perceptions may have been formed as a result of Nigeria's past history as a haven for military juntas, with the consequent political instability, social unrest and disorder.

Such views and perceptions may have been valid in the 80s and 90s but things have since changed in Nigeria. The country became a civilian democracy in 1999 and since then, a strong wind of political, social and economic change have been blowing all over the country. The Olusegun Obasanjo government has put in place measures aimed at rebuilding and regenerating the economy. The government's economic diplomacy program is finally paying off; public enterprises are being privatized with core investors coming from outside Nigeria. Also, external investors are now very active in the lucrative banking, telecommunication, agriculture and technological sectors. Leading the way are companies such as MTN, Standard Chartered Bank, Microsoft etc. This is in addition to multinational companies such as Shell, Chevron, Mobil and Total who remain the major players in both the downstream and upstream petroleum sector.

However, this paper will focus on the fast rising fast-food sector, by attempting to identify the trends as well as the major players in the sector and their competitive strategies, the challenges they face will also be analyzed.

The Beginning

What may today be regarded as the organized fast-food industry in Nigeria has always existed in one form or the other. Although there are no official records available which chronicles the origin or history of the Nigerian fast-food sector, one can safely make certain assumptions.

Long before the discovery of oil and the consequent reliance on petrodollars by Nigeria as a major source of revenue, Nigeria was primarily an agrarian economy, with more than 80 percent of the population earning a living from and working in the agricultural and related industries. Most of the farmers during this period were mainly subsistence farmers, who normally brought any unwanted or excess produce to the local market to sell; firstly to avoid wastages, and also to earn extra cash which they would then use to purchase household supplies. When the village market squares then became a regular meeting place of sorts for the rural dwellers while all the transactions went on in the markets, there also arose the need for the buyers and sellers to be able to buy light snacks pending when they got home for the regular family meals. Such light snacks were usually in the form of fried bean cakes, known as *akara* and also fried kneaded dough that is known as *bons* or *kpof-kpof*. There are also several others that are called by different names in the thousands of villages in Nigeria, where over 250 native dialects and languages are spoken.

At this time, what could also be regarded as the local fast-food trade was largely dominated and operated by women, who also recruited their young children and relatives into the trade. For the children, their job was primarily to hawk the wares, which are usually carried on their heads as they walked around the market squares or village announcing their goods in loud voices to passers-by. Because the markets in the rural communities operated only on certain days in the African native week, the women discovered the lucrative nature of the trade and expanded and branched out to include local schools, government buildings, building sites and other such public places where there was a more regular and constant demand.

As development continued all over Nigeria, more and more people became educated and moved out of the villages to major cities where there were job opportunities. This is how the fast-food sector entered its next stage of growth, firstly with the setting up of what is known locally as *mama-put* or *bukas* (local eating shacks) to cater for the taste of the fast emerging working class, who may find eating in the standard hotels a bit expensive. Interestingly, the *mama-put* and *buka* concept is growing stronger; there are now hundreds of thousands of *bukas* in Nigeria, providing employment to both men and women, while also fulfilling a need in both the urban and rural centers. *Bukas* are quite easy to set up, requiring very minimal start-up costs, and while their customer services may not particularly be the best, they offer their customers a wide variety of local food, which they can mix and match at very reasonable and affordable prices. This mix and match concept is known as *orishirishi* or *gbogbori* in local parlance, and customers get to choose from different selections of the local delicacy on offer; in the Nigerian context these will include rice, beans, fried plantains (known as *dodo*), spaghetti, *moin-moin* (cooked ground beans), fried or cooked yams and potatoes etc. These are normally served with fried, roasted or cooked beef, chicken, turkey etc.

Emerging Trends

Nigerians rank as one of the most educated people in the world. They are also widely traveled, as both the oil boom and gloom contributed to Nigerians leaving Nigeria for America, Europe and other developed countries originally to study, with the intention of returning back to Nigeria to contribute to national development. However, the economic downturn of the 80s made the majority of Nigerians stay in the countries where they had originally gone to study, and subsequent emigrants actually left to escape the economic hardship of the 80s and 90s. Naturally, as Nigerians traveled, they also acquired western tastes. There was a craving for western standard of life especially amongst the Nigerian elite living in the big cities such as Lagos, Port Harcourt, Ibadan, and Enugu.

On hand to satisfy such cravings were multinational companies such as Leventis, UTC, and Kingsway, which at the time, especially in the 80s and 90s, had supermarkets and snacks bars in the big cities. These companies that were products of the colonial period also catered for the large Caucasian population, known locally as *Oyinbo*. So it can be argued that at this time, the 60s, 70s and the early 80s, the organized fast-food sector in Nigeria was predominantly controlled by the multinational companies. There were however, independently owned fast-food restaurants or shops at this period, mainly targeting Nigerians who may consider the UTC Snacks, Leventis Stores, or Kingsway Stores a bit up-market or expensive. Most of them were small scale, operating from "kiosks", and the owners had very limited knowledge of marketing, and therefore made limited or no attempts at branding their businesses, which were usually called after the names of the owners.

Mr. Bigg's

The Nigerian fast-food industry entered another major phase in 1985, when the United African Company (UAC) launched the Mr. Bigg's brand, Nigeria's biggest fast-food franchise. With the advent of Mr. Bigg's, the fast-food industry as we knew it changed. Mr. Bigg's was like a fast-food revolution, an idea that was long overdue: it was modeled after McDonalds; the restaurants are well decorated with ample seating and car parking facilities; and it was known for their famous meat pies, *jollof rice* and chicken. Nigerians embraced the Mr. Bigg's concept wholeheartedly; who needed McDonalds or Burger King anymore when there was Mr. Bigg's catering to local tastes? The franchise, which opened in Nigeria quickly grew and branches sprang up in Nigeria's other major cities. Currently there are about 130 Mr. Biggs restaurants all over Nigeria, and the planned African expansion has also seen Mr. Bigg's opening in Ghana, where there are now 2 franchises in the country, with plans for more.

So what did Mr. Bigg's do right that its predecessors (Leventis, Kingsway, and UTC) didn't? Mr. Bigg's bought into the theme restaurant concept, just like McDonalds, providing good ambience and a relaxing family atmosphere. Mr. Bigg's went a step further though, by combining cultural and local food in their menu, especially jollof rice, moin-moin, salad and chicken. They must have done their research to come out with a winning business plan, and seem to have listened to Paul A. Herbig (1998), who in writing about culture and marketing, advised that marketers should seek to understand the cultural mores of the country to which they are attempting to market. An over-worn cultural marketing cliché you may say; maybe, but one that is oftentimes not adhered to and which, according to Herbig, has cost many firms dearly, especially unwearied and careless ones.

Some of the previously mentioned restaurants may have fallen into that trap of cultural negligence, as they were often regarded as up-market and elitist, catering for the interests of the few, to the neglect of the wider population (a form of niche marketing). Mr. Biggs, on the other hand, could be said to be for the "average Nigerian", irrespective of their income. Mr. Bigg's made it possible for low income earners to "feel among and have a sense of belonging"; they could walk into a Mr. Bigg's restaurant, not minding the way they were dressed, and enjoy a snack meal of meat pie and a bottle of soft-drink, and come out with the double satisfaction of the snacks, and the extra satisfaction of having been to a Mr. Bigg's restaurant. Mr. Bigg's also offered couples and lovers a good and decent "hang-out", different from conventional hotels. Without having to spend so much money on advertising and marketing, the Mr. Bigg's success story was buoyed and sustained mainly by word-of-mouth.

In all Nigeria's major commercial and urban cities, it will be difficult to find anyone who hasn't at least visited a Mr. Bigg's restaurant, the same way it will be difficult to encounter anyone who hasn't stopped by a McDonalds restaurant in Europe and America. The Mr. Bigg's franchise is now a major cash cow for UAC Nigeria Plc, whose other activities have been adversely hit by competition, as well as the general economic conditions.

The Mr. Bigg's success story has inspired later entrants into the sector, who would also like to have a taste of the profit pie. According to nigeriabusinessinfo.com, there are currently over 70 different indigenous fast-food franchises in Nigeria. This estimate though may be conservative, as the numbers will rise sharply if the other less known outlets, and owner-operated restaurants are taken into consideration. Matanmi and Awodun write that out of the 80 branded players in the Nigerian fast-food industry, only 10 could be said to be major players, and they account for about 75 percent of the market, with Mr. Bigg's having the majority market share of 45 percent, and Tantalizers coming second with only a 10 percent share.

There are however fast-food outlets that are emerging as market leaders such as *Tantalizers, Mama Kas, Favorites, Hunger Busters, Frenchies, Domino* and *Tetrazzini*. This classification is based on the number of their outlets and spread, their increasing brand visibility and equity, as well as by their turnover and customer numbers. There are also some which can only be classified as regional franchises, operating only one or a small number of outlets in particular towns, where they also compete strongly against the fairly established and more national brands: *Dreams* and *Southern Fried Chicken* (*SFC*) operate in Abuja, *Munchies* in Aba, *Big Treat, Tastee Fried Chicken,* and *Sweet Sensation* in Lagos, *O'Neal* operates in Enugu and Abuja, etc.

These regional brands are very popular in the towns where they operate and are also major players in the fast-food market in the towns, to the point of being market dominant. *Tastee Fried Chicken* (*TFC*) for instance operates multiple locations in Lagos, a city of over 10 million residents, and has not established any other outlet anywhere in Nigeria. In Lagos, TFC is a major player and rank as one of the market leaders, alongside Mr. Bigg's and Tantalizers. TFC, just like Tantalizers and Tetrazzini could easily use their brand reputation as leverage and set up branches in other major cities such as Abuja and Port Harcourt, Nigeria's other cosmopolitan cities, but surprisingly the company has chosen as part of its strategy to domicile only in Lagos, and be the big fish in the big ocean.

The Competitive Strategies of Nigeria's Fast-food Restaurants

For Nigeria's fast-food restaurants, the need to compete against one another is borne out of a desire to attract new customers, and also to satisfy and keep their existing customer base. Mark Stewart (1996) writes that successfully implemented customer retention strategies are a point of competitive advantage, which means that the customer should always be treated as king, and should be at the core or heart of the operations of every business. For some of the fast-food restaurants, customer service is a key competitive strategy, while for some others, customer service is not very high on their agenda, and while the latter operate as if it is still a seller's world, this may be the case for those restaurants operating in towns where there is less competition.

Matanmi and Awodun list the competitive weapons of Nigerian fast-food restaurants as including taste, prices, environment, class sensation, visibility and availability of parking space. They conclude by saying that for the restaurants, the critical factor remains the quality of products provided to customers at affordable prices. These classifications would appear to be consistent with the strategies adopted by the major players in the sector; this is because lesser-known operators are not so much concerned with long-term brand building efforts that may be eroded by poor product and service offerings.

A more detailed analysis of the competitive strategies of Nigerian fast-food restaurants is presented as follows:

Customer Services

Customer services in the Nigerian fast-food restaurant context is a bit different from what it is in Western countries where customer services has already moved on to the stage of relationship management, with companies introducing several loyalty schemes to attract and retain their customers. Almost every Nigerian fast-food restaurant uses doormen and women, their main job being to open the doors for customers and give them a welcoming smile. These "front office" personnel are usually dressed in standard uniforms with matching caps. This is a beautiful concept since the big Western fast-food restaurants such as McDonalds and Burger King do not offer such five star services customary to hotels such as The Ritz and the Waldorf Astoria. However, this doorman concept which was originally hailed by customers, is now being abused by the doormen, and as a result customers normally leave the restaurants with complaints and "bad tastes in their mouths" as a result of the antics and attitudes of the doormen, who have now converted the front doors to begging spots. It is now usual to see them beg and sometimes harass customers to give them money, which is not helped by their rude attitude that can sometimes be unfriendly. Customers no longer receive the expected welcome smiles, and those customers who have not succumbed to the pleas for a tip are sometimes thrown a mean look, and that's if he or she has not already been sworn at or cursed in the doorman's native language.

Nigerian fast-food restaurants provide parking facilities in their restaurants, and there are usually parking attendants to help and direct customers when driving in or out of the premises. This is a good concept but like their doormen counterparts, the parking attendants now also concentrate on squeezing tips out of customers, rather than on their jobs. It is not uncommon to find the parking areas in chaotic states, because a parking attendant has vacated his or her place of work and have gone to pursue a customer, who may have promised the attendant a tip on the way out.

The staffs in these restaurants dress in standard uniforms, usually in the corporate or house colors of the restaurants. Tetrazzini is different in this regard because it portrays an "ethnic and natural look"; its sales attendants are dressed in African print clothes in shades of green. Between the doormen, parking attendants and sales attendants, there is still much to be desired amongst all the restaurants; service delivery from these front line personnel can be better improved with additional training, and also with an improvement in their working conditions, which will enable them to appreciate their strategic importance to the survival of the business. It is also worth mentioning that the sales attendants need extra training in speedy order taking and how that translates into efficient service delivery; they sometimes mix-up customers' orders and do not normally take kindly to customer complaints, most times refusing to change a customer's order.

It may be that the customers have not much choice at the moment, as they continue to patronize the restaurants, as it is still a seller's market in the Nigerian fast-food sector. According to Folu Ayeni of Tantalizers, *'There is no cut-throat competition in the fast-foods sector; the operators don't see themselves as rivals"*. He concludes by saying that what exists amongst operators is co-operation rather than competition. This cannot be imagined in the Western countries where consumers rule, and therefore all the major fast-food companies use several strategies to outsmart each other.

However, in the case of Nigeria, as competition increases and new players enter the market, those restaurants which have been ignoring their customers may find their customer numbers decreasing. The restaurants that will thrive in the future will be those that focus on their customers more, rather than on the products and services which they sell. There should be a conscious effort at not only attracting new customers, but also in making existing customers enjoy their current experience which will help the different restaurants to actually begin to build a customer-focused brand. The top managers should aim to manage customer relationships rather than products and services, because at the end of the day it is customers and not products/services that provide the business with revenues and profit.

Products

Nigeria is a multi-ethnic country, and each of the many ethnic regions has its peculiar tastes and indigenous food and recipes. However, there are some standard dishes and menus which almost all Nigerians have in common, such as rice; cooked in many ways and called by different names - fried rice, jollof rice, white rice etc. In addition, Nigerians are united by another common staple food *Garri* or *Eba, which* is processed locally from cassava plant. These are normally eaten with different types of locally prepared soups such as *Egusi* soup, *Ogbono* soup, *Okra* soup, *White* soup, *Nsala* soup etc. Nigerians like their soups to contain lots of meat (cow, goat, bush meat, chicken, turkey etc) and fish (dried or fresh). The soups may also be eaten with pounded yam (yam flour), or with other ground meals such as maize, plantain etc that are molded into balls and dipped in the soup bowls. The other delicacies which are served in the Nigerian fast-food restaurants include *Boli* (roasted plantain) and *Epa* (ground-nuts), *Isu Esun* (roasted yam) and *Epo* (palm oil) with dry pepper, *Dundun* (fried yam), fried plantain (*Dodo*), boiled and roasted corn, *Eko* (congealed, unflavored custard) and *Akara* (beans cake), *Ogi* (unflavored custard) and *Moin Moin*, *Eran Igbe*, *Asun* (barbecued goat meat), *Suya* (grilled cow meat) and many others.

In the beginning, Nigerian fast-food restaurants sold mainly meat-pies, fish pies, cakes, egg rolls, sausage rolls and other such pastries that were culled from foreign cuisine books. They had adapted a standardized approach at this time, offering fairly similar products to the customers. This strategy was justified by Paul Herbig who also listed several reasons why firms may seek such an approach to marketing their products. These include:

- High costs of adaptation and differentiation of products;
- Perceived convergence in taste in diverse markets;
- Predominant use in urban environments;
- Marketing to predominantly similar countries and cultures;
- Centralized management;
- Economies of scale in production, R&D, and marketing;
- Toeing the line of competitors ("a- me" too approach).

While the above classifications may not exactly apply to Nigerian fast-food companies and the fast-food market however, some of the classifications do, especially those of economies of scale, toeing the line of competitors and use in urban environments.

Over time however, came the need to adapt the products to meet local needs, tastes and culture. This was in recognition of the fact that marketing should only aim to satisfy the needs and wants of customers, which in the Nigerian context was very much culturally biased. The shift from standardization to adaptation may also have been influenced by:

- Variations in consumer needs,
- Variations in conditions of use,
- Variations in ability to buy and differences in income levels,
- Strong cultural differences,
- Environment-induced adaptation, differences in raw materials availability, government requirements and regulations,
- Need for a competitive strategy,

Nigerian fast-food companies have since incorporated local Nigerian cuisine into their menu. It may then be this understanding of the needs of the customers in the society that is driving the success of Nigerian fast-food restaurants. In the global context, firms now adopt this adaptation strategy buoyed by the concept of *glocalization* - thinking globally but acting locally. Customers of these Nigerian fast-food restaurants can now enjoy their native delicacies in most of these restaurants, and they can mix and match the food they want because the restaurants usually have the different food on offer well displayed in their glass show cases; the customer can see what he or she is buying first before ordering. Knowing that most of the buying decisions take place at the point of purchase, and that this process is further influenced by the way the food "looks" or the way that it is presented, the restaurants endeavor to arrange the dishes in very appetizing and enticing ways.

As Nigerians generally prefer hot meals to cold meals (sandwiches etc), the fast-food restaurants in recognition of this hot meal culture are also able to serve their food hot to the customers; the foods which are displayed in giant showcases have inbuilt warmers which help to keep them mildly heated up.

Sales Promotion

Unlike the fast-food sector in Western countries, Nigerian fast-food restaurants do not engage in many sales promotions to encourage sales. If any, the sales promotions they normally undertake are one-off activities rather than planned and orchestrated campaigns that are tied into the overall marketing plan. The reasons may be as a result of the fact that the sector is still driven by the fast-food operators, rather than by the customers, so there is not yet a need to actively attract, keep and reward both new and existing customers.

There are some restaurants though who have done some sales promotions in the past, especially Mr. Bigg's, but these are usually done during festive ceremonies such as Christmas and Easter when families are targeted and encouraged to visit any of the Mr. Bigg's restaurants as part of their holiday outings. Such promotions occur during the school resumption period, and books, pens, papers and school bags are given away. Another popular sales promotion method in the Nigerian fast-food sector are the draws and give-away prizes where customers are automatically entered into a draw if they make purchases exceeding a certain amount; these will normally run over a few months and are heavily advertised through the television, radio, billboards and press.

However, it is doubtful if the customers feel that the restaurants are creating any kind of value for them with these promotional tactics. This may be because the prizes and rewards are usually not substantial, and may therefore be regarded as 'intangible', and most customers have consequently ignored such promotions in the past, and have only been pulled to the restaurants not because of the sales promotions, but by the convenience of the restaurants, or by the fact that they have no other choice, as they would visit the restaurants anyway, whenever they are hungry.

It may be an idea therefore for the restaurants to think genuinely of the customers, in planning and executing these sales promotion campaigns. Customers would actually love a buy-one-get-one free kind of offer, which is more tangible and beneficial to them, and which makes every customer a winner.

Currently there is no form of student discount for purchases in any Nigerian fast-food restaurant. It is therefore ideal for such student offers and discounts which are easily obtainable in McDonald's, Burger King and some of the other fast-food restaurants in Europe and America to be introduced by the Nigerian restaurants.

Branding and Media Advertising

Although there are many types of advertising media in Nigeria, including several national and regional television and radio stations, hundreds of newspaper and magazine titles etc, Nigerian fast-food restaurants have not yet started to take advantage of this by incorporating them in their brand building efforts.

This may be as a result of what I earlier mentioned about the sector still being operator-led. The sector has not yet reached the stage where the customers dictate what happens just like in the Western countries, so there is still not the urgency to carry out sustained media advertising campaigns aimed at attracting new customers or at reassuring existing customers. Mr. Bigg's appears to be the only company that often advertises on some of the media, especially during its sales promotion campaigns.

Even so, all the restaurants use outdoor advertising; the billboards are usually erected in strategic places in the towns where the restaurants operate, and also at the exact locations of the restaurants. Billboards may be the preferred medium of choice amongst the restaurants because it may be considered to be cheaper in costs compared to the other media, and produces more direct customer-pull mileage, as customers could be encouraged to come into the restaurants just by seeing the billboards at the different locations where the restaurants are situated. Tastee Fried Chicken (TFC), one of the major players in the sector, uses billboards in the Lagos metropolis to advertise its services, with a funny catch line phrase *'We do chicken right'*. This is featured in all their chicken outdoor advertisements, although such a testimonial may annoy animal rights activists and vegetarian campaigners in the Western countries, who may argue that there is no such thing as doing a chicken right, if the chicken is to be slaughtered for human consumption.

There is a need for better understanding of the value of branding in the operations of Nigerian fast-food restaurants, as only a few of them could be said to be actually pursuing a strategic brand building effort; the rest just come up with a name, logo and corporate colors, and then fail to actually go any further in building and sustaining their brands. Rita Clifton (2004) writes that the reason why businesses do not take brands and branding seriously is probably because of a lack of understanding by senior managers of what branding is, and also ignorance of the value branding will add to shareholder investments.

Another reason may be because of the fact that branding can be expensive, and so the operators are not so willing to make the association between investing in an "intangible" branding program and the benefits it will bring to the business.

Tetrazzini has consistently marketed itself as an "ethnic and cultural" restaurant. This is reflected in their choice of colors (green and yellow), and also in the uniforms worn by their staff (locally made Nigerian wax fabrics). This concept is complimented by their menu offerings, including wrapping *moin-moin*, (cooked ground beans) in local leaves. Mr. Bigg's has also managed to sustain a strategic branding effort, along the lines of McDonald's, but has become a victim of its own success, as its size has meant that the vision of the managers at the top is no longer being played out by the staff in the restaurants. Customer complaints continue to increase, ranging from reducing quality in their food to poor customer services in the restaurants, and as a result the new entrants are now encroaching on the market that they once dominated.

To complement any brand-building program, it is also important that Nigerian fast-food restaurants establish a strong presence in cyberspace; while researching this paper, I discovered that most of the restaurants do not have any functional website. The importance of a well designed and maintained website in the internal and external communications of a firm cannot be over emphasized, and this is another area that should be improved upon, as it will add value to the restaurants' businesses, especially in a connected and global village, such as the one we live in now.

Corporate Social Responsibility

There are no actual figures to determine the extent that Nigerian fast-food sectors invest as part of their corporate social responsibility roles, but it is already obvious that they are doing a lot, especially by creating employment opportunities in an economy that has one of the highest unemployment figures in the world; conservative estimates based on the1992 census put the figure at 28 percent. What needs to be improved upon is the working conditions, including salaries paid to workers in the sector, as the practice of paying meager wages to staff in the sector appears to be a universal practice. The Nigerian fast-food sector can do better in this regard, as this may actually be the reason why their staff resort to begging and harassing customers for tips, thus damaging their brand image further.

Restaurants in the fast-food sector also contribute to other social causes: they donate money and equipments to local schools; some of them have built local roads, especially roads leading to their restaurants; the reputable firms pay substantial taxes as good corporate citizens, while others evade and avoid taxes, probably as a result of a lack of strict tax regime in Nigeria, a situation that most firms (not only in the fast-food sector) have exploited fully, hence the huge profits they declare annually.

The current global trend amongst fast-food restaurants is the introduction of healthier meals in their menu. This decision was influenced by the outcry from government officials and also members of the public over the worsening situation of obesity, which is attributed to the fatty foods served in most restaurants. McDonald's and Burger King have introduced healthy meals such as salads and fruits due to this demand, and they also promote healthy living as part of their corporate social responsibility. Nigerian fast-food restaurants have not yet started doing this, probably because they want to maximize profits which would drop if any such healthy living is promoted; the reason being that about 80 percent of the meals they serve are full of fat, starch and carbohydrates. One would therefore wish that they would start living up to these societal roles, because if the fast-food restaurants in Europe and America can do it, then the Nigerian restaurants can do the same too.

Government and Regulatory Agencies

In the Nigerian fast-food sector, it is no longer a case of restaurant operators working like fly-by-night cowboys, since the advent of the National Agency for Food and Drug Administration and Control (NAFDAC), the government agency responsible for the regulation of the food and allied industries. The agency's website (www.nafdacnigeria.org) provides guidelines on compliance requirements for operators in the food industry, and there are also a myriad of other government laws to comply with, especially the different state and local government health, sanitation and environmental edicts, laws, rules and regulations. Complying with these various laws can sometimes be frustrating, time consuming and expensive for the operators, and the picture is best captured by Folu Ayeni of Tantalizers:

"From day one, you are harassed from every where. Federal, state and local government officials hound you. It's like me against the world. The 'area boys' and different community leaders are after you. On the day we opened the outlet on Lagos Island, in the evening of the same day, the authorities 'welcomed' us with a bill of N614, 000 for signpost charges. How much could we have made between morning and evening of our opening day to pay such bill? That was from state government. We had to deal with up to 16 different councils from federal, state and local governments. And if you build anything on Lagos Island, you have to pay "area boys", even if your generator develops fault and you want to repair it, you must settle them because they claim they are the owners of the land."

"The day we started to renovate the property we had leased, some people came to seize the implements of workers, insisting that we settle them. It was a helpless situation. We had to take care of community leaders and all that. They also insisted that we sign a memorandum of association with them giving the ruler the right to nominate all the workers we intended to employ in the outlet. And that every year, we would pay a tribute of N500,000 and a cow to the ruler because they are the owners of the land. All that had to be negotiated and appeasement made. But the demands continued. Some youths from one division would come and say 'Some of the people you hired are not from our area, so you must take people from our own place'. They would come in a team of about 20 and when they sensed that you would not play ball, they would insist that we pay for their transportation back home. And if you asked them how much, they would tell you N500, 000. They talk about money as if you mint it. Perhaps, it is because they have been dealing with oil companies.

"The other day, we were trying to effect repairs on the road to one of the communities in collaboration with one of the commissioners. Then, one of the chiefs of the community insisted that his people be employed to do the job. Two were hired as a result. But the chief came back later to argue that the N100 we paid them was not enough. He again insisted that we hired two more people and that we pay each of them N4,000 a day. His people promptly confiscated the implements for the road repairs to enforce his will. If they could do that to government, you can imagine what they will do to investors. I don't know what the NDDC is doing, but something has to be done to better the lives of the people of the Niger Delta."

Although the above story is disheartening, but with regards to the governmental regulations, this is actually good for the consumers because if left on their own without such strict controls, there is a tendency that the operators may begin to compromise in a lot of ways, leading to environmental abuse, and even selling expired products. However it is also necessary that the government show a human face in the implementation and enforcement of the laws, so as not to scare away potential investors in the sector.

Most of the fast-food restaurants in Nigeria are sole trader, partnership and incorporated private limited companies; ownership is mainly in the hands of few individuals. Therefore there are no pressures from a board of directors, or shareholders to comply with other stakeholder interests, as would have been the case in the case of public limited companies where corporate governance procedures may be in place.

The Future of the Nigerian Fast-food Sector

The future looks rosy for operators and potential investors in the sector, especially as the Nigerian economy continues to be on the upswing, as a result of the social, political and economic reforms currently being implemented by the President Obasanjo government. As the Nigerian economy opens up, it will begin to attract the interests of global fast-food restaurants such as Burger King, McDonald's, and Pizza Hut etc. In part, this is already happening: South Africa's *St Elmo's* (the wood fried pizzeria) has already established franchises in Lagos. Ian Halfon, the Managing Director, justifies their African focus and strategy in these words, "Instead of breaking into the competitive and expensive European and US fast-food markets, we have our sights set on Africa. With start-up costs similar to South Africa's, we consider Africa as a huge untapped market with unlimited potential and very little competition".

Hunger Busters (formerly Big Macs), an indigenous Nigerian fast-food chain, has also recently invested the sum of $10 million in its fast-food business in Nigeria and other parts of Africa (Cote d'Ivoire, North and South Africa), an apparent show of faith in the Nigerian and African fast-food industry.

The consumer movement is still largely underdeveloped in Nigeria; hence some of the fast-food restaurants still exploit and take the customers for granted. However, with the rising trend of globalization, quicker communications, as well as developments in information technology including the Internet, Nigerian consumers will eventually become more aware of their rights; they will eventually feel so enabled and empowered to start mass actions against companies that are not customer friendly and focused. Sadly, the many non-governmental organizations (NGOs) which abound, have not been able to do much in this regard, maybe as a result of lack of resources to pursue the consumers' causes, or as a result of the selfish and self-serving motives of the NGO founders.[21]

Case Discussion Questions

1. With the help of the material discussed in this chapter, how would you describe the industry life cycle in which the Nigerian fast-food restaurant presently finds itself?

2. Using the five-forces model of competition discussed in this book, how would you explain the forces driving the Nigerian fast-food industry? How is the competition when you use the five-forces model to explain the competitive forces shaping the fast-food industry in Nigeria?

3. What factors are driving change in the Nigerian fast-food industry and what impacts will they have for new comers?

4. What strategic moves are rivals in the Nigerian fast-food industry likely to make next?

5. What are the key factors for competitive success in the Nigerian fast-food industry?

6. Based on the discussions in this chapter, what are the dominant economic features in the Nigerian fast food industry?

7. What are the competitive strategies of the fast-food industry?

8. Evaluate the marketing strategies (especially advertising and promotional strategies) of the fast-food industry in Nigeria. What would you recommend?

Chapter 9

STRATEGY FORMULATION FOR THE ENTREPRENEURIAL FIRM

"Suppose a king is going to war against another king, He will first sit down and consider whether with 10,000 men he can oppose the one coming against him with 20,000, won't he?" (Jesus Christ, Luke 14:31).

CHAPTER LEARNING OBJECTIVES
After studying this chapter, you should be able to:

1. Understand the types of entry and competitive strategies at the disposal of an entrepreneur.

2. Understand the differences between low cost and differentiation strategies.

3. Understand the nature of the competition in an industry and make an appropriate decision regarding the competitive strategy to match those of the competitors.

3. Understand the basis for and the usefulness of cooperative strategies.

5. Understand the basis for and the usefulness of offensive and defensive strategies.

6. Understand what a distribution strategy means and how to apply distribution strategies in order to be competitive in the marketplace.

7. Understand an industry's and a firm's value chain and how to use it as a competitive strategy.

INTRODUCTION: DESIGNING APPROPRIATE STRATEGIES

The preceding chapter tells us what we should do in order to understand our businesses, our business environment and firms before we can consider launching a business venture. As an entrepreneur, understanding your capabilities and your weaknesses and the conditions that shape your industry are one of the crucial steps that must be taken in the strategy-making process. This important step serves as the means to one particular end and that is, what strategies you can adopt in light of your understanding of your present standing. The reason why we do this is to help us design our competitive strategies. The purpose of this chapter is to help you achieve this. The best indicators of a company's strategy are its actions in the marketplace and the statements of its owners/managers about the company's current business approach, future plans, and efforts to strengthen its competitive performance.[1]

As this chapter will indicate, there are several types of strategies at the disposal of the entrepreneur or the owner of a small business in terms of the decisions about entering a particular market or an industry. The choice of each of these strategies depends on the nature of the business, the stage at which the industry finds itself, the nature and competition in the industry and the resources at the disposal of the entrepreneur or business owner (financial, human, technology, etc.) We will start with entry and competitive strategies, what we call in strategic management *"generic strategies."* Second, we will discuss the logic of cooperative strategies as a way of entering the market and as a strategy for competing effectively. These strategies include strategic alliances and joint ventures with other firms that are not necessarily in your core business area. Third, the chapter examines the differences between an offensive strategy and a defensive one and the conditions under which an entrepreneur can apply anyone of the two. Fourth, the chapter examines the concept of distribution and the strategies associated with it. Producing or offering a good product or service is not the final answer; it must be delivered to the end-user, and that is where distribution strategy comes in. This chapter also examines the different stages your product or service must go through. In each of these stages, a value is created (in strategic management, this is known as value-chain management). Knowing the different stages helps when to perform certain activities yourself or when to outsource them in order to achieve a competitive advantage. It helps you to concentrate on those activities that you are good at and allow others to do those activities that you are not so good at.

ENTRY AND COMPETITIVE STRATEGIES

Now that you have chosen to enter the market, the next question becomes "how do I enter the market and how do I intend to compete with the existing or potential competitors? What strategies do I use to enhance the profitability of my business?" As an entrepreneur, you need what is called a competitive strategy or *business strategy*. A competitive strategy focuses on improving the competitive position of the business within the specific industry or market segment that the company serves or intends to serve. As an entrepreneur, your business strategy can be competitive (battling against all competitors for advantage) and/or cooperative (working with one or more firms or competitors to gain advantage against other competitors). A competitive or business strategy asks how the company or its units should compete or cooperate in the industry in which it operates. In this section, we will examine the issue of competitive strategy.

Competitive (or business) strategies, according to Michael Porter, raise the following questions:

> ➢ Should we compete on the basis of low cost (and thus price), or should we differentiate our products or services on some basis other than cost, such as quality or service?
> ➢ Should we compete head to head with our major competitors for the biggest but most sought-after share of the market, or should we focus on a niche in which we can satisfy a less sought-after but also profitable segment of the market?

Michael Porter proposes two "generic" competitive strategies for outperforming other companies in your particular industry: lower cost and differentiation strategies. These strategies are called generic because they can be pursued by any type or size of a business firm; small, medium or large firms, even by nonprofit-organizations.[2] In the following pages, we will discuss these generic strategies and see how they are applicable to your own business situation.

Low Cost Strategy

A low cost strategy is the ability of a firm or business to source materials, design, produce and market a comparable product or service more efficiently than its competitors. This can be achieved through a number of ways. If you source your raw materials at a cheaper rate than those of your competitors, you adopt a lower cost strategy. If you are located at a place where you pay lower rents and still maintain good quality compared to your competitors, you can compete on the basis of a lower cost strategy. Similarly, if you are able to market your services or goods at a lower rate compared to that of the competitor, you can compete on the basis of lower cost strategy. Lower cost strategy is not about selling your goods or services at lower prices *per se*. Rather; it is about producing and delivering your product or service to the end user more efficiently than those of the competitors without compromising the quality of your goods and services. In management, we call this *performance efficiency*, which is a measure of the resource cost associated with goal accomplishment. It tells you how much you have spent in producing something and how much you realize in its output. Cost of labor is a common efficiency measure. Others include equipment utilization, distribution and so on.

The cost leadership strategy is exactly that - it involves being the leader in terms of cost in your industry or market. Simply being amongst the lowest-cost producers is not good enough, as you leave yourself wide open to attack by other low cost producers who may undercut your prices and therefore block your attempts to increase market share.

You therefore need to be confident that you can achieve and maintain the number one position before choosing the cost leadership route. Companies that are successful in achieving cost leadership usually have:

- Access to the capital needed to invest in technology that will bring costs down.
- Very efficient logistics.
- A low cost base (labor, materials, facilities), and a way of sustainably cutting costs below those of other competitors.

The greatest risk in pursuing a cost leadership strategy is that these sources of cost reduction are not unique to you, and that other competitors copy your cost reduction strategies. This is why it's important to continuously find ways of reducing every cost.

Differentiation Strategy

A differentiation strategy is the ability of a firm to provide unique and superior value to the buyer in terms of product quality, special features, or after-sale service. What is required here is the ability of the firm to compete by making its products or services different from those of the competitors. Differentiation strategy comes in several forms such as services, innovation, promotion, location, distribution, etc. Firms pursuing a differentiation strategy seek competitive advantage through uniqueness. They try to develop goods and services that are clearly different from those made available by the competition. The objective is to attract customers who become loyal to the firm's products and lose interest in those of competitors. This strategy requires organizational strengths in marketing, research and development, technological leadership, and creativity. Its success is highly dependent on its ability to respond to customers' perceptions of the quality and uniqueness of the products or services that are offered.

Generally speaking, a firm's competitive advantage in an industry is determined by its *competitive scope*, that is, the breath of the firm's target market. As an entrepreneur, before you use one of the two generic competitive strategies (low cost or differentiation), your firm must choose the range of product varieties it will produce, the source of its supplies, the distribution channels it will employ, the types of buyers (customers) it will serve, the geographic areas in which it will cover, and the array of related industries in which your business will also compete. This should reflect an understanding of your firm's unique resources. Simply put, your company can choose a broad target (when you aim at the middle of the mass market) or a narrow target (when you aim at a market niche, a small portion of the mass market).

A combination of these two types of target markets (broad and niche markets) with the two competitive strategies, (low cost and differentiation) results in the four variations of generic strategies depicted in Figure 9-1. If your firm, for example, operates on the basis of lower cost and differentiation strategies and has a broad mass -market target, it is occupying the position of *cost leadership* and *differentiation*. However, if your firm is focused on a market niche (narrow target), the strategy is called *cost focus* and *differentiation focus*.[3]

The terms "Cost Focus" and "Differentiation Focus" can be a little confusing, as they could be interpreted as meaning "A focus on cost" or "A focus on differentiation." Remember that Cost Focus means emphasizing cost-minimization **within a focused market**, and Differentiation Focus means pursuing strategic differentiation **within a focused market**.

Figure 9-1:
Porter's Generic Competitive Strategies

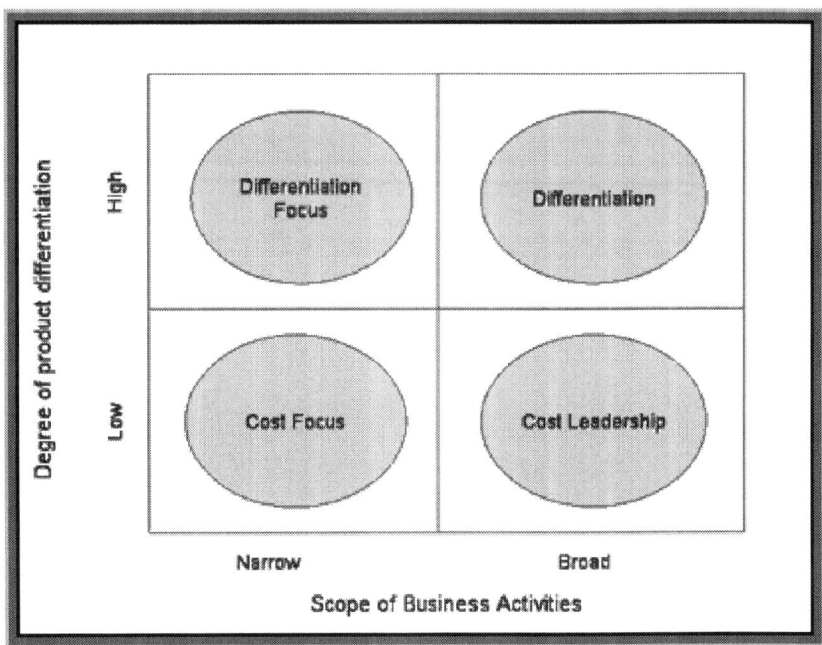

Porter's Generic Competitive Strategies

Source: Michael E. Porter, *Competitive Advantage* (New York, NY: Free Press, 1985). 1985, p.39

Competing on the Basis of Cost Leadership Strategy

Cost leadership is a low-cost competitive strategy that aims at the broad mass market. According to Michael Porter, cost leadership requires "aggressive construction of efficient-scale facilities, vigorous pursuit of cost reductions from experience, tight cost and overhead control, avoidance of marginal customer accounts, and cost minimization in areas like R&D, service, sales force, advertising, and so on." Thus, because of its lower costs, the cost leader is able to charge a lower price for its products and services than its competitors and still make a satisfactory profit. Some large companies in the developing countries such as UACN and others are able to compete in the fast-food market because they are able to lower their costs in relation to the procurement of their goods and services. For instance, the Fast Food Division of UACN has one of its competitive advantages by having its own Food Division that supplies Mr. Bigg's its raw materials at a lower cost. Having a low-cost position also gives your firm or business a defense against rivals. Your company lowers costs to allow it to continue to earn profits during times of heavy competition. Its high market share means that it will have high bargaining power relative to its suppliers (because it buys in large quantities). Its low price will also serve as a barrier to entry by other prospective competitors because few new entrants will be able to match the leader's cost advantage. As a result, cost leaders are likely to earn above-average returns on investment.

Competing on the Basis of Differentiation Strategy

Differentiation is aimed at the broad mass market and involves the creation of a product or service that is perceived throughout the industry as unique. As an entrepreneur, your firm may then charge a premium for its product or service because it is perceived as unique and different in quality from other products in the market. This uniqueness or specialty can be associated with design or brand image, technology, features, dealer network, or customer service. Differentiation is a viable strategy for earning above-average returns in a specific business because the resulting brand loyalty lowers customers' sensitivity to price. Example is the *Guardian* newspaper in Nigeria; whose above industry price has not deterred the patronage of its readership. Increased costs can usually be passed on to the buyers. Buyer loyalty also serves as entry barriers because new firms must develop their own distinctive competence to differentiate their products or services in some way in order to compete successfully.

Competing on the Basis of Cost Focus Strategy

Cost focus is a low-cost competitive strategy that focuses on a particular buyer group or geographic market and attempts to serve only this niche, to the exclusion of others. In using cost focus strategy, your business seeks a cost advantage in its target segment. What you are doing, in essence, is to offer your products or services to a particular segment of the broad market that is price sensitive. A good example is Dana Air's entry into the Nigerian aviation industry. When Dana Air, a new subsidiary of the Dana Group, entered the Nigerian aviation market in 2008, it did so with low-cost strategy with a focus on bringing aviation services to Nigerians, combining the best elements of low-cost carriers – world-class safety and on-time reliability – with the latest on-line services and operational efficiency. The airline focuses on attracting leisure and business travelers from within Nigeria. In addition, it "targets travelers who desire safe, quality, affordable air transportation". Dan Air achieves cost focus by keeping overhead and R&D to a minimum and by focusing its market efforts strictly on its market niche that is sensitive to price. The airline does not offer its services to expensive customers, only to those that can afford its fare. It does, however, require a tradeoff between profitability and overall market share.

Competing on the Basis of Differentiation Focus Strategy

Like cost focus, *differentiation focus*, concentrates on a particular buyer group, product line segment, or geographic market. This is the strategy successfully followed by most health food stores, exclusive designers and up-scale newspapers. In using differentiation focus, the company or business unit seeks differentiation in a targeted market segment. The firms that adopt this strategy are those who believe that a business that focuses its efforts is better able to serve the special needs of a narrow strategic target more effectively than can its competition.

Such differentiation focus strategy may include emphasis on engineering design and performance (Mercedes in the auto industry), prestige and distinctiveness (Rolex in watches), top-of-the-line image and reputation (Gucci, Ralph Lauren, and Chanel in fashion and accessories), writing instruments (Monte Blanc), and selected, sophisticated and educated business decision-makers as readers (*BusinessDay* in Nigeria).

Choosing the Right Generic Strategy

Your choice of which generic strategy to pursue underpins every other strategic decision you make, so it is worth spending time to get it right. But you **do** need to make a decision: Porter specifically warns against trying to "hedge your bets" by following more than one strategy. One of the most important reasons why this is wise advice is that the things you need to do to make each type of strategy work appeal to different types of people. Cost leadership requires a very detailed internal focus on processes. Differentiation, on the other hand, demands an outward-facing, highly creative approach.

So, when you come to choose which of the generic strategies is for you, it is vital that you take your organization's competencies and strengths into account.

Use the following steps to help you choose.

Step 1: For each generic strategy, carry out a **SWOT analysis** of your strengths and weaknesses, and the opportunities and threats you would face, if you adopted that strategy.

Having done this, it may be clear that your organization is unlikely to be able to make a success of some of the generic strategies.

Step 2: Use Five Forces Analysis to understand the nature of the industry you are in.

Step 3: Compare the SWOT analyses of the viable strategic options with the results of your Five Forces analysis. For each strategic option, ask yourself how you could use that strategy to:

- ➢ Reduce or manage supplier power.
- ➢ Reduce or manage buyer/customer power.
- ➢ Come out on top of the competitive rivalry.
- ➢ Reduce or eliminate the threat of substitution.
- ➢ Reduce or eliminate the threat of new entry.

Select the generic strategy that gives you the strongest set of options.

COMPETITIVE STRATEGIES FOR THE NEW VENTURE

To be able to compete successfully, a new business venture must adopt one or more of the strategic options discussed above. As an entrepreneur, your strategic options, however, depend on the uniqueness of your competitive situation. No matter how different is your situation; most entrepreneurial ventures follow a focus strategy. The successful ones differentiate their product from those of other competitors in the areas of quality and service, and they focus the product on customer needs in a segment of the market, thereby achieving a dominant share of that part of the market. By adopting guerrilla warfare tactics, entrepreneurial companies go after opportunities in market niches too small to justify retaliation from the market leaders. N. Brodsky argues that it is often much easier for a small company to compete against a big company than against a well-run small company. "We beat the giants on service. We beat them on flexibility. We beat them on location and price."[4] What does this mean to you as an entrepreneur? It means that, before you go into business, you must identify and create a place in the market where no one else is serving. This niche provides you with a piece of the market where you can establish the standards and create your own brand. It allows you to dance with the giants and defeat them at their own turfs.

The *competitive structure of the industry* can also affect the kind of competitive strategies you adopt. Competitive structure refers to the number and size distribution of companies in an industry. Two types of competitive structures in an industry help us to know what competitive strategies are appropriate. These are (i) a fragmented industry, and (ii) a consolidated industry.

Competition in a Fragmented Industry

A *fragmented industry* contains a large number of small or medium-sized firms, none of which is in a position to dominate the industry. A good example is the "church business" in Nigeria and in the United States of America. In this business, there are so many operators or church owners that it is difficult for one church to dominate that particular industry because it is a growing one. Thus, what most owners of the churches do is to compete for relatively small shares of the total religious market, and focus strategies tend to dominate. The same can be said in terms of the restaurant business where there are many players. To be successful, the owner of a restaurant tries to focus on a specific market or customer group or a specific menu that appeal to a specific group. In fact, competition in a fragmented industry seems to be weak as everyone enjoys the benefits of a growing market.[5]

In Nigeria for example, there are numerous industries that can be termed as fragmented. The fast-food industry, for instance, has become a fragmented one as a result of competitors coming in with new innovative menus. Although first movers such as *Mr. Bigg's* still enjoy their own competitive advantages, new comers such as *Tantalizers* still benefit from the opportunity offered by a growing industry or market because, at this stage competitors do not see themselves as rivals as there is something for everyone. They cooperate to reap the benefits of a growing market. For example, the chairman/CEO of Tantalizers, Nigeria's fastest growing food chain (Mr. Folu Ayeni) has this to say about competition in the Nigerian fast food industry: "The operators don't see themselves as rivals. There is co-operation (not competition) in the industry," he explained. " … The potential of the fast food industry is enormous. We estimate the market to be worth N190 billion. At the moment, what the operators tap from this is less than N50 million. So, there is a great deal of potentials there. A lot of people will still join the market. If we get our acts right, the McDonald's of this world will come."[6]

Fragmented industries are typical for products in the early stages of their life cycle. It is important to note that many fragmented industries, such as the restaurant industry, the real estate industry, the film and video producing and rental industry and the religious industry in Nigeria are characterized by low entry barriers and commodity-type products that are hard to differentiate as everyone produces and markets the same service, product or concept. The combination of these traits tends to result in boom-and-bust cycles as industry profits rise and fall. Low entry barriers imply that whenever demand is strong and profits are high there will be a flood of new entrants hoping to cash in on the boom. There are several examples of this phenomenon: The explosion in the number of privately run schools in Nigeria is one, the emergence of the film and video producers and rental industry is another, the proliferation of newspapers, magazines and other publications exemplify this situation. In a fragmented industry, every firm seems to be reaping the fruits of a growing industry.

A fragmented industry structure can constitute a threat rather than an opportunity. Most booms will be relatively short-lived because the ease of new entry will be followed by price wars and bankruptcies. For example, we saw in the eighties the proliferation of banks and other financial or mortgage institutions in Nigeria. Back then, it was easy to set up a financial or mortgage company as a result of a free-for-all policy of deregulation within the context of a structural adjustment program. The result was that there was a boom-and-bust situation with an ensuing price war and only a few were able to survive. This bust part of the cycle continued until the overall industry capacity was brought into line with demand (through bankruptcies) and government regulation.

Competition in a Consolidated Industry

A Consolidated industry emerges when the flood of new entrants into a booming fragmented industry creates excess capacity. Once excess capacity develops, firms start to cut prices in order to utilize their spare capacity. The difficulties firms face when trying to differentiate their products from those of the competitors can worsen this tendency. The result is a price war, which depresses industry profits, forces some companies out of business, and deters potential new entrants. In Nigeria, for example, this was the case in the auto importation business in the late eighties and early nineties when most importers of used vehicles (Tokunbos) decided to exploit the lucrative business of auto-importation. This also explains the demise of the clearing and forwarding industry in Nigeria because the entry barrier is low. At this stage, the fragmented industry reached the age of maturity.

As an industry matures, fragmentation is overcome and the industry tends to become a consolidated one dominated by a few large companies. Although many industries begin fragmented, battles for market share and creative attempts to overcome local or niche market boundaries often increase the market share of a few companies. After product standards become established for minimum quality and features, competition shifts to a greater emphasis on cost and service. Slower growth, overcapacity, and knowledgeable buyers combine to put a premium on a firm's ability to achieve cost leadership or differentiation along the dimensions most desired by the market. At this stage competitors either merge with each other or acquire a rival. This is the case with the Nigerian banking industry in 2004-2005.

As an illustration, the consolidation phase of the Nigerian banking industry enable Nigerian banks to merge with other ailing banks, thus becoming more competent and competitive players in the regional and global financial markets. Among other gains, the consolidation phase also helped in driving down cost structure of banks, improving banks efficiency and encouraging competition thereby lowering interest rates and providing affordable credit to the economy.

COOPERATIVE STRATEGIES FOR THE NEW VENTURE

As noted in the preceding section, competitive strategies and tactics are used to gain competitive advantage within an industry by battling against other firms and as ways to gain an entrance into the market. As an entrepreneur, these are not, however, the only business strategic options available to you for competing successfully within your industry. Neither are these the only strategic options at your disposal to gain an entrance into a market. *Cooperative strategies* can be used to gain entrance into the market and to gain competitive advantage within an industry by collaborating with other firms. The most important type of a cooperative strategy as far as a new venture is concerned is through a strategic alliance. In today's highly competitive business environment some companies, in order to survive, have either joined forces with like-minded firms or decided to dine with the enemy (entering into partnership with a competitor) and they do this through strategic alliances.

Strategic Alliances

A strategic alliance is a partnership of two or more firms or businesses to achieve strategically significant objectives that are mutually beneficial.[7] Alliances between companies or businesses have become a fact of life for many entrepreneurial ventures. Some alliances are very short-term, only lasting long enough for one partner to establish a beachhead in a new market. Overtime, conflicts over objectives and control often develop among partners. As an entrepreneur, you may decide to form a strategic alliance for a number of reasons, including:

(i) To obtain technology and/or manufacturing capabilities.
(ii) To obtain access to specific markets.
(iii) To reduce financial risk.
(iv) To achieve or ensure competitive advantage.
(v) To achieve name recognition.
(vi) To achieve distribution opportunities.
(vii) To gain access to sources of supplies.[8]

Examples of these strategies abound everywhere. For example, John wanted to establish a gas station and Paul wanted to establish a fast-food restaurant. John and Paul can pool their limited resources together to get their ventures going. Customers who want to fill their vehicles with gas might want to eat something and drivers who are hungry might just want to fill their vehicles with gas while getting their snacks. In the United States, the major fast-food restaurants such as McDonalds, Burger King, etc are located in the same outlet with Shell, ChevronTexaco and other gas service stations. Cooperative arrangements between companies can take several forms and arrangements such as mutual service arrangement, joint venture arrangement, licensing arrangement and value-chain partnership are very prevalent.[9]

Mutual Service Arrangement: A mutual service arrangement is a partnership of similar companies in similar industries who pool their resources to gain a benefit that is too expensive to develop alone, such as access to advanced technology. The mutual service arrangement is a fairly weak and distance alliance, which is appropriate for partners who wish to work together but not share their core competencies. There is very little interaction or communication among partners. Example is the alliance between a business newspaper in Nigeria, *BusinessDay*, and the *Financial Times* of London. The benefit of this arrangement is that while the Nigerian partner gains access to international business news, The Financial Times gets exposure into the growing market for European products and services in the Nigerian market.

Joint Venture: A joint venture is a "cooperative business activity, formed by two or more separate organizations for strategic purposes, that creates an independent business entity and allocates ownership, operational responsibilities, and financial risks and rewards to each member, while preserving their separate identity or autonomy."[10] Along with licensing arrangements, joint ventures are formed to pursue an opportunity that needs a capability from two companies such as the technology of one and the distribution channels of the other.

Let us assume that Paul has a hotel and found out that several of his customers are always in need of a business center within the vicinity of the hotel so that they do not need to go out for their printing, photocopying, faxing and Internet services. Let us also assume that James has a printer, a photocopying machine, a fax machine and computers and wanted to open a business center but did not have the finances to rent a place and get the business going? The logical answer to Paul's problems and that of James' is to join hand together and make their dreams come true. This is the essence of a joint venture. In order to make their dreams come true, Paul and James can pool their resources together and form a business entity with a different name (e.g., P & J Cybercafe).

It is worth stressing that joint ventures have their own disadvantages such as loss of control, lower profits, probability of conflicts with partners and the likely transfer of technological advantage to the partner. Joint ventures are often meant to be temporary, especially if you view it as an easier way to enter the market or as a way to rectify a competitive weakness until they can achieve long-term dominance in the partnership.

Licensing and Franchising Agreement: A licensing arrangement is an agreement in which the licensing firm gives another firm the rights in a market to offer, produce and/or sell its products or services. The licensee (you, the entrepreneur) pays compensation to the licensing firm (the firm that allows you to produce or sell its products/services) in return for technical expertise.

Franchising, on the other hand, is an arrangement whereby the manufacturer or sole distributor of a trademarked product or service (e.g., Mr. Bigg's) gives exclusive rights of local distribution to independent retailers (a restaurateur) in return for payment of royalties and conformance to standardized operating procedure. A good example is the franchising arrangement offered by the Redeemed Christian Church of God in Nigeria. Since its inception in 1952, The RCCG has provided rights to thousands of church planters worldwide with the mandate to operate according to the core beliefs, operating principles, vision and mission of the mother church in Lagos, Nigeria.

Licensing is an especially useful strategy if the trademark or brand name is well known, but if the licensing company does not have sufficient fund or knowledge it needs to enter the market. Companies such as Sheraton Hotel, Hilton Hotel, were able to enter the Nigerian hospitality business through franchising arrangements with Nigerians (the franchisee) who have the financial resources, including the local knowledge necessary to run a successful business in the hospitality industry. The foreign partner (usually the franchisor) provides the technical resources needed to run the enterprise. For example, when the Tourist Company of Nigeria decided to change the corporate identity of the Federal Palace Hotel in Lagos, its owners entered into a licensing arrangement with Sheraton International and the name of the hotel was changed to Federal Palace Sheraton Hotel and Towers. The chairman of Tourist Company of Nigeria, Mr. Goodie Ibru, pointed to the benefit of this arrangement: "The hospitality industry is dynamic and requires specialized management for business survival. In view of this demand and our desire to make our hotel the reference hotel in Nigeria, we have since engaged Sheraton Overseas as technical partner in the on-going effort to resuscitate and reposition the Federal Palace Hotel."[11]

Value-Chain Partnership: The value-chain partnership is a strong and close alliance in which the entrepreneurial venture forms a long-term arrangement with its key suppliers or distributors for mutual advantage. Another way of understanding this relationship as an entry or competitive strategy is to look at what you have been doing internally in your company and how profitable it is for you to allow these activities to be performed by other companies while you are making your money. As will be shortly explained in another chapter, you could do everything if it is cheaper for you. On the other hand, you could allow others to do them for you if it is cheaper for you through outsourcing. Outsourcing is a viable competitive way to solve the problem that arises when you do not have enough resources to undertake all of the activities necessary for you to deliver the product to the final consumers. It implies that if those activities that you have been doing, such as production, marketing, accounting, are cheaper for you when other companies do them, it is better for you to give these activities to them and you will be able to concentrate your energy in providing those things that you are good at doing. With outsourcing as a strategy, your business venture has the chance of not falling into the victim of "jack of all trade and good at nothing."

Strategic Alliance Success Factors

As was pointed out earlier, all forms of strategic alliances are filled with uncertainties. There are many issues that you need to deal with when the alliance is initially formed and others that emerge later. Many problems revolve around the fact that your firm's alliance partners may also be your competitors, either now or in the future. It is therefore important that if your company is interested in joining or forming a strategic alliance, you must seriously consider the strategic alliance factors listed below:

- You must have a clear strategic purpose. You must also integrate the alliance with your partner's strategy. You must ensure that mutual value is created for all partners. Ensure that you are not felt cheated and your partner does not feel cheated.

- You should find a partner with compatible goals and complementary capabilities.

- You should identify likely partnering risks and deal with them when the alliance is formed.

- You should allocate tasks and responsibilities so that each partnering firm can specialize in what it does best.

- You should create incentives for cooperation to minimize differences in corporate culture or organization fit.

- You should agree upon an exit strategy for when the partner's objectives are achieved or the alliance is judged a failure.

OFFENSIVE AND DEFENSIVE STRATEGIES

Before we discuss how to formulate and implement your competitive strategy through offensive and defensive tactics, it is appropriate we understand the concepts of *first movers* and *late movers*. The first company to manufacture and sell a new product or service in a market is called the **first mover** (or pioneer). Some of the advantages of being a first mover are that the company is able to establish a reputation as an industry leader, move down the learning curve to assume the cost leader position, and earn temporarily high profits from buyers who value the product or service very highly. One of the advantages of being a first mover comes from establishing a brand name such as the fast-food giant in Nigeria, Mr. Bigg's.

Being a first mover does, however, have its disadvantages. These disadvantages can be, conversely, advantages enjoyed by late mover firms. **Late movers** may be able to imitate the technological advances of others (and thus keep R&D costs low). This may be similar to the concept of creative imitation discussed in chapter one. In the case of the fast-food industry in Nigeria, late movers such as Tastees Fried Chicken, Quarter Jack and The Triangle, for example, were able to capitalize on the technology and services of Mr. Bigg's. Late movers also keep risks down by waiting until a new market is established, and take advantage of the first mover's natural inclination to ignore market segments. First movers will likely adopt defensive strategies while late movers prefer offensive ones.

A business venture can implement a competitive strategy either offensively or defensively. An **offensive tactic** usually takes place in an established competitor's market location. Here, a new comer to that market uses competitive tactics to take market share from the dominating firm. A **defensive tactic** usually takes place in the firm's own current market position as a protection against possible attack by rivals. Here, the existing firm tries to defend its market share.[12]

Offensive Tactics

Some of the methods you, as an entrepreneur, could use to attack your competitor's position are:

Frontal Assault: This is when a firm goes head to head with its competitors as it matches them in every category from price to promotion to distribution channel and to location. As a new venture, the entrepreneur is attacking the competitors in the areas that they are best at. When a firm assumes this type of an attack as a competitive strategy, it must not only have superior resources, but also the willingness to persevere. The entrepreneur must also know that this strategy is generally a very expensive tactic and may serve to awaken a sleeping giant. In Nigeria, for example, it is difficult to stage a frontal attack at Mr. Bigg's in the fast-food industry. It is difficult simply because Mr. Bigg's, with the backing of UACN, can fight back at smaller firms so hard with its financial resources.

Flanking Maneuver: Rather than going straight for a competitor's position of strength with a frontal assault, one may attack a part of the market where the competitor is weak. In effect, one is going outside of the competitor's domain. As pointed out in a preceding section, an entrepreneur must know and understand the strengths and weaknesses of the firm. In most cases, there is nothing one wants to supply to the market that others are not supplying. However, everyone has a weakness. And it is duty of an entrepreneur to capitalize on the weaknesses of the competitors or rivals. In the hospitality business, for example, there is nothing any new entrant can offer to upscale clients that perhaps Sheraton or Hilton hotels are not offering in terms of upscale type of hospitality. The customers of these hotels are those we define as "upscale customers". Attending to this group of customers, one will have to provide something that Sheraton or Hilton is not providing to them. In other words, one would be flanking the big guys in areas where they are weak within the range of the same customer group or segment. To be successful, you, as a flanker, must be patient and willing to carefully expand out of the relatively undefended market niche or else face retaliation by an established competitor.

Guerrilla Warfare: Instead of a continual and extensive resource-expensive attack on a competitor, your firm may choose to "hit and run." As a guerrilla, you are a member of an irregular unit operating in small bands to undermine the larger and more powerful enemy. In the Nigerian courier and freight industry where there are large multinational players such as DHL and UPS, one way a new entrant can compete is to look at niches that are not adequately served by them -- a hit and run strategy. For example, Mr. Oluwole Adeyemei, the Managing Director of Broadline Services Ltd, Lagos was able to succeed in the courier business by going directly to clients he had served while working for DHL and UPS and providing them with personalized services such as delivering consignments within 24 hours through a good network system. What the entrepreneurial firm of Broadlink did was adding a new service to the freight forwarding and courier business by offering services that the larger established companies are unwilling to offer, thereby taking customers from them.[13] Guerrilla warfare as discussed in chapter ten is characterized by the use of small, intermittent assaults on different market segments held by the competitor. In this way, a new entrant or small firm can make gains without seriously threatening a large, established competitor and evoking some form of retaliation. To be successful, if a firm decides to conduct guerrilla warfare, it must be patient enough to accept small gains and to avoid pushing the established competitor to the point that it must respond or else lose face. Guerrilla tactics are good if the firm has something unique to offer, to draw customers from the large competitive enemy.

Defensive tactics

The foremost purpose of defensive strategy is to protect competitive advantage and fortify the firm's competitive position. This strategic approach is good for companies that are well established in the market or industry. According to Michael Porter, defensive tactics aim to lower the probability of attack, divert attacks to less threatening avenues, or lessen the intensity of an attack. Instead of increasing competitive advantage per se, they make a company's competitive advantage more sustainable by causing a challenger to conclude that an attack is unattractive. These tactics deliberately reduce short-term profitability to ensure long-term profitability. In order to achieve this, you could (i) offer a full line of products in every profitable market segment to close off any entry points; (ii) block channel access by signing exclusive agreements with key distributors; and (iii) avoid suppliers that also serve competitors, if possible.[14]

DISTRIBUTION AND SUPPLY CHAIN MANAGEMENT STRATEGIES

Distribution is about logistics: the movement of goods and services from producers to buyers. Distribution is also about the way you market your product or service within your *distribution channel* – deciding, for example, how much of the channel you want to cover. As we shall see in this section, a firm has many options to choose from in deciding on the appropriate way to distribute its products or services in order to gain a competitive advantage. A firm may distribute its products to an independent distributor, which in turn distributes them to retailers and the retailers distribute them to the ultimate consumer. Alternatively, it might distribute its products directly to retailers or even to the final customer. In Europe and in North America, many firms have turned to the later alternative by marketing their products or services directly to the consumer through the Internet.

Looking back at what we've learned so far in this chapter, an entrepreneur who intends to enter a consolidated industry must know that the industry consists of few large companies. These large companies gain strengths over their suppliers and customers as a result of their distribution strategies, among other things. In a consolidated industry, suppliers become dependent on the few large buyers left in the industry for buying their inputs and on customers for obtaining the industry's outputs. As the industry matures, and companies try to consolidate their operations, protect their market share and improve product quality, many firms want to take over more of the distribution of their products and control the source of inputs crucial to the production process. This is possible because the large companies in a consolidated industry have the resources to do so. But for a new venture with limited resources this approach is a difficult one. That is why the new venture must take into consideration decisions regarding the distribution of its products or services.

A couple of reasons explain why distribution has become such an important part of the entrepreneur's competitive strategy. Because manufacturers needed a way to sell directly to the customer, e-commerce has thus become the newest form of direct marketing via direct channels to the customer. The Internet has precipitated massive consolidation in many industries by getting rid of intermediaries and collapsing distribution channels. This is the case of the Nollywood, the Nigerian movie industry. In the industrialized countries, the way in which e-commerce has revolutionized a whole industry is illustrated by the PC industry. The second largest PC manufacturer in the world today, as at 2008 (Dell Computers) was able to take market shares from its rivals (Compaq Computers, IBM, Gateway, etc) by shortening the time and points in the distribution channel it takes to manufacture the product and take it to the end-user, by removing its intermediaries. An intermediary is the conduit between the producer and the consumer. *Intermediaries* are suppliers, distributors, wholesalers, and retailers who come between producer and customer. Because the Internet is an open channel of communication with access to information at its source, customers connect directly with the source rather than paying more to an intermediary.

An increase in the popularity of low cost distribution methods is the second explanation why distribution or supply chain management is gaining such prominence. Large corporations in the United States of America and in Europe pioneered a price-based distribution model, forcing manufacturers to change their operations so that they produce at lower costs and still make a profit. To many manufacturers, particularly those that deal in commodity products, survival means going directly to their customers via warehouse, factory direct, or e-commerce versions of themselves. Even companies that deal in information have come to realize that their survival hinges on the effective use of the Internet. This is particular true with respect to newspapers that now turn to online version of their print. For the printing industry, this trend has become necessary as it reduces overhead costs associated with newsprint, ink and paper.

The Role of Logistics in Distribution

If you are a manufacturer, do you want to reach every possible distributor of your product? Alternatively, do you want to reach only retailers in a defined geographic area? If you are trying to project an image of luxury, for example, you might limit distribution to upscale boutiques, period. Although one cannot escape decisions about distribution channels, one can probably sidestep many of the details involved in the logistics, at least for a while. For most entrepreneurial start-ups, having their own shipping department – a distribution center – is not within the realm of possibility because of limited funds. Consequently, most start-ups outsource their logistics needs to companies that specialize in providing that service.

Logistics consists of transportation, storage, and materials handling. Working with a good logistics service provider can ensure that you get the best rates and the most reliable carriers. When it comes time to decide on your firm's distribution or logistic strategies, ask yourself the following questions:

- Can the company provide the services you need when you need them?
- How do this company's costs compare with other companies in the industry?
- What kinds of services do they provide?
- Does the company already deal with products like yours?
- What kind of guarantees does the company provide to ensure that your products arrive at their destination in good shape?

Your distribution strategy not only provides an enormous competitive advantage to your business in a market where everyone is innovating on the product/service side, but it also can be a matter of life and death.

CASE IN POINT: WHEN CHRISTMAS DELIVERY GOT STUCK IN THE STORE ROOM

Ladipo Designs Limited was a small printing firm employing about nine employees and located on Allen Avenue, Ikeja Lagos in the early nineties. Its business was that of printing calendars, Christmas greeting cards, ceremonial invitational cards, business cards and associated services. The company designed and produced these products with its own personnel and in-house. However, it left the service of distribution to a firm located in Yaba, Lagos. Over the years, Ladipo Designs Limited had operated without any problem and has had a trouble-free business relationship with its distributor in the past and so the firm never thought of delays in delivering its finished products to their clients even during the busy Christmas season. Ladipo Designs Limited derived its revenues from large clients who were willing to pay whatever it cost as long as their goods and services were delivered to them on time and with the appropriate quality.

Chief Taiwo Oladipo, the owner of the business, with his employees, had received huge amount of offers from several clients and they decided to make sure that they were able to deliver these products before December 2nd. They all went to work as far back as October that year. They worked through three months to make sure that the calendars, the Christmas greeting cards and other Christmas celebration products (pens and diaries) were delivered on time. After working so many months, weeks, days and hours, mostly at overtime, the calendars were ready, so also were the clients' Christmas greeting cards. They successfully met the deadline they had set for themselves. After the products have been packaged, it was delivery time!

While working on these products, Ladipo Designs Limited was not thinking about the delivery. They knew, from past experience, that delivery is a given, all they had to do was print and meet the deadline and delivery would be taken care of. Ladipo Designs waited two days in vain for the delivery company to come. It did not. Panic griped Chief Ladipo, the owner after waiting a week in vein. His customers started calling for their products, and Chief Oladipo would tell them not to worry, "I trust my distributor". At last, Chief Oladipo found out that the distribution company no longer existed. Its owner, for one reason or the other, was compelled to sell his company and had gone to Europe.

Oladipo's customers were furious. Their Christmas orders were received after Christmas. Their calendars were delivered when it was too late. These clients had to cut their relationship with Ladipo Designs Limited. In the end, Ladipo Designs Limited ran into financial difficulties because it could not get paid for all its efforts. The owner could not pay his employees; he could not pay for the rent, he could not pay for utilities and he could not pay himself, because the budget was based on its Christmas sales and delivery. At the end, Chief Taiwo Oladipo had to close his business.

THE VALUE CHAIN AND A FIRM'S COMPETITIVE ADVANTAGE

A firm performs several activities before its product or service gets to the consumer. In each of these activities, money is spent and value created in order to get the product or service to the consumer. From a strategic management perspective the firm can develop its competitive advantage in any of these activities.

To better understand the activities through which a firm develops a competitive advantage and creates value, it is useful to separate the business system into a series of value-generating activities referred to as the **value chain**. In his 1985 book *Competitive Advantage*, Michael Porter introduced a generic value chain model that comprises a sequence of activities found to be common to a wide range of firms. In the model, Michael Porter identified primary and support activities as shown in the following diagram:

Figure 9-2
Porter's Generic Value Chain Model

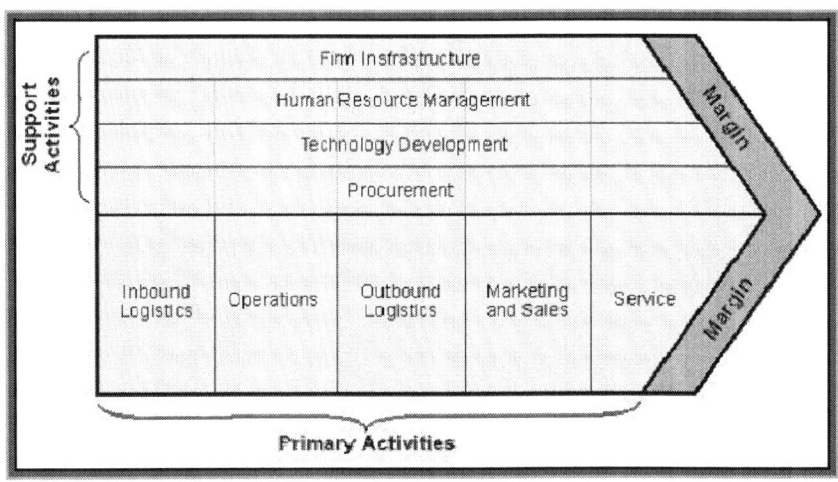

Figure 9-2, Porter's Generic Value Chain Model

The goal of these activities is to offer the customer a level of value that exceeds the cost of the activities, thereby resulting in a profit margin.
The primary value chain activities are:

(i) Inbound Logistics: the receiving and warehousing of raw materials and their distribution to manufacturing as they are required.
(ii) Operations: the processes of transforming inputs into finished products and services.
(iii) Outbound Logistics: the warehousing and distribution of finished goods.
(iv) Marketing & Sales: the identification of customer needs and the generation of sales.
(v) Service: the support of customers after the products and services are sold to them.

These primary activities are supported by:

(i) The infrastructure of the firm: organizational structure, control systems, company culture, etc.
(ii) Human resource management: employee recruiting, hiring, training, development, and compensation.
(iii) Technology development: technologies to support value-creating activities.
(iv) Procurement: purchasing inputs such as materials, supplies, and equipment.

The firm's margin or profit then depends on its effectiveness in performing these activities efficiently, so that the amount that the customer is willing to pay for the products exceeds the cost of the activities in the value chain. It is in these activities that a firm has the opportunity to generate superior value. A competitive advantage may be achieved by reconfiguring the value chain to provide lower cost or better differentiation.

Thus, we can analyze an industry in terms of the profit margin available at any one point along the value chain activities. In analyzing the complete value chain of a product or service offering, note that even if a firm operates up and down the entire industry chain, it usually has an area of primary expertise where its primary activities lie. Where a firm's primary activities lie is known as the firm's center of gravity. A firm's **center of gravity** is the part of the chain that is most important to the company and the point where its greatest expertise and capabilities can be located. In short, a firm's center of gravity lies in its **core competence**. As we pointed out in chapter six, the company's core competence or center of gravity is usually the point at which the company started. After a firm has successfully establishes itself at this point by obtaining a competitive advantage, one of its first strategic moves is to move forward or backward along the value chain in order to reduce costs, guarantee access to key raw materials, or to guarantee distribution. As noted above, these core activities are supported by other activities that are crucial in enhancing your core competence or they may be insignificant in the overall process of producing and delivering your product or service to the final consumer. A support activity such as accounting may better have been outsourced than your core area of operation.

In strategic management, one of the decisions a firm must make is whether or not to integrate forward or backward in the industry value chain in order to remain competitive. As an entrepreneur, you are trying to integrate the activities in your value chain or to disengage from them in order to remain competitive. Take for example, a furniture manufacturing company we will now call ABC Furniture Limited. The company's core competence is to design beautiful furniture that is needed by the ultimate user. A typical industry value chain would be: *lumber producers – wood finishing – furniture designing – furniture manufacturing – wholesalers – retailers – consumers*. ABC Furniture is faced with the choice of producing the lumbers, making them into woods, treating them, designing the furniture, manufacturing them, delivering them to the wholesaler or retailer or taking them directly to the ultimate user. If ABC Furniture buys woods from local lumber producers (or produces the wood), treats this to match the specification before assembling them into furniture, the firm is integrating backward (backward integration) in the value-chain. If ABC Furniture decides to plant the iroko trees that produce the lumber, the firm is integrating further backward. This is what we call *backward integration* in the value chain. Backward integration is going backward on an industry's value chain.

On the other hand, if our furniture manufacturer decided to acquire its source of distribution such as the wholesalers or retailers of the firm's furniture so that it can distribute its furniture directly to the consumer, this is *forward integration*, going forward on an industry's value chain. It is essential that owners and managers of businesses know where their firm's core competence, capabilities and distinctive competence reside in the industry value-chain. The big question to answer is: Do you want to do every thing yourself or do you want to do the things that you are capable of doing and leave the rest to others to do? The answer rests upon one important consideration, which is the ability to achieve a competitive advantage while minimizing costs.

The value chain model is a useful analysis tool for defining a firm's core competencies and the activities in which it can pursue a competitive advantage are as follows:

Cost advantage: by better understanding costs and squeezing them out of the value-adding activities.

Differentiation: by focusing on those activities associated with core competencies and capabilities in order to perform them better than do competitors.

Cost Advantage and the Value Chain

A firm may create a cost advantage either by reducing the cost of individual value chain activities or by reconfiguring the value chain. Once the value chain is defined, a cost analysis can be performed by assigning costs to the value chain activities. The costs obtained from the accounting report may need to be modified in order to allocate them properly to the value creating activities. Michael Porter identified 10 cost drivers related to value chain activities:

- ✓ Economies of scale
- ✓ Learning
- ✓ Capacity utilization
- ✓ Linkages among activities
- ✓ Interrelationships among business units
- ✓ Degree of vertical integration
- ✓ Timing of market entry
- ✓ Firm's policy of cost or differentiation

- ✓ Geographic location
- ✓ Institutional factors (regulation, union activity, taxes, etc.)

A firm develops a cost advantage by controlling these drivers better than do the competitors. A cost advantage also can be pursued by reconfiguring the value chain. Reconfiguration means structural changes such as a new production process, new distribution channels, or a different sales approach.

Differentiation and the Value Chain

A differentiation advantage can arise from any part of the value chain. For example, procurement of inputs that are unique and not widely available to competitors can create differentiation, as can distribution channels that offer high service levels.

As we pointed out earlier in this chapter, differentiation stems from uniqueness. A differentiation advantage may be achieved either by changing individual value chain activities to increase uniqueness in the final product or by reconfiguring the value chain. Porter identified several drivers of uniqueness:

- ✓ Policies and decisions
- ✓ Linkages among activities
- ✓ Timing
- ✓ Location
- ✓ Interrelationships
- ✓ Learning
- ✓ Integration
- ✓ Scale (e.g. better service as a result of large scale)
- ✓ Institutional factors

Many of these also serve as cost drivers. Differentiation often results in greater costs, resulting in tradeoffs between cost and differentiation.

There are several ways in which a firm can reconfigure its value chain in order to create uniqueness. It can integrate forward in the industry value chain in order to perform functions that once were performed by its customers. It can integrate backward in order to have more control over its inputs. The firm may implement new process technologies or utilize new distribution channels. Ultimately, the firm may need to be creative in order to develop a novel value chain configuration that increases product differentiation.

Technology and the Value Chain

Because technology is employed to some degree in every value creating activity, changes in technology can impact competitive advantage by incrementally changing the activities themselves or by making possible new configurations of the value chain. Various technologies are used in both primary value activities and support activities:

Inbound Logistics Technologies
- ✓ Transportation
- ✓ Material handling
- ✓ Material storage
- ✓ Communications
- ✓ Testing
- ✓ Information systems

Operations Technologies
- ✓ Process
- ✓ Materials
- ✓ Machine tools
- ✓ Material handling
- ✓ Packaging
- ✓ Maintenance
- ✓ Testing
- ✓ Building design & operation
- ✓ Information systems

Outbound Logistics Technologies
- ✓ Transportation
- ✓ Material handling
- ✓ Packaging
- ✓ Communications
- ✓ Information systems

Marketing & Sales Technologies
- ✓ Media
- ✓ Audio/video
- ✓ Communications
- ✓ Information systems

Service Technologies
- ✓ Testing
- ✓ Communications
- ✓ Information systems

Note that many of these technologies are used across the value chain. For example, information systems are seen in every activity. Similar technologies are used in support activities. In addition, technologies related to training, computer-aided design, and software development frequently are employed in support activities. To the extent that these technologies affect cost drivers or uniqueness, they can lead to a competitive advantage.

Linkages Between Value Chain Activities

Value chain activities are not isolated from one another. Rather, one value chain activity often affects the cost or performance of other ones. Linkages may exist between primary activities and also between primary and support activities. Consider the case in which the design of a product is changed in order to reduce manufacturing costs. Suppose that inadvertently the new product design results in increased service costs; the cost reduction could be less than anticipated and even worse, there could be a net cost increase.

Sometimes however, the firm may be able to reduce cost in one activity and consequently enjoy a cost reduction in another, such as when a design change simultaneously reduces manufacturing costs and improves reliability so that the service costs also are reduced. Through such improvements the firm has the potential to develop a competitive advantage.

Outsourcing Value Chain Activities

A firm may specialize in one or more value chain activities and outsource the rest. The extent to which a firm performs upstream and downstream activities is described by its degree of vertical integration.

A thorough value chain analysis can illuminate the business system to facilitate outsourcing decisions. To decide which activities to outsource, managers must understand the firm's strengths and weaknesses in each activity, both in terms of cost and ability to differentiate. Managers may consider the following when selecting activities to outsource:

- ➢ Whether the activity can be performed cheaper or better by suppliers.

- ➢ Whether the activity is one of the firm's core competencies from which stems a cost advantage or product differentiation.

- ➢ The risk of performing the activity in-house. If the activity relies on fast-changing technology or the product is sold in a rapidly changing market, it may be advantageous to outsource the activity in order to maintain flexibility and avoid the risk of investing in specialized assets.

- ➢ Whether the outsourcing of an activity can result in business process improvements such as reduced lead-time, higher flexibility, reduced inventory, etc.

The Internet and a Firm's Value Chain

As we noted earlier, a value chain is a chain that links the various activities undertaken by the producer of a product or service before it gets to the final consumer. It is the highway for delivering your product or service to the end user. In the 1990s, we saw the shortening of the value chain in the music industry. Musicians are now trying to market their productions directly to the consumers rather than going through labeling companies, producers and distributors. This is possible thanks to the Internet or what we call e-business. The Internet has now taken out the distributor as well, reducing a complex channel to a direct one where the consumer or end-user deals directly with the producer. In Western Europe as in the U.S., the services provided by intermediaries in many industries such as travel, real estate, education and financial services are now been eliminated through the efficacy of the Internet. Businesses everywhere have started to reinvent themselves to meet the challenges of the e-commerce revolution before they found they are out of business.

CHAPTER SUMMARY

A competitive strategy focuses on improving the competitive position of a business within the specific industry or market segment that the firm serves or intend to serve.

Entry strategies answer two important questions: how a business wants to enter the market and how it intends to compete in the market.

A competitive strategy raises two important questions: (i) competing on the basis of a low cost strategy or (ii) competing on the basis a niche strategy.

The low cost strategy is the ability of a firm to source materials, design, produce, and market a comparable product or service more efficiently than the competitors.

A differentiation strategy is the ability of a firm to provide unique and superior value in terms of product quality, special features, innovation, promotion, location or distribution.

Cost leadership strategy is a competitive strategy that requires aggressive construction of efficient-scale facilities, vigorous pursuit of cost reductions from experience, tight cost and overhead control, avoidance of marginal customer accounts, and cost minimization in the areas of R&D, service, sales force, advertising, etc.

Differentiation strategy involves the creation of a product or service that is perceived throughout the industry as unique.

Cost focus strategy is a low-cost competitive strategy that focuses on a particular buyer group or geographic market and the attempts to serve only this niche to the exclusion of others through offering products or services at a relatively lower cost compared to the competition.

A differentiation focus strategy concentrates on a particular buyer group, product line segment, or geographic market.

Most successful ventures follow a focus strategy because they are able to differentiate their products or services from those of other competitors in the area of quality and service.

A fragmented industry is one that contains a large number of small or medium-sized firms, none of which is in a position to dominate the industry.

A consolidated industry is one which is dominated by a few large companies.

A strategic alliance is a partnership of two or more firms or businesses to achieve strategically significant objectives that are mutually beneficial. Strategic alliances can take several forms such as (1) mutual service arrangement, (2) joint venture, (3) licensing agreement, and (4) value-chain partnership.

A strategic alliance is successful when (1) the partners have clear strategic purpose, (2) the partners have compatible goals and complimentary capabilities, (3) the partners identify likely partnering risks and deal with them when the alliance is formed, (4) responsibilities and tasks are allocated according to each partner's area of specialization, (5) the partners create incentives for cooperation, and (6) there is an agreement on an exit strategy.

Offensive tactics include (1) frontal assault, (2) flanking maneuver and (3) guerrilla warfare.

Defensive tactics include (1) offering a full line of products in every profitable market segment to close off any entry points, (2) block channel access by signing exclusive agreements with key distributors, and (3) avoid suppliers that also serve competitors, if possible.

First movers are the firms that introduce a product or service into a market before anyone else does it. As a first mover, the firm establishes a reputation as an industry leader, earns temporarily high profits from experience and learning effects.

Late movers are firms that capitalize on opportunities established by the first mover in the market. Late movers compete on the basis of identifying market niches ignored by first movers.

Distribution is the movement of goods and services from producers to the end-users. Two reasons why decisions about distribution strategy are important are (1) the supremacy of

E-commerce over traditional methods of marketing and (2) competitive pressures for low-cost distribution methods.

Logistics consists of transportation, storage and material handling.

A value chain is a linked set of value-creating activities beginning with basic raw materials coming from suppliers, moving out to a series of value-added activities involved in producing and marketing a product or service, and ending with distributors getting the final goods or services into the hands of the ultimate consumer.

A company's center of gravity is the part of the value chain that is most important to the company and the point where its greatest expertise and capabilities are located. A firm's center of gravity lies in its area of core competence.

CHAPTER DISCUSSION QUESTIONS

1. What is a competitive strategy? What questions does a competitive strategy raise?

2. What are the two generic strategies proposed by Michael Porter? Why are they called generic strategies?

4. Why would your firm compete on the basis of cost leadership strategy, differentiation strategy, cost focus strategy, or a differentiation focus strategy? Provide examples for each instance.

5. What is a strategic alliance? What are the factors dictating the success of a strategic alliance?

6. What are the major differences between offensive and defensive strategies? Provide example of each strategy.

7. What do you understand by the concept "value chain" in strategic management as it relates to a firm's ability to compete effectively? Chose an industry with which you are familiar and give an example of how the "value chain" process works out.

CASE STUDY 9: ABIODUN STUDENT IMPRESSIONS: DEVELOPING AN ENTREPRENEURIAL GROWTH STRATEGY[15]

"I think that there's plenty of opportunity out there and I don't think we're scratching the surface in our main target market, the university students," suggested Abiodun Ogundare, owner and managing director of *Abiodun Student Impressions Nigeria Limited (ASI Nig. Ltd)*. "But the reality is that students in Nigerian universities and colleges of higher education constitute about 85 percent of our market and customer base. I want the whole thing, I want to provide our products to other segments of the growing fashion industry, I mean, those guys out there who want to look hippie, other customer groups that our products might appeal to. You know what I mean, the men and women who want to look younger."

Abiodun Ogundare was both excited and optimistic about the future of the company he has created. *ASI* was a rapidly growing direct seller of affordable fashion wears targeted at university and college students in Nigeria. The firm had a plan to achieve sales of N75 million in 2008. In the year 2006, the educational industry in Nigeria was growing very fast as a result of the emergence of private universities and colleges of higher learning. As a result, the company had its sales to students increased more than 110 percent in the past three years.

ASI, with corporate offices and distribution center in Yaba, Lagos, Nigeria, sold jeans wears, tennis shoes, T-shirts, baseball caps, cosmetics, underwear, magazines (such as Ebony) and other related products imported directly from Europe and the United States. Abiodun's products are supposed to reflect the hip-hop culture in the U.S. and Europe. Most of the company's products bear the logo of Levi Strauss, Nike, Reedbuck and other well-known designers and carry the signatures of such popular Black artists such as 50 cents, Ludacris, P. Diddy, Jay-Z, Snoop Doggy Dogg, etc.

To save costs, the company does not carry large inventories. Rather, it has a large sales team that consists mainly of students who are employed on a commission basis. *ASI Nig. Ltd*. has more than 1,500 salespeople in over twenty states in Nigeria, primarily students. The selling is done by means of students bringing the products to their colleagues in their homes or halls of residence (student dormitories), and especially when students have parties or other social gatherings – a form of the direct marketing strategy. *ASI's* strategy is based on a perceived market need by students and a compensation system designed to reward salespeople with substantial commissions while pursuing their studies and "looking good" in the eyes of their colleagues. Abiodun was certain he had positioned the firm for future growth for two main reasons: The global convergence and appeal of the youth culture from America (as exemplified by MTV), the changing demographics and the accompanying changes of consumer and entertaining products. Nigerians as a whole, not only university and college students are becoming more globalized in their pattern of consumption. The youth, in particular, have become more Americanized in outlook and Nollywood (the Nigerian movie industry) has helped to shape this demographic outlook. The future is bright and full of opportunities both local and in neighboring West African markets of Ghana and Cameroon. Abiodun called a meeting of his staff to discuss repositioning the firm for the future. He asked the staff to respond to the following issues:

"What do we need to do to get us where we want to go, to reach other customers we have always wanted to reach and have not been able to reach, and to recruit and maintain the kind of sales force that will grow the business?"

Who is Abiodun Ogundare?

Abiodun Ogundare had graduated from the A & M University of Texas in the United States with a degree in management. In 1993, he was making N40, 800 a year as a supervisor in a local bank in Nigeria. Four years later, he earned N120, 000 a year as a manager in one of the financial and mortgage companies in Lagos, Nigeria, supervising a team of salespersons who directly meet with prospective customers. In the late nineties, this form of marketing was very popular in Nigeria as the mortgage and financial industry had reached its maturity stage and was declining. Aggressive marketing strategies were thus employed by firms on the brink of bankruptcy. Mr. Abiodun had also worked with several manufacturing and advertising companies as a marketing consultant. For the last four of those years, he held the position of an executive vice president for marketing in a major oil and gas company and was sent abroad for further training by one of the defunct banks in Nigeria.

> "I went through the Birmingham Business School Programme for a Master's degree in Marketing. As part of the degree programme, I traveled around Europe and the United States … that was an exciting phase in my educational and managerial experience. Most importantly, I wanted to go back home and apply this experience in the business of direct marketing. When I came back to Nigeria, I knew that university and college students have needs that have not been adequately served. I have contacts in the United States and I could contact them for information about the latest fashion over there. But the company that sent me to the United States was liquidated when I came back from the U.S. My folk told me to look for another job with my credentials. I was not ready for that. The problem was that I had no money to set up my own business, but I knew that there is an unfulfilled need in the university community. More importantly, I was not politically adept at dealing with the paternalistic business environment in Nigeria. I wasn't comfortable and I decided to move on, get my own show and see what I can do with my life, even though my folk were not happy about my decision. That's why I decided to become an entrepreneur."

Abiodun next entered the loan consulting business on a freelance basis, by starting a small but profitable financial planning company. He left after a short period of time to become a consultant for a major financial and accounting consulting firm. Tiring again of the corporate environment, he left after six months because "we could not agree on how we were going to salvage [the company] … it was going way down. At that point, I said, 'hey, who was I kidding?' I'm too rambunctious to report to someone else."

After additional experience in training and recruiting programs, Abiodun decided to return to direct selling and marketing as a profession. "I missed direct sales and the psychic rewards the business offers," he recalled. "I looked into the possibilities and capital requirements." He surveyed the field to identify an unsatisfied market need. He felt that he wanted to "control his destiny" at that mid career point in his life. A number of fields in direct sales are relatively crowded but there are very few successful businesses catering for the fashion needs of Nigerian university and college students. Most of the students do their shopping on the eve of their going back to school because that is when they are given money by their parents. He also knew that most students going back to school always carry along with them large sum of money and by the time they are back home with their parents, they are already broke. What a better way to give them what they want while they "are still loaded," he reasoned. He also knew that many firms provide direct marketing services to students on-campus. But he was determined "to change the way others have been doing business."

When Ogundare started *Abiodun Student Impression*, he intended to become the dominant supplier of student fashion wears in that particular industry. "Success is intentional," he said. While studying business administration in the United States and Europe, Abiodun was fascinated about how successful businesses were started from the "nowhere." He said, "Successful business must be based on a sound business idea and a dream based on who you are and what you want to become. " The idea of starting his business was ingrained in him from that period.

The Direct Sales Environment in Nigeria

The direct selling industry in Nigeria consisted of several participants such as established companies and individual salespeople that sell a broad range of products such as clothes, shoes, electronics, computer software, financial services and cosmetics, drugs, etc. Unlike in Europe and in the United States where direct sales is made through the telephone or the World Wide Web, in Nigeria, direct marketing occurs through contacts with individuals on a face-to-face basis. This is made possible through (i) network with colleagues and (ii) public transportation. The possibility for this contact is made possible through relationships built with colleagues at the place of work, friends and family members. This is a semblance of the *Mary Kay* (cosmetics) business model where cosmetics are sold through a process of sellers' relationship with prospective customers. In recent years, the Nigerian direct sales industry has also included religious visits by pastoral agents and promoters of vitamins and health foods. Other small operators were already using students to sell magazines in college and university campuses nationwide. Second, the popular means of transportation (the bus, also known as molue) has been one of the cheapest and popular means of direct marketing where sellers hawk and announce their products inside the moving vehicle.

From the perspective of the students, earning extra income was very alluring. Growth in the direct sales industry was spectacular in Nigeria, but in recent years it has faced a number of problems such as the fraudulent practices of some of the marketers, which have made potential buyers to go directly to established and recognized retail stores to do their purchases. Secondly, the importation of fake products from China, India, Taiwan, Thailand and other developing countries has made those who patronize the direct sales business shun the industry. But for Abiodun, the concept of direct marketing was not a new one. It is Nigerian version of "relational marketing" where buyers buy from those they know – not some impersonal salesperson in a boutique. He only needed to refocus the concept and capitalize on its potentials in spite of the above problems. What is new was how to capitalize on the growing student market with the addition of more privately owned universities. In addition, he must convince the public that his products and labels are genuine.

As Abiodun saw it, *Abiodun Student Impressions* offered a part-career in direct sales that would appeal to individuals who are either unemployed or who wanted to make extra money while traveling across the country to different university campuses. Furthermore, students who need extra income would also become beneficiaries of Abiodun's business concept. "Our people, who are independent contractors, see our company as a vehicle for obtaining financial independence," he suggested.

The Organization

Abiodun Student Impressions was a privately held, multilevel direct sales organization in which a hierarchical network of distributors is created to sell and distribute a product line such as DVDs, CDs, fashion wears, electronics, newsmagazines, beauty products, etc.

The organizational structure of *ASI* can be described as multilevel. What distinguishes a multilevel organizational structure from that of a traditional organizational structure is the fact that each distributor in the network is not only seeking to make retail sales of goods and services to the final consumer, but is also looking for distributors to join his or her distribution network. In the case of *ASI*, a regional distributor (who represents the North zone) and who gets goods directly from the firm can either chose to sell the products directly to the final consumers (the students) with his or her own sales force, or he or she can get another distributor who hires salespersons to distribute the goods to the students.

The organization has three major regional distribution centers located in Kaduna (Northern zone), Ife (Western zone) and Port-Harcourt (Eastern zone), in addition to its headquarters in Lagos. As at 2006, the company was planning to open a distribution center in Benin City to cater to the needs of students at the Universities of Benin, Ambrose Ali and Delta State. By recruiting and training new distributors, the recruiter becomes a regional distributor who earns sales commissions and bonuses on the retail sales of all distributors within the network. Through the Internet, *ASI* has plans now to sell its products directly to the consumers. At the same time, the firm has plans to keep its traditional marketing strategy. This method of on-campus-retailing requires a salesperson to make presentations at students' social gatherings. A student member in such social occasions who is affiliated with *ASI* would come and make presentations of the products he or she want to sell to the colleagues.

According to the company's mission statement, *"Abiodun Student Impressions* exists to provide quality state-of-the-art needs of Nigerian students." But Abiodun noted, the primary goal of his firm was to survive, and the second goal was to be consistently profitable - "profit is not something that is left over." He noted. Although Abiodun Ogundare was no longer a student, he knew that Nigerian students made up 70 percent of his company's sales force, as well as 85 percent of its customers. As He explained, "Going into this business was not intentional. It just went that way, because of the direction in which Nigerian students is going. You want to study abroad; our magazine provides you with the necessary information. Our magazine also gives you information about the best schools in Europe and America based on our research. The magazine also provides you with information regarding financial and visa assistantship both in Europe and in North America. We give to the students what they want and what is in vogue. That is our business objective. MTV kind of tells us the trend in our youth culture. ... We provide to the students what MTV gives us on our television."

The organization's training program, called "The System Works" was provided free to distributors in the three zonal regions and their representatives. Representatives, also known as sub distributors, can also train their sales persons with the same training material supplied by the head office.

Another emerging market niche that the company was beginning to explore was the "old boy associations" of known universities and colleges in Nigeria. The idea was to get in touch with alumni of Nigerian universities and colleges both in Nigeria and in abroad. Abiodun believed that getting in contact with this group would enable him promote and sell products and services that make them feel connected to their roots and make him ventures into foreign markets in Europe and in the United States of America. Abiodun noted that

> "We are booming in the number of recruits coming in and the number of states we are in Nigeria. We also know that there is a huge market potential in Europe and North America. That is why we are trying to establish a very strong group of direct sellers in North America. They are asking for more and more Nigerian goods such as newspapers, foodstuffs, art objects and others. This is a new business area for us. But the opportunity is there. There are stores in America and in the United Kingdom that provide some of the things Nigerians need in these foreign lands. What we want to do, however, is to be able to supply these things directly to them. Our plan is to locate people in these countries that can supply our products directly to the end-users. That is our expansion plan."

The Process

Developments in the late nineties indicated that the educational system in Nigeria would be privatized and more importantly, Nigerians would continue to achieve their educational needs abroad as a result of the problems associated with labor strikes, the closure of institutions of higher education in Nigeria and the menace of cultism in university campuses. "I made a mental note at that time that the field was hot and was going to continue to be hot, if only one can provide something to the field," Ogundare recalled. "I made lists of what business I could be in. Later that factor plus my several years of experience of recruiting, training, and developing direct sales people combined to show me a way to capitalize on my assets."

While he was studying in Europe and North America, Abiodun was fascinated with what he saw in student organizations and the way student organization leaders market goods to their colleagues. "In America, you have student organizations that promote the well-being of its members and promote their profession. In Nigeria, we have student organizations that are occult. But what we are trying to do is to get good people who represent a good image of an organization … we then employ this person to market our goods." Abiodun felt that he could provide products to the Nigerian university and college students that would enhance their quality of life – getting what they want on-campus. Hence, he defined the nature of the business as "helping students get what they want while they are in school at a cheaper price and high quality." The core of Abiodun's strategy was: (i) finding a need or niche, (ii) developing a product to fill it, and (ii) developing a marketing strategy and a compensation system that would allow the firm to fulfill its objectives and at the same time provide above income for its sales force. The marketing program at *ASI* was based on "consultants who take pride in making students feel good by offering them products and services they need while they are on-campus at affordable prices." Abiodun feels that he has started a process and marketing to students is just the beginning.

Case Discussion Questions

1. What is the business strategy adopted by *Abiodun Student Impressions*?

2. Do you think that the company has a solid business idea? If yes, why? If no, why not?

3. What is the future of the direct sales business in Nigeria? Why would you want to go into it? Why wouldn't you go into it?

4. What are the forces driving the fashion industry particularly as it relates to the student segment of the market?

5. What are the key success factors as they relate to the student segment of the fashion industry in Nigeria?

6. What problems do you think *Abiodun Student Impressions* will be confronted with in the future and how do you think the company can overcome these problems?

PART IV: COMPETITIVE STRATEGIES FOR THE ENTREPRENEURIAL FIRM

Chapter 10: Marketing Strategies for the Entrepreneurial Firm

Chapter 11: Growth and Organizational Strategies for the Entrepreneurial Firm

Chapter 12: Financial Strategies for the Entrepreneurial Firm

Chapter 13: Ownership Strategies for the Entrepreneurial Firm

Chapter 14: Ethics and Social Responsibility Strategies for the Entrepreneurial Firm

Chapter 10

MARKETING STRATEGIES FOR THE ENTREPRENEURIAL FIRM

"Lack of market focus is typically a disease of the 'neonatal', the infant new venture. It is the most serious affliction of the new venture in its early stages – and one that can permanently stunt even those that survive" (Peter Drucker).

CHAPTER LEARNING OBJECTIVES
After studying this chapter, you should be able to:

1. Describe the principles of building a guerrilla marketing plan and explain the benefits of preparing one.

2. Explain how entrepreneurial firms can pinpoint their target markets.

3. Discuss the role of market research in building a guerrilla marketing plan and explain the market research process.

4. Describe how an entrepreneurial firm can build a competitive edge in its industry and marketplace using guerrilla marketing strategies.

5. Discuss the "four Ps" of marketing: product, place, price, and promotion and their role in building a successful marketing strategy for the entrepreneurial firm.

6. Understand the concept of positioning and how the entrepreneurial firm can position itself.

7. Apply the lessons from this chapter in the preparation of a business plan.

INTRODUCTION: THE CUSTOMER AS THE EPICENTER OF BUSINESS

As we shall see in this chapter and in chapter fifteen, the culmination of the practice of entrepreneurship is the marketing plan, that is, how to achieve success in the marketplace. The essence of a marketing plan is how to situate the customer at the epicenter of business operation – how to satisfy the customer. Every strategy must be accompanied with a marketing plan that works. As we observed in chapter five, some of the major problems confronting business owners in Sub-Saharan Africa are marketing related. Specifically, marketing related challenges include inability to keep up with market developments; inability to adequately identify market niches and how to exploit them; lack of information on a number of issues, such as market, technology and suppliers; inability or unwillingness on the part of the business owner to put the customer at the epicenter of business activities and poor marketing effort. We also noted that in many Sub-Sahara African countries, there is a pervasive socio-cultural belief that a good product or service automatically sells itself. Consequently, most small business owners are often unwilling to invest in marketing their products or services through promotion and advertisement. Furthermore, the inability to perform adequate market research before plunging into the business is a fundamental cause of business failure in Sub-Saharan Africa. Many small business owners are unable to define their target market, the special needs of their prospective customers or the attractiveness of the market overtime.

Building a growing base of customers requires a sustained, creative marketing effort. Keeping customers coming back requires providing them with value, quality, service, and timely deliveries. Unfortunately, the typical African business owner operates in a business culture that pays too much attention on financial objectives, and pay little, if any attention, on the strategies to achieve that goal; that is, how to bring his or her services to the end-user in a way that is appreciated by the customer. Sometimes, too many small business owners squander enormous effort pulling together capital, people, and other resources to sell their products and services because they fail to determine what it will take to attract and keep a profitable customer base. Sometimes, small business owners fail to determine if a profitable customer base even exists.

To be successful, a business must have a marketing plan that focuses on the *customer* and recognizes that *satisfying* the customer is the foundation of every business success. Customer satisfaction is the mantra of business. To be successful, a business must be customer-driven. Indeed, the customer is the central player in the cast of every business venture. It is an open secret that the primary purpose of a business is not to earn a profit; instead, it is to create and keep a customer. The rest, given reasonable sense, will take care of itself. From a strategic management perspective, every area of business must practice putting the customer first in planning and actions.

The purpose of this chapter then is to place the entrepreneur's actions within the context of the customer: that is, determining what to sell, to whom and how, on what terms, and at what price, and how to get the product or service to the customer. In short, this chapter helps the reader to identify the company's target customers and describes how that business will attract and keep them. In line with the strategic management orientation of this book, the primary focus is to help you, as a reader, learn how to capture and maintain a competitive edge for your business venture. Because a small business is competing in a business terrain where there are large companies offering the same product or service, we will start with how the small business can compete with the larger ones through a guerrilla marketing plan.

GUERRILLA MARKETING PLAN FOR THE ENTREPRENEURIAL FIRM

As we know it, marketing is the process of creating and delivering desired goods and services to customers and it involves all of the activities associated with winning and retaining loyal customers. Marketing, as a concept, can be defined from several perspectives. The American Marketing Association, for example, defines **marketing** as "the process of planning and executing the conception, pricing, promotion, and distribution of ideas, goods, and services to create exchanges that satisfy individual and organizational objectives."[1] Philip Kotler, one of the acknowledged experts in the discipline of marketing, looks at the subject from a social perspective and defined marketing as "a societal process by which individuals and groups obtain what they need and want through creating, offering, and freely exchanging products and services of value with others."[2] The secret to successful marketing is to understand what your target customers' needs, demands, and wants are before your competitors can; offer them the products and services that will satisfy those needs, demands, and wants; provide customers service, convenience, and value so that they will keep coming back and attract more. Marketing should be seen as a way through which a firm comes up with strategies that enables it win customers from the competition.

In a small business, the marketing function cuts across the entire company, affecting every aspects of its operation - from finance and production to hiring and purchasing, as well as the company's ultimate success. Although small businesses may be small in size and cannot match their larger rivals' marketing budgets, entrepreneurial firms are not powerless when it comes to developing effective marketing strategies. To be successful in the market, the small business owner must wage guerrilla warfare in its marketing strategy. But first, what is guerrilla marketing?

What is Guerrilla Marketing?

The concept of "Guerrilla Marketing" was first developed by Jay Conrad Levinson in his marketing book *Guerrilla Marketing*, as an unconventional system of promotions on a very low budget, by relying on time, energy and imagination instead of big marketing budgets. Guerrilla marketing is also a term used in describing aggressive, unconventional marketing methods aimed at drawing customers away from larger organizations.[3] When implementing guerrilla marketing tactics, small size is seen as an advantage instead of a disadvantage. According to Jay Levinson, small businesses and entrepreneurs are able to obtain publicity more easily than large companies; they are closer to their customers and considerably more agile. Guerrilla marketing is especially geared for the small business and entrepreneur.

In *The Guerrilla Marketing Handbook*, Levinson states: "In order to sell a product or a service, a company must establish a relationship with the customer. It must build trust and support. It must understand the customer's needs, and it must provide a product that delivers the promised benefits." Some of the principles of a guerrilla marketing approach include:[4]

(i) The primary investments of marketing are time, energy, and imagination, instead of money.
(ii) The primary statistic to measure a business is the amount of profits, not sales.
(iii) The guerrilla marketer concentrates on how many new relationships are made each month.
(iv) The guerrilla marketer creates a standard of excellence with an acute focus instead of trying to diversify by offering too many diverse products and services.
(v) The guerrilla marketer aims for more referrals, more transactions with existing customers, and larger transactions instead of concentrating on getting new customers.

Guerrilla Marketing Strategies

Guerrilla marketing strategies are a type of marketing warfare strategy designed to wear-down the enemy by a long series of minor attacks. Guerilla marketing is also known as an unconventional marketing intended to get maximum results from minimal resources. Guerilla marketing involves being original, breaking the rules, and looking for alternatives to traditional marketing methods. In fact, guerrilla marketing is more about matching wits than matching budgets. It is low-cost driven and innovative. Guerrilla marketing warfare strategies consists of attacking, retreating, hiding, then doing it again, and again, until the competitor moves on to other markets. It may also include "flanking" marketing warfare strategies, whereby the small business operates in areas of little importance to the competitor. Third, it may also consist of alliance strategies, involving the use of alliances and partnerships to build strength and stabilize situations. A guerrilla marketing strategy works best under the following conditions:

(i) Knowledge of the Market: Know your market. Know who your customers are, how they think, and where they go.
(ii) Working with the press.
(iii) Educating the market.

(iv) Putting E-marketing to work for you.
(v) Getting a prime spot on the Web's search engines.
(vi) Giving talks and presentations at industry association meetings and conferences.
(vii) Networking.

> **CASE IN POINT: LUNCH FOR THE OFFICE**
>
> Tope Ogunlola used the network of connections she had developed at her job with a large restaurant chain in Victoria Island, Lagos to launch her business venture: **Lunch for the Office**, a Lagos-based catering service that delivers lunch to executives in Lagos who do not have the time to dine outside. At the large restaurant, where she had worked, Tope had seen clients rushing in and out of the restaurant as a result of time factor. Some had even asked if it were possible to deliver their lunch to their offices. Her employer was not prepared to offer this kind of services to the customers, as it would dilute their main business focus. Thus, Ms. Tope Ogunlola decided to satisfy this particular market segment: "The executives who are in a hurry and who want their lunch to be delivered to their offices." For a start, she did a survey by administering questionnaires to those who patronize the restaurant and other business executives around Lagos Island, Victoria Island, Ikoyi and Lekki Peninsula. The result of the survey indicated that there was a need for customers who wanted their lunch to be delivered to their offices.
>
> Tope understood that one of the reasons for this demand was the traffic problem in the Lagos metropolis. It takes some executives an hour to drive to and from their favorite restaurants during lunch hours. For Tope, there was a huge segment to cater for and setting up her own lunch delivery service to cater for the needs of this segment would be a logical step in realizing her entrepreneurial dream. Her firm specializes in the delivering of custom-made lunch to executives with large and small companies in major business areas in Lagos.
>
> In her first year of operation, Ms. Ogunlola convinced a friend who worked in the marketing department at Federal Palace Hotel, Victoria Island, Lagos to introduce her to the prime clients of the hotel. In the meeting, she pitched the idea of collaborating with her to sponsor "Eat at your convenience" fair aimed at the elite and business professionals. Tope believed that this segment did not have the time to go out and lunch. She saw this group as a niche market to provide her services. Tope's friend agreed and provided her with the names and addresses of those who lunch at Federal Palace Hotel. Tope Ogunlola even went to the management of Federal Palace Hotel to request for the use of their lobby for the fair and they agreed. With a fee, she was provided with a space to promote the fair and the rights to use the logo of a major business magazine in her own promotional materials. The fair was a huge hit, and its success earned Ms. Ogunlola an interview with a Lagos daily newspaper. Today, **Lunch for the Office** is a growing successful business thanks to Ms. Tope Ogunlola's guerrilla marketing tactics.

Guerrilla warfare and Guerrilla Marketing Plan

Guerrilla warfare also consists of waging small, intermittent attacks to harass and demoralize the opponent and eventually secure permanent footholds. The guerrilla challenger uses both conventional and unconventional means of attack to beat the big guys in the market such as low or high cost strategies and other creative marketing techniques that we will discuss in this chapter.

The guerrilla marketer understands positioning as he or she knows that challenging the market leader on his or her turf is foolish. The guerrilla marketer also is aware that challenging the big players in the open market is an invitation to disaster. Instead, he or she maneuvers the leader, repositioning the leader to his or her advantage. To be successful, a guerrilla marketing plan should accomplish eight important objectives:

(i) It should determine customer needs and wants through market research.
(ii) It should pinpoint the specific target markets and a niche market the small company will serve.
(iii) It should know where the competitor is most vulnerable and weak.
(iv) It must know the roots, nature and capabilities of the competitor's strengths.
(v) It should understand competitors' core competencies and how they are sustained.
(vi) It must understand the source of the competitor's competitive advantage.
(vii) It should help create a marketing mix that meets customer needs and wants.
(viii) It should analyze the firm's competitive advantages and build guerrilla tactics as an attack and marketing strategy.[5]

DETERMINING CUSTOMER NEEDS THROUGH MARKET RESEARCH

The changing nature of Africa's population is a potent force altering the landscape of business. Shifting patterns of age, income, education, the composition of the family and other population characteristics (which are the subject of demographics) will have a major impact on companies, their customers, and the way they do business with those customers. Businesses that ignore demographic trends and fail to adjust their strategies accordingly run the risk of becoming competitively obsolete.

A demographic trend is like a train; a business owner must find out early the direction it is heading and decide whether or not to go on board. Waiting until the train is roaring down the tracks and gaining speed means that it is too late to get on board. Small businesses that spot demographic trends early and act on them can gain a distinctive edge in the market.

The goal of an entrepreneur is to make sure his or her company's marketing plan is on track with the most significant trends that are shaping the industry. The entrepreneur must be able to determine the needs and wants of customers through a comprehensive market research. The celebrated success of firms and organizations such as Redeem Christian Church of God, MTN and Mr. Bigg's in Nigeria and BusyInternet in Ghana was based on their ability to understand and capitalize on the demographic trends in the Sub-Sahara African region such as the heightened need for spirituality; the privatization trends in the communication industry; changes in demographics, which have witnessed more working women in the labor force; and changes in the culture of dinning and entertainment. Also, changes in people's attitude to existential issues and religion have seen the rise of Pentecostal movement and the proliferation of churches in many countries in Sub-Saharan Africa. These changes, as we pointed earlier, are most prominent in the labor market and the structure of the family. Change in the structure of the family is easily noticed through the transition from an extended family relationship to a nucleus one. Second, the typical "African Child" has now become "the Global Child" through demographic changes manufactured and imported by culture-carrying organizations such as Coca Cola, McDonald's, MTV, CNN, Levi Strauss, Hollywood and others.

Trends are powerful forces and can be a business owner's greatest friend or enemy. The restaurant and fast-food industry in Nigeria has experienced the challenges associated with a shift in demographics. In Sub-Saharan Africa, the traditional restaurants are facing challenges from fast-food outlets. In the United States and Europe, however, fast-food restaurants are having a difficult time competing. Several factors are driving this trend: consumers who are "burned out" on burgers and concerned about the health considerations of fast-food diets. The most significant factor driving this trend is a growing global concern about obesity. For entrepreneurs who are observant and position their firms to intercept these factors, trends can be to their companies what the perfect wave is to a surfer. For entrepreneurs who ignore them or discount their importance, trends can leave their firms stranded like a boat stuck in the mud at low tide.

The Importance of Market Research

Market research is defined as the systematic design, collection, analysis, and reporting of data and findings relevant to a specific marketing situation facing a company.[6] According to Roberta Maynard, "Market information is just as much a business asset and just as important as your inventory or the machine you have in the back room."[7] The research you do on your target market is probably the most important of all, because it helps you determine who your primary customer is. It also helps you determine the level of demand for your product or service. Many new business concepts have failed because small business owners misjudged their marketplace, envisioning more demand than actually existed. That is a costly error that you can avoid, maybe not totally, but substantially. By performing some basic market research, small business owners can detect key demographic and market trends. Indeed, every business can benefit from a better understanding of its market, customers, and competitors.

In the field of entrepreneurship, market research is understood as the vehicle for gathering the information that serves as the foundation for the marketing plan. It involves systematically collecting, analyzing, and interpreting data pertaining to a company's market, customers, and competitors. The objective of market research is to learn how to improve the level of satisfaction for existing customers and to find ways to attract new customers. Market research answers questions such as: Who are my customers and potential customers? What are they looking for? What kind of people are they? Where do they live? How often do they buy these products or services? What models, styles, colors, or flavors do they prefer? Why do or don't they buy from my business? How do the strengths of my product or service serve their needs and wants? What hours do they prefer to shop? How do they perceive my business? Which advertising media are likely to reach them? How do customers perceive my business versus my competitors? Answers to these questions provide information that is an integral part of developing a marketing plan that produces sales. When marketing their goods or services, small companies must avoid mistakes because there is no margin for error when funds are scarce and budgets are tight. Small businesses simply cannot afford to miss their target markets, and market research can help avoid this costly problem.

One of the worst and most common mistakes small business owners make is assuming that a market exists for their product or service. Market research can tell the owner of the business whether or not a sufficient customer base exists and how likely those customers are to purchase their products or services. In addition to collecting and analyzing demographic data about people in a particular geographic area and comparing the results to the profile of a typical customer, the owner of the business can learn much by actually observing, mingling with, and interviewing customers as they shop. This process is what is known as "hands-on-marketing". For example, the founder of one snack-food venture in Lagos says that he brought a business concept from Europe where he has lived for nine years and he wanted to establish a snack-food restaurant. But before he did that, he learned a great deal about packaging, design and product placement by hanging around the aisles of grocery stores and watching shoppers' buying behavior, and their needs and what they have not been provided to satisfy their needs. In Europe and in the United States, many business owners learn about consumer behaviors by videotaping them while they are shopping to get a clear picture of their buying habits. Hands-on-marketing research techniques such as these allow entrepreneurs to get past the barriers that consumers often put up and to uncover their true preferences and hidden thoughts when interviewing them for information.

As a guerrilla marketing strategy, market research does not have to be time consuming, complex, or expensive to be useful. Many small business owners who do not appreciate the benefits of market research complain about how expensive and how time consuming it can become. As an entrepreneur, you do not have to seek the help from an experienced marketing firm to do your own marketing research, if you do not have the financial resources to do it. By applying the same type of creativity to market research that the above example shows when creating their businesses, entrepreneurs can perform effective market research without investing much capital. That is an aspect of the guerrilla marketing strategies discussed in this chapter.

Many entrepreneurs are discovering the power, the speed, the convenience, and the low cost of conducting market research over the World Wide Web. Online surveys, customer opinion polls, and other research projects, although relatively new in Sub Saharan Africa, are easy to conduct, cost virtually nothing, and help companies connect with their customers. By observing their customers' attitudes and actions, small business owners can shift their product lines and services to meet changing tastes in the market. To spot significant trends, the following actions are suggested:

(i) Read as many current publications as possible, especially the ones you normally would not read.
(ii) Watch the top 10 TV shows because they are indicators of consumers' attitudes and values and what they're going to be buying.

(iii) See the top 10 movies because they also influence consumer behavior, from language to fashions.
(iv) Talk to at least 150 customers a year about what they're buying and why. Make a conscious effort to spend time with your customers, preferably in informal settings, to find out what they are thinking.
(v) Talk to the 10 smartest people you know. They can offer valuable insights and fresh perspectives that you may not have considered.
(vi) Shop from your competitors so that you can learn how they attend to customers and what they offer.

Next, small business owners should make a list of the major trends spotted and should briefly describe how well their products or services match these trends. Companies, whose products or services are diverging from major social, demographic, and economic trends rather than converging with them, must change their course or run the risk of failing because their markets can evaporate before their eyes. How small business owners can find the right match among trends, their products or services, and the appropriate target market can be found in the conduct an appropriate market research.

Figure 10-1:
The Market Research Process

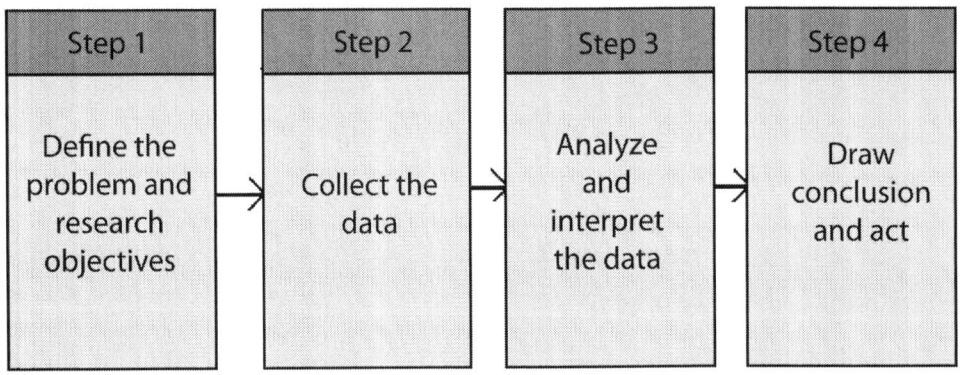

CONDUCTING MARKET RESEARCH FOR THE NEW VENTURE

The goal of market research is to get the facts straight before you launch your product or service in the marketplace. It is to reduce the risks associated with making business decisions. It can replace misinformation and assumptions with facts. Hearsays are not viable foundations on which to build a solid marketing strategy. Because someone says a product or service is hot in the market does not make your venture into that business a successful one. Successful market research consists of four steps: Knowing the problem and defining the objective of the market research, collecting the data, analyzing and interpreting the data, and drawing conclusions and acting on the basis of the information. As indicated earlier, market research involves the gathering of data in order to determine such information as who will buy the product or service, what size of the potential market, what price should be charged, what is the most appropriate distribution channel, and what is the most effective promotion strategy to inform and reach potential customers.[8] Figure 10-1 below describes the process of market research.

Step 1: Define the Problem and Research Objective. The first and most crucial step in market research is defining the problem and objective of the research clearly and concisely. In a market research, the goal is to provide answers to a very important question: "What is it you need the research for?" A common error at this stage is to confuse a symptom with the true problem. For example, dwindling sales is not a problem; it is a symptom. To get to the heart of the matter, the owner of the business must list all the possible factors that could have caused it. Do we face new competition? Are our sales representatives impolite or unknowledgeable? Have customers' tastes changed? Is our product or service line too narrow? Do customers have trouble finding what they want? Is our Website giving customers what they want? Is it easy to navigate? One Alhaji Omar wanting to discover the possible causes of his company's poorly performing Website asked surfers what they like or dislike about the site. After listening to their comments, he redesigned the site to make it easier for users to maneuver through its pages, and he refocused its content.

In some cases, the entrepreneur may be interested in researching a specific type of question. What are the characteristics of my customers? What are their income levels? What radio stations do they listen to? Why do they shop here? What factors are most important in their buying decisions? In either case, you must be able to demonstrate what you need the research or its data for. Do you need the data to

(i)   Demonstrate demand for your product or service?
(ii) Describe the primary customer?
(iii) Describe the buying patterns of your customers?

Other objectives of your market research may include:

(i) How much potential customers would be willing to pay for the product or service.
(ii) Where potential customers would prefer to purchase the product or service.
(iii) Where the customer would expect to hear about or learn about such a product or service.

The point is that each of these questions requires a different type of data. For example, demonstrating demand for your product or service may require you to find a similar product or service and use its history to estimate demand figures for your enterprise.

Step 2: Collect the Data. For most business owners, collecting useful information about their customers and potential new products and markets is simply a matter of sorting and organizing data that are already floating around somewhere in their companies. The key to success is to mine the data that most companies have at their disposal and turn it into useful information that allows the company to "court" its customers with special products, services, ads, and offers that most appeal to them. The way small business owners can collect valuable market and customer information falls into two basic methods: conducting *primary research* (data collected and analyzed by the company) and *secondary research* (data that have already been compiled and available, often at a very reasonable cost). In other words, you can gather data from primary sources (your own data) or from secondary sources (other people's data).

Gathering Information from Primary Sources
As one who intends to gather or collect data through a primary source, you have different types of methods at your disposal: customer surveys and questionnaires, focus group, observation, networking and interviewing. These methods are discussed below.

1. *Customer surveys and questionnaires*: When using customer surveys and questionnaires, these should be kept short and questions should be worded carefully so that the results are not biased. A simple ranking system should be used, if possible. Mr. Ade Balogun operates a local pharmaceutical shop where he sells drugs to patients. In most countries of Sub-Saharan Africa, it is common that patients go to a pharmacy for drugs rather than visiting the hospital for diagnosis. In order to keep track of his customers, Mr. Balogun developed a database. Everyday he goes through the list of customers and visits them to see if their ailment is cured or ongoing.

2. *Focus groups*: Focus groups are a more informal method for gathering in-depth information. A focus group is a sample of 5 to 12 potential customers who are invited to participate in a discussion relating to the entrepreneur's research objectives. The focus group discusses issues in an informal, open format, enabling

the owner to ascertain certain information. Small business owners should enlist a small number of customers to give them feedback on specific issues in their businesses such as quality, convenience, hours of operation, credit, service, and so on. An entrepreneur should listen carefully for new market opportunities as customers or potential customers tell him or her what is on their minds. As some experts have correctly pointed out, you gain unbiased information from a focus group when someone other than the entrepreneur or an experienced monitor leads it.

3. *Observation*: Observation is the simplest approach. The entrepreneur might observe potential customers and record some aspect of their buying behavior. As already pointed out, an entrepreneur can simply go to the competitor's shop and observe what it is been offered or why the customer needs the product or service. At the same time, the entrepreneur can observe other patterns of behavior associated with the customer's needs and requirements.

4. *Networking*: This is an informal method to gather primary data from experts, prospective customers and acquaintances. You get the information you need through the help of those you know. One advantage with the networking method is that it is less expensive. The opening profile on Tope Ogunlola described in this chapter illustrates the importance of networking as a viable tool for collecting primary data. Ms. Tope Ogunlola was able to establish her venture, Lunch for the Office, through the information she obtained from her friends and former employer.

5. *Other Ideas*: Ideally, the owner of a business should set up a suggestion system for customers and employees (such as a suggestion box) and use it. An entrepreneur should establish a customer advisory panel to determine how well the company is meeting various needs. Business owners should talk to customers and suppliers about trends they have spotted in the industry. They should also contact customers who have not bought anything in a long time and find out why and contact people who are not customers and find out why. They should teach employees to be good listeners and then ask them what they hear.

Gathering Information from Secondary Sources
The issue of secondary data or information has already been discussed in this chapter. The source of secondary data and information, which is usually less expensive to collect than primary data, includes the following:

1. *Business Directories*: To locate a trade association and suppliers, use business directories.

2. *Direct-mail lists.* An entrepreneur can compile mailing lists from prospective customers from his or her own data base using the network approach discussed in the preceding section.

3. *Demographic and Census Data*: Many government ministries in Africa or elsewhere have large data base on the demographics of a particular population group. In Africa, in general, the World Bank has been publishing, annually, data on the demographical changes occurring in many parts of the world. Central banks in the region have numerous publications about the census data of their countries and their consumption patterns. These data are readily available to assist you in knowing the kind of information you are looking for.

5. *Market Research*: Someone may already have compiled the data or information you need in your market research. All what you need is to get access to this data, convert them to information and see how they are relevant to the objectives of your market research. You must bear in mind that such information is not free.

6. *Articles*: Magazine and journal articles pertinent to your business are a great source of information. For example, many countries have *"Entrepreneur"* publications that provide a wealth of data and information about entrepreneurship and how to run a business. Many such publications provide information on customers, demographic data, industry analysis, laws and regulations that the prospective business owner can use for decision-making.

7. *World Wide Web*: Most business owners are astounded at the marketing and market information that is available on the World Wide Web (WWW). Using one of the search engines, an entrepreneur can gain access to a world of information that may be useful in making informed decisions.

For an effective individualized marketing campaign to be successful, some experts in this area suggest the following three types of information that an entrepreneur must collect:

(i) *Geographic*: Where are my customers located? Do they tend to be concentrated in one geographic region?

(ii) *Demographic*: What are the characteristics of my customers (age, education levels, income, gender, marital status, and many other features)?

(iii) *Psychographic:* What drives my customers' buying behavior? Are they receptive to new products or are they among the last to accept them? What values are most important to them?

Step 3: Analyze and Interpret the Data. The results of market research alone do not provide a solution to the problem; business owners must attach some meaning to them. What do the facts mean? Is there a common thread running through the responses? Are there new opportunities the owner can take advantage of? There are no hard-and-fast rules for interpreting market research results; business owners and entrepreneurs must use judgment and common sense to determine what the results of their research mean.

Step 4: Draw Conclusions and Act. The market research process is not complete until the business owner acts on the information collected. In many cases, the conclusion is obvious once a small business owner interprets the results of the market research. Based on her or his understanding of what the facts really mean, the owner must then decide how to use the information in the business. For example, the owner of a retail shop discovered from a survey that her customers preferred evening shopping hours over early morning hours. She made the schedule adjustment, and sales began to climb.

IDENTIFYING THE TARGET MARKET

One of the major reasons for conducting a market research is for the business owner to point to the target market and to be able to define a niche market for the business. Similarly, one of the first steps in building a guerrilla marketing plan is to identify a small company's **target market** - the specific group of customers at whom your firm aims its goods and services. The more a business learns about its local markets, its customers and their buying habits and preferences, the more precisely it can focus its marketing efforts on the group(s) of prospective and existing customers who are most likely to buy its products or services. As pointed out by Philip Kotler, a marketer can rarely satisfy everyone in a market. Not everyone likes the same soft drink, hotel room, restaurant, automobile, college, and movie.[9] Therefore, small business owners and marketers start by diving up the market by identifying and profiling distinct groups of buyers who might prefer or require varying product and service mixes. Failure to target a market leads one to try and satisfy all segments at the same time using what is called a "shotgun approach." In other words, many small businesses fail in their marketing efforts because they follow a "shotgun approach" to marketing by firing marketing blasts at every customer that they see, hoping to capture just one of them. Although this approach can work to get a small business established, it can lead to serious problems for a company using it to try to grow.[10]

The shotgun approach to marketing exhibit many of the features associated with traditional marketing which are centered on fuzzy message, product-focused, investing money, enhancing revenue, creating media perception, telling and selling, one size fits all and taking marketing share. On the other hand, guerrilla marketing focuses on the message, it is insight-based, builds intellectual assets, builds client relationships, enhances profits rather than revenue, reveals reality rather than creating media perception, listens to serve rather than telling and selling, adopts the principle that one size fits none rather than saying that one size fits all. Finally guerrilla oriented market research and marketing strategy creates markets; it does not pretend to take market share.[11]

In the context of developing countries, where most of economic activities are directed at the large and medium-scale firms, small business owners and entrepreneurs simply cannot use a shotgun marketing techniques and compete successfully with larger rivals with their deep pockets. In many parts of the world, marketing efforts of many entrepreneurs tend to be unsuccessful because they develop new products or services that do not sell. The reason for this is that these products or services are not targeted at the needs of specific audience; they broadcast ads that attempt to reach everyone and end up reaching no one; they believe a good product or service can sell itself without adequate marketing effort; they spend precious time and money trying to reach customers who are not the most profitable; and many of the customers they attract leave because they do not know what the company stands for.

Why, then, is the shotgun approach so popular? It is popular because it is easy and does not require market research or a marketing plan. The problem is that shotgun approach is a sales-driven rather than a customer-driven strategy. Successful entrepreneurs know that they do not have the luxury of wasting resources; they must follow a more targeted approach to marketing by using a guerrilla principle.

To be customer-driven, an effective marketing program must be based on a clear, concise definition of a company's target customers. Failing to pinpoint their target markets is especially ironic because small firms are ideally suited to reaching small, often concentrated market segments that their larger rivals overlook or consider too small to be profitable. A target-focused marketing strategy can be a powerful strategic weapon for any company that lacks the financial and physical resources of its larger competitors. Customers respond when companies take the time to learn about their unique needs and offer products or services designed to satisfy them.

CASE IN POINT: J&N HOUSE OF BEAUTY

When Julius and Nneka launched **J & N House of Beauty in** 1998, the couple targeted women who had plenty of purchasing power and wanted state of the art hairdressing and other beauty products brought to them at their homes. Their customers were busy upscale women who did not have the time to visit the traditional beauty salons for their make-ups or for the supply of their beauty products. This clientele consisted of rich women who belonged to social clubs where the latest fashion was always the major topic for discussion. Julius and Nneka knew also that this group would not want their clothes to be seen in other women or in the available fashion stores in Lagos. They wanted their European-styled dresses to be brought to them directly from Italy or their local attire made exclusively for them. **J & N House of Beauty** decided to add clothing lines to their business. They knew that if they could provide advice on beauty products they could as well convince these customers to purchase their clothes. **J & N House of Beauty** focused on clothing designed for what they called "real women" with all their curves and imperfections, rather than styles that only supermodel and pop stars could wear. The line of clothing is exclusive to the firm's customers because they understand their preferences. They train their own sales clerks extensively in identifying the needs of their customers.

Like *Lunch for the Office* and *J & N House of Beauty*, most successful small businesses have well-defined portraits of the customers they are seeking to attract. From market research, they know their customers' income levels, lifestyles, buying patterns, likes and dislikes, and even their psychological profiles. These firms establish prices appropriate to their customers' buying power, product lines that appeal to their tastes, and the service they expect. In essence, the target customer permeates the entire business – from the merchandise sold to the location, layout, and décor of the store. They have an advantage over their larger rivals because the images they have created for their companies appeal to their target customer, and that is why they prosper. Without a clear picture of its target customers, a small company will try to reach almost everyone and usually ends up appealing to no one.

Africa's increasingly diverse population: college students, company executives, the emerging middle class, etc, offers businesses of all sizes tremendous market opportunities if they target specific customers, learn how to reach them, and offer goods and services designed specifically for them. Because of this diversity, a "one-size-fits-all" approach no longer works. Most specifically, in the Sub-Sahara African region, we cannot classify all women as a target group. As a result of shifts in demographics, more and more women are now in the labor market. Consequently, what we have traditionally classified as a homogenous group has now become a heterogeneous one with diverse needs and wants. Sometimes new target markets emerge on their own, much to the surprise of a small business owner. The challenge for the entrepreneur now becomes how to meet the needs of these emerging sub-groups.

DEFINING THE NICHE OF A FIRM

One of the results of a market research is a definition and knowledge of the niche or target market. As a small business owner, it is often difficult for one to compete head-on with the big players in a chosen industry without the knowledge of the target market or creating a niche for the firm in its business terrain.

Identifying a target market – the customers who are more likely to purchase from you – is critical. You do so by conducting a thorough feasibility analysis of your business concept. Everything else about your business may appear viable, but if you cannot demonstrate that sufficient customer demand exists, the concept will not fly. To be able to understand the target market, one must first understand what the chosen industry consists of. We understand from the previous chapter that an *industry* consists of groups of businesses that have things in common, do transactions with each other, and compete with each other. This is followed by an understanding of the market, which consists of groups of customers inside an industry. Thus, in conducting the market research (i.e., determining whether your business concept is viable), you work your way down from the broad industry to the narrower market niche.

Narrowing your Market: Market Segmentation
As an entrepreneur, you can narrow your market within each broad market in order to achieve a segment that appeal to your product or service. The process of narrowing down the broad market to suit your product or service is called market segmentation. *Market segmentation is the process of analyzing one market to find out if it should be viewed as more than*

one market. For example, the broad market of people who buy books contains segments for:

- College or educational books
- Research books
- Travel books
- Children books
- Fictions
- Religious books
- Audio books
- Cooking books

Within a market segment, you can find *niches* - specific needs that are not being served, such as:

- Educational books that are directed at elementary (primary) schools, secondary schools, tertiary schools, undergraduate education, or post-graduate education.
- Research books that are geared toward specific disciplines such as management, sociology, the social sciences, the physical sciences, etc.
- Religious books directed at Christians or Christian books directed at Catholics.
- Children books that target the underprivileged, according to age, and according to their interests.

If a business or an organization, for example, had control of the only water supply in a country, its sales volume would be huge. This business would not be concerned about differences in personal preferences for taste, color, or temperature. It would consider its customers to be *one* market. As long as the water product was "wet," it would satisfy everyone. However, if someone else discovered a different way of satisfying the taste for water or create a situation where preferences for water become different, the view of the market would change. The first business might discover that sales were drying up and turn to a modified marketing strategy. The new approach could well emerge from an understanding of consumer behavior.

In the real world, a number of preferences for water exist. What may seem to be a homogenous market is actually heterogeneous. The different preferences may take a number of forms. Some preferences may relate to the way consumers react to the taste or to the container. Other preferences may relate to the price of the liquid drink or to the availability of "specials" such as bottled water. Preferences might also be uncovered with respect to different distribution strategies or to certain promotional tones and techniques. In other words, markets (such as the water market) may actually be composed of several submarkets (such as bottled water market). Consequently, to be competitive, a business owner should try as much as possible to identify these submarkets in order to identify a niche market. Market niches provide a place for entrepreneurs to enter a market and gain a foothold before bigger companies take notice and begin to compete. Having a niche for a business gives the owner or manager a quiet period during which the business alone serves a need of the customer that otherwise is not being met. Similarly, the business is in a position to set the standards for the niche. In short, the entrepreneur with a niche is ultimately the market leader for that particular niche.

As you zero in on your market, take care that the niche you ultimately choose is big enough to allow your business to make money. The niche you select must have enough customers willing to buy your products or services from you, enabling you to pay your expenses and turn a profit. If your niche is in the bottled water business, you must be sure that there are enough consumers who prefer bottled water as against tap water.

Defining your market, as pointed out, is about identifying the primary customer for your products or services - the customer most likely to purchase from you. You want to identify a niche market because creating customer awareness of a new product or service is time-consuming and costly, requiring lots of marketing expenses that few start-ups have at their disposal. So, instead of using a shot-gun approach and trying to bag a broad market, aiming at the specific customers who are likely to purchase from you is far more effective. More important still, is going to the customer who is easiest to sell and will help you gain a foothold quickly and start to build a brand recognition for you. This initial brand recognition will gain you access to other potential customers easier. As an entrepreneur, your first definition of a target customer will probably be fairly loose - an estimate. Suppose your target customers are book buyers. That is a fairly broad estimate. But as you conduct market research, you come to know that your primary customers in the book-buying industry or market are educational books geared toward elementary (primary) schools; this becomes your niche in the business of book supply.

In order to understand the process of market segmentation and how it helps you to define and create a niche for your business, we need to understand three types of market segmentation strategies. These are the unsegmented strategy, the multisegmentation strategy, and the single-segmentation strategy.[12]

An **Unsegmented Strategy** occurs when a business defines the total market as its target market. This strategy assumes that all buying units desire the same general benefit from the product or service. This may hold true for water supply but probably not for shoes, which satisfy numerous needs through many styles, prices, colors, and sizes. This may also hold true for the supply of electricity but not for a fashion or restaurant business.

A *multisegmentation strategy* views the market as composed of individual segments that have different preferences and where a firm is in a position to tailor its offering and marketing strategies according to the different groups of buyers in that industry. For example, if your firm feels that two or more homogenous market can be profitable, it will follow a multisegmentation strategy by developing a unique marketing mix for each segment. A beauty salon may decide to offer hair dressing for ladies, barbering service for men, and manicure for other groups of customers. The owner of the salon can develop the same marketing mix such as products and services offered, promotion, etc. to these different customer groups.

A *Single-Segmentation Strategy* occurs when a firm recognizes that distinct market segments exist but chooses to concentrate on reaching only one segment. The segment selected will be one which the business feels will be most profitable. The single-segmentation approach is probably the best for small businesses during their initial stages of growth. This approach allows them to specialize and make better use of their limited resources. When a reputation has been built, it is easier for them to enter new market segments.

As far as the issue of niche identification and market segmentation is concerned, some of the basic questions to answer about your potential customers are:

- What are their demographics: age, education, religious affiliation, life style, income level, size of family, etc.
- What are their buying habits? What do they buy? When? How?
- How do customers hear about your products and services? Do your customers buy based on word-of-mouth-referrals, ads or Internet advertising?
- How can your new business meet customers' needs? What customer need is your product or service now meeting?

Where do you find answers to these important questions? As already mentioned in the beginning of this chapter, your market research is the answer. Actually talking with your potential customers provides answers. From the perspective of guerrilla marketing principle, you should see your firm as a small player in the pack. The pack consists of bigger players who occupy all aspects of the market. They adopt unsegmented or multisegmentation strategies. As a little player on the block, you have to identify areas where they are not satisfying. In order for you to survive, you have to hit and run. To be successful in this strategy, you must know the weak points in your enemies' strategy and marketing practices (that is, where your competitors are weak). One primary reason to define and analyze a target and a niche market is to find a way into the market so that you have a chance to compete with your competitors. As a small business owner, you cannot afford to compete with the same weapons the big players bring to the business terrain. As an entrepreneur, if you enter a market without a niche strategy, you are setting yourself up for failure. As a new kid on the block, it is imperative that you hit competitors where they are least vulnerable so that they have to come at you with huge resources at their disposal. If customers cannot distinguish you from your competitors, they are not likely to buy from you. People generally prefer to deal with someone they know. Customers will know you if you have something to offer that is different from the available offerings.

CREATING A MARKETING MIX FOR YOUR PRODUCTS OR SERVICES

Until now, we have been discussing the environment you find yourself in as far as the knowledge about your customer is concerned. Now it is time to turn our attention to the other half of the equation – the environment you create for your self in the practice of marketing. If the market analysis deals with "what is going on in the market place or in the industry," then marketing mix deals with your marketing strategy. It is about what you bring to the market place.

For many years, marketers have described "what you bring to the market place" as the marketing mix, which consists of four elements usually referred to as the "four Ps" of product, place, price, and promotion. A full marketing strategy consists of decisions regarding each of these elements. The marketing mix shifts your focus from the environment to the components that *you* control.

P= PRODUCT AND SERVICE OFFERING

A product can be a physical thing such as menu offered by the owner of a restaurant, a movie that is released to the public or an idea. A product may be a tangible thing, a combination of tangibles and intangibles mixing products with services, or solely existing in the dimension of service. That is why some marketing experts use the term "offering" to describe both a product and a service. The value of the term "offering" is that it is inclusive. A dress off the rack is a product. A dress altered to fit you is a product combined with a service. A specialist who creates a wedding dress to your order is delivering more service than product. A person who teaches sewing so you can make your own dress is providing a service – no products attached. In our service oriented society of today, the boundaries between products and services are fast fading away. Product companies offer services; service companies develop products. For example, Millelium Business Center (now a cyber café) located in the heart of Lagos originally started with the provision of copy services, bookbindery and Internet services. Overtime, it began also to merchandise some office supplies as well because it made sense that customers might want to see this firm as a one-stop shop. For this Millelium Business Center, the line between a product and a service is blurred. However, and in whatever form you define your company, try to think about developing both products and services to offer your customers. Selling products or providing services that do not require continuous interaction with your customers is not a good idea in today's business world. Just making sales and forgetting about the customer is a dangerous way of marketing your products and services.

The Product Life Cycle and Its Marketing Implications

As in human beings and industries, products and services typically have a life cycle. Products are invented, introduced, and the demand for them grows. At some point, they reach maturity, and eventually pass into decline and exist no more as new products and services replace them. For example, the fax machine was introduced, gained wide acceptance, and is already in decline, not even 20 years later. A new innovation came along – the Internet – and drove a stake through the fax machine's heart.

Thus, one of the most useful concepts in marketing, insofar as strategic management is concerned, is that of the **product life cycle**. As depicted in Figure 10-2, the product life cycle is a graph showing time plotted against sales of a product as it moves from introduction through growth, maturity, decline and eventual death.

Marketing Strategies for a Product in Its Introduction Stage: Entrepreneurs are usually faced with the problem of being the first movers: profits are negative in the first year, pressure from promotional activities, securing distribution in retail outlets, and making their presence felt. As an entrepreneur, introducing your product into a new market implies that you are a pioneer. If you are good, early users will recall your brand name.

The pioneer's brand establishes the attributes the product class possesses. Innovation is the essence of being a pioneer in your industry. Many studies have found out that market pioneers enjoy a substantially higher market share than do early followers and late entrants.[13]

As a pioneer, one should know that competition would eventually enter and cause prices and its market share to fall. When will this happen? What should you, as the pioneer, do at each stage? Some answers to these questions include:

(i) Relentless innovation,
(ii) Financial commitment, and
(iii) Analyzing the profit potential of its market.

Marketing Strategies for a Product in Its Growth Stage: When your product is in the growth stage, your firm uses several strategies to sustain its growth momentum such as:

(i) Improving the quality of your product or adding new product features.
(ii) Adding new models and flanker products (i.e., products of different sizes, flavors, etc.)
(iii) Entering new market segments.
(iv) Increasing your distribution coverage and entering into new distribution channels, and
(v) Lowering prices to attract the next layer of price-sensitive buyers.

Figure 10-2:
The Product Life Cycle and Its Marketing Implications

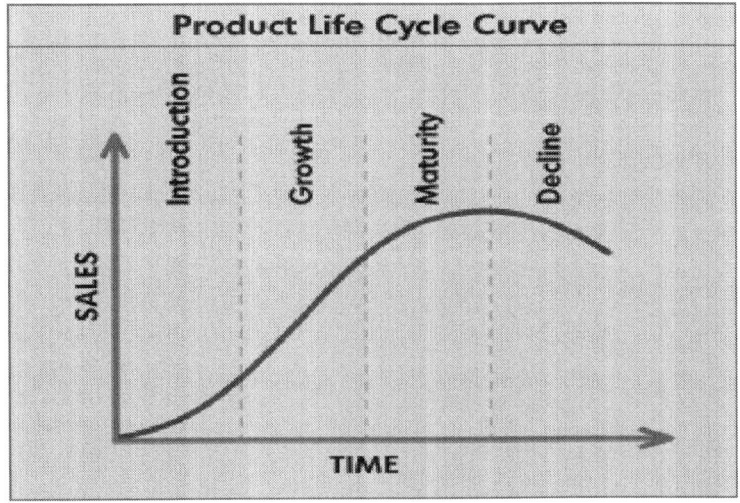

These market expansion strategies strengthen the firm's competitive position. A firm in the growth stage faces a trade-off between high market share and high current profit. By spending money on product improvement, promotion, and distribution, it can capture a dominant position. It forges maximum current profit in the hope of making even greater profits in the next stage.

Marketing Strategies for a Product in Its Maturity Stage: it is possible that your product or service has entered a stage in which rates of sales are slowing down. At this stage, your firm might try to expand the market for its mature brand, modify the product or by modifying the marketing mix. As a business owner, you modify the marketing mix by doing the following:

(i) Deciding whether a price cut will attract new buyers.
(ii) Deciding whether your firm would obtain more product support and display in existing outlets.
(iii) Deciding whether advertising expenditure should be increased or whether your firm's sales promotion should be stepped up.
(iv) Deciding on whether you should improve your services in delivering your product or service offering.

Marketing Strategies for a Product in Its Declining Stage: Your sales may decline for a number of reasons, including technological advances, shifts in consumer tastes, and increased domestic and foreign competition. As the sales and profit of your product or service decline, you might want to withdraw your products from the market. Other firms might want to withdraw from smaller market segments and weaker trade channels, and they may cut their promotion budgets to reduce prices further. Thus, developing a strategy for handling aging products or services is crucial in the marketing mix. As pointed out by Philip Kotler, unless strong reasons exist, carrying a weak product is very costly to the firm as there are many hidden costs. Weak products often consume a disproportionate amount of the owners' time; require frequent price and inventory adjustments; generally involve short production runs in spite of expensive setup times; require both advertising and sales force attention that might be better used to make the healthy products more profitable; and can cast a shadow on the company's image. Your marketing strategy must consider your products/service offering in terms of their life cycles. Whatever you are offering, expect it to evolve in tune with customers needs. Failing to eliminate weak products delays the aggressive search for replacement products, because "the weak products create a lopsided product mix, long on yesterday's bread-winners and short of tomorrow's.[14]

The product life cycle concept enables the entrepreneur or marketing manager, to examine the marketing mix of a particular product or groups of products in terms of their position in the life cycle model. Not just products, but whole product categories go through this cycle. Think about those business owners in the hair market. In the late 1990s, Black men both in the United States and in Nigeria, and elsewhere began having their hair shaved off. Many of them were shaving their hair off themselves or by their friends: they did not need the services of barbers. As a result, barbers experienced a corresponding lack of demand for their services. Thus, some traditional barbers either went out of business or adapted to the new challenges by learning what beauty parlor operators knew about other types of hairstyles. Consequently, what had been an industry strictly segregated by gender became largely unisex. And it happened pretty quickly. Few barbers had business plans and more than a few went under or began attending to both male and female customers.

When the "P"-word is a service: In today's knowledge economy, your offering is more likely to be a service than a product. The majority of offerings combine elements of both. Restaurants provide a tangible product, but the service they provide, from food preparation in the kitchen to waiters at your table, add the elements that distinguish one restaurant from the next. The whole experience of dining in a specific establishment becomes the "service" as chains such as McDonald's everywhere and Mr. Bigg's in Nigeria have proved.

Service-only offerings exist everywhere you look. While all offerings, both products and services, exist to fill customer needs, services have characteristics that make them very different from products. Consider the following characteristics of services:

(i) *Intangibility*: Purchasers cannot touch, taste, see, or feel a service before they agree to buy it. It is difficult for them to measure its quality. What they get in the buying exchange is initially a promise of satisfaction. Once they can determine whether the promise has been fulfill, the water is pretty much under the bridge. It is hard to return a bad haircut. There is a heavy requirement that the buyer trust the seller when services are involved. You can counter this by stressing competence, professionalism, and experience in your selling messages.

(ii) *Inseparability*. Services are typically delivered by people. Have you ever followed your hair stylist when she or he has moved from one salon to another? It is the person you trust - not the institution she or he works for. Employers in service businesses must respond to inseparability with an emphasis on collaboration and teamwork. The Internet is changing this dynamic for some of us since it enables us to provide services without face-to-face contact. Keeping personal touch, without encouraging inseparability, will force some service providers to master this high-wire balancing act.

(iii) *High perishability*. Products sit on shelves waiting for buyers; services don't. If you are a psychic and you expect a client at 4:00 p.m., and that client fails to show, you cannot resell that 4:00 p.m. slot to someone else (unless you are extraordinarily good psychic, in which case you already knew this would happen). You may respond to perishability via several strategies, including offering early-reservation discounts and charging for no-shows. In selling services, timing is everything.

(iv) *Difficulty of Quality Control*. It is impossible to standardize a service offering, especially once you hire employees to help you deliver your service. Your management of personnel becomes critical at this stage. You must set performance standards, perform appraisals to make sure standards are being met, and find other ways of ensuring quality control wherever possible.

(v) *Involvement of Customer*. When you are having your hair cut, do you chat with the person cutting your hair? Over time, we become friendly with the people who provide services to us. If service slips, we are likely to feel uncomfortable complaining because of this involvement. It is psychologically easier for us to find another supplier than to approach the problem head-on. Unfortunately, this is costly for the business we leave behind. Replacing a customer costs much more than retaining one.

Each of the above characteristics is a factor to consider when an entrepreneur is offering a product or a service. A firm must deliver not only a high quality of service, but also be in a position to manage the service encounter so that the process is as satisfying as its eventual result. As an owner of a business, the good news for you in the service business is that you are typically in closer touch with your customers than those who offer products. This gives you a constant source of feedback, new ideas, and inspirations that will help your service offering evolve.

For new businesses, and for existing businesses considering new offerings, a key element is determining the *feasibility* of the offering. Are there customers who want to buy this offering? Are there enough of them to make you financially viable? If this offering were already available elsewhere, why would people buy from you instead of your competitors? As an entrepreneur, you must look at the trends around you, as discussed in the section on market research, for objective proof that your offering has a compelling reason to exist. This means finding your competitive edge - that thing you do particularly well. Some of my colleagues in the banking sub sector have also emphasized this point:

For instance, a loan officer at a bank situated in Lagos, Solomon Adidi contributed, "There are two powerful motivations for businesses to get started and succeed - the consumer must believe that business will either save them time, or provide them knowledge. If you save the consumer time, or provide them knowledge, you will have a successful business."

Another bank official, also located in Lagos, Ernest Chukwu said, "As an entrepreneur, make sure you are really offering something that has value added. You must really be providing value that was not there before. Unfortunately in Nigeria, most business owner copy what others have been providing. In terms of marketing, you must come with your own edge to be a successful entrepreneur."

Features and Benefits: As a prospective business owner or one already operating an existing business, it is important that you take into consideration that your customers value products and services not for what they are, but for what they do (the utility). So, you should concentrate on the benefits or the utility of your product or service. What makes it useful? What problem does it solve? And most important, what makes your offering deliver the benefit better than any competing offering can? As pointed out in chapter seven, customers purchase goods or services for the benefits they offer. We do not buy a pair of shoes because they are shoes. We buy shoes because they offer us comfort ability or a way of dressing. We do not buy grilled chickens from Mr. Bigg's because we are hungry. We go there to eat because of convenience, time and probably because it is fashionable to dine there. Again, in chapter seven, we present examples of features translated into benefits (or utility) for most common products or services. Here, we refresh your memory by using the credit card as an example.

Features and Benefits of a Product or Service: The Credit Card

Feature   *Benefit*

Accepted at many locations .... Freedom, flexibility
Large credit line............................. Purchasing power
Works like cash.............................. Convenience and safety
Compact size .... Easy to take anywhere
You do not carry large cash................ Security
Picture ID..................................... Security
One monthly bill............................ Saves time

From the above example, it is easy to see why banks offer credit card to their customers. A credit card (or value card) can be accepted at many locations and the benefit the customer gets is his or her freedom and flexibility. When you live and work in Nigeria, you do not want to go through the hassle of going to the black market to buy dollars or pound sterling anytime you are traveling abroad. The credit card gives you the freedom to buy anything you want to buy in a foreign country without carrying foreign cash on you. Secondly, those who qualify for credit card are usually provided with credit line. The benefit of this is that you have purchasing power when you do not have the cash on you. Third, rather than carrying large cash with you while traveling from Lagos to Kano, you hold on you a little plastic card and you are safe. Fourth, we live in a society where armed robbery is rampant. Your security is partly guaranteed when robbers do not find cash on you. In some countries, picture identity cards are required before you can use your credit card for your purchases or any other transaction using the credit card. The benefit of this is that no one can take your money from the bank if your card is stolen because the thieves have to provide proof of their identity. If you are prudent, it is easy for you to organize your payments better, using a credit card. In fact, the global economy has been moving toward a cashless economy in an amazing rate. And Sub-Saharan Africa, as a participant in the global economy, cannot avoid this trend. As it is happening in most industrialized countries of the West and the developing ones in Southeast Asia, there will be a time in Africa when the credit card will the medium for commercial transactions. Entrepreneurs better take this development into consideration.

P= PLACE (LOCATION AND DISTRIBUTION)

The research done concerning your market position, your product, and your customer will greatly influence the location and/or place from which you conduct business. What does *place* mean anymore, in this era of the global village and Internet commerce? This *P* is really ready to retire. Or, it is evolving into a more relevant letter when one considers the impact of e-commerce. This *P* stands for all the aspects of getting product or service offerings to their end users. The right goods must get to the right place, in the right quality and quantity, at the right time, for the lowest possible cost, without sacrificing quality or customer service. This requires planning, and that is what this *P* has become so crucial in the entrepreneur's marketing mix and marketing strategy.

As we pointed out in chapter eight, the importance of location varies according to the product or service offering. For example, retailers are highly concerned with locations convenient to customers, unless they have chosen to locate on the Internet. Manufacturers and distributors are also concerned with location, but their concerns are different. Convenience to customers, availability of raw materials, access to suitable employees and support services, impact of existence of government regulations will be important to relative degrees, depending on the business category in which you operate.

As an entrepreneur, how much you emphasize the *place* aspect in your marketing strategy will depend on the unique challenges facing your business. "Place" is likely to be either highly critical or unimportant to you because there does not seem to be much middle ground. Sometimes the issue of "place" is really about connecting places - connecting buyer and seller. If your product and/or product mix is such that your customer is a retail consumer, location becomes very important. If your customer is an institution and you reach that customer through an outside sales force, location of the office and warehouse is less important.

Decision about location (place) is important because the more accessible the location, the more expensive will be the occupancy costs associated with that location. In a sense, a trade-off exists; prime location will, by its nature, attract and draw in customers. A less desirable location will cost less to occupy. However, due to its poorer accessibility and convenience, customers must be drawn to that location through more aggressive advertising and promotion. To maintain an equivalent level of sales, the cheaper location, from the perspective of occupancy, may in fact cost more when the costs of the additional advertising and promotion are factored in.

P= PRICING STRATEGY

Pricing a product or service offering requires the entrepreneur or the small business owner to know both the fiscal break-even point and the nature of market demand for that offering. As an entrepreneur, if you set your price at or below the break-even, you will have no profits. If you set your price too high above that point, you may be out of reach of many buyers. Your customer's goal is to obtain the most benefits for the price paid for a product or service. An entrepreneur's goal is to obtain the most price for the benefits. Somewhere in the middle, the entrepreneur and the customer meet for mutually profitable buying exchange.

Many small business owners think that price is a function of mathematics - you take what it costs you to produce a product, you estimate and put in a percentage for profit, and that is your price. But that does not work if the price does not meet the value expectations of the customer who is going to buy the product or service you are offering.

Another way of pricing is to look at what the customer expects to pay, you then work out what you can afford to deliver at that price, while protecting your percentage for profit. Either method requires that you know your break-even point on each product/service line.

The issue of pricing puts the entrepreneur in the land of supply and demand. If there is high demand for what you sell, and relatively few alternatives or substitutes available, then you will be able to charge a high price. Marketers and economists term this *inelastic demand*. If, on the other hand, there is less demand for what you sell, and/or plenty of alternatives and substitutes available, then you are facing *elastic demand*. If your price is too high, your customers will simply choose an alternative or do without it. The nature of elastic demand limits your ability to charge a price higher than that of your competitors.

As purchasers of goods and services, the issue of price has become the customers' most quantifiable and qualitative way of measuring the value of an offering. Customers believe that "one gets what one pays for." Thus, when making purchasing decisions, the customer is suspicious of low-price offerings. At the same time, the customer is suspicious of high-price offerings. The value of your product or service offering determines the price the customer is willing to pay based on his or her perception of the value offered by the product or service.

How do we define value? As customers, we weigh the benefits of a purchase against its cost to us. The benefits may be tangible, or intangible - the status that the purchase conveys, for example. The cost is only partly monetary because the customers must also factor in the time and energy it took to decide on that purchase. Many customers are willing to pay more to avoid unpleasant experiences and tasks because they value their time more than money. In short, in today's service economy, many customers pay more attention to convenience as they do to price.

All the elements of an offering contribute to the value customers perceive it to have. The form of the product (stylish or utility), its functionality, its availability, added niceties like free assembly or packaging, will lend value to the offering. If you want to raise your price (and your profits), look for an aspect of the offering that can be tweaked to increase its value in the potential buyer's mind.

In today's "save me time or give me knowledge business and social environment," service is often the component that adds the value that allows you to charge a higher price. For example, a customer who wants a TV set has two options. He or she could buy the product from a discount store or from a hawker of electronics on the street with a lower price. Alternatively, the buyer could choose to buy from a reputable dealer in electronics at a higher price. In the same manner, the customer could purchase a TV set from the street market (the hawker) and spend hours trying to assemble it at home. On the other hand, the buyer who had chosen to buy from the more expensive dealer who provides extra service such as assembling and programming would benefit more in the long-run. This customer will also feel that he or she has a place to go when questions about programming, repair, warranty, etc come up. It is unlikely that a provider who hawks his or her wares on the street or a discount shop owner will offer such services. Service, and the perception of value it conveys, makes the difference in setting your price. The value of this service must, as a matter of importance, be conveyed to the customer, thereby justifying the price set for the offering.

As an entrepreneur, there is a warning here: Don't compete on price if you can help it. As we stated in chapters eight and nine, most entrepreneurs go into business because they have something unique to offer and an identifiable niche to fill. What does this mean for the entrepreneurial firm? It means that the firm cannot afford to compete on the basis of price discounts. That area is left for large companies that have the advantage of economy of scale. Most new ventures are successful because they are providing something the customer wants, better than their larger competitors. For example, you can compete on the basis of price if your firm is able to source its raw materials and deliver the end product or service at a cheaper rate than what the competitor does. This is to say that, if you are able to manage the industry value-chain efficiently, competing on the basis of price is an attractive competitive strategy for the entrepreneurial firm.

What are the alternatives to competing on price? From the point of view of guerrilla marketing strategy, an entrepreneur has several alternatives in place for competing on the basis of price: As an entrepreneur, you can personalize, you can customize, you can specialize, you can offer better financing or better guarantees, you can offer more convenience, you can raise the perception of value by promoting an upscale image, you can even raise your price, and communicate that you charge more because you are worth it.

Price is more than the figure you print on a tag. Price is a strategy that includes discounts, surcharges, payment terms, negotiability, and more. Your pricing strategy can help you achieve your strategic and financial objectives such as increasing your market share, maximizing profits, building up a new product line, or remaining competitive. Your pricing policies will affect your sales volume goals, and thus affect the projections in the financial section of your marketing strategy and business plan.

P=PROMOTION, ADVERTISING AND POSITIONING

This "**P**" covers promotional activity from advertising to promoting your product or service and positioning. The purpose is to position your product or service in the eyes and minds of prospective customers. Promotion and advertising are the elements that communicate the availability and desirability of whatever it is you are offering and why people should buy what you are offering. Depending on the situation in which you find yourself, this section of your marketing strategy might mention your plans to use paid advertising media, or to offer sales promotions like contests and coupons, or to rely on personal selling or public relations activity to "get the word out." You will get a chance to expand on the promotional strategy you plan to adopt when you come up with the marketing strategy and plan.

A CASE IN POINT: NWUCHE'S PEOPLES' LIBRARY
Mr. John Nwuche decided to establish a secondary school in Aba, Nigeria, after spending over ten years in the United States. With a master's degree in education counseling, John Nwuche's dream has been to own and operate a secondary school. After completing a business plan, Mr. Nwuche found out that he did not have enough financial resources to compete with the existing secondary schools in the Aba region and its environs. There

> were more well-financed schools in Abia state, offering the same curriculum Nwuche's school had intended to offer. The owner had no financial means needed to promote the school in media outlets such as the local television and newspaper. He came up with a solution. Most of the books he brought from the United States were placed in a building he calls "The People's Library." In his "People's Library", families were coming from the surrounding villages and towns in the city of Aba just to read. The scarcity of textbooks in Nigeria has long been seen as one of the greatest obstacle to education in the country. With his library, Nwuche was able to promote his business. Gradually, the "word" went out and with his reputation, Nwuche was able to secure a market niche and to obtain initial start-up capital from a local bank. The point here is that a little community service can help you promote and or position your business and compete successfully with the established larger companies.

In my opinion, the key to this "P" – meaning "promotion" lies in yet another "P": the concept of *positioning*. Positioning is the component that keeps your promotional activity coordinated - dancing to the same music, pulling in the same direction, and, above all, making your products or services visible. Positioning takes your product or service and promotes its uniqueness in the marketplace.

The Idea of Positioning

Nowadays, the "**P**" in marketing has also been used to describe "Positioning", which defines the position of a product in the mind of its buyers. Thus, a products' position is how potential buyers see the product, and is expressed relative to the position of competitors. In marketing, positioning is the process by which marketers or organizations create an image or identity in the minds of their target market for a product, brand, or organization. It is the relative competitive comparison of a product or service in terms of the position it occupies in a given market as perceived by the target market. In a similar manner, "Re-positioning" involves changing the identity of a product, relative to the identity of competing products, in the collective minds of the target market. De-positioning involves attempting to change the identity of competing products, relative to the identity of your own product, in the collective minds of the target market.[15]

The logic of positioning is that any brand is valued by the perception it carries in the prospect or customer's mind. Each brand has thus to be "Positioned" in a particular class or segment. For example, Mercedes is positioned as a luxury brand, and Volvo is positioned for safety. In Nigeria, the *Guardian* Newspaper is positioned as an elitist paper dedicated to the educated middle- and upper class. The position of the brand has to be carefully maintained. The *Guardian* newspaper costs above the market average to buy. As a result of its positioning, if the *Guardian* decides to reduce its price to that of its competitors, sales will definitely drop because its readers will associate it with other newspapers in the country. Rolex watches are even more dramatically positioned as a luxury items, and have become a symbol for accomplishment in life. If Rolex reduces its prices, it will reduce brand cachet and sales.

Positioning is also about perception that happens in the minds of the target market. It is the aggregate perception the market has of a particular company, product or service in relation to their perceptions of the competitors in the same category. Perception occurs whether or not the owner of the business or management is proactive, reactive or passive about the on-going process of evolving a position. However, the entrepreneur or business owner can positively influence the perceptions through enlightened strategic actions. Generally, product positioning process involves the following steps:

- Defining the market in which the product or brand will compete (who the relevant buyers are),
- Identifying the attributes (also called dimensions) that define the product "space",
- Collecting information from a sample of customers about their perceptions of each product on the relevant attributes,
- Determine each product's share of mind,
- Determine each product's current location in the product space,
- Determine the target market's preferred combination of attributes.

The process involved in product positioning is similar for positioning a firm's services. As we pointed out earlier, services, however, do not have the physical attributes of products - that is, we can't feel them or touch them or show nice product pictures. So you need to ask first your customers and then yourself, "what value do clients get from my services? How are they better off from doing business with me?" Also ask: "is there a characteristic that makes my services different?" Answers to these questions serve as a guide on how to properly position your product or service.

In the process of positioning a product or service, it is also important to write out the value customers derive and the attributes your services offer to create the first draft of your positioning. In addition, it is recommended that you hit on people who don't really know what you do or what you sell, watch their facial expressions and listen for their response. When they want to know more because you've piqued their interest and started a conversation, you will know you are on the right track.

For the business owner and or entrepreneur, there are three types of positioning, namely, functional positioning, symbolic positioning and experiential positioning.

Functional Positioning is about the functions a customer derives from the product or service. It answers questions such as what problems are solved by the product or service. What benefits do the product or service provides for the buyer? What favorable perceptions do investors and lenders get when they see the product or service?

Symbolic Positioning deals with intrinsic values associated with the product or service and include issues such as self-image enhancement, ego identification, belongingness and social meaningfulness, and affective fulfillment. For example, Sheraton Lagos Hotel and Towers is positioned as "an oasis of luxurious comfort, a relaxing haven, designed for the business and leisure traveler."

Experiential Positioning depicts what the brand stands for. It is an image-driven depiction of the experience that the brand stands for. For Mr. Bigg's, the experiential positioning is "delicious experience – great food, friendly place, lovely place"! According to Bernd H. Schmitt, the author of "Customer Experience Management", experiential positioning is equivalent to the functional positioning, but it replaces the functions performed by the product/service with an insightful and useful multi-sensory strategy component that is full of imagery and relevant to the buyers and users of the brand.[16]

Positioning (within the context of marketing a firm's product or service) is usually seen as the act of designing the company's offering and image to occupy a meaningful and distinct position in the customer's mind of the target market.[17] Positioning is how potential customers differentiate you and your products and services from those of your competitors. Positioning is by its nature competitive because it is always chosen relative to positions held by competitors.[18]

There are different positioning possibilities that your firm can choose from:

(i) Attribute positioning: you can position your firm on an attribute, such as size or number of years in existence.
(ii) Benefit positioning: Your product or service is positioned as the leader in a certain benefit.
(iii) Use or application positioning: You position your product or service as best for some use or application.
(iv) User Positioning: You position your product as best for some user group.
(v) Competitor Positioning: Your product claims to be better in some way than a named competitor.
(vi) Product Category Positioning: Your product or service is positioned as the leader in a certain product category.
(vii) Quality or Price Positioning: You position your product as offering the best value.

Positioning works as a promotional strategy for a simple reason: Your customers are human beings. Basic psychological insight teaches us that we humans cannot hold two conflicting beliefs. As humans, we refuse to believe that two different detergents can provide the same solution to our washing needs, even if both products state that in their advertisements. Consequently, developing a promotional strategy for your business should start with choosing the position you want to hold in potential customers' minds. As a business owner, you must consider the positions held by your competitors: On what dimensions are they considered "best"? They might be known for product features, brand name recognition, selection, or convenience - you get the idea. Positioning is about finding or creating a dimension in which you can become the "best."

Positioning reflects the personality you have created for your business. This personality comes from the tone of your advertising, your customers' experiences with you, what they tell others about you, what your employees say about you, the appearance of your store, your Web Site, and your personnel, etc. In other words, practically everything you do has the potential to strengthen the position you hold in pubic perception.

A new business has the opportunity to create a position from scratch. An existing business already has a position, whether it has proactively chosen that niche, or simply been assigned it by the community's experience of that business. The success of your promotional activity absolutely depends on controlling your position and using it to your advantage. Every communication and experience customers have with your company should be consistent with the image and position you have chosen to project.

Brand identity is an extension of the idea of positioning. In Nigeria, for example, Mr. Bigg's, through its promotional activities, has established a brand identity for itself as the de facto "market leader in the quick service restaurant business in Nigeria". A brand consists of the associations and expectations that come to mind when exposed to a name, or a logo, or a package. Through repeated exposure, brand identity comes to represent the positioning you want your customers to think of when they see your brand. Branding is absolutely essential if you want to stand out in an ever-more-crowded marketplace.

Building a brand and a position is relatively simple if you are doing business in a centralized geographic area, easily reached by mass media advertisement. Building a brand is much more difficult if your market is geographically dispersed, or you dream of conquering the national scene. You can take the hard road, and build your own brand name and credibility, or you can take a shortcut and buy an existing franchise. Part of what a franchise gets you is a leg up on that long process of gaining a position in public awareness.

A main purpose of advertising is to build brand identity. Dot-com companies advertise in the traditional media to publicize their brands; traditional companies advertise on the Internet to reach consumers where they work and play. To participate in this high-stakes competition for consumer awareness, everything you do must reinforce your brand and the positioning behind it.

Message distribution. If the promotion (the "P"-word) is about communicating the availability and desirability of your product or service offering, how do you do that? You may rely on yourself and your staff in personal selling situations. You may also find yourself turning to mass media, including broadcast, print, and the Internet vehicles (depending, of course, on your budget) to distribute your message beyond the ground you and your staff can cover in person. When planning your message distribution strategy, think about what goes on as an individual is converted from an ordinary person who is not aware of your offering to a buyer of your product or service. Let us call this process a "sales conversion process."[19] Your prospective customer does not know you. He or she is expected to go through different stages to be aware of what you are offering and then make the crucial decision of whether or not to buy your offering. In fact, you are converting someone who does not know your product or service offering to a position where he or she can make the decision to make a purchase. Some promotional activities are better at motivating a person from a state of unawareness of your product or service to becoming aware of them; other activities are more successful at convincing that person to want your offering, and then act on that desire. Broadcast advertising, trade shows, and conventions are good at creating awareness and positioning your firm. Print advertising and direct mail are good at building comprehension. Personal contact is excellent in the final stages of convincing and closing the sale. When you plan the distribution of your marketing message, keep this process in mind. As a business owner, one must not assume that a sale postcard or a business card will take the average person from not knowing you to buying your offer in one move.

PROMOTIONAL AND ADVERTISEMENT STRATEGIES

Promotion and advertising are usually considered separate. But, in some ways, both terms are mutually supportive. They are related because the two concepts are about how you make people buy your product or service. The real difference between the two concepts is the road you want to go. Advertising is viewed more from the perspective of "out there someplace," as an activity or process of getting the word out that your firm exists, while the message you wish to convey is broadcasted to a target audience through selected media. Thus, advertising offers a *reason* to buy your product or service. Promotion, on the other hand, is designed to stimulate purchase of your product or service by the consumers and deals more with in-store merchandising and marketing activities. While advertising offers the buyer the reason to buy your product or service, promotion, on the other hand, offers the *incentive* to buy. Promotion and advertising are marketing activities that are mutual in achieving the overall objective of the marketing plan.

Promotion:
As a business owner, promotion is multifaceted ways of making people buy your product or service. Promotion deals primarily with a visual presence: eye appeal and the attention-getting aspects of the physical structure, equipment, merchandise, and personnel who make up the physical elements of your enterprise. Promotion begins with the facility itself and the grounds surrounding the facility. Many major retailers spend enormous time and energy to attract customers into their stores through the attractive use of window displays. In high-traffic retail settings such as a mall or shopping center, many prospective customers walk by the stores and observe the items on display. It is the window and merchandise displays within the potential customer's line of sight that attract and influence store traffic. Window banners, signs, posters, etc. which influence a store's image, are all a part of developing the customer's first impression.

Many retailers have spent enormous amounts of money attempting to maximize sales through store layout, shelf and other types of arrangements to provide incentives to buy their products. This is an example of promotional activities. When product salespersons or company representatives are available to provide information, assistance, and support for you, they are performing the promotional activity. Many manufacturers will supply stationery and sometimes moving displays and end-of-aisle displays. Other suppliers will offer to set up end-of-aisle displays in your store. These are all promotional activities.

How you display your merchandise reflects on the image of your store. Keeping your merchandise looking fresh and clean is a time-consuming task. Keeping an inventory that appears to be new and bright can be assisted with adequate light, wide and spacious aisles. Keeping your inventory interesting often requires that displays be moved and changed frequently. Even a store's price tag is part of the promotional effort and conveys a message to the patron. It is easy to see the extensive use of point-of-sale displays near the checkout counters of nearly every major retailer. In Europe, North America and Asia, point-of-purchase displays tend to offer impulse items and account for substantial increase in sale levels. Even a business such as a machine parts store or automotive replacement parts store can increase sales at the point of purchase by emphasizing merchandising. Another avenue used to increase the level of impulse buying of patrons is through the use of vending machines. Their presence and appearance are also a part of the promotional activity and contribute to the image of the business.

Whatever the promotional mix employed, it should support the firm's image, not contradict or detract from the positioning strategy that it has adopted. Keeping a retail outlet as fresh and appealing as the plate layout of a five-star restaurant is a demanding activity. It requires a great deal of energy and a lot of creativity to maintain a good promotional mix. In general, promotional tools are made to bring in customers. Firms do this through introductory samples, coupons; cash refund offers, prices off, premiums, prices patronage reward, and free trials.

Advertising

What advertising is really about is information. Like promotion, advertising is simply an exercise devoted to enhancing the image of your firm or advancing some issues or cause that you or your firm is passionate about. However, unlike promotion, advertising is the impersonal presentation of an idea, which is identified with a business sponsor and is projected through mass media. The primary goal of advertising is to draw attention to the existence or superiority of your product or service. Doing business without advertising is like winking at a girl in the dark. You know what you are doing, but no one else does. Somehow, the entrepreneur must get the word out and inform the public, particularly the target market. The advertising message should contain information about whom and what the business is about and what product or service is offered. The presentation of this information should create at least an interest and ultimately a desire in the consumer to try that product or service.

After a name and logo are developed to help create a specific image, probably the best promotional tool is the product or service itself. One of the most effective marketing tools is word of mouth from one satisfied customer to that person's circle of family, friends, and associates. Quality of product or service is best established before the first day of business. If you can imagine a business where the service became a fiasco and the product quality ebbed to a low level, the damage to the firm's image could be irreparable. We have pointed out consistently in this book that it is much easier and cheaper to keep existing customers than to replace customers continually with new ones. A product and/or service with a high level of quality can be a real asset in maintaining customer loyalty.

Choosing the Medium for Promotion and Advertising

There are several media options at the disposal of the small business owner to promote and advertise the firm's product or service. The choice of media depends on the type of business, common practices in the industry and the financial resources at the owner's disposal. In general, a business owner chooses between print and broadcast media as discussed below.

The Local Newspaper: Many areas in the world today have some type of a local newspaper. The local newspaper is the inhabitants' prime medium for getting news from the outside world. Every area, no matter how remote, in the global economy, has one form of communicating among them and such a medium is the peoples' local newspaper. Such a medium is an appropriate means to place the firm's promotional or advertisements activities because it covers its geographical area and it is relatively inexpensive. The disadvantage is that the advertisement has a short life span. To be successful, the owner of the business must look for specialized newspapers for better targeting and try to locate his or her ad on the right-hand above the fold. Many local newspapers have set aside certain days of the week and pages for ads, news and information for certain industries and markets. The implication is that the business owner must know when the local newspaper carries issues and ads about specific industries and markets involving the firm's product or service.

The Periodical News Magazine: There are certain news magazines that are called periodicals. We call them periodical because they do not come out daily. Advertising in a periodical magazine can help you target customers with special interest and it is more credible than newspapers. The disadvantages with placing your ads in news magazines are (i) it is expensive to design, (ii) it is expensive to produce and place and (ii) it does not reach as many people at once compared with your local newspaper. For an ad to be effective in a news magazine, you should look for regional edition. Use a media buying service; use color effectively and choose the particular magazine that the prospective customers in your industry read. You can also turn to trade magazines, but these are expensive and are targeted at professionals in a specific field.

Direct Marketing: As a medium for advertisement, direct marketing includes direct mail, mail order, coupons and telemarketing. Direct marketing helps you close the sale when the advertisement takes place, it targets specific customers, you get more sales with the least cost, more information is provided and you get the highest response rate per person. The disadvantage with direct marketing is that not all products or services are suitable for it. For your ad to be successful through direct marketing, it is important that you create a personalized mailing list and database from responses. You should also use several repeat mailings to increase the response rate of your respondents. Somehow, it is good to entice customers to open the envelop through offers placed right on the envelop.

The Yellow Pages: This is another medium through which a business owner can advertise his or her products/services. The advantage with yellow pages is that it is good in the early stages for awareness and it is good for retail and service types of businesses. The disadvantages are that yellow pages are relatively expensive and target only the local market. For your ad to be successful, it is advisable that you create one that stands out on the page and you should always look at what attracts your attention on a page.

The Radio: This is an important medium for advertising your product and service. It is good for local or regional advertising. It is also good if you have a product or service that is quickly and easily understood. The disadvantage is that for the advertisement to be successful it must be done several times in a series and it can be very expensive in high demand time slots. To be successful, it is advisable that you advertise on more than one station to saturate market. You should try to sponsor a national radio program, if you have the means. You should also try as much as possible to provide the station with finished recorded commercials. Most importantly, you must know who the audience of the station is, their preferences, their demographics and their buying patterns. For example, if your products or services are for the "hip-hop" generation, do not put your ad on a radio station that plays only classical music or the "oldies".

The Television: The TV has become one of the most popular forms of advertising and promotion in today's "go to work-or-sit-at-home-culture." For the kids and teenagers, TV ad is also about "you are either at school, or you're at home watching the TV." People (whether adults, teens, or kids) can see and hear about products and services through the TV ad and it can be used to target national, regional and local audience all at once. The television, as a medium of advertisement, is good for large-scale companies. But for entrepreneurial firms, one must factor in the cost. Thus, the disadvantage with using the television as a medium is that it is very expensive for both production and on-air time. Like the radio, ads on the television must be repeated frequently to be effective. The television, as a medium of advertisement, is very expensive and the message and how it is packaged is the work of professionals. As an entrepreneur, you must consider your advertising budget against other financial obligations before you decide on advertising your service or product on the television.

The Internet: This has become one of the most popular media for advertising as a result of several advantages associated with it. The advantages with advertising on the Internet are that the ads can reach customers on a global level less expensively than direct marketing or mass marketing. It is also a good way to create repeat customers by providing added value at the Web site. The disadvantages are that it can be difficult to target your audience; it is difficult to capture the attention of Web surfers and it can be expensive to do well. Another disadvantage is that a business owner needs to do offline advertising to get customers to his or her site. As a business owner, it is important that you look for Web partners who will let you place links on their sites. You should also try to put your Web address on your business card and all offline advertising for your company.

Community Volunteering: Community volunteering is an initiative in which the firm supports and encourages employees, retail partners and even customers to volunteer their time to support local community organizations and causes. Community volunteering enhances the image of your business, provides you with an opportunity to showcase your products or services and helps you build genuine relationships in the community.

Free Publicity: As the owner of a small business, the best and cheapest way to promote your company is through free publicity, which is basically free advertising for a product or business through various forms of media. The key to getting free publicity is having a product or company that is newsworthy, that has a great story. Take for example, the case of Mr. Festus Bamiyo, who introduced himself as an "Industrial, Financial and Management Consultant at Projects for Entrepreneurs WA Ltd". He wrote an article in the *Guardian* of Saturday, May 29, 2004 about "Micro Scale Palm Kernel Crushing."[20] In the article, he describes in a detailed manner, the process of starting a business on small scale vegetable oil processing. He did a very thorough research about what it costs to start one. At the end of the article he puts his name, the name of his company, and his e-mail address. What he did was to publicize and advertise not only his company, but also more importantly, his competencies and skills without paying for it. He has written a similar article prior to this one and many people have responded by contacting him directly about how they can go into that particular business. If you believe that your company has an important story to tell, try the following:

- Writing to a reporter, suggesting an idea and then following up with a phone call. It is better if you initially get to the reporter through a referral. Networking is very important in terms of your company's publicity.

- Issuing a press release that answers who, what, where, when, and why.

- Participate in community services where you can offer the community your services or products free.

By making the reporter's jobs easier, you are more likely to get them write something about your company. If an article is written, be sure to get reprints that you can use in your advertising and promotion. To get your company noticed through guerrilla marketing approach, the following tactics should be adopted:

1. **Sponsoring a special event**. For example, one company presented a "sport-after-the-hour" event after a major football contest in Ibadan, Nigeria, where the owner, who sells sport wears, displayed his products to an invited group of athletes who can enjoy drinks and free food. Another educational company sponsored "a children-reading day" gala in a local town hall, where children of all ages and their parents were invited for free lunch and to meet celebrities. The matron of the school was advertising her school.

2. **Demonstrating your expertise in a particular area**. A management consulting firm in Lagos, Nigeria, created awareness by developing a newsletter focusing on accounting practices for managers in large organizations. Another firm that operates a restaurant for the busy executives (in South Africa) puts its newsletter in a Web site. The newsletter discusses issues about weight watching and the type of meals one can eat to improve and maintain his or her health.

3. **Give your products to role models and public opinion shakers**. Giving your products or services away to people who can get you free publicity is a cheaper and an effective way to advertise your products. For example, giving your

products to celebrities and role models especially those with access to the media is a useful way to make your products or services known to the public.

CHAPTER SUMMARY

To be successful, a business must have a marketing plan that focuses on the customer and recognizes that satisfying the customer is the foundation of every business.

Marketing is the process of creating and delivering desired goods and services to customers and it involves all of the activities associated with winning and retaining loyal customers.

Marketing can be defined as the performance of business activities that affect the flow of goods and services from producer to consumer or user.

A guerrilla marketing strategy is a marketing tactic that can help small business owners to: (i) learn how and why clients buy products or services, (ii) overcome and capitalize on clients' skepticism, (iii) compete for client relationship, (vi) demonstrate what the clients want – results, (v) wield the right mix of marketing tactics to build and sustain the business.

A guerrilla marketing plan must accomplish five objectives: (i) pinpoint the specific target market, (ii) understand the strengths and weaknesses of competitors, (iii) know where the competitor's weaknesses lie, (iv) determine customer needs and wants through market research, and (v) analyze and understand the firm's competitive advantages.

A target market is the specific group of customers at whom a firm aims its products or services.

A shotgun approach to marketing puts the small company in dangerous competitive position because it has fuzzy messages, product-focused, telling and selling. The shotgun approach to marketing is sales-driven rather than customer-driven.

Guerrilla marketing is insight-based, builds intellectual assets, builds client relationships, enhances profits rather than revenue, reveals reality, listens to serve the customer better, be flexible and creates markets.

The needs and wants of customers can be ascertained through market research.

Because of the changes in demographics, customer needs and wants are not static but change constantly. By performing some basic market research, entrepreneurs can detect key demographic and market trends.

Market research involves systematically collecting, analyzing, and interpreting data pertaining to a company's market, customers, and competitors. The goal of market research is to get the facts straight before a product or service is launched in the market place. Market research is a process that consists of four steps: (i) defining the objective of the research, (ii) collecting data, (iii) analyzing and interpreting the data, and (vi) drawing conclusions and acting on them.

Market segmentation is the process of analyzing one market to find out if it should be viewed as more than one market.

An unsegmented strategy is when a business defines the total market as its target market.

A multisegmentation strategy views the market as composed of individual segments that have different preferences. In a multisegmentation strategy, the firm is in a position to tailor-make different strategies.

A single segmentation strategy is when a firm recognizes that distinct market segments exist but chooses to concentrate on reaching only one segment.

A marketing mix consists of marketing practices such as product or service offering, place or location, pricing strategy, and promotion.

A product life cycle is a graph showing time plotted against sales of a product or service as it moves from introduction through growth, maturity, decline, and eventual death.

The characteristics of a service offering are: (i) intangibility, (ii) inseparability, (iii) high perishability, (vi) difficulty of quality control, and (v) involvement of the customer.

A pricing strategy is determined by several factors such as: (i) the fiscal break-even point and (ii) the nature of market demand for the product or service offering. A pricing strategy must meet the value expectations of the customer. An entrepreneur can charge a higher price if there is a high demand for what he or she sells or produces.

Setting a price for a product or service means that the entrepreneur must know the value (or utility) provided by the product or service. As an entrepreneur, it is not advisable to compete on the basis of a lower-cost strategy. The alternatives for competing on the basis of lower cost strategy is personalizing and customizing your offering, specializing on what your core competencies, you can raise your price and let your customers know why you are raising your price.

Promotion communicates the availability and desirability of what the firm has to offer. Promotion is about "getting the word out." Promotion offers an incentive to buy the product or service.

The promotional activities of a firm are all about positioning the firm, its products or services and its image.

Positioning is the process by which marketers or organizations create an image or identity in the minds of their target market for a product, brand, or organization. It is the relative competitive comparison of a product or service in terms of the position it occupies in a given market as perceived by the target market.

Positioning is the act of designing the firm's offering and image so that they occupy a meaningful and distinct position in the customer's mind. Positioning is about how potential customers differentiate you or your products and services from those of the competitors.

Advertising is about providing information about a product or service. Unlike promotion, advertising is the impersonal presentation of an idea, which is identified with a business sponsor and is projected through the mass media. Advertising offers a reason to buy a product or service.

There are seven types of media to choose from when advertising a product or service: (i) the local newspaper, (ii) direct marketing, (iii) the yellow pages, (vi) the radio, (v) the television, (vi) the Internet, and (vii) free publicity.

The product or service offering of a business venture can be noticed through guerrilla advertising approaches such as when the business owner (i) sponsors a special event, (ii) demonstrates his or her expertise in a particular area, (iii) gives the products or services to role models and public opinion shakers, and (vi) being the first person to do innovate.

CHAPTER DISCUSSION QUESTIONS

1. What do you understand by the term "guerrilla marketing strategies?" As an entrepreneur, how do you build a guerrilla marketing strategy to achieve a competitive advantage?

2. Why do you think conducting market research before going into business is crucial for the success of your business? How do you, as an entrepreneur, determine customer needs and wants through market research?

3. What do you understand by the concept of a "product life cycle?" Describe the different stages in the life of a product or service and the applicable marketing issues in each stage.

4. What is product positioning? Why is positioning necessary for your product or service? Explain the three types of positioning available to you, as an entrepreneur.

5. How do you get your company noticed through guerrilla advertising and promotional approaches?

CASE STUDY 10: JIDE'S INTERIORS: DEVELOPING A PROMOTIONAL STRATEGY[21]

Sade Olajide, age 41 and married for 20 years, was born and raised in Abeokuta, Nigeria. Her husband Dayo Olajide, age 43, had been working for one of the oil multinational companies in Lagos, Nigeria. Five years ago, Dayo came from abroad where he had spent two months in a course on computer applications. Together, Sade and Dayo pulled their resources and founded an interior decorating business located on one of the business streets in Ikeja, Lagos, Nigeria.

Sade's Background

During her early years of marriage, Sade tried several jobs but was mainly at home being a housewife. Tired working for someone else, Sade and a friend opened a store on the busy Balogun Street in the main business district of Lagos. There, she sold imported fashion wears such as handbags, perfumes, and dresses. Many of her customers were the housewives of her husband's colleagues. But in time Sade and her partner began to develop a customer segment that was based on her own marketing skills: word of mouth. During this time she was combining her job at the store with that of a housewife. In the main, she was a housewife, with three children (two sons and a daughter), Abiodun, Toyin and Bisoye. After two years in the retail business, her partner moved back to Ibadan with her husband and Sade found it difficult to operate the business herself. Sade soon found out that without her partner, she was not cut out to be a retailer. Coupled with the demand at home raising her children, she felt it was too much for her to run the business. In her words, "Selling clothes was difficult for me. I feel I know how to do something but not in retailing. You know, what gives joy is helping at home, decorating the house, taking care of my children, and making sure that the home looks good when my family comes home." She sold her inventory and decided to concentrate on raising her children.

When her husband, Dayo, came back from the United States, he was given a promotion and a pay raise and the couple decided to build their own house, rather than "paying rents for someone else," Sade said. Because her children have grown, Sade was very much involved in the building of the house, and when the construction was completed, she was personally responsible in designing the interiors, choosing the type of curtains and furniture, including the flora needs of the exterior. Her husband was spending a lot of hours at the office, so Sade was busy helping with the construction project. "If I wasn't busy with a hammer and nails, wallpaper, or helping the plumber, I was running back and forth to Yaba or Lagos Island picking out interior decorations. My neighbors and relatives thought I was doing something crazy. After all, building a home is a job for the man." Through this, Sade gained some experience in interior designing and decoration.

Working for a Large Chain in Lagos Island

Sade began helping friends with their interior decorating. A friend of her husband, Kemi Olufemi, suggested that she works in a departmental store located in the business district of Lagos that was just expanding into the provision of interior decorations and affiliated products. Incidentally, Sade had gone to that shop on several occasions while doing her purchases and the general manager had noticed her. Kemi, the family friend, also was impressed by the well-organized clippings and folders that she brought to their house. One day Kemi took her to the general manager of the departmental store. Sade also brought with her the clippings and folders she had made. The general manager was impressed and offered Sade an opportunity to work with the store in the newly created interior decorating department. Sade was not interested at that time because she had just enrolled for a course in basic accounting at a local private tutorial college. "I have been watching you for four months, and I know you are what I need," the manager said. Finally, Sade consented to work on Saturdays beginning in December after the semester concluded. The manager agreed, and Sade continued for two months under this arrangement. Then in March, she began working full time and set up the interior design department. During the next five years, she was highly successful and reached the point where she was earning a very handsome salary including commission and bonus. For the Ikeja area where they built their house and the costs of their three children' education, this was a high income and an excellent supplement to Dayo's salary.

One day, Sade realized she was "working around the clock for another company." She would get up at 5 a.m. to figure bids, report to the store at 8 a.m., oversee installations, and then come home to figure more bids at night. She was also very concerned about the transportation problem driving from her Ikeja residence to Lagos Island with her car. The daily journey from Ikeja to Lagos and the return journey have already affected the durability of her car. "I really had too much clients and transportation was a very big problem," she recalled. She was overloaded and uncomfortable with carrying heavy carpet samples and wallpaper samples in and out of customers' houses. The weight of these samples was also wearing on her personal car. Finally, she requested a company van and an assistance to carry these samples. The request was received favorably, but the company never did buy the van.

Sade was also been asked to train interior decorators from other stores in the chain organization. Also, her husband's friends have introduced her to Nollywood (Nigerian film industry) directors in Lagos where she could provide her services as a stage decorator and earn extra income. "When I was training these salesmen and women, I was missing out on store sales. I was also getting behind in my work. It was a nice compliment from the store, but I got to looking at it and decided they would have to compensate me or get me some help. The strange thing was that I was feeling more fulfilled anytime I did a job for people not affiliated with my employer. I thought about resigning," Sade recalled. Later, Sade was told the company was about to promote her to the position of a regional manager. This would have meant she would be teaching even more, something she didn't enjoy. Sade decided, "I like decorating because that's my talent and my passion. That's the talent God gave me, so I'm going to stay with it."

Sade's Business Idea and Her Plan for Starting Her Own Business

Sade's passion for interior decorating was contagious and overpowering. She also felt that her employer was not catering to her needs. "At this time, I was not fulfilled in what I was doing," she blurted out. That was why Sade "decided to quit and be on her own." Other precipitated reasons, according to Sade, were the lack of a van and an assistance to help her transport decorating samples to customers' homes. She left a well-paid job to start her own business from the scratch. Dayo and Sade started their own business with a used Toyota van. The van was furnished in a way that displayed the company's merchandize. Jide's Interiors Nigeria Ltd. was thus born in 2002. The business began smoothly. All of Sade's suppliers were eager to help because they had observed her success with the departmental store. She had no trouble opening accounts with them because they knew she would be able to deliver.

After six months in business, the Toyota van became crowded. Sade told Dayo, "If we are going to do this, let's do it big." So they bought a bigger van and Sade personally designed a plush interior in the new van. Dayo, with assistance from his friends, built the interior, and they had a decorating studio on wheels. "The type of customers I want need to see what you can do the minute they step into your place," Sade commented. "I want them to think, 'If she can do this in a van, she can do my home to please me.'"

Jide's Interiors' store was located in Ikeja and occupied a large space for store and warehousing. The store allowed for increased display of many items, which were also for sale to walk-in customers. The location was leased and had three neighbor tenants: Prestige Reality, Zenith Jewelers, and Duro's Travel Services. Although, all these four businesses cater to different types of customers, they all had one thing in common, namely, upscale customers who wanted the best, whether in choices of homes or apartments, home decoration, jewels, or traveling to and from abroad. In this, Jide's Interiors was able to tap into the same clientele.

For Sade, business had been good. In fact, Sade said, "I am so busy; I cannot take everything which comes off the street. The first question I ask is: Have you been recommended? I cannot physically get to all the potential business. Therefore, I consider only those jobs I know I can get. I am really wasting time going out to bid on a job if they don't know whether they want me to do it or not. I thank Jesus for my blessings. Lately, my husband and his friends have introduced me to another business niche, which is decorating the stages and studios where they shoot films. I know this is a lucrative business area, but do I have the time and energy to do it?"

Sade was a strong believer in bringing the personal touch to a business. She always tried to bring this to her clients. Even Dayo, who found time to install all drapes and supervised carpet installation, believed in the personal touch. Sade said, "I hope our business never gets so big that we cannot personally oversee our entire job."

Sade saw her customers as upper-middle class and upper class Nigerians, 35-56 years old, both Christians and Moslems, and especially the rich educated ones who want "good taste in their homes." She believed that the city of Lagos and its suburban areas would provide the customers she is looking for.

The Product/Service Mix

Contract sales provided about 75 percent of the total business volume of Jide's Interiors. Contract sales were those sales made to interior decorating clients - individual homeowners or business owners. Sade occasionally contracted with builders for the decorating of new houses. Recently, because of the high growth rate of residential construction and new property development in the surrounding areas and Lekki Peninsula, the business has expanded into areas that are outside of Jide's core competencies. The main products, which sold in contract jobs, were carpet, vinyl floor covering, draperies, and wallpaper. Because of its involvement in the film or video producing business, furnishing became another service offered by the company. Drapery sales and furnishing contracts constituted 60 percent of the contract sales, and Sade was happy with this situation because of the higher markup associated with draperies. Since competition was much greater in carpeting and furnishing, these products produced a much lower markup. The remaining 25 percent of business volume came from in-store sales of tables, flora items, lamps, ceiling fans, paints, wallpapers, and other decorative accessories.

Promotional Practices:

Most of Sade's promotion had been accomplished through the recommendations of satisfied customers (referrals). Customers who had known Sade when she worked for the departmental store recommended her to their friends. When Jide's Interiors was initially "garaged" at Dayo and Sade's home, few people knew that the business existed. Sade did not advertise in the local newspapers. Nor did she advertise on the local radio. For one, she did not have the means to do so.

Sade, however, was using direct mail advertising because it was cheaper. She had done all the design work for the firm's stationery and for print advertising. She felt very strongly that this was an effective medium for her business. These were either mail out or where hand-delivered to selected upper class prospective customers. These mail-outs were primarily a reminder that her store was there and that she was available. The mailing lists came mainly from an internal file of satisfied customers and prospective ones suggested by friends and existing customers. This file was updated to remove customers who had not visited the store after about three mail-outs.

More importantly, Sade offers exceptional customer service, making people feel comfortable and appreciated. "I've known my customers so long, I can go on buying trips, see a drapery or a dinning table, or a carpet and say, 'That's for the Segun family, and that's for Ike's house,'" she said. "We can spend a couple of hours just visiting my customers. There I would discuss with them the latest designs and fashion in interior decoration. I would suggest to them when their chairs, carpets, wallpapers, and other home accessories are due for replacement." Sade also offers her customers free evaluation and delivery. Four times a year the Olajide family hosts parties where existing customers are invited. These customers were encouraged to come along with their friends. According to Sade, "There is a danger of going overboard and becoming too friendly and generous with customers and you forget you are in business," Sade commented. "But if my prices can allow me to provide that level of service and get more customers, I think I'm doing the right thing. Unlike most people, we take customer satisfaction very seriously. We know that without customers, we have no business."

Jide's Interiors' yearly promotional expenditures were planned at the beginning of the year when the master budget was finalized. Sade, with the help of an accountant, forecasted the expenses and the sales needed to meet these expenses. Break-even sales were around N650, 000 per month. In the master budget, Sade included an advertising budget because she believed that advertising was important. In 2003, she allowed approximately N50, 000 of the total budget per month for promotion. Most of her promotion emphasized home decoration items. Sade reasoned, "I want people to come in and buy home decoration items. I want my customers to get used to having a home with latest brand in furnishing. My involvement with the film producing industry in Nigeria has helped a lot to sell my ideas to my customers," she said.

Employees of Jide's Interiors

The business had only three full time employees and four part-time helpers. According to Sade, "Funke and Martin are the only persons beside me who get outside the business and work with clients." Sade wanted to remain as the designer-buyer for the store but willing to take on another designer. She was also looking for someone to manage the home accessory department of the store and someone to help in fixing accessories in customers' residences. She wanted one of the full-time employees to pre-interview other employees, but she wished to make the final decisions.

Case Discussion Questions

1. What type of promotion would "fit" Jide's Interiors' customers?

2. Evaluate the promotional practices of Jide's Interiors. What is your opinion?

3. Should Sade continue to advertise when she already has more business than she can handle? If yes why? If no, why not?

4. Evaluate the source of Sade's business idea and how it relates to the promotional activities adopted by Jide's Interiors.

5. How can Jide's Interiors grow and also retain the personal touch that is so important to Sade?

Chapter 11

GROWTH AND ORGANIZATIONAL STRATEGIES FOR THE ENTREPRENEURIAL FIRM

"The sure path to oblivion is to stay where you are" (Bernard Fauber).

CHAPTER LEARNING OBJECTIVES
After studying this chapter, you should be able to:

1. Understand the factors that affect the growth of a business.

2. Understand the concept of the organizational life cycle and how to manage a business according to the stage it finds itself in the cycle.

3. Understand the types of competitive strategies suitable in the organization's process and stages of growth.

4. Understand and manage growth strategies when a business grows outside of its market or industry.

5. Understand human resource practices and strategies as they apply to the entrepreneurial firm.

6. Understand how to manage succession in a firm as it grows.

INTRODUCTION: THE CHALLENGE OF MANAGING TRANSITION

You will recall that one of the stated problems facing entrepreneurial development in Sub-Saharan Africa is that of managing growth. This is to say that sometimes it is easy to start a business. However, it can become extremely difficult to manage the transition from an entrepreneurial firm to medium-sized or large corporation. The difference between an entrepreneurial firm and a small business lies in the area of managing growth and the transitional strategies adopted. As we pointed out in chapter five, many organizations owe their existence to the individual efforts of entrepreneurs. New organizations are formed as entrepreneurs devote time and effort and assume personal financial, psychological, and social risks to introduce innovations. The formation and the survival of an organization during its formative stages might depend on the individual efforts, leadership characteristics and personality of its founder. The problem with entrepreneurial leadership, however, is that it is personalized. Although entrepreneurs are visionaries who value the autonomy to make decisions as they see fit and to take personal responsibility for those decisions in order to realize their visions, this kind of leadership may not be useful during the growth and transitional stage of the firm.[1]

The breed of successful entrepreneurs consists of business owners who successfully managed the growth of their businesses through various types of growth and competitive strategies. For example, Aliko Dangote, the chairman of Dangote Group started small and his business empire is seen today as one of the largest in Africa. He was able to achieve this feat because he successfully transformed a small trading business, which he started in 1977 at the age of 21, to a global company in many industries through the adoption of inward looking and growth strategies. Unlike Aliko Dangote, many small business owners remained small business owners because they were unable to plan for the growth of their business or were unable to manage the growth of their businesses. Vernon Ellis, the international chairman of Accenture (the global accounting firm) noted that the Nigerian business owner lacks what it takes to become an entrepreneur. He says, "Every entrepreneurial individual who have a bright idea and have something going make often-start-ups. Often, however, these same people do not have the qualities to manage the growth of their businesses."[2]

The challenges of growth, as have been pointed out, define entrepreneurship. There are circumstances in the business environment that force entrepreneurs to face growth such as new emerging markets and new product or service development. In such situations, rigidity is the last baggage an entrepreneur would want to carry along. As a business owner, one thing is certain: You cannot be too rigid in the way you manage your business. You will be faced with the challenge of growth. Success in your business calls for sound entrepreneurial leadership. On the other hand, you might be faced with the challenges of decline. Whichever way, your organizational and management practices must not be built on rigidity. As a founder of a business, it is your dream to expand.

Expansion creates both managerial and organizational problems for the owner, for management, and for the employees. To understand the problems of transition, one must be able to understand how organizations grow and the stages they pass through.

Remember that in chapter eight, we talked about the life cycle of an industry and in chapter ten we talked about the product life cycle. In this chapter, we will discuss the concept of the organizational life cycle: the different stages your firm must through in its process of development. Within each stage of the growth process, there are appropriate strategies for managing growth. Thus, this chapter examines the concept of organizational life cycle in order to properly understand the types of strategies appropriate for each stage in the growth process. Second, an entrepreneur must be able to understand the factors that affect growth in order to manage growth successfully. Third, entrepreneurs must also understand the mechanisms involved in growing within a given industry and the idea of expanding beyond ones' given markets. Fourth, expansion involves the issue of staffing and managing the human resources in your firm. If you manage it well, it can become your strength. On the other hand, if your human resources (the people who work in your organization) are not well managed, consider this as a big weakness. Especially in a family owned and operated business, the idea of staffing and managing succession is very crucial in terms of entrepreneurial success.

Numerous studies indicate that if you start and run your own business and do all the things that have been discussed in the preceding chapters, there are good chances that you will not be among the large number of entrepreneurs who fail or who start small and remain small. You are on your way to success, reaching the stage that causes the worst problems for many business owners – how to manage growth. The way an entrepreneur manages the small firm at its start-up stage is fundamentally different from the way he or she manages the firm at its growth stage. Remember that solutions to yesterday's problems might not be applicable in providing answers to the challenges of today.

In as much as change is inevitable, so too is resistance to change. In any organizational setting, people have many reasons to resist change. Small business owners, for instance, resist change for fear of the unknown, insecurity, lack of a felt need to change and lack of resources. Entrepreneurs and managers must thus know how to manage resistance to change especially during periods of growth. One approach to dealing with resistance is through education and communication; another is through facilitation and support.

Growth is an inevitable outcome of a business start-up. Now, the big question becomes why business owners do not often plan for the growth of their businesses? There are several reasons: they are either too busy with the day-to-day effort of running their businesses that they do not stop long enough to raise their periscopes to see what is coming, they simply want to remain small, or they lack the expertise to manage growth. Thus, when the demand for their products or services grows, they failed to deliver because they do not have the systems and personnel in place to handle growth on demand. Small business owners who do not prepare for growth fumble around with growth, and before they know it, the business is in trouble.

As we have already pointed out, the competitiveness of a business depends on the resources at its disposal. One of those resources is the leadership and managerial skills needed to manage the growth of the business. Because managing growth is mostly affected by the ownership of the business, we will start the discussion of this chapter by examining the role of partners in the start-up process.

FINDING START-UP PARTNERS

Before we start discussing the issue of managing the growth of a business, it is important that a discussion of the type of individuals an entrepreneur brings into his or her team in the start-up stage be made. The people one brings into the business are crucial in terms of how successful a firm will become in the future. As indicated in the case of Jide's Interiors (in chapter ten), sometimes you would want to do it alone and there are times you would want to come on board with a team. An entrepreneur needs a team for several reasons. Either he or she could not provide the necessary financial resources needed to finance the business or the human resources needed to manage the business. In the first case, you will need someone as a partner who is willing to invest his or her money in the business. In the second case, you form a start-up team because the skills residing on the individual members of a team provide a synergistic effect that gives your business a competitive advantage.

If an entrepreneur decides to use a team to start a venture, the first place to begin looking for help is among people you know (friends, colleagues from your present or former employer, college friends, family, and so on). The practice of hiring the people you know can be good, but it can also be bad. As an entrepreneur, one obviously needs to know his or her partners well so one can trust them. Similarly, friends and family members definitely fit that criterion. On the other hand, the entrepreneur is also constrained by this criterion, as he or she must choose people who bring the skills and expertise needed to complement the ones the entrepreneur has. Sometimes, it is difficult to find such qualifications among friends or relatives.

Starting a new business can be a stressful and tiring experience even with family members and close friends to share the burden. Many entrepreneurs will tell you that they were able to start their businesses through assistance from friends or relatives who believed in their business ideas. When the venture is going well as planned, everyone is happy. If things start going wrong, you may lose more than your business; you may lose a friend. Those who want to be entrepreneurs should beware! The old saying rings true: Money from family or friend is the most expensive money you will ever get, because if you lose it, you will pay for it for the rest of your life.

Having said that, there are many successful entrepreneurs who have started their businesses with their wives or husbands and they are still married and others who have established successful businesses with their friends and still remained friends. For example, some of the most successful newspapers and newsmagazines in Nigeria such the *Newswatch* and *Tell* magazines are the products of friends or colleagues coming together to produce something great. The celebrated success of the Ibru Organization in Nigeria is a product of four brothers and spouses working together as a cohesive team. So, it can work out if you know the rules. The question becomes what are the rules?

Whatever the case, the first test of a durable start-up hinges on the quality of the individuals that make up the firm's workforce and effective human resources planning. Human resource planning, as we shall see later in this chapter, is the process of analyzing an organization's human resource needs and determining how best to fill them.

The Rules with Family and Friends

When going into business with family or friends, an entrepreneur must try as much as possible to separate business issues from social ones. In other words, an entrepreneur must leave business issues at the business and family issues at home, friendly issues at a social place, charity issues at a charity house and religious issues at the church or mosque. Many business owners experiencing a problem with the business do not intend to put it behind them when they go home. They would rather discuss it with the spouse, a friend at the club or with a church member at the church. There is nothing wrong with the owner of a business doing all these, because as a business owner, you must trust someone. But when it comes to trusting people in a business relationship (those you do business with), trust is a critical issue here. It goes beyond trusting and relying on your friends and members of your family. Here are some tips about deciding whether to include friends and family on your start-up:

> *Synergistic effect*: Make sure that you all have someone in your team whose skills add to or complement your skills. Choose friends or family members as your business partners because they have skills and expertise you need or contacts that can help make the business successful, not because they are your friends or family members.

> *Choose Partners with similar work ethics*: Most successful entrepreneurs have very strong work ethics – ready to work eighteen hours a day. As an entrepreneur it is important that one chooses someone as a partner that has the same or similar work ethics. If one of the partners is a workaholic and the other is a slacker, they are not going to work well together.

> *Choose partners with objective views:* Remember that friends and family do not view you or your business objectively, so if they are part of your start-up team, make sure that your advisory board is comprised of people who have more objective views.

> *Defining responsibility*: Agree on whom is responsible for what. For example, if your expertise is money, then your decision is the one that counts when you cannot agree with your partner on an issue related to money. Similarly, if your partner's expertise is marketing and you have a disagreement on a strategy, your partner's wishes should take precedence over yours. That way you will not have any stalemates and you will not argue so much.

> *Separate business issues from your home*: If you are working with a spouse, make it a rule never to bring the business into the bedroom (for that matter, into any part of your home). Spending extra time at the office helps settle differences before going home. Your home represents a haven for you, not another battle ground.

> *Third party*: If a friend or family member is not working out as you had hoped, then it is time to bring in a third party who can either help you resolve the issue or be the one to suggest that this person needs to leave the business. That way, you at least have a chance of saving the personal relationship.

Putting Everything in Writing
There are several instances in which many business owners go into business with people they like and trust only to have things go the opposite direction because of one reason or the other. Most people will agree that none of us can predict what life may throw at us tomorrow. That is why it is important that a partnership agreement must always be signed before any business undertaking is formulated and implemented. In many business relationships, such a document is known as "Memorandum of Understanding" and it stipulates the obligations, duties and responsibilities of all parties to a business venture. It is for the parties to sign a partnership agreement because treating your business relationship in a business manner helps you avoid the grief that lurks down the road. In fact, such a business agreement is just like prenuptial agreements. You may flinch at suggesting a written agreement to a friend or family member, but do it anyway, especially if you are not equal partners in the venture.

Forming a Board of Advisors
In the developing countries, most people live in societies where the success of an individual depends, in most cases, on the contribution provided by others, without compensation. There is the saying that it "takes a village to bring up a child". There are several people in your community who are ready to bring up your business without expecting payments as you have in a modern corporation with board of directors.

In the beginning, you typically do not have all the resources necessary to hire all the expertise you need. You certainly cannot afford an in-house attorney or accountant, and you may be relying on your brother, uncle, or aunt, or your former college teacher, who is willing to donate services for a time. A board of advisors comes in handy in these situations, bringing together people who believe in you and in what you are trying to do. The board members provide experience, guidance, information, services, network, and many times play devil's advocate, pointing out potential flaws in what you are doing. They are, essentially your reality check.

In general, members of an advisory board should consist of people in high places in the society such as attorneys, accountants, bankers, professors, consultants, politicians in various specialties, and others who are willing to provide you the advice you need to get your business running and to help you find the people and resources you need to tap into.

For the most part, boards of advisors serve without compensation (although that is certainly not always true). Many entrepreneurs offer a great dinner at meetings, which may be from two to four times a year. If possible, offering to cover your advisors' expenses for attending the meetings is expected, especially if they travel a great distance. Advisors expect that you may be calling them for advice from time to time, but do not abuse the time they are essentially donating. Unlike a board of director, members of your board of advisor are there to help you. They have no stake in your business in terms of financial reward.

IDENTIFYING FACTORS THAT AFFECT GROWTH

When an entrepreneur plans to design an effective growth strategy, he or she must understand all of the factors that affect the firm's ability to grow. As an entrepreneur it is important to start with the following areas:

The Intentions About the Business
As an entrepreneur, you may be surprised to discover that business owners do not always want to grow their businesses substantially. They are perfectly happy running their little shops just the way they are. Probing a little deeper, you may find that the decision not to grow is rooted in fear. With a small business, you can pretty much control everything, but when your business grows rapidly, you begin relying on other people. For some entrepreneurs, delegating authority for their businesses to others is hard, like handing your child over into the care of someone else. Before your business can grow, you must want it to grow; it does not normally happen by itself.

The Ability to Pull Together the Right Team for Growth
No matter how much you believe in your growth strategy, you cannot do it alone. You need a team of people as committed to your business as you are. Conveying your vision of company growth and convincing everyone to buy into it is critical to the successful execution of your growth plan.

The Nature of the Target Market
How much your company can grow is a function of the size of your market and the buying power of your customers. If your market is small and not showing signs of growth, achieving high levels of growth may be impossible. On the other hand, if your product or service has global potential, substantial growth is definitely within the realm of possibility.

The Nature of the Competition in Your Industry or Market
Why would anyone enter a market where giants play? Going head-to-head with the big guys is not a good strategic plan in most cases; unless you can create a niche in that market that no one is serving. That way you can gain a foothold before the big companies find you. Older stable industries are tough to grow unless you introduce an innovative product, service, or new technology.

How Innovative is the Industry
If your industry is not known for its innovations, your firm can gain a competitive advantage by introducing something new. On the other hand, if you are in a highly innovative industry like software, you must quickly produce a constant stream of innovations to grow.

The Importance of Intellectual Property Rights

Not many industries exist today where intellectual property is not critical to long-term success. Owing patents, trademarks, and copyrights is the key to entering some industries and providing barriers to entry for others. If you cannot gain access to the intellectual property you need through licensing, it may be difficult to grow. Innovation is the key word here. A product or service that can easily be duplicated by potential competitors does not provide the competitive advantage you need to grow in the long run.

Barriers to Entry

Your ability to grow your firm is also affected by barriers to entry that others in the industry set up to keep you out. Those barriers can take the form of intense research and development, heavy expenditures in plant and equipment, contracts with key supply channels, or regulations, to name but a few. In general, there are two ways to grow your business. On the one hand, you can grow within your industry or market. On the other hand, you can grow outside of your market or industry.

GROWTH STRATEGIES WITHIN THE MARKET

Most new businesses attempt to grow as much as possible within their current markets before taking on new markets. That kind of growth makes sense financially and in the owner's ability to concentrate his or her core competence within a particular industry or market. Growing within a firm's current market implies increasing the number of customers and volume of sales to those who patronize the market. In strategic management, we call this *market penetration* and *focus strategy*. Let us now look at the methods or strategies for doing that.

Market Penetration

One of the first growth strategies that businesses use is *market penetration*. You increase sales to current customers by doing a better job of advertising and promotion. You are gradually increasing the number and type of customers you serve. Suppose, for example, that your firm provides distilled water to households. You may extend your product to small and mid-sized companies or extend your reach beyond your current geographical area. After solidifying each customer group, you move on to the next group. Another way of achieving market penetration is by finding additional uses for your product, luring customers away from your competitors, and educating nonusers the benefits of your product or service.

When you use *market development* as your growth strategy, you are expanding your product or service market into a broader geographic area. For example, if your company starts in the Lagos area, you may begin moving into the Abuja area. One of the more popular ways of growing geographically is by franchising. You are no doubt familiar with the popularity of this strategy considering such famous franchises as Mr. Bigg's, McDonald's, Sheraton Hotel, Hilton Hotel, etc. Another way of expanding geographically is to build offices or branches in other parts of the country, as you know you are serving the same type of customer groups although they are located outside of your immediate geographic area.

A third way to grow in the current market is developing new products and services for the customers you have. The goal is selling more to your current customers because they are the easiest sales you have. For example, John Bamiyo opened a hotel in 2001 providing simply room services. Over the years he learned that his customers wanted more services and products. He opened a bar to serve their needs. Even those who are not regular guests now come to have their drinks at the hotel. Later, he added a club where regular customers and others can come and dance. Finally, he added a sport bar, where customers and non-customers can come and watch games. What Mr. Bamiyo tried was to regularly upgrade his product and services to newer versions, thereby attracting new customers.

Your present customers are the best source of ideas for product and service innovations. Most of these ideas come in form of improvements to existing products (*incremental innovation*), but once in a while you uncover an idea for an entirely new product that can be a tremendous source of growth for your company. These breakthrough products are not something you can plan. They usually surface during intense brainstorming sessions or when customers, suppliers, or employees suggest them. Breakthrough products usually require a much longer product development cycle and cost more to develop than incremental products.

One of your more important products or services – and many entrepreneurs do not realize this – is your company and what it stands for (your brand). Too many entrepreneurs focus exclusively on promoting their products and services and forget their company images – their brands, which are far more valuable assets than any products or services. If you establish brand recognition for your firm, marketing any new products or services that you develop is by far easier. When customers associate the name of your company with quality, service, reliability, and great products and services, that brand becomes an umbrella under which you can add new ways of serving the customer.

The classic examples of the effectiveness of branding are apparel companies that do not design their own clothes but put their branding on articles of clothing they purchase from a commodity apparel manufacturer. Nike, for example, purchases T-shirts from apparel manufacturers such as Hanes and prints their logo on them. This company, and many others, finds that customers actually pay more for the same T-shirt with a Nike design on it than for the same T-shirt with no design or the design of a lesser-known company.

As we discussed in chapter ten, creating a brand is crucial for marketing your product or service. Creating a brand is thus an essential part of developing new products and services. Actions you can take to start creating brand recognition for your company include:

> *Brainstorming all of the things that your company is good at doing.* What is special about your company? Do you offer the highest quality products or services? Do you have a better service? Is your company culture unique?

> *Selecting your biggest strengths to serve as the focus of all your marketing efforts.* Make sure customers see the strengths associated with your company's name again and again so that the two become synonymous.

> *Decide how your brand name will be used.* You must create rules for the consistent use of your brand name. For example, make sure that the company name is always displayed with the product or service that you are promoting. If you want your company to be associated with the highest quality, you probably would not promote it in an environment that is not perceived as such.

> *Getting feedback from your customers.* Conduct blind tests with customers to see how they are responding to your branding efforts. Then adjust your strategy based on what you find out.

Growing Within an Industry through Acquisitions

Within an industry or market, a firm can grow or expand by acquiring or teaming with other companies in the industry and in its distribution channel. One way to expand and achieve growth is through a process known as *vertical integration*. In vertical integration, the growth of a company can occur either through moving upstream or downstream in the process of delivering its product or service to the end user. As we pointed out in chapter nine, vertical integration is the degree to which a firm operates vertically in multiple locations on an industry's value chain from extracting raw materials to manufacturing and retailing.

When a firm moves upstream in its channel, it gains control of its suppliers by acquiring them, by securing exclusive contracts, or by starting a supply outlet of its own. Gaining control of upstream activities in the channel is popular with firms using a just-in-time approach to production. Doing so enables them to receive raw materials and supplies exactly when they are needed without carrying an inventory. This control saves time and money and significantly reduces the cost of production.

When gaining control of downstream activities in a firm's value chain, management is controlling the distribution of the firm's product or service by either selling directly to the customer (for example, it purchases a retail or wholesale outlet) or acquiring the distributors of its products or services.

What the owner and/or management can control is a function of two factors: where the firm's expertise or core competence lies in its value chain and how profitable it is for the firm to perform certain activities rather than paying others to perform them. As a retailer, for example, the firm already controls the downstream portion because it sells directly to the consumer. The firm can control its sources of supply upstream as a way of growing within its industry. Likewise, if the firm is a supplier, the only upstream activities it is able to control are the actual sources of raw material (in other words, lumber mills for lumber and paper goods or the production of its own meat to resell) or the distributors from which it gets its supplies for resale.

Moving Horizontally in The Channel

A business can also grow within its own industry through *horizontal integration* or by acquiring its competitors or starting a competing business. A horizontal integration is the degree to which a firm operates in multiple geographic locations at the same point in an industry's value chain. Suppose you own a theme restaurant catering to customers who like sports and your restaurant is located in the northern part of the city. One way you can grow into other areas of the city is to acquire one or more of your competitors that are located where you want to be.

Another way to grow horizontally in the channel is for the firm to manufacture its product under another label, reaching a different customer segment. For example, some established high-end apparel designers reach the mass markets by producing a line of apparel under a different label, a strategy that is also common in the major appliance and grocery industries. Major retailers put their brands on products made by others expressly for that purpose.

Creating a Network in the Industry

The newest way to grow is developing strategic alliances with other actors in the industry, so that the owner or management can focus on what the company does best and rely on its network for everything else that the company needs. These alliances enable the firm and its management to work with the best suppliers and distributors, grow more rapidly, keep its unit costs down, and develop new products more quickly. Another benefit is that, because investing heavily in fixed assets no longer is a necessity, the owner and management of the firm can devote those resources to finding new competitive advantage. Even if the owner and/or management have a service business, they can take advantage of this strategy by forming strategic alliances with companies that are the best in accounting, payroll, telemarketing, and data processing.

STRATEGIES FOR DIVERSIFYING OUTSIDE THE INDUSTRY

Many successful entrepreneurs in the developing countries seem to be those that have diversified outside of their core industry. As we pointed out in chapters one and two, entrepreneurs are those who are able to identify new business opportunities and capitalize on them. For example, successful Nigerian entrepreneurs such as Aliko Dangote and Michael Ibru have all diversified outside of their core business areas as a result of their entrepreneurial ability to identify opportunities in a developing and emerging market. When you see, for example, an entrepreneur who started and build his or her business within the food industry (e.g., Ibru) and latter expand to different industries such hotel/hospitality, banking and publishing, you have a good picture of what we call diversification outside of ones' core industry (or unrelated diversification). Take for example, an entrepreneur who is in the business of interior designing, the business is growing and wants to branch out into real estate business. These two businesses are unrelated and we call this diversifying outside of your industry. As a rule, one must exploit all of the opportunities in his or her current market and industry before moving into areas that are unrelated in the form of a new industry. However, entrepreneurs have succeeded in using a diversification strategy early in the growth process. Situations in which such a strategy makes the most sense include the following:

- The company has excess capacity or spare resources that are not in use. Making use of them provides a new revenue stream for it.
- Existing or potential customers are asking the company to provide them with products or services that are outside of its current industry.
- The owner and/or management foresee major changes in the industry forcing them to look outside for growth.

Capitalizing on the Synergy of Like Businesses

The easiest way of diversifying so that a firm makes the most of what it already has is to find products, services, or businesses that are technologically similar and complimentary to its existing business. This is called *synergistic diversification*. For example, a restaurant chain may acquire a bakery to bring down the costs of supplying baked goods to its chain. A sporting goods store may go into the pub business in order to draw more customers during major sport events such the world cup, the African Nation's Cup, or other major league soccer events. Such a store provides itself not only promotional opportunity, but also drawing more customers to its base.

Acquiring an Unrelated Business

When a business owner acquires a business that has no relationship to his or her core business area, the growth strategy adopted is called *conglomerate diversification*. The idea of expanding a business outside of an entrepreneur's core competence is worth discussing because acquiring a business that is unrelated to your core competence can be a source of success or failure in your entrepreneurial goal. You do not want to become a conglomerate without ensuring your core business is in a healthy position. Because no synergies exist between the two businesses, they operate like two completely different entities. Large corporations, such as UACN and the Dangote Group in Nigeria have diversified into unrelated business units for two reasons: they were able to identify a niche and they have the resources to fill the identified niches. As indicated in chapter six, many of the business units within the UACN conglomerate are not related. They have no synergistic effects (with the exemption of a few such as the food divisions and the transportation divisions). So, why do many entrepreneurs try conglomerate diversification? The answer is that entrepreneurs do it because they have found new areas of doing business and it sometimes enables them to gain control of a business function that can ultimately help them.

Whenever you acquire another business, particularly one that is completely different from yours, working with someone who is experienced in mergers and acquisitions are a necessity. You will also want to ask the following questions:

> Are the cultures of the two companies compatible? Do not focus only on financial and operational synergies?
> Are the leadership styles of management compatible?
> Will you be better off a year from now having acquired this business?

Going Global to Grow

As was pointed out in chapter one of this book, we are all living in a global economy. Whether one lives and does business in Lagos, Johannesburg, London, Singapore, or Houston, there is no way one can escape the hands of global competition and global business; the reality of today's business competition demands that companies go global in order to survive and to remain competitive. The reason is simple: E-commerce. And if a firm does business on the Internet, it has already become a global business whether its owners or management wanted to or not. Similarly, the point is not whether a firm should go global, but rather when should it should go global? Several reasons why the owner(s) and/or management need to consider the global marketplace in planning and managing the growth are as follow:

a) The Internet brings the world to the firm's doorstep. The owner/management may find that their best suppliers, distributors, and customers are located in other countries.

b) The Internet also brings the firm's competitors to its doorstep. Today, even if you have a local business, your competitors can pounce on your market from anywhere in the world with the click of a mouse button and the overnight delivery capability of companies like global postal firms.

c) Shortened product lives and costly research and development force a company to enter more than one major market to start out just so it recap the costs of product development more quickly. The global marketplace is a major supporter of businesses introducing new products.

d) The owner or management may find new markets for the firm's products that are already losing their luster here in its geographical market area (the furniture industry in Nigeria is an example). Management may also find complementary products or services produced in other countries that it can add to the firm's product line.

e) Exporting to countries is now easier than before if one knows the laws governing trade in other countries. One can find untapped markets in new areas like the former Communist Europe, China and the United States of America where there is a growing population of immigrants from the African continent and Southeast Asia.

Never before in the history of the world have there been such interesting and exciting business opportunities. The opening of the once-controlled economies of Eastern Europe and Central Europe, the former U.S.S.R., and the People's Republic of China to market-oriented enterprise provides a myriad of possibilities for entrepreneurs wanting to launch businesses in a foreign country. Presently, many Western multinationals are seeking suppliers of input from the developing countries. Thus, the internationalization of entrepreneurship has created opportunities also for the African entrepreneur.

The Readiness to go Global

Most new businesses do not begin exporting until they establish their businesses domestically, because global markets present entirely new issues that must be dealt with. Likewise, most entrepreneurs with start-ups are busy enough just establishing their products and services in the domestic market. In the case of African Independent Television (AIT) discussed in chapter two and six, a huge potential in the international market was projected and it was realized that Nigerians and Africans in North America and Europe have demand for Nigerian television programming. But before taking that leap to go international, the management of *AIT* in Nigeria had to perform serious market research, search for distributors or agents who understand the broadcasting practices in the international markets. Doing that right took important resources away from their focus on building their presence in the Nigerian domestic market.

There are certain business attributes that serve as precursors of greater success for businesses deciding to go global. Ask yourself whether you or your business has the following attributes:

- Do you have a global vision from the inception of your business?
- Do you have a management team with international experience?
- Do you have a strong international network of contacts you can tap?
- Do you have a product or service that is in great demand in other countries?
- Do you have a unique intangible asset in your business such as know-how that no one else has?
- Can you derive additional products and services from your core business area by going international?
- Do you have systems and controls in place that will work in the international environment?

Going global also demands that one knows that exporting or importing is a long-term commitment. An entrepreneur who intends to go global may not make money for some time, so he or she must be in a position to suffer some losses for a while.

ORGANIZING FOR GROWTH

In a business world running at Internet speed, how an entrepreneur organizes the company and how it is staffed with the right people become critical issues that can either facilitate the growth of the company or ensure that it does not grow. As we discussed in chapter five, when a company goes beyond survival stage and enters a rapid growth stage, not only that cash flows remains a vital issue, but also staffing and management systems begin to compete for the owners' attention. The challenge becomes how to balance limited resources against the need to take on more staff. Needless to say, in planning for growth, the owner(s) must also plan for the potential addition of employees and management to the team.

Furthermore, as the business grows, the owner or management must maintain the entrepreneurial spirit that got them to this point, because that spirit is essential to the company's ability to navigate in a fast-moving global environment. By now the owner(s) or management should be aware that there are fundamental shifts and changes in the way management is practiced, including leadership styles. In this era of globalization and rapid technological changes, more and more companies have abandoned the top-down, chain-of-command hierarchical structure for more fluid structures that encourage employee empowerment, participation, and open-book management styles. As we noted earlier, many businesses have found out that rigid structures do not respond well to fast-changing environments. In fact, one of the problems facing organizational transition is the rigidity with which owners manage their firms. A rigid approach to management does not work well in an ever-changing business environment of today.

Moving from Entrepreneurship to Professional Management

The success of the growth strategy of a business depends on the ability to move from entrepreneurial style of management to a professional one. This is what we call adapting to changing circumstances, such as growth in your organization. Adapting to changes in the environment does not mean that you leave your entrepreneurial spirit behind – far from it. Changing to professional management implies that the skills you need to rapidly grow your company are quite different from the skills you need to start your company. In fact, sometimes the skills that launch your venture – taking a risk, controlling attitude, being a deviant person, following your dreams, and so forth – can propel it out of control during a rapid growth cycle.

Many entrepreneurs do not have strong enough professional management skills; rather, they are by nature resource gathers, when what the company needs most as it grows are people who can manage resources. The reality is that most entrepreneurs do not enjoy the management aspect of business, so they leave it to others who are better at it. An entrepreneurial firm requires an entrepreneurial mindset and a growing business requires both entrepreneurial and managerial mindset.

In general, entrepreneurs are driven by an opportunistic attitude, while managers are generally driven by the need to manage resources that have been put together. Entrepreneurs work with limited budget, while managers are typically given a budget within which they must strive to stay. Entrepreneurs tend to break the rules and create brand-new ways of doing things. Managers, for the most part, work in a more evolutionary fashion, building on what already exists, improving and refining it. Entrepreneurial organizations are generally flat, which means that they do not involve layers of management. Everyone works together as a team, quite unlike the layers of management found in most large organizations.

If you are making the transition from entrepreneurial management style to a professional one:

> ➤ Recognize that a change in your management structure must take place before growth begins.
> ➤ Get help putting formal decision systems in place that give more people authority and responsibility over major decisions for the company.
> ➤ Make sure that any functions of your business that are critical (life and death) to the success of the business are not in the hands of only one person. If that person left, you would be in big trouble.
> ➤ Carefully evaluate your growth strategy and make sure that the systems and procedures you have put in place match your strategies.
> ➤ Establish a board of directors, if you do not already have one.

THE CULTURE OF A COMPANY: DISCOVERING THE SOUL OF YOUR BUSINESS

Every company has values, a personality, and distinct way of doing things that you recognize the minute you spend any time at all inside that company. Any visitor to a company will immediately recognize the way things are done in that company. As a company grows, its culture or the ways things are done must be properly managed. A chief executive officer of a large American company (Wayne Leonard, CEO of Entergy) says, "The biggest levers you've got to change a company are strategy, structure, and culture. If I could pick two, I'd pick strategy and culture."[3] As an entrepreneur or a small business owner, the way you do things in your company affect the way you put your strategy together and make your company competitive. The importance of strategy has been so much discussed in this book. However, your strategy means nothing if the internal work climate and the personality of the company do not support it. That is why we should talk about the way you do your business (not your strategy). We will call this your corporate culture. The concept of corporate culture has been defined and explained in many ways, but for our purpose in this section, corporate culture refers to the character of a company's internal work climate and personality – as shaped by its core values, beliefs, business principles, traditions, ingrained behaviors, and style of operating.[4] As an entrepreneur or a small business owner, you bring your values, your belief system, your ideology, and your personality and personal convictions to bear on the way your company is managed. This corporate culture becomes an important competitive advantage for your company. While you describe the culture of your company in a handbook or allude to it in your promotional activities, and in your mission and value statements, you see it mainly in the daily interactions of the people who work in your company.

Knowing and understanding the culture of your company is important for two reasons:

> - It gives people in your company a sense of purpose and identity and propels them to achieve the goals of your company.
> - It is a reflection of the implementation of your company vision, mission, and goals.

Many of the successful companies in the world today have a strong corporate culture that is built around the value and benefit of customers' satisfaction. For example, there are many firms that epitomize the benefits of a strong corporate culture. These companies are fanatically customer-driven. Anything they do is termed in these words: "The customer comes first." The founder of one company, located in Lagos, Nigeria believes that the only way he could compete successfully is to satisfy the customer in order for him or her to come back for business. Newly employed workers are drilled in the value of customer satisfaction. Everyone in the company, from the janitor to the CEO, knows what he or she must do to contribute to customer satisfaction. They all know that it is the customer who pays their bills.

In some of the successful entrepreneurial firms, the personality, values and belief systems of the founders are mirrored in the way business is done. Whatever the business you find yourself, as a founder or a manager, the way your company is managed is a reflection of your image and your personality. As a business owner you are required to build a cult-like culture that promotes the execution of your business strategy. That kind of cult-like culture is found in many successful Nigerian organizations like Zenith Bank (under the leadership of Jim Ovhia), Africa Independent Television (with Chief Dokpesi as a visionary leader), the Ministry of the Federal Capital Territory (under the visionary leadership of Mallam El – Rufai), the Lagos Business School (under the leadership of Professor Pat Utomi), to name a few. When employees are committed to the vision and culture of the company, they can accomplish nearly impossible feats.

How do you know what your company culture is if it is not obvious? One way to know the culture of your company is to look for the stories that get told over and over again to illustrate to new comers the importance of certain values and the depth of commitment that various company personnel have displayed. Make sure that what you *find* out matches what you *want* your culture to be. In general, the culture of your company is manifested in the values and business principles that you preach and practice, in the official policies and procedures of your firm, in your firm's revered traditions and oft-repeated stories, in the attitudes and behaviors of your self and your employees, in the peer pressures that exist to display core values, in the politics that is played in your company, in the manner in which your company approaches people and solve problems, in your company's relationships with its external stakeholders, and in the "chemistry" and the "personality" that permeate its work environment.

How Compatible is Your Culture With Your Strategy?

Your company's present culture and work environment may or may not be compatible with what is needed for you and your company to devise and implement your chosen strategy. When it does not, it is time to do something about it. Asking the following questions can help you begin to think about the kind of culture you have in your company.

> Does your company work in teams or individually? Are you someone who prefers to work individually in order to solve problems? Do you prefer to work with others whose ideas might be different from yours? Do you think that a problem can be solved by seeking ideas from your employees or by deciding on the solution yourself?

> How does your company deal with change? Are you afraid of change? Do you want things to run the way they are and not to rock the boat?

> How does your company deal with failure? Do you see failure as end of the road or as something to learn from? Would you fire your employees because they have failed?

> How does your company make decisions? Who makes the critical decisions? Do you, as the owner of the company, make all the necessary decisions or do you allow (delegate) some other persons to make some decisions? How do you share information inside and outside your company? Who do you share your information with regarding the performance of your company? Your friends? Your family members? Or your employees?

> Do you take a long-term or short-term view of decision-making? When you make decisions about your company's activities, do you look at what you can gain now or what your company can gain in the future in terms of financial gains?

> How do you make sure you have competent employees? What are the criteria you use in employing people? Competence and integrity or family and types of connections? Do you employ those who share the same value with you or those who do not?

> How do you encourage diversity? Do you employ people based on their affiliation to your family, your ethnic background, your gender belongingness or your religious affiliation? Do you employ people based on their work-related qualifications?

> How are employees treated? What does your company's vision say about employees? Do you see your employees as tools to accomplish your goals? Or do

you see them as a team working together for the benefits of your firm and for their own benefits as satisfied individuals in your company?

Your company's culture is part of its tools for competing in the market. Management and employees need to recognize and promote your company's culture in order to achieve a competitive advantage in your business. If it is strong like the culture at Zenith International Bank, which makes the satisfaction of its customers and technology the center of management philosophy and management orientation, it is your responsibility to maintain it! If does not, it your responsibility to change it.

DEVELOPING A HUMAN RESOURCE POLICY

People or the human capital side of your business is a precious organizational resource. For a company to achieve high performance on a continuing basis, no one's talents can be wasted. Successful business owners everywhere are those who take steps to unlock the full potential of those who work for them. The people who you employ make the difference on whether your company succeeds or looses in its effort to be competitive. In principle, at least, the following organizational slogans say it all; "People are our most important asset;" "Its people who make the difference;" "It's the people who work for us who ... determine whether our company thrives or languishes."[5] Such testimonials are found in newspaper and television ads, annual reports, corporate mission and values statements, corporate recruiting literature, executive speeches, and company newsletters. They communicate a very specific understanding: Even with the guidance of a clear mission and the best strategies, and even with the support of appropriate organizational structures, your firm must be well staffed with capable and committed human resources if it is to achieve the objective of the business. Today, and perhaps more than ever before, the pressure to compete in your chosen industry or market demands that you have capable people in your firm and that is why the issue of human resource management concerns you and your ability to manage your firm successfully.

Human resource management (HRM) is a term used to describe the wide variety of activities involved in attracting, developing, and maintaining a talented and committed organizational workforce. This involves a managerial responsibility not only for staffing organizations with capable workers, but also for ensuring that their performance potential is fully realized. The major elements in the human resource management process are:

> *Attracting a quality workforce*: managing human resource planning, recruitment, and selection.
> *Developing a quality workforce*: managing employee orientation, training and development, and career planning and development.
> *Maintaining a quality workforce*: managing retention and turnover, performance appraisal, compensation and benefits, and labor-management relations.

The changing role of the management of organizations whether large or small also impacts the way you as the entrepreneur make decisions in terms of who you employ and how you make them to become committed members of your organization. While a detailed discussion of all the principles of human resource management is not possible in this book, I suggest that as an entrepreneur, the following principles should promote your success in the marketplace:

- Using self-directed teams rather than departments, functions, or specific tasks. *A self-directed team* is a work group that uses consensus decision making to choose its own team members, solve job-related problems, design its own jobs, and schedule its own break time.[6] As an entrepreneur, one should not look for an employee whose knowledge is specific within a functional area. Rather, it is important to seek an employee who can apply his or her expertise across your company's functional areas. An entrepreneur should look for an employee who is literate in areas such as marketing, accounting, finance, computer, and every other essential management aspects. The reason is that you would want your employees to work as a team. To work as team, one should know the basics of general management. This strategy empowers employees and focuses everyone's energies on company goal.

- Focusing on core competencies. Those things the company does well to create value must be taken into consideration when hiring someone and see if the new employee has the qualifications that matches the company's core competence.

- Hire people who believe that the customer is supreme: Your human resource management policy should also be built around the notion that everyone you hire should be able to treat your customers as the reason why you are in business. Your recruits must accept that every thing they do, from product design to marketing to service must take the need of the customer as a priority. As pointed out earlier, the customer must always be the focus of your activities. There is no short cut to success. If that happens, it does not last long. The only way to remain in business for a long time is for you to attend to customers' demand in ways that he or she is satisfied. Similarly, everyone in your company needs to know the customer and what his or her needs are.

- Providing rewards based on team effort above rewards based on individual efforts. If you reward individuals when trying to encourage teamwork, your employees become confused. In the business world, for instance, one of the problems facing employee productivity is when an employer chooses one out of the many for promotion. This practice breeds jealousy and animosity among colleagues. One important way to provide an equitable reward system is to encourage employees to work in teams, and reward should be distributed equally according to the result accomplished by the team. The African culture, like the Chinese one, embraces collective efforts as against individual ones. Encourage your employees to work as a team.

- Providing company information with employees so they can use it to provide input and feel that they have a vested interest in the success of the company. It is in the human sense that we do not act on the basis of what we do not know. Your employees should know all that is happening in your company. In that way they know that their interest in the company is aligned with whatever they are called upon to do.

RECRUITING THE RIGHT PEOPLE

Ask any business owner what the most difficult issue he or she faces and you will hear, "finding and retaining good employees." Some business owners will tell you, "I hire him because he is my relative, and someone I know from my village recommended him." Or "I hire him because he is my friend, and I have known him for a long time, and I trusted him." Managing your business should not be a problem if you recruit the right people. Recruiting the right people can become a problem if the recruitment strategy is not properly formulated and executed. In today's career oriented society, good employees are those who want to pursue their career, earn money, while working for you. As a business owner, one problem in the management of your firm is about recruiting and keeping good employees who share the vision, mission and objective of your firm.

Second, many entrepreneurs are not effective at recruiting and hiring top talent because during the start-up, they usually had a closed-knit team that satisfied all the functions of the organization and worked well together under a common goal. Bringing new people on board is sort of a shock to the system, because they do not always fit neatly into the culture and ways things are done. But, bringing new people into the organization does not have to be such a culture shock if you spend the necessary time and effort to find the right people. Bringing new people is an added advantage if they are able to bring new ideas to the way you do your business. The culture of your company may have been detrimental to the way you do your business and everyone may have accepted this way as the fact of life in your business. New employees with new and innovative ideas can change this. The question of when to add new people to the team is extremely important for the survival and profitability of your business. Some companies take the approach of doing it when it becomes obvious that they have to. They employ new people when it is clear that it is time to delegate authority and bring in professional management to give the organization a new direction.

Recruiting is the task among all aspects of the hiring process on which entrepreneurs probably spend the least amount of time. And that is surprising because the recruiting process determines whether you ultimately get the right person for the position you want to fill. Entrepreneurs often find someone to fill a job rather than someone with the potential to fit in well and grow with the organization. Part of the fault for that slipup lies in the way they announce the opening for the position. If you describe a position solely in terms of skill requirements and function, you will probably find someone who is looking for a job rather than a career. Newly formed entrepreneurial companies need people who can perform several functions and work as a team. To recruit effectively, the entrepreneurial firm must know where and how to secure qualified applicants. The sources are numerous, and one cannot generalize about the best source in view of the variations in personnel requirements and quality of sources from one locality to another. The following tips can help one to effectively find the right people for your needs:

Have a strategic plan for attracting talent. Just like a strategic plan creates awareness for a business and gives it direction, an entrepreneur needs a similar plan to catch the attention of the best candidates for the positions he or she wants to fill. That plan spells out your strategy for proactively going after the type of people you need in simple terms: what kind of person you are looking for, where you can find him or her, and how you are going to approach that person. Help-wanted advertising serves two purposes: it advertises your company as well as it helps you gain access to numerous candidates with diverse talents. The "Help-Wanted" sign in the window of a business establishment is one form of recruitment used by small firms and a way of showcasing what your business is all about.

Identify your best employees. Most entrepreneurs can profile their best customers, but can they profile their best employees? Knowing the characteristics, skills, experience, and attitude of your best employees helps you look for those traits in your new hires. If you know what you are going after, you are more likely to find it. The small business owner or manager should analyze the functions required and determine the number and kinds of jobs to be filled. Knowing the job requirements and the capacities and characteristics of the individual applicants allows for a more intelligent selection of persons for specific jobs. In particular, the small business owner should attempt to obtain individuals whose capacities and skills complement those of the owner-manager. Again, it is worth stressing that the owner-manager should not select personnel simply to fit a rigid specification of education, experience, or personal background. Rather, the employer must concentrate upon the ability of an individual to fill a particular position in the business. The identification and evaluation of applicants, from the perspective of the small business owner, should be done on a step-by-step basis such as: (i) use of application forms, (ii) interviewing the applicant, (iii) checking references and further investigation, (iv) testing the applicant, and (v) physical examination of the applicant.

Be creative about where you find talent. Finding the required talent for a position in your company can also be accomplished when you look for it inside your company. Some companies are so concerned about hiring new people who immediately fit in with their corporate culture that the first place they look is through their current employees. If the opportunity for employees to grow and move up in your company exists, then there is no problem in hiring from inside your firm. This approach not only improves the morale of current employees but also offers an inducement for outsiders to accept employment. However, choosing this strategy means that the existing employee must be trained. In view of the fact that personal development and advancement are prime concerns of able employees, the small business can profit from paying careful attention to this phase of the management of the human resource program. To achieve this goal, on-the-job-training of current employees can facilitate in-house personnel development without bringing in outsiders who are not in sync with the culture of the firm.

Training and Development

If you are used to being a sole proprietor, training your first employee can be a challenge, says Nichole L Torres, a management consultant and author.[7] Will your new hire fit in with your business culture? How can you make sure he or she completes tasks correctly and efficiently? The biggest mistake many entrepreneurs make, says Torres, is throwing everything at the new employee at once and expecting that person to get up to speed immediately. As an employer, you need to organize the information that you are going to teach your new employees. Before a new employee's first day on the job, it is essential that a detailed list of his or her duties is created. Included in the list are: what to be expected of that person, how his or her performance will be evaluated, etc. All these are important so that the employee knows the parameters when he or she starts.

Although it can be a challenge to find the time to list all the new employee's duties, it can really help the entrepreneur or trainer to communicate clearly during the training. It may not be easy also because, as an entrepreneur, you did not probably have much prior training experience. Overall, it is important to take enough time to train, so you do not assume your new employee knows things innately. Though creating a list of duties is important, do not think you have to create a 100- page manual. What is important is hands-on training where you should demonstrate what a task looks like, and give them a chance to try it while you watch. Finally, give your newly hired employees feedback about what went well. Most adults learn quickest when there is a model of good performance.[8]

MANAGING GROWTH AND THE ORGANIZATIONAL LIFE CYCLE

As pointed out in previous chapters, human beings have a life cycle: the course of developmental changes through which a human being passes from its birth as a fertilized zygote to the mature stage and eventually death are inevitable in our lives. In the same manner, your firm has similar stages of life, or its life cycle: a progression through a series of differing stages of development. In Management and Organization Theory, we call this progression, "**the organizational life cycle.**"[9] The organizational life cycle is the evolution of an organization over time through different stages of growth. The organizational life cycle approach places the primary emphasis on the dominant issue facing the firm, as it describes how organizations grow, develop, and eventually decline (see figure 11-1). It is also the organizational equivalent of the product life cycle in marketing. These stages are Birth or start-up (stage I), Growth (stage II), Maturity (stage III), Decline (stage IV), and Death (stage V).

Figure 11-1
The Organizational Life Cycle

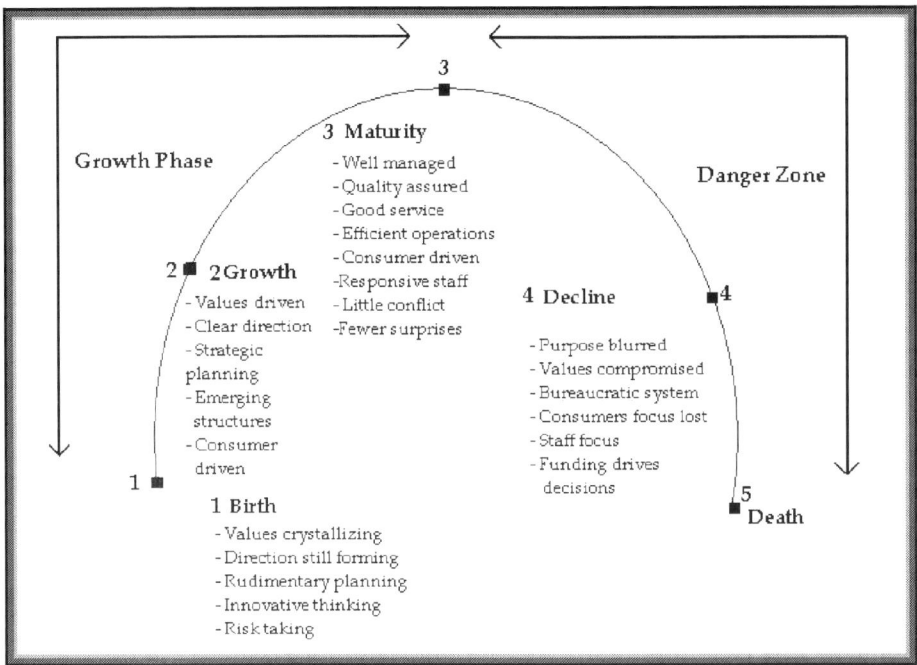

The management of each of the stages shown in figure 11-1 and described below requires a specific type of **organization structure**. Organization structure is the system of tasks, reporting relationships, and communication that links together the work of individuals and groups. Any structure should both allocate work through a division of labor and provide for the coordination of performance results so that the objectives and goals of your firm (organizational objectives) are best served. An appropriate structure that does both of these things well can be an important asset to your firm.[10]

We can understand the concept of structure best in the form of an **organization chart**, which is a diagram describing the formal arrangement of work positions within an organization. A typical organization chart shows how various positions are linked to one another through lines of authority and communication. This is the formal structure of the organization in its official state. It also represents the way the organization is intended to function.

Figure 11-2
The Simple Structure and Job Descriptions of a Small Firm (An Extra Hand)

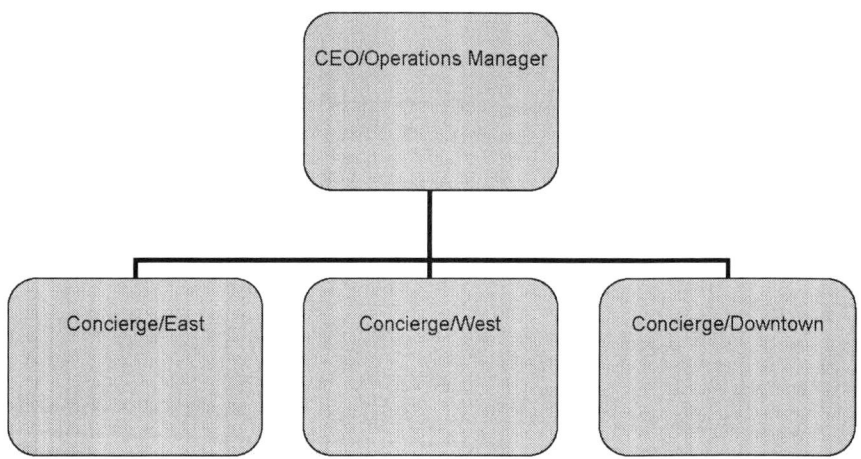

The Birth or Start-up: The Entrepreneurial Stage

The first stage in the organizational life cycle is typified by the entrepreneurial firm (the **birth stage**). The entrepreneurial stage typifies the personality of the founder of the company who is trying to promote and sell an idea (product or service). The firm in the birth stage has little formal structure, which allows the entrepreneur to directly supervise the activities of every employee. There is no clear direction yet in terms of structure and processes and planning is rudimentary without any strategic focus. The entrepreneurial stage of the organization normally exhibits an entrepreneurial culture. **Entrepreneurial culture** typifies high levels of risk taking, dynamism, and creativity. There is a commitment to experimentation, innovation, and being on the leading edge. Decision-making sessions among owners and employees with entrepreneurial mindset are characterized by debates and arguments because of absence of clear-cut policy and decision-making procedures. At this stage, the concerns of the owner are centered on securing enough start-up capital, seeking customers, and designing an effective way to deliver product or service. The role of the owner is that of doing almost everything (including, some times, the janitorial work). Cash is important, because you never have enough of it. A venture in the entrepreneurial stage normally adopts the simple structure.

The simple structure of an entrepreneurial firm (An Extra Hand Limited), as shown in figure 11-2, consists of one top manager (the CEO/Operation Manager), who is the founder or owner of the firm and three non-managerial employees who do operating work. This is a "lean" structure common to entrepreneurial organizations.[11] Because of its simplicity and small size, the owner-manager can exercise central control while still allowing others a great deal of freedom in their work.

An Extra Hand Limited is an errand service offered through large area employers and professional practices as a concierge benefit to their employees. This benefit is low cost to the employer and they provide a nominal space for **An Extra Hand** to operate and help promote the service. Employees, who are the clients, pay for the services used. Services or errands include, but are not limited to, pick-up and delivery of such items as dry cleaning, post office, and packages, and shopping for groceries, gifts, hardware, transportation of children to and from schools and other miscellaneous errands. There are no other services similar to those offered by **An Extra Hand** in the city for members of the workforce. Through this service, the firm reduces clients' gas costs, save them time in running errands, and reduce frustration at the traffic patterns and discomfort in the daytime heat and rainy days. In order to facilitate service, delivery times are scheduled with the employer and some locations may have multiple times in order to benefit employees who work second and third shifts. The company's owner serves as the CEO and Operations Manager with three concierges working under him.

Job Title: CEO/Operations Manager
Reports To: Board of Directors
Summary: Plans, organizes, directs, and coordinates the day-to-day operations of **An Extra Hand**.
Duties And Responsibilities include the following, other duties as required.
➢ Marketing:
  ✓ Develops and implements marketing plans and programs to ensure the growth of the company.
  ✓ Makes initial contact and conducts meetings with prospective clients; provides follow-up and ensures that service was provided as guaranteed.
  ✓ Solicits feedback from employers and clients to improve customer services.
➢ Operations:
  ✓ Responsible for the recruiting, training, supervising, and providing performance reviews of the concierges, taking disciplinary action when required.
  ✓ Plans, organizes, directs, and controls activities of organization.
  ✓ Resolves complaints and operating problems as needed and uses these to continually improve efficiency and effectiveness of operations.
➢ Administration:
  ✓ Responsible for cash management, accounts receivable, and accounts payable as well as coordinating with the accountant for tax reporting.
  ✓ Reconciles all client receipts with fees to ensure that concierges submit all fees on a daily basis.
  ✓ Prepares and distributes payroll.
  ✓ Insures that all insurance coverage, as required by law and recommended by the Board of Directors, is maintained.
  ✓ Responsible for the maintenance and security of vehicles and all equipment.
➢ Purchasing:

✓ Responsible for obtaining vehicles and equipment needed to accomplish the activities of the company.
✓ Responsible for obtaining contracts with grocers, dry cleaners, etc. that An Extra Hand uses. The purpose is to establish more advantageous payment terms.

Job Title: Concierge
Reports To: CEO/Operations Manager
Summary: Accumulates, consolidates, and fills clients' orders as well as collecting and remitting all fees to the Operations Manager.
Duties And Responsibilities include the following, other duties as required.
- Responsible for providing service to employers in their geographical area.
- Collects orders through electronic ordering system and ensures that all orders are recorded on receipts. If pick-up is required for same day delivery, the concierge picks up the item and collects fees, providing receipt for item and fees.
- Combines orders by store into one master list per concierge and fills the orders on their master list.
- Separates all individual client orders and completes the clients' receipts.
- Delivers filled orders and collects fees from the clients.
- Reconciles clients' receipts and fees collected and submitting them to the Operations Manager on a daily basis.

The typical managerial functions of planning, organizing, leading, and controlling are usually performed to a very limited degree, if at all. The greatest strengths of stage one are its flexibility and dynamism. The drive of the entrepreneur energizes the organization in its struggle for growth. Its greatest weakness is the extreme reliance on the entrepreneur to decide general strategies as well as detailed procedures. If the entrepreneur falters, the company usually flounders and we call this, the *crisis of leadership*.

The Growth (Youth) Stage

At this stage, the entrepreneur knows he or she has made it through the first phase if there are enough customers to keep the business running with a positive cash flow. Now the question becomes, do the owners have enough cash flow to sustain the business while it is growing? Although the business is still small during this phase, the owners are still doing a lot of the work because they are keeping employees to a minimum. Nevertheless, it is stable, and if they wanted to, they could actually keep it running this way indefinitely.

If you are an entrepreneur, you probably will not be satisfied maintaining your business at the level of initial growth, which is essentially where most small, lifestyle businesses remain. You probably want to expand and grow the business to the next level, but that takes a much more intense level of growth. Attaining high growth usually does not happen when using internal cash flows, so you must consider finding the resources you need to do it.

At this stage, you must:

- ❖ Plan carefully for this type of growth, because it can quickly get away from you, depleting your resources before you achieve your goals.

- ❖ Delegate more responsibility and perhaps even bring professional management on board. In high growth business, it is common to find a management team in place that is different from the one that founded the company.

The growth stage is also known as the "youth stage" when the organization starts to grow rapidly, when management responsibilities begin to spread among more people. Here, your simple structure begins to exhibit the stress of change, prompting it to adopt a new structure, preferably the functional structure as indicated in figure 11-3.

Figure 11-3:
The Functional Structure

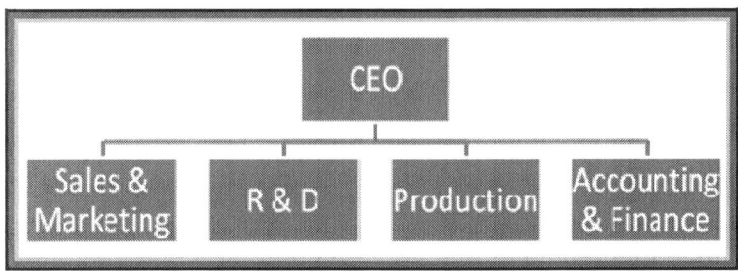

As the volume of business expands, the entrepreneurial structure outlives its usefulness. The need arises for specialized skills and delegation of authority to managers who can look after different functional areas. The functional structure seeks to distribute decision-making and operational authority along functional lines. The organization at the growth stage is value-driven with a clear direction. During this stage, most firms begin to plan strategically as lessons are learned from mistakes through trial and error leading to refinement of organizational processes. Typically, the organization experiencing growth is consumer-driven and service oriented.

The emerging structure is a **functional structure**, where people with similar skills who perform similar tasks are placed together in formal groups. These groups are typically made up of employees who shared technical expertise, interests, and responsibilities. In figure 11-3, all production activities are the responsibilities of the head of the manufacturing or production department, whereas sales and marketing problems are the province of the head of the marketing department.

Figure 11-3 above typified the functional structure of a firm that is departmentalized into functional units for sales and marketing, research and development, production, and finance and accounting. Functional structures typically work well for smaller and less complex organizations dealing with only one product or service. They also work best in relatively stable environments that allow your firm to pursue relatively stable strategies. One of the major advantages of the functional structures is that task assignment is consistent with technical training.

The growth stage then is when the entrepreneur may be replaced by a team of managers who have functional specializations. The transition to this stage requires a substantial managerial style change for the chief officer of the company, especially if he or she was the stage one entrepreneur. He or she must learn to delegate; otherwise, having additional staff members yields no benefits to the company. The great strength of the growth stage lies in its concentration and specialization in one industry. Its greatest weakness is that all of its eggs are placed in one basket.

By concentrating on one industry while that industry remains attractive, a firm in the growth stage can be very successful. Once a functionally structured company diversifies into other product or services in different industries, however, the advantages of the functional structure break down. A *crisis of autonomy* can now develop in which people managing diversified product lines need more decision-making freedom than top management is willing to delegate to them. The company needs to move to a different stage and structure.

The Maturity Stage

If the owners/managers succeed in passing through the growth stage, the company can probably achieve a more or less predictable level of stable growth. The company now has all the systems and controls found in a larger company and it is well managed. Typically, quality is assured as a result of accumulated experience over the years. During the maturity stage, the organization has put in place a good service system, efficient operation and responsive to staff demands. In particular, there is little conflict, few surprises with a focus on customers.

The danger at this point is complacency. Sometimes the owners/managers falsely assume that stable growth can continue indefinitely. Unfortunately, the market does not agree with them. If the company is not in a relatively constant state of change, responding to and leading in the market, it may begin to lose market share. Companies can and do fail at this stage.

In the corporate world, the stage of maturity is typified by the company's attempt to manage diverse product or service lines in numerous industries. Or to manage the same business in geographically dispersed areas. Take for example, you have been so successful in the printing business and as a result of growth and pressure from competitors you decided to expand and reach out into other product areas or geographical areas.

Figure 11-4
The Divisional Structure

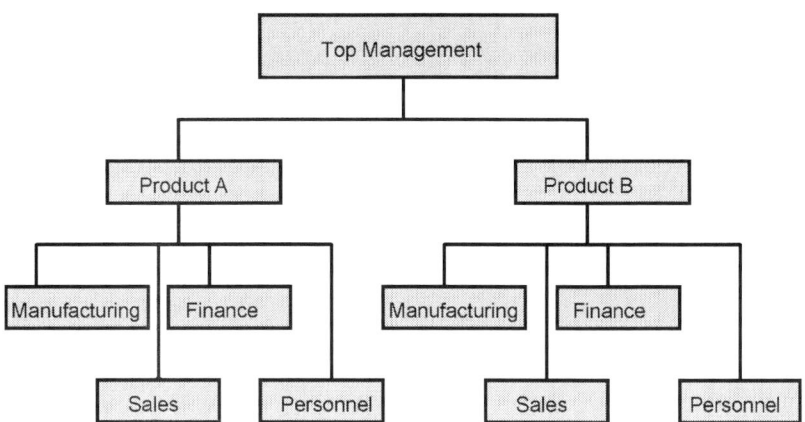

You decided to go into the publishing, newspaper or magazine business. Although, these are different markets, they are nevertheless somehow related as a result of certain things (raw-material or technology) they all share in their value chain. Your business now has different product areas (product divisions). Or your printing business in the Southern part of Nigeria (Lagos) is growing and as a result of competitive pressure and new customers' demand for your products in the Northern part of the country, you decided to establish a branch in Kano in another geographical area. Your company now has geographical divisions. In these particular cases, your normal functional structure does not work anymore. In either case, you need a different structure that can take care of the different products or geographical areas. In management, we call this the divisional structure.

A divisional structure groups together people with diverse skills and tasks but who work on the same product, with similar customers or clients, or in the same geographical region. In a divisional structure, you are managing different strategic business units (SBUs) or profit centers. Similarly, a new management style and organizational structure is needed to cope with the new challenges. The example of UACN discussed in chapter six exemplified a high-level divisional structure otherwise known as conglomerate structure or *group*. Such an organization is made up of a group of companies that are relatively independent but answerable to a corporate board. They operate in different markets or industries, therefore they adopt different strategies, and hence they are known as strategic business units (SBUs).

As a divisional company, you grow by diversifying your product lines and expand to cover wider geographical area. Previously, you were satisfied having your offices or your operations located in Lagos. Now you want to expand into the Abuja area or to the West African sub-region. This is called geographical divisionalization, that is, when your organization is grouped into different units based on the geographical or regional presence. Mr. Bigg's expansion into Ghana is an example of a regional diversification. *Thisday* Newspapers, as a result of growth, expanded to South Africa from Nigeria. A company can thus have different types of divisional forms such as product divisions, geographical division and customer divisional structures.

Some companies grow through diversification by creating a network in their industry. Others grow by diversifying outside their industry. We know that an entrepreneur must exploit all of the opportunities in his or her current market and industry before jumping outside to foreign territory in the form of a new industry. However, entrepreneurs have succeeded in using a diversification strategy early in the growth process. As we observed in chapter two, this is the typical growth strategy (unrelated diversification) adopted by many successful African entrepreneurs. Situations in which such a strategy makes sense include when you have excess capacity or spare resources are not in use, your customers are asking you to provide them with products or services that are outside of your current industry, you have foreseen major changes in your industry forcing you to look outside of your current industry, and there are major opportunities and you have the resources to invest in them. This is when a divisionalized structure comes into the picture.[12]

Divisionalized companies move to a divisional structure with a central headquarters and a decentralized operating division, where each division or business unit is a functionally organized form as in stage 2 form of structure. It is not uncommon that during this stage, a *crisis of control* can develop in which the various units act to optimize their own sales and profits without regard to the overall corporation or firm, whose headquarters seems far away and almost irrelevant. In some cases, there is always a conflict between corporate strategic objectives and those of the divisions.

The Decline Stage

The point has been consistently made that as an entrepreneur or the owner of a business venture, one must recognize the fact that there will be a period at which your business finds itself on a declining stage when so many competitors have entered the market, when your product or service has been copied and duplicated by new entries, and most importantly, when you are losing your market share as a result of new comers into your domain. A declining stage describes a situation when sales are going down, when your devoted customers are going somewhere else, and when your firm can no longer compete with the very instrument you have used initially to conquer the market.

This stage also typifies a company that has been plagued with managerial problems because of its large structure, when everything is out of control and your profits are declining. Some of the factors that precipitate organizational decline are (i) blurred vision, purpose, mission and goals, (ii) compromised values, (iii) aging leaders without capable successors, (iv) a bureaucratic system of management, (v) lost of consumer focus, etc. One of the features of organizations at this stage is that decisions are driven by politics and how to fund weak competitive businesses.

Everything can be out of control for several reasons: your dealings with the public can be out of sync, other competitors are offering more quality products, the government is on you because of taxes or other businesses practices that are not in line with current regulations, you are behind innovative practices, and you are not in touch with anyone else who comes in contact with your business. A particularly troublesome reason for the decline of organizations is when the entrepreneurial culture becomes a bureaucratic one. A **bureaucratic culture** (or culture of rigidity) occurs when an organization values formality, rules, standard operating procedures, and hierarchical coordination. Something is bound to happen that you will rather did not happen. Circumstances like that are almost laws of nature that challenge your business from time to time. Sadly, most businesses suffer more than they need to when bad things happen, because owners did not understand the challenges out there and did not have a plan for dealing with change, regardless of whether the change was positive or negative. Whatever the case, such changes can bring your firm towards the declining stage. If these circumstances are not handled well, a business can find itself in the death stage.

The Death Stage

Unless a company is able to resolve the critical issues facing it in the Decline stage, it is likely to move into stage five: the death stage, which is also known as *bankruptcy*. The death stage is when everything in your business has gone wrong. As will be observed in a following section, there are several reasons when your company can be seen as approaching the point of liquidation or bankruptcy. These include the inability to pay off debts because of a lack of cash, poor management, problems with your suppliers, poor financial management, and problems with regulatory agencies such as tax authorities. When your business arrives at this stage, what can you do? The following are some alternative actions that business owners can take:

Selling out your business: If you are ready to move on to something else, or you are ready to make a change in your life or where you live because your business is not doing well and there is no way you can savage it, selling the business may be the right to do. Doing so leaves you free mentally and financially to do whatever you want. Unfortunately, many entrepreneurs or business owners do not consider this as an option. Many successful businesses have been sold when their owners consider it is time to quit, when they know they can not manage the business themselves. But do not think that selling the business that you sweated blood and cried real tears to create will be easy. On the contrary, selling is one of the more difficult decisions you will ever make about your business. Some entrepreneurs experience a sense of loss much like losing a loved one. Others experience a sense of exhilaration from the freedom of not having to think about the business everyday, but then they realize they have lost their focus and do not know what to do next. Thus, never sell your business without knowing what you are going to do the next day, the next month, and the next year.

    If it comes to the point when you must sell, remember that you do not have to sell all the assets of your business. For example, you may sell all the equipment but choose to maintain ownership of the building and lease it to the new owner. Your buyer may not want to purchase all the equipment you have, so you will have to find another buyer for what is left. Accounts receivable, inventory, and accounts payable are negotiable items, too. You may also reach a point when you want to take some of your investment out of the business to enjoy some things you have always wanted to do, yet you are not ready to completely leave the business. You can accomplish this in several ways:

One choice is for you to sell some or all of the stock you hold in your company. Remember that selling stock applies to corporations and limited liability companies. If you are in a partnership, you can sell your interest back to the partnership. If your company is privately held, you are probably governed by a shareholders' agreement that was drawn up when you formed the company, specifying how much of your stock you can sell at a given time, to whom you can sell it, and how its value is determined.

Liquidation: When your business does not have the resources to pay its debts or any hope of securing them anytime soon, you will probably resort to liquidating all assets of the business and discharging most of your debt.

NEW FORMS OF ORGANIZATION STRUCTURES

Changes in the global economy have witnessed the emergence of new forms of organization structures. These structures are fundamentally different from the traditional ones (simple, functional, and divisional) in terms of the ability for the firm to make the best use of its resources in a highly competitive and dynamic business environment. New technological development has ushered in the Internet, virtual organizations and virtual shopping malls, electronic commerce and more. The implication is that traditional forms of organization structures have become inadequate in dealing with challenges brought about by a dynamic global economy. For the purpose of entrepreneurial firms, one particular form of organization structure - the network structure demands special attention as it is very much in vogue today among entrepreneurs.

The Network Structure

Firms using **network structures** consist of a central core that is linked through "network" with outside suppliers of essential business services in the management of the value chain. Sometimes called **virtual firms** or corporations, these firms use a variety of strategic alliances and business contracts to operate without having to "own" all of its supporting functions. They are accessed as the need arises through electronic networks. This creative approach allows firms to operate as smaller and less complex basic systems, even while maintaining extensive operations. A good example of such networking can be found among small and large companies in Europe, Japan, the U.S., and in many other developed economies. The importance of network structures has witnessed the growth of professional employer organizations (PEOs). The U.S. National Association of Professional Employer Organizations (NAPEO) estimates that 2 million to 3 million Americans are co-employed in professional employer organization (PEO) arrangements.[13] The idea is to put personnel, administration, and other duties that require professionals to perform into the hands of professionals so that the entrepreneur can concentrate on the core areas of the business. In the U.S., as in several Western European countries, the professional employer organization (PEO) handles workers' compensation and other benefits much cheaper than when they are handled by the small firm because the PEO can get volume discount. Indeed, many small business owners sign on because they want to offer benefits to their employees that they could never afford on their own.

In addition to the area of staffing, the practice of networking or **outsourcing** is increasingly been used in a firm's logistics: from the supply of raw materials, production processes and to the distribution of the finished goods or services. Such arrangements are increasingly more common in the international arena, where networks bring the advantages of global operations into the reach of many firms. They are also increasingly popular as managers and business owners seek ways to gain competitive advantage through reduced overhead and increased operating efficiency.

As an entrepreneur, the network structure is particularly useful when the environment of your firm is unstable and is expected to remain so. Under such conditions, there is usually a strong need for innovation and quick response. Moreover, it will be unwise to invest heavily in employees, equipments and other materials when the business environment is unpredictable. In such a scenario, outsourcing or networking provides the temporary relief needed for firms to run smoothly without interruption as a result of logistics. Thus, instead of having salaried employees on your payroll, you may contract with people for a specific project or length of time. Long-term contracts with suppliers and distributors replace services that you could provide for yourself through your firm's vertical integration.

Figure11-5 describes a network structure as it might work for a mail-order company selling furniture through a catalog. The firm itself is very small, consisting of relatively few full-time employees working from a central headquarters. Beyond that, it is structured as a series of business relationships. Merchandise is designed on contract with a furniture design firm; its manufacturing and packaging are contracted to "off-shore" companies; stock is maintained and shipped from a contract warehouse; and all of the accounting and financial details are managed on contracts with an outside accounting firm. The quarterly catalog is designed, printed, and mailed as a strategic alliance with two other firms selling different home furnishings of a related price appeal.

Such network structures can make a broad range of operations possible for smaller businesses including those in their stages of growth and maturity. An important foundation for their success lies with developments in information technology. Electronic computer networks greatly facilitate the links necessary for a network structure to function, even across great distance. This is one of a network structure's major advantages - flexibility in responding to changing conditions. And, within the operating core of the network, a variety of interesting jobs are created for managers who must coordinate the entire "system" of relationships to serve a common purpose. According to John Schermerhorn, network structures are lean and streamlined. They help organizations stay cost competitive through reduced overhead and increased operating efficiency.[14] Network concepts allow small businesses to employ outsourcing strategies and contract out specialized business functions rather than maintain full-time staff to do them. The network structure, like most structures, has its own disadvantage, which is the difficulty in controlling the many systems components that are involved in the network. If one part of the network breaks down or fails to deliver, the entire system suffers the consequences.

Figure 11-5
The Network Structure for a Web-based retail business

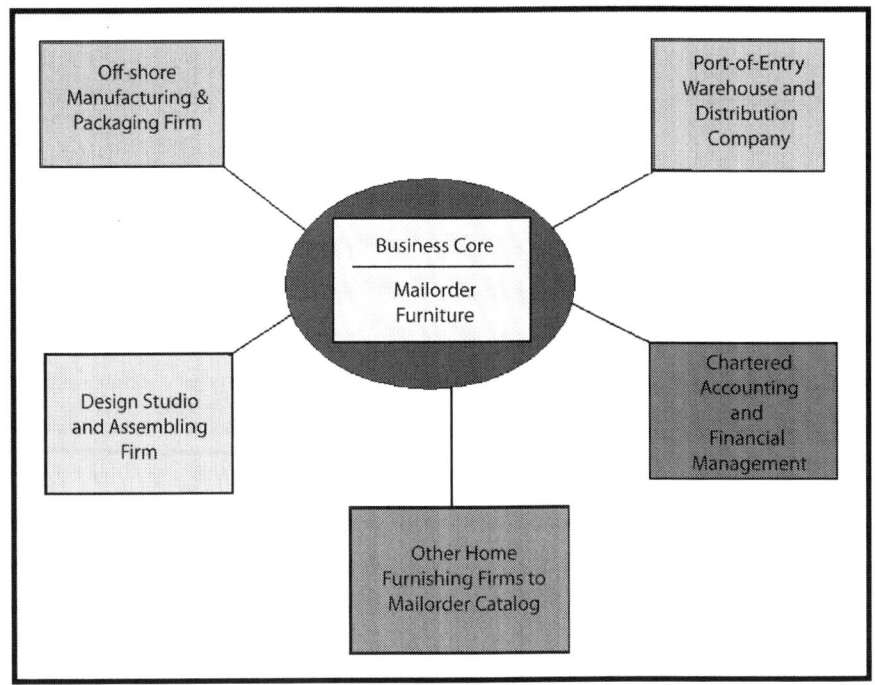

Source: Adapted from John Schermerhorn, *Management,* Hoboken, NJ: John Wiley & Sons, 2008, p. 245.

As information technology continues to develop, and as the concept of network structures become better understood, the future will very likely see them grow in number and in applications. In the developed economies of North America, Western Europe and Japan, the quest for greater efficiency and competitive advantage helps, too. For example, many larger firms are moving in the direction of more networks as they contract out specialized business functions; many others, especially smaller firms, are benefiting from these opportunities to step in and provide them.

The organizational form or structure of the future is the virtual organization. A virtual organization operates in a shifting network of external alliances that are engaged as needed using IT and the Internet. The boundaries that traditionally separate a firm from its suppliers, customers and distributors are largely eliminated, temporarily and in respect to a given transaction or business purpose. According to John Schermerhorn, virtual organizations came to being "as needed" when alliances are called into action to meet specific operating needs and objectives. When the work is complete, the alliance rests until next called into action. The virtual organization operates in this manner with the mix of mobilized alliances, continuously shifting and with an expansive pool of potential alliances always ready to be called upon as needed.

THE EXIT PLAN

Although a discussion of an exit strategy may seem strange in a book about starting and running a company, an exit or harvest plan is part of the overall strategic planning for your business. Using such a strategy certainly is a major change in the business, but if you do not know where you are headed, how will you know when you have arrived? Some entrepreneurs plan to never leave their businesses; others just enjoy the start-up phase and like to leave the management to other employees. Still others do not plan for the inevitable to happen when they may be forced to leave the business at a time when they did not prepare for it.

We noticed in chapter five that one of the reasons for the high mortality rate among African businesses is the fact that many business owners do not have an exit strategy. First, most people do not imagine that circumstances, such as untimely death, can force them exit the business. Africans live in a culture where it is a taboo to think of the death of the founder. As a result of human's propensity to deny the inevitability of death, most Africans refuse to plan for it. In a strange way, many of us think that we are immortal. The fact that most small business owners and entrepreneurs refuse to even consider that failure is a possibility proves they are the eternal optimists of the world. What you will find when looking at most books about entrepreneurship is the slightest hint of a discussion of the topic of failure. It is almost as though talking about it will start a virus, causing many more businesses to fail. One of the more often quoted stories about the late Nigerian politician and businessman, Chief Moshood Abiola, was that at the time of his death, there was a bitter feud among his family members over the distribution of his estate. As a result, many of his business holdings, creditors, suppliers and so forth could not be easily ascertained. No one thought death was inevitable and they failed to prepare for it.

The problem is not failure, because business failure is an integral part of entrepreneurship; the problem is failing to know when to recognize circumstances that cause business failure and how to walk away. The shame is not in having a business fail; rather it is in taking your family down with it, all because your pride would not allow you quit and prepare for it. Failure is an option, and sometimes the ability to prepare for it when it occurs is the only option.

Ask entrepreneurs and small business owners if they understand the risks they are taking when they start a business, and they always say yes. Ask if they realize they can lose their homes, family, their cars, and their savings accounts, and they say yes. But ask them if they believe that failure can happen to them, and their answer is a resounding no.

During the life cycle of a business s we discussed earlier, an entrepreneur or management will face adversity, perhaps because of external factors (the economy, competition, changes in consumer needs, technology, or unpredicted acts such as war, strikes, or weather); or the adversity may be self-inflicted (that is, due to poor management). The severity of the adversity can result in bankruptcy or in a need to refocus the business and strive for a turnaround. First and foremost it is important for the entrepreneur to recognize the warning signs of bankruptcy in order to act in appropriate manner. When things are beyond repair; when turnaround is no more an option, the entrepreneur must prepare for an exit strategy. There are several options in an exit strategy, including an initial public offering (IPO), private sale of stock, succession by a family member or a nonfamily member, merger with another company, or liquidation of the company. In the next sections, we examine the set of remedies that are available when a business is on the brink of failure.

Facing Bankruptcy

The term *bankruptcy* sends shivers up the spine of entrepreneurs, because they want to avoid it at all costs. Contrary to the popular notion that you can solve all your problems by bankrupting out of your company and walking away, it just is not that easy. Besides, if you have any ethics, you do not want to leave your vendors and shareholders high and dry, because it really is a small world, and you may need their help in the future.

What causes a business to reach the point of considering bankruptcy is not easy to identify. Typically, the immediately precipitating cause is the inability to pay off debt because of a lack of cash. But that lack of funds is only a symptom of a much deeper and more complex problem. There is a saying that goes thus: "The tree grows from the bottom up, but it dies from the top down." How right is that saying when applied to the high rate of business failure? Whenever a business suffers or dies, look to top management to find the problem. The main source of bankruptcy always is poor management – when the entrepreneur allows excessive debt to occur and overhead to explode, when he or she does not monitor the market, when things are done the way they have always been done, or when the business has marketing problems, supplier problems, problems from regulators, and poor financial management.

Avoiding Bankruptcy

Sometimes business owners have more control over a bankruptcy than you may think, because creditors naturally would rather be paid and they usually fare better in a structuring of the debt than they do in liquidation.

If you want to try your best to avoid bankruptcy, follow these tips:

- ➢ Do not rely on one major customer to generate the majority of your revenue. In other words, do not put all your eggs in one basket.
- ➢ Keep your overhead down to the essentials- those things that contribute to the generation of revenues.
- ➢ Stay as liquid as possible. A good rule-of-thumb is to have several months of overhead expense on hand.
- ➢ Pay attention to your relationships with your creditors. Be honest and forthright with them.
- ➢ Before you consider taking the bankruptcy route, seek the advice of a turnaround consultant who specializes in bringing businesses back from the brink of disaster.

Stepping Back from the Brink of Collapse

Business turnaround consultants, like medical doctors, specialize in making unhealthy - even dying businesses healthy again. They are experts who find positives in your business that you never thought about. They put your firm on a diet, help you establish small goals, and make sure you stay on track. The following suggestions can be helpful when you are facing failure in your business:

> **Seek advice**. Find entrepreneurs who have *been there* and get their advice. Unfortunately, when your business is failing, your family and friends can probably be the last people who can help you. So you need to talk with people who have gone through what you are experiencing. Ask around. In general, entrepreneurs who fail and come back to experience success are more willing to talk about what they found out and to help you get back on your feet.

> **Fail fast**. Do not drag your feet if things are going very badly. There are business owners who stuck with a dying business for years while it sucked the life out of their families, friends, and their own health. You must focus on the fact that the business failed, that you did not, and that you still have the talent and skills to start again. That is important.

> **Give yourself a deadline**. Tell yourself that if your business is not making a profit or generating a positive cash flow by next year, you are going to quit. That is not easy to do, because entrepreneurs, you remember, are optimists, always thinking that a big order is just around the corner and agreeing with people who are telling that their business is terrific. But when the numbers do not add up (and that is the real indicator), give yourself a deadline and stick to it.

> **Never mingle personal and business funds or assets.** If you lend your personal funds to your failing company and the company goes bankrupt, you must hop in line with the other creditors. Moreover, you may even have to return any repayment money you received in the year prior to the bankruptcy.

> **Pay back your debts**. Do whatever it takes to pay back your investors. Your investors took the risk, yes, but if you pay them back, even if it takes a long time, they will respect you and be there for you the next time you need them to fund an opportunity.

Before any bankruptcy attempt is contemplated, the entrepreneur should look first at the turnaround strategy. In any turnaround strategy, it is essential that the entrepreneur identify the roots of any issues that are contributing to the threat of bankruptcy or to the need to successfully resurface from bankruptcy.

CHAPTER SUMMARY

When hiring among family and friends make sure that you are hiring the skills and expertise needed in your firm. Other things to consider include similar work ethics.

Among your partners, put everything in writing whether they are your friends, relatives or close acquaintances.

You should form an advisory board made up of people who can help you.

The factors that affect growth are the intentions of the business, the ability of the entrepreneur to pull together the right team for growth, the nature of the target market, the nature of the competition, how innovative the industry is, the importance of intellectual property rights, the predictability of the industry and barriers to entry.

A firm can grow in its current market by building a customer base, developing the market through geographical expansion, developing the product by adding more utilities to existing ones, and by branding the company. A firm can also grow within an existing industry by moving vertically in its channel (vertical integration), moving horizontally in its channel Horizontal integration), and by creating a network in the industry. A firm can grow by diversifying outside its industry by capitalizing on the synergy of like businesses, acquiring an unrelated business, and by going global.

The success of an entrepreneurial firm depends on the ability of its owners, leaders, and managers to move from entrepreneurial to professional styles of management. Entrepreneurial views of management are different from managerial views.

The culture of a firm is the values, personality, and distinct ways of doing things that are peculiar to that firm. The culture of the firm becomes an important advantage because it gives people in the company a sense of purpose and propels them to achieve the goals of the firm.

A good human resource policy should include (i) the use of self-directed teams, (ii) a focus on core competencies, (iii) the customer in every thing the firm does, and (iv) providing rewards based on team efforts above rewards based on the efforts of individuals.

An entrepreneur's need to bring additional skills to the company is a function of (i) the ability of the entrepreneur to delegate responsibility and authority, (ii) the resources available for hiring the best, and (iii) the company's need for more structure and the skills of professional management.

Strategies for recruiting the right people include (i) having a strategic plan for attracting talented people, (ii) identifying the best employees in the firm, and (iii) creativity about where one finds talented people.

The organizational life cycle is the evolution of an organization over time through different stages of growth. It consists of five stages: (i) the start-up stage, (ii) the growth stage, (iii) the maturity stage, (iv) the decline stage, and (v) the death stage. There is an appropriate organization structure suitable for each stage.

An organization structure is the system of tasks, reporting relationships, and communication that links together the work of individuals and groups.

An organization chart is a diagram describing the formal arrangement of work positions within an organization.

A simple entrepreneurial structure consists of a top manager (the founder or owner) of the firm and non-managerial employees who do operating work and it is suitable for start-up stage.

Entrepreneurial culture typifies high levels of risk taking, dynamism, and creativity.

A functional structure places together people with similar skills who perform similar tasks in formal groups. Functional structures are suitable for firms in their growth stage.

A divisional structure groups together people with diverse skills and tasks but who work on the same product, with similar customers or clients, or in the same geographical region. A divisional structure is most appropriate for firms in the maturity stage.

An organization finds itself in a declining stage when sales are declining; losing customers and the firm is no longer capable of competing with the competitors. Such firm can also use a network structure to cut overheads. Declining stage can also occur when the entrepreneurial culture becomes a bureaucratic one.

A bureaucratic culture occurs when an organization values formality, rules, standard operating procedures, and hierarchical coordination.

The death stage is when the organization has reached the point of liquidation or bankruptcy and nothing can be done to save it.

A network structure consists of a central core that is linked through networks with outside suppliers and distributors of essential business services.

An exit plan prepares the entrepreneur to face future challenges if things should go wrong.

An entrepreneur can avoid bankruptcy by (i) not relying on a single customer to generate majority of the firm's revenue, (ii) keeping overhead down to essentials, (iii) staying liquid as possible, (iv) paying attention to relationships with creditors, and (v) seeking the advice of a turnaround consultant who specializes in bringing businesses back from disaster.

DISCUSSION QUESTIONS

1. What rules must you follow and take into consideration when teaming with other persons to form your business?

2. What factors must you consider that can affect the growth of your business?

3. What strategies are available to you if you intend to grow your business within your current market or industry?

4. How do you diversify outside your industry?

5. What do you understand by the term "organization or corporate culture". How is managing the culture of your company crucial to its competitiveness?

6. According to the textbook, what principles must you consider when developing a human resource policy for your firm?

7. What strategies must you adopt in order to recruit the right people?

8. What is an "organizational life cycle?" Why is the concept of "organizational life cycle" applicable to the management and growth of your company?

9. Is the network structure suitable for an entrepreneurial firm in the hospitality and restaurant business? Explain how this might work.

10. What is an exit strategy? Do you think that entrepreneurs or small business owners should consider an exit strategy while forming or managing their business ventures? Why or why not?

CASE STUDY 11: IYARE'S FURNITURE: UNCHARTED ORGANIZATIONAL RELATIONSHIPS

Iyare's Furniture Limited was founded in 2002 by Mr. Emmanuel Iyare. The original store occupied a space of about 3,000 square meters and was operated by the Iyares and three other employees. Ben Emeruwa joined the business in 2004 as a store manager and then was elected as the general manager in 2006. Ben Emeruwa was a cousin to Emmanuel Iyare.[15]

Business Growth

In 2004, Iyare's Furniture Ltd. had a sales volume of about N9 million and operated with 8 employees, including the Iyares and Ben Emeruwa. Merchandise was warehoused in a separate location where the firm leased 6,000 square meters of space. The business was incorporated in May, 2004 as a limited liability company.

Construction began on a second store location to be named Iyare's Home Furnishing in June, 2006. This location opened for business on December 23, 2006. By November, 2007, all administrative and accounting offices had been moved to the new location and all paperwork was being processed at Iyare's Home Furnishing. Together, the 2 store locations had a total 14,000 square meters of sales space and 18,000 square meters of warehousing space. In addition to retail furniture and accessory sales, the business included an interior design sales division and a contract furniture sales division. As a result of increasing demand for "Bini-made" furniture and related goods in the international market, Iyare Furniture began to receive orders for export. Unfortunately, the company was not prepared to handle such growth. Management decided to wait until they have qualified personnel to handle a growing order from countries in Western Europe and the Middle East.

The total annual sales volume of Iyare's Furniture Limited had grown from N9 million in 2004 to N32 million in 2007; and the number of employees had grown from 8 to 54 (including 8 part-time employees) in the same period. The firm's departments and number of employees were as follows:

Department	Number of Employees
Sales	16
Design	4
Accounting	5
Warehousing (including drivers and loaders)	11
Administrative and Support	4
Carpentry and Assembly	7
Upholstery, etc	3
Janitors	2
Security	2

Organizational Structure

No formal organizational chart had been created for the firm. The lines of power, authority, responsibility, and delegation were defined only in the minds of each employee. However, each employee realized that Ben Emeruwa was the general manager and that all decision-making authority came from him. Ben hired Frank Imafidon, who is a relative of one of the major stockholders of the firm, in September of 2006 as company manager and general merchandise manager. Prior to this period, Frank had been employed as senior designer in a major engineering firm upon his graduation from the University of Benin. Frank's responsibility as a general merchandise manager was to oversee daily operations and coordinate the purchase of inventory. A very good working relationship had existed between Ben and Frank from the very beginning. In 2006, when Ben was elected as the general manager, Emmanuel Iyare had retired from active management of the firm due to ill health. His daughter, Josephine Iyare, however, retained the position of company treasurer. This position was actually under the control of her father, in addition to that of an accountant, which was given to an outsider. The principal stockholders of Iyare's Furniture Limited were:

Stockholders (%)	Position
Emmanuel Iyare (40)	President and Managing Director
Josephine Iyare (25)	Secretary-Treasurer
Ben Emeruwa (10)	General Manager
Innocent Imafidon (25)	Non-official

Innocent Imafidon, who held the position of chairman of the board, had no active role in the daily operations of the company. He was active in the state's local politics and had several businesses that are unrelated to Iyare's Furniture Limited. He was chosen as the chairman of the board as a result of the financial investment he made in the company and his networking relationships with the local and national business communities. He acted as a voting member of management only and was active in the operation of his own other businesses.

Management Style

Ben Emeruwa retained total control of daily operations in all phases of the furniture firm. It was not uncommon to see him building merchandise displays, moving inventory on the sales floor, and loading delivery trucks on any given day. He actively participated in the sale of merchandise and in routine housekeeping duties. Ben was also actively involved in making sure that their furniture suppliers located in different parts of Benin City and its environs were designing and producing the furniture according to the company's specification. He also instructed new sales personnel in sales techniques and helped store designers in color and fabric coordination and display. Ben was very concerned with building and keeping a reputable firm with a good image for Iyare's Furniture.

Frank Imafidon participated in the selection of merchandise and coordinated its delivery to the display floors and warehouse. Frank was also involved in the training of new sales personnel and all general activities of the firm. He would also observe loading and unloading delivery trucks, moving displays, selling merchandise, and answering the phone.

It can be said that each of these managers became totally involved in each facet of daily operations and that each gave daily directions to the other employees. Ben and Frank were the type of individuals who were motivated by self-competition and do not need outside feedback or reinforcement concerning their job performance.

Organizational Problems

The lack of a formal organizational structure created an overlap of power and authority centers within the firm. Employees at Iyare's Furniture Limited were unable to identify who their immediate supervisors were and whose directions and instructions should be followed. One person employed as a merchandise stocker identified nine individuals who gave him job instructions. This situation was shown to exist at all levels within the firm. The impression of the majority of employees was that no one really knew to whom he or she was accountable.

Mrs. Iyare, Mrs. Emeruwa and Mrs. Imafidon, the wives of the owner and managers, frequently visited the two store locations. When they visited, they would suggest methods of merchandise display, fabric coordination to the design administrator, or raise questions about the company's accounting procedure and how much had been made by the company. They would tell the merchandise stockers what needed to be done and what displays were to be arranged. They would also assist the sales personnel in attending to customers, explaining merchandise and indicate which product lines should be promoted. Recently, rumors of misunderstanding and infighting among the wives have spread to the two locations. The wife of Imafidon was heard complaining to a friend that her husband was been used as a slave without due compensation. The matter was taken to the chairman of the board, Mr. Innocent Imafidon, who incidentally is a major stockholder and a senior brother to Frank Imafidon. Innocent had threatened to resign his position if Frank was not properly promoted and compensated accordingly. Meanwhile, rumors of voodoo and witchcraft by the wife of Ben were spreading. It was rumored that Mrs. Emeruwa had gone to a witch doctor to accelerate the death of the founder, Iyare, so that her husband could take over the affairs of the business.

Meanwhile, there were also rumors of financial misappropriation in the firm. Josephine, the daughter of the owner, who was also the treasurer, was befriending the company accountant. The accountant was reported to have no knowledge of accounting and bookkeeping. He was there because Emmanuel Iyare was doing a favor to a man who had helped him won a lucrative contract from the State government in the late nineties.

The employees within this company did not know how their job performance was viewed by top management (Ben and Frank). No formal evaluation or job reviews were utilized, and little verbal feedback was given. This frustration was evident when Ben was asked how he viewed John Omokaro (a top salesperson) and when Omokaro was asked about his perceived status within the firm. Their respective comments illustrated the situation when Ben said, "John is one of our best. I could not be more pleased. I hope that he will be with us for a long time because we need him." And John Omokaro's reply was: "I feel that if I make a mistake today, I'm gone. I try to do my job, and the money is not bad. But I'm not too sure if they like me. I would like to know if I'm doing a good job or not. I may leave at the end of the month." It must be noted that this was not an isolated case because this situation existed at all levels within Iyare's Furniture Limited.

Case Discussion Questions

1. Evaluate the culture of Iyare's Furniture Limited and discuss how it has affected the organizational structure and morale of its employees.

2. Evaluate the overall performance of Iyare's Furniture Limited. What does this show about the effectiveness of its management?

3. Identify the various organizational problems in this business. Which appears most serious? Why?

4. What are the probable causes of Ben Emeruwa's practices regarding delegation of authority? As a consultant, what changes, if any, would you recommend? How would you suggest that these changes be affected?

5. Outline an organizational plan and chart for the firm, and defend any changes you propose. Should the firm adopt the practice of outsourcing as a way of dealing with the identified organizational problems?

6. Should Iyare's Furniture expand into the international market? If yes, why and how? If no, why not?

Chapter 12

FINANCIAL STRATEGIES FOR THE ENTREPRENEURIAL FIRM

"Suppose one of you wants to build a tower. He will first sit down and estimate the cost to see whether he has enough money to finish it, won't he?" (Jesus Christ in the Holy Bible, Luke 14:28).

CHAPTER LEARNING OBJECTIVES
After studying this chapter, you should be able to:

1. Understand income statements, balance sheets, and cash flow statements and to use them in preparing a business plan.

2. Plan for the financial future of a firm.

3. Understand the various sources of financing a business and how to meet the conditions of investors and loan providers.

4. Understand why and how financial institutions screen an application for loan through a 5 Cs' screening process.

5. Understand how to prepare financial statements, budgets, and balance sheets that are useful to the firm.

INTRODUCTION: THE IMPORTANCE OF FINANCIAL PLANNING AND CONTROL

As we observed in chapter five, one of the biggest problems facing entrepreneurial development in developing countries is lack of knowledge about financial planning and control. So often, the typical small business owner in Sub-Saharan Africa fails to understand the differences between investing profits in the business and using the same for conspicuous consumption: The "I have arrived" syndrome, which is pervasive among business owners is a problem we have to face squarely if entrepreneurship is to be developed in Sub-Saharan Africa. Small business owners also face cash flow problems, which result from the inability to separate business accounts from personal ones. In one study, a researcher points out that during the early stages of some business start-ups, owners were unable to separate their business and family/domestic situations. Business funds were put to personal use and thus used in settling domestic issues. This has a negative impact on profitability and sustainability.[1]

The purpose of this chapter is partly to address this issue. Individuals in Sub-Saharan Africa are seen to possess business acumen based on their enterprising traditions. However, the financial environment and the manner in which finances are allocated and managed remains a big problem. For this reason, this chapter is made up of two parts: the first part examines how an entrepreneur or the small business owner can master his or her own finances. The first part of the chapter shows you how to prepare an income statement, a balance sheet, a cash flow statement, and how to forecast and prepare budgets. The second part deals with how to finance a business and what financiers such as banks and other financial institutions demand from an entrepreneur or a small business owner.

Entrepreneurs and small business owners are being asked to show the money all the time; in their business plans, in their financial statements, and in their budgets and forecasts. Why? The reason is that while there is certainly more to being in business than money, without money the owner cannot stay in business. Thus, this chapter will help you keep close tabs on your money by helping you master three fundamental building blocks of financial planning and management: an income statement, a balance sheet and a cash flow statement. These three areas give you a complete picture of how you are doing in your business.

The income statement: An income statement is a statement (or written document) that starts with how much money the firm earned in a given period of time (most often, a year) and then subtracts all the costs of doing business over that same period to arrive at its *net profit*. Sometimes a business owner may hear the income statement referred to as an *earnings report or a profit-and-loss statement*. They are all one and the same.

The balance sheet: A balance sheet is a form that captures a financial snapshot of a business at a particular moment in time, usually the very end of the year. The top half of the balance sheet tallies up the company's *assets*, all the things it owns that have monetary value. The bottom half combines all the money the business owes (its *liabilities*) together with what the company is actually worth (its *equity*). The top and bottoms halves must always balance each other out, hence the name, *balance sheet*.

The cash flow statement: A cash flow statement is a form that tracks the money as it flows in and out of the business over any given period of time (weekly, monthly, quarterly, or yearly.) The top half of the cash flow statement looks in detail at the funds coming in and the funds going out of the company over the period. The bottom half shows the resulting changes in the firm's cash position. Like the balance sheet, the top and bottom halves must match up.

PUTTING TOGETHER AN INCOME STATEMENT

A firm's income statement compares expenses against revenue over a certain period of time to show its net profit (or loss). Your company's income statement is designed to reveal your proverbial bottom line. The income statement is also known as the profit and loss statement, or the statement of operations. This statement summarizes the operations of a company over a specified time period in financial terms. The purpose of the income statement is to compute the net income (profit and loss) of the operation between the opening and closing dates of the chosen time period. By adding up all the revenue you receive from selling your products and services, and then subtracting all the costs associated with doing business over a certain period of time, the income statement comes up with your net profit for the period:

Net profit = Revenue - costs

For those just new in business, it is really a simple calculation. No matter how complicated the financial experts out there sometimes make it seem, it is just a basic measure of how well your company is doing. The time period you choose for your income statement depends on the type of business you are in and what you are using the income statement for. Various regulatory agencies such as the tax authority, for instance, are interested in your income statement for the taxable year. As the owner of a small business, you would also want to look over the firm's profits by quarter if, for example, the business is seasonal. As a business owner, you also get a more complete picture of where the company has headed by reviewing the income statements over a number of years.

To get a better idea about how an income statement is constructed, take a look at the books for *Onome Gift Shoppe*, a gift shop specializing in handicrafts and imported fashion wears, shoes and bags. Apart from selling in-store, the shop also makes sales through catalogs and through the Internet. The store has been in business almost 6 years, and Figure 12-1 shows an income statement as of December 31st for the most recent year, as well as the year before that. By comparing two years in a row, the owner of the gift shop, Ms. Onome, can see how revenues, costs, and profits are changing overtime.

The income statement for *Onome Gift Shoppe* is made up of five different sections. Since each one says something important about the shop's financial condition, it is important that we take a look at them section by section.

Figure 12-1:
Income Statement for Onome Gift Shoppe

	Year End, 31 Dec 2005	Previous Year 2004
Receipt on in-store sale	$626,000	$596,000
Receipt on catalog sale	106,000	96,000
Gross Revenue	**732,000**	**692,000**
Costs of goods sold	-461,000	-442,000
Gross Profit	**271,000**	**250,000**
S, G & A	-127,000	-109,000
Depreciation expenses	-20,000	-20,000
Operating Profit	**124,000**	**121,000**
Dividends & interest	+3,000	+3,000
Interest expenses	-24,000	-25,000
Profit Before Tax	**103,000**	**99,000**
Taxes	-18,000	-17,820
Net Profit	**84,460**	**81,180**

Section 1: Gross revenue
Gross revenues are the sum total of all money that the company takes in as a direct result of operating the business. The gross profit is the total revenue subtracted by the cost of generating that revenue. It tells you how much money a business would have made if it didn't pay any other expenses such as salary, income taxes, etc. Gross Profit should be broken out and clearly labeled on the income statement.

Revenues are the inflows from the routine operations of the company, commonly referred to as sales. In the case of *Onome Gift Shoppe*, those revenues are broken down into two major sources: money taken in by the store itself and money collected on the store's catalog and Internet sales. Any time a company has money coming in from different lines of business; the owner(s) must track the amount separately so that they know at a glance where the revenues are really coming from.

Depending on the type of business one is in, revenues may be based on sale of a single product, entire product lines, or the delivery of a whole array of services. Revenues can take the form of simple purchase transactions, leasing arrangements, subscription services, or any number of financing options. Together, these sources all get totaled up and entered on the income statement as *gross revenue*. The word "gross" implies that the revenue is as large as it can get, without subtracting any costs whatsoever.

Section 2: Gross Profit

In general, profits refer to the money from the company's revenues that the owners get to keep after all the bills have been paid. But as you can see from *Onome Gift Shoppe's* income statement, there are different kinds of profit. By taking time to analyze the company's profit at various stages of the business, the owners gain a clearer idea of where the company is making money and where the costs may be too high.

The first stage profit is typically referred to as *gross profit*. Gross profits starts with gross revenue and subtracts only those costs that can be directly associated with producing, assembling, or purchasing what the firm has to sell. In the case of *Onome Gift Shoppe*, the cost of goods sold refers to the whole-sale costs that the store must pay out for the gifts and handicrafts found on its shelves and in its catalog.

If a business offers a service, its gross profit will subtract only the costs directly related to supplying or delivering that service. If the business actually produces a product from raw materials, its gross profit reflects only those material costs as well as the labor, utilities, and facilities needed to put the product together. As a business owner, one may have to make judgment calls as to which costs should or should not be included here. No matter what one decides, it is better to be consistent over time. Otherwise, one will not know whether he or she is adding and subtracting apples or oranges.

Section 3: Operating Profit

All sorts of costs associated with doing business are not directly related to assembling a product or delivering a service. These costs include everything from the ads you run and the sales force you hire to travel expenses, telephone bills, and office supplies. Operating costs also include your own office space if you rent and even the salary you pay your self - at least the part of it that is often referred to as *overhead*. All of these indirect costs are usually added together into a category simply titled *SG&A* (*sales, general, and administration*) expense.

A business owner must keep a careful eye on all the SG&A expenses. Because they are not all tied directly to the firm's products or services, these expenses do not directly contribute to the firm's revenue. If they should get out of line, the profits of the firm can rather turn into losses.

In addition to the firm's SG&A expenses, there is the possibility that the owner of the firm will invest in at least one or two big-ticket items in the course of doing business. Maybe the business owner needs a car to call on clients, some sort of a computer system, and perhaps even a building or two for offices, a warehouse, or other facilities. If a business owner thinks about it, each of these big purchases is really an exchange of one asset (cash in the bank or on hand) for another asset (the car, computer, or building). The business assets the owner acquires all have useful life spans, so one way to spread out the costs of these assets over the number of years they are actually in service is to calculate *depreciation expenses* each year.

Operating profit is the money you make as a business owner from your actual business operations. It is calculated by subtracting your SG&A and depreciation expenses from gross profit. For *Onome Gift Shoppe*, the bulk of the SG&A expense is tied to the salaries of the sales staff, advertising and the production and delivery of the store's catalog three times per year. In addition, to SG&A expense, the company is taking depreciation expenses on its storefront building, the store's computer system, and a delivery van.

Section 4: Profit before taxes
Managing a company's finances (money) is part of running almost every business. The owner of a business is likely to have a business checking account, for example, maybe a business savings account, and perhaps even an investment portfolio to make sure that the cash the business keeps on hand is working for the owner. A business owner may need to borrow money to finance a car, a building, business equipment, or ongoing operations.

The money a business owner makes on his or her invested cash as well as the interest on any business-related loans the owner has must be included in the business income and expense tally. But the owner will want to keep these amounts outside the company's operating profit because the income that is made on investments is not really a part of your business operations - unless the business owner is an investment banker. And the interest expenses the business owner pays out are different from other expenses he or she has. For one thing, interest payments depend on how one has structured his or her company financially, not in the business itself. And for another thing, they absolutely, positively have to be paid on a strict and unforgiving schedule.

Profit before taxes takes into account all the income the company makes on investments of any sort and subtracts any interest expenses the company pays out. Onome Gift Shoppe has dividend and interest income amounting to $3,000 for the current year, but the company also paid out $24,000 in interest expenses, most of that going toward the mortgage for the store itself.

Section 5: Net Profit
Net profit refers to the company's bottom line - the amount the company has left after every last one of its expenses is subtracted from all the income available. Till now we have not considered every conceivable cost a company will incur. There is one important one left: taxes.

Depending on the structure of the company, the business may or may not have to pay taxes directly on the profits it has earned. If the business is a sole proprietor or it is structured as a partnership, for example, the business profits are funneled straight down to the individual owners for tax purposes, so no profit is left to be taxed. Of course, the owners can't escape the tax agencies so easily and must still pay individual income taxes on the money. Even if the business is not taxed on its profits, the owners may still find themselves owing money to various government agencies in the form of taxes.

Putting all sections together

Now it is time to put together the company's own version of an income statement. Maybe the owner(s) are already using accounting or financial software that does much of the work for them. That is great. However, it's more appropriate for the owner of the business to print out a copy of the most recent income statement to date and look over it carefully.

He or she should make sure that each entry is well understood and that they are convinced that the overall financial picture makes sense.

Entrepreneurs and small business owners should not let software program do all the number crunching for them and assume everything must be okay. In the end, it is the business owner that must know what all the numbers mean. After all, it is the owner of the business that is responsible for knowing what the income statement says about the financial health of his or her own company.

If one is not using a computer to track his or her company's finances, one should assemble all the relevant income and expense figures. If one is not yet in business, no problem: The income statement is also used to project what one expects to earn in the future and, for this reason, is the basis for putting together budgets as the business will look like in the future.

An income statement is an essential part of a written business plan as we will show in chapter fifteen. If a venture is already up and running, business owners should include numbers for the last year or two for the purpose of comparison. No matter how long one has been in business (even if one is just starting one) the income statement is used to show what the owner(s) plan to do in the future. A year or two ahead is usually an appropriate projection to make.

PUTTING TOGETHER A BALANCE SHEET

A company's balance sheet gives the owner a snapshot of what the business is worth, captured at a particular moment in time. In order to make the calculation, the business owner needs to calculate and add up the monetary value of everything the company owns and then subtract the money the business or company owes to others. What the business owns is usually referred to as *assets*. The amounts the business or company owes others are called *liabilities*. The difference, or what is left over, is the company's worth, sometimes referred to as the *equity* in the business.

A business owner can represent what the balance sheet is telling him or her about the company in a really straightforward equation:

Equity = Assets - Liabilities

Sometimes, accountants have decided to confuse things further by rewriting the equation as follows:

Assets = Liabilities + Equity

It is the very same equation, only it no longer makes common sense. Any way, the layout of your company's balance sheet is based on this second equation. The top half of the balance sheet is a list of all your business assets, divided into a number of basic categories. The bottom half of the balance sheet lists all your liabilities by category and then tacks on all of the equity in the business. Given the equation we just looked at, the top half's total and bottom half's total must be equal. In other words, they must balance each other out. How they balance each other tells the owner(s) a lot about their company's financial health. How often should you create a balance sheet for your company? Well, you can do it as often as you like, of course. At the very least, one should put together a balance sheet on the last day of the year. This particular balance sheet can also show the numbers for the end of the previous year, so one can compare how the assets, liabilities, and equity have changed over the year.

To see how a balance sheet is put together, take a look at *Onome Gift Shoppe*, the specialty gift shop. Figure 12-2 shows the company's balance sheet on December 31st for the most recent year and includes the numbers for the end of the previous year for comparison purposes.

The top and bottom halves of the balance sheet for the *Onome Gift Shoppe* are each made up of four different sections. Each section totals up a different category of assets, liabilities or owners' equity. Let us now take a look at them section by section.

Section 1: Current assets
A company's assets are made up of all the things the company owns that have monetary value. On the balance sheet, the owners are interested not only in how much each asset is worth, but how long it would take them to sell it off, converting it into cold, hard cash. The length of time needed to dispose of an asset is often described in terms of *liquidity*. The more *liquid* an asset, the faster one can sell it off.

Current assets represent all the items your business owns that are liquid enough to be converted into cash within a year, including the following:

1. **Cash**: You cannot get more liquid than cash. Cash can be anything from the bills and change in the cash register or the petty cash drawer to the money you or the company has in a checking or savings account at the bank.

2. **Investment portfolio**: Cash is nice, but it is even nicer to see your money working a bit harder for you. Your investments may include money market accounts, government bonds, or any other reasonably safe security. You probably won't want to make high-risk investments with these particular funds.

3. **Accounts receivable**: This asset consists of the money your customers owe you for products or services you have already delivered to them. If you bill your clients, for example, you may give them 30, 60, or 90 days to pay. Keep an eye on your accounts receivable. One deadbeat customer, after all, can throw your numbers for the loop.

4. **Inventories**: The equivalent cash value of the products or supplies you have on hand. It is often tricky to come up with a realistic number for the value of your inventories. My advice: stay on the conservative side. Your balance sheet should reflect what you can reasonably expect to receive if you should have to liquidate these assets.

5. **Prepaid expenses**: At any given time, your company may have paid for services you have not received yet. Maybe you have paid retainers or insurance premiums ahead of time, for example. These should be considered as part of your current assets.

Current assets, especially the most liquid ones, are extremely important to your business. They represent the readily available reserves you have to fund your day-to-day operations and to draw on in case of an unforeseen financial emergency. Onome Gift Shoppe had a total of $196,000 in current assets as of the end of the most recent year.

Section 2: Fixed assets

Fixed assets are fixed in the sense that they are usually big, expensive, meant to last a long time - and not very liquid at all. Buildings, machinery, cars, and computers fall into this category. As a rule, expect to take a year or more to dispose of these assets, turning them into cash in the bank. In general, fixed assets include the following:

1. **Land**: If your company happens to own a land - the ground under your office building, for example - it is listed separately on the balance sheet. Unlike other fixed assets, land cannot be depreciated overtime, so its value remains the same on the books year after year.

2. **Buildings**: As far as your balance sheet is concerned, the value of the buildings your company owns is equal to the original price you paid for them plus whatever you have spent on improving them over the years.

3. **Equipment**: Equipment includes anything and everything you buy for the business that is meant to last more than a year. Machinery, cars, office equipment, computers, telephones, and furniture all fall into this category. Their value is the original price you paid for them. If, for some reason, you didn't pay cash for one of these fixed assets, you should assign a reasonable value to it on your balance sheet.

4. **Accumulated depreciation**: All the big-ticket items you acquire as part of doing business each have a useful lifespan. *Depreciation* measures the decline in the useful value of these fixed assets over time. As a small business owner, don't worry, you do not have to come up with the numbers here. The tax agencies or any other organization interested in financing your business have a standard set of depreciation schedules, depending on the kind of assets your company owns. Accumulated depreciation sums up these numbers up over all your assets and your years of ownership, and then reduces the total value of your fixed assets accordingly.

Figure 12-2
Balance Sheet for Onome Gift Shoppe

Assets	Year End (2005)	Previous Year (2004)
1. Current Assets		
Cash	$45,000	$36,000
Investment portfolio	20,000	17,000
Accounts receivable	20,000	18,000
Inventories	110,000	97,000
Prepaid expenses	1,000	1,000
Total current assets	196,000	169,000
2. Fixed Assets		
Land	100,000	100,000
Building	295,000	295,000
Equipment	15,000	10,000
Accumulated depreciation	65,000	45,000
Total fixed assets	475,000	450,000
3. Intangible (goodwill)	10,000	10,000
4. Total assets	**681,000**	**629,000**
Liabilities & Owners' Equity		
5. Current Liabilities		
Accounts payable	19,000	13,000
Accrued expense payable	12,000	8,000
Total current liability	31,000	21,000
6. Long-term Liabilities		
Building & Mortgage	210,000	214,000
Total long-term Liabilities	210,000	214,000
7. Owners' Equity		
Invested capital	280,000	200,000
Accumt. retained earning	160,000	194,000
Total Owners' Equity	440,000	394,000
8. Total Liability & Equity	**681,000**	**629,000**

The value of a fixed asset is really quite arbitrary, at least as far as it is defined on the balance sheet. After all, the amount is based on the original price you paid minus any accumulated depreciation schedule. The resulting figure may in fact have very little to do with the market value you could receive if you decided to sell the asset or the price you would have to pay if you needed to replace it for some reason. *Onome Gift Shoppe* now has fixed assets valued at $475,000 after accumulated depreciation is taken into account.

Section 3: Intangibles
Intangibles are assets that, by definition, are hard to get your arms around. They can turn out to be extremely important to your business, however. Intangible assets include things like an exclusive contract to supply services, a franchise ownership, or hard-to-get license or permit to do business. An intangible asset can also be a patent protecting some invention, software technology, or production process. All these assets are clearly valuable to the company that owns them, but the question is, what are they really worth? Some companies don't even try to place a monetary value on their intangible assets. Instead, they allocate symbolic dollar amount toward them on the balance sheet, indicating that these assets are there and are valuable, but are not measurable.

Under the category of intangible assets, you find an item with an odd name: *goodwill*. Goodwill represents the amount of money your company may pay for something above and beyond its fair market value. Why would anyone do that? In fact, entire companies are often purchased at prices above market value, simply because they are worth a lot more to the buyer than to anyone else. *Onome Gift Shoppe* bought an existing gift shop a number of years ago and paid $10,000 more than what was considered the fair market value of the business at the time. The company now carries that goodwill entry on its balance sheet.

Section 4: Total assets
The *total assets* entry on the balance sheet sums up the total value of all the assets your company owns including current assets, fixed assets, and intangibles. This completes the top half of the balance sheet. In the case of *Onome Gift Shoppe*, the company has increased its assets over the most recent year by $52,000 to $681,000.

Section 5: Current Liabilities
Your company's liabilities are the various amounts of money you owe to creditors in the form of bills that are due, bank loans you have taken out, and bonds or warrants you may have issued to raise money. Many of these so-called financial instruments can get quite complex. The basic idea is always the same: You receive money or something else of value in exchange for the promise to pay the money back over a certain period of time (usually with interest, of course.) Sometimes these debts are secured by an asset that you own. (If you don't pay back as promised, the creditor can come in and take that asset away from you.) Sometimes the debts are unsecured. Sometimes the payback period is very long; other times, it is very short.

Current liabilities represent the short-term debts your company takes on that have to be repaid within one year. These liabilities are closely tied to your current assets listed on top half of the balance sheet, because your current liabilities have to be paid off using those assets. In most cases, current liabilities fall into two groups.

1. **Accounts payable**: At any given moment, your company typically owes money to various providers and suppliers that you do business with on a regular basis. The liabilities are usually in the form of outstanding bills that are due but have not yet been paid for such things as utilities, telephone services, office supplies,

professional services, or raw materials or wholesale goods that you resell to customers.

2. **Accrued expenses payable**: In addition to outside accounts that come due, your business is continuously accruing liabilities related to salaries or wages (if you have employees), insurance premiums, interest on bank loans, and taxes you owe. To the extent that these current obligations are unpaid, at the time your balance sheet is put together, they are grouped together here.

What is left over after you subtract your current liabilities from your current assets is typically called *working capital*: It is the money you have to work with on a day-to-day basis to keep your business up and running. On the balance sheet, *Onome Gift Shoppe* has a strong working capital position of $165,000.

Section 6: Long-term liabilities
Long-term liabilities usually represent the large financial obligations you take on either to get your company up and running or to expand your business operations. As such, these liabilities are often at the very heart of your company's financial structure. Perhaps you have taken a ten-year business loan directly from the bank. Or you have issued bonds to a group of investors to be repaid in 15 years. Or maybe you have a real estate mortgage on the buildings you use.

Onome Gift Shoppe has only one long-term liability: A mortgage of $210,000 on the building housing its store, which will be completely paid off in 26 years.

Section 7: Owners' Equity
When you own something, it is all yours, isn't it? Well, not always. Lots of people say they own their own homes, but what they really mean is that they own a piece of their own homes and banks or mortgage companies own the rest. In the same way, lots of people own their own businesses - or at least a part of their own businesses.

The term "owner(s) of a company" can come in any number, from a single individual to tens of thousands of investors in a large, publicly traded company. How much the owners actually own are referred to as their *equity*. The equity in a company can be distributed in all sorts of ways and have various strings attached concerning when it can be sold or how it can be used. When you strip away all the complexity, however, you are left with two basic sources of equity: money coming from outside investors and money generated from profits that are kept inside the company:

Invested capital: The money that is invested in your company comes from various sources, including the cash you put up as a principle owner of the business. You can also raise cash by selling off small pieces of the company to outside investors. The stock those investors receive in exchange represents their equity in your business. This outside equity may be privately held, or when you get big enough, you may decide to go for an IPO (Initial Public Offering). As part of an IPO, shares of your company are offered for sale to the general public. These shares are then traded on a public stock exchange. No matter how you exchange equity for cash, it is all added together as invested capital. The owners of *Onome Gift Shoppe* have invested their own $280,000 in the business.

Accumulated retained earnings: If you are lucky enough to make a profit on your business (meaning that the revenues you take in during the year exceed all the costs and expenses you incur), you are in the happy position to decide what to do with all the excess dough. You may decide to give some of it back to the owners and investors: That is what *dividends* are for. Or you may invest some of the extra cash back into the business so that you can grow bigger and, as a result, create more equity for everyone who has a stake in your company. Accumulated retained earnings represent all the profits you have poured back into the business year after year.

Total owner's equity sums up invested capital and accumulated retained earnings to come up with the value of the part of the company that all the owners actually own. The owners of *Onome Gift Shoppe* have invested $280,000 in the business and have poured another $160,000 of profits back into growing the company over the years. Total owners' equity now stands at $440,000.

Section 8: Total Liabilities and equity
Total liabilities and equity sums up the total value of all the liabilities your company is responsible for, including both current and long-term liabilities, and then adds on the total owner's equity. This completes the bottom half of the balance sheet. As you can see, the top and bottom halves of *Onome Gift Shoppe's* balance sheet are in balance at $681,000 at the end of the most recent year.

Putting all sections

You need to make a balance sheet of your own. If you are using accounting software of any kind, you can probably push a button to create an instant balance sheet out of financial information you have already entered into the program. But do not assume that that is all you have to do. Your computer-generated balance sheet is only as good as the numbers you put into it in the first place. So print out a copy and make sure it makes sense. If you want to get a head-start on your company's balance sheet and don't yet have business software in place (or you just want to understand what the darn thing really means) think about putting together your own version the old fashioned way: on a paper. Even if you are not in business yet, you can use the basic balance sheet format to total up the set of assets you think you will need to get your business off the ground, as well as the liabilities and equity capital you will require to get your hands on those assets.

Your company's balance sheet will appear in your written business plan as another important part of your financial picture, producing a snapshot of what you own, what you owe, and what you are worth. If you are already in business, include year-end numbers for the most recent two years as a useful comparison. And no matter how long you have been in business - even if you are just starting out - use the balance sheet to show exactly how you plan to grow to meet the income statement projections you have developed.

Figure 12-3:
Cash Flow Statement for Onome Gift shoppe

Assets	Last Year (2005)	Previous Year (2004)
1. Funds in		
Receipts on in-store sale	$626,000	$596,000
Receipts on catalog sale	106,000	96,000
Dividends and interest	3,000	3,000
Invested capital	5,000	10,000
Total Funds in	**$740,000**	**$705,000**
2. Funds out		
Costs of goods acquired	$ 461,000	$442,000
SG & A	127,000	109,000
Interest expenses	24,000	25,000
Taxes	22,000	19,000
Buildings & equipment	5,000	1,000
Long-term debt reduction	4,000	3,000
Distribution to owners	85,000	65,000
Total Funds out	**$728,000**	**$664,000**
3. Net Changes in Cash Position	+12,000	+41,000
Changes by Account	Last year (2005)	Previous Year (2004)
4. Changes in Liquid Assets		
Cash	9,000	28,000
Investment portfolio	3,000	13,000
Total Changes	12,000	41,000
5. Net Changes in cash position	+12,000	+41,000

PUTTING TOGETHER A CASH FLOW STATEMENT

Especially for companies that are small or have just started out, cash flow statements can be as important as the income statement and balance sheet combined. Why? Well for one thing, it shows you where the money is. Paper profits and a healthy balance sheet, after all, don't necessarily mean that you have money in the bank. And you cannot do business very long without cash.

The cash flow statement monitors the money flowing into and out of your business over a period of time. The typical statement is divided into two halves: the top half keeps track of where the money comes from and what it goes out for. The bottom half traces where the funds end up with after they are inside the company. Just like the two halves of the balance sheet, the top and bottom halves must be in balance.

If the cash flow statement is so important, how often should you look at it? If you are starting up a business, you probably cannot look at it often. At the very least, you review your monthly cash flow report. A well-designed cash flow report presents side-by-side numbers for two periods, so you can easily track changes in your cash position.

To see how a cash flow statement is constructed, we check with *Onome Gift Shoppe*. Figure 12-3 shows the cash flow statement as of December 31st for the most recent year, as well as the year before that. By comparing two years in a row, the owners of the gift shop can monitor how their cash positions have changed over time.

The two halves of *Onome Gift Shoppe's* cash flow statement are divided into five sections. The top half lists where the cash funds come from and what they are used for over the statement period. The bottom half looks at where the money ends up, tracking changes in the company's liquid asset accounts. We look at each section individually.

Section 1: Funds in
The cash flow statement keeps track of all the money coming into your company, no matter where it originates. That is why you find more entries listed in this section than just the revenues reported on your income statement. You may notice another important difference, too. The cash flow statement is more honest than the income statement. You can show the revenue on sales, for example, only when you actually have the money in hand. Yes, we really are talking about the flow of cash here. Take a look at the list of sources for funds coming into the company:

Receipts on sales: The money you take in from sales of your products or services belongs in this section, but only when it is actually deposited in the bank. While billing a customer may be enough to generate revenue on your income statement, the amount of your invoice will not be included here until you have the deposit slip to show for it. From figure 12-3 above, receipts on sales consist of in-store sales and receipts on catalog sales.

Dividend and interest income: The interest income you make on the money in your business bank accounts and your investment portfolio earnings are recorded on your company's income statement. As long as you receive the money during the period covered by the cash flow statement, the funds appear here, as well.

Invested capital: The money that is invested in your company shows up on your balance sheet as owners' equity. Because this may represent an important source of cash, it also makes an appearance on the cash flow statement when you receive it. This invested capital has nothing to do with the revenues your company generates from business operations, however, so you will not see these amounts appearing anywhere on your income statement.

When totaled together, the funds in this section of the cash flow statement represent every last dollar that comes into your company during the period. *Onome Gift Shoppe* took in $740,000 cash during the most recent year. The receipts on sales entry include all the revenue recorded on the income statement, as well as $3,000 in accounts receivable (see "section 1: Current assets" section, earlier in this chapter) that were paid off. Along with the dividend and interest income, additional $5,000 of equity was put into the company by its owners.

Section 2: Funds out:
When you are in business, you can spend money in a lot of ways. In this section of the cash flow statement, you can see where all that money goes. Only the money that is actually spent is included here. You may notice a number of entries that do not appear as expenses on the income statement. That is because certain cash outlays are not directly related to the cost of doing business. The following is a review of the complete list:

Cost of goods acquired: The difference between this entry and the cost of goods sold on your income statement has to do with when you actually spend the money. For example, the cost of goods sold on the income statement includes only the items you actually sell and may include items out of inventory that you may have paid for years ago. Cost of goods acquired, on the other hand, covers all the products and materials that you actually purchase and pay for during the period that is covered by the cash flow statement, whether or not they are sold or go into inventory.

Sales, general, and administration: These are the so-called *overhead expenses* that you write checks for day after day, including everything from paperclips to payroll. These are close to the same expenses that appear on your income statement, differing only if you put off bill-paying or decide to pay down your accounts and expenses payable. The difference is based on timing, that is, when the money actually leaves your hands.

Interest expense: Interest expense also shows up on your income statement. The amount here, however, reflects the interest you actually pay during the cash flow statement period.

Taxes: Taxes are unavoidable part of doing business, so they show up on your income statement. Again, the amount here reflects the taxes you actually pay during the cash flow statement period.

Buildings and equipment: Any big-ticket item that you purchase and pay for shows up on the company's cash flow statement. It also shows up on the balance sheet. However, you will not find it as an expense on your income statement. Why? Because you are really just trading one asset (cash) for another and your business expense shows up when this brand new asset begins to lose its value over time. To account for that, you are allowed to take a depreciation expense on your income statement every year that the assets are in service, reflecting the slow decline in its value.

Long-term debt reduction: You need cash to pay any of the business debts you owe and reducing your liabilities often makes for a healthier balance sheet. You cannot include these debt reduction payments as business expenses, however. That is why they do not appear on your income statement.

Distribution to owners: If your company makes a profit and your balance sheet is strong, you are probably in a position to give some of the financial rewards back to the owners of the business. For any outside owners, these distributions are the dividends they receive as return on their equity in the business. For small business owners and companies of one, these funds often represent the only paycheck for working long and hard hours. In either case, the distributions come out of your business funds but are not a cost of doing business, so you will not find them referred to on your income statement.

The funds tallied up in this section of the cash flow statement represent absolutely all the money that goes out of your company coffers over the period. *Onome Gift Shoppe* used up $728,000 cash during the most recent year. The cost of goods acquired entry includes all the cost of goods sold on the income statement, plus an increase in inventories of $13,000. Sales, general, and administration reflect a pay down of $1,000 in current liabilities. $5,000 was spent on equipment and $4,000 on long-term debt reduction, increasing equipment assets and decreasing long-term liabilities on the balance sheet. Finally, $85,000 was distributed back to the owners of the gift shop over the year.

Section 3: Net change in cash position
If you subtract all the funds going out of the company from all the funds coming in, you end up with the net change in your cash position over the period. *Onome Gift Shoppe* increased their cash position by $12,000 during the most recent year.

Section 4: Changes in liquid assets
The bottom half of the cash flow statement monitors where the money ends up while it is inside your company, including everything from the petty cash box and the business checking account to the investment portfolio you may set up to manage your funds:

Cash: Whether in a cash register or a checking account, this is the place you go first to receive payments and pay your bills. Cash is an asset, so you can find a similar entry on the balance sheet. Here, however, the cash entry tracks only the total change in your cash reserves over the period.

Investment portfolio: If your company owns money market accounts, government bonds, or other securities, they represent assets and can be found on the balance sheet. The entry here tracks only the change in the value of your investment portfolio over the period.

By adding up the individual changes in all your liquid asset accounts, you can determine the net change in your company's overall cash position. *Onome Gift Shoppe* increased its cash account by $9,000 and its investment portfolio by $3,000 for a total increase of $12,000 in the most recent year. By the way, if you look at the previous and last year's entries under current assets, you see these changes reflected on the balance sheet.

Section 5: Net change in cash position
Because the top and the bottom halves of the cash flow statement must be in balance, Section 5 should be identical to Section 3. In other words, a net change in cash position can be determined either by subtracting money going out from money coming in, or by monitoring changes to the accounts where the money is coming and going from.

Putting all sections together

As you begin to assemble a cash flow statement of your own, you may notice that many of the entries are based on the figures that appear on your income statement and your balance sheet. That is nothing surprising. After all, your company's cash flow is closely tied to your revenues and costs, as well as the assets you own and the debts you have taken on.

If you are already using an accounting package to manage your business finances on the computer, find the appropriate menu and create a cash flow statement. If you know how to read it, you can find out all sorts of important information about where and when the money comes into and goes out of your business. You may find out even more by putting together a cash flow statement from scratch – at least one time.

In your written business plan, the cash flow statement shows how you intend to manage your one indispensable resource: cash. If your business is already up and running, you are required to include year-end numbers for the most recent two years. If you are just getting started, the balance sheet becomes a particularly important piece of evidence to show exactly how you plan to grow to meet the income statement projections you have developed.

FORECASTING AND BUDGETING

After your business is in operation, you can use the three basic financial building blocks – your income statement, balance sheet, and cash flow statements – to paint a financial portrait of your company. By definition, this picture captures only what you once were, and maybe what you are today. It says almost nothing about what your finances will look like tomorrow, next month, or next year. And yet the future is where we are all headed.

There is nothing quite as hard as peering forward and constructing a financial portrait of what your business will look like at some point down the road. Ever heard the saying, "The future is not what it used to be?" That is exactly why forecasting is so important. Unfortunately, if you are just starting up a business, the task can be especially difficult, because you don't have a financial history to look back on as a guide. It is difficult for someone to be able to fill in the numbers for you, but the steps you have to take as you start to look ahead can be outlined for you. This is done in the following pages.

Your financial forecast is created around the same three financial building-blocks covered in the preceding sections of this chapter. Only this time, the numbers are projected into the future. Based on what you see in your financial future, you can then develop a master budget for your company. This budget sets out the major guidelines for where and how you plan to spend all the money you see coming in. Your budget is really a financial blueprint for carrying out your business plan, allocating your company's resources in directions that are most likely to see your business succeed.

The financial forecast you put together will end up containing all sorts of numbers: revenue predictions, expense projections, and cost estimates. As a business owner, you are predicting what the future of your business will be. Thus, financial forecast are the same kinds of figures that appear on the financial forms covered in the preceding sections of this chapter. But in this case, the numbers are not really real. Instead, they are based on your best guess about the future. They are based on a set of assumptions about what you expect to happen down the road. Carefully consider all the business assumptions that go into your financial forecast. Make sure you know what each is based on. For example,

> If you are assuming that the economy will grow at a given rate, state it.
> If you believe you can raise the cash you need from at least three different funding sources, be specific.
> If you are almost certain that a new technology is going to completely change the way your industry does business, explain the basis for your reasoning.
> If you think competition will increase in a certain segment of your market, say so.

In other words, spell out what is behind the numbers, because the assumptions you make are just as important as the financial forecast itself.

In the three following sections, we go over exactly what your financial forecast should look like. In addition to the assumptions you make, the forecast consists of three basic financial forms.

Pro forma income statement

Pro forma is one of those strange Latin phrases that sound pretty fancy but actually means something quite simple; in this case, it refers to anything you are going to estimate in advance. So your pro forma income statement is meant to estimate your business revenue, expenses, and profit ahead of time; looking out one, three, or even five years. In fact, you may want to sub-divide the first two of these years into quarterly projections, if you can. It is a big undertaking, so take time to prepare for it by doing the following:

❖ If you have been in business for a while, get together your company's income statements for the last several years. If your history does not go back that far, use whatever financial information you can get your hands on. Your past income statements can serve as a starting point for the pro forma income statements you are about to create.

❖ If you are starting up your business and do not have a company history to fall back on, think about other sources of information in your industry. Search out people in similar businesses, go to trade shows, get on the Internet, and find out if consultants can give you guidance. You may have to invest some real effort here, but if your financial projections end up close to the mark, the results will definitely be worth it in the end.

You may also want to review the description of each of the entries on the income statement by referring to the "Putting Together an Income Statement" section, near the beginning of this chapter. When you are finished, your pro forma income statements should look quite similar in format to their real counterparts. That way, you will have an easy time comparing the future you projected with the future as it really happens.

Remember, the more these projections you make, the better you will get at them. To learn from your previous attempts, take time to go back over your pro forma income statements after the quarter or the year is finished. Make notes on where you were right as well as those areas where you need to work on your crystal ball.

Estimated balance sheet

An estimated balance sheet looks very similar to the real thing, which is discussed in the "Putting Together a Balance Sheet" section, earlier in this chapter. Rather than taking a snapshot of your company at some point back in time, however, the estimated balance sheet tries to take a picture of what your company will look like sometime in the future. In other words, your estimated balance sheet attempts to project what you will own, what you will owe, and what your company will be worth year-by-year, looking ahead three or five years. We know it sounds tough, and it is. But make a stab at this estimate, anyway: Even if it proves to be less than perfect, your estimated balance sheet will provide you with a financial roadmap into the future.

While a pro forma income statement tells you something about what you expect to earn over the next few years, your estimated balance sheet lays out how you expect the company to grow so you can meet those income projections. To put it together, you first look at what assets you think you will need to support the growth you are looking forward to. Then you have to make some decisions about how to pay for those assets. That means you have to consider how much debt you are willing to take on, what company earnings you will be able to plow back into the business, and how much equity you need to invest in the future. Needless to say, these are all major decisions.

Projected cash flow

The projected cash flow statement will help you ensure that you will always have money around when you need it. Your projected cash flow statement is put together just like a normal cash flow statement. But rather than focus on what happened to the cash last year or the year before, the projection tries to predict where the cash will come from and how it will be used looking ahead anywhere from three to five years. If you can make your cash flow projections quarterly, so much the better. And if your business has built-in seasonal variations, you may want to make your projections monthly.

When you start looking closely at your future cash needs and sources, you may want to take advantage of the company cash flow statement in Figure 12-3. That way, you are able to compare your projected cash flow with your actual cash flow statements. In addition to guiding you how you run your business, you will also need a pro forma cash-flow statement for your business plan. In that case, your business plan would not be a plan at all without some sort of a financial forecast. So make sure to include your pro forma income statement, estimated balance sheet, and projected cash flow statement along with the business assumptions that go into them. Be prepared to review and revise this financial forecast on a regular basis. Your financial forecast just happens to be one of the most important and fragile parts of a business plan and you have to be able and willing to change it when the business circumstances around you change.

THE MASTER BUDGET

The various parts of your financial forecast create a moving picture of your company as it goes forward into the future. While this picture is clearest in the near-term, it can get extremely fuzzy the farther you look out ahead. Fortunately, you can use the sharpest parts of your financial forecast to create a master budget, which is a detailed spending blueprint that not only reflects your financial picture, but also reinforces what you would like to see happen. The master budget you put together for your company allows you to do two extremely important things:

> ➢ **Live within your means**. When the rough outlines of your company's budget are defined by your projected cash flow statement, your spending guidelines are based on the most realistic financial picture you have. The budget, of course, fills in all the details.

> ➢ **Use your money wisely.** The master budget allows you to plan your spending so that it is in line with both your strategy and your business plan. That way, you make sure that funds are allocated in the most efficient and effective way possible to achieve your larger, long-term goals.

To begin your own budgeting process, start with copies of your projected cash flow statement for the next year or two. In particular, review the section that shows where you expect the cash to be used. The categories in your projected cash flow statement are very broad, including cost of good acquired; sales; general, and administration expenses; buildings and equipment; and distribution to owners. Your job is to break down these broad categories into more manageable pieces, as you begin the process of assigning exactly how much money should be spent on what service or what piece of equipment.

If your company is large enough, you may want to get a few of your colleagues involved in the budgeting process at this point. After all, it is a big job. Working with the key people around you not only spreads some of the effort around but also improves the odds that your management team will buy into the master budget you finally come up with.

While your master budget is a key operational part of your business planning efforts, you have to decide whether you want to include it as a formal part of your written business plan. For the majority of your readers, your financial forecasts: the pro forma income statement, estimated balance sheet, and projected cash flow statements are usually enough to make them feel comfortable with your future finances.

FINANCING THE BUSINESS

Recall that in chapter four we pointed out that the lack of access to and cost of finance remain a binding constraint on establishment and expansion for small-scale enterprises. We also noted that it is not uncommon for small-business owners to have insufficient working capital for day-to-day operations. In chapter five, we noted that one of the obstacles confronting the development of entrepreneurship in Sub-Saharan Africa is weakness in financial management. Thus, although these shortcomings, such as financial constraints, may be explained as products of market imperfections or symptomatic of supply conditions, they are nevertheless rooted in managerial shortcomings and the inability on the part of business owners to understand basic principles of financial management – including banks' conditions.[2] For many business owners and entrepreneurs, the potential for growth is also hampered precisely because their needs for additional finance are not easily met from the banks. This inability to secure finances from the bank is the result of the inability to fulfill requisite lending and/or credit conditions inherent in bank financing.

Once a prospective business owner has made a decision to start a business venture, the next step is about how to obtain the necessary capital to make that decision a reality. For most people that entails some type of financing. We know that in Sub-Saharan Africa, it is difficult to obtain the necessary financial support from the financial institutions as a result of the negative trust built between lenders and borrowers and the underdeveloped nature of the region's financial markets. As indicated in chapters four and five, the rate of default is astronomically high in many developing countries compared to most other developed countries. For that reason, banks and other lenders are very careful about whom they entrust their money. If a guarantee could be given here, it would be that this phase is one of the most frustrating and trying phases of a new business startup. Most of us have bright business ideas. We would be millionaires if only someone can help us with the finances to start the business. In the context of Sub-Saharan Africa, many business ideas have died prematurely as a result of lack of funding. So, see how this section can help you.

Obtaining financing is hard. It is also hard to make money and it is equally difficult to hang onto money once you have made it. As a small business owner a degree of humility is required. It is also important to maintain a perspective that the financial institutions have seen hundreds of applicants like you and have a degree of competence in spotting trouble before it starts. It is also imperative to maintain the perspective that a bank's principal priority is to make money. If you are an acceptable fit from the bank's position, you will be granted a loan based on the bank's conditions. It is also helpful to realize that rejection is not the end; it is only a temporary setback. Persistence and adaptability will help you prevail.

I have mentioned before and will mention again that after the idea-generation phase, multiple steps in the business concept are progressing simultaneously. This development is constrained by the availability of capital, and unless acceptable financing can be obtained, all previous expenditures are often wasted. The financing stage is therefore critical.

For most aspiring entrepreneurs one of the first steps in the quest for financing is at the local bank or some other financiers he or she knows. For most banks in any country, all loan applicants are viewed from the perspective of five C's:

1. Character
2. Collateral
3. Cash flow
4. Capital
5. Competence

Most banks view these five C's as a screening process and reject some 75 percent of the applications they reviewed based on the five C's.

Character

Before extending a loan to or making an investment in a small business, lenders and investors must be satisfied with the **character** of the loan applicant. The first **C**, *character*, is given the heaviest weight. To quote verbatim from one bank manager: "If we are not comfortable with the applicant's character, nothing else matters. We believe the bank cannot make a bad loan to a good person, nor can it make a good loan to a person of poor character." The bank manager continues: "The bank would first of all appraise the person to know whether he is worthy or not." All this helps to convey the message that character (or integrity) is the key to getting a loan from the banks.

To become a productive member of the business community means being a person of your word: being able to manage the resources at your disposal to fulfill the commitments you have made to those around you. If you are unable, for instance, to pay your mortgage or your rent or your utility bill on time, how would you be able to pay a bank loan? If you were to view a small business or a major corporation from the perspective of its stakeholders, the ideal thing to do is to look at the relationships you have with your internal and external stakeholders. Internally, the employees, including management are your stakeholders. Externally, your customers, suppliers, creditors, stockholders, governmental agencies, and the community at large are your stakeholders. The firm maintains its character and credibility by fulfilling the commitments made such as paying taxes. If payday is established as being on the 15th or 30th of the month, from employees' perspective it is not acceptable for payday to be on other days. A lack of trust begins to ensue if financial commitments are not kept. It is no different for the small business owner. When a person walks into a financial institution and asks for a loan of $50,000, the bank will not take the request lightly. The bank also has made financial commitments to their stakeholders; the bank is a for-profit institution. They loan money to make money; therefore, they loan money only to those from whom they can reasonably expect payment. The bank community generally will only loan to people of high moral character.

Collateral

The second **C** is *collateral*. The bank must protect its own interest and will require that you have sufficient collateral to cover the loan. What is sufficient depends on the institution and the specific situation and your character. Collateral includes any assets the owner of the business (or any loan applicant) pledges to a lender as security for repayment of a loan. Very often in the developing countries, loan applicants use their landed property as collaterals. In a general range the bank will usually require that you have at least a 25 percent equity stake in your venture. The amount of equity required will depend on the bank's degree of confidence in a particular business. If the financial institution is comfortable with this loan, it will tend to be on the lower end of the spectrum. Other factors will play into this scenario, but in the end if a loan is granted, the equity required will depend on the bank's comfort level with that type of loan in that type of industry or enterprise.

A CASE IN POINT: REJECTION AND ACCEPTANCE
One of my clients in the United States was planning to launch a venture - a Nigerian who migrated to the United States to start and run a church. After about five years, the growth of the church was great and my client wanted to expand the church with other facilities such as a day-care center and a sport facility. The proposal made the bank uncomfortable. The bank was skeptical to the loan application because it believed that the church was going into an area with which it had no experience; thus 40 percent equity was requested from this church by the financial institution. My client went home and raised the 40 equity percent and had it available in cash as requested. He met with the loan officer who had originally set the condition, only to have the loan denied the second time. In this case, the loan officer was less credible. He arbitrarily set a high equity stipulation to discourage further pursuit of this venture. Having met the bank's request, the loan officer seemed at first surprised and then irritated that the church owners were back. The second loan request did not even make it to the loan committee stage; the loan request was rejected immediately. The bank was simply not interested in making that type of loan. In my interview with the loan officer, he said that the "church business" was getting saturated and the bank is not sure if they will ever recover their money back. Fortunately, my client and I went to the next bank across the street and the loan was granted.

From the above case, a valuable lesson was learned and never forgotten concerning bankers and financial institutions. First and foremost, the small business owner needs a good banker. In order to get a good banker he or she must be trustworthy. Second, when dealing with bankers and banks, a personal relationship must be developed. The banker needs to know you and your business and needs to feel comfortable that you are, indeed, serious, credible, and trustworthy. Third, the bank is a for-profit institution and the loan officer will always operate from a perspective of what is best for the bank. Fourth, the bank will consider the nature of your market or industry in terms of its attractiveness to be profitable over time. In many cases, banks will not lend money for businesses in a saturated or declining industry, except the owners come up with a very winning strategy. Fifth, and most importantly, the banks would want to know the extent of your "stake" in the business. You have to convince that lenders that you've got something invested in the business that matters very much to you: what you've invested is your collateral. A personal note: Ironically, the bank that initially turned down my client's loan request sent a loan officer to call on him three years later in an attempt to solicit his business account. Obviously, this occurred after his business was established and had proven itself. The bank was then comfortable with granting a loan. That seems to be typical: that when you don't need a loan, it is easy to get one. From the bank's perspective I suppose it is the reverse of the issue. When they are ready to grant a loan to a business, the business does not seem to want one. In the same way, the loan officer mentioned met with little success in granting a loan to my client's business. It was too late; the account remained with their competitor.

If the bank were forced to call a loan, the type of assets and the liquidity of those assets are prime determinants concerning the level of debt the bank will allow a business to carry. Single-purpose highly specialized equipment will require more equity than generic types of business such as an application for a housing loan or a pickup truck. The bank can sell a pickup truck to recover monies owed, but if an asset pledged as collateral is something like a cassava processing machine, the amount of money they can recover will be limited. Thus the loan limits associated with that type of business will reflect that liquidity limitation.

For existing businesses that are looking for financing or additional financing, accounts receivables can be pledged as collateral and are usually granted as a loan value of about 75 percent. However, an accounts receivable aging list may be required, which in turn may reduce the loan value if collection problems exist.

Cash Flow

The Third **C** is *cash flow*. According to banks and other lending institutions, character, collateral and cash flow are the most critical stages in the loan screening process. The cash flow phase is where detailed business plan is imperative, backed by a marketing plan with realistic obtainable forecasts and projections. You must demonstrate unequivocally to the financial institution that you can repay the debt. That means answering questions concerning whether a market exists for your product or service, how big that market is, and how much of that market you can reasonably expect to obtain. The second part of the question requires that the business owner demonstrates that he or she can make a profit. For a small business owner, this becomes a much larger issue.

Outside source of income can be a major consideration in a bank's decision as to whether or not to grant a loan. Some banks consider it as a safety net when an applicant has another source of income outside the proposed business venture. This, however, raises a crucial question. Should one start a business on a part-time basis? From consultancy experience, some banks' response was not in support of a part-time venture, the biggest reason being that the proprietor demonstrates a lack of commitment and a lack of focus. One of their reasons is that "it is easy to quit"; therefore, the business venture is not given the effort required to make it successful. Others have shown that as a result of divided and sometimes conflicting obligations, the returns of a business in which the owner has other business commitments are substandard because one cannot devote the time and energy required to make things work properly. Whatever the case, it is important that prospective entrepreneurs state in clear terms how money will be realized in order to run the business venture.

Capital

For a business to operate, it must have *capital*, the fourth **C**. We are not talking about collateral; we are referring to cash and/or liquid assets. It means that a small business must have a stable capital base before any lender is willing to grant a loan. As pointed out earlier in this chapter, the current asset portion of the balance sheet is what you use to pay the current liability portion of the balance sheet within the current period. The bank or your lender is concerned that adequate cash is available to meet those current obligations. From the perspective of the small business, a lack of current assets will cause a business to begin to violate both internal and external relationships by not meeting its obligations or commitments to employees, creditors, suppliers, and others. From the perspective of banks and other lenders, your firm or business would not be the first one to go broke with orders on the desk. To meet the financial obligations adequately on a day-to-day basis, the small business owner needs an operating budget. The year's projected cash inflows and outflows are broken down into a month-by-month budget. This operating budget facilitates planning and provides a basis for making decisions concerning purchases, inventory levels, equipment purchases, employee hiring and scheduling, sales activity, and short- and intermediate- term cash management.

   The bank or any lender is going to be very concerned with your ability to repay. As a business owner, you, on the other hand, must also be concerned with being able to make a living. You must consider such important issues such as the cash flow requirement for the growth of your firm because growth can severely strain a firm's financial resources. You can, in fact, go broke if your finances are not aligned with your growth potentials and experience. The demands on cash from purchasing new equipment, expanding inventory, increasing payroll and the accompanying increase in payroll taxes, including increasing accounts receivables can all drive up your operating expenses and can quickly outstrip your ability to raise cash. If you are out of cash and simultaneously exceed your ability to borrow, the entire firm will come screeching to a halt. Growth is good but must be a planned and managed growth. The budget plan, which you must always have in hand, helps control and monitor cash flows so that the firm's current financial position does not become critical.

Competence

The bank or any other lender will not loan money to someone unless they feel confident that this person has the required competence and capability to operate this business. The fifth C, then, is *competence*. In short, lenders are going to want to see a demonstrated ability to manage this type of business. The financial institution is going to be very interested in your past experience. As a small business owner, you are responsible for all the functions of the enterprise. Experience goes well beyond the ability just to perform the work, so to speak, or the production function. It entails the marketing, accounting, pricing, personnel, sales, finance, risk management, and every other issue the fledging firm encounters. A bank will grant you a loan if it knows that your firm has the necessary competence to perform these management functions.

The importance of experience was stressed to me by an employee at the U.S. Small Business Administration (SBA) in the following words: "If you are entering into a business in a particular industry, you enter into a field that is first, filled with competition, and second, one that has been littered with the corpses of failed businesses. Those who succeed do so for a reason – and that reason is the experience they previously had."

As a small business owner, you can get experience in a particular field by obtaining an education and by working for someone in that industry. If you want the best kind of experience, it is important that you seek out the best in the industry in your region and work for this person. In fact, go to that person, tell them of your aspirations, and ask them if they will mentor you and train you – even if you worked for nothing, even if you had to pay the business owner to acquire this type of experience. It would be worth it to avoid the "If I only knew then what I know now" and to retain and apply the "I have learned so much." To say that such experience is invaluable would be an understatement. Such experience could well be the difference between success and failure or possibly make the difference between moderate success and great success.

A Final Note on Why Businesses Fail

There are many reasons why so many businesses fail. As we pointed out in chapter 11, the reasons for business failure can be either externally generated factors or internally generated ones. Externally, factors of business failures can be rooted in the economy, (e.g., national or global economic recession), intense competition from rival firms or substitute products, changes in consumer needs, the arrival of new technology, or unpredicted acts, such as war, strikes, or weather. In this section, we will focus more on the internally generated factors for business failure especially when it comes to financial management or factors due to poor management in general.

The problems related to financial management can be seen as one of the major causes of business failures in Sub-Saharan Africa. We noted in chapters four and five that there is a prevailing attitude and cultural practices whereby profits are used for prodigious expenses that have no bearing with the business. The typical African business owner rarely has plans for reinvesting profits to help the company grow, either by buying equipment, building facilities, or funding new hires etc. Thus, it is not uncommon that many businesses run out of cash just when the cash becomes essential to facilitate business growth and then die down to fierce competition later on. Among African business owners, cash-flow problems are quite common. In addition, there are several financial leakages as a consequence of poor credit management, theft/fraud and not using resources efficiently enough. In general, the financial management problems boils down to a lack of systematic use of record-keeping and being able to monitor and interpret these records so that the appropriate action may be taken. This problem is compounded by what appears to be a relatively poor understanding of the macroeconomic context among the majority of business leaders.

Another internally generated cause of business failure is lack of experience. First, business failed because the owner did not have a sense of business savvy, and second, because they were unwilling to get some help to supplement their limited or lack of experience. Lack of experience can also lead to cash flow problems: perhaps too much inventory, poor control over accounts receivable, or lack of financial discipline, spending funds that should be marked for other financial commitments. Before one realizes, the firm and/or the business owner has gone broke.

Another reason why firms go broke centers around the owner's refusal to seek help when help is required, which is most closely related to the accounting function. As we pointed out in chapter five, many small business owners have a difficult time distinguishing between cash flow and profit. Demands on cash in the early stage of a business are generally great. This lack of understanding goes beyond just a lack of financial aptitude, and also implies a lack of financial discipline. The danger is that the business owner spends cash that should be committed to financial obligations incurred. A new luxury car or the most recent office equipment in the market is purchased because cash seems to be available. Often, the business owner does not realize that other current obligations have already been incurred, which will take that cash. The owner looks in the checkbook and spends the money he thinks he has. The next thing he knows he must file a sales tax return, or make a payroll deposit or workers' compensation premium, and is completely surprised by these expenses. This type of business owner is operating financially blind and cannot make good and informed decisions.

Having once been stung by the unexpected, the entrepreneur compounds his or her mistake by failing to recognize or admit his or her limitation. He does not seek help. When the business owner is finally forced to get help, it is too late. The accrued financial obligations have wiped out his equity and the bank will not extend credit to satisfy the multitude of creditors who are exerting pressure for payment. As it turns out, profit was not what the owner thought, and the doors swing shut on yet another business startup. "If only I knew what I know now" becomes a way of thinking by the business owner.

CHAPTER SUMMARY

For a small business owner, the three areas he or she must deal with in terms of finances are the income statement, the balance sheet, and the cash flow statement.

An income statement (aka profit and loss statement) compares expenses against revenue over a certain period of time to show the firm's net profit or loss.

A balance sheet provides a summary of a firm's financial position, providing owners with an estimate of the worth of the business on a given date.

A cash flow statement shows the changes in a firm's working capital from the beginning of the year by listing both the sources of funds and the uses of these funds.

A gross profit is when a small business owner subtracts only those costs that can be directly associated with producing, assembling, or purchasing what the firm has to sell.

Operating expenses are those costs that contribute directly to the manufacture and distribution of goods and services.

Net Profit is the company's amount that is left after all expenses are subtracted from the income available.

A company's current asset consists of cash, investment portfolios, accounts receivable, inventories and prepaid expenses.

Fixed assets involve the long-term commitments and large investment for the new venture and include land, buildings, equipment and accumulated depreciation.

Intangible assets include such things as brand-name, image, patent, company reputation, buyer goodwill, or a motivated and energized workforce.

Liabilities represent money that is owed to creditors. Current liabilities represent the short-term debts a company takes on that have to be paid within one year. Long-term liabilities represent large financial obligations a firm takes on to get it running.

Owners' equity represents the amount owners of a venture have invested and/or retained from the operations of the business venture. Owners' equity can take on several forms such as invested capital or accumulated retained earnings.

A cash flow statement monitors the money flowing into and out of a business. It consists of money that flow in (such as receipts on sales, dividend and interest income, invested capital, etc) and money that flows out (such as costs of goods acquired by the company, sales, general and administrative costs, interest expenses, taxes, building and equipment, etc).

Loan applications are viewed from the perspective of the applicant's character, the collateral the business owners have, the possibility of cash flow, the cash that comes in and goes out of the business, the capital the business owner has at his or her disposal and the competence needed to run a business venture.

Reasons why many businesses are unable to get financial support is their lack of experience. Experience can be gained through education or working for someone else.

DISCUSSION QUESTION

1. What is the purpose of your company's income statement?

2. What is an operating profit?

3. What are the differences between a gross profit and a net profit?"

4. What is a balance sheet?

5. What do we mean by a company's assets?

6. What do we mean by a company's liabilities?

7. What is a cash flow statement?

8. What is a pro forma income statement?

9. Chief Olu Falade approached his bank in order to apply for a loan to finance the growth of his business. When he met the loan officer, he was asked to come back with an income statement, a balance sheet for the current year and a cash flow statement. Unfortunately, the Chief has no idea of what the loan officer was talking about. Chief Olu Falade wants you to help him. Now, you have been called upon to explain to him what income statement, balance sheet and cash flow statement imply. As you're doing this, be sure to include the elements contained in each of these documents.

10. When you try to finance your business through outside sources, your credibility and worthiness is always judged based on what we call the "Five C's". Explain what is meant by this statement?

CASE STUDY 12: PROJECTING CASH FLOWS AT AJAYI AND OSUNDE CONSULTING (NIG) LTD[3]

Mr. Wole Ajayi and Lare Osunde, former roommates while pursuing their university education, had each been employed by very reputable chartered accounting firms for eight years. While at school, they had all majored in accounting and Wole had been promoted to chief auditor while Lare to senior accountant in their respective firms. Each was making very good salary, having been hired in their mid-twenties and having received pay raises once each year. Each lived rather frugally, and between them they had more than N300, 000 to invest in a small accounting or consulting firm. Each consulted his recent past account and principals and discovered that several would give their business to the new firm rather than remaining with the previous one. Advertising cards would be mailed to professional acquaintances and personal friends once the firm had been established.

The firm was initiated on July 1, 2000. Both partners had remained with their respective firms through May of that year, giving themselves substantial overtime from doing audits and tax returns for corporate and partnership clients. They knew that it would probably take about six months before the firm would reach a break-even. It was their plan to hire an office manager the first year. It would be necessary to add a junior executive, they both believed, in the second year. As revenues increased and as the clientele became larger in size, it would be desirable to add even more staff persons. The two principals, who decided to form a professional corporation for liability and other reasons, would elect the limited liability option. Moreover, it would be possible to expense a greater part of the payroll taxes and fringe benefits than if operating as a partnership.

Wole Ajayi and Lare Osunde sought a location intermediate in distance from the two communities that they planned to serve. Thus they would be about 20-kilometer radius of expected clients. A busy consultant in Lagos Island, Ikoyi and Victoria Island axis charges more naira per hour for the time billed than any other location. It was desirable to bill not less 6 hours per day to clients if expenses were to be covered, adequate compensation was to be paid to the consulting partners, and any profits were to be left as a return on capital. It was decided that the initial charge would be N6000 hourly, but the clients were told that this was introductory and hourly billing rate would likely advance by about N50 per hour each thereafter. At this rate, each accountant or consultant might generate about N6000 X 30 hours X 50 weeks = N9,000,000 in annual revenues. Junior partners serving on an assignment billed at lesser rates, such as N3000 to N4000 hourly customarily. The work of secretarial staff was not billed separately. Neither was the cost of office materials, if used in moderate amounts. However, only a dozen copies of the final report were presented to the client. If more copies were needed, it was an extra printing charge.

It was decided that a large, four-bedroom house with ample parking space located on the highway intermediate between the three areas (Lagos Island, Ikoyi and Victoria Island) would be leased for the office space. The living room would be used as the outer office, reception area, the secretary's office, and the bookkeeper's office. Each of the principal consultants would have a separate room to be used as an office. Another room would be used as a study, conference room, or storage space. The fourth bedroom would be needed by other consultants being added in the third and subsequent years of operations. The den would be the normal conference room/library, and the kitchen would be used as a snack area. The two bathrooms would be assigned one each to gentlemen and ladies.

The actual income statements for the first 18 months of operation and projected for the third year is shown below:

Ajayi and Osunde Consulting Nigeria Limited
Actual and Projected Income Statements

	Second-Half 2000	2001	2002 (projected)
Revenues billed	N10,563,500	N22,125,500	27,922,000
Expenses:			
Compensation of officers	3,169,100	6,637,700	8,376,600
Costs of operations	164,790	345,160	203,830
Wages expenses	110,920	295,920	502,600
Continuing education cost	30,000	45,000	75,000
Lease rental expense	106,150	106,150	106,150
Taxes	48,590	101,780	122,860
Depreciation	73,600	84,080	94,930
Liability insurance	39,080	75,230	111,690
Pensions and Benefits	26,410	55,310	125,650
Books	12,500	14,000	18,000
Interest expenses (auto, etc.)	16,500	16,500	30,710
Professional dues	10,670	19,190	27,920
Repair expenses	7,390	15,490	23,960
Donations	8,000	12,500	22,500
Advertising expenses	8,980	13,280	10,890
Bad debt expense	2,110	4,430	8,380
Miscellaneous expenses	2,640	5,530	6,980
Total expenses	N9,852,400	18,740,400	23,297,100
Net profits	711,100	3,385,100	4,624,900
Dividend withdrawal (taxes)	24,890	95,620	118,120
Reinvested capital	46,220	242,890	344,370

In the first year, a secretary was hired at an annual wage of N110,920. A staff assistant was hired in the second year, and another was planned for the third year at a beginning salary of N185,000. Wage increase increments would be made yearly to the experienced persons, averaging about 3 per cent to 5 per cent above the rate of inflation.

Initially, some N450,000 would be invested in fixed assets, such as furniture and fixtures, leasehold improvements, and partial payment on two autos for use by the principals in visiting their clients. The furniture would be depreciated at 10 per cent yearly, the autos over 5 years. About N120,000 in office equipment would be acquired, which would have an estimated life of 3 years. The balance of the funds would be held in cash until needed for operating expenses. Following are the balance sheets at the beginning of business yearend 2000, and yearend 2001.

Ajayi and Osunde Consulting
Balance Sheets

	Initial	Yearend 2000	Yearend 2001
ASSETS			
Cash	N411,270	N324,620	N387,640
Accounts receivable	-	228,280	388,400
Other (prepayments)	-	106,080	130,000
Total current assets	411,270	708,980	906,040
Long-term Assets:			
Fixed assets	459,260	401,550	531,170
Office equipment	129,470	113,200	141,470
Total assets	1,000,000	1,173,730	1,578,680
DEBTS AND NET WORTH			
Accounts payable	-	42,620	41,090
Dividends payable	-	24,890	95,620
Wages payable	-	-	39,860
Total current debts	-	67,510	176,570
Installment notes, long-term	-	60,000	110,300
Total debts	-	127,510	289,570
Common stock (N100 par)	1,000,000	1,000,000	
Retained earnings	-	46,220	289,110
Total debts and equity	1,000,000	1,173,730	1,578,680

By the end of the second year, Ajayi and Osunde Consulting felt that they had a good grasp of the monthly billings.

Case Discussion Questions

1. As the newly hired junior executive in Ajayi and Osunde Consulting Nigeria Limited, you have been asked to prepare a cash flow statement by month for the first six months and by quarter for the last two quarters of the third year. Make any needed assumptions, but state them.

2. Prepare a pro forma balance sheet as of December 31, 1995, that ties together the previous balance sheet and the cash budget.

3. Suggest more appropriate use of idle funds.

Chapter 13

OWNERSHIP STRATEGIES FOR THE ENTREPRENEURIAL FIRM

"Two heads are better than one" (unknown author)

CHAPTER LEARNING OBJECTIVES
After studying this chapter, you should be able to:

1. Find the right legal form for any type of business.

2. Understand the meaning of sole proprietorship, partnership and a limited liability structure.

3. Understand the advantages and disadvantages in buying an existing business and the process involved.

4. Understand the concept of franchising, its types, advantages, and limitations.

5. Understand when the services of an attorney are needed in the process of starting and managing a business.

INTRODUCTION: DECIDING ON THE BEST LEGAL FORM FOR THE BUSINESS

Should a new firm be organized as a sole proprietorship, a partnership, or a corporation? Anyone who buys or starts a business faces this question at once. Moreover, the problem reappears as a business grows. In the world of business venture and entrepreneurship, firms started as proprietorships (when the owner is the individual who started the business) later may find it desirable to become partnerships, limited liability companies or publicly quoted corporations – depending on the particular circumstances under which the firm is founded. There are other firms that may decide to grow through a franchising option. The first major decision that a new business owner must make is that of the form of ownership. Most small businesses operate under one of four broad legal classifications: sole proprietorship, partnership, a limited liability entity, and a franchise. Many entrepreneurs assume that the best entity is always one that allows the ability to reap unlimited profits and the ability to exercise control in the business operation. These assumptions can be wrong for some entrepreneurs and for some businesses.

In this chapter, we will examine the major forms of business organization and also the areas of law relevant to the small business. In view of the need for legal counseling both in forming the organization and in dealing with various legal issues, we will conclude the chapter by discussing the choice of an attorney for the small firm. Understanding the factors that affect your choice of business form is very important. Five factors or relevant questions should be considered when the decision is made in going into business:

1. *Who will be the owners of the company?* If more than one individual owns the company, you can eliminate sole proprietorship as an option. If many people own the company, the limited liability form is often the choice because it has an unlimited life and free transferability of interests. If you intend to have many employees, the limited liability corporation also lets you take advantage of pension plans and stock option plans.

2. *What level of liability protection do you require, especially for your personal assets?* Some forms protect you; others do not. It is a sad fact that too many businesses ignore the risks they face and do not acquire the correct forms of insurance. Just as you want to see the advice of an attorney and accountant as you develop your business, you also want to consider the advice of an insurance broker.

3. *What level of freedom do you need to develop and manage the company?* Some business forms give you absolute freedom; others do not. If you need absolute freedom, the sole proprietorship is the ideal option. If freedom to manage the business the way you feel is not an issue, then a franchise option can be an appropriate form. You will recollect that one of the discussions we encounter in chapter two is that some individuals leave salaried employment because they dislike working under the direct supervision and control of others. Similarly, your choice will depend on how much control you are willing to exert in the management of the business.

4. *What are your ambitions in terms of growth?* Most successful entrepreneurial firms end up as large corporations. A basic principle of business growth is to expand the existing sales territory. If your ambition is to take the company to a higher growth and sale level, the limited liability form where stocks are sold and the public can invest in the company is an appropriate form. On the other hand, many franchising organizations develop contracts that restrict you to a defined sales territory, thereby eliminating this form of growth.

5. *What are the startup capital requirements and cost of formation?* Forms of ownership differ in their ability to raise start-up capital. Depending on how much capital an entrepreneur needed and where he or she plans to get it, some forms are superior to others. In the same manner, some ownership forms are much more costly to create. An entrepreneur must weigh carefully the benefits and the costs of the particular form he or she chooses.

THE SOLE PROPRIETORSHIP

The sole proprietorship is a business owned and managed by one individual. In many countries, majority of small businesses fall under the sole proprietorship form of ownership. For example, 75 percent of all businesses operating in the United States are sole proprietorship.[1] Many business owners begin as sole proprietorship because they are the easiest to form. A sole proprietorship is a business where the owner is essentially the business; that is, he or she is solely responsible for the activities of the business and is the one to enjoy the profits and suffer the losses of the business. Why do so many business owners start this way? Sole proprietorship is the easiest and least expensive way to form a business. Particularly in the context of Sub-Saharan Africa where the informal sector predominates, sole proprietorship offers the easiest route to transitioning from informal sector survivalist business undertaking to the formal sector. If you are using your own name as the name of the business, all you need is a business license, some business cards, and you are in business! The individual proprietor has title to all business assets, subject to the claims of creditors. He or she receives all profits but must also assume all losses, bear all risks, and pay all debts of the business.

Advantages of Sole Proprietorship

As already mentioned, the sole proprietorship is the easiest to start and least expensive form of organization, but it also gives the owner complete control of the company. You make all the decisions and suffer all the consequences, but the income from the business is yours and you are taxed only once at your personal income tax rate. In summary, the advantages associated with the sole proprietorship as a form of ownership include:

(i) The ease with which the business is created. Many professionals, such as consultants, authors, and many home-based business owners, operate as sole proprietors. Chances are the owners of your neighborhood restaurant, shoe repair shop, beer parlor, or tailoring shop are sole proprietors. Thus, one of the most attractive features of a proprietorship is how fast and easy it is to begin.

(ii) It is the least costly form of ownership to begin.

(iii) There is profit incentive because the proprietor keeps all the money once taxes and debts are paid.

(iv) The proprietor has total decision-making authority. Because the sole proprietor is in total control of operations, he or she can quickly respond to changes, which is an asset in a rapidly changing business environment.

(v) No special legal restrictions compared to other forms of ownership, and

(vi) It is easy to discontinue. If the proprietor decides to discontinue operations, he or she can terminate the business quickly.

Disadvantages of Sole Proprietorship

For most entrepreneurs, the sole proprietorship form of organization is not satisfactory for several reasons.

(i) As a sole proprietor, you have unlimited liability for any claims against the business. In other words, you are putting your personal assets at risk - your home, car, bank accounts, and any other assets you may have. So, having business liability insurance is extremely important. If you are producing a product, you will need product liability insurance to protect you against lawsuits over defective products. If your company does work for other people (for example, if you are in the construction business) you may be required to have bonding insurance to ensure that you complete the work specified in your contract. Because there are so many areas of liability and so many different types of insurance, you should talk to a good insurance broker. Remember that in a proprietorship, *you*, as the owner, *are the business*. You own all of the business assets. Consequently, if the business fails, creditors can force you to sell all your assets.

(ii) Raising capital is much more difficult, because you are relying only on your financial statement. You are, for all intents and purposes, the business, and most investors do not like that situation. As pointed out in chapter twelve, most banks and lenders have well-defined formulas for determining borrower's eligibility and your character is seen by your bank as a decisive factor in making their decisions. If you do not have enough capital or your credit worthiness is not good enough for the banks and lenders, sole proprietorship is not the appropriate route to business ownership. Limited access to capital can thus become a great disadvantage for the sole proprietor.

(iii) As a sole proprietor, you probably will not have a management team with diverse skills helping you grow in your business. You may have employees, but that is not really the same thing. Putting together an advisory board of people with skills you need helps compensate for the skills you lack.

(iv) Because the survival of your company depends on you being there, if something happens to you, the company no longer exists. Legally, if the sole proprietor dies, so does the business, unless its assets are willed to someone.

If you intend to grow your business, organizing as a sole proprietorship is not a good idea, unless you are taking advantage of income and control benefits during the early stages of your business - for example, through product development.

THE PARTNERSHIP

A partnership is usually formed when two or more people enter into a business relationship or venture together, when they decide to share assets, liabilities, and profits of their business. Under a partnership agreement, the members come together to carry out a business activity. The formation of a partnership is set forth in a partnership agreement. Partnering is an improvement over the sole proprietorship because people are sharing the responsibilities of the business and bouncing ideas off each other. Additionally, you now have multiple sources of finance on which to rely and an entity that usually survives if one of the partners dies or leave.

In terms of liability, however, you are raising the stakes, because each partner becomes liable for the obligations incurred by other partners in the course of doing business. In a partnership, each partner uses any property owned by the partnership and shares in the profits and losses of the partnership unless otherwise stated in the partnership agreement. Partners do not have to share equally in the profits and losses. Ownership in the partnership can be divided in any manner the partners choose. The biggest issue with partnerships is that they often are fraught with conflict in much the same way as family businesses.

You do not have to have a written agreement when forming a partnership; a simple oral agreement works. In fact, in some cases, the conduct of the parties involved implies a partnership. Accepting a share of the profits of a business is *prima facie* (legally sufficient) evidence that you are a partner in the business, meaning that you may also be liable for its losses. Ideally, every partnership agreement should be put into a written document.

Partnerships come in several forms. In most partnerships, entrepreneurs are general partners, meaning they share in the profits, losses, and responsibilities, and are personally liable for actions of the partnership. But, other types of partners have more limited liability, including: (i) limited partners (these partners' liability is generally limited to the amount of their investment); (ii) secret partners (these partners are active in the ventures but are unknown to the public), and (iii) silent partners (these partners are usually inactive with only a financial interest in the partnership).

The Partnership Agreement: Rights and Duties of Partners

The importance of a partnership agreement cannot be strongly emphasized enough. I often see people who claim, "We have been the best of friends for years; we know what we are doing," How can I ask my father to sign a partnership agreement?" How can you not? As I pointed out earlier, it is essential that business affairs are separated from friendship and family, at least when it comes to structuring the firm. This is a serious deal. No matter how well you know your partner, you probably have not worked with him or her in this particular kind of situation. You have no way of predicting all the things that can cause a disagreement with your partner. The partnership agreement gives you an unbiased mechanism for resolving disagreements or dissolving the partnership, if it comes to that.

Of course, consulting an attorney is necessary when drawing up an agreement, so that you are not inadvertently causing yourself further problems by the way a phrase is worded in the agreement or leaving something important out. The partnership agreement addresses the following:

1. The legal name of the partnership.
2. Date of formation of the partnership.
3. The nature of the business. That is, statement of the business purpose or purposes.
4. Names and addresses of all partners.
5. Statement of fact of partnership.
6. Duration of the business.
7. Name and location of the business.
8. How long the partnership is to last. Just like any contract, it needs a stop date.
9. What each of the partners is contributing to the partnership – capital, in-kind goods, services, and so forth. This is the initial capitalization.
10. Any sales, loans, or leases to the partnership.
11. Provision for accounting records and their accessibility to partners.
12. Specific duties of each partner: Who is responsible for what – the management of the partnership?
13. The sale of a partnership interest. This clause restricts a partner's right to sell his or her interest to third parties. It provides, however, a method by which a partner can divest his or her interest in the partnership.
14. Provision for dissolution and for sharing the net assets. How the partnership can be dissolved.
15. What happens if a partner leaves or dies?
16. How disputes will be resolved.

Unless specified otherwise in the articles, a partner is generally recognized as having certain implicit rights. For example, partners share profits or losses equally if they have not agreed on a profit-and-loss-sharing ratio. In a partnership, each partner has *agency power*, which means that a partner can bind all members of the firm. Good faith, together with reasonable care in the exercise of management duties, is required of all partners in a business. If you do not execute a partnership agreement, all partners are equal under the law.

Termination of Partnership

Death, incapacity, or withdrawal of a partner terminates a partnership and necessitates liquidation or reorganization of the business. Liquidation often results in substantial losses to all partners. It may be legally necessary, however, because a partnership is a close personal relationship of the parties that cannot be maintained against the will of any one of them.

This disadvantage may be partially overcome at the time a partnership is formed by stipulating in the articles of partnership that surviving partners can continue the business after buying the decedent's interest. This can be facilitated by having partners carry mutual life insurance. Or the executor might act as a partner until the heirs become of age. In the latter case, the agreement should also provide for liquidation in the event of unpredictability or in the event of major disagreements with the executor as partner.

The Limited Partnership

A small business sometimes finds it desirable to use a special form of the partnership called the limited partnership.[2] This form consists of at least one general partner and one or more limited partners. The *general partner* remains personally liable for the debts of the business, but all *limited partners* have limited personal liability as long as they do not take an active role in the management of the partnership. In other words, limited partners risk only the capital, which they invest in the business. Because of this feature, an individual with substantial personal assets can invest money in a limited partnership without exposing his or her total personal estate to liability claims that might arise through activities of the business.[3]

In the United States, for example, the limited partnership form is frequently used to provide real estate tax shelters to the limited partners. Thus, the limited partnership may acquire a piece of undeveloped real estate, apartment houses, or commercial buildings. Most of the interest and other costs of the partnership are prorated to the limited partners, who report them as tax-deductible expenditures on their personal income tax returns. When the property is finally sold, it may produce a capital gain, which is taxed at a lower rate than ordinary income.

THE LIMITED LIABILITY COMPANY

The limited liability company is a different form of organization because it is a legal entity under the law. Chartered or registered by the country or the state in which it resides, a limited liability company can survive the death or separation of all its owners. It can sue, be sued, acquire and sell real property, and lend money. Owners of a limited liability company are stockholders (or shareholders) who invest capital into the business and receive shares of stock usually proportionate to the level of their investment. Much like limited partners, shareholders are not responsible for the debts of the corporation (unless they have personally guaranteed them), and their investment is the limit of their liability.

There are two types of limited liability companies – the closely held and the publicly quoted corporation. Most limited liability companies are closely held companies or corporations, which means that their stock is held privately by a few individuals. A closely held company operates as any type of corporation – general, professional, or nonprofit. In a close corporation, the number of shareholders you may have may be limited or restricted. In addition, holding directors meetings is not required. Such meetings are a requirement for a general corporation. The closely held limited liability company operates much like a partnership.

By contrast, in a public corporation, stock is traded on a securities exchange like the Nigerian Stock Exchange or the New York Stock Exchange. Shareholders own the company but they don't manage it. Shareholders exert influence through the directors they elect to serve and represent them on the board. The board of directors, in turn, manages affairs of the corporation at a policy level and hires and fires the officers who are responsible for the day-to-day decisions of the company.

The Benefits of a Limited Liability Company

The advantages of a limited liability company definitely outweigh the disadvantages. In another section, I mention that the owners enjoy limited liability to the extent of their investment. By selecting the limited liability form, an owner of a business can

(i) Raise capital through the sale of stock in the company.

(ii) Own a business without the public being aware of your involvement. So, if you want anonymity, it's the way to go.

(iii) Create different classes of stock to help you meet the various needs of investors. For example, you may want to issue *non-voting preferred stock* to conservative investors wanting to be first to recoup their investment in the event the business fails. Most stock issued is *common stock*, whose owners enjoy voting rights and share in the profits after the preferred stock has been paid.

(iv) Easily transfer ownership. In a private corporation, you want assurances that your shareholders can't sell their stock to just anyone. In other words, you want to know who owns your stock. You can protect yourself by including a buy-sell clause in the stockholder's agreement. Usually, this clause specifies that the stock must first be offered to the firm at an agreed-upon price.

(v) Enter into corporate contracts and sue or be sued without the signatures of the owners.

(vi) Enjoy more status in the business world than other legal forms because limited liability companies survive apart from their owners.

Disadvantages of a Limited Liability Company

Every legal form has disadvantages and risks, and the limited liability form is no exception. Here are the disadvantages or risks worth considering when contemplating using the limited liability form.

(i) Limited liability corporations are much more complex, cumbersome, and expensive to set up. This explains why most entrepreneurs and small business owners start with the sole proprietorship in the beginning.

(ii) Registered limited liability companies are subject to more government regulation.

(iii) A limited liability company pays taxes on profits regardless of whether they are distributed as dividends to stockholders.

(iv) Shareholders of limited liability corporations do not receive the tax benefits if a company losses.

(v) By selling shares of stock in your company, you are effectively giving up a measure of control to a board of directors. The reality, however, is that the entrepreneur determines who sits on that board of directors in privately held corporations.

(vi) As an entrepreneur, you must keep your personal finances and the firm's finances completely separate. You must conduct directors' meetings, and maintain minutes from those meetings. If you don't, you may leave your company open to what is known as *piercing the corporate veil*, which makes you and your officers liable personally for the company.

BUYING AN EXISTING BUSINESS

For logical reasons some would-be entrepreneurs choose to buy an existing business rather than create a new venture. An existing sole proprietorship business, a partnership or limited liability company can be bought by any one.

Reasons for Buying an Existing Business

One reason for buying an existing business is that it reduces the uncertainties involved in launching an entirely new venture. A successful going concern has demonstrated an ability to attract customers, to control costs, and to make a profit. Although future operations may be different, the firm's past record shows what it can do under actual market conditions. For example, the satisfactory location of an on-going business venture eliminates one major uncertainty. Although traffic counts are useful in assessing the potential value of a location, the litmus test comes when a business opens its doors at that location. And this test has already been met in the case of an existing firm, with the results available in the form of sales and profit data.

Another reason is that the buyer of an existing business typically acquires its personnel, inventories, physical facilities, established banking connections, and ongoing relationships with suppliers. Consider the time and effort otherwise required in acquiring them from "scratch." Of course, this situation is an advantage only under certain conditions. For example, the firm's skilled, experienced employees constitute a valuable asset only if they will continue to work for the new owner. The physical facilities must not be obsolete, and the relationships with banks, customers and suppliers must be healthy.

Still another reason is that an on-going business may become available at what seems to be a low price. Whether it is actually a "good buy" must be determined by the prospective new owner. The price may appear low, but several factors could make the "bargain price" anything but a bargain. For example, the business may be losing money; the location may be deteriorating; or the seller may intend to reopen another business as a competitor. However, the business may indeed be a bargain and turn out to be a wise investment if the buyer has a plan for turning these around.

Finding a Business to Buy

Frequently in the course of day-to-day living and business contacts, a would-be buyer comes across an opportunity to buy an existing business. For example, a sales representative for a manufacturer or a wholesaler may be offered an opportunity to buy a customer's retail business. In other cases, the would-be buyer may need to search for a business to buy. Advertisements in local newspapers provide some leads.

Other sources of business leads include suppliers, distributors, trade associations, and even bankers, who may know of business firms available for purchase. In addition, realtors, particularly those who specialize in the sale of business firms and business properties, can also provide leads. Moreover, these realtors, or brokers, can assist in closing the transaction. Naturally the buyer would wish to deal with a reputable broker and be aware of a broker's motivation in making the sale.

Investigating and Evaluating the Existing Business

Regardless of the source of business leads, each opportunity requires a background investigation and careful evaluation. As a preliminary step, the would-be buyer needs to acquire information about the business. Some of this information can be obtained through personal observation or discussion with the seller of the business. Also important is the need to talk with other parties such as suppliers, bankers, and possibly customers of the business. Although some of this investigation requires personal checking, the would-be buyer can also seek the help of outside experts. The two valuable sources of assistance in this regard are accountants and lawyers.

Reasons Why People Sell Their Businesses

The seller's real reasons for selling an existing business may or may not be disclosed. The buyer must be wary, therefore, of taking the seller's explanations at face value. Here, for example, are some of the reasons why owners offer their businesses for sale:

(i) Old age or illness.
(ii) Desire to relocate in a different section of the country or migrate to a different country.
(iii) Decision to accept a position with another company.
(iv) Unpredictability of the business.
(v) Discontinuance of an exclusive sales franchise.

The buyer will also be interested generally in the history of the business and the direction in which it is moving. To form a clear idea of the firm's value, however, the buyer must eventually examine the financial data pertaining to its operation. This calls for an independent audit of the firm offered for sale.

The major purpose of an **independent audit** is to reveal the accuracy and completeness of the financial statements of the business. It also determines whether the seller has used acceptable accounting procedures in depreciating equipment and in valuing inventory. To accept statements prepared by the seller's bookkeeper without an independent audit would be dangerous. Therefore, the would-be buyer should contact a competent, independent auditor for this purpose. Of course, the would-be buyer may refer to an audit report prepared by an independent chartered accountant if this report is available and can be obtained directly from the auditor. If audit reports are available for the past two or three years, or even longer, the would-be buyer can obtain some idea of trends for the business.

Even audited statements may be misleading and require adjustment to obtain a realistic picture of the business. For example, business owners sometimes understate business income by concealing receipts from the tax collector. This illegal practice consists in receiving cash payments from customers without recording them on the books or including them in the firm's income tax returns. Adjustment may also be required if the pricing of goods and/or services is abnormally low, that is, lower than necessary to attract a satisfactory volume of business. Other items in audited income statements may also need some adjustment including personal or family expenses and wage or salary payments. For example, costs related to the family use of business vehicles frequently appear as a business expense. And in some situations, family members receive excessive compensation or none at all. All these items must be examined carefully to be sure that they relate to the business and are realistic.

Valuation of the Business

Prior to negotiating with the seller of a business, the worth (or value) of the business must be estimated by the buyer. The basis for the buyer's estimate is the adjusted financial statements described above. Two simple approaches to calculating the value of a business are explained below.

(i) *Value Based on the Balanced Sheet:* The balance sheet of a firm shows its total assets and total liabilities, or obligations. The difference between the total assets and total liabilities is the **net worth**, or **book value**, of the business. Difficulties arise, however, when one estimates the value of a business based on its balance sheet. First, asset values shown on the balance sheet often differ from their current value. The historical costs of assets shown on the books may bear little resemblance to the current value of the assets. Second, the real value of individual assets is often different from their combined value as part of a going concern. The total is more than the sum of its parts. This situation can be compared, for example, to a hungry person who enjoys eating a piece of cake much more than eating the individual ingredients. In a similar manner, many individual assets are combined in a productive pattern to form a more valuable existing business.

(ii) *Value Based on the Income Statement*: Because of the difficulties associated with valuing a business on the basis of its balance sheet, it is proper here to suggest another simple method of valuation, which is based on net income or profit, as reported in the income statement. In most cases this method provides a reasonably accurate value for negotiating purposes.[4]

Another valuation system, which is based on net income, requires the use of a process known as **capitalization of profit**. Using this process, the buyer first estimates the profit that may be expected and then determines the amount of investment, which should logically earn the estimated profit.

As an illustration, suppose that the adjusted income statement of a business shows that its annual net income is $60,000. What should a buyer be willing to pay for such a business? To answer this question, the buyer should follow four logical steps:

Step 1: Estimate the probable *future* profit on the basis of *past* profit data. In doing this, the buyer must adjust past profit figures to eliminate nonrecurring gains or losses, for example, a loss from a fire. The buyer must ask what profit the business can be expected to earn in the future.

Step 2: Allow for personal time invested in the business. In the case of a sole proprietorship, see whether the expenses shown on the income statement include a proper salary for the owner-manager. If no allowance has been made for the owner-manager's salary, a reasonable amount should be deducted before capitalizing the profit. Of course, this assumes that the buyer intends to devote personal time to the business, time that might otherwise be spent productively elsewhere. In the case of a partnership, the "salary" for a partner is not identified as an expense but is included as part of the firm's net profit.

Step 3: Estimate the degree of risk involved in the business. One might expect a 30 to 40 percent return in businesses that entail considerable risk; in a less hazardous venture, 20 or 25 percent might be quite satisfactory.

Step 4: Determine the existence and amount of goodwill, if any. Goodwill derives from the reputation of the firm, from the loyalty of customers or other advantages that cause earnings to be exceptionally high in view of the physical resources involved. Goodwill tends to be less durable than other assets and thus is worth proportionately less to the buyer.

How Do You Calculate the Value Based on Net Income?

Following the four steps discussed above, let us now calculate the value of a business whose annual income is estimated to be $60,000.

According to step 1, we must decide whether $60,000 can be expected to continue in the future. An examination of the income statement may show no unusual expenses or income items. A general review of business prospects, moreover, may suggest no drastic changes in the foreseeable future. We might assume, therefore, that the $60,000 constitutes a reasonable prediction of future profit.

Following step 2, we may find that no salary expense has been shown for the owner-manager in arriving at the $60,000 profit. If the buyer places a value of $25,000 on personal time and effort, this amount should be deducted from the $60,000, leaving $35,000 to be capitalized. This $35,000 is the profit, which will compensate the buyer for the amount invested in the business.

When estimating the degree of risk involved in the business as prescribed in step 3, we assume that the buyer considers the business to be moderately safe and feels that a 20 percent profit would be a good return on investment (ROI) in comparison with alternative investment opportunities. We can then calculate the value of the business as follows, assuming that no goodwill exists:

$$\text{Value of business} \times \text{Desired rate of return} = \text{Net profit}$$
$$\text{Value of business} \times 20\% = \$35,000$$
$$\text{Value of business} = \$35,000/.20$$
$$\text{Value of business} = \$175,000$$

Thus, the $175,000 provides a benchmark for use in negotiating the purchase price of the business.

In following Step 4, the buyer inquires about the existence of goodwill. If the profit is unreasonably high in view of the physical resources of the business, the buyer will be purchasing goodwill along with the physical assets of the business. And if a substantial amount of the firm's profit is attributable to goodwill, the buyer should value the firm more conservatively due to the intangible and somewhat fragile nature of goodwill. Under these circumstances the buyer needs to use a higher rate for capitalizing the profit. Assuming that the higher rate, adjusted for goodwill, is 30 percent rather than 20 percent, the value of the business can then be calculated as follows:

$$\text{Value of business} \times \text{Desired rate of return} = \text{Net profit}$$
$$\text{Value of business} \times 30\% = \$35,000$$
$$\text{Value of business} = \$35,000/.30$$
$$\text{Value of business} = \$116,667$$

Clearly, the estimated value of the business is lower when we assume that we are paying for goodwill, which may soon disappear.

Other Factors to Evaluate: A number of other factors remain to be explored when evaluating an existing business. Some of these factors include the following:

(i) *Competition*: The prospective buyer should look into the extent, intensity, and location of competing businesses. In particular, the buyer should check to see whether the business in question is gaining or losing in the race with competitors.

(ii) *Market*: The adequacy of the market to maintain all competing business units, including the one purchased, should be determined. This entails market research and personal, on-the-spot observation at each competitor's place of business.

(iii) *Building*: The quality of the buildings housing the business should be examined to see if the buyer would spend additional money in renovation or expansion.

(iv) *Legal commitments*: These include contingent liabilities, unsettled lawsuits, delinquent tax payments, missed payrolls, overdue rent or installment payments, and mortgages of record against any of the real property acquired.

(v) *The present and future social, economic, and political development of the area*: The political stability of the area must be examined as well as present and future economic potential of the area. You would not want to buy a business in an area where there is constant social and political unrest and the area's economy is on the downturn.

(vi) *Product prices*: The prospective buyer should compare the prices of competing products or services in the locality. This is necessary to assure full and fair pricing of goods and services whose sales are reported on the seller's financial statements.

Finally, the purchase of a business must be done in such a way that both parties (the seller and the buyer) do not run into legal problems after the deal has been closed. As in the purchase of real estate, the purchase of a business is closed at a specific time. The closing may be handled, for example, by a title company or an attorney. Preferably, the closing should occur under the direction of an independent third party. If the seller's attorney is suggested as the closing agent, the buyer should exercise caution. Regardless of the closing arrangements, the buyer should never go through a closing without extensive consultation with a qualified attorney. A number of important documents are completed during the closing. These include a bill of sale, certifications as to taxing and other governmental authorities such as certificate of occupancy, and agreements pertaining to future payments and related guarantees to the seller.

FRANCHISING

In *Franchising*, an independent business owner (the franchisee) pays fees and royalties to a parent company (franchisor) in return for the right to become identified with its trademark, to sell its products or services, and often to use its business format and system.[5] Entrepreneurship carries a double-edged sword: risk and independence. As an entrepreneur, you have the freedom to pursue any strategy you want, but you run the risk that what you want to do is a mistake. Franchises offer the opportunity to minimize your risk of mistakes in exchange for a degree of independence. Franchising is a creative form of business, which helps thousands of entrepreneurs realize their business-ownership dreams. The franchising concept is an attractive option for operating a small business. The term *franchising* is defined in many ways. In this book, we use a broad definition to encompass its wide scope. As a form of business ownership, franchising is a marketing system that revolves around a two-party legal and management agreement whereby one party is granted the privilege to conduct business as an individual owner but is required to operate according to certain methods and terms specified by the other party. The legal agreement is known as the **franchise contract**, and the privileges it contains are called the franchise. The sponsor of the privileges is the **franchiser**. A company that creates and sells franchises is called **franchiser**. The party receiving the privileges is called the **franchisee** (that is, the person who has purchased a franchise).

The potential value of any franchising arrangement is determined by the rights contained in the franchise contract, and the extent and importance of these rights are quite varied. For example, a potential franchisee may desire the right to use a name.

Alternatively, the potential franchisee may need an entire marketing system, often with a new retail store and a standardized method of operation. Regardless of the specific need, a franchise is the mechanism, which gives birth to an independently owned business, with the franchisee hiring the employees and assuming the operating responsibilities.

"Look before you leap" is an old adage, which should be heeded by potential franchisees. Entrepreneurial enthusiasm should not cloud the eyes to the realities, both good and bad, of franchising. Let's first look at the advantages of buying a franchise and then examine the weaknesses of this decision.

Advantages of Franchising

A franchise is attractive for many good reasons. Three advantages in particular warrant further discussion. A franchise can offer (i) managerial guidance and formal training, (ii) financial assistance, and (iii) marketing benefits. Naturally, all franchises may not be equally strong on all these points. But it is these advantages which cause many persons to consider the franchise arrangement.

Formal Training and Managerial Guidance: The importance of formal training and managerial guidance received from the franchiser is underlined by the generally glaring weakness in managerial ability of small business owners and entrepreneurs. As pointed out in chapter five, one of the reasons why businesses fail is managerial, marketing, financial and organizational incompetence on the part of the owner/manager. Franchising provides solutions to this problem. To the extent that this weakness can be overcome, therefore, the training program offered by the franchiser constitutes a major benefit. Franchises are great for people who want systems. With the franchise you get guidance and parameters within which to work. You can get into business, get some training, and by virtue of the franchise's reputation, get your operation properly positioned right from the start.

The value and the effectiveness of training are evident from the records of business failures, a large majority of which is caused by deficiencies in management. For example, in the United States, there is a high failure rate among businesses in the fast-food industry. However, franchisees with such franchisers as McDonald's, Burger King, and Kentucky Fried Chicken have reputedly never experienced a failure. There appears to be little question that the failure rate for independent small businesses in general is much higher than for franchised businesses in particular. In Nigeria, for example, the consulting branch of the University of Lagos, Unilag Consult, has been in the business of providing effective training to those who use its brand name. Thus, *Wisdom Gate High School* located in Ikeja is able to provide services under the technical supervision of Unilag Consult.

These advantages do not mean that operating as a franchise is a short road to entrepreneurial success. There are several factors that can inhibit the success of a franchise business. For example, a particular franchiser may offer unsatisfactory training, or the franchisee may not apply the training or may fail for some other reasons.

Financial Assistance: The costs of starting a business are often high and the prospective entrepreneur's sources of capital quite limited. The entrepreneur's standing as a prospective borrower is weakest at this point. But by teaming up with franchising organization, the aspiring franchisee will enhance the likelihood of obtaining financial assistance. If the franchising organization considers the applicant to be a suitable prospect with a high probability of success, it frequently extends a helping hand financially. For example, the franchisee seldom is required to pay the complete cost of establishing the business. In addition, the beginning franchisee is normally given a payment schedule that can be met through successful operation. Also, the franchisor may permit delay in payments for products, services or supplies obtained from the parent organization, thus increasing the franchisee's working capital.

Marketing Benefits and Brand-Name Appeal: A licensed franchisee purchases the right to use a nationally or globally known and advertised brand name for a product or service. Thus, the franchisee has the advantage of identifying his or her business with a widely recognized trademark, which usually provides a great deal of drawing power. Most franchised products and services are widely known and accepted. For example, customers will readily go to Sheraton Hotels, Holiday Inn or Hilton Hotels in Nigeria because they know the reputation of the services offered by these franchisees. Thus, franchising offers both a proven successful line of business and product or service identification.

The entrepreneur who enters a franchising agreement acquires the right to use the franchisor's advertised trademark or brand name. For example, wholesale distributors of *Panasonic* product lines in Nigeria are proud to be associated with the Panasonic brand name. This serves to identify the local enterprise with the widely recognized product or service. Of course, the value of product identification differs with the type of product or service and the extent to which it has received widespread promotion. In any case, the franchisor maintains the value of its name by continued advertising and promotion. The franchise organization's investment in marketing and advertising goes a long way in building brand identity, positive associations in consumers' minds that benefit each franchisee. These are important advantages for the small retailer who doesn't mind trading some independence for a greater chance of success.

In addition to offering a proven successful line of business and readily identifiable products and services, franchisers have developed and tested their methods of operation. The standard operating manuals and procedures they supply have permitted other entrepreneurs to operate successfully. This is one reason why franchisers insist upon the observance of standardized methods of operation and performance. If some franchisees were allowed to operate at substandard levels, they could easily destroy the customer's confidence in the entire system.

Without well-standardized operating methods, an independent business owner is often inclined to do what comes naturally and throw effective management to the wind. Recall that many small-business owners tend to disregard financial planning, records, and control (see chapter five). Observing operating methods that have proven successful elsewhere, therefore, should strengthen the new franchisee and offer some assurance of success.

The existence of proven products and methods, however, does not guarantee that a franchised business will succeed. For example, what appeared to be a satisfactory location as a result of the franchisor's marketing research techniques may turn out to be inferior.

Or the franchisee may lack ambition or perseverance. Yet the fact that a franchisor can show a record of successful operation proves that the system can work and has worked elsewhere.

Limitations of Franchising

Franchising, according to some experts, is like a coin - it has two sides.[6] Given the positive side of the coin of a franchise, as we have discussed above, the negative side should not be flipped over hurriedly, but rather examined with the same detail. A few limitations to franchising keep it from being a perfect form of business-ownership. In particular, we can identify three shortcomings that permeate the franchise form of business. These are: (i) the cost of a franchise, (ii) the restrictions on growth, which can accompany a franchise contract, and (iii) the inherent loss of absolute independence on the part of the franchisee.

Cost of a Franchise: Fees of various types must be paid to the franchisor. Generally speaking, the higher fees will be asked by the more successful and well-known franchisers. If entrepreneurs could earn the same income independently, they would save the amount of these fees and royalties. However, this is not a valid objection if the franchisor provides the benefits previously described. In that case, franchisees are merely paying for the advantages of their relationship with the franchisor. And this may be a good investment, indeed.

Restrictions on Growth: As an entrepreneur, there is this idea of growth. Growth can take several forms such as geographical expansion, product or service mix, additional customer groups, forward or backward integration, etc. Many franchise contracts restrict the franchisee to a defined sales territory, thereby eliminating this form of growth. However, the franchisor usually will agree not to grant another franchise to operate within the same territory. In the United States, for example, if you operate a pizza restaurant under the PepsiCo Company, your product mix such sodas and soft drinks are restricted to those under the PepsiCo brand name. You are literally forbidden to carry any product under the Coca-cola label.

Loss of Absolute Independence: The main idea behind franchising is that it allows individually owned businesses to operate as part of a large chain. The products and services offered, and many other aspects of the operation, are prepackaged and held to a standard imposed by the franchisor. As pointed out by Joan Gillman, "People buy franchises because they remove much of the possibility of failure. The 'school of hard knocks' lessons that entrepreneurs experience in their start-up years are handed to the franchisee, neatly packaged."[7] Thus, franchises work well for people who want to be part of a larger chain team effort. Not for those who want to run their businesses independently. Meaning that if your motive of becoming an entrepreneur is becoming an independent person, doing what you like to do, a franchise form of business-ownership is not the prescribed route. The reason is that you are going to surrender a considerable amount of your independence upon signing a franchise agreement. The franchisor's regulation of business operations may be unpleasant to an entrepreneur who cherishes independence. In addition, some franchise contracts may go to extremes by specifying practices that are more helpful to others in the chain than to the local operation.

Evaluating Franchise Opportunities

Once an interest in becoming a franchisee emerges, much remains to be done before the dream materializes. The prospective franchisee must locate the right opportunity, investigate a franchise offer for possible fraud, and examine the franchise contract carefully. The following steps are suggestions in the overall process for evaluating the merits and shortfalls of franchising, rather than individual ownership, in a line of business.

1. *The Willingness and Ability to run a Franchise*: You must evaluate your own strengths in selling, management, and willingness to devote long hours and years of endeavor to the franchising business. As has already been pointed out, a franchise business is good for those who are ready to delegate responsibilities to others. Most importantly, the willingness to work within the confinement of the rules and regulations contained in the franchise contract is very important.

2. *Growth and Expansion Possibility*: As a prospective franchisee, you must assess the likelihood of a growing demand for the product or service offered in the operating territory of the planned franchisee firm over the terms of the proposed lease. If demand does not appear to be expanding geographically, the possibility of expanding the territory or types of goods/services offered should be written into the franchise contract before it is signed.

3. *Beware of Franchising Frauds*: Every industry has its share of shady operations, and franchising is no exception. Unscrupulous fast-buck conmen offer a wide variety of fraudulent schemes to attract the investment of unsuspecting individuals. The franchisor in such cases is merely interested in obtaining the capital investment of the franchisee and not in committing to a franchise relationship. The growth of the franchising industry and the substantial opportunities in legitimate franchising create an opportunity for illegitimate operators who attempt to fleece the public.

   As one example of the fraudulent operator, a group of persons in Lagos, Nigeria, put out an advertisement in which they are supposedly representing two universities: one in England and the other in Hungary. The "franchisee" is supposed to offer degrees on behalf of these universities. Many Nigerians paid the initial registration fee only to find out that the outfit was a fraudulent one. These colleges and universities have no such franchise relationship or contract with the Nigerian office: they were set up as a front to dupe those who want to get services from a franchise organization. In a more serious note, others have been deceived into investing their money in nonexistent businesses by buying into this scheme. In Nigeria, some fraudulent franchise practitioners in England would advertise the possibility of offering someone in Nigeria the opportunity to have his other own business through a franchise option. In most cases, the would-be franchisee, after paying the initial "registration fee" or "application fee" does not know where to go because there are no franchisers. Thus, it is important that you, as a prospective franchisee, review the franchisor's profile for any shady business practices in the past, such as bankruptcies, lawsuits brought or defended, and so on, and evaluate their merits. You should also evaluate the chances that problems could be on the horizon that involve you as a prospective franchisee and your ability to operate profitably.

4. *Examining the Franchise Contract*: The basic features of the relationship between the franchisor and the franchisee are contained in the franchise contract. The contract is typically a complex document, often running to several pages. Because of its extreme importance in furnishing the legal basis for the franchised business, no franchise contract should ever be signed by the franchisee without legal counsel. As a matter of fact, many reputable franchisers insist that the franchisee have a legal counsel before signing the agreement. An attorney would be useful in anticipating trouble and in noting objectionable features of the franchise contract.

In addition to consulting an attorney, it is important that the prospective franchisee makes use of as many other sources of help as possible. In particular, you should discuss the franchise proposal with a banker, going over it in as much detail as possible. You should also obtain the services of a professional accounting firm in examining the franchisor's statement of projected sales, operating expenses, and net income. The accountant can be of invaluable help in evaluating the quality of these estimates and in discovering projections, which may be unlikely to occur. Among the many other items to be examined in any franchise contract are the following:

- Fees that are involved.
- Geographical limits of the franchise.
- Training provisions.
- Restrictions upon the purchase of materials.
- Control of operations and performance standards.
- Quota clauses.
- Prohibitions against the sale of competing lines.
- Price requirements.
- Record-keeping requirements.
- Necessary hours and days of operation.
- Advertising provisions.

In essence, as a prospective franchisee, you should evaluate the level of support services for reasonableness in light of the size of the franchise fee, and determine with several personal interviews how managers/franchisees view their past relationships with the managers of the franchiser. You should review the cost estimates and estimates of return on investment or equity capital suggested by the franchisers for reasonableness in comparison to independently operated firms in the industry. You must also review provisions for protecting the operating territory of the franchisee from other franchised operations to know, for example, if there is any provision for relocating in the event that a major competitor locates a similar firm nearby.

Protecting Oneself against Franchise Frauds

Dishonest franchisers tend to follow certain patterns, and well-prepared franchisees who know what to look for can avoid trouble. The following clues should arouse the suspicion of an entrepreneur about to invest in a franchise:

- Claims that the franchise contract is a standard one and that "you don't need to read it."
- A franchiser who fails to give you a copy of the required disclosure document at your first face-to-face meeting.
- A marginally successful prototype store or no prototype at all.
- A poorly prepared operations manual outlining the franchise system or no manual (or system) at all.
- Oral promises of future earnings without written documentation.
- A high franchisee turnover rate or a high termination rate.
- An unusual amount of litigation brought against the franchiser.
- Attempts to discourage you from allowing an attorney to evaluate the franchise contract before you sign it.
- No written document to support claims and promises.
- A high-pressure sale that forces you to either sign the contract now or lose the opportunity.
- "Get-rich-quick schemes," promises of huge profits with only minimum effort.
- Reluctance to provide a list of present franchisees for you to interview.
- Evasive and vague answers to your questions about the franchise and its operation.

Not every franchise failure or bad story is the result of dishonest franchisers. More often than not, the problems that arise in franchising have more to do with franchisees who buy legitimate franchises without proper research and analysis. They end up in businesses they don't enjoy and that they are not well suited to operate. How can you avoid this mistake? The following steps will help you make the right choice.

Evaluate Yourself

Before looking at any franchise, an entrepreneur should study his or her own traits, goals, experience, likes, dislikes, risk orientation, income requirements, time and family commitments, and other characteristics. Will you be comfortable working in a structured environment? What kinds of franchises fit your desired lifestyle? What is your ideal job description? Knowing what you enjoy doing (and what you don't want to do) will help you narrow your search. The goal is to find the franchise that is right for you.

THE NONPROFIT ORGANIZATION

Let us dispel the biggest myth about nonprofit organizations (or not-for-profit organizations) first. You can make a profit in a nonprofit company; in fact, doing so is a good idea. What you can't do is distribute those profits in the form of dividends the way other legal forms do. A nonprofit organization is one that, by law, is unable to hold or distribute profits like a "for-profit" organization can. This means that the nonprofit company is required by law to redistribute any "profits" back into the company (in the form of salaries, new capital, etc), or to other nonprofits or to charity. This also means that nonprofit companies do not have the ability to issue or sell stock/shares and, therefore, cannot pay dividends on any earnings. Furthermore, nonprofit companies may be required to have an unpaid (volunteer) board of directors with a larger number of directors than a business corporation. Although some nonprofits may run very similar to some for-profit companies, the laws restricting the two are very different. Nonprofit organizations are mainly those that are set up for philanthropic purposes. Social organizations that collects money and utilize for some social work, is one example, but there are thousands of others. Ideally, a nonprofit organization or entity is formed for charitable, public, education, religious, or mutual benefit (as in trade associations).

Like the limited liability company, the nonprofit is a legal entity with a life of its own and offers its members limited liability. Profits that it generates from its nonprofit activities are not taxed as long as the company meets the state and federal requirements for exemption from taxes (as I point out in the following section, it is very necessary to consult an attorney for these issues).When you form a nonprofit organization, you actually give up proprietary interest in the corporation and dedicate all the assets and resources to tax-exempt activities. If you choose to dissolve the corporation, you must distribute those assets to another tax-exempt organization. In effect, you cannot take the assets with you. Any profits you make from for-profit activities are taxed the same as any other corporation. Financial Institutions Training Centre in Papa, Lagos, Nigeria is nonprofit organization. But when it holds a seminar and decides to charge fees for participants, the seminar is seen as a for-profit activity and profits derived from it are taxed as in any other corporation.

Nonprofit organizations derive their revenues from a variety of sources. They receive donations from corporations (these donations are tax deductible to the corporation) and others, conduct activities to raise money, or sell services (a for-profit activity). As entrepreneurs, founders of nonprofit, tax-exempt corporations can pay themselves a good salary, provide themselves with cars, and generally do the kinds of things you would do with a normal business firm, except distribute profits. Most entrepreneurs who start nonprofits do so for reasons other than money. Some of those reasons include a driving need to give back to the community. For example, the Sunshine Foundation was set up by the late publisher of *Classique Magazine* in Nigeria, May Mofe-Damijo, in order to "keep faith with her dreams to reach out to the underprivileged." The mission of this nonprofit organization is to "assist the old and the neglected in the society."⁸

The rise and growth of nonprofit organizations has become a trend in the developing countries. We witness this in the proliferation of religious organizations, schools and trade associations. But most of these ventures or establishments lack the legal requirements necessary to run such outfits. As the Sub-Saharan Africa region develops, the time will come when the law will be fully applied to their operations. From the perspective of an entrepreneur going into a nonprofit outfit, the best advice is to consult legal experts in this area.

CHOOSING AN ATTORNEY

A review of legal organizational forms and areas of business law makes evident the need for proper legal counsel. Unless the entrepreneur is trained in law, he or she cannot be expected to know the law sufficiently well to avoid the use of professionals. Nor should the small business owner wait to establish a working relationship with a competent attorney until an emergency arises. The small firm's team of advisors and counselors should include an attorney, a chartered accountant, a banker, and other specialists.

The entrepreneurial firm needs an attorney experienced in legal practice related to small business. Lawyers might be selected by using the Yellow Pages of a telephone directory, but an informed choice requires a recommendation based on some acquaintanceship with the legal profession. Suggestions of possible attorneys may be obtained from the firm's banker, other business owners and friends. Because your friend or family member is an attorney does not qualify him or her to assist you in issues concerning the legal aspect of your business. What factors should be considered in selecting an attorney to represent the business? Following is one set of recommended criteria:

1. *Size of Practice.* Even though a small firm can offer personalized attention, a large firm may have a broader range of expertise. Either way, satisfy yourself that the lawyer is not too busy to be accessible, and not so available that you cannot help wondering why.

2. *Client Base.* Find out if representing other small-business owners is a major part of the lawyer's practice.

3. *Experience and Specialty.* The lawyer's background should qualify him or her to advise you on routine matters, as well as on major decisions.

4. *Sounding Board.* A cautious lawyer will consult other lawyers, both generalists and specialists, for your benefit. Find out whom the lawyer consults, and when.

5. *Philosophy.* You won't learn everything in one interview with your lawyer, but try to assess his or her basic attitudes toward the law and the conduct of business. It is

important that the lawyer's views be compatible with yours so that you can feel comfortable in relying on his or her judgment.

6. *Style*. You will want a lawyer who can clearly, objectively, and logically present both sides of an issue. Avoid the highly opinionated, the pedantic, the overly glib, and the paternalistic.

7. *Fee Structure*. Minimum fee schedules have been jettisoned, so you are left to informal comparisons and your own judgment of what is reasonable. Fees are a big source of attorney-client conflict, so discuss them openly at your first meeting.

The relationship of your firm or your relationship with its attorney is most effective when courtroom battles are unnecessary. Much of an attorney's contribution is made by providing information when specific questions arise, when contracts or other documents are reviewed, and when counseling is needed. The relationship should preferably be a continuing one. Once an attorney-client relationship is established, the client should utilize the attorney's services promptly whenever the need arises.

CHAPTER SUMMARY

The factors that affect the form and structure of business ownership are: (i) Who will be the owners of the company, (ii) The level of liability protection sought by the owner or owners, (iii) The level of freedom in managing the company sought by the owner or owners, (iv) The owners ambitions in terms of growth, (v) The startup capital requirements and cost of formation.

A sole proprietorship is a business owned and managed by one individual. A sole proprietorship is a business where the owner is essentially the business.

A partnership is usually formed when two or more people enter into a business relationship or venture together, when they decide to share assets, liabilities, and profits of their business. A partnership agreement is important because it gives the partners an unbiased mechanism for resolving disagreements or dissolving the partnership.

In a limited liability company, owners invest capital into the business and receive shares of stock usually proportionate to the level of their investment. A limited liability company is a legal entity.

One of the many reasons for buying an existing business is that it reduces the uncertainties involved in launching an entirely new venture. Another reason is that the buyer of an existing business typically acquires its personnel, inventories, physical facilities, established banking connections, and ongoing relationships with suppliers.

A business can be valued through (i) value based on the balance sheet, (ii) value based on the income statement, (iii) capitalization of profit. Other factors that must be considered include: competition, market, building, legal commitments, social, economic and political development in the area and the prices of the product.

Franchising is a form of ownership in which an independent business owner (the franchisee) pays fees and royalties to a parent company (the franchiser) in return for the right to become identified with its trademark, to sell its products or services, and often to use its business format and system.

The advantages of franchising include (i) formal training and managerial guidance, (ii) financial assistance, and (iii) marketing benefits and brand-name appeal.

The disadvantages of franchising include (i) high cost, (ii) restriction on growth, and (iii) loss of absolute independence.

Issues to consider when evaluating franchising opportunities include (i) the willingness and ability to run a franchise, (ii) growth and expansion possibility, (iii) avoid franchising frauds, and (iv) examine the franchise contract.

A nonprofit organization is formed for charitable, public, religious, educational, or mutual benefit (as in trade associations). Profits can be made in a nonprofit organization but it cannot be distributed in the form of dividends the way other legal forms do.

The criteria for selecting an attorney for the purpose of your business include (i) the size of the practice, (ii) the client base, (iii) experience and specialty, (iv) sounding board, (v) philosophy, (vi) style, and (vii) fee structure.

DISCUSSION QUESTIONS

1. Explain the major factors that can affect an entrepreneur's choice of forms of business ownership structure. Give examples, please! Discuss the relative importance of the four major legal forms of organization.

2. What is a partnership agreement? What issues does a partnership agreement address? Suppose a partnership is set up and operated without formal articles of partnership. What problems might arise? Explain.

3. Evaluate the four major forms of organization from the standpoints of management control by the owner and the sharing of the firm's profits.

4. What is the significance of the seller's real reasons for selling his or her business? How might you discover them?

5. Alhaji Ibrahim Dankori is a dealer in used cars. The store is located in the city of Kano, Nigeria. At the age of 67, Dankori believes that it is time for him to retire and enjoy the fruits of his labor. All of his two children are in England and are not ready to take over the business because they have their own businesses. So Dankori decided to sell the business. Chief Sam Okoh who has a car dealership in the city of Jos was at that time thinking of expanding his business and he believes that the city of Kano would be an ideal location. Chief Okoh saw Dankori's advertisement in the local newspaper and decided to negotiate with him. Dankori Enterprises (as the business is called) had posted an annual income for the past two years in the amount of 8,000,000 and 10,000,000 Naira respectively.

    As a valuator, how would you help Sam Okoh in the valuation of Dankori Enterprises following the four steps discussed in this chapter? What other factors would you take into consideration in evaluating Dankori's Enterprise as a buyer?

7. Discuss the advantages and limitations of a franchise business. As a prospective entrepreneur, why would you consider the franchising option as a form of business ownership?

CASE 13: BUYING A FRANCHISE: LOOK BEFORE YOU LEAP![9]

Bamidele Ogunaike almost rushed into their two-bedroom apartment holding a bottle of Gulder beer and a can of malt drink, struggling to put the drinks on the table, "Honey, I think I've found it!" he blurted out to his wife Funke. "This is just what I've been looking for, waiting for. Honey, it's about time. I told you, God will answer our prayers one day. My severance package with our savings will run out in three months time. The man said that that if we invested in this franchise now, we could be bringing in good money by then. It's that easy!" By this time Dele was already shaking as he could no longer control his excitement. His words were becoming incoherent.

Funke knew that Dele had been working very hard at finding another job since he had been a victim of the restructuring and down-sizing policy at his former employer. Dele had put over twenty-five years of service with the Nigerian Ports Authority. As far as his career was concerned everything was going well – he had a good job with good pay until he was laid off in 2004 as a result of the government's policy to "right-size" public sector organizations by adopting a cost-saving approach. Dele received a handsome severance package. Jobs were scarce even for someone with his supervisory background in handling good clearance in Nigerian ports. "Without any connection, nobody wants to hire a 51-year-old man when they can hire 23-year-old college graduates at less than half the salary and teach them what they need to know," Dele told Funke after months of fruitless job hunting. During this time, Dele had tried everything humanly possible. He had gone from one church to the other. The payments he has been making to the spiritualists for promised miracles have run deep into his pockets. He did not know what else to do.

Dele is a man who is very optimistic. He has been told several times that he would "hit the jackpot one day." However, the money from his former employer was fast running out and he was dipping his fingers into their savings. That was when Dele got the idea of setting up his own business. Rather than start an independent business from scratch, Dele felt more comfortable, given his 26-year career in business, opening a franchise. When he was laid off from his job, Dele had initially contemplated going into the "clearing and forwarding business". But he thought this was not going to be feasible as result of police crackdowns on the operators. A franchise can give me the support I need," he told Funke.

"Tell me about this franchise," Funke said.

"It's a phenomenal opportunity for us," Dele said, barely able to contain his excitement. "God has really answered my – our prayers this time. I saw this booth for Romanian Express Print Services at Lagos International Trade Fair. You know I told you I was going to attend the fair this morning and see what business opportunities they have? There were all kinds of business opportunities including this franchise company, but this one really caught my eye," Dele said as he pulled a rather plain-looking photocopy of a brochure from his briefcase.

"Is that their brochure"? Funke asked.

"Well, the company is growing so fast that they have temporarily run out of their normal literature. This is just temporary."

"Oh my God … You would think that a printing franchise could print flashier brochures even on short notice, but I guess …," said Funke.

"The main thing is the profit potential this business has," said Dele. I met one of their franchisees. I tell you honey, the guy was wearing designer suits from Milan, Italy, and he had expensive jewelry dripping from his fingers. He even showed me the picture of his jeep as we were talking. He is making a mint with this franchise, and he said we could too! I told him how I had prayed for this moment. Guess what he said. He said God has answered my prayers!"

Dele continued, "With the money I got from NPA and our savings, we could pay the one million Naira (N1,000,000) franchise fee and lease most of the equipment we need to get started. It will take every kobo of my savings and, but hey, it is an investment in our future. The representative said the company would help us with our grand opening and would help us compile a list of potential customers. They have solid market research teams.

"But they are located in Romania," Funke added.

"That is right, they are not local, they are international. But honey, they have local representatives here in Lagos, those who know the local market," Dele added, confidently.

"What would you print?" Funke inquired.

"Anything!" Dele answered. "The franchise I talked to does flyers, posters, booklets, newsletters, advertising pieces, cards … you name it!"

"Wow! It seems like you will need lots of specialized equipment to do all that. How much does the total franchise package cost?" Funke asked.

"Well, I am not exactly sure. He never gave me an exact figure, but we can lease all the equipment we need from the franchisor!"

"Is this all of the material they gave you? I thought franchisers were supposed to have some kind of information packet to give to people," said Funke.

"Yeah, I asked him about that," said Dele. "He said that Romanian Express Print Services is just a small franchise. They would rather put their money into building a business and helping their franchisees succeed than into useless paperwork that nobody reads anyway. It makes sense to me."

"I guess so …," Funke said reluctantly.

"I think we need to take this opportunity, Honey," Dele said, with a look that spoke of determination and enthusiasm. "Besides, he said that there was another couple in this Ojuelegba district, where I intend to put our own that is already looking at this franchise and that the company will license only one franchise in this area. They don't want to saturate the market. He thinks they may take it. I think we have to move on this now, or we will lose the opportunity of a lifetime."

Funke had not seen Dele exhibit this much enthusiasm and excitement for anything since he had lost his job at the port authority. Piles of rejection letters from his job search had sapped Dele's zest for living. He had even turned to drinking of recent. Funke was surprised that Dele was talking for over an hour without opening the bottle of beer he brought home with him. She was glad to see "the old Dele" return, but she had her doubts about the franchise opportunity Dele was describing.

"It might just be the opportunity of a lifetime, Honey," she said. "But don't you think we need to find out a little more about this franchise before we invest that much money? I'm afraid of all these 419ers (business fraudsters), you know. I mean … Please let's look before we leap."

"Honey, I would love to do that, but like the man said, we may miss out on the opportunity of a lifetime if we don't sign today. I think we've got to move on this thing now!"

Case Discussion Questions

1. What advice would you offer Dele about investing in this franchise?

2. Map out a plan for Dele to use in finding the right franchise for him. What can Dele do to protect himself from making a bad franchise investment?

3. Summarize the advantages and disadvantages Dele can expect if he buys this particular franchise.

Chapter 14

ETHICS AND SOCIAL RESPONSIBILITY STRATEGIES FOR THE ENTREPRENEURIAL FIRM

"The houses of those who do what is right hold great wealth. But those who do what is wrong earn only trouble." (The Book of Proverbs, 15:6)

"I decided that a man who wants to reach the top must keep his record clear. He cannot do anything of which he is ashamed or that might bob up at some future time to embarrass him."
(A.P. Giannini, founder Bank of America)

CHAPTER LEARNING OBJECTIVES
After studying this chapter, you should be able to:

1. Understand the meaning of ethics and how it relates to business ethics.

2. Understand how to make sound strategic decisions from an ethics perspective.

3. Understand why acting socially responsible as a business owner gives you a competitive edge in the marketplace.

4. Understand the concept of stakeholder and how it relates to the management of your business.

INTRODUCTION: ETHICS, SOCIAL RESPONSIBILITY AND BUSINESSES COMPETITIVENESS

In this chapter, we now turn our attention to how the entrepreneur can use good business ethical behavior and socially responsible business actions to compete successfully in the chosen market. More than any other part of the world, Sub-Saharan Africa has suffered the most economically and socially from the prevalent of unethical business practices and the lack of social responsibility by economic and business organizations; whether small or large. Thus, similar to the call for profit maximization in the conduct of business, ethics in the conduct of business has slowly taken root in people's consciousness due to its importance to the economic health of business organizations, and hence to society as a whole.[1] At a more fundamental level, it is important that companies adopt a code of ethics that promotes professional integrity, business ethics, transparency, respect for contracts and commitments, while acting in a socially responsible manner. Adherence to acceptable ethical conduct in business engenders higher profitability, better company performance, improved efficiency and higher market valuation of companies. It is against this background that Peter John Opio suggests that "If an enterprise is to succeed, and to maintain its success, every aspect of its existence has to be considered as being potentially good or bad for its standing in the eyes of the public, which is reflected in profit or loss. A manager, who keeps his eyes on the 'bottom line,' turning his back to the customers, can therefore hardly be considered responsible."[2]

In this chapter, our focus will be on the responsibility of the owner of a business venture to do the right thing while making profit. Our point here is that there is a fundamental relationship between economic development, entrepreneurship and business ethics. We noted in chapter four that one of the biggest problems facing economic development, in general, and entrepreneurial development, in particular, has to do with the unethical social and business environment prevailing in Sub-Saharan Africa. The reason for this is multifaceted: (i) a pervasive culture of bribery, favoritism, and corruption, (ii) an inefficient and corrupt bureaucratic system of governance, (iii) a corrupt political system, (iv) a corrupt class of bureaucrats and business elites, (v) a corrupt, ill-equipped and unmotivated law enforcement system, and (vi) an inept and corrupt judicial system. Add all these together and you get a highly corrupt and an unethical business environment. Needless to add, the problem of corruption has militated against foreign investments in Sub-Saharan Africa, particularly in Nigeria. Swedish Minister of International Economic Affairs, leading a Swedish trade delegation to Nigeria points out that one of the major reasons why Swedish investors are not interested in Nigeria is because of the problem of corruption. "Once this issue of corruption is sorted out, investors and the foreign business community will be able to come to the long ball. It is a signal that is needed outside for investment flow." The Swedish Minister told reporters in Abuja (the Nigerian capital) that "Sweden will love to have agricultural exports from Nigeria but the country needs to address the scourge of corruption to make for a direct investment flow into the country."[3]

At the macro level, corruption reduces the returns on business investment and leads to low economic growth. In a country where corruption is common, unproductive bureaucrats who demand side payments for granting the enterprise permission to operate may siphon off the profits from a business activity. Corruption, as an unethical business practice "corrupts" both the bribe giver and the bribe taker. Corruption feeds on itself, and once a society has started to walk down the road of corruption, pulling back may be difficult if not impossible.

In many cases, the forces and mechanisms that engender corruption in a society are outside of the control of individual business owners and entrepreneurs. In such a case, there is nothing the owners of business can do to insulate themselves from the vagaries of corruption. In Sub-Saharan Africa, particularly in Nigeria, however, the culture of corruption that pervades society has also bred an unethical business culture to which business owners are both the practitioners and the victims. We noted in chapter five how the institutionalization of illegality among businessmen in Sub-Saharan Africa has become detrimental to the development of a viable entrepreneurial culture. In general, the issue of business ethics and social responsibility is crucial to the emergence of a modern entrepreneurial class of business owners in the context of Sub-Saharan Africa. Questions of ethical strategic management, accountability, transparency, responsibility to stakeholders (especially customers, creditors and shareholders), social responsibility, and compliance with incorporation regulations such as disclosure rules remain problematic among the emerging African entrepreneurial class. To develop economically, there must be established and acceptable mechanisms for improving the ethical business climate by promoting entrepreneurial accountability, transparency, responsibility and fairness. At the very least, the success of a business remains in the hands of the owner.

In this chapter, we will focus our attention on two important areas: (i) how to manage the business from an ethically accepted behavior by developing and applying a code of ethics in the pursuit of a profitable business operation and (ii) an examination of the responsibility of business owners to the stakeholders of the firm.

The issue of ethics in businesses is a global one and not restricted to certain geographical areas. However, the developing countries seem to be the regions where ethics and other forms of malpractices have come to impinge on the development of the region. For example, in the year 2000, KPMG, the international accounting firm, surveyed 3,075 working adults. Nearly half reported seeing unethical or illegal conduct of a serious nature at their jobs during the past year, and 76 percent said they had observed a "high level" of illegal or unethical conduct. The most common legal and ethical breaches reported by the survey respondents were deceptive sales practices, unsafe working condition, and mishandling of confidential or proprietary information.[4]

The fact that nearly all countries in the developing regions of the world are classified as corrupt nations naturally demands that any discussion about entrepreneurship and economic development must take the issues of ethics and social responsibility as an integral part in the discussion. I believe that the issue of ethics and social responsibility within the context of business and economic development in the developing countries must be accorded an urgent attention for the simple reason that many of these nations' authorities have not invested enough in the promotion of sound business ethics and corporate or business social responsibility. The purpose of this chapter, then, is to examine the mechanisms available for the creation of an enabling ethical environment conducive for entrepreneurial and economic growth. The chapter also proposes models and frameworks for acceptable ethical practices capable of enhancing the profitability of a business venture while doing the right thing. Although we cannot learn ethics solely from what is written in a textbook, it is possible to provide guidelines to how ones' ethical and moral behavior can be applied to the management of a business.

Our ethical conduct is written and/or imprinted inside us, written on the hearts and in the minds of humankind. It got there through the socialization process and was influenced by family or lack of family, friends, school, neighborhood, religion or lack of religious upbringing, as well as a myriad of other factors that make us who and what we are today. Another important factor that affects our ethical behavior is our professional belongingness. In other words, our ethical and moral behavior can also be shaped by what we have learned through the socialization process in our various professional fields. For example, auditors are imbibed with a set of professional ethics, so also are accountants, medical practitioners, bankers, and managers. The point is that if we expect high ethical standards from another profession such as the medical, law, and government agencies, small business owners must exercise the same characteristics in their dealings with stakeholder groups.

The purpose of this chapter is thus to examine the link between the efforts of entrepreneurial firm to develop and implement a winning strategy and its duties to (i) conduct its activities in an ethical manner and (ii) demonstrate socially responsible behavior by being a committed corporate citizen and attending to needs of other stakeholders apart from those of the owner such as employees, the communities in which it operates, the disadvantaged, and society as a whole. Business firms are economic entities, to be sure, but they are also social institutions that must justify their existence by their overall contribution to society.

THE MEANING OF ETHICS

For our purpose, *ethics* can be defined as the code of moral principles that sets standards of good or bad, right or wrong, in one's conduct and thereby guides the behavior of a person or group. Ethics tells us whether our behavior is moral or immoral and deals with fundamental human relationships – how we think and behave toward others and how we want them to think and behave toward us.[5] *Ethical principles or codes of conduct* are guides to moral behavior. For example, in most societies, lying, stealing, deceiving, and harming others are considered to be unethical and immoral. Honesty, keeping promises, helping others, and respecting the rights of others are considered to be ethically and morally desirable behavior. Such basic rules of behavior are essential for the preservation and continuation of organized life everywhere. In concept, the purpose of ethics is to establish principles of behavior that help people make choices among alternative courses of action. In practice, *ethical behavior* is what is accepted as "good" and "right" as opposed to "bad" or "wrong" in the context of the governing moral code.

Sources of Ethics

These notions of "right and wrong" come from many sources. The religious beliefs system one holds tends to guide ones' definition and interpretation of what is considered right or wrong in certain behaviors. The family institution (whether two parents, a single parent, or an extended family with brothers and sisters, uncles, aunties, nieces, grandparents, cousins and other kin) imparts a sense of what is right or wrong to children as they grow up. Schools and school teachers, neighbors and neighborhoods, friends, and admired role models are other sources that shape the way we differentiate between what is right or wrong. Our ethnic background (including the cultures or mores, traditions, etc.,) also constitutes another important source of our conception of what is good or bad.

As adults, we somehow want to be identified to a particular association or a group of persons that shares some goals and aspirations. These associations may include professional associations (e.g., the medical, accounting, bar associations), social clubs, and philanthropic associations such as the Rotary Club International. In each of these associations, there are elaborate rules or laws that govern the behaviors or actions of its members. The purposes of these rules or laws are to guide members towards behaving in an acceptable ethical manner. These professional bodies have their own set of codes of ethical behavior (or rules that govern the actions of members) that everyone must abide by.

Developments in the society in general tend to affect the ethical conduct in that society in terms of what is considered right or wrong in a business transaction. For example, if doing contracting business with the government requires a ten percent fee as kickback and every one sees this as the way to do business this will be accepted as "the way things are done." Finally, the legal system in a country, the enforcement of the law, and the respect accorded to the rule of law can also promote what we considered as right or wrong in our business interactions with other stakeholders. The totality of these learning experiences creates in each person a concept of ethics, morality, and socially acceptable behavior. This core of ethical beliefs then acts as a moral compass that helps to guide a person when he or she is faced with an ethical dilemma.

The underlying theme in this chapter is that as an entrepreneur, your firm should pursue the positive figure for its bottom line with a long-term perspective in mind. This book suggests that there are solid reasons to adopt business strategies based on a strong ethical foundation even if most business managers and business owners are not of strong moral character and personally committed to high ethical standards. For one, rehabilitating a company's shattered reputation is time-consuming and costly. Customers shun companies known for shady behavior. Companies with reputations for unethical conduct have considerable difficulty in recruiting and retaining good and talented employees. For example, a 1997 survey revealed that 42 percent of the respondents took into account a company's ethics when deciding whether to accept a job.[6] Other studies have also shown that firms that perform better financially over time are those with a commitment to ethical behavior. For example, a study in the *Academy of Management Journal* concludes that firms involved in ethical difficulties experience earnings declines for at least five years following the public announcements of their problems.[7]

WHAT IS BUSINESS ETHICS

Business ethics can be defined as the application of general ethical ideas to the conduct of business. Business ethics does not really involve a special set of ethical standards applicable only to business situations. Ethical principles in business are not materially different from ethical principles in general because business must draw its ideas of "the right thing to do" and "the wrong thing to do" from the same sources as anyone else. If dishonesty is considered to be unethical and immoral in a given society, then anyone in business who is dishonest with stakeholders (employees, customers, stockholders, suppliers, distributors, government agencies, competitors) is acting unethically and immorally. If protecting others from harm is considered to be ethical, then your firm or business that recalls a dangerously defective product is acting in an ethical manner. If society deems bribery to be unethical, then it follows that it is unethical for a company personnel to make payoffs to government officials to facilitate business transactions or bestow gifts and other favors on prospective customers to win or retain their business.[8]

In business, rightness of behavior is closely associated with honesty and being trustworthy, being a man or woman of your word, committed to doing the right thing or to treating the customer right. When you stop and think about this for a moment, it is not a strange concept. The marketing concept is not far from the definition of ethics: to give customers what they want. As a vendor to the government, you are obligated to provide what you have been paid to do because the government is your customer. What does the customer want? He or she wants to be treated fairly. Customers do not want to be deceived concerning price, product quality, or timeliness and quality of service. They do not want to pay for something they did not receive. In short, they do not want to be ripped off. Treating the customer right has for years been the mantra of business practices in the developed countries. In the developing countries, there is a culture and ethics that say that people should be treated fairly. Business ethics should not be different from that accepted cultural practice.

In business ethics, the importance of treating a firm's stakeholder fairly is seen as the foundation for a firm's long term profitability. Most importantly, treating the customer right has been upheld as the gospel of ethical business transactions. Thus we have the saying that "the customer is always right," "the customer is king." These sayings also help to convey the importance of this concept to other stakeholders, especially the employees of the firm, its regulators, suppliers, investors and competitors. Making profit by treating the customer right is not enough. One must deal with the firm's communities, suppliers, employees, competitors, distributors, creditors and the government in an acceptable ethical manner.

In a just society, the relationship between a business and a customer requires that these conditions be reciprocal. That is, the customer is also expected to be ethical, to be honest and trustworthy, a man or woman of his or her word. As customers, we will naturally guard against unscrupulous and unethical businesses that attempt to prey upon us and the rest of the trusting public. In the same manner, business owners expect the customer and the public to act in an acceptable ethical manner and they are also required to guide against unscrupulous customers, suppliers, regulatory agencies and the public at large.

Thus, an **acceptable business ethical environment** is one that protects the interests of all participants in the business relationship. In some instances, this might not be the case because customers, employees, the public and the authorities are unable to do their duty in an ethical manner. The types of unethical behavior exhibited by a firm's customers are varied. The same is applicable to the unethical behavior that arises from the employees of a firm. The types of unethical customer behavior your firm will be exposed to will depend in part on the type of business you are in, your business principles/values, your business culture, your mission statement, and especially, the manner with which all these are communicated to your employees and the way they are implemented. If you run a retail establishment or any type of business where you have inventory, internal and external theft from employees and shoplifters is always a threat. In a survey of *Harvard Business Review* subscribers, most of the ethical dilemmas reported by managers involved conflicts with superiors, customers, and subordinates. The most frequent issues are related to honesty in advertising and communications with top management, clients, and government agencies. Problems in dealing with special gifts, entertainment, and kickbacks were also reported.[9] These issues are not restricted to particular national or geographical areas; they manifest themselves in the global economy.

Another important point to note is that there is clearly a legal component to ethical behavior. This implies that any behavior considered ethical should also be legal in a just and fair society. This does not mean that simply because an action is not illegal it is necessarily ethical. Just living up to the "letter of the law" is not sufficient guarantee that one's actions can or should be considered ethical. However, a well-functioning market economy requires laws protecting private property rights and providing mechanisms for contract enforcement. Without a functioning legal system, the incentive to engage in economic activity can be reduced substantially by private and public entities, including organized crime, that expropriate the profit generated by the efforts of private-sector entrepreneurs. This has become a problem in many developing countries where some government agencies take the law into their hands without due process; without protecting the rights of an entrepreneur and bribery is openly solicited by bureaucrats without legal repercussions.

Most ethical problems arise when people are asked to do or find themselves about to do something that violates their personal conscience. For some of them, if the act is legal, they proceed with confidence. For others, however, the ethical test goes beyond the legality of the act alone. The issue extends to *personal values* – the underlying beliefs and attitudes that help determine individual behavior. To the extent that values vary among people, we can expect different interpretations of what behavior is ethical or unethical in a given situation. The idea is that when we are faced with an ethical dilemma, unable to determine what is right or wrong in a given situation, the legal environment can help in defining what is considered as good or bad in the conduct of business interactions. From a legal perspective, we are talking about fairness and impartiality in the decision making process. As John Ogbor has pointed out, the legality of an action is viewed from a justice perspective. This implies that an action is judged on the basis of how it is impartial, fair, and equitable in treating people.[10]

As pointed out earlier, most professions have their own formal code of ethics. *A code of ethics* is a written document that states values and ethical standards to guide the behavior of the members of an organization. The accounting profession, for example, is an organization that has a formal code of ethics that guides the behavior of its members. The same is true in the legal profession, the banking profession, the medical profession, etc. The codes try to ensure that individual behavior is consistent with the historical and shared norms of the professional group. Management as a profession has no specific or widely established and accepted code of ethics. But we have what can be termed as *managerial ethics*. **Managerial ethics** come into being because each organization must develop its own code of ethics that reflects the values advanced by the founders or owners and are shared by all members, that is the employees. It is the duty of managers at all levels of the organization to adopt and communicate these codes of ethics to all employees. Although interest in management and business codes of ethical conduct is growing, it must be remembered that the codes have limits; they cannot cover all situations, and they are not automatic insurance of universal ethical conduct. That is why managers are encouraged to join professional organizations where they can apply the ethics of their profession in the management of their business organization.

As far as business is concerned, the value of any formal code of business ethics still rests on the underlying human resource foundations of the organization – the values of its founders, the managers, and the employees. There is no replacement for effective hiring practices that staff your firm with honest and moral people to do the work in line with the code of ethics you set forth. And there is no replacement for your leadership and those of your managers who are willing to set the examples and expectations and then act as positive role models to ensure desired results.

John R. Boatright, in his book "Ethics and the Conduct of Business," suggests, "One of the features that distinguish business activity from non-economic ones is its *economic* character."[11] In the world of business, we interact with each other not as family members, friends, or neighbors but as buyers and sellers, employers and employees, regulators and the regulated, the producers and the consumers, the suppliers and the supplied, etc. In these activities, trading or commercial exchange is often accompanied by bargaining, in which both sides conceal their full hand and perhaps engage in some bluffing. A skilled salesperson who is well versed in the art of arousing a customer's attention (sometimes by a bit of puffery) will clinch the sale. A supplier to a producer also has his or her own ways of closing the deal. In all of these "wheeling and dealing", looms the E-word (Ethics). For example, there is an "ethics of trading" that prohibits the use of false or deceptive claims and tricks such as "bait-and-switch" advertising. The issue of business ethics, for example, comes in when a seller sells fake products to his or her customers. In May 2004, the Nigerian National Agency for Food and Drug Administration and Control (NAFDC) published a list of genuine and counterfeit products marketed in the Nigerian market ranging from skin-toned creams to vitamin capsules. The list is exhaustive and the names of the companies included, showing that the issue of deceptive marketing practices is an endemic one in the Nigerian business environment.[12]

Employment, as a business practice and as a contractual agreement between employers and employees, is also recognized as a special relation between a firm and its employees in terms of business ethics with its own standards of right and wrong. Although employers are generally entitled to hire and promote whomever they wish and to terminate the employment of workers without regard for the consequences, this right is being increasingly challenged by those who hold that employers ought to fire only for cause and to give employees an opportunity to defend themselves in the developed societies. In the least industrialized countries, unions have traditionally served as a preventing mechanism for the abuse of this right.

Employees also have some protections, such as a right not to be discriminated against or to be exposed to workplace hazards. There are many controversies in the workplace, such as the rights of employers and employees with regard to drug testing, at least in the industrialized nations of the world. The ethics of business then is, at least in part, the ethics of *economic relations* - such as those involving buyers, sellers, suppliers, communities, the government, employers and employees. In other words, the question becomes: (i) what are the rules that ought to govern these kinds of relations? (ii) How do these rules differ from those that apply in other spheres of life? And (iii) how can a business owner conduct the economic relations in an acceptable ethical manner?

The answer to the first question is addressed in this chapter. An organization, whether small or large, entrepreneurial or bureaucratic, must follow a set of rules or code of ethics that guides the conduct of its business. The customer is more likely to accept a product or service from a firm that he or she perceives to be ethical if he or she has the means to pay for it. In short, customers want to do business with someone they can trust. Suppliers would want to be treated fairly, the government requires you and your firm to abide by the rules, employers requires employees to follow company rules, employees need to be treated fairly and investors require acceptable returns on their investments.

The answer to the second question is somehow more complicated to provide because what is ethical depends on your perspective, your professional obligation and the value structure of all the participants involved in a decision making process. It is almost a foregone conclusion that the stakeholders of a business will have varying sets of values. To meet everyone's expectations completely will be almost impossible. The best outcome could be how a firm is able to arrive at equilibrium on how to satisfy the needs of its diverse stakeholders. Finally, the answer to the third question is simple: As an entrepreneur or the owner of a small business, it is important that one develops a code of ethical conduct that others in the organization must follow.

The purpose of business ethics is not so much to teach the difference between right and wrong as to give people the tools for dealing with moral complexity, tools that they can use to identify and think through the moral implications of strategic decisions. Most of us already have a good sense of what is right and wrong. We already know that it is wrong to lie, cheat, and steal. We know that it is wrong to take actions that put the lives of others at risk. Such moral values are instilled in us at an early age through formal and informal socialization. The problem, however, is that although most business owners and managers of large corporations rigorously adhere to such moral principles in their private life, some fail to apply them in their business life, occasionally with disastrous consequences.

ETHICAL DILEMMA IN BUSINESS DECISIONS AND THE PERSISTENCE OF UNETHICAL BUSINESS PRACTICES

The difficulties in making the right ethical judgment come in when we try to rationalize our actions in order to justify an unethical decision. Business owners and their employees do face ethical dilemmas when they are confronted with a difficult decision that has ethical implication. An **ethical dilemma** is a situation with a potential course of action that, although, offering potential benefit or gain, is also unethical. There are situations forcing someone to decide on a course of action that, although offering the potential of personal or organizational benefit or both, may be considered potentially unethical. Sometimes, we found ourselves in situations to decide whether or not what we are about to do is good or bad (either for you as a person, or for the organization as a whole). In situations such as this, we normally try to convince ourselves that the course we have taken is proper one regardless of how it affects others. In short, we tend to rationalize our actions or behaviors. Examples of such rationalizations include:

(i) *"Everybody else does it. If we don't do it, someone else will."* Every profession has its own code of ethics. Everyone who followed the drama of Enron including its rise and fall will agree that most participants in the Enronian saga are seasoned corporate and financial gurus in their own rights. The drama covers the most respected financial institution in the world (Morgan Chase, City Corp) and the accounting firm (Arthur Andersen). Everyone in the Enronian saga did what he or she had to do because "everybody else does it". At the end, this way of explaining an action (or rationalization) caught up with everyone not only within Enron, but almost every participant in the U.S. energy industry.[13]

(ii) *"It's not really illegal. We'll wait until the lawyers tell us it's wrong."* Although the court of law is the last place to judge your rights and privileges, this same medium can also be incapable in restoring your dignity and your pride. Ask O.J. Simpson. The legality of your behavior and action should be seen as meeting the law. On the other hand, your actions, as a business owner, are judged in the marketplace. Legal judgments can sometime be at odd with social and public opinion. The advice is that when confronted with the legal implication of your course of action; consider the opinion of the public as well. There is a place for the law and there is a place for ethics and your morality.

(iii) *"It doesn't really hurt anyone and the behavior is really in everyone's best interests."* This rationalization involves the mistaken belief that because someone can be found to benefit from the behavior or action, it is also in the individual's or the organization's best interests. Overcoming this rationalization depends in part on the ability to look beyond short-term results to address longer term implications and to look beyond results in general to ways in which they are obtained. Sometimes it is important to know that the end might not justify the means. The means may come to hurt you in the long run.

(iv) *"The system is unfair and I must do it to get at the system."* Many employees make the erroneous ethical decision that the prevailing system has not been fair to them and therefore they feel they have a score to settle. Because some government official requires you to pay bribe, and you are angry, you may feel that the society or the government owes you something. In the contemporary business practices and environments, many business owners and employees have a score to settle. Remember that if every one of us that the system has treated unfairly decides to fight back, there would be no system in which to operate our businesses in an ethical manner. In a similar manner, just because your employer refuses to give you promotion and a pay raise and you want to fight back by behaving unethically, you will be the looser at the end.

(v) *"Nobody will ever find out what I've done."* One of the reasons why many of us engage in unethical business practices is that we erroneously think and believe that no one will ever find out because of our skill in concealing the "evidence." The advise is that, those evidence you have skillfully concealed will come back to hunt you. The Holy Bible reminds us that "there is nothing hidden that will not be revealed, and there is nothing secret that will not become known and come to light" (Luke 8:17).

The Persistence of Questionable Business Practices

Part of the ethical problems associated with businesses stems from the perspective of how we, as members of the society, measure success and whose perspective or position is protected within the context of the stakeholders. When a bank diverts foreign exchange sourced from the official market to the parallel or black market, even though most people are doing the same, this bank is engaging in an unethical business practice, because other stakeholders in the banking industry get hurt in the process. Although, a fiduciary responsibility exists between management and the stockholders (or investors) of a corporation and it is management's job to make decisions that are in the best interests of the stockholders, we must not lose sight of demands by other stakeholder groups. Some of the courses many of us teach in most business schools seem to adopt a Milton Friedman's view that the primary objective of the manager is to maximize wealth to the stockholder; in so doing, he or she is expected to maximize the utility to everyone.

From the perspective of business ethics and the social responsibility of managers, maximizing shareholder wealth is not enough. Many "successful" business firms, including large corporations such as Enron, have gone into bankruptcy by simply pursuing the profit motive and negating the demands of other stakeholder groups. In Nigeria, for example, the problems confronting many transnational oil corporations are partly rooted in their inability to manage the stakeholder aspect of their business operations in an all-inclusive manner. Similarly, many small business owners have gone out of business simply because, while focusing on maximizing profit, they overlooked their relationships between other stakeholder groups: government agencies, suppliers, distributors, the immediate community and even the competitors.

Perspectives and loyalty to a specific group can create a bias in what is deemed unethical. With the current trend in business practices such as mergers and acquisitions in an era where many industries are consolidating, management will often strive to widen profit margins through personnel cuts. The correct term is *downsizing*. With downsizing in place, management can often create an atmosphere where those who remain will be willing to go without pay increases, and in some cases, pay cuts. One could understand these types of concessions if a joint decision were being made between management, employees and unions to save a company from financial ruin (as it is done in the more developed Western European countries such as Germany and Sweden). Yet, at the same time that this trend in downsizing is occurring, corporate profits have helped drive the stock market to record levels, not only in Sub-Saharan Africa, but also in the stock markets all over the world, even while supporting huge pay increases for top executives.

Although most managers think of themselves as ethical persons, some still question whether ethics is relevant to their role as a manager or a business owner. It is important for people in business to be ethical, they might say, but being ethical in business is no different than being ethical in private life. The implication is that a business owner or manager need only be an ethical person. There is no need, in other words, to have specialized knowledge or skills in ethics. Your personal moral and the way you are brought up and socialized can shape your business ethics; that is, the way you, as a person, undertake the economic transaction between producers, distributors and consumers.

Nothing could be further from the truth. Although others will say that there is a demarcation between ethics in business and personal morality, situations arise when your personal morals will dictate your responses when faced with ethical dilemma in a business situation. Your ethics as a business owner or manager is affected by your personal experiences and background. We point out earlier that family influences, religious values, personal standards, and personal needs (financial and otherwise) will help determine a person's ethical conduct in any given circumstance. Managers or business owners who lack a strong and consistent set of personal ethics will find that their decisions vary from situation to situation as they strive to maximize self-interests. Managers and business owners who operate with strong ethical frameworks, personal rules or strategies for ethical decision making, will be more consistent and confident since choices are made against a stable set of ethical standards developed overtime.

As noted in a preceding discussion, doing the right thing always pays off in the long-run and this simple principle applies more in the business world than any where else. We do not have to be philosophers to know the simple rule that doing good is *good* and doing bad is *bad*. Faced with critical decision moment, we have the dictates of our morality to follow either wisely or blindly. Since each profession has its own codes of ethics that its members must follow, your business firm must have a set of codes of ethics that must guide the behaviors and actions of your employees. In the next section, we will examine some of the factors that may affect the ethical climate of a business firm.

FACTORS SHAPING THE ETHICS OF AN ENTREPRENEURIAL FIRM

No matter how much we teach or preach about good ethical behavior in business, an entrepreneur or the owner/manager of a small business is often challenged to put in place necessary organizational structures and policies that promote an acceptable ethical environment in the firm. Increased awareness of factors influencing ethical behavior in a firm may help you better deal with situations of ethical dilemmas in the future. In general, the factors that shape the ethical environment of a firm come from (i) the entrepreneur as a person, (ii) the firm he or she sets up and manages, and (iii) the social environment.

The Entrepreneur as a Person

The tone of the business ethics comes, first and foremost, from the entrepreneur (the founder) as a person. Because the system of your beliefs can be carried over to your firm, it is thus important to understand that the influence of the entrepreneur's family, religious belongingness, personal standards, and personal needs (financial, esteem, or otherwise) will help determine the influence and the "personality" you as person bring into your firm. As pointed out elsewhere, if you are "an easy going type of a person," your employees will try to emulate that. If your religious belief tells you that it is wrong to take bribe and you abide by that belief and practice it in your organization, you are creating an ethically acceptable environment in your business. In other words, who you are as a person will determine the ethical behavior of those who work in your little or large entrepreneurial firm. The Bible says that we reap what we sow. Significantly, we are reminded that "A good tree doesn't produce rotten fruit, and a rotten tree doesn't produce good fruit. For every tree is known by its own fruit. ... A good person produces good from the good treasure of his heart, and an evil person produces evil from an evil treasure" (Jesus Christ, The Bible, Luke 6: 43-45). If you put in the seeds of good ethical behavior, your organization, including those who work for you, will reap the fruit of good ethical behavior. There is no two ways about it. If you want to know why a business or firm is ethically rotten, look at the behavior or morality of its founders or those who run it.

The Entrepreneurial Firm and Its Culture

The firm that you have set up and the ways things are done there can also influence the ethical environment in that organization. Although the values or belief systems of an entrepreneur can shape the culture of the firm, it is possible that, once created, the actions of those in managerial or supervisory position can also create an ethical business environment in your firm. The expectations and reinforcement provided by peers and group norms are likely to influence the ethical behavior of those that work in your firm. The official policies and procedures of the firm, mission statements, the values, which the firm stands for, and written or unwritten rules are also very important in establishing an ethical climate for the firm as a whole.

If a company's management truly aspires for a company to behave ethically, they must personally see to it that strong and effective procedures for enforcing ethical standards and handling potential violations are put in place. Even in an ethically strong company, there can be bad apples – and some of the bad apples may be top management. So it is rarely enough to rely on the exhortations of the owner or top management to achieve an ethically principled organization, one must also rely on an ethically principled culture to produce ethics compliance.

As we discussed in chapter eleven, every organization, whether small or large; entrepreneurial or bureaucratic, has a culture. The culture of a company, also known as organizational or corporate culture, refers to the character of a company's internal work climate and personality, as shaped by its core values, beliefs, business behavior, traditions, ingrained behavior, work practices, and styles of operating. A company's corporate culture is mirrored in the character or "personality" of its work environment – the factors that underlie how the company tries to conduct its business and the behaviors that are held in high esteem.

According to Arthur Thompson, A. Strickland and John Gamble, the more managers succeed in making the espoused values and ethical principles the main drivers of "how we do things around here," the more that the values and ethical principles function as cultural norms.[14] Over time, a strong culture grounded in the display of core values and ethics may emerge. As the authors indicated, cultural norms rooted in core values and ethical behaviors are highly beneficial in three aspects. One, the advocated core values and ethical standards accurately communicate the company's good intentions and validate the integrity and above-board character of its business principles and operating methods. Second, the values-based and ethics-based cultural norms steer company employees toward doing things right and doing the right thing. Third, they establish a "company conscience" and provide yardsticks for gauging the appropriateness of particular actions, decisions, and policies.[15]

The External Environment

A business venture, like all other forms of organizations, operates in an external environment that is made up of customers, competitors, suppliers, distributors, government laws and regulation, including social and business norms. Laws interpret social values to define appropriate behaviors for firms and other types of organizations and their members; regulatory laws help governments monitor these behaviors and keep them within acceptable standards. The competitive climate within an industry and what is accepted as means of competition among rival firms also set a standard of behavior for those firms who wish to prosper in it. Sometimes the pressure for competition contributes to the ethical dilemmas of entrepreneurs and the business managers. Not surprisingly, a corrupt sociopolitical and cultural environment will beget corrupt business culture, managers, and employees.

ETHICAL ISSUES IN BUSINESS PRACTICES

Business ethics, as defined earlier, can be applied to any aspect of a firm's business activity. In this section, we will discuss some of the more important areas where the issue of business ethics matters most for the entrepreneurial firm: Marketing (such as advertisement and promotion) and production (such as product safety). In several instances, a firm's business practice within the context of business ethics goes through its marketing function. The production process also matters in terms of what the producer delivers to the customer. A third important consideration in the context of developing countries is the relationship between employers (owners of businesses) and their employees. We will examine various types of managerial orientations toward employees, including the important human resource management issues of employee rights, the right to due process and fair treatment.

Ethical Issues in Marketing

Almost all aspects of marketing (from the development of new products to pricing, promotion, and sales) raise ethical questions that do not always have an easy answer. Marketing, according to one often-cited definition, "consists of the performance of business activities that direct the flow of goods and services from the producer to consumer or user."[16] Within this broad definition, there is a number of distinct functions, including product development, distribution, pricing, promotion, and sales. Selling an inferior product and labeling it as a superior one does not constitute a good marketing practice or good business ethical practice. In a similar manner, when a contractor is awarded a contract to construct a road and did the job in a manner that deviates from the term of the contract the business relationship between producer and customer does not constitute good business ethics.

Packaging and Labeling:
To be ethically responsible, customers need a certain amount of information to make rational choices. In some countries' business culture, very often, this is not easily provided, and in most cases it is deceptive. Consider the plight of a customer who went to a distributor and purchased packaged fabric purportedly containing bails of clothing materials imported from Holland. He was told by the distributor that the contents of goods in the package were the genuine ones. The customer went home, opened the package and found out that the fabric were different from what he was told. The customer went back to the distributor and lodged his complaints. The distributor insisted that his customer was provided the goods as requested and the matter was taken to the court. Without information on the label, customers have no practical means for determining the content and quality of the products he or she is offered.

Packaging and labeling are deceptive when the size, shape or content of a container, a picture or description, or the use of terms such as *new and improved* misleads consumers in some significant way. Warranties that cannot easily be understood by the average consumer are also deceptive. Another form of deceptive and manipulative marketing practice is when producers and advertisers label the origin of their products differently from where they were produced. Certainly, the more information consumers have, the better they can protect themselves in the marketplace, and conversely the better the supplier, producer, or distributor can protect himself or herself in the court. The ethical question, though, is, how much information is a manufacturer obligated to provide? To what extent are consumers responsible for informing themselves about the product or service for sale? [17]

Deceptive and Manipulative Marketing Practices
Roughly, marketing practices are deceptive when customers are led to hold false beliefs about a product or service.[18] Examples of some common deceptions are markdowns from a "suggested retail price" that is never charged, "introductory offers" that incorrectly purport to offer savings, and bogus clearance sales in which inferior goods are brought in.

In the developing countries such as Nigeria, deceptive and manipulative marketing practices occur in several forms. For example, a product made in Nigeria is shipped to a foreign country and labeled as made in that country. Then the same product is shipped back to Nigeria as a product manufactured in another country. Although, this can be seen as a practice of "giving the customer what he or she wants," it is nevertheless and unethical business practice that affects business relationship in the country in general.

CASE IN POINT: DECEPTIVE MARKETING PRACTICES[19]
It is now confirmed that Aba shoemakers who are very prominent in the industry produce their shoes and sandals, send them to Dubai and other countries under foreign labels and bring them back to Nigeria as foreign shoes to make Nigerians buy them. The story which has been held as rumor over time was confirmed by the national president of the shoemakers or better put, leather workers, Chief Ebenezer Ibiam in a discussion with Saturday Sun.

The reason for this act by the shoemakers which some may conclude portrays inferiority, is as a result of the attitude of Nigerian consumers who snub products with 'made in Nigerian labels', said Ibiam. "Until the Nigerian consumer takes pride in products manufactured by our people, that practice may continue".

AGOA frowns at the practice
Chief Ibiam in further explanation on this trend said that although it is what obtains, it is not a proper way to encourage industrial growth in any society. According to him, "the act is contrary to the provisions of the African Growth and Opportunity Act (AGOA), but the attitude of our people does not encourage the manufacturers to abide by this rule. Moreover, some of the manufacturers are not members of AGOA and they don't feel bound by the law. But for people like me, I do not and cannot put a false label on my products because I am a beneficiary agent of the AGOA. So, as one that operates a company that is recognized by AGOA, I mark my shoes 'made in Nigeria'."

Why Nigerian shoes are inferior
Chief Ibiam said made-in-Nigeria shoes are inferior to those of developed economies because the raw materials used here are of inferior quality. "Good quality product is an outcome of good quality raw materials and there is nowhere you will have a very advanced product quality from inferior raw materials. Also, the equipment and tools we use in our factories here are inferior, outdated and poorly maintained. The infrastructure level has also not helped matters. For instance, while mixing chemicals for a particular work, the power supply must be assured, and if electricity fails while the chemical is still in the mix, the required good quality is tampered with and will never be regained. The tannery in Nigeria, all of which are located at the northern part of the country have this habit of exporting the best of their products and selling the inferior ones to manufacturers in Nigeria. That also affects the quality of our products, so if the nation wants something better, the government should have a policy in place that stops this practice and also encourages better infrastructural development."

Aba shoes, best in Africa
No matter the flaws of Aba shoes as seen by Nigerians, Chief Ibiam is emphatic that it is the best in Africa and Aba shoemakers produce and supply up to 80 percent of the African shoes used in Africa. According to Chief Ibiam, the outside world knows of the unique quality of Aba shoes and also the potentials of the area. As a result, the United Nations Industrial Development Organization (UNIDO) has approved the establishment of leather production cluster region in Aba where thousands of shoe manufacturers will have their business base. And to compliment this effort and international recognition of the quality, potentials and future benefits of the Aba shoe industry, the Abia State government has donated some acres of land to establish the industrial estate. One of the major conditions in the joint venture development is that Aba leather products must be marked made in Nigeria.

Ban, not final solution
The man popularly known as 'Mr. Leather' in the leather workers union in Nigeria said one of the good things the present government has done is the ban on importation of inferior and expired leather products that have been contributing to the poor growth of Nigerian industries. But according to Ibiam who is a member of the Presidential Committee on Leather, Wood and Furniture whose chairman is the Minister of Industries said the best step towards stabilizing the leather industry is to provide all the necessary incentives required to make the industry what it is in other parts of the world. The industry needs real encouragement, and that should be more that mere partial remedies.

Manipulation is distinguished from deception in that it typically involves no false or misleading claims. Instead, it consists of taking advantage of consumer psychology to make a sale. More precisely, manipulation is coercively shaping the alternatives open to people or their perception of those alternatives so that they are effectively deprived of a choice. Examples of relatively harmless forms of manipulation include multiple pricing, such as "3 for $1" and "buy two get one free," and odd-even pricing, $2.99 instead of $3.00. When customers are accustomed to paying a certain price for a product, such as a candy bar, manufacturers often reduce the amount in order to maintain the same price, a practice known as customary pricing.

A more objectionable form of manipulation is "bait and switch," which is a generally illegal practice in which a customer is lured into a store by an advertisement or word of mouth recommendation for those paid to do so for a low-cost item and then sold a higher priced version. Often the low-cost item is not available, but even if it is, the advertised product may be of such low quality that customers are easily "switched" to a higher priced product. Bait and switching is manipulative not only because consumers are tricked into entering the store but because they enter in a frame of mind to buy. Manipulation can also take place when salespeople use high-pressure tactics. The sales force of one traveling agency and airline booking office located in Tafawa Balewa Square in Lagos, Nigeria, used deception to attract travelers to its sales office. According to their ad, it costs about U.S. $1,500 to book a return ticket from Lagos to New York. However, prospective travelers found out that it would cost them about $2,000 dollars to get into the plane. The other U.S. $500 was not revealed to the customers. After a customer has paid the advertised U.S. $1,500, he or she is committed to the deal, because other hidden expenses are revealed.

Advertising

In our modern society, advertising pervades our lives. It is impossible to read the daily newspapers or magazines, watch a television show, or travel the streets of our cities without being bombarded by commercial messages. Although some ads may be irritating or offensive, many advertising efforts have been geared towards entertainment. We also derive benefit from information about products and services and from the boost that advertising gives to the economy as a whole. On the other side of the fence, firms with products or services to sell regard advertising as a valuable, indeed indispensable marketing tool.

A typical definition of advertising, from a marketing textbook, is that it is "a paid non-personal communication about an organization and its products that is transmitted to a target audience through a mass medium."[20] So defined, advertising is only one kind of promotional activity. The others are *publicity* (press releases and other public relations efforts that do not involve the purchase of air time or space in the print media), *sales promotion* (contests, coupons, free samples, and so on, strictly speaking, forms of communication), and *personal selling* by shop clerks and telephone solicitors (which, of course, is not impersonal and also does not take place through a mass medium). Although most advertising is for a product or a service, some of it is devoted to enhancing the image of the firm or advancing some issues or cause. Thus, a distinction is commonly made between product or service advertisement on the one hand and advocacy advertising on the other.[21] The issue of ethics and morality comes into play within the context of advertising when an ad has a tendency to deceive, or when an ad merely takes advantage of people's ignorance. Consider health claims in food advertising. The word *natural*, which usually means the absence of artificial ingredients, evokes images of wholesomeness in the minds of consumers. Yet many food products advertised as natural contain unhealthy concentrations of fat and sugar and are deficient in vitamins and minerals.[22]

Deception in advertising is thus a crucial issue when discussing ethics in marketing a product or service. As pointed out by John Boatright, central to any definition of deception in advertising is the concept of rational choice. Deception is morally objectionable because it interferes with the ability of consumers to make rational choices, which generally depend on adequate information. Deception occurs when a false belief, which an advertisement either creates or takes advantage of, substantially interferes with the ability of people to make rational consumer choices.[23]

Ethical Issues in Production and Delivery

Product Liability: The right of consumers or customers to be protected from harmful products raises innumerable problems for manufacturers, wholesalers and retailers. Many products can injure or kill people, especially if the products are used improperly. The ethical question here is "Do business owners have a responsibility to ensure that a product is safe before it is placed on the market? Do retailers conceal the real benefits of a product from their customers and exaggerate its uses? Consider a drugstore operator who got a visit from someone with fever. The drugstore operator wanted to make quick profit, and so he did not care about knowing the symptom of the fever. He then gave some tablets of aspirin to the sick man. The man took the tablets, believing that he would be cured. He went home and a day later he was found dead. Should our drugstore operator be held responsible for the death of the patient? Yes, because according to some theorists, a producer or deliverer of goods and services must exercise due care. Their obligation is to take all reasonable precautions to ensure that products they put on the market are free of defects likely to cause harm. Thus, if the drugstore operator had persuaded the patient to visit a doctor, perhaps he would have helped in saving his life. In ethics, we call this *negligence* on the part of the drugstore operator. In the United States of America, for example, some courts have held companies responsible not only for foreseeable misuse but also for misuse that is actively encouraged in the marketing of a product.[24]

Ethical Issues in Employer-Employee Relationships

In the context of entrepreneurship, any discussion of business ethics must also take into consideration the relationship between business owners and the employees. Job-related ethical issues have received increasing attention in Sub-Saharan Africa due in large part to employee exploitation, child labor and various forms of harassments, (such as sexual harassment) in many firms. In the context of Sub-Saharan Africa, job-related ethical issues most commonly discussed involved the rights of the employee, which include (i) the right not to be fired without just cause; (ii) the right to due process and fair treatment; and (iii) the right to privacy, safety, and health in the wok-place. We will start the discussion of ethics in the context of employer-employee relationship with an examination of different managerial approaches to employee management. In terms of employer-employee relationship, three management approaches have been identified in the literature: (i) moral management, (ii) amoral management, and (iii) immoral management.[25]

Moral Management: Managers who adopt a moral management approach see their employees as a human resource that must be treated with dignity and respect. Employees' rights to due process, privacy, freedom of speech, and safety are maximally considered in all decisions. Management seeks fair dealings with employees. The goal is to use a leadership style, such as consultative/participative, that will result in mutual confidence and trust. Commitment is a recurring theme.

Amoral Management: Employees are treated as the law requires. Attempts to motivate focus on increasing productivity rather than satisfying employees' growing maturity needs. Employees are still seen as factors of production, but a remunerative approach is used. The organization sees self-interest in treating employees with minimal respect. Organization structure, pay incentives, and rewards are all geared toward short- and medium-term productivity.

Immoral Management: Employees are viewed as factors of production to be used, exploited, and manipulated for gain of individual owner, manager or the firm. No concern is shown for employees' needs, rights or expectations. The relationship between employers and employees is short-term focus. The working environment and relationship is coercive, controlling, and alienating.

Employee Rights

Employee rights refer to legitimate and enforceable claims or privileges obtained by workers through group membership that entitle or protect them in specific ways from the prevailing system of governance. In this light, employee rights are seen as individual's legitimate and enforceable claims to some desired treatment, situation, or resource.[25] Richard Edwards has argued that employee or workplace rights serve to provide workers with either (i) desired outcomes or (ii) protection from unwanted outcomes.[26]

Employee rights may be afforded on the basis of economic, legal, or ethical sources of justification. In a limited number of cases, companies even use philanthropic arguments as the bases for providing employee rights or benefits. For example, some companies have justified day-care rights and benefits to employees on philanthropic grounds.

Management Ethics and Employee's Job Claims

With respect to employees' claim concerning their jobs, management needs to be aware of two important points from an ethical point of view: (i) It is now appropriate stakeholder management policy to treat workers fairly and to dismiss them only for justifiable cause, and (ii) in many countries, the law protects workers who do not get fair treatment. Therefore, management has an added incentive not to get embroiled in complex legal entanglements over wrongful discharges. Four specific actions that management might consider in dealing with this issue include the following:

(i) *Stay on the right side of the law.* As an employer, it is your responsibility or that of your management to know the law and to obey it. This is the clearest, best, and most effective position to take. The company that conducts itself honestly and legally has the least to fear from disgruntled workers.

(ii) *Investigate complaints fully and in good faith.* Well-motivated complainers in organizations are likely to report problem or concerns to someone within the company first. Therefore, employee complaints about the activities of your company should be checked out. If there is substance to the problem, management has time to make corrections internally, with a minimum of adverse publicity.

(iii) *Deal in good faith with your employees.* Honor commitments, including those made in writing and those that employees have a reasonable right to expect as matters of normal policy, behavior, and good faith.

(iv) *When you fire someone, make sure it is for a good reason.* This is the best advice possible. Also make sure that sound records and documentation support the reason. Effective performance appraisals, disciplinary procedures, dispute-handling procedures, and employee communications are all keys to justifiable discharges. You or your management needs to be attentive to abusive or retaliatory firings that are supported by thin technicalities. If the need arises to fire someone, it should not be difficult to document sound reasons for doing so.

The Right to Due Process and Fair Treatment

In many parts of Sub-Saharan Africa today, one of the most frequently proclaimed employee rights issues (or generally, the right of the citizen) of the past decade has been the right to due process. Basically, **due process** is the right to receive an impartial review of one's complaints and to be dealt with fairly. In the context of the workplace, due process is thought to be the right of employees to have decisions that adversely affect them to be reviewed by objective, impartial third parties. In general, it is widely accepted that due process is consistent with the democratic ideal that underpins the universal right to fair treatment. It could be argued that, without due process, employees do not receive fair treatment in the workplace.

Patricia Werhane, a leading business ethicist, contends that, procedurally, due process extends beyond simple fair treatment and should state, "Every employee has a right to a public hearing, peer evaluation, outside arbitration, or some other open and mutually agreed-upon grievance procedure before being demoted, unwillingly transferred, or fired."[27] Thus, we see due process as ranging from the expectation that employees be treated fairly to the position that employees deserve a fair system of decision-making.

Only in the past few years have some leading companies and governments in Sub-Saharan Africa given special consideration to employees' rights to due process. Historically, managers and employers have had unlimited freedom to deal with employees as they wished. In many cases, unfair treatment was not intentional but was the result of inept or distracted supervisors inflicting needless harm on subordinates. It can also be easily seen how unethical managers and employers may have failed to provide employees with acceptable due process and fair treatment. By failing to institute alternative ways to resolve disputes, the managers lost an opportunity to avoid the time, energy, and money that is often lost in protracted administrative and judicial processes.

Due Process and Employee Constitutionalism

David Ewing, an authority on the question of employee rights, has argued that employee due process should be regarded as but one part of **employee constitutionalism**. He suggests that employee constitutionalism "consists of a set of clearly defined rights and a means of protecting employees from discharge, demotion, or other penalties imposed when they assert their rights."[28] He goes on to enumerate the main requirements of a due-process system in an organization:

(i) It must be a procedure; it must follow rules. It must not be arbitrary.
(ii) It must be sufficiently visible and well-known that potential violators of employee rights and victims of abuse are aware of it.
(iii) It must be perfectly effective.
(iv) It must be institutionalized – a relatively permanent fixture in your organization.
(v) It must be perceived as equitable.
(vi) It must be easy to use.
(vii) It must apply to all employees.

Ewing further defines corporate due process as: A fair hearing procedure by a power mediator, investigator, or board with complaining employee having the right to be represented by another employee, to present evidence, to rebut the other side's charges, to have an objective and impartial hearing, to have the wrong corrected if proved, to be free from retaliation for using the procedure, to enjoy reasonable confidentiality, to be heard reasonably soon after lodging the complaint, to get a timely decision, and so forth.[29]

A MODEL OF ETHICAL DECISION MAKING

Ethical decision-making is not always easy. Some dilemmas do not fit nicely within the guidelines of an ethical code. Others create such strong emotions within us that it is difficult for us to remain objective, or at least to give our emotions no more due than they deserve. Some decisions require us to consider the conflicting claims of different parties. Besides establishing the right kind of ethical climate in your firm, business owners and managers must be able to think through the ethical implications of strategic decisions in a systematic way. A number of different frameworks have been suggested as aids to the decision-making process. The four-step model shown in Figure 14-1 is a compilation of the various approaches recommended by several authorities on this subject.[30]

Figure 14-1
A Model of Ethical Decision Making

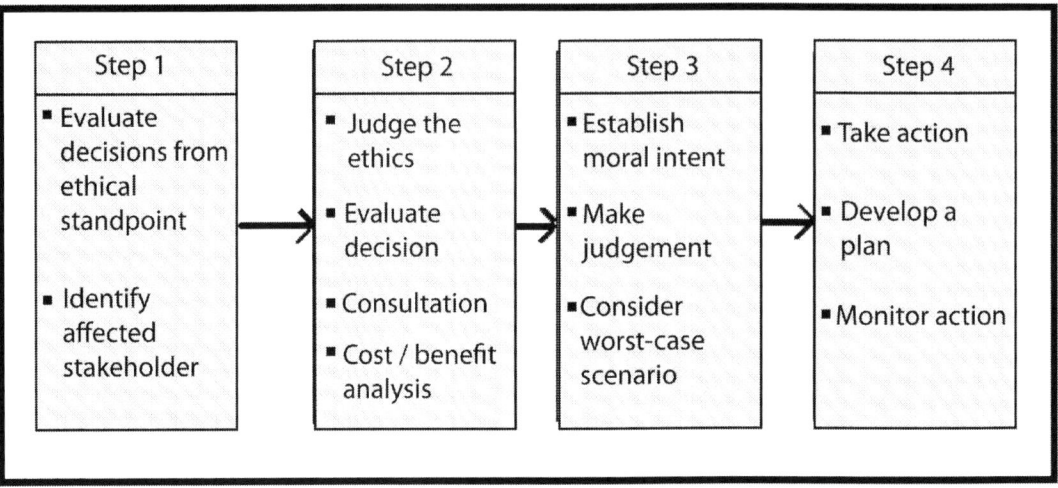

Step 1: Assess and Evaluate a Situation for its Ethical Dimension
Evaluating a proposed strategic decision from an ethical standpoint requires business owners and managers to identify which stakeholders the decision would affect and in what ways. Most importantly, entrepreneurs and managers need to determine whether the proposed decision would violate the rights of any stakeholders. The term *rights* refer to the fundamental entitlements of a stakeholder. For example, we might argue that the right to information about health risks in the workplace is a fundamental entitlement of employees. It can also be the fundamental rights of the employer to refuse it.

At this stage, the decision-maker gathers information in an effort to add definition and meaning to the situation and decide if there are indeed ethical dimensions to the problem. This requires a deliberateness on the part of the decision-maker, first to be conscious that some difficulty exists, and then to investigate its meaning. Sometimes, making a list of facts and problematic circumstances can help to organize one's thinking. Specifically, some issues to consider at this stage are:

➢ Determining precisely what must be decided.
➢ Formulating and devising the full range of alternatives.
➢ Eliminating patently impractical, illegal and improper alternatives.
➢ Forcing yourself to develop at least three ethically justifiable options.
➢ Examining each option to determine which ethical principles and values are involved.

Step 2: Judging the Ethics
This involves judging the ethics of the proposed decision, given the information gained in step 1. This judgment should be guided by various moral principles that should not be violated. The principles might be those articulated in your firm's mission statement or

other documents, such as employee handbook or the company's employee code of conduct. In addition, certain moral principles that we have adopted as members of society (for example, the prohibition on stealing - should not be violated).

Ultimately, it is the decision-maker's responsibility to review all applicable laws and guidelines. In many cases, existing guidelines speak directly to the issue at hand with clarity, and contradictory or complicating concerns do not arise. When the guidelines are clear, following the rules should lead to resolution. When resolution doesn't occur, and even when it does, it may be important to review the principles that underpin ethical rules of conduct. The judgment at this stage will also be guided by the decision rule that is chosen to assess the proposed decision. Although long-term profit maximization is rightly the decision rule that most business owners stress, it should be applied subject to the constraint that no moral principles are violated.

At the stage, consultation may actually be considered in the decision-making process. It may be considered as soon as one experiences the uncomfortable feeling signaling that a situation is emerging. Indeed, consultation with another peer or a superior may even help define exactly what the problem is. Seeking consultation with valued colleagues is one of the most important things a decision-maker can do at any time during the process of decision-making. There are several reasons consultation is important. The outside help or colleague will add a measure of objectivity that you, who is personally involved, in the case will not have. The objective colleague or superior can often help you define the problem more accurately and, in the decision-making phase, can help you evaluate competing courses of action and choose the course of greatest integrity. This stage is practically a stage of evaluation:

> ➤ If any of the options requires the sacrifice of any ethical principle, evaluate the facts and assumptions carefully.
> ➤ Distinguish solid facts from beliefs, desires, theories, suppositions, unsupported conclusions, opinions, and rationalizations.
> ➤ Consider the credibility of sources, especially when they are self-interested, ideological or biased.
> ➤ With regard to each alternative, carefully consider the benefits, burdens and risks to each stakeholder.

Step 3: Establishing Moral Intent and Deciding
Establishing moral intent means that your firm must resolve to place moral concerns ahead of other concerns in cases where either the rights of stakeholders or key moral principles have been violated. At this stage, input from your board of advisors might be particularly valuable. Without the proactive encouragement of your board of advisors, you and your employees might tend to place the narrow economic interests of your firm before the interests of other stakeholders.

At this stage, the decision-maker considers the options to take and the possible consequences of each option. Essentially, the decision-maker considers both the costs and benefits, social or economic nature as well as long-term and short-term consequences. The decision-maker also takes appropriate responsibility for the consequences. Taking appropriate responsibility acts as an additional check, encouraging the decision-maker to look carefully at the potential consequences to all parties involved of any action he or she might take to solve the dilemma.

This is the stage at which decisions are made and you must:

- Make a judgment about what is not true and what consequences are most likely to occur.
- Evaluate the viable alternatives according to personal conscience.
- Prioritize the values so that you can choose which values to advance and which to subordinate.
- Determine who will be helped the most and harmed the least.
- Consider the worst-case scenario.
- Consider whether ethically questionable conduct can be avoided by changing goals or methods, or by getting consent.

Apply three "ethics guides."
- Are you treating others as you would want to be treated?
- Would you be comfortable if your reasoning and decision were to be publicized?
- Would you be comfortable if your children were observing you?

Step 4: Taking Action and Engaging in Ethical Behavior
After establishing moral intent and making the decision, the next stage is for the organization to take action. This requires your business venture to engage in ethical behavior. At this stage, you must proactively engage in making sure that your ethics principles are enforced. The result of their enforcement must be seen and judged by you or your management. This is the stage at which your actions are implemented and results monitored. Specific actions include:

- Developing a plan of how to implement the decision.
- Maximizing the benefits and minimizing the costs and risks.
- Monitoring the effects of decisions.
- Be prepared and willing to revise a plan, or take a different course of action.
- Adjust to new information.

Ethical decision-making involves the process by which a person evaluates and chooses among alternatives in a manner consistent with his or her core ethical values or principles. Thus when you make an ethical decision you: (a) perceive and eliminate unethical options and (b) select the best from several competing ethical alternatives.

Ethical decision-making requires more than a belief in the importance of ethics. It also requires sensitivity to perceive the ethical implications of your decisions; the ability to evaluate complex, ambiguous and incomplete facts and the skill to implement ethical decision making without jeopardizing your career and the reputation of the firm. Ethical decision-making requires three things; ethical commitment, ethical consciousness and ethical competence. The task of business ethics in the management of a business venture, therefore, is to make two central points: (i) that business decisions do have an ethical component and (ii) that owners and managers of business ventures must weigh the ethical implications of strategic decisions before choosing a course of action.

CREATING AND MAINTAINING HIGH ETHICAL BUSINESS STANDARDS

Companies that practice good ethical standards in their business relationships with their stakeholders support a variety of methods for creating and maintaining high ethical standards in their businesses. Some of the most important efforts in this area involve ethics training, whistleblower protection, top management support, formal codes of ethics, and strong ethical business cultures.

Ethics Training

Ethics training in the form of structured programs to help employees understand the ethical aspects of decision-making is designed to help people incorporate high ethical standards into their daily behaviors. In the academics, an increasing number of college curricula now include courses in ethics, and seminars on this topic are popular in the business community. In Europe, Japan and North America, companies have increasingly put in place programs for ethical training. It is important to keep the purpose of ethics training in perspective. In our world we know what is right or wrong, and nobody needs to teach you that. However, in the business world, ethics training is important because it helps employee to solve ethical problems when they are confronted with situations of ethical dilemma. Many of these dilemmas, as pointed out earlier in this chapter, arise as a result of the difficulties decision makers are faced with in choosing between what is wrong or right. Most ethics training is designed to guide the employee in dealing with issues that they do not understand the ethical implications of their actions and how it affects the business and its stakeholders. Secondly, most ethics training helps employees avoid the common rationalizations for unethical behavior that were discussed earlier.

Many companies choose to design their own ethics-training program for the advantages it provides over other options such as consultant-led purchased program. Doing so allows the organization to tailor the ethics training-program to the industry, market, and company-specific factors that either exist within the organization or exert influence from outside. Regardless of the direction taken, some key considerations for designing an ethics-training program include:

(i) Define terms. What is an ethics-training program?
(ii) Define objectives. What are the objectives of an ethics-training program?
(iii) Decide what to include. What makes up an ethics-training program?
(iv) Decide where to start. How does the organization implement an ethics-training program?
(v) Decide on training methods. Who provides ethics training?

(vi) Define your audience. Who is the ethics training directed at?
(vii) Avoid roadblocks. What issues are commonly encountered in designing ethics training programs?
(viii) Test training effectiveness. How does an organization evaluate the effectiveness of its ethics-training program?
(ix) Follow up on training. What follow-up should take place after the ethics training program is initiated?

Even if your organization is already an ethical-value-based one that is managing for ethical compliance internally and for good stakeholder relations, adopting an ethics-training program offers the opportunity to enhance the content and ensure greater influence in the direction and focus points of the training. As ethics training drives, among other things, the establishment and reinforcement of your organization's value and culture, designing an effective ethics-training program to communicate the organization's ethics strategy pays dividends well beyond simply encouraging compliance.

Whistleblowing and Whistleblower Protection

As a form of principled organizational dissent, whistleblowing is the disclosure by current or former employees of illegal, immoral, or illegitimate organizational practices to people or organizations that may be able to change the practice. According to Archie Carroll and Ann Buchholtz, "a whistleblower is an individual who reports to some outside party (e.g., media, government agency) some wrongdoing (illegal or unethical act) that he or she knows or suspects his or her employer of committing."[31] The whistleblower lacks the power to change the undesirable practice directly and so appeals to others either inside or outside the organization. One important way a firm can create and maintain a high ethical standard is to protect those who report wrongdoing in the firm. To create an ethical business environment, it is the responsibility of business owners and managers to protect an employee who exposes the misdeeds of others in organizations. Experience in the world of business points to a situation in which whistleblowers face the risks of impaired career progress and other forms of organizational retaliation up to and including termination.[32]

In any situation of whistleblowing, what is at stake is the employee's right to speak out in cases where she or he thinks the company or management is engaging in an unacceptable practice. Whistleblowing is contrary to our cultural tradition that an employee does not question a superior's decisions and acts, especially not in public. The traditional view holds that loyalty, obedience, and confidentiality are owed solely to the employer. The emerging view of employee responsibility holds that the employee has a duty not only to the employer but also to the public and to her or his own conscience. Whistleblowing, in this latter situation, becomes a viable option for the employee should management not be responsive to expressed concerns.

Most whistleblowers seem to be engaging in these acts out of a genuine or legitimate belief that the actions of their organizations are wrong and that they are doing the right thing by reporting them. They may have learned of the wrongful acts by being requested or coerced to participate in them, or they may have gained knowledge of them through observation or examination of company records. The genuinely concerned employee may initially express concern to a superior or to someone else within the organization. Other potential whistleblowers may be planning to make their reports for the purpose of striking out or retaliating against the company or a specific manager for some reason. Research conducted in the United States has indicated that the average whistleblower turns out to be a family man, in his mid-40s, who was motivated by conscience, or what might be termed "universal moral values."[33]

The main point here is that whistleblowing occurs when there is an unethical culture and climate prevailing in an organization, when management refuses to act in ways that prevent unethical behaviors, and when the company or management is engaging in an unacceptable practice. The issue then becomes how organization can work with its employees to reduce their need to blow the whistle. One researcher in business ethics, Kenneth Walters,[34] has suggested five considerations that might be kept in mind:

(i) The company should assure employees that the organization would not interfere with their basic freedom.
(ii) The organization's grievance procedures should be streamlined so that employees can obtain direct sympathetic hearings for issues on which they are likely to blow the whistle if their complaints are not heard quickly and fairly.
(iii) The organization's concept of social responsibility should be reviewed to make sure that it is not being construed merely as corporate giving to charity.
(iv) The organization should formally recognize and communicate respect for the individual consciences of employees.
(v) The organization should realize that dealing harshly with a whistleblowing employee could result in needless adverse public reaction.

Companies are learning that whistleblowing can be averted if visible efforts are made on the part of management to listen and be responsive to employees' concerns. One specific approach is the use of an **ombudsperson** as a due-process mechanism. "Ombudsman", the word from which ombudsperson is derived, is a Swedish word that refers to one who investigates reported complaints and helps to achieve equitable settlements. The ombudsperson can also be used to deal with employee grievances against the company. Research conducted in the United States confirmed that the companies that have put money into ombudsperson programs say that they were worth the investment.[35]

Whether or not an ombudsperson is used, management should respond in a positive way to employee objectors and dissenters. At a minimum, companies that want to be responsive to such employees should engage in the following actions:

(i) *Listen*. Management must listen very carefully to the employee's concern. Be particularly attentive to the employee's valid points, and acknowledge them and show that you have a genuine respect for the employee's concerns. It is recommended that you attempt to "draw out the objector's personal concerns."

(ii) *Delve into why the employee is pursuing the complaint or issue.* Determining the objector's motives may give you important insights into the legitimacy of the complaint and how it should be handled.

(iii) *Look for solutions that will address the interests of both the objector and the company.*

(iv) *Attempt to establish an equitable means of judging future actions.* Objective tests or criteria that are agreeable to both sides are superior to perseverance or negotiation as a means of resolving an impasse.

(v) *Shout it from the rooftops.* The company should aggressively publicize a reporting policy that encourages employees to bring forward valid complaints of wrongdoing.

(vi) *Face the fear factor.* Employee fear may be defused by directing complaints to someone outside the whistleblower's chain of command.

(vii) *Get right on it.* The complaint should be investigated immediately by an independent group, either within or outside the company.

(viii) *Go public.* The outcomes of investigations should be publicized whenever possible so that employees can see that complaints are taken seriously.

The desire of employees to speak out will increasingly become a right in their eyes and in the eyes of the courts as well as African countries become increasingly democratized and the citizens more enlightened. In particular, African governments are now calling attention to due process, justice and social responsibility as a response to the injustice deriving from the authoritarian regimes of the past. It is to be expected that this wind and calls for change will also blow through the business and corporate environment. Although the courts and the judicial system in many parts of Sub-Saharan Africa are still battling with a corrupt and autocratic socio-political system, it is likely that whistleblowers and employees' rights to free expression will increasingly be protected in the future, again as a result of the forces of democratization and globalization. This being the case, management needs to assess carefully where it stands on this vital issue. It is becoming more and more apparent that respecting an employee's right to publicly differ with management may indeed serve the longer-term interest of the organization. We should also remember, however, that companies need and deserve protection from employees who do not perform as they should.

Steps for Creating a Whistleblowing Culture

As a summary to the foregoing discussion, the following steps are important for organizations that genuinely want to include sound ethics in their overall organizational culture.

Create a Policy
A policy about reporting illegal or unethical practices should include:
- Formal mechanisms for reporting violations, such as hotlines and mailboxes,

- Clear communications about the process of voicing concerns, such as a specific chain of command, or the identification of a specific person in the organization, such as an ombudsman or a human resources professional,
- Clear communications about bans on retaliation.

In addition, a clear connection should exist between an organization's code of ethics and performance measures. For example, in the performance review process, employees can be held accountable not only for meeting their goals and objectives but also for doing so in accordance with the stated values or business standards of the company.

Get Endorsement From Top Management

Top management, starting with the CEO, should demonstrate a strong commitment to encouraging whistleblowing. This message must be communicated by line managers at all levels, who are trained continuously in creating an open-door policy regarding employee complaints.

Publicize the Organization's Commitment

To create a culture of openness and honesty, it is important that employees hear about the policy regularly. Top management should make every effort to talk about the commitment to ethical behavior in memos, newsletters, and speeches to company personnel. Publicly acknowledging and rewarding employees who pinpoint ethical issues is one way to send the message that management is serious about addressing issues before they become endemic.

Investigate and Follow Up

Managers should be required to investigate all allegations promptly and thoroughly, and report the origins and the results of the investigation to a higher authority. For example, many organizations have a long-standing open-door policy which requires that any complaint received must be investigated within a certain number of hours. Inaction is the best way to create cynicism about the seriousness of an organization's ethics policy.

Assess the Organization's Internal Whistleblowing System

Find out employees' opinions about the organization's culture vis-à-vis its commitment to ethics and values. For example, in the United States, many corporations and small business organizations are conducting an annual employee survey related to ethics. Some questions are: Do you believe unethical issues are tolerated here? Do you know how to report an ethical issue?

Top Management Support

As an entrepreneur, you have the opportunity to set an ethical standard for your employees to follow. Your employees may be honest people or persons of high moral character, but examples set by you and your management team may cause them to overlook the unethical practices in your business venture, or even to adopt some of the unethical business practices showed by you or your top management team. As the owner of a business venture including your top managers, you have the power to shape the policies of your firm and to set the moral tone of your business in terms of which it relates to its stakeholders. To create and maintain a high ethical standard for your business, you and your management team must serve as models of appropriate ethical behavior for your firm. Not only must your behavior and the actions of your management team be the epitome of high ethical conduct, you must also communicate similar expectations throughout your business and firm. For example, if you and your top management team are known to use the firm's resources for personal pleasures, your employees may expect to do likewise.

Developing and Establishing a Code of Ethics or Conduct

As we pointed out earlier, a code of ethics is a document describing what your company stands for and the general rules of conduct it expects of its employees (e.g., to avoid conflicts of interests, to be honest, and so on). Most codes of ethical behavior identify expected behaviors in terms of general organizational citizenship, the avoidance of illegal or improper acts in one's work, and good relationships with customers and other stakeholder groups.

Codes of conduct are statements, which identify and define (i) strategic options and target behaviors which contribute to an organization's quality aims; (ii) a set of values and creeds; and (iii) specific guidelines for acceptable and unacceptable behavior among employees, with a view to fostering the strategic goals of the firm. Perhaps more than any other aspect of business ethics, ethical codes of conduct have been accepted and adopted, at considerable cost, by competitive businesses and corporations all over the world. These ethical codes represent an important breakthrough in the development of business ethics, and this for two reasons.

Firstly, as "practical techniques" for moral decision-making, they are more useful than moral principles drawn up in the studies of "business ethics professionals". They provide clear guidelines for specific courses of action in situations where neither of the available alternatives seems ethically acceptable.

Secondly, they provide "blueprints" for decisions: in the absence of codes, it is simply not possible for managers and employees to resolve dilemmas, which do not fall into their spheres of competence. This can lead to businesses operating not in a more or less ethically structured atmosphere but in one of corruption.

It should be understood that ethical codes of conduct do not always or necessarily ensure ethical behavior. The effectiveness of any ethical code of conduct in any organization presupposes that leaders and managers not only adhere strictly to them but must also serve as good example. In order not to be construed as window dressing devices, an organization's ethical code of ethics must be enforced without any exception and must follow a due process. Secondly, without the personal integrity of leaders and managers, codes of conduct must remain a show and, therefore, ineffective in effecting the real cultivation of an ethical organization and business practice. Without critical reflection upon the practical meaning of codes, principles and ideals, values such as justice, fairness, honesty and responsibility lose their binding force. As Vincete Montes rightly points out:

"Strictly speaking, the only realistic way to promote ethics within the company is through the practice of personal and social virtues. It is excellent for a company to have codes of ethics, and even some have a 'creed'! But these solemn statements are ineffective if they do not reflect the ethical behavior of the people who belong to it, especially managers and the powers behind the veil."[36]

Aligning Your Strategy to Your Ethical Principles and Core Values

As a business owner, you are who you are and you will run your business accordingly. Your strategy can be a product of your ethical upbringing and the values you hold so dear in your life. That is why many firms have adopted a code of ethics and a statement of company values. But there is a huge difference between having a code of ethics and a value statement that serve merely as a public window dressing and having ethical standards and business values that truly paint a different scenario. As an entrepreneur, if your ethical standard and statement of core values are to have more than a cosmetic role, your advisory board is a necessary place to go to for an informed advice.

What You Should Guide Against

In the process of creating and maintaining a high ethical standard in your organization, there are certain areas you should take into consideration, including:

(i) Do not adopt a "bottom-line" strive for financial success at all cost. Because society places a high value on economic success does not mean that you must make money at all cost. When your company's culture spawns an ethical corrupt or amoral work climate, your employees will have a business-approved license to ignore "what's right" and engage in most any behavior or employ most any strategy they think they can get away with.

(ii) Do not create an organization culture that encourages people to do whatever is necessary to be profitable. Because intense competition occurs between people, departments, or companies does not mean that your company must compete at all costs. The pressures to conform to the norms of the corporate culture can prompt otherwise honorable people to make ethical mistakes and succumb to the many opportunities around them to engage in unethical practices.

(iii) Your business policies regarding ethical behavior must not be ambiguous. One of the major reasons your employees will behave unethically is because your codes of ethics are vague and provide little guidance regarding appropriate and inappropriate behavior.

(iv) Do not create a lax control systems that allow your employees to "get away with" behaving unethically. Lax accounting systems and the absence of security procedures make behaving unethically all too easy for some people.

(v) As the owner of your business, do not fail to comprehend the public's ethical concerns. There are situations in which you or your employees can forget that the public at large is increasingly intolerant of unethical behavior.

(vi) Do not succumb to the idea that it is acceptable to behave unethically because others expect you to do so (e.g., in buyer-seller relationships as in kickbacks for contracts).

CASE IN POINT: ENRON

A perfect example of a company gone awry on ethics is Enron.[37] Enron's leaders encouraged company personnel to focus on the current bottom line and to be innovative and aggressive in figuring out what could be done to grow current revenues and earnings. Employees were expected to pursue opportunities to the utmost in the energy industry that at the time was undergoing looser regulation. Enron executives viewed the company as a laboratory for innovation; the company hired the best and brightest people and pushed them to be creative, look at problems and opportunities in new ways, and exhibit a sense of urgency in making things happen. Employees were encouraged to make a difference and do their part in creating an entrepreneurial environment where creativity flourished, people could achieve their full potential, and everyone had a stake in the outcome. Enron employees got the message – pushing the limits and meeting one's numbers were viewed as survival skills. Enron's annual "rank and yank" formal evaluation process where the 15 to 20 percent lowest-ranking employees were let go or encouraged to seek other employment made it abundantly clear that bottom-line results and being the "mover-and –shaker" in the marketplace were what counted. The name of the game at Enron became devising clever ways to boost revenues and earnings, even if it sometimes meant operating outside established policies and without the knowledge of superiors. In fact, outside-the-lines behavior was celebrated if it generated profitable new business. Enron's energy contracts and its trading and hedging activities grew increasingly more complex and diverse as employees pursued first this avenue and then another to help keep Enron's financial performance looking good.

As a consequence of Enron's well-publicized successes in creating new products and businesses and leveraging the company's trading and hedging expertise into new market arenas, the company came to be regarded as an exceptionally innovative company. It was ranked by its corporate peers as the most innovative U.S. company for three consecutive years in Fortune magazine's annual surveys of the most admired companies. A high-performance/high-rewards climate came to pervade the Enron culture, as the best workers (determined by who produced the best bottom-line results) received impressively large incentives and bonuses (amounting to as much as $1 million for traders and even more for senior executives). On Car Day at Enron, an array of luxury sports cars arrived for presentation to the most successful employees. Understandably, employees wanted to be seen as part of Enron's star team and partake in the benefits that being one of Enron's best and smartest employees entailed. The high monetary rewards, the ambitious and hard-driving people that the company hired and promoted, and the competitive, results-oriented culture combined to give Enron a reputation not only for trampling competitors at every opportunity but also for internal ruthlessness.

The company's super-aggressiveness and win-at-all-costs mind-set nurtured a culture that gradually and then more rapidly fostered the erosion of ethical standards, eventually making a mockery of the company's stated values of integrity and respect. When it became evident in the fall of 2001 that Enron was a house of cards propped up by deceitful accounting and a myriad of unsavory practices, the company imploded in a matter of weeks – the biggest bankruptcy of all time cost investors $64 billion in losses (between August 2000, when the stock price was at its five-year high, and November 2001), and Enron employees lost their retirement assets, which were almost totally invested in Enron stock.

STRATEGY, ETHICS AND SOCIAL RESPONSIBILITY

Should business owners be responsible only to making profits or do they have broader responsibilities? This is an important question because your strategic actions (the actions you undertake in order to be competitive in your chosen industry) carry with them an ethical consequence: for good or bad. Similarly, your strategic actions will affect, in one way or the other, those who have stakes (interests) in your business. We should have learned, from the discussion in chapter seven that the mission statement of your firm is not about making money *per se*. It is also about doing what is right while making your money and giving something back to society. As an entrepreneur, you will feel good about yourself making money and giving something back to your community.

Although discussions in management and business textbooks talk about corporate social responsibility, the term is not restricted to large corporations: It could equally be applied to small businesses. Hence, Keith Davis and Robert Blomstrom define social responsibility as "the obligation of decision makers to take actions which protect and improve the welfare of society as a whole along with their own interests."[38] This definition suggests two active aspects of social responsibility – *protecting* and *improving*. To protect the welfare of society implies the creation of positive benefits for society. The second characterization – improving – is perhaps vague and might permit managers wide latitude in interpreting how to improve society.

A definition provided by Archie Carroll helps to understand the components that make up corporate social responsibility (CSR): "The social responsibility of business encompasses the economic, legal, ethical, and discretionary (philanthropic) expectations that society has of organizations at a given point in time."[39] The economic dimension of social responsibility is required of business by society and presupposes that businesses should be profitable; maximize sales; minimize costs; make sound strategic decisions and be attentive to dividend policy.

The legal component is required of business by society and implies that a business must obey all laws; adhere to all regulations; adhere to environmental and consumer laws; fulfill all contractual obligations, etc. The ethical dimension is expected of business by society and implies that businesses should avoid questionable practices, respond to spirit as well as letter of the law; assume law is a floor on behavior and operate above minimum required; do what is right, fair, and just; assert ethical leadership. The philanthropic dimension of social responsibility is desired and expected of business by society and implies that a business should be a good corporate citizen; make corporate contribution; provide programs supporting community – education, health/human services, culture and arts, civic; provide for community betterment, engage in voluntarism, etc.[40] Stated in more practical and managerial terms, the socially responsible firm should strive to:

- Make a profit.
- Obey the law.
- Be ethical.
- Be a good corporate citizen.

Whether you are an executive of a large multinational corporation or the owner of a small business, making your profit without meeting the requirements or needs of other stakeholders is detrimental to the long-term profitability of your business. There are several arguments supporting why your business must be socially responsible:

- One of the most widely accepted arguments in favor of corporate social responsibility (CSR) is that it is in business's long-range self-interest to be socially responsible. Some theorists have argued that it was partially business's fault that many of today's social problems arose in the first place, and, consequently, that business should assume a role in remedying these problems. It must be inferred from this that deterioration of the social condition must be halted if business is to survive and prosper in the future.[41] According to Archie Carroll and Ann Buchholtz, the long-range self-interest view holds that if business is to have a healthy climate in which to exist in the future, it must take actions now that will ensure its long-term viability. It is sometimes difficult for managers who have a short-term orientation to appreciate that their rights and roles in the economic system are determined by society. Business must be responsive to society's expectations over the long term if it is to survive in its current form or in a less restrained form.[42]

- One of the most practical reasons for business to be socially responsible is to ward off future government intervention and regulation. Today, there are numerous areas in which government intrudes with an expensive, elaborate regulatory apparatus to fill a void left by business's inaction. To the extent that business polices itself with self-disciplined standards and guidelines, future government intervention can be somewhat forestalled.

- Another argument in favor of corporate social responsibility is that business has the resources to do just that. This argument maintains that because business has a reservoir of management talent, functional expertise, and capital, and because so many others have tried and failed to solve general social problems, business should be given a chance. This argument has some merit, because there are some social problems that can be handled, in the final analysis, only by business. Examples include a fair workplace, providing safe products, and engaging in fair advertising.

> Another argument is that "pro-acting is better than reacting." This position holds that pro-acting (anticipating and initiating) is more practical and less costly than simply reacting to problems once they have developed. Environmental pollution in the Niger Delta of Nigeria is a good example, particularly business's and government's experience with attempting to clean up rivers, creeks and pay compensations for environmental and social damages resulting from years of pollution. The cost in human, financial, economic, and social loss far exceeds what it would have cost the oil corporations had they acted proactively in guarding against oil pollution. In the long-run, it would have been wiser to have prevented the environmental deterioration from occurring in the first place.

In general, the unethical business practices of a few business owners, and their lack of attention to social responsibility, will not only hurt their businesses in the long run; such actions will also hurt their customers, employees, suppliers, business community, profession, shareholders (if there is any) and society in general. As the Nigerian experience has indicated, the problems of "419-iers" have, more than any other factor, imperiled the business reputation of the country in the global economy. Prospective foreign investors have years shunned the Nigerian business environment because of its culture of frauds cultivated by the actions of few individuals.

THE STAKEHOLDERS OF THE ENTREPRENEURIAL FIRM AND ITS SOCIAL RESPONSIBILITY

The stakeholder concept has become a central idea in understanding business and its relationship to society. First, to appreciate the concept of stakeholders, it helps to understand the idea of a stake. A **stake** is an interest or a share in an undertaking. A stake is also a claim. A claim is an assertion to a title or a right to something. A claim is a demand for something due or believed to be due. We can see clearly that an owner or a stockholder has an interest in and an ownership of a share of a business.

The idea of a stake, therefore, can range from simply an interest in an undertaking at one extreme to a legal claim of ownership at the other extreme. In between these two extremes is a "right" to something. This right might be legal right to certain treatment rather than a legal claim of ownership, such as that of a shareholder. Legal rights might include the right to fair treatment (e.g., not to be discriminated against) or the right to privacy (not to have one's privacy invaded or abridged). The right might be thought of as a moral right, such as that expressed by an employee: I've got a right not to be fired because I've worked here 30 years, and I've given this firm the best years of my life." Or a consumer might say, "I've got a right to a safe product after all I've paid for this."

When a person or group will be affected by a decision, it has an interest or stake in that decision. Thus, there are several types of stakes. A fisherman in the Niger Delta area of Nigeria whose waters have been polluted would assert his stake in any decision made by an oil exploration firm operating in the Niger Delta area. For an example of an interest: when the closure of a plant affects a particular community or when a TV commercial demeans women. Example of legal right: Employees expect due process, privacy, customers or creditors have certain legal rights. Example of moral right: When a person or group thinks it has a moral right to be treated in a certain way or to have a particular right protected (e.g., the right to earn a legitimate living, the right to fairness, justice, equity, etc). Example of ownership right: "This company is mine, I founded it, and I own it," or "I own 1,000 shares of this company."

A **stakeholder**, then, is an individual or a group that has one or more of the various kinds of stakes in a business. Just as stakeholders may be affected by the actions, decisions, policies, or practices of the business firm, these stakeholders may also affect the organization's actions, decisions, policies, or practices. With stakeholders, therefore, there is a potential two-way interaction or exchange of influence. In short, a **stakeholder** may be thought of as "any individual or group who can affect or is affected by the actions, decisions, policies, practices, or goals of the organization."[43]

In today's competitive, global business environment, there are many individuals and groups who are business's stakeholders. From the business point of view, there are certain individuals and groups that have legitimacy in the eyes of management. That is, they have a legitimate interest in, or claim on, the operations of the firm. The most obvious of these groups are stockholders, employees, and customers. From the point of view of a highly pluralistic society, stakeholders include not only these groups, but other groups as well. These other groups include competitors, suppliers, the community, special-interest groups, the media, government and its agencies, and society or the public at large. Many observers, such as Mark Starik, have argued that the natural environment and future generations should also be considered among business's important stakeholders.[44]

To understand the concept of a stakeholder, we must connect it to the concept of business social responsibility as previously discussed. The responsibility of your firm to its constituencies must thus be discussed within the context of its stakeholders, that is, those who have a stake in your business. The concept of **social responsibility** proposes that a firm has responsibilities to society including its stakeholders that extend beyond making a profit. The essence of socially responsible business behavior is that a company should strive to balance the benefits of strategic actions to benefit the owners against any possible adverse impacts on other stakeholders (employees, suppliers, customers, local communities, and society at large).

As an entrepreneur, your strategic decisions ought to be shaped by your responsibility to your stakeholders. Any strategic action taken by the owner of a business and the manager of a business inevitably affects the welfare of its stakeholders: employees, suppliers, customers, investors and stockholders, the local communities in which it does business, the government, and the general public, and many others. The social responsibility of your business is a society-wide issue. It is worth emphasizing that while a strategy may enhance the welfare of some stakeholder groups, it might harm others.

That is why it is important to understand the interests of the major stakeholders of your business.

The idea that your business must act in good ethical manner invariably brings us to the issue of social responsibility. The question then becomes: "Responsible to who?" The environment in which your firm exists includes a large number of individuals or groups with interest in the activities of your business. These individuals or groups are referred to as your firm's stakeholders because they affect or are affected by the achievement of your firm's objectives. Paying attention to their stakes or demands will help your firm avoid many of the unethical practices prevalent in our business culture today. In any one strategic decision, the interests of one stakeholder group can conflict with another.

The concept of a stakeholder highlights the fact that the activities of a business venture are not merely a series of market transactions but also a cooperative (and competitive) endeavor involving large numbers of people organized in various ways. The business venture is an organizational entity through which many different individuals and groups attempt to achieve their ends. The business firm interacts continually with its stakeholder groups, and much of its business success depends on how well all of these stakeholder relations are managed. Managing stakeholder relations, rather than managing inputs and outputs, may provide a more adequate model for understanding the business, its owners and managers and employees actually do to maintain an acceptable business ethical behavior. Such an approach for understanding the conduct of a business firm can help business owners pay attention to the demands of those who have a stake in their businesses. Second, the stakeholder approach can be used as a *normative* account of how the firm *ought* to treat their various stakeholder groups. The stakeholder approach would have business owners recognize the interests of employees, customers, and others as worth furthering for their own sakes. Thus, even if making profit is the ultimate goal of your firm, this goal does not provide much help in the conduct of your business. In order to avoid ethical problems in the conduct of your business, you must pay attention to demands of your stakeholders.

In a nutshell, the survival of your business depends on the quality of its interaction and relationships with its various stakeholder groups. Your duty and obligation to your **customers** is the de facto reason why you are in business. Customers must be provided with the best quality of goods and services available. The **shareholders** in your company and **investors** (the owners) are another important stakeholder groups. People may have invested their money in your company, so you must make sure that they receive their dividends. The **employees** of your business are a major stakeholder group. Effective stakeholder management suggests that your organization seriously consider its obligations to your employee stakeholders and their rights and expectations with respect to their jobs. As pointed earlier, your responsibility includes dealing with your employees in good faith, giving them the right to due process, maintaining their rights to privacy, and providing a safe working condition. The **government and its agencies** constitute an important stakeholder group. For example, the government provides infrastructures in order for your business to operate properly and so you must pay your taxes and other fees. Government has a significant impact on business by virtue of the fact that it regulates its conduct. The **community** in which the business exists demands that your business activities are in sync with its best interests. Most firms in Sub-Saharan Africa exist in industries that are regulated by **trade associations** or **interest groups** with their own code of conduct. These trade associations are there to protect your firm's interest and their own interests. In turn, you are expected to abide by the code of conduct established by your association. Your **suppliers** provide you with what you sell or produce and their demands must be attended to in a manner that enhances your profitability and their profitability. You must compete with your **competitors** within the limit of the law. There must be an obligation to deal fairly with your **distributors**. An important stakeholder of your business is the natural environment. The activities of your business must not be detrimental to the natural environment. The **natural environment**, commonly referred to simply as the **environment**, comprises all living and non-living things that occur naturally on the planet. The natural environment include all ecological units that function as natural systems without massive human intervention, including all vegetation, animals, microorganisms, rocks, atmosphere, natural resources and physical phenomena that lack clear-cut boundaries, such as air, water, and climate, as well as energy, radiation, electric charge, and magnetism, not originating from human activity.

Unfortunately, and especially in Sub-Saharan Africa, businesses have played a major role in contributing to natural environmental degradation, pollution and depletion. Virtually, every sector of business in every country is responsible for consuming significant amounts of materials and energy and causing waste accumulation and resource degradation. For instance, forestry firms and companies that process raw materials have caused major air, water, and land pollution problems in their extraction, transportation, and processing. From meat processing factories, to restaurants and oil refineries, the natural environment has been a victim of business activities. Although manufacturing and operations processes are the most visible contributors to air, water, and land pollution, virtually every other business activities in all sectors potentially plays some role in affecting the natural environment. Thus, in order to act responsibly with the natural environment, a firm must have a strict environmental policy.

MANAGING STAKEHOLDER RELATIONS AND THE CONSTRUCTION OF ORGANIZATION'S VALUES

The values of an organization play a significant role in its leadership ability to manage the organization's relationship with its external and internal stakeholders. In other words, an organization must be value-based, one in which the espoused values are adhered to. The values of an organization, if properly adhered to, provide members the moral compass with which to navigate in their daily actions and behaviors with stakeholders. Some of the ways organizations have used to develop a value-based organization are: (i) managing stakeholder relations and (ii) creating a value-based organization by constructing a set of values that guide the ethical behavior of all members of the organization.

Managing Stakeholder Relations

Organizations become increasingly sophisticated and see the long-term value to be gained from maintaining good relations with key stakeholders. Self-interest drives the organization to monitor its reputation among these stakeholders and to initiate programs to address their ethical concerns. The primary objective of managing stakeholder relations for your firm is to create value by meeting stakeholder expectations. Such an approach serves as a standard for judging behavior including stakeholder demand and expectations. The advantage of such an approach is stakeholders can be surveyed for expectations and attitudes. Action steps include:

- (i) Define organizations' stakeholders.
- (ii) Evaluate the attitudes and opinions of stakeholder groups.
- (iii) Design programs to address stakeholder concerns.
- (iv) Audit the effectiveness of stakeholder programs.

Creating a Values-based Organization: The Elements of Value - construction

Many organizations have found it difficult to manage compliance or stakeholder relations without creating a genuine change in their organizational culture. As a result, instinct rather than strategy dominates responses to the breadth of ethical issues held important by stakeholders. Value-based organizations define their values and invest considerable efforts and expense in making those values permeate all aspects of their work. They find it productive to make decisions consistent with these values even when short-term payoffs are not apparent. In reality, every few organizations reach this stage. The primary objective is to create an organization that has enduring value. The approach serves as standards for judging behavior, including the company's own values and beliefs. The strengths of the approach include bolstering the firm's own culture, with desired behavior becoming instinctive. Action steps include:

- (i) Define the organization's values.
- (ii) Communicate the organization's values.
- (iii) Create systems that support the organization's values.
- (iv) Ensure supervision of the organization's values.
- (v) Establish an ethics or organization's values function.
- (vi) Assign responsibility for interpreting values.
- (vii) Recruit and promote employees of strong moral character.
- (viii) Train employees in ethical decision making and application of the values.
- (ix) Encourage employees to report behavior inconsistent with the values.
- (x) Reward managers and employee behavior consistent with the values.
- (xi) Renew the values.
- (xii) Conduct policy and practice reviews.

The establishment of an ethical culture within an organization is essential, not only for the achievement of desired business goals, but also necessary for the proper management of key risks in its business environment.

CHAPTER SUMMARY

Ethics is the code of moral principles that sets standards of good or bad, right or wrong in one's conduct and thereby guides the behavior of a person or group. Ethics tells us whether our behavior is moral or immoral and deals with fundamental human relationships - how we think and behave toward others and how we want them to think and behave toward us. Ethical principles are codes of conduct that guide human behavior.

Sources of ethical behavior are a person's religious beliefs, the institution of the family, schools and school teachers, neighbors and the neighborhood, friends and role models, ethnic groups, the media, professional belongingness, society and its legal institutions.

Business ethics is the application of general ethical ideas to the conduct of business. The ethical conduct of business must draw its principles from the same sources as everyone else. What is considered right or wrong in a society is equally applicable to the conduct of business.

The importance of business ethics comes into the fore when we consider how the actions of a business venture affects its stakeholders. An acceptable business ethical environment is one that protects the interests of all participants in the business relationship.

An ethical dilemma is a situation with a potential course of action that, although, offering potential benefit or gain, is also unethical.

Ethical rationalization is a process in which people try to explain their decisions as ethically right when they know that they are ethically wrong.

Ethical issues in business practices include (i) marketing practices (such as packaging and labeling, deceptive and manipulative marketing practices, advertising), (ii) production and delivery (such as product liability), (iii) accounting and financial malpractices (such as kickbacks), and contract inflation.

Rationalization occurs when people explained their actions because everyone else does the same thing, because the action is not illegal, because it does not really hurt anyone and the behavior is really in everyone's best interests, the system is unfair and one needs to get at it, nobody will ever find out what one has done.

A model of ethical decision making is a process that consists of four major steps: evaluation of a proposed strategic decision from an ethical standpoint, judging the ethics of the decision made, establishing the moral intent of the decision, and engaging in the decision that has been made.

Due process is the right to receive an impartial review of one's complaints and to be dealt with fairly.

Employee constitutionalism consists of a set of clearly defined rights and a means of protecting employees from discharge, demotion, or other penalties imposed when they assert their rights.

A stakeholder is any individual or group who can affect or is affected by the actions, decisions, policies, practices, or goals of the organization.

Business social responsibility is as an obligation of a business entity, whether large or small, to act in ways that serve both its own interests and the interests of its stakeholders while formulating and implementing a firm's competitive strategy.

The concept of social responsibility proposes that a firm has responsibilities to society including its stakeholders that extend beyond making a profit.

The ability to manage your entrepreneurial firm depends on how you manage yourself. How you manage your self is about how (i) you manage your finances, (ii) you treat your family in relationship to your business, (iii) you develop personal discipline, (iv) know your weaknesses, (v) align your priorities with your values, and (vi) you value people.

Ombudsperson is derived from the Swedish word "ombudsman" and refers to one who investigates reported complaints and helps to achieve equitable settlements.

Companies can create and maintain high ethical business standards by (i) pursuing a program of ethics training in their firms, (ii) protecting whistleblowers, (iii) behavioral support from top management, (iv) developing a code of ethics, (v) aligning the business strategy to the firms' ethical principles and core values.

Whistleblowing is the disclosure by current or former employees of illegal, immoral, or illegitimate organizational practices.

In order to guide against unethical practices in your firm, the following actions should be avoided (i) Do not adopt a "bottom-line" mentality to guide your business operation, (ii) Do not create an organization culture that encourages people to do whatever it takes to be profitable, (iii) Do not adopt an ambiguous business policy regarding ethical behavior, (iv) Do not fail to listen to the concerns of the general public, (v) Do not create a lax control systems that allows your employees to get away with behaving unethically, and (vi) Do not act unethically because others are doing it.

In order to create a value-based organization, owners and managers should properly define the organization's values, communicate the organization's values, create systems that support the organization's values, ensure supervision of the organization's values, assign responsibility for interpreting values, recruit and promote employees of strong moral character, train employees in ethical decision making and application of the values, encourage employees to report behavior inconsistent with the values, reward employee behavior consistent with the values, renew the values, and conduct policy and practice reviews.

DISCUSSION QUESTIONS

1. What do we mean by the concept of "ethics?" What are the sources of a person's ethical behavior?

2. What is business ethics? What is an acceptable business ethical environment?

3. What is an ethical dilemma? What is ethical rationalization and how do people rationalize their behaviors ethically?

4. What and who is a stakeholder?

5. What is the meaning of social responsibility as it applies to an entrepreneur's business?

6. What is a values-based organization? What must an entrepreneur do in order to create a values-based organization? Be sure to describe the steps that must be followed.

7. What must you do in order to create and maintain high ethical business standards in your business?

8. What must you do to guide against unethical business practices in your firm?

CASE 14: FOREIGN EXCHANGE MALPRACTICES: WHY PERPETRATORS CHEAT ON REGULATORY AUTHORITIES[45]

In the context of economic development in a country, it is assumed that the accumulation of external reserve is the secret for maintaining and sustaining a stable exchange rate. Despite the obvious significance of this matter, over the years, the Nigerian foreign exchange has acquired a pervasive influence on consumption and production in the economy.

In Nigeria, foreign exchange (forex) is used for purposes other than they are applied for by most users. Experts claim that the malaise is currently endemic, and is responsible for major adverse economic indicators such as the non-growth of the real sector. For most observers, it is difficult to see why the individual offender cannot be picked out and subjected to established penalties. Forex malpractice is made possible by a network of collaboration, and it usually takes the consent of an entire institution to hatch, even though, not everyone in the institution may have been involved at the initial plot. Forex malpractice includes any act, with fraudulent intent, of omission, commission, falsification, collaboration, in the application for, utilization, exportation, importation, declaration or documentation relating to the use of foreign exchange in the market negating the letter or spirit of subsisting and applicable statuses and regulations.

At the 2004 quarterly forum of Bank Directors Association of Nigeria held in Lagos in February 2004, many of the directors aired their views concerning the problems of foreign exchange in the country. In the conference, papers were presented on the theme: "Malpractices in Foreign Exchange Operations." The view from the presentation was that foreign exchange (forex) malpractices include: over invoicing of imports, under invoicing of exports, round tripping, falsification of documents, trading in "free funds', fake judgment debts, duty evasion, aiding laundering of foreign currencies etc. What are the motivational factors and how is government dealing with the situation? The following are excerpts taken from the views of some of the participants.

Mr. Ernest C. Ebi, Deputy Governor, Policy, Central Bank of Nigeria: "An economic system is never devoid of distortions. The Nigerian economy is no exception to this rule. Malpractices thrive more in an economy characterized with fundamental economic disequilibrium, an economy that fosters arbitrage and speculative attack on currency. The job of curbing malpractices should not be left for the Central Bank alone; it is the task of all the stakeholders. What we need is convertibility of the exchange rate. We need the cooperation of the banks. We want the banks to be self-policing. To a large extent, banks' unrealistic targets can induce its staff to take undue advantage of certain loopholes in the system. Staff should be properly trained and retained to update their knowledge, be properly remunerated to discourage poaching and properly rewarded to have the courage to maintain a good ethical standard and to abstain from forex malpractice. The managements of the banks cannot say they are not aware of the plot and perpetration of forex scam committed by their staff. It is a network and if the banks become self-regulatory and discipline their staff, it cannot happen. At a time in this country, between 1999 and 2000, we were spending over 25 percent of our foreign exchange for travels. 25 percent on business and traveling allowances, so, how can we grow? People are just buying money for one reason and using it to bring in goods into the country, for another reason. They gain but this will distort data that we give out. Trade statistics are falling because you buy foreign exchange for holiday for traveling, which is invisible and at the end of the day, you bring in merchandise. How can we plan with these statistics?"

Mr. Aigboje Imoukhuede, Managing Director/CEO Access Bank Plc. "The administration of foreign exchange in this country has a long history with the various market tier regimes. Apart from the first and second tier which were basically transitional, the second tier foreign exchange made the banks the conductor between the Central Bank funds and the end-users' funds. This period saw the first major devaluation of the currency from a naira quoted equal to the dollar and becoming N4 to the dollar. Operators began to go crazy because of the excessive freedom, excessive rent system. We are a wholly import-dependent country and the type of forex we operate have very pervasive influence on the consumption pattern and production of our economy. Over the last 15 years, most banks have used their business model in exploiting the forex market. The Central Bank of Nigeria under Joseph Sanusi was able to largely remove the wide rent opportunities. But the CBN has not been able to eliminate the opportunities. To control abuse, there was an attempt to ensure there was a direct relationship between the CBN and the end-users. This established the pattern which exists today whereby banks act on behalf of end-users vis-à-vis getting dollars from the CBN. Banks should not buy dollars from the CBN directly. There is also low level of ethical standard and professionalism in the industry coupled with weak government policy and weak deterrence measures."

Mrs. Onwu Phillips, former Managing Director, Gateway Bank Plc: "The problems of abuse in the forex market seem to me, varied. A government official gets a 10 days event abroad. He is given estacodes and he spends two days. Does he come back to change his money at the official rate? Does he send it to the open market and is this round tripping? The purchase of the naira by the Mallam who buys and sells indicate there are patrons, who are the big people in this country. The CBN said last year, through its report, that Nigerians have the largest money in foreign accounts. If the disparity is not too much between the official and parallel market rate, if the gap is not too wide, over a period of time, people will be discouraged from storing money abroad or buying houses there. Also, if we are able to implement a policy that will attract people to bring back these monies without questions asked, maybe, this imbalance between the supply and demand of forex will be corrected. Until we try to correct it, there will be disparity."

Mrs. Onasanya, Member, Board of Prudent Bank Plc: "If parallel market is a malpractice, why is it official? Today, there is public knowledge about the rate of exchange, published in the newspapers. Year back, this was not so and we appreciate the current development. But which market is Yaba and which one is Lagos Mainland? You cannot pass through Marina/CMS bus stop and around the corners of the Central Bank without being hailed by Mallams: Dollars! Dollars!! And we say these things are illegal. What is the authority doing about it? If people are not able to buy and sell this illegally acquired forex, it will reduce their appetite for such trade. The suspension of the trading licenses of banks found guilty of forex crimes is not enough. They should be made to face criminal charges, because, if you don't do that, the problem will continue.

Case Discussion Questions

1. From a stakeholder perspective, discuss the actions of Nigerian banks in foreign exchange malpractices. Mr. Ernest Obi said that "the job of curbing (foreign exchange) malpractices should not be left for the Central Bank alone; it is the task of all the stakeholders." In your view, who are the stakeholders? What claims do they have on the foreign exchange market?

2. What did Ernest Obi mean when he said that the banks should be "self-policing and self-regulatory?" Based on materials discussed in this chapter, how can an organization such as a bank police and regulate itself?

3. In your opinion, why do you think that most banks in Nigeria have used their business model in exploiting the foreign exchange market?

4. Mr. Aigboje Imoukhuede pointed out that "There is also low level of ethical standard and professionalism in the industry coupled with weak government policy and weak deterrence measures" in curbing the unethical practices of foreign exchange sellers and buyers. In your view, what are the solutions to these problems?

5. From the perspectives of Mrs. Onwu Phillips, what are the roots of the unethical practices in the Nigerian foreign exchange market?

*PART IV: IMPLEMENTING
              ENTREPRENEURIAL STRATEGIES*

Chapter 15:   Crafting a Competitive Business Plan

Chapter 15

CRAFTING A COMPETITIVE BUSINESS PLAN

"Strategies most often fail because they aren't executed well"
(Larry Bossidy and Ram Charan, CEO Honeywell International; author and consultant).

CHAPTER LEARNING OBJECTIVES
After studying this chapter, you should be to:

1. Understand the meaning of a business plan and how to prepare one from a strategic management perspective.

2. Understand the purposes for which a business plan is often prepared.

3. Understand what a business plan can do for you.

4. Understand the outline and contents of a typical business plan.

5. Understand the process and steps involved in preparing a business plan.

INTRODUCTION: THE NEED FOR A BUSINESS PLAN

Let's start the discussion by saying that for every business to be successful in the long-term, there is a need for a business plan. The main reason is simply that the business plan forces the owner to implement the business ideas and strategies. Strategies are plans, words, and ideas that only become meaningful when they are put into action; that is, when they are implemented. Without a business plan to follow, it becomes extremely difficult to implement and evaluate the strategies. The experience of most business owners in Sub-Saharan Africa illustrates a situation where the business failure rate is high as a result of the refusal or the apparent inability on the part of business owners to have viable business plans. As important as a business plan for the successful operation of a business venture, there is no ideal format for one. Each plan is as unique as the business owner that creates it, and each audience for a plan has unique needs of its own, as well. A successful business plan should be able to have those ingredients that make the business owner to be competitive in the market place.

The purpose of our discussion here is to illustrate the importance of a business plan written from of a strategic management perspective and to provide the strategy for writing a winning business plan. I see a business plan as the compass leading you to the successful destination of your business goals as it navigates your journey in realizing your entrepreneurial dreams. I see a business plan in terms of the strategic plans a firm must use in order to remain competitive in the marketplace. A business plan, like a business strategy, consists of the competitive moves and the business approaches that you must employ to attract and please customers, compete successfully, grow your business, conduct its operations, and achieve its targeted objectives. I also see a lack of business plan as a lack of direction. A business owner without a business plan is like a blind person groping his or her way through the dark; he or she does not know where the road will take him or her. Like a strategy, an entrepreneur without a business plan is like a ship without a rudder.

Your business plan gives meaning to your strategy because it is your commitment to undertake one set of actions rather than another. A business plan gives the owner of the business a competitive advantage when it is prepared from a strategic management perspective. For a business plan to function as a competitive tool, it must provide understanding of what the business owner wants its business to look like and provide him or her with a reference point in making strategic decisions and preparing the business for the future.

Note that not all business plans are alike. A business plan for a home-based sole proprietorship business differs from a business plan for a large corporation with offices in many cities. But all business plans have the same purposes described below. Because all business plans have the same purposes, they all have the same basic elements. As a rule, do not include unnecessary or irrelevant information taken from a textbook. Use simple language that will give your readers a clear idea of what you want to do and how you plan to do it.

WHAT IS A BUSINESS PLAN AND FOR WHAT PURPOSE?

First, a business plan is a written document that details a proposed or existing venture. It will typically explain the vision, current status, expected needs, defined markets, and projected results of the business. A business plan is a comprehensive document that helps an entrepreneur analyze and understand the market and plan a business strategy. It details an entrepreneur's proposed business venture, its operational and financial details, its marketing opportunities and strategy, and its managers' skills and abilities. There is no substitute for a well-prepared business plan, and there are no shortcuts to creating one. A business plan serves as an entrepreneur's compass on the journey toward building a successful business. It describes the direction the firm will take (or is currently taking), what its goals are, where it wants to be, and how it's going to get there. A business plan is a written proof that the entrepreneur has performed the necessary research and has studied the industry, the market and the business opportunity adequately.

As an entrepreneur, or a prospective one, you may be amazed to see how many would-be entrepreneurs set out to start a business without a plan. It is possible that these would-be entrepreneurs reasoned that a great idea is all that they need. Or may be they believed that they just do not have the time to prepare one. Whenever these two reasons prevail, a business barely survives the forces of competition. In fact, not having a solid business plan in place is the number one reason why businesses fail. The bottom line is this: A new business or an existing one cannot afford *not* to have a plan. If you still need convincing, the following section gives you the reasons why a business plan is essential.

> *A Business Plan Puts your Business Ideas to the Test*: The best way to test whether your business idea is as good as it sounds is to create a business plan. The planning process forces you to think about who is going to buy your product or service, who your competitors are likely to be, and how much time and money you need to get your company going. Chances are you will find yourself refining or even retooling your idea as you go through the process of planning, and that is good, too. The more fine-tuning you do upfront, the better your odds of success down the road.

> *A Business Plan Turns a Good Idea into a Viable Business*: The heart of business planning involves taking a good idea and turning it into a working venture - laying out exactly where and how the money is going to be made. If you cannot figure out where your revenues will come from, for example, it is back to the drawing board. Nonprofit organizations such as charity homes do not have to worry about making money, of course, but they do have to make sure there are contributors out there willing to support a worthy cause - and clients to serve. In either case, a business plan helps you to come up with a way to make your business work.

> *A Business Plan Shows You What You Are Up Against*: You are probably not the first person along your street to dream of striking it rich by offering a beer parlor,

a day-care center, a secondary school, a fishery venture, water bottling outfit, a printing shop, an internet café, or whatever your very cool new product or service happens to be. And that means you better have a really good idea of who your competitors are before you get started. Putting together a business plan gives you the chance to analyze your market and scope out the competition, gathering critical intelligence data that will allow you to prepare upfront and avoid pitfalls later. It also requires that you create a detailed action plan describing exactly what you need to do to keep one competitive step ahead.

- *Specify What You Need To Start Your Business*: Beginning entrepreneurs often underestimate how much they need (in terms of time, equipment, personnel, and sheer determination) to get a business up and running. A business plan helps you develop a no-nonsense list of equipment you need and the chores to do to get your business off the ground. In addition, your plan's goals and objectives, along with an action plan, provide a timetable for when you need to finish the items on your to-do list.

- *A Business Plan Helps You To Know How Much It is Likely to Cost:* Something else that would-be entrepreneurs often underestimate is how much getting their businesses going will cost. When you take the time to create a detailed business plan, you provide yourself with financial guidelines. In addition, your plan's financial review increases the likelihood that you will have the cash available when you need it.

- *A Business Plan Gets Funded:* As we shall see in the next section, one of the major objectives of a business plan is that it enables you secure the necessary finances needed to run your business. The bottom line is that if you need money to get your business started, you need a business plan. Period. To persuade a venture capitalist or your local banker to put up cash today, you have to convince him or her that you not only have a solid idea, but also that you know exactly how you are going to turn it into a successful business. A strong and convincing business plan can do just that.

- *Your Business Plan Tells The World Who You Are*: A business plan is like your resume or curriculum vitae that introduces you to your prospective employers when you are looking for job. A big part of marketing your new business involves telling anyone and everyone who is interested exactly who you are and what you do. Your business plan provides a great resource here. In fact, your mission and vision statements, along with the company overview, form the basis for your entire business identity - the way you describe yourself and your company to the world. Your business plan also serves as the basis for communicating directly with your stakeholders, everyone from your prospective investors and shareholders to regulators and the business press.

- *Inspire Your Employees*: A business plan with a compelling mission statement, vision, and values tells your employees not only what your company is but what it stands for. Just as important, a business plan describes exactly how the company will accomplish its mission through specific goals and objectives. By sharing your business plan with employees at all levels - and better yet, making them part of the planning process - you create a strong sense of team work and *esprit de corps*. If you are putting together a business completely on your own, a business plan can still inspire, convincing you that you have what it takes to make it work.

> *A Business Plan Helps You Monitor Your Progress:* A good business plan provides reliable benchmarks to measure your progress over time. Part of your plan contains a description of where you are right now. Part of it describes where you would like to be at the end of six months, a year, or even farther down the road. After you reach these milestones, you can look back at your plan to assess how your business has performed. And if you do not reach them? By having a business plan in place, you know exactly where - and why - you have fallen short.

> *A Business Plan Prepare You for the Unexpected:* There is nothing better for us to see that our path to a successful business is smooth and free of obstacles. But the real world seldom works out that way, so chances are good you will hit a few potholes along the road to successful entrepreneurship. You may even find yourself on a dead-end street, trying to figure out how in the world you got there. Never fear. A good business plan helps you to find your bearings if you lose your way. A good business plan is a like a compass that prepares you to face the unknown course of your entrepreneurial journey. Finally, the best business plan includes contingencies to provide direction, just in case things go wrong.

IMPORTANT AREAS WHERE A BUSINESS PLAN IS REQUIRED

We can summarize the purpose of a business plan into two areas from the preceding discussion: A business plan serves two essential purposes. First, and more important, it guides the company's operations by charting its future course and devising a strategy for following it. The plan provides fundamental elements to guide entrepreneurs toward success such as mission statements, goals and objectives, budgets, strategic actions, target markets, financial forecasts - to help entrepreneurs lead a company successfully. It gives the owner and his or her employees a sense of direction. Having a business plan also forces entrepreneurs to subject their ideas to the test of reality. Can this business idea actually produce a profit? This is the biggest question. Without profit there is no way you can run the business.

The second broad function of the business plan is to attract lenders and investors. Too often small business owners approach potential lenders and investors without having prepared to sell themselves and their business concept. Simply scribbling a few rough figures on a note pad to support a loan application is not enough. Applying for loans or attempting to attract investors without a solid business plan rarely attracts needed capital. A business plan must prove to potential lenders and investors that a venture will be able to repay loans and produce an attractive rate of return. For this purpose, you, as an entrepreneur, must pay attention to detail because it is germane to your sales presentation to potential lenders and investors. The quality of your business plan is very important in the decision to lend or invest funds in your firm. It is also potential lenders' and investors' first impression of the company and its owners and managers. The plan should be highly polished and professional in both form and content.

The discussion in this section is based on the principles of strategic management as the point of departure. The difference between a successful and an unsuccessful business lies in the extent to which owners and/or managers adopt a strategic management approach, which is the ability to survive in the face of a competitive environment. The goal of setting up and managing an entrepreneurial firm from a strategic management perspective is to create for the small business a competitive advantage, which is the aggregation of factors that sets your small business apart from its competitors and gives it a unique position in the market. No business can be everything to everyone. In fact, one of the biggest pitfalls many entrepreneurs stumble into is failing to differentiate their businesses from the crowd of competitors. Following the outline provided below will help you stand out from the crowd of would-be entrepreneurs or small business owners as someone who knows his or her mission and objectives, including the necessary strategies needed to accomplish the entrepreneurial dream.

Although, the outline of a business plan provided here does not guarantee success, it does raise your chances of succeeding in business venture. Your final plan may vary according to your specific needs or individual requirements of your lender or investor. Writing a business plan is something that must be done from your heart. Your first test of becoming a successful entrepreneur is the development of passion for your "entrepreneurial call". Therefore, a business plan must be prepared with a passion, commitment, challenge, and having fun from preparing it.

An acceptable business plan ranges from 20 to 40 pages in length. Shorter plans usually are too sketchy to be of any value and those much longer than 40 pages run the risk of never getting used or read. The following pages provide a suggested outline of the material to be included in your business plan, using the principles of strategic management as a framework. I call this a competitive business plan in the sense that it pushes the entrepreneur to act in a manner that strengthens the competitiveness of the business in a chosen market or industry. Below is an outline of a business plan.

OUTLINE OF A BUSINESS PLAN

An ideal business plan should include the following areas:

1. **Executive Summary** (not to exceed three pages)

    A. Brief description of the business
    B. Overview of the market of your product or service
    C. Brief overview of the industry (such as trends, etc)
    D. Brief overview of the strategy to make your firm a success
    E. Brief description of the managerial and technical experience of your key people

    F.   Brief statement of what the financial needs are and planned use for the money.

2. **Vision and Mission Statement**

    A.   Your vision and mission statements (and your values)
    B.   Performance goals and objectives needed to accomplish the mission
    C.   What makes your business unique? What are the sources of your firm's competitive advantage?

3. **Detailed Business Description**

    A.   Brief history of your business.
    B.   Who are your customers?
    C.   How does your company create value for customers?
    D.   Describe the key factors that will dictate success for your business (i.e., price competitiveness, quality, durability, dependability, technical superiority, etc)
    E.   How do you intend to satisfy the needs of the customers?

4. **Industry Analysis**: How does each of the following external forces affect the sale or profitability of your product or service?

    A.   Industry background and overview
    B.   Trends in the industry
    C.   Growth rate
    D.   The drivers of the industry
    E.   Outlook for the future
    F.   Economic factors affecting your business
        i.   Inflation
        ii.   Recession
        iii.   High or low employment
        iv.   Interest rates
    G.   Social factors affecting your business
        i.   Demographics
        ii.   Income levels
        iii.   Size of household
        iv.   Social attitudes

    H.   Laws and regulations affecting your business
        i.   Import control laws
        ii.   Export promotion or control laws
        iii.   Environmental laws
        iv.   Special licenses needed to run the business
    I.   Technological factors affecting your business
        i.   The Internet

    ii. Computer software and hardware

5. **Market Analysis**

  A. Your company's target market
    i. Demographic profile
    ii. Other significant customer characteristics
  B. What motivates customers to buy?
  C. Which product features influence customers' buying decision?
  D. How many customers does the market contain? (How large is the market?)

6. **Competitor Analysis:** Describe each of the following factors and discuss how these factors will influence your success.

  A. Existing competitors
    i. Who are they?
    ii. Why do potential customers in your target market buy from them now?
  B. Future competitors
    i. Who are they?
    ii. What would be the impact in your target market segment if they enter?
  C. What are the strengths and weaknesses of each key competitor?

7. **Strategic Analysis and Plan**

  A. What are your core competencies?
  B. What will be your market positioning and image?
  C. SWOT analysis
    i. What are your strengths?
    ii. What are your weaknesses?
    iii. What are the opportunities for the growth of your business?
    iv. What are the potential threats facing your business?
  D. Business strategy (How are you going to compete?)
    i. Will you be a low cost provider? If so how?
    ii. Will you differentiate your product or services from those of the competitors? If so how?
    iii. Will you focus on a particular segment of the large market? If so how?

8. **Marketing and Promotional Strategy**

  A. Your pricing strategy
  B. Your advertising strategy

  C. Your promotion strategy (How will you generate publicity for your product or service?)
  D. What other sales techniques and incentives will you offer?
  E. Which media are most effective in reaching your target audience? Why?
  F. Which media will you use and why?
  G. Media costs
  H. What are your channels of distribution?
  I. How will you get your product or service into the hands of the customers?

9. **Organizational Plan**

  A. How is your business organized? (Ownership structure)
    i. Legal structure (sole proprietorship, partnership, franchise, etc)
    ii. Functions (What are the different functions or activities to be performed in the organization?)
  B. Who are the key people in your organization?
    i. What are their backgrounds, and what do they bring to the business that will enhance the chance of success?
    ii. Resumes of key managers and employees
  C. Organization chart

10. **Financial Plans**

  A. How much money do you need to make this product and your business a long-term success?
    i. Tie the response to this question to your production, marketing, and management plans
    ii. Be realistic and specific
  B. Create a budget. Show the lender or investor how much money you need, why you need it, when you need it, and how and when you plan to generate revenues from operations and sales
  C. Have a realistic projection of the cost of operating the business
    i. Materials
    ii. Labor
    iii. Equipment
    iv. Marketing
    v. Other (i.e., unique start-up costs)
  D. Present actual balance sheets and income statements (for existing business only)
  E. Present projected balance sheets and income statements (for both existing and planned ventures)
  F. Prepare a breakeven analysis
  G. Create cash flow projections.

11. **Loan Proposal**

   A. If you are requesting a loan, state the purpose for it
   B. Amount request
   C. Repayment or "cash out" schedule (exit strategy)
   D. Timetable for plan implementation

12. **Appendixes** (Documentation)

   A. Market research
   B. Financial forecast
   C. Letters from business associates, prospective customers, suppliers, etc.
   D. Resumes of key personnel
   E. Other relevant documents.

THE CONTENTS OF A BUSINESS PLAN

The following pages contain detailed discussion of the contents of your business plan as outlined above.

1.   THE COVER SHEET FOR YOUR BUSINESS PLAN

The cover sheet serves as the title page of your business plan, and should include the following information:

a) Name, address, email, and phone number of the company (or proposed company).
b) Name, title, addresses, phone numbers of owners/corporate officers.
c) Month and year your plan was prepared.
d) The recipient (audience) of your business plan.

2.   THE TABLE OF CONTENTS

It is very important that you put a table of content immediately after the cover sheet. The table of content tells your reader what page to go immediately he or she needed pertinent information. Most investors are very busy. They might not have the time to read through your 20 to 40 page business plan. If they are interested in your business idea from the executive summary (discussed below), the probability is that they would jump to the areas that most interest them (such as your mission statement, your financial plans, etc). The best way to make it easier for them is to have a table of contents. Having a table of contents is not enough. You must include the page numbers of any important topic or section that is relevant to the business plan and areas you think that your reader will be interested in.

EXECUTIVE SUMMARY

Because the business plan is usually a very large document, an executive summary is necessary. The executive summary, which is approximately three pages long, provides the reader with an overview of all of the most important facts contained in the business plan. Although the executive summary is placed in the front of the business plan, it is actually easier to write it after you have written the entire business plan. You should bear in mind that an executive summary highlights the key points of each section of your business plan. This is the summary of who you are, what your business is about, how you hope to compete, how much it will cost you to compete, and what your firm will be in the future in order to stay in business. In writing the executive summary of your business plan, you should try to include the following information:

a) *A Brief Description of the Business (Your Offering)*: Give a brief description of the business (proposed business or an existing one) and the product or service it will provide. For an existing business, describe the products and services currently offered and any new products and services that will be offered in the future.

b) *List the most important trends in your industry*: Here, you will provide a brief description of the structure of the industry in which you want to be or currently engaged in. You will provide brief information concerning the attractiveness of the industry or market, the competition in the industry, and most importantly, what is driving the industry.

c) *The Opportunity*: Here, you will briefly point out what opportunities are there for you when you intend to enter the industry. You should be able to summarize here why you think the industry is a profitable one and why you think your business can make a profit in the industry or market.

d) *Your Objectives (Strategic and Financial):* The purpose of this section is for you to list what you hope to accomplish by entering into this business. If you are going into the business because of financial motive state it here. If you are entering the market because of any other reasons (e.g., strategic) put it here. Remember that financial motives are about making profit and strategic motive is about how to compete successfully in the marketplace. Whatever motive you chose, investors must know that your business will be profitable either financially or otherwise. Remember too, that for non-profit organizations, donors will judge your firm's profitability not on the basis of how much money you make, but how you are able to contribute in the promotion of their mission and vision and the ideals they stand for.

e) *Marketing and Promotional Strategies*: State the type of advertising and promotion that will be implemented. (For an existing business, state the type of advertising and promotion that has been used in the past and any new methods that will be used in the future).

f) *The People*: This is where you must describe briefly the people running the business. You are expected to provide a brief description of their backgrounds, experiences, and qualifications. Here, you will also describe in a brief form those people in your management team, including their strengths.

g) *Financial Information*: Here, you have to give a summary or a brief description of your sale projections, your profit potentials, and growth potentials. In this section of the executive summary, you are not expected to provide tables and figures. What is required here is a statement pointing out your sales projections, how much you will make and how you will make it. If the purpose of the business plan is to get people invest in your business, try as much as possible to put in here how much you need and how long it will take you to pay back your investors, again, in a very brief form. In this section, give the projected sales and profits for the next three years. For an existing company, give the sales and profits of the last three years and the projected sales and profits for the next three years. Give a brief statement such as a sentence about why you need the money and how you intend to use it. You must remember, again, that you cannot do all these without completing the whole business plan.

VISION AND MISSION STATEMENT

Following the executive summary, but entirely in a new page, is your mission or vision statement. State the purpose of your business and how it relates to what you intend to accomplish in life. The mission statement tells people your vision of what your company hopes to become. Your mission statement should be able to provide answers to a simple question: What business are you in? Answering this question means thinking carefully about the products or services you offer and how these relate to your beliefs and values in life; who you are, who your customers are, and the reason you want to provide this product or service. When writing this aspect of the business plan try hard to answer these following questions: (a) Why am I in business? (b) What does my business do? (c) What do I want to become? (d) How do I get there?

OBJECTIVES AND GOALS OF THE BUSINESS

You probably do not need to be convinced what goals are and why setting goals is important. But it is important for you to know how and why you set your goals and the reasons for setting up those goals. The reasons why goals are set are that they help you achieve your objectives. Goals established where you intend to go, and they tell you when you have gotten there.

The simplest way to make your goals achievable is to break them down into parts or specific objectives. Objectives act as **milestones** along the way, showing you how far you've come in reaching your goal and how much farther you need to travel. After you've set up a goal for yourself or your business, you must specify what specific actions that must be performed in order to achieve the goal. It will be difficult to achieve these goals without stating in clear terms what you must do.

Now, there are reasons why you would want to reach that goal. As an entrepreneur, like a soccer team, you must have a goalpost. The goals of your firm specify where it wants to be. Your goals or those of your firm represent a commitment to achieving specific outcomes and results. The objectives of your firm function as yardsticks for your firms' performance and progress, they must be stated in quantifiable or measurable terms and they must contain a deadline for achievement. Your objectives must spell out how much of what kind of performance and by when. At this point, you are different from the soccer teams. Now it is your life and it means that you must avoid generalities like "maximize profits," "reduce costs," "become more efficient," or "increase sales," which specify neither how much or when. You should try as much as possible to put your objectives under two categories: (1) strategic objectives and (2) financial objectives in the following order.

1. *What are your strategic goals and objectives, for example:*

a) The market share you want to capture: If possible, you should discuss the share of the market you need to capture within a time frame.

b) Higher product quality than rivals: From your industry and market analysis, you are aware of the quality of products that the existing firms offer. You are expected to state if your product and service offer a better quality than those currently offered by your current or prospective rivals.

c) A stronger reputation with customers than rivals: If you have a good reputation through your career, your education, your connection with important persons in the society, it is advisable that you state it in this section of your business plan. If you know that you have a good brand name that others do not have put it here. For example, if your competitors or rivals import their goods from Taiwan and you import yours from Europe and you know that customers' perception concerning the origin of the products or services is important, then your reputation of where you import your goods becomes a competitive advantage. A strong reputation is about branding and differentiating your product or service from those of the competitors.

d) Superior customer service: If you intend to improve the technology available in the industry in terms of providing superior services to your customers. You should know that technology is ever-changing. State in this section how you intend to improve the technology in the manufacturing or delivering of your product or service as against the way the existing firms are doing it. Similarly, if you know that you are entering the market with new products, that is, innovation, state it here.

e) Wider geographic coverage than rivals: If your competitors only cover a limited geographical area and you want to cover a larger geographical area in order to be more competitive and profitable, state it here.

2. *What are your Financial Objectives?*

a) Growth in revenue and earnings: Your objectives in growth in revenue tell people how much your firm or you intend to make in the years ahead running your business. In other words, it is important that you provide information about your firm's financial objective in this section of your business plan.

b) Higher dividends: If someone invests money in your company, you should be able to predict how much he or she will earn at the end of your financial year. If your business is incorporated, you should state how the stock price will rise or decrease, or how you plan to diversify the revenue base of your firm.

BUSINESS DESCRIPTION

Describing your business is one of the most important steps you must undertake in order to convince yourself and others who are interested in your business that you know what you are doing or where you are heading. Your business description is simply about describing (i) the needs of your customers or what is being satisfied, (ii) the type of customers you intend to serve, customer groups, or who is being satisfied, and (iii) the technologies used and functions performed, or how customers' needs are satisfied.

a) *Customer Needs*: The needs of your customer are not the product or service you are providing. Rather it's what they get from your product or service. If you are a retailer, a producer, or a wholesaler you should describe what the product or service provides for the customer. You are required to describe the *utilities* your product or service provides to your customers. Most importantly, state the benefits of your product or service to your customers. Here, you should try to state, if possible, why you think that your customers need your product or service.

b) *Customer Groups*: It is not enough to know the needs of your customers; it is as important to be able to describe who the customers are. A new business must understand the nature of its customers. It is not enough to know the needs of everyone; it is much more important to know the group of persons that need what you've got to offer. To know who your customers are, you should be able to answer these questions: Who are my customers? What is the market I intend to serve? What is the geographic domain I intend to serve (or presently serving)? What type of customers am I going after?

c) *Technology and Functions Performed*: How do you intend to satisfy the needs of your customers? In this aspect of the business plan, you should state how you intend to do this. If it is shorter delivery chain, state it. If it is through the Internet state it. If it is through importation state it. What is needed in this aspect of your business plan is *how* you intend to meet the needs of your customers.

ANALYSING INDUSTRY, BUSINESS, MARKET AND COMPETITION

In preparing a business plan, you or your readers should be able to understand how familiar you are with the industry in which you are staking yourself. Most importantly, you would want to know the competitive position of your competitors. Analyzing the industry and the competition requires answers to the following questions:

a) *What are the Trends Affecting the Industry?* List and explain any changes in the demographic trends that will affect your business or market. For example, if the Internet business is going to affect your business, you should state it. If government regulation policies, such as trade de-regulation are going to affect the way you compete in the industry, state it. In a similar manner, you are required to discuss how the political developments in your country will affect the way you conduct your business.

b) *What are the Dominant Economic Characteristics of the Industry Environment?* Here, you should list (1) the size of the market and its growth rate; (2) the geographic scope of the market; (3) the number and sizes of buyers and sellers; (4) the pace of technological changes and innovation; (4) the scale economy; (5) the experience curve effects; (6) the capital requirements, and (7) others.

c) *What is the Nature of the Competition in the Industry?* In order for you to understand how intense the competition is in your industry, you should try to state in your business plan the following pertinent points and answer the questions that they raise:

- Is the rivalry among competing sellers (your existing or potential competitors) strong, moderate, or weak?

- Are there any threats from potential entry? What is meant by potential entry is the ease with which others can come into the business and become your competitors. You should state whether or not the potential for others to come into the industry is strong, moderate, or weak. If it's easy to enter your particular chosen industry, it is good you explain why. If it's hard, you should also explain why.

- Competition from substitutes. Remember that everything from a product or a service that you want to supply has a substitute. To rent a movie and watch it at home is a substitute to going to a movie theater. If, for example, you are providing limousine service, the cab can be seen as a substitute. If you are providing a coffee shop, a restaurant can serve as a substitute place for your coffee shop. In other words, it's important for you to know what substitute products are available out there that can affect how you compete in the market. One way to do this is to state the power of competition from substitute products as either strong, moderate, or weak.

- Power of suppliers: Does the survival of your business depend on those who supply certain inputs to your business? Inputs can take several forms such as what you must get from your suppliers in order to make your business competitive. Inputs are about anything you need to make your service or product available to your customers. These inputs can take the form of money, labor, knowledge, connections or networking, Internet capability, services, etc. If you know that the existence of your business does not so much depend on who supplies you with the necessary inputs, state it here. If your suppliers' power to influence the way you compete is great, state it here. The most important thing is that the reason why you depend or do not depend on your suppliers in any aspect of the process of delivering your product or service to the end-users is clearly stated. Your dependence can be stated in terms strongly, moderately, or weakly dependent on whom and why.

- Power of customers: Your ability to succeed, as a business owner, depends on how much control you have over those who buy your product or service or how much control they have over you. The point to consider here are (1) whether some or many buyers have sufficient bargaining leverage to obtain price concessions and other favorable terms and conditions of sale, and (2) the extent to which buyers (your customers) can influence the way you compete with your competitors.

d) *Industry Driving Force*

- All industries and markets are characterized by trends and new developments that gradually or speedily produce changes important enough to require a strategic response from participating firms. Industry conditions change because important factors are driving industry participants (competitors, customers, or suppliers) to alter their actions. The driving forces in an industry are the major underlying causes of changing industry and competitive conditions. The areas to look for while writing your business plan are as follow:

- The Competitive Position of Major Firms/Strategic Groups: Here, you have to show whether the firms in your market or industry occupy favorable competitive position and the reason why they are so. You will also say something about the firms who do not occupy favorable competitive position and why.

- Competitor Analysis: What is required from you here is (1) a discussion of the strategic approaches of the competitors; (2) the predicted moves of the competitors; and (3) whom to watch and why.

- Key Success Factors (KSFs): As indicated in chapter eight, an industry's key success factors are those things that most affect the ability of firms within a particular industry to prosper. They are the important strategic elements such as product attributes, resources, competencies, competitive capabilities, and business outcomes that spell the differences between profit and loss. Key success factors concern what every industry member must be competent at doing or concentrate on achieving in order to be competitively and financially successful. Preparing your business plan implies that you must know the key success factors in your industry. Some of the key questions to answer include the following: (1) technology-related KSFs; (2) distribution-related KSFs; (3) marketing-related KSFs; (4) skills-related KSFs; (5) organizational capabilities; (6) financial resources; and (7) any other factor that you think might be crucial to the success of any firm operating in the industry.

➢ Industry Prospects and Overall Attractiveness: Here, you should try and provide answers to the following questions:

- ✓ What are the factors that make the industry attractive?
- ✓ What are the factors that make the industry unattractive?
- ✓ Are there any special industry issues or problems?
- ✓ What is the profit outlook of the industry (favorable/unfavorable) and why?

COMPANY STRENGTHS, WEAKNESSES, OPPORTUNITIES AND THREATS

One of the crucial areas in the preparing your business plan is how you are able to evaluate your firm's resource capabilities, relative cost positions, and competitive strengths versus rivals. The purpose is to prepare the groundwork for matching your firm's strategy both to its external market circumstances and to its internal resources and competitive capabilities. As we have seen in chapter eight, this is known as SWOT analysis, encompassing analysis of your strengths, weaknesses, opportunities, and threats. This part of your business plan should provide answers or information to the following questions:

What are your Potential or Existing Strengths and Competitive Capabilities?

- ✓ A powerful strategy supported by good skills and expertise in key areas?
- ✓ A strong financial condition? Do you have ample financial resources to grow the business?
- ✓ A strong brand-name image or company reputation?
- ✓ Ability to take advantage of economies of scale and/or learning/experience curve effects?
- ✓ Propriety technology/superior skills or important patents?
- ✓ Strong advertising and promotion?
- ✓ Product innovation skills?
- ✓ Good customer service?
- ✓ Location and/or geographical coverage?
- ✓ Strategic alliances/joint ventures with other firms?

Potential Resource Weaknesses and Competitive Deficiencies? In this part of your business plan you should discuss those things that you are not good at, that is, your weaknesses. Try to answer the following questions if you think they are related to the success of your business:

- ✓ Do you have a clear strategic direction?
- ✓ Do you have obsolete facilities?
- ✓ Do you have weak brand image or reputation?
- ✓ Are you plagued with internal operating and management problems?
- ✓ Do you have a narrow product line relative to rivals?
- ✓ Do you have a weaker dealer or distribution network than key rivals?
- ✓ Do you have poor marketing skills relative to rivals?
- ✓ Do you have poor financial resources to fund necessary strategic initiatives?
- ✓ Are you behind on product or service quality?
- ✓ Are you missing some key skills or competencies necessary for business success?

What are your Firm's Opportunities? You are required to discuss the opportunities that are available in the industry that your firm can tap into. To provide such information, try and provide answers to the following questions.

- ✓ Opportunity to serve additional customer groups or expanding into new geographic markets or product segments?
- ✓ Opportunities to expand the company's product line to meet a broader range of customer needs?
- ✓ Opportunities to integrate forward or backward?
- ✓ Falling trade barriers in attractive foreign markets?
- ✓ Openings to take market share away from rival firms?
- ✓ Ability to grow as a result of increases in market demand?
- ✓ Opportunity to acquire rival firms?
- ✓ Opportunities and openings to exploit emerging new technologies?

Potential External Threats to Your Firm's Competitiveness? Provide answers to the following questions.

- ✓ How likely is it for potential new competitors to enter the market?
- ✓ Are there any likelihood for losing sale to substitute products?
- ✓ Are there any possibilities for slowdowns in market growth?
- ✓ Costly new regulatory requirements?
- ✓ Is there any vulnerability to recession and business cycle?
- ✓ What is the nature of the growing bargaining power of customers or suppliers? Is it a threat to your business?
- ✓ How do you intend to counter these threats?

What are your Firm's Distinctive Competencies or Competitive Advantage? After you have examined your strengths, weaknesses, opportunities and threat in your business environment, it is now time for you to state in simple terms what you are good at.

With this knowledge, you must now decide what is it that you possess in order to compete successfully in the market. A distinctive competence is a competitively important activity that a company performs well in comparison to its competitors. It answers the question of what separates your firm from the pack. Answer to this question lies in examining what your company intends to offer that others are not offering. This question thus goes directly to the heart of your business venture. What can you do better than the competitors in the market or industry? Answers to this question demand that you perform the following analysis:

- Describe your competitive advantage in as much detail as possible. This might include quality, price, selection, location, service, etc.

- Provide an explanation of how you will achieve your competitive advantage. For example, how do you intend to provide better quality? What will make your service better? Why is your location better? Try to combine several advantages, if possible.

DEVELOPING THE STRATEGIC PLAN

Your strategic plan provides the groundwork for your marketing plan. Your firm's strategy or strategies are its plans of action, its tactics in the industry. Based on your knowledge of the industry, the competitors and their strategies, your strengths and weaknesses, the available opportunities and environmental threats, it is now time for you to indicate your own entry or competitive strategies. Several possible strategic moves or strategic alternatives are available to choose from. Are you going to compete or enter the market on the basis of

- A low-cost/ low price strategy? Why?
- A Differentiation strategy? What kind of differentiation strategy you intend to use?
- A focus strategy in which you target a specific market niche? Why?
- Collaborative partnerships and strategic alliances with others? How and why?

DEVELOPING THE MARKETING PLAN

A marketing plan is your firm's link to your customer and the competition. The plan must, therefore, be concerned with (a) your pricing strategy, (b) advertising and promotional strategy, (c) the market position and market segmentation, and (d) the marketing mix of the firm. This aspect of your business plan deals with how you are going to deliver your product or service to the end-users. Most importantly, it deals with the question of why and how customers should buy your product or service. The following points will help you produce or examine your marketing plan.

Setting your Price: What is the most important thing you want your price to do for you?

- To maximize sales?
- To discourage competition?
- To maintain an image?
- To increase profits?
- To attract customers?

How do you intend to determine your Price?
- Price to be determined by how much customers are willing to pay?
- Price to be determined by cost?
- Competition-based pricing?

Product or Service: Your marketing message should at least look at one or more of the following areas

- Quality? Is the quality of your product or service better than those of the competitors?
- Features? What other features you are providing to your product or service that your competitors are not providing?
- Style? This answers the question of how you intend to design or package your product or service.
- Brand? If you intend to market your product or service through name recognition you should write it here.

Promotional Plan: This is where you are expected to discuss how you intend to promote your product or service. Remember that a good product or service, cannot sell itself. It must be talked about, it must be known and its usefulness must be communicated to the outside world. In a nutshell, your product or service must be promoted! How are you going to do that? The following points should be able to help you write your promotional plan.

- List the types of promotion you will use such as sales and direct marketing, advertising, publicity and public relations, sales promotion.
- State your promotional goals. This might include: a specific sales volume, a percentage increase sales, an increase awareness, to inform customers of a sale, etc.
- Provide information on your inside and/or outside sales force. State whether you will hire only experience sales people or if you will hire inexperience personnel and train them
- If you will use telemarketing, state whether you have your own telemarketing staff or if an outside telemarketing firm is used.
- Describe any direct mail, catalogs, or direct response ads that will be used.
- Identify any trade-oriented or consumer-oriented sales promotions that will be implemented. State the objective of the promotions and the total annual cost.

> Will you have a Web site? If so, describe the site and what will be offered to consumers.

Public Relations: Doing something good to your community in order to create awareness for your product or service is a very powerful way to market your product or service. How do you achieve this? Provide answers to the following issues:

> State whether you will sponsor a youth sports team. If so, identify which one. Is it possible for your firm to participate in local activities such environmental protection? There are so many things you and your firm can do in helping your community as a way of show-casing your product or service to the public. As an entrepreneur, this is one of the easiest and least costly ways to market your product or service.
> If you will participate in local business organizations such as a local chamber of commerce, identify those organizations.
> If you will donate time or funds to charitable organizations, identify them.
> Will you write an article for the local newspaper concerning the grand opening, expansion plans, new products or services that you offer? Is it possible for you to feature any of your business activities on the local newspaper, radio or television stations?
> Are there any other public relations activities the company will engage in?

DEVELOPING THE ORGANIZATION PLAN

An organization plan tells you how you intend to run your firm or how your firm is going to be managed. Most importantly, your organization plan tells the public the caliber of persons you intend to hire to run your business. If your business plan is written for the purpose of securing finances, your audience will also be interested in the qualifications of your employees. You can provide this information by answering the following questions:

> *Who Are the Owners of The Business?* Here, you will list the owners and/or corporate officers of your firm.

> *What is the composition of Management and Personnel?* Here, you will include a paragraph describing the education and work experience of the owner or owners and all key personnel. Emphasize any management experience and any experience in the industry of the proposed business. Include complete resumes if they are available.

> *Number of Employees?* Here, you will include the number of employees you have and in what positions (e.g., driver, secretary, etc.).

> *What are the necessary qualifications?* There are certain positions that need special qualification. For example, if you intend to have your own accountant, you

should state his or her qualifications and the qualifications required for that position in the industry.

- *How many hours will they work and at what wage?* If possible, try and write down how many hours each of your employees will work and what you intend to pay them hourly, weekly, monthly, or yearly.

- *What are your future plans and needs for adding employees?* You should be able to project the needs for more employees in the future, especially if you intend to expand your business by adding more products, services, or expanding into other geographical areas.

- Provide an organizational chart to show all personnel needed and their areas of responsibility.

DECIDING ON THE BUSINESS LOCATION

In preparing your business plan, it is essential that you take into consideration the location of your business because it plays a decisive role in the success or failure of your business venture. Your location should be built around your customers, it should be accessible and it should provide a sense of security. Some of the questions you should consider include the following:

- What are your location needs? What kind of space do you need?

- Why is the area desirable? Is the building desirable?

- Is the area easily accessible? Is public transportation available? Is street lighting adequate?

- Are market shifts or demographic shifts occurring? Are more people moving to the area or are they moving out? Who are those moving in or moving out and how would this affect the profitability of your business?

EXAMINING LEGAL ISSUES

The legal requirements of your business are those things that you must do to meet what the law requires from you to run your business. The areas to look at are described below. Try to provide information that will make you not to run into trouble with the authority.

- *Have you registered your Business*? Have you registered your business with the appropriate authorities? This is the first step you must take. You do not want to be raided for not paying your taxes. Experience has shown that many small business owners think about how they can make money without properly registering their businesses. Remember that those who would want to help you (financially or otherwise, and in any form) would demand that the business is properly registered. Remember, too, that they would like to see the certificate of registration issued by the appropriate authority. When preparing your business plan, a copy this certificate must be attached as an appendix.

- *What is the Legal Status of your Business*? You must state whether the business you have registered is a sole proprietorship, a partnership, or a limited liability company. If you can, put the names of your partners or those who have significant shares in your business.

- *Who will you use for a tax accountant*? As an entrepreneur the chances are that you do not know the fundamentals of accounting principle. In that case, you will need an accountant who is knowledgeable in this area.

- *Who will you retain for an attorney*? Like an accountant, an attorney represents you in case you get into problem. These problems can arise from your inability to deliver your products or services as you have promised. A problem can also arise from your insurance obligations. An attorney will represent you while you are running your business.

- *What kinds of insurance will you carry (Property & Liability, Life & Health)?* You never know what would happen tomorrow to you or your business. People interested in your business would want to know if they can get their money back if anything happened to you. So, you must state the type of insurance you are carrying in this section.

- *Intellectual Property Issues?* If you an inventor, you must make sure your service or product is not copied without your permission. Your attorney should be able to take care of this area. If you are an author, and you want to market your book, it is important that your work is not copied by others without your prior permission. For your investors or banks to know about the viability of your business in terms of intellectual property such as copyrights, trademarks, and patents, you must back this up with supporting documents such as registrations, photos, diagrams, etc.

FINANCIAL REQUIREMENTS

This section of your business plan deals with how you manage the finances that come in and go out of your business. As a start-up business, it is important to have a very good idea of how much it will take to start and run your business for a defined period of time before the money starts rolling in. The amount of capital required to start a business is made up of two components: (i) the amount needed before the first sale is made, and (ii) the amount needed to cover day-to-day operation until profitability is reached. In this section, you must be able to show in your business plan the amount you need to start your business, that is, the start-up costs before the first sale is made. An example is provided below showing the start-up costs for a firm:

START-UP COSTS

Complete a Checklist for Furniture/Fixtures and Machinery/Equipment

Furniture/Fixtures

Item (sample)	Quantity Needed	Price for each	Total price
Desk	3	150	450
Shelving	7	100	700
_____	_____	_____	_____
_____	_____	_____	_____
_____	_____	_____	_____
_____	_____	_____	_____

Total for Furniture and Fixtures   =======

Machinery and Equipments (sample)

PC and Software	1	1,200	1,200
Telephone/Fax	1	600	600
_____	_____	_____	_____
_____	_____	_____	_____
_____	_____	_____	_____

Total for Machinery and Equipments   _____

Checklist for Start-up Costs

Inventory   _____
Furniture and Fixtures   _____
Machinery and Equipments   _____
Prepaid Expenses   _____
Insurance   _____
Grand Opening Advertising   _____
Legal Fees   _____
Accounting Fees   _____
Employee Wages   _____
Other (specify)   _____

Total Prepaid Expenses   _____

Deposits
    Lease   _____
    Utility   _____
    Tax   _____
    Other (specify)   _____

Total Deposits   _____

Building and Renovation
If Purchased
    Sales Price   _____
    Construction/Renovation   _____
If Leased
    Leasehold improvements   _____

Total Location Costs   _____

Working Capital
                                                  Cost per year
    Owners' Salary   _____ x 3= _____
    Employees' salary   _____ x 3= _____
    Employee taxes   _____ x 3= _____
    (App. 11% of owner and employee wages)
    Rent   _____ x 3= _____
    Advertising   _____ x 3=_____
    Utilities   _____ x 3= _____
    Supplies   _____ x 3= _____
    Telephone   _____ x 3= _____
    Legal/Accounting Fees _____ x 3= _____
    Loan Payment_____ x 3= _____
    Repairs/Maintenance_____ x 3= _____
    Auto/Travel Expenses_____ x 3= _____
    Inventory   _____ x 3= _____
    Miscellaneous   _____ x 3 = _____
    Other (specify)   _____ x 3 = _____

Total Working Capital   _____

Total Start-up capital   _____

SOURCES OF FINANCING

This section deals with how you intend to finance your business. The following figure tells you how to go about preparing this important aspect of your business plan.

    a)   What are your total start-up costs?   _____

    b)   How much will you need from personal funds?   _____

    c)   How much will you obtain in other equity?   _____

          *   Family and Friends   _____

          *   Venture capital   _____

          *   Other (specify)   _____

It is also important to state their ownership share in terms of the amount they are willing to invest in your business.

    d)   How much will you borrow? _____
        *   Friends and family _____
                Borrowed for ____years at _____% interest
                Monthly payments of _____
        *   Bank loans _____
                Borrowed for ____years at ____% interest
                Monthly payments of _____

        *   Finance companies _____
                Borrowed for ___years at ____% interest
                Monthly payments of _____

        *   Other (specify) _____ _____
                Borrowed for _____ years at_____ % interest
                Monthly payments of _____

FINANCIAL PLAN AND PRO-FORMA STATEMENTS

This aspect of the business plan is very important because it determines the potential investment commitment needed for the new venture and indicates whether the business plan is economically feasible. Generally, three areas are covered in the financial plan section of the business plan:

a) *Forecasted Income Statements*: First, the entrepreneur should summarize the forecasted sales and the appropriate expenses to arrive at income statements for at least the first three years, with the first year's projection provided monthly. It should include the forecasted sales, cost of goods sold, and the general and administrative expenses. Net profit after taxes can then be projected by estimating income taxes. The income statement (or profit and loss statement) compares expenses against revenue over a certain period of time to show your firm's net profit (or loss).

b) *Pro Forma Cash Flow Statement (Budget)*: The second major aspect of financial information needed is cash flow figures for three years, with the first year's projections provided monthly. Since bills have to be paid at different times of the year, it is important to determine the demands on cash on a monthly basis, especially in the first year. Remember that sales may be irregular, and receipts from customers also may be spread out, thus necessitating the borrowing of short-term capital to meet fixed expenses such as salaries and utilities.

c) *Projected Balance Sheet*: The last financial item needed in this section of the business plan is the projected balance sheet. This shows the financial condition of the business at a specific time. It summarizes the assets of a business, its liabilities (what is owed), the investment of the entrepreneur and any partners, and retained earnings (or cumulative losses). Any assumptions considered for the balance sheet or any other item in the financial plan should be listed for the benefit of the potential investors.

d) *Break-even Analysis*

The break-even point is the point at which your firm's expenses exactly match the sales or service volume. It can be expressed in: (1) when revenue is exactly offset by total expense, or (2) Total units of production (cost of which exactly equals the income derived by their sales). This analysis can be done either mathematically or graphically. Revenue and expense figures are drawn from your three-year income projection.

Complete the following to determine your break-even point

1. Categorize all of your operating expenses as "fixed" and "variable" in the lists below:

Sample Expense	Fixed	Variable
Rent	3,000/yr	
Office Supplies		1,200/yr

Expense	Fixed	Variable
-------------	------------	------------
------------	------------	------------
-------------	------------	------------
-------------	------------	------------
-------------	------------	------------

Total	-----------	-----------

2. Determine Your Contribution Margin
   A. Projected Sales for the First Year _____
   B. Projected Gross Margin for the First Year _____
   C. Divide b by a (b/a) to obtain a percentage _____

   Sample: Sales   200.000
   Gross Margin   50,000
   Contribution Margin   50,000/200,000 = .25

3. Determine Your Break-even Point
   A. Total Fixed Expenses _____
   B. Contribution Margin _____
   C. Divide a by b (a/b) _____

   Sample: Fixed Expenses for the First Year   70,000
   Contribution Margin   .25
   Break-even Point   70,000/.25 = 280,000 in sales the first year.

4. Number of Customers Needed to Reach Break-even
   A. Break-even Point in amount (3c) _____
   B. Average Amount of a customer per day _____
   C. Divide a by b (a/b) to get number of customers for the first year _____
   D. Divide answer in c by the number of days the

company is open to get the number of customers
per day   _____

Sample: Break-even Point =   280,000
           Average Customer Purchase   10
           Number of customers per year = 280,000/10 = 28,000.

If your business is open 360 days per year, the number of customers needed per day is 28,000/360 =   77.8

HISTORICAL DOCUMENTATION

Historical statements are actual performance statements. They reflect the activity of your business in the past. Historical statements do not apply to you if your business is new and has not yet begun operations. If your business is an established one, you will include the following:

a) *Profit and Loss Statement (Income Statement)*: The income statement shows the financial activity of your business over a period of time (monthly, annually). It is a moving picture showing what has happened in your business and is an excellent tool for assessing your business. Your ledger is closed and balanced and the revenue and expense totals transferred to this statement.

b) *Balance Sheet*: The balance sheet shows the condition of the business as of a fixed date. It is a picture of your firm's financial condition at a particular moment and will show you whether your financial position is strong or weak. It is usually done at the close of an accounting period. A typical balance sheet contains (1) Assets, (2) Liabilities, and (3) Net worth.

c) *Cash Flow Statement*: A cash flow statement is a form that tracks the money as it flows in and out of the business over any given period of time (weekly, monthly, quarterly, or yearly.) The typical statement is divided into two halves: the top half keeps track of where the money comes from and what it goes out for. The bottom half traces where the funds end up with after they are inside the company. Just like the two halves of the balance sheet, the top and bottom halves must be in balance.

SUPPORTING DOCUMENTS OR ASSUMPTIONS

Your business plan is not complete if you fail to include materials upon which you have prepared your plan. We call these "supporting documents" or "assumptions." They are assumptions because what your business plan says is an assumption of what you intend to accomplish. If possible, your supporting documents should include the following materials:

- Your resumes and those of the key personnel in your company.
- Sources of your materials.
- Letters of intent or sales agreement.
- Lease and purchase agreement.
- Copies of leases.
- Any form of contract you have entered into.
- Permits and licenses, such as your certificate of registration.
- Certificate of insurance.
- Letters of reference.
- Business development plan.
- Your exit plan.

CASE 15: THE DILEMMA OF IYA 'JOKO'S MOIN MOIN BUSINESS

When Stella Olagbaju (aka Iya 'Joko) became a widow, she was left with a large house located along Badagry Road, Lagos, Nigeria. Her late husband also left behind an ailing mother and five children: the elder, Bamijoko, is in the university, two in secondary schools and two in elementary schools. The house was a very large one by local standard. It contained six units of three-bed-room flats built by her late husband with about five tenants who have lived in the house for almost six years without rental problems. The Olagbaju family occupied the largest of the six flats with five bedrooms. Stella, her ailing mother and the five children moved to a smaller flat in the house to save money after the death of her husband. They rented the large one out to a new tenant. Their income was based mainly on the rent from the tenants. To supplement their income, they began baking and supplying bean cakes, fried meat, fried fish and soft drinks to neighborhood restaurants, offices, and artisan workshops. Later, they added other staple menus such as rice, dodo (fried plantain), pounded yam, amala and assorted soups. Because the venture started with baked bean cakes (moin moin) the business was fondly referred to as "Joko's Moin Moin".

After eight months, Stella's customers consisted of about six restaurants, three factories and several workshops. In addition to that, customers were coming directly to their kitchen either to eat there or take their orders with them to their offices or homes. The business was growing in a way that the Olagbaju family never anticipated. They had purchased a delivery van and hired three bike riders who served as delivery boys and operated much like the pizza delivery system in the United States. The family venture was netting about $2,300 a month (about 300,000 Nigerian Naira, the local currency as at September 2005). Because, the family never expected growth in this magnitude, they were taken by surprise. Stella was confronted with a decision and the family must choose between two alternative courses of actions: either to rent a commercial space or build a modern facility that could cater for cooking, delivery and restaurant needs for those customers who decide to have their meals right on the spot. There was no doubt that the business must move out of their present residence.

Without a business plan, the Olagbajus bought ovens and other equipment before scrambling to find a location for rent, line up commercial ovens, obtain licenses, and applied for a business loan. However, with no financial records for the business and real business plan, the banks turned down the loan application. Meanwhile all of their savings had been spent in buying kitchen equipments, renting the new place and purchasing inventories. They had no money to pay the builders and other construction workers who were working on the new facility. The old place (which was their residence) was too small for the business. Customers were coming in without getting their orders on time. The operation was very chaotic by this time and Mrs. Stella and her few workers did not know where to start from or where to head. The business has simply lost all sense of direction and this was bearing on her health. It was during this time that she also lost her ailing mother. She went back to the loan officers at the banks; they told her to go home and put her house in order: to prepare a plan for her business.

When Mrs. Stella finally found a consultant to prepare a business plan for her ailing business, most of her customers had turned to other food suppliers to meet their growing needs. To add to her difficulties, two fast food restaurants (Mr. Bigg's and Tantalizers) opened up in her neighborhood. After the initial success of Joko's Moin Moin business, many copycats have also sprung up in the neighborhood. It was to the new comers that Mrs. Stella's customers turned. Had this venture put in place a solid business plan, it is doubtful whether Joko's Moin Moin would have been confronted with its dilemma.

Case Discussion Questions

1. You have been called as the consultant for Mrs. Stella. What are the major problems confronting Joko's Moin Moin?

2. As a consultant using the elements of a business plan discussed in this chapter, how would you go about preparing a business plan for Mrs. Stella?

GLOSSARY

A

Achievement-oriented cultures. In highly achievement-oriented cultures, social status is largely derived from a person's achievements. Cultures that are high on the achievement end of this dimension value competition, assertiveness and materialism. Whether competing as individuals or as members of a group (i.e., individualistic versus collectivist), achievement-oriented cultures value winning and the rewards that accompany success.

Advertising. Providing information regarding your product or service. Unlike promotion, advertising is the impersonal presentation of an idea, which is identified with a business sponsor and is projected through the mass media. Advertising offers a reason to buy a product or service.

Amoral Management. Managers who treat employees as the law requires. Attempts to motivate focus on increasing productivity rather than satisfying employees' growing maturity needs. Employees are still seen as factors of production, but a remunerative approach is used.

Ascription-oriented cultures. In highly ascription-oriented cultures, social status is largely derived from personal attributes such as age, experience, social connections, or gender.

B

Balance sheet provides a summary of a firm's financial position, providing owners with an estimate of the worth of the business on a given date.

Bribery. This is the practice of offering something (usually money) in order to gain an illicit advantage.

Bureaucratic corruption. The misuse of the power of public office for personal gain in breach of laws that govern public servants and moral principles.

Bureaucratic culture occurs when an organization values formality, rules, standard operating procedures, and hierarchical coordination.

Business definition explains the nature of the industry in which an entrepreneur intends to operate the business.

Business environment. The environmental setting in which a competitive engagement with an adversary (a competitor) takes place.

Business ethics. The application of general ethical ideas to the conduct of business.

Business plan. A business plan is a written document that details a proposed or existing venture. It will typically explain the vision, current status, expected needs, defined markets, and projected results of the business.

Business Social Responsibility. An obligation of a business entity, whether large or small, to act in ways that serve both its own interests and the interests of its stakeholders while formulating and implementing a firm's competitive strategy.

Business Strategy (business-level strategy). The managerial or entrepreneurial game plan for a single business.

C

Capabilities. A set of company's skills at coordinating its resources and putting them to productive use.

Cash flow statement monitors the money flowing into and out of a business. It consists of money that flow in (such as receipts on sales, dividend and interest income, invested capital, etc) and money that flows out (such as costs of goods acquired by the company, sales, general and administrative costs, interest expenses, taxes, building and equipment, etc).

Center of gravity a company's center of gravity is the part of the value chain that is most important to the company and the point where its greatest expertise and capabilities are located. A firm's center of gravity lies in its area of core competence.

Code of ethics is a written document that states values and ethical standards to guide the behavior of the members of an organization.

Competitive advantage. The aggregation of factors that sets a business firm apart from its competitors and gives it a unique position in the market superior to its competition. **Competitive strategy** focuses on improving the competitive position of a business within the specific industry or market segment that the fir m serves or intend to serve.

Conditionalities (or IMF conditionalities). The conditions generally relating to macroeconomic policies, which countries have to meet to qualify for international loans as a way of ensuring that borrowed resources are used to assist balance of payment adjustment; as a way of encouraging private capital inflows; as a way of retaining scarce IMF resources; as a mechanism for counter-cyclical world economic management.

Consolidated industry. An industry that is dominated by a few large companies.

Core competence. A unique set of capabilities that a company develops in key areas, such as superior quality, customer service, innovation, team building, flexibility, responsiveness, product design, low cost manufacturing, proprietary technology, superior distribution, etc.

Corporate governance. The system by which companies are directed and controlled, including the roles of the board of directors, management, shareholders, and other stakeholders.

Corporate strategy. Actions and initiatives a company uses to establish business positions in different industries, the approaches corporate executives pursue to boost the combined performance of the set of businesses the company has diversified into, and the means of capturing cross-business synergies and turning them into competitive advantage

Cost focus strategy. A low-cost competitive strategy that focuses on a particular buyer group or geographic market and the attempts to serve only this niche to the exclusion of others through offering products or services at a relatively lower cost compared to the competition.

Cost leadership strategy is a competitive strategy that requires aggressive construction of efficient-scale facilities, vigorous pursuit of cost reductions from experience, tight cost and overhead control, avoidance of marginal customer accounts, and cost minimization in functional areas of operation.

Culture. The historically transmitted patterns of meanings embodied in symbols, a system of inherited conceptions expressed in symbolic forms by means of which men communicate, perpetuate, and develop their knowledge about and attitudes toward life.

Current asset consists of cash, investment portfolios, accounts receivable, inventories and prepaid expenses.

D

Death stage is when the organization has reached the point of liquidation or bankruptcy and nothing can be done to save it.

Declining stage when sales are declining; losing customers and the firm is no longer capable of competing with the competitors. Such firm can also use a network structure to cut overheads. Declining stage can also occur when the entrepreneurial culture becomes a bureaucratic one.

Defensive tactics (offensive strategy). A strategy that include (i) offering a full line of products in every profitable market segment to close off any entry points, (ii) block channel access by signing exclusive agreements with key distributors, and (iii) avoid suppliers that also serve competitors, if possible.

Deregulation. The reduction or elimination of specific governmental rules and regulations that apply to private business including removal of regulations that prevented the private sector from competing with a nationalized monopoly.

Differentiation focus strategy. A strategy that concentrates on a particular buyer group, product line segment, or geographic market.

Differentiation strategy is the ability of a firm to provide unique and superior value in terms of product quality, special features, innovation, promotion, location or distribution.

Digital divide. Is a term that is often used in describing disparities in access to, and usage of, the telephone, personal computers and the Internet across demographic groups, within the same country, or between countries.

Distinctive competence. A unique strength that allows a company to achieve superior efficiency, quality, innovation, or customer responsiveness and thereby create superior value and attain a competitive advantage.

Distribution. The movement of goods and services from producers to the end-users.

Divisional structure. An organizational structure that groups together people with diverse skills and tasks but who work on the same product, with similar customers or clients, or in the same geographical region. A divisional structure is most appropriate for firms in the maturity stage.

Drivers of an industry (or industry drivers) are all the relevant factors and influences outside the company's boundaries that shape the behavior or state of that industry. These drivers emanate from the economy at large, population demographics, societal values and life styles, governmental regulation, technological factors and the industry and competitive arena in which the company operates.

Due process is the right to receive an impartial review of one's complaints and to be dealt with fairly.

E
Employee constitutionalism consists of a set of clearly defined rights and a means of protecting employees from discharge, demotion, or other penalties imposed when they assert their rights.

Employee rights. Employee rights refer to legitimate and enforceable claims or privileges obtained by workers through group membership that entitle or protect them in specific ways from the prevailing system of governance.

Entrepreneur. One who identifies an opportunity in an economic system, assembles the resources necessary to successfully exploit that opportunity and creates and delivers a value in an economic system.

Entrepreneurial competencies. The total sum of the entrepreneur's requisite attributes: attitudes, values, beliefs, knowledge, skills, abilities, personality, wisdom, expertise (social, technical, organizational, managerial), mindset, and behavioral tendencies needed for successful and sustaining entrepreneurship.

Entrepreneurial culture. A culture that typifies high levels of risk taking, dynamism, and creativity.

Entrepreneurial firm. An innovative firm that follows an entrepreneurial process.

Entrepreneurial process consists of (i) identifying and evaluating business opportunity, (ii) developing a business plan, (iii) determining resources, (vi) developing a management system, and (v) managing the entrepreneurial transition.

Entrepreneurship. The process of combining scarce resources in new ways to respond to opportunities or provide solutions to a problem.

Ethical dilemma. A situation with a potential course of action that, although, offering potential benefit or gain, is also unethical.

Ethical environment. An organization's environment that protects the interests of all participants in the business relationship.

Ethical rationalization is a process in which people try to explain their decisions as ethically right when they know that they are ethically wrong.

Ethics. The code of moral principles that sets standards of good or bad, right or wrong in one's conduct and thereby guides the behavior of a person or group.

Ethics training. This is a structured training program that helps employees understand the ethical aspects of decision-making and is designed to help people incorporate high ethical standards into their daily behaviors.

Experiential Positioning. Type of market position that depicts what the brand of a product or service stands for. It is an image-driven depiction of the experience that the brand stands for.

Expropriation. The surrender of a claim to exclusive property and the act of dispossessing a person or entity of ownership or propriety rights usually by the government.

F

Factor endowment. The extent to which a country is endowed with such resources as land, labor, capital, raw materials, technology, infrastructure, etc.

First movers. Firms that introduce a product or service into a market before anyone else does it. As a first mover, the firm establishes a reputation as an industry leader, earns temporarily high profits from experience and learning effects.

Five Forces Model of Competition. A model that helps us to understand the structure of an industry and the application of appropriate competitive strategies. It is an appropriate tool for understanding the competition within an industry. The model helps industry participants to understand the intensity of rivalry among existing firms, the threats from substitute products or services, the threat from potential new comers to the market, and the bargaining power of suppliers and buyers.

Fixed assets. Company assets that involve the long-term commitments and large investment for the new venture. Fixed assets include Land, buildings, equipment and accumulated depreciation.

Fragmented industry. An industry that contains a large number of small or medium-sized firms, none of which is in a position to dominate the industry.

Franchising. A form of ownership in which an independent business owner (the franchisee) pays fees and royalties to a parent company (the franchiser) in return for the right to become identified with its trademark, to sell its products or services, and often to use its business format and system.

Functional Positioning. This is a type of market positioning that focuses on the functions a customer derives from the product or service.

Functional Strategy (or functional-level strategy). The managerial game plan for a particular functional activity, business process, or key department within a business.

Functional structure. An organizational structure that places together people with similar skills who perform similar tasks in formal groups. Functional structures are suitable for firms in their growth stage.

G

Globalization. A process of interaction and integration among the people, companies, and governments of different nations, a process driven by international trade and investment and aided by information technology.

Gross profit (or gross profit). The gross profit is the total revenue subtracted by the cost of generating that revenue. It tells you how much money a business would have made if it didn't pay any other expenses such as salary, income taxes, etc. Gross Profit should be broken out and clearly labeled on the income statement.

Guerrilla marketing. An unconventional system of promotions and other marketing activities on a very low budget, by relying on time, energy and imagination instead of big marketing budgets.

I

Immoral Management. Employees are viewed as factors of production to be used, exploited, and manipulated for gain of individual owner, manager or the firm. No concern is shown for employees' needs, rights or expectations. The relationship between employers and employees is short-term focus. The working environment and relationship is coercive, controlling, and alienating.

Income statement. A financial statement that compares expenses against revenue over a certain period of time to show the firm's net profit or loss.

Indigenization policy. A government policy that aims at the wholesale take-over of enterprises or a policy of linking government supervision in the extent of expatriate or foreign participation in various economic activities.

Industrial clusters. Geographic concentrations of interconnected companies, specialized suppliers, service providers, firms in related industries and associated institutions in particular fields that compete but also cooperate.

Industry. A group of companies offering products or services that are close substitutes for each other. Close substitutes are products or services that satisfy the same basic consumer needs. An industry is a group of firms whose products or services have so many of the same attributes that they compete for the same buyers.

Industry driving-forces. Driving forces in an industry are the major underlying causes of changing industry and competitive conditions that have the biggest influence on how the industry landscape will be altered.

Industry Key Success Factors (KSFs). Those things that a firm in an industry must do in order to succeed in a particular market. In order to design appropriate competitive strategies in an industry, an entrepreneur must also understand what it takes to be successful overtime within an industry.

Industry life cycle model is an explanatory model that is used for analyzing and understanding the effects of industry evolution on competitive forces. The success of a firm in understanding the forces driving change depends on the firm's understanding of the developmental stage in which the industry finds itself. Understanding these stages directs us to see an industry in evolutionary stage or the industry life cycle. **The life cycle of an industry** starts with its birth, growth, shakeout, maturity, and decline to the death stage. Each of these stages demands an appropriate entry and/or exit strategy.

Informal financial sector. Includes *non-formal* financial activities and transactions that are undertaken in and by such institutions as credit unions, savings and credit co-operatives; less formalized, smaller-scale group arrangements such as savings groups, mutual aid associations, non-rotating savings and credit associations (SCAs), rotating savings and credit associations (ROSCAs); commercial lenders such as individual savings (*esusu*) collectors, estate-owners, landlords, traders, shopkeepers, and professional and non-professional money lenders; friends, relatives and business associates among whom transactions take place on a non-commercial basis.

Informal sector is the portion of a country's economy that lies outside of any formal regulatory environment and is rarely reflected in official statistics on economic activity.

Infrastructural provisions. The provision of public utilities such as energy, telecommunications, water supply, sanitation, sewage and waste disposal; public works, such as irrigation systems, schools, housing and hospitals; transport systems, such as roads, railways, ports, waterways and airports; and educational facilities.

Infrastructure. The facilities, structures, associated equipments, services, and institutional arrangements that facilitate the production and flow of goods and services between individuals, firms, and governments.

Intangible assets include such things as brand-name image, company reputation, buyer goodwill, or a motivated and energized workforce.

Intangible resources include such things as the firm's brand name, reputation, patents, and technological or marketing know-how.

Interventionist financial policies. When governments play a major role in regulating the financial markets in an economy such as determining credit flows through a system of subsidies, interest-rate ceilings, policy-based credit allocation, high reserve requirements, and restricting entry into banking and capital account transactions.

Innovation. The successful exploitation of a new idea.

L

Late movers. Are firms that capitalize on opportunities established by the first mover in the market. Late movers compete on the basis of identifying market niches ignored by first movers.

Liabilities represent money that is owed to creditors. Current liabilities represent the short-term debts a company takes on that have to be paid within one year.

Liberalization (trade liberalization). The removal of or reduction in the trade practices that thwart free flow of goods and services from one nation to another. It includes dismantling of tariff (such as duties, surcharges, and export subsidies) as well as non-tariff barriers (such as licensing regulations, quotas, and arbitrary standards).

Limited liability company. Owners invest capital into the business and receive shares of stock usually proportionate to the level of their investment. A limited liability company is a legal entity.

Logistics consists of transportation, storage and material handling.

Long-term liabilities. Liabilities that represent large financial obligations a firm takes on to get it running.

Long-term orientation (LTO) a cultural value that stands for the fostering of virtues oriented toward future rewards – in particular, perseverance and thrift.

Low cost strategy is the ability of a firm to source materials, design, produce, and market a comparable product or service more efficiently than the competitors.

M

Managerial (leadership) succession. The process by which key officials, especially the top managers, are replaced by others in the organization.

Market research involves systematically collecting, analyzing, and interpreting data pertaining to a company's market, customers, and competitors and consists of four steps: (i) defining the objective of the research, (ii) collecting data, (iii) analyzing and interpreting the data, and (iv) drawing conclusions and acting on them.

Market segmentation. The process of analyzing one market to find out if it should be viewed as more than one market.

Marketing. The performance of business activities that affect the flow of goods and services from producer to consumer or user.

Marketing mix. A marketing strategy that consists of marketing practices such as product or service offering, place or location, pricing strategy, and promotion.

Microfinance. refers to the provision of financial services to low-income clients, including the self-employed.

Mission of a firm is the purpose or reason for its existence. It tells what the firm is providing to the customer or society.

Moral Management. Managers who adopt a moral management approach see their employees as a human resource that must be treated with dignity and respect.

Multisegmentation strategy views the market as composed of individual segments that have different preferences.

N

Nation-state. Refers to a single or multiple nationalities joined together in a formal political union. The nation-state determines an official language(s), a system of law, manages a currency system, uses a bureaucracy to order elements of society, and fosters loyalties to abstract entities like "Nigeria", United States", "United Kingdom", etc.

Net Profit. The company's amount that is left after all expenses is subtracted from the income available.

Network structure. An organization's structure that consists of a central core that is linked through networks with outside suppliers and distributors of essential business services.

Nonprofit organization. A nonprofit organization is one that, by law, is unable to hold or distribute profits like a "for-profit" organization can. This means that the nonprofit company is required by law to redistribute any "profits" back into the company (in the form of salaries, new capital, etc), or to other non-profits or to charity.

O

Objective. Objective of a firm is the commitment of the owners or management to achieve specific performance targets and results within a specific time frame. Objectives are the results of a firm's activities.

Offensive tactics (see also offensive strategy). Competitive strategies that include (i) frontal assault, (ii) flanking maneuver and (iii) guerrilla warfare.

Ombudsperson is derived from the Swedish word "ombudsman" and refers to one who investigates reported complaints and helps to achieve equitable settlements.

Operating expenses. Expenses and costs that contribute directly to the manufacture and distribution of goods and services.

Operating strategy. An operational strategy deals with the strategic initiatives and approaches for managing key operating units such as procurement in the production department, advertising in the marketing department, payroll in the human resources department, debt collection in the accounting department.

Organization chart is a diagram describing the formal arrangement of work positions within an organization.

Organization structure is the system of tasks, reporting relationships, and communication that links together the work of individuals and groups.

Organizational citizenship. The extent to which an individual's voluntary support and behavior contributes to the organization's success.

Organizational life cycle is the evolution of an organization over time through different stages of growth. It consists of five stages: (i) the start-up stage, (ii) the growth stage, (iii) the maturity stage, (iv) the decline stage, and (v) the death stage. There is an appropriate organization structure suitable for each stage.

Owners' equity represents the amount owners of a venture have invested and/or retained from the operations of the business venture. Owners' equity can take on several forms such as invested capital or accumulated retained earnings.

P

Particularistic cultural orientation. In a particularistic culture, people develop their expectations of others based on their personal relationships with them and their trust in them rather than on rules.

Partnership is usually formed when two or more people enter into a business relationship or venture together, when they decide to share assets, liabilities, and profits of their business. A partnership agreement is important because it gives the partners an unbiased mechanism for resolving disagreements or dissolving the partnership.

Political culture is the set of attitudes, beliefs and sentiments which give order and meaning to a political process and which provide the underlying assumptions and rules that govern behavior in a political system. It encompasses both the political ideals and the operating norms of a polity.

Political environment consists of all laws, the political system, system of government, government agencies, and lobbying groups that influence or restrict individuals or organizations in the society.

Political risk is the chance that political decisions, events, or conditions in a country will negatively affect the profitability or sustainability of economic and business investment. It is the likelihood that political actions will affect the business environment in ways that lead investors and owners to lose some or all of the value of their investment or be forced to accept a lower than projected rate of return.

Positioning is the process by which marketers or organizations create an image or identity in the minds of their target market for a product, brand, or organization. It is the relative competitive comparison of a product or service in terms of the position it occupies in a given market as perceived by the target market.

Privatization. A process that entails the reduction of the role of the government in asset ownership and service delivery and a corresponding increase in the role of the private sector.

Product life cycle is a graph showing time plotted against sales of a product or service as it moves from introduction through growth, maturity, decline, and eventual death.

Pro forma income statement is a statement of a firm's future projections, showing how the firm targets a profit and then determines what sales level the firm must achieve.

Promotion communicates the availability and desirability of what the firm has to offer. Promotion is about "getting the word out." Promotion offers an incentive to buy the product or service.

R

Regional trade blocs. These are intergovernmental associations that manage and promote trade activities for specific regions of the world.

S

Short-term orientation (STO). A cultural value that stands for the fostering of virtues related to the past and present – in particular, respect for traditions and fulfilling social obligations.

Shotgun approach. A marketing approach that puts the small company in dangerous competitive position because it has fuzzy messages, product-focused, telling and selling. The shotgun approach to marketing is sales-driven rather than customer-driven.

Simple entrepreneurial structure consists of a top manager (the founder or owner) of the firm and non-managerial employees who do operating work and it is suitable for start-up stage.

Single segmentation strategy is when a firm recognizes that distinct market segments exist but chooses to concentrate on reaching only one segment.

Small business owner. One who starts a business undertaking and remains small without a clear plan for growth.

Sole proprietorship is a business owned and managed by one individual. A sole proprietorship is a business where the owner is essentially the business.

Stakeholder. Any individual or group who can affect or is affected by the actions, decisions, policies, practices, or goals of the organization.

Strategic alliance is a partnership of two or more firms or businesses to achieve strategically significant objectives that are mutually beneficial. Strategic alliances can take several forms such as (i) mutual service arrangement, (ii) joint venture, (iii) licensing agreement, and (iv) value-chain partnership.

Strategic entrepreneur. One who makes all the strategic as well as operational decisions in the firm.

Strategic group consists of those rival firms with similar competitive approaches and positions in the market, adopting similar strategies, and tends to be affected by, and respond to competitive actions and external events in similar ways

Strengths and weaknesses can be found by examining the company's R&D, operations, sales and marketing, distribution and delivery, customer service, management, organization and the financial condition of the firm.

Strategic planning. This is a management approach concerned with the long-term mission and objectives of a firm, the resources used in achieving those objectives, and the policies and guidelines that govern the acquisition, use, and disposition of those resources. Strategic planning at the firm level must also take into account the Opportunities available to the firm, and an assessment of its ability to exploit those opportunities with a view to gaining a distinct competitive advantage.

Strategy. The game plan management is using to stake out a market position, conduct its operations, attract and please customers, compete successfully and achieve organizational objectives.

Structural Adjustment Program. A program of economic development and restructuring consisting of economic policies which countries must follow in order to qualify for new World Bank and International Monetary Fund (IMF) loans and help them make debt repayments on the older debts owed to commercial banks, governments and the World Bank.

SWOT analysis. An acronym for analyzing the strengths, weaknesses, opportunities and threats facing a company. Success in an industry demands that an entrepreneur knows the strengths, weaknesses, opportunities and threats facing the company. Strengths and weaknesses reside within the company and opportunities and threats exist in the firm's environment.

Symbolic Positioning. A type of market position that deals with intrinsic values associated with the product or service and includes issues such as self-image enhancement, ego identification, belongingness and social meaningfulness, and affective fulfillment.

T

Tangible resources. Include such things as land, buildings, plant, equipment, human, finance, technological, and organizational.

Target market. The specific group of customers at whom a firm aims its products or services.

Theory X Management. Management assumes employees are inherently lazy and will avoid work if they can. Because of this, workers need to be closely supervised and comprehensive systems of controls developed. A hierarchical structure is needed with narrow span of control at each level. According to this theory, employees will show little ambition without an enticing incentive program and will avoid responsibility whenever they can. Managers that subscribe to Theory X, tend to take a rather pessimistic view of their employees. A Theory X manager believes that his or her employees do not really want to work, that they would rather avoid responsibility and that it is the manager's job to structure the work and energize the employee. The result of this line of thought is that Theory X managers naturally adopt a more authoritarian style based on the threat of punishment.

Theory Y Management. Management assumes employees *may be* ambitious, self-motivated, and anxious to accept greater responsibility, and exercise self-control, self-direction, autonomy and empowerment. It is believed that if given the chance employees have the desire to be creative and forward thinking in the workplace. There is a chance for greater productivity by giving employees the freedom to perform at the best of their abilities without being bogged down by rules. A Theory Y manager believes that, given the right conditions, most people will want to do well at work and that there is a pool of unused creativity in the workforce.

Trade bloc. A trade bloc is a large free trade area formed by one or more tax, tariff and trade agreements.

Transport infrastructure. Transport infrastructure refers to roads, railways, bridges, tunnels, ports (for maritime and inland water transport), airports, urban transport infrastructure (mass transit systems), dry ports and inland container depots.

U

Ujamaa. A socialist development policy based on family-hood, self-help and mutual cooperation, which is derived from African tradition of family and clan self-help.

Uncertainty avoidance. The extent to which the members of a culture feel threatened by ambiguous or unknown situations.

Universalism. Universalism is the degree to which people believe that various ideas and practices can be effective in all circumstances.

Universalistic cultural orientation. In a universalistic culture, people believe they can develop rules and standards that can be reasonably applied to everyone in every situation. They tend to use contracts, formal systems, and procedures to convey what they expect from others.

Unsegmented market strategy. A market strategy that defines the total market as its target market.

V

Value. An organization's values are the operating philosophies or principles that guide an organization's internal conduct as well as its relationship with the external world.

Value chain. This is a linked set of value-creating activities beginning with basic raw materials coming from suppliers, moving out to a series of value-added activities involved in producing and marketing a product or service, and ending with distributors getting the final goods or services into the hands of the ultimate consumer.

Value Statement. The statement of a firm that tells the public its creed statement, a statement of purpose, the firm's guiding belief systems, a statement of philosophy, and a statement of business principles.

Vision. The vision of a firm is what the company is trying to achieve over the long term as formally declared in the dreams or purposes of their owners. The vision statement of a firm answers the question: "What do we want to become?"

W

Whistle-blowing. The disclosure by current or former employees of illegal, immoral, or illegitimate organizational practices.

ENDNOTES

CHAPTER 1

1. Peter F. Ducker, *Innovation and Entrepreneurship* (New York, NY: HarperCollins, Inc. 1985).
2. For a detailed understanding of the entrepreneurial activities of BusyInternet in see these sites: www.busyinternet.com; www.ghanacybergroup.com/newsletters John Yarney, "Ghana gets wired," (*The Industry Standard*, April 4th, 2005); Michael M. Philips, "On Ghana's Tech Frontier: Internet Start-up Flourishes," *The Wall Street Journal* (Wednesday, May 22, 2002).
3. R. D. Hisrich, M. P. Peters, and D. A. Shepherd, *Entrepreneurship* (Boston, MA: McGraw-Hill, 2005), pp. 5-6.
4. John O. Ogbor, "Mythicizing and Reification in Entrepreneurial Discourse: Ideology Critique of Entrepreneurial Studies," *Journal of Management Studies* (Vol. 35, No. 5, July, 2000), pp. 605-637.
5. Joseph Schumpeter, *Can Capitalism Survive?* (New York: Harper and Row, 1952), p. 72. See also Joseph Schumpeter, *The Theory of Economic Development: An Inquiry into Profits, Capital, Credit, Interest, and Business Cycle* (Cambridge, MA: Harvard University Press, 1934).
6. Robert Hisrich, Michael Peters and Dean Shepherd, Ibid, p. 7.
7. For a brief discussion of Andrew Carnegie and how his innovation led the U.S. into the steel age, see William J. O'Neil, *Business Leaders Success: 55 Top Business Leaders and How they Achieved Greatness* (New York: McGraw, 2004), pp. 15-18.
8. For more information on Michael Dell and Dell Computer Inc., see Kathryn Jones, "The Dell way," (*Business 2.0,* February 2003), pp. 60-66; Stephen Prichard, "Inside Dell's Lean Machine", *Works Management* (December 2002), pp. 14-17; and Dell's website, www.dell.com, (Accessed on June 24, 2006).
9. Ibid.
10. See Kenichi Ohmae, "Managing in a Borderless World," *Harvard Business Review* (May/June 1989).
11. See Alex Taylor, "A Tale of Two Factories," (*Fortune* magazine, September 18, 2006). http://money.cnn.com/magazines/fortune/fortune_archive/2006/09/18/8386187/index (Accessed December 21, 2006).
12. The discussion in the section is based on Peter Drucker's examination of the concept of innovation and how it relates to entrepreneurship in *Innovation and Entrepreneurship* (New York, NY: HarperCollins Inc., 1985).
13. John Bessant and Joe Tidd, *Innovation and Entrepreneurship* (West Sussex, UK, 2007), p. 13.
14. See Peter Drucker, Ibid.
15. Arthur. A. Thompson, A. J. Strickland and John E. Gamble, *Crafting and Executing Strategy: The Quest for Competitive Advantage* (New York: McGraw-Hill, 2007).
16. *Tell* Magazine (No. 1, Jan. 7, 2002), p. 78.
17. See A. Gibb, *Effective Policies for Small Business* (OECD/UNIDO, 2004).

18. Kristin Hallberg, "A Market-oriented strategy for small and medium-sized enterprises," *International Finance Corporation, World Bank, Discussion Papers* (No. 40: Washington, DC), http://ifcln1.ifc.org/ifcext/economics.nsf/attachmentByTitle/dpd40/ (Accessed on June 24, 2006).
19. The World Bank, *Doing Business in 2004: Understanding Regulation* (The World Bank, the International Finance Corporation and Oxford University Press, Washington, DC, 2004).
20. Central Bank of Nigeria, *Revised Small and Medium Enterprises Equity Investment Scheme (SMEEIS) Guidelines* (Abuja, Nigeria, August 8, 2005).
21. For definitions and statistical classification of small business in South Africa, see: South Africa Government Gazette, *White paper on National Strategy for the Development and Promotion of Small Business in South Africa* (Cape Town: Government Printer, 357/16317, 1995); Stats SA, *Demography: Employment and Unemployment in South Africa, October House Hold Survey* (Pretoria: Government Printer, Statistical Release P0317.10, 1998); "Census of Manufacturing" (Pretoria: Central Statistical Services, Government Printer, 1997); Kobus Visser, *The Export and Growth Potential of Small and Medium-sized Enterprises in the Clothing Industry* (University of Edinburgh, Centre for African Studies, papers in Education, Training and Enterprise, No. 15, 1998).
22. Dalitso Kayanulu and Peter Quartey, *The Policy Environment for Promoting Small and Medium-sized Enterprises in Ghana and Malawi* (University of Manchester, IDPM, Finance and Development Research Program, Working Paper Series, #15, May 2000).
23. Ibid.
24. Robert Hisrich, Michael Peters and Dean Shepherd, Ibid.
25. Peter Drucker, Ibid, pp. 32-36.
26. Ibid. p. 323.
27. Charles Tushabomwe-Kazooba, "Causes of Small Business Failure in Uganda: A Case Study from Bushenyi and Mbarara Town," *African Studies Quarterly* (The Online Journal of African studies, (Volume 8, No. 4 Summer 2006), http://web.africa.ufl.edu/asq/v8i4a3. (Accessed on November 23, 2007).
28. Helsinki School of Economics, *Regional Program on Enterprise Development: Development and Growth of Industrial Enterprises in Tanzania* (Helsinki, World Bank, 1994); L. C. Kimbi, *Women Entrepreneurs in Dar es Salaam: A profile Study* MBA Research Projects (Dar es Salaam, University of Dar es Salaam, 1989); T. Malyamkono and M. S. D Bagachwa, *The Second Economy in Tanzania* (London, James Currey, 1990); A. Tibaijuka, "Women and Structural Adjustment in Sub-Saharan Africa," *Seminar Paper* (ERB University of Dar es Salaam, 1992, Mimeo).
29. See M. C. de Jantscher: Administrating the VAT: in *Value Added Taxation in Developing Countries* (Washington, DC, World Bank, 1990), p.179; Tony Land, "Developing Capacity for Tax Administration: The Rwanda Revenue Authority", *ECDPM Discussion Paper* (No. 57D, November 2004), p. 3; A. Sindzingre, "Political economy of taxation and international financial institutions in sub-Saharan Africa: reforms as problems and solutions," *Paper presented at the Annual Conference* (Windhoek, 4-5 April 2002).
30. Source: Desmond Utonwen, "A Dogged Trailblazer," *The News* (March 26, 20080, http://thenewsng.com/article/242 (Accessed on April 02, 2008).

CHAPTER 2

1. Robert D. Hisrich, Michael Peters and Dean A. Shepherd, *Entrepreneurship* (New York, NY: McGraw-Hill, 2008), p. 33.
2. The growing interest in managing religious organizations from an entrepreneurial perspective is anchored on the fact that churches like most organizations take in a lot of money and spend a lot of money. Therefore, more and more churches are reinventing themselves and are engaging in strategic planning to ensure effectiveness in achieving their vision and mission.
3. O. F. Collins and D. G. Moore, *The Enterprising Man* (East Lansing, MI: Michigan State University Press, 1964) p. 244.
4. Jon P. Goodman, "What makes an Entrepreneur," *Inc.*, (Oct. 1994), p. 29.
5. Cited in "Animator Walt Disney: His Innovation and Persistence gave Birth to Magic," by J. Barnes, *Investor's Business Daily* (October 24, 2000).
6. Taiwo Amodu, *Daily Sun* (Sat., July 31, 2004).
7. Source: William O'Neil, *Business Leaders Success: 55 Top Business Leaders and how they Achieved Greatness* (New York: McGraw-Hill, 2004); pp. 45-49.
8. David McClelland, *The Achieving Society* (New York: The Free Press, 1961).
9. David McClelland and David Winter, *Motivating Economic Achievement* (New York, NY: The Free Press, 1969).
10. Robert D. Hisrich, Michael P. Peters, and Dean A. Shepherd, *Entrepreneurship* (New York: McGraw-Hill, 2008), p. 9.
11. See R. H. Brockhaus, "Risk Taking propensity of Entrepreneurs," *Academy of Management Journal* (Vol. 23, September, 1980) pp. 509-520.
12. Robert D. Hisrich, Michael P. Peters, and Dean A. Shepherd, Ibid, p. 8.
13. Curt Schleier, "Intel Co-founder Robert Noyce: He Invented His Way to the Top," *Investor's Business Daily* (November 5, 2001).
14. Source: Black Herald African Magazine, http://blackherald.egoon.com (Accessed on February 12, 2008).
15. T.W. Zimmerer and N. M. Scarborough, *Essentials of Entrepreneurship and Small Business Management*, (Upper Saddle River, NJ: Prentice Hall, 2003) p. 64.
16. Source: *Black Herald African Magazine*, http://blackherald.egoon.com. (Accessed, February 12, 2008).
17. Tom Forrest, *The Advantage of African Capital: The Growth of Nigerian Private Enterprise* (Edinburgh, Scotland, Edinburgh University Press, 1994) p. 234.
18. Source: Vincent Ukpong Kalu, "How Ifeanyi Muokwe finds his niche," *Daily Sun Enterprise* (Saturday, September 25, 2005).
19. Source: Dominic Eluemunor, "How Steers Fast Food Steers the Ship of Nourishment," *Daily Sun Enterprise* (Sat., Sept. 16, 2006).
20. Source: Olatunde Owolabi, "He left Leventis Group 10 Years ago, now he manufactures freezers and ice-block making machines," *Daily Sun* (Saturday, August 14, 2004).
21. Lavern S. Urlacher, *Small Business Entrepreneurship: An Ethics and Human Relations Perspective* (Upper Saddle River, NJ: Prentice Hall, 1999), p. 11.
22. T.W. Zimmerer and N. M. Scarborough, Ibid, p. 72.

23. Source: "When I left banking for art, people thought I was Mad," *Daily Sun Enterprise* (Saturday February 05, 2005).
24. Source: Curt Schleier, *Investor's Business Daily* (December 16, 1999).
25. Source: William J. O'Neil, Ibid, pp. 69-74.
26. Ibid, pp. 25-30.
27. Source: Chima Jupadim, "World of a female painter," *Daily Sun, Women in Business* (Tuesday July 6, 2004).
www.Sunnewsonline.com/webpages/features/womenbusiness/2004/July/06. (Accessed on June 8, 2006).
28. *Tell* Magazine, (No. 16, April 19, 2004), p. 40.
29. Source: Nancy Njoku, "He started card Making as a result of poverty. Now, he employs graduates," *Daily Sun* (Saturday, October 16, 2004).
30. Peter Barlas, "AOL's Steve Case: He built an online empire by keeping the customer in mind," *Investor's Business Daily* (February 10, 2000).
31. D. C. Mead and C. Liedholm, "The dynamics of micro and small enterprises in developing countries", *World Development* (Vol. 26, No. 1, 1998), pp., 61-74; M. Keyser, M. de Kruif and M. Frese, "The Psychological strategy process and socio-demographic variables as predictors of success for micro-and small-scale business owners in Zambia," In M. Frese (ed.), *Success and failure of micro business owners in Africa: A psychological approach* (Westport, CT: Quorum Books, 2000), pp. 31-54; G. Godsell, "Entrepreneurs embattled: Barriers to entrepreneurship in South Africa," In B. Berger, ed., *The culture of entrepreneurship* (San Francisco: ICS Press, 1991).
32. M. Frese (ed.), *Success and failure of micro business owners in Africa: A psychological approach* (Westport, CT: Quorum Books, 2000); Samuel K. Buame, *Entrepreneurship: A contextual perspective* (Lund, Sweden: Lund University Press, 1996).
33. Samuel K. Buame, Ibid.
34. M. Keyser, M. de Kruif and M. Frese, Ibid, p. 44.
35. Moses N. Kiggundu, "Entrepreneurs and entrepreneurship in Africa: what is known and what needs to be done," *Journal of Development Entrepreneurship* (Vol.7, No. 3, 2002), pp. 239-259.
36. M. Frese, (ed.), Ibid.
37. Moses N. Kiggundu, 2002, Ibid.
38. See S. K. Buame, Ibid; K. M. Kallon, *The economics of Sierra Leone Entrepreneurship* (Lanhan, MD: University Press of America, 1990).
39. M. Dia, African management *in the 1990s and beyond: Reconciling indigenous and transplant institutions* (Washington, D.C.: The World Bank, 1996).
40. P. Kennedy, *African capitalism: The struggle for ascendancy* (Cambridge: Cambridge University Press, 1998).
41. See S. K. Buame, Ibid; F. Ng and A. J. Yeats, "On the recent trade performance of Sub-Saharan African countries: Cause for hope or more of the same?" *African Region Working Papers Series, #7* (Washington, DC: The World Bank, 2000); J. Svensson, "The cost of doing business: Firms' experience with corruption in Uganda", *African Region Working Paper Series, #6* (The World Bank: Washington, D.C., 2000); M. J. Dia, Ibid; M. A. Sam, "Exploring the link between customary inheritance practice and discontinuity of indigenous enterprises in Nigeria," *Canadian Journal of African Studies* (Vol. 32, No. 2, 1998), pp. 349-377; M. N. Kiggundu, *Managing Organizations in*

developing countries: An operational and strategic approach (West Hartford, CT: Kumerian Press, 1989); P. Trulsson, *Strategies of entrepreneurship: Understanding industrial entrepreneurship and structural change in Northern Tanzania* (Linkoping University, Linkoping, Sweden, 1997); J. J. Jorgensen, T. Hafsi and M. N. Kiggundu, "Towards a market imperfections theory of organizational structure in developing countries," *Journal of Management Studies* (Vol. 23, No. 4, 1986), pp. 417-442.

42. W. Elkan, "Entrepreneurs and entrepreneurship in Africa," *Finance & Development* (Vol. 25, No. 4, 1998), pp. 41. K. M. Kallon, Ibid; F. Ng. and A. J. Yeats, Ibid; J. Svensson, Ibid; S. Koop, T. de Reu and M. Frese, "Socio-demographic factors, entrepreneurial orientations, personal initiative, and environmental problems in Uganda," In M. Frese (ed.), Ibid.

43. See Samuel K. Buame, Ibid; K. M. Kallon, Ibid.

44. Moses N. Kiggundu, 2002, Ibid.

45. Cited in Moses Kiggundu, 2002, Ibid.

46. See K. M. Kallon, Ibid; D. C. Mead, "MSEs tackle both poverty and growth but in different proportions," In K. King & S. McGrath (eds.), *Enterprise in Africa* (London: Intermediate Technology, 1999), pp. 61-71; D. C. Mead and C. Liedholm, "The dynamics of micro and small enterprises in developing countries," World Development, (Vol. 26, No. 1, 1998), pp. 61-74; H. W. Stewart, *Psychological correlates of entrepreneurship* (New York: Garland Publishing, Inc., 1996).

47. B. Benedict, "Family firms and firm families: A comparison of Indian, Chinese, and Creole firms in Seychelles," In S. M. Greenfield, A. Strickon, & R. T. Aubey, (eds.), *Entrepreneurs in cultural context* (Albuquerque: University of New Mexico Press, 1979).

48. D. C. Mead and C. Liedholm, Ibid.

49. L. Rutashobya, "Female entrepreneurship in Tanzania: Constraints and strategic considerations," *Proceedings of the International Academy of African Business and Development* Washington, D.C., April 4-7, 2001), pp. 31-37; M. Frese, Ibid.

50. M. Keyser, M. de Kruif and M. Frese, Ibid, pp. 31-54; E. M. Rathgeber and E. O. Adera, (eds.), *Gender and the information revolution in Africa* (Ottawa: International Development Research Center, 2000); M. P. Van Dijk, "Regulatory restrictions and competition in formal and informal urban manufacturing in Burkina Faso," In P. English & C. Henault (eds.), *Agents of change* (London: Intermediate Technology, 1995), pp. 106-125.

51. W. Elkan, Ibid; S. Koop, T. de Reu and M. Frese, "Socio-demographic factors, entrepreneurial orientations, personal initiative, and environmental problems in Uganda," Ibid; K. M. Kallon, *Ibid*; A. Strickon, & R. T. Aubey, (eds.), *Entrepreneurs in cultural context* (Albuquerque: University of New Mexico Press, 1979); M. Keyser, M. de Kruif and M. Frese, Ibid; B. C. Mitchell, "Motives of Entrepreneurs: A Case Study of South Africa," *Journal of Entrepreneurship* (Vol. 13, No. 2, 2004), pp. 167-183.

52. B. C. Mitchell, Ibid.

53. John O. Okpara and Pamela Wynn, "Determinants of small business growth constraints in a sub-Saharan African economy", *SAM Advanced Management Journal* (March 22 2007).

54. Tom Forrest, *The Advantage of African Capital: The Growth of Nigerian Private Enterprise* (Edinburgh, Scotland, Edinburgh University Press, 1994), p. 234.

55. For a discussion of Aliko Dangote's entrepreneurial spirit and the strategies he adopted for expanding in a developing economy such as Nigeria, see *Newswatch* June 29, 1998 and Oluwatoyosi Ogunseye, "Dangote: A brand in transit," *The Daily Sun* (Thursday, June, 3, 2004).
56. Tom Forrest, Ibid, p. 234.
57. This case is reproduced from materials in these sources: *Tribune*, "The rise and and rise of Dr. Mike Adenuga Jnr." Sunday, February 11, 2007; Source: Mike Awoyinfa and Dimgba Igwe, "Mike Adenuga: What you don't know about this man" Tuesday, March 20, 2007 (Accessed on November 1, 2007), http://nm.onlinenigeria.com/template; Uche Nworah, "Nigerian Matters," 05/07/2006; Nigeriabusinessinfo.com, "Revisiting Nigeria's Telecoms Industry,"www.nigeriabusinessinfo.com/telecoms08093.htm (Accessed on May 21, 2008); BBC News, "Nigeria's digital mobile bonanza," http://news.bbc.co.uk/2/hi/business/1512949.stm (Accessed on May 21, 2008).

CHAPTER 3

1. Jorn Madslien, "No quick fix for Zimbabwe's economy" (BBC, April 14, 2008), http://news.bbc.co.uk/2/hi/business/7346042.stm (Accessed on April 24, 2008).
2. Ibid.
3. Michael Clemens and Todd Moss, "Cost and Causes of Zimbabwe's Crisis," *Center for Global Development* (Washington, DC, July 2005), p. 2; See S. Power, "How to Kill a Country: Turning a breadbasket into a basket case in ten easy steps – the Robert Mugabe way," *Atlantic Monthly* (December 2003).
4. See Michael Clemens and Todd Moss, Ibid. p. 7.
5. *The Economist* (March 18th-24th 2006), p. 50.
6. *The Economist* "South Africa's Economy," (September 24th 2005), p. 58.
7. Lindiwe Hendricks (South Africa's Deputy Minister of Trade and Industry), "The Building Blocks of Economic Development," *Trade and Investment Journal from South Africa* (No. 15, February 24, 2005), pp. 4-10.
8. See Gerry Rodgers, "The Pattern of globalization and some implications for pursuit of social goals," *Working Paper No. 55* (Policy Integration Department, International Labor Office, Geneva, February 2005); Mark Weisbrot, Dean Baker, Egor Kraev and Judy Chen, "The Scorecard on Globalization 1980-2000: Twenty Years of Diminished Progress," *Center for Economic Policy and Research* (July 11, 2001).
9. Cited in Deborah Bräutigam, "Local Entrepreneurship in Southeast Asia and Sub-Saharan Africa: Networks and Linkages to the Global Economy," *Conference Paper*, (School of International Service, American University Washington, DC, July 14, 1998).
10. See M. Sheila Nicholas, "The State and Capitalism in Zimbabwe," in Bruce J. Berman and Colin Leys, eds. *African Capitalists in African Development* (Boulder, CO: Lynne Rienner Publishers, 1994).
11. John Rapley, "The Ivorian Bourgeoisie," in Bruce J. Berman and Colin Leys, eds. *African Capitalists in African Development* (Boulder, CO: Lynne Rienner Publisher, 1994).

12. David Himbara, "Domestic Capitalists and the State in Kenya," in Bruce J. Berman and Colin Leys, eds. *African Capitalists in African Development* (Boulder, CO: Lynne Rienner Publishers, 1994).
13. Frederick Cooper, *Africa since 1940: The Past of the Present* (Cambridge: Cambridge University Press, 2002), p. 21.
14. For a detailed discussion of colonial administrative practices and consequences for economic development during this era in Nigeria, see I. W. Zartman (ed.), *The Political Economy of Nigeria* (New York: Praeger, 1983). About Africa, see J. Iliffe, *The Emergence of African Capitalism* (Minneapolis, MN: University of Minnesota Press, 1983); R. Austen, *African Economic History* (London: The Periplus, 1987).
15. Anthony Baah, "History of African Development Initiatives," *Africa Labor Research Network Workshop* (Johannesburg, 22 - 23 May 2003).
16. Ibid.
17. IMF, *International Financial Statistics*, 1969, p. 138.
18. Source: Benjamin Asare and Alan Wong, "An Economic Development of Two Countries: Ghana and Malaysia," *West Africa Review* (No. 5, 2004). www.africaresource.com/war/issues5/asare-wong.htm (Accessed on October 13, 2006).
19. Clive Crook, "Third World Economic Development." http://www.econlib.org/library/ENC/ThirdWorld/EconomicDevelopment. (Accessed on December 10, 2006)
20. Ibid.
21. Anthony Baah, Ibid.
22. Benjamin Asare and Alan Wong, Ibid.
23. Ibid.
24. A detailed discussion of the origins, magnitude and the corresponding effects of these crises is contained in the following volumes edited by various authors: T. Killick, ed. *The Quest for Economic Stabilization: The IMF and the Third World*, Vols. 1 and 2, (London: Heinemann, 1984); G. K. Helleiner, ed., *Africa and the International Monetary Fund* (Washington, DC: IMF, 1986);
25. See World Bank, *Accelerated Development in Sub-Saharan Africa: an Agenda for Action* (Washington, DC, 1981); World Bank, *Towards Sustained Development in Sub-Saharan Africa: A Joint Program of Action*, (Washington, DC, 1984); World Bank, *Financing Adjustment with Growth in Sub-Saharan Africa, 1986-90* (Washington, DC, 1986); World Bank, *Report on Adjustment Lending*, (Washington, DC, 1988).
26. See R. L Parker, R. Riopelle, and W. F. Steele, "Small Enterprises Adjusting to Liberalization in Five African Countries," *World Bank Discussion Paper/Africa Technical Department Series, No. 271* (World Bank, Washington DC, 1995), see also ILO (1999), p. 14.
27. For a detailed discussion of the effect of trade liberalization and deregulation on the Nigerian Dairy Industry, see John Ogbor, *Structural Adjustment and the Politics of Adjustment* (Stockholm, Sweden: Norstedt, 1994).
28. Yilmaz Akyüz, "The WTO Negotiations on Industrial Tariffs: What is it at Stake for Developing Countries?" *Third World Network* (May, 2005), pp. 7-17
29. See Africa Action, "Call for Development Policy Shift," Africa Action (June, 2005), http://www.Africapolicy.org. (Accessed on December 12, 2006).

30. J. W. Smith, *The World's Wasted Wealth 2* (Institute for Economic Democracy, 1994), pp. 127.
31. Ibid, p. 139.
32. Richard Robbins, *Global Problems and the Culture of Capitalism* (Upper Saddle River, NJ: Prentice Hall, 1999), p. 95
33. Celine Tan, "Tackling the Commodity Price Crisis Should Be WSSD's Priority," *TWN Briefings for WSSD No.14* (Third World Network, August 2002).
34. J. W. Smith, Ibid, pp. 141
35. Susan George, *A Fate Worse Than Debt* (New York: Grove Weidenfeld, 1990), pp. 143, 187, 235.
36. Matthew Lockwood, "We must breed tigers in Africa," *The Guardian* (June 24, 2005).
37. Ann-Louise Colgan, "Hazardous to Health: The World Bank and IMF in Africa," *Africa Action* (April 18, 2002).
38. The European Union, "The European Statute for SMEs," http://ec.europa.eu/enterprise/entrepreneurship/craft-priorities. (Accessed on March 15, 1996).
39. The European Union, Enterprise and Industry, "Women Entrepreneurs and Co-Entrepreneurs." http://ec.europa.eu/enterprise/entrepreneurship/craft/craft-women. (Accessed on March 15, 1996).
40. Geri Smith and Cristina Lindblad, "Mexico: Was NAFTA worth It?" *Business Week*, (December 22, 2003), BW Online version).
41. Raymond, J. Keating, "The Entrepreneurial View," (Small Business and Entrepreneurship Council), http://www.sbsc.org/content/display (Accessed on Dec. 14, 2006).
42. Robert A. Pastor, "Wanted: A Real NAFTA Partnership," *Worth* (March 10, 2004), http://www.worth.com/Editorial/Wealth-Management/Business. (Accessed on Dec. 14, 2006).
43. The discussion in this section is based on materials from ASEAN Policy Blueprint for SME Development (APBSD) 2004-2014.
   www.aseansec.org/pdf/sme_blueprint. (Accessed on February 9, 2006).
44. The phrase, "Global Digital Divide," seems to have its origin in the United States of America. Many considered Andy Grove, one of the creators of digital divide network, to have coined the term. Few others say the credit goes to Larry Irvin. According to Benton Foundation, former President Bill Clinton first used the term in the discussions of the National Information Infrastructure in 1993. Though there are controversies existing as to the origin of the term, there is a wider acceptance on the increasing gap between information have-s and Information have-nots -what we call the digital divide.
45. Source: United Nations ICT Task Force Working Group on the Enabling Environment, "Open Access for Africa. Challenges, Recommendations and Examples," 2005; United Nations ICT Task Force, "Information and Communications Technologies (ICTs) in Africa – A Status Report, Prepared by Mike Jensen, 2002; United Nations ICT Task Force, UNICTTF III/2002/12, "Background paper on ICT-for-Development in Africa," Prepared by Dr. Joseph Opaku, Sr., 2002; Dr. Nii Narku Quaynor, "Africa's Digital Rights", United Nations ICT Task Force UNICTTF III/2002/16.

46. S. Onyeiwu, "Inter-Country Variations in Digital Technology in Africa. Evidence, Determinants and Policy Implications," *United Nations University, World Institute for Development Economics Research* (July 2002).
47. United Nations ICT Task Force Working Group on the Enabling Environment, "Open Access for Africa. Challenges, Recommendations and Examples," 2005; United Nations ICT Task Force, "Information and Communications Technologies (ICTs) in Africa – A Status Report, Prepared by Mike Jensen, 2002.
48. George Clarke, Naomi Halewood, and Rob Henning "Technology and African Entrepreneurship," (World Bank/IFC, Archive Discussion-July 2006), http://rru.worldbank.or/Discussions/Topics/Topics75. (Accessed August 22, 2006).
49. A more detailed historical comparison between the experience of Sub-Saharan Africa and Southeast Asia within the context of foreign direct investment arising from contacts with multinational enterprises is contained in Deborah Bräutigam, "Local Entrepreneurship in South-east Asia and Sub-Saharan Africa: Networks and Linkages to the Global Economy," *Research Paper* (School of International Service, American University, Washington: DC, July 14, 1998).
50. Ibid.
51. Source: C. C. Edordu, Speech Delivered at the 10th Meeting of the Advisory Group on "Trade Finance Export Development in Africa." Held in Abidjan, Cote d'Ivoire (August 27, 2004. www.afreximbank.com/press (accessed on November 23, 2006).
52. Michael Porter, "Clusters and the New Economics of Competition," *Harvard Business Review* (November/December, 1998).
53. This case is developed from materials in G. Robbins, "Strategies and Policies on TNC-SME Linkages Country Case Studies: South Africa", (*UNCTAD*: Research Report, No. 70, 2006).
54. Source: Trade and Investment Journal of South Africa (No. 15, February 24, 2005).
55. The materials in this section are taken from John Ogbor, "Understanding the Global Economy and its Competitiveness as Relations of Power," *Competitiveness Review* (2003, Vol. 12, no. 2, pp. 24-56) and Michael E. Porter, *The Competitive Advantage of Nations* (New York: The Free Press, 1990).
56. This case is based on materials in Amos Safo, "Ghana: From Commodities to Technology," (*AfricaNews*, Dec. 2001); Bridges.org, "ICT-Enabled Development Case Studies Series: Geekcorps of Ghana," http://www.bridges.org/case_studies/140; Michael M. Philips, "On Ghana's Tech Frontier: Internet Start-up Flourishes" *The Wall Street Journal* (Wednesday, May 22, 2002); Linda Cashdan, "Internet Company Takes Off in Ghana," *Voice of America News* (Washington DC, Nov. 29 2001); Hiawatha Bray, "The Wiring of a Continent: Entering the Queue," (The Boston Globe, July 23, 2001); Jophus Anamuah-Mensah, "The impact upon local Development of Digital inclusion for small and Medium Business," *Connect World*. http://www.connect-world.com/Articles. (Accessed September 22, 2006); Brony Hale, "In search of profitable connection," *BBC News Online* (Monday, 9 June, 2003). http://bbc.co.uk/1/hi/business/2974418.stm (Accessed on June 24, 2006); Matthew Clarke, "Are the development policy implications of the new economy, new? All that is old is new again," *Journal of International Development* (Vol. 18, No. 5, 2006), pp.

639-648; Development Data Group, World Bank, http://www.worldbank.org/data/countrydata/ict/gha_ict.pdf; International Telecommunications Union,
 http://www.itu.int/ITU-D/ict/statistics/at_glance/basic01.pdf; See the ITU World Telecommunication Development Report: Reinventing Telecoms - World Telecommunication Indicators, 2002, pA-36; See the ITU World Telecommunication Development Report: Reinventing Telecoms - World Telecommunication Indicators, 2002, pA-66.

CHAPTER 4

1. There are a large number of studies with a focus on the cultural aspect of entrepreneurship. For these studies, the general discourse has held the opinion that the behavior of entrepreneurship is rooted in the particular cultural context under which it is practiced. Hence, notions such as the "American entrepreneur" or "the African entrepreneur" are used to denote particular cultural attributes among certain entrepreneur located in these "cultures". Other studies have also focused on ethnicity and race as a constructs to explain the behavioral pattern of entrepreneurs across cultures.
2. Clifford Geertz, *The Interpretation of Cultures* (New York, Basic Books, 1973), p. 89.
3. See R. K. Mitchell, B. Smith, K.W. Seawright and E.A. Morse. "Cross-Cultural Cognitions and the Venture Creation Decision," *Academy of Management Journal* (Vol. 43, No. 5, 2000), pp.974-993; P. B. Robinson, D.V. Stimpson, J.C. Huefner, and H.K. Hunt, "An Attitude Approach to the Prediction of Entrepreneurship," *Entrepreneurship Theory and Practice* (Summer, 1991), pp. 13-31.
4. See L. W. Busenitz and C. M. Lau, "A Cross-Cultural Cognitive Model of New Venture Creation." *Entrepreneurship, Theory and Practice* (summer, 1996), pp. 25-39; J. C. Hayton, G. George, and S.A. Zahra, "National Culture and Entrepreneurship: A Review of Behavioral Research." *Entrepreneurship Theory and Practice* (Summer 2002) pp. 33-52; K. Hindle and M. Lansdowne, "Brave Spirits on New Paths: Toward a Globally Relevant Paradigm of Indigenous Entrepreneurship Research," *Journal of Small Business and Entrepreneurship* (Vol. 18, No. 2, Spring 2005), pp.131-141; A. L. Carsrud and R.W. Johnson, "Entrepreneurship: A Social Psychological Perspective," *Entrepreneurship Theory and Regional Development: An International Journal* (Vol. 1, No. 1, 1989), pp. 21-31.
5. Ibid.
6. L. W. Busenitz and C. M. Lau, Ibid; J. C. Hayton, G. George, and S.A. Zahra, Ibid. K. Hindle and M. Lansdowne, Ibid.
7. Geert Hofstede, "Motivation, Leadership and Organizations: Do American theories apply abroad?" *Organizational Dynamics* (Vol. 9, No. 1, 1980), pp. 42-63; Geert Hofstede, "McGregor in Southeast Asia?" In D. Sinha and H. S. R. Kao eds. *Social Values and Development: Asian Perspectives* (New Delhi, India: Sage Publication, 1988).
8. Geert Hofstede, *Culture's Consequences - International Differences in Work-Related Values*, (Beverly Hills, Sage Publications, 1980); G. Hofstede, "Organizing for Cultural Diversity," *European Management Journal* (Vol. 7, No. 4, 1989); pp. 390-397;

G. Hofstede, *Cultures and Organizations: Software of the Mind* (London: McGraw-Hill, 1993).

9. See S. Shane, "The Effect of National Culture on the Choice between Licensing and Direct Foreign Investment," *Strategic Management Journal* (Vol. 15, 1994), pp. 627-642; S. Shane and S. Venkataraman, "The Promise of Entrepreneurship as a Field of Research," *The Academy of Management Review* (Vol. 25, No. 1, 2000) pp. 217-26; J. Tan, "Culture, Nation, and Entrepreneurial Strategic Orientations: Implications for an Emerging Economy," *Entrepreneurship, Theory and Practice* (Summer 2002), pp. 95-111; J. H. Tiessen, "Individualism, collectivism, and entrepreneurship: a framework for international comparative research," *Journal of Business Venturing* (Vol. 12, 1987) pp. 367-384.

10. See F. Erdem, "A cultural approach toward risk taking propensity and tolerance for ambiguity of entrepreneurs," *Akdeniz IIBF Dergisi* (Vol. 2, 2001), pp. 43-61; P. N. Khandwalla, "Pioneering innovative management: An Indian Excellence," *Organization Studies* (Vol. 6, 1985), pp. 161-83; G. S. Saffold, "Culture traits, strength and organizational performance: Moving beyond strong culture", *Academy of Management Review* (Vol. 13, 1988), pp. 546-68; S. Shane, "Cultural influences on national rates of innovation," *Journal of Business Venturing* (Vol. 8, 1993), pp. 59-73.

11. Ibid.

12. See Kabeya Tshikuku, *Culture, Entrepreneurship and Development in Africa*, Paper presented at the International Conference on the Cultural Approach to Development in Africa (Dakar, Senegal: 10-14 December 2001).

13. See Max Weber, *The Protestant Ethic and the Spirit of Capitalism* (New York, Charles Scribner's Sons, 1930).

14. Kabeya Tshikuku, Ibid.

15. Geert Hofstede, 1980. *Ibid*; G. Hofstede, "Organizing for Cultural Diversity," *European Management Journal* (Vol. 7, 4, 1989), pp. 390-397; G. Hofstede, 1993, Ibid; G. Hofstede, 1980, *Ibid*; G. Hofstede, 1989, Ibid.

16. See A. Mamman and K. Saffu, "Short-termism, control, quick-fix and bottom line," *Journal of Managerial Psychology* (Vol. 13, 1998), pp. 291-308.

17. See Geert Hofstede and Geert Hofstede, Ibid.

18. P. Marris, Ibid; P. Marris and A. Somerset, Ibid; K. Madsen, *African Entrepreneurs: Pioneers of Development International Finance Corporation - Discussion Paper No. 9*. (Washington D. C. The World Bank, 1990); J. Herskovits and M. Haritz, *Economic Transition in Africa* (London, Routledge & Kegan, 1964).

19. Kenneth, R. Gray, William Cooley and Jesse Lutabingwa (1996) "Small Scale Manufacturing in Kenya: Characteristics, problems and sources of finance." http://sbaer.uca.edu/research. (Accessed on April 21, 2005).

20. See Retha Scheepers, "How innovative are South Africa's firms," In Marlese von Broembsen, Eric Wood, and Mike Herrington, eds. *Global Entrepreneurship Monitor: South African Report 2005* (UCT Center for Innovation and Entrepreneurship, University of Cape Town, South Africa, 2006), p. 33.

21. P. Davidsson, "Culture, structure and regional levels of entrepreneurship," *Entrepreneurship and Regional Development* (Vol. 7, 1995), 41-62; A. Etzioni, "Entrepreneurship, adaptation and legitimation: A macro-Behavioural Perspective," *Journal of Economic Behaviour and Organization* (Vol. 8, 1987), pp. 175-189.

22. E. W. Nafzinger, Ibid; Paul Kennedy, "Political Barriers to African Capitalism," *The Journal of Modern African Studies* (Vol. 32, N. 2, 1994), pp. 191-213; R. Rajan and L. Zingales, 1999 *Politics, Law and Financial Development* (Chicago, IL: University of Chicago Working Paper, 1999).
http://gsblgz.uchicago.edu (Accessed on January 24, 2005).
23. A. Etzioni, Ibid.
24. P. Davidsson, P. & J. Wiklund, "Values, beliefs and regional variations in new firm formation rates," *Journal of Economic Psychology* (Vol. 18, 1997), pp. 179-199; P. Davidsson, "Culture, structure and regional levels of entrepreneurship," *Entrepreneurship and Regional Development* (Vol. 7, 1995), pp. 41-62; D. Huisman, "Entrepreneurship: Economic and cultural influences on the entrepreneurial climate," *European Research* (Vol. 13, No. 4, 1985), pp. 10-17.
25. For a discussion of the cultural values of achievement/ascription and universalism/particularism and how they relate to gendered management practices, see Fons Trompenaars, *Riding the Waves of Culture: Understanding Diversity in Global Business* (New York: Irwin, 1994; See also Geert Hofstede, et al. *Masculinity and Femininity: The taboo dimension of national cultures* (Thousand Oaks, CA: Sage, 1998).
26. This section is based primarily on studies by R. Daumont, F Le Gall and F. Leroux, "Banking in Sub-Saharan Africa: What went wrong?" *IMF Working Paper* (IMF, Washington, DC, 2004), pp.1-47; Machiko Nissanke and Ernest Aryeetey, *Financial Integration and Development: Liberalization and Reform in Sub-Saharan Africa* (London and New York: Routledge, 1998); Ernest Aryeetey and Charles Udry, "The characteristics of informal financial markets in Sub-Saharan Africa," *Journal of African Economies* (Vol. 6, No. 1, 1997), pp. 161-203; Ernest Aryeetey, A. Baah-Nuakoh, T. Duggleby, H. Hettige and W. F. Steel, "The Supply and Demand for Finance among SMEs in Ghana," *World Bank Discussion Paper 251, Africa Technical Department* (World Bank: Washington, DC, 1994); Machiko Nissanke, "Financing enterprise development in Sub-Saharan Africa," *Cambridge Journal of Economics* (Vol. 25, 2001), pp. 343-367. For a detailed discussion of the nature of the credit industry in developing countries, including the roles of credit bureaus, credit regulations, and credit protection, etc., see The World Bank, Doing Business in 2004, pp. 55–80.
27. Some of the available literature on the financial sector in Sub-Saharan Africa include: Hassanali Mehran et al, Financial Sector Development in Sub-Saharan Africa Countries," *IMF Occasional Paper No. 196* (Washington DC: International Monetary Fund, 1998); Jo Ann Paulson, "Some Unresolved Issues in African Financial Reforms," in *African Finance: Research and Reform*, ed. by Lawrence White (San Francisco, CA: ICS Press, 1993); Martin Brownbridge, "The Causes of Financial Distress in Local Banks in Africa and Implications for Prudential Policy," *UNCTAD Discussion Papers No.* 132 (Geneva: United Nations Conference on Trade and Development, 1998).
28. The discussion here derives from the work of Machiko Nissanke and Ernest Aryeetey, Ibid; Machiko Nissanke, *Ibid*; B. Levy, "Obstacles to developing indigenous small and medium enterprises: an empirical assessment, *World Bank Economic Review* (Vol. 7, No. 1, 1993), pp. 65-83.
29. World Bank, "Adjustment in Africa: Reforms, Results and the Road Ahead," *World Bank Policy Research Paper* (World Bank, Washington DC, 1994).

30. See R. Daumont, F. Le Gall and F. Leroux, *Ibid*; John Ogbor, *The Implementation of Structural Adjustment Programmes and the Politics of Adjustment: The Case of the Nigerian Foreign Exchange System* (Stockholm, Sweden: Norstedt Tryckeri AB, 1994); Frederic Mishkin, "Understanding Financial Crises: A Developing Country Perspective," *NBER Working Paper No. 5600* (Cambridge, MA: National Bureau of Economic Research, 1996).
31. G. Caprio, I. Atiyas, and J. Hanson (eds.), *Financial Reforms: Theory and Experience* (Cambridge: Cambridge University Press, 1994); R. Daumont, F. Le Gall and F. Leroux, "Banking in Sub-Saharan Africa: What Went Wrong?" Ibid.
32. See A. Soyibo, "Financial Linkage and Development in Sub-Saharan Africa: the Role of Formal Financial Institutions in Nigeria," *ODI Working Paper 88* (London: Overseas Development Institute, 1996); Brownbridge and Harvey, Ibid.
33. See Gerald Caprio and Daniela Klingebiel, "Bank Insolvencies: Cross-Country Experience," *Policy Research Working Paper No. 1620* (Washington, DC: World Bank, 1996); Gerald Caprio and Daniela Klingebiel, "Bank Insolvency: Bad Luck, Bad Policy, or Bad Banking?" in *Annual World Bank Conference on Development Economics 1996*, ed. by Michael Bruno and Boris Pleskovic (Washington, DC: World Bank, 1997).
34. World Bank, "Adjustment in Africa: Reforms, Results and the Road Ahead," *World Bank Policy Research Report,* (Washington, DC: World Bank, 1994); World Bank, *Implementation Completion Report, Kenya, Financial Sector Technical Assistance Projects and Financial Parastatals Technical Assistance Project, Report No. 14246* (Washington, DC: World Bank, 1995).
35. W. F. Steel and L. Weber, "Small Enterprises under Adjustment in Ghana," *World Bank Technical Paper No. 138, Industry and Finance Series,* (Washington, DC: The World Bank, 1991); B. Levy, "Obstacles to developing indigenous small and medium enterprises: an empirical assessment," *World Bank Economic Review* (Vol. 7, No. 1, 1993), pp. 65-83; Machiko Nissanke, *Ibid*; Aryeetey et al., 1994, *Ibid*; X. Blanc, 1997, Ibid.
36. For comparison with other developing regions and emerging economies, see C. Bell, "Interaction between institutional and informal credit agencies in rural India," *World Bank Economic Review* (Vol. 4, no. 3, 1997), pp. 297-327; P. B. Ghate, "Informal credit markets in Asian developing countries," *Asian Development Review* (Vol. 6, No. 1, 1988), pp. 64-85.
37. The discussion in this section is based on A. Graziosi "Microfinance in Africa: Rethinking the role of the actors."
http://www.microfinancegateway.com (Accessed on June 27, 2007); Joanna Ledgerwood, *Microfinance Handbook: an Institutional and Financial Perspective* (Washington DC: The World Bank, 2000), p. 1.
38. Robert Peck Christen, Richard Rosenberg & Veena Jayadeva. *Financial institutions with a double-bottom line: implications for the future of microfinance*, (CGAP Occasional Paper, July 2004), pp. 2-3.
39. See Hernando de Doto, *The Other Path: The Economic Answer to Terrorism* (New York: Basic Books, 1989); Douglas R. Snow and Terry F. Buss, "Development and the Role of Microcredit," *Policy Studies Journal* (Vol. 29, No. 2, 2001), pp. 296-307; Nitin Bhatt and Shui-Yan Tang, "Delivering Microfinance in Developing Countries:

Controversies and Policy Perspectives," *Policy Studies Journal* (Vol. 29, No. 2, 2001), pp. 319-333; Simeen Mahmud, "Actually how Empowering is Microcredit?" *Development and Change* (Vol. 34, No. 4, 2003), pp. 577-605; Gary M. Waller and Warner Woodworth, "Microcredit and Third World Development Policy," *Policy Studies Journal* (Vol. 29, No. 2, 2001), pp. 265-266.

40. Marguerite Robinson, *The Microfinance Revolution: Sustainable Finance for the Poor* (Washington, DC: World Bank, 2001), pp. 199-215.
41. Brigit Helms, *Access for All: Building Inclusive Financial Systems* (Washington, DC: The World Bank, 2006).
42. A. Land, "Structured Public-Private Sector Dialogue: The Experience from Botswana," *ECDPM* (Discussion Paper 37, ECDPM, Maastricht, May, 2002).
43. F. Mantero and N. Santos, Ibid.
44. A. Land, Ibid.
45. See John. Daniels, Lee H. Radebaugh and Daniel P. Sullivan, *International Business* (Upper Saddle River, NJ: Prentice Hall, 2007), p. 99.
46. For a detailed discussion of the meaning of political risk, see Mark Fitzpatrick, "The Definition and Assessment of Political Risk in International Business: A Review of the Literature," *Academy of Management Review*, (Vol. 8, No. 2, 1983), pp. 249-254.
47. The materials under this section are based on the work of Professor Kabeya Tshikuku, *Culture, Entrepreneurship and Development in Africa*, Paper presented at the International Conference on the Cultural Approach to Development in Africa (Dakar, Senegal: 10-14 December 2001).
48. See Kabeya Tshikuku, Ibid.
49. A.M. Yahie, "Poverty Reduction in sub-Saharan Africa: Is there a Role for the Private Sector?" *Economic Research Papers, No. 52, 2000* (The African Development Bank, Abidjan, Côte d'Ivoire).
50. Papa Demba Thiam, "The Role of the Private Sector in Advancing Democratic Development: What works, what doesn't and why?" World Bank Institute, (Washington, DC: World Bank, November 2007), http://www1.worldbank.org/devoutreach/article.asp?id=448 (Accessed on Dec., 2007)
51. Ibid.
52. The materials for this discussion are based on the work of Kabeya Tshikuku, Ibid.
53. World Bank/IFC, *Doing Business in 2005: Removing Obstacles to Growth* (Washington, DC: World Bank/IFC, 2004).
54. A. Brunetti, G. Kisunko, and B. Weder, "Institutional Obstacles to Doing Business: Region-by-Region Results from a Worldwide Survey of the Private Sector," *World Bank Policy Research Working Paper 1759* (Washington, DC: The World Bank, 1997).
55. Brett D. Schaefer, "How Economic Freedom Is Central to Development in Sub-Saharan Africa," Ibid.
56. John Ifediora, "The Effects of Bureaucratic Corruption on Economic Development: The Case of Sub-Saharan Africa," Published in the Nigerian Village Square, April 2005, www.nigeriavillagesquare1.com/Articles/Guest/2005/04/ (Accessed on August 23, 2007).

57. Ibid.
58. E. Harch, "Accumulators and Democrats: Challenging State Corruption in Africa," *Journal of Modern African Studies* (Vol. 31, No. 1, 1993), pp. 31-48.
59. John Ifediora, Ibid.
60. S. T. Akindele, "A Critical Analysis of Corruption and its Problems in Nigeria," *Anthropologist* (Vol. 7, No. 1, 2005), p. 11.
61. Ibid, p. 11
62. See D. J. Gould, *Bureaucratic Corruption and Underdevelopment in the Third World: The Case of Zaïre* (New York: Pergamon Press, 1980); J. S. Nye, "Corruption and Political Development: A Cost-Benefit Analysis," *American Political Science Review* (Vol. 6, No. 2, 1967), pp. 417-427.
63. J. D. Wolfensohn, "The true impact of corruption," *Crossroads* (Vol. 5, No. 9, October 1999), pp. 15-16, cited in S. T. Akindele, Ibid.
64. Source: Anti-Corruption Resource Centre, "Causes and Consequences of Corruption," http://www.u4.no/helpdesk/faqs1.cfm#22 (Accessed on April 3, 2008).
65. Reinikka and J. Svensson, "Confronting Competition Investment Response and Constraints in Uganda," *World Bank, Development Research Group* (Washington, DC, 1999).
66. World Bank/IBDR, *World Development Report 2006: Equity and Development* (Washington, DC: The World Bank/Oxford University Press, 2005).
67. N. Limão and A. J. Venables, "Infrastructure, Geographical Distance, Transport Costs and Trade," *World Bank Economic Review* (Vol. 15, No. 3, 2001), pp. 451–79.
68. World Bank World Bank, *Transport Sector Overview*, http://www.worldbank.org/transport/whytsimp.htm (Accessed on April 23, 2008)
69. S. Radelet and J. Sachs, "Shipping Costs, Manufactured Exports and Economic Growth" (1998). http://www.earthinstitute.columbia.edu/about/director/pubs/shipcost.pdf (Accessed on July 13, 2007); N. Limão and A. J. Venables, "Infrastructure, Geographical Distance, Transport Costs and Trade," *World Bank Economic Review* (Vol. 15, No. 3, 2001), pp. 451–79.
70. D. Dollar, X. Clark and A. Micco, "Maritime Transport Costs and Port Efficiency," World Bank Policy Research Working Paper Series No. 2781, (The World Bank, Washington, DC, 2000); ECA, *Economic Report on Africa 2004: Unlocking Africa's Trade Potential* (Economic Commission for Africa, Addis Ababa, September 2004).
71. Wim Naudé and Marianne Matthee (2007), *High transport costs pose a significant barrier to development in Africa* (Helsinki, Finland, United Nations University, 2007).
72. FAO *Bioenergy*. (13-16 April, 2005. www.fao.org/docrep/meeting /009/j4313e.htm. (Accessed on July 5, 2006).
73. World Bank/UMACIS, "Competing in the Global Economy: An Investment Climate Assessment for Uganda," *Investment Climate Assessment* (The World Bank and Uganda Manufacturers Association Consultancy and Information Services, Washington D.C., 2004).
74. J. Saghir, *Energy and poverty: myths, links and policy issues*. Energy Working Notes. Energy and Mining Sector Board (Washington, DC: The World Bank, The World Bank Group, 2005).

75. S. McGrath & K. King, *Education and Training for the Informal Sector* (London, UK: Overseas Development Administration, 1995); D. W. Kent and P. S. D. Mushi, *The education and training of artisans for the informal sector in Tanzania* (London, UK: Overseas Development Administration, 1995); L. A. Honny, "Reshaping vocational training: challenges for Ghanaian development," *Paper presented at the conference Enterprise in Africa: Between poverty and growth* (Centre for African Studies, Univ. of Edinburgh, 1998); B. W. Kerre, "The role and potential of technical and vocational education in formal education systems in Africa," *Paper presented at the conference "Enterprise in Africa: Between poverty and growth* (Centre for African Studies, Univ. of Edinburgh, 1998).

76. See R. Palmer, *Beyond the Basics: Post-basic Education and Training and Poverty Reduction in Ghana*, Post-Basic Education and Training Working Paper Series No 4, (Centre of African Studies, University of Edinburgh, 2005); Hans C. Haan, "Training for Work in the Informal Sector: new evidence from Eastern and Southern Africa," *Occasional Papers* (International Training Centre of the ILO, Turin, 2002).

77. Alan Gelb, et al. *Can Africa claim the 21st century?* (Washington, D.C.: World Bank, 2000), p. 136; Commission for Africa, *Our Common Interest* (Report of the Commission for Africa, London, 2005).

78. See John Ogbor, *The Implementation of Structural Adjustment and the Politics of Adjustment* (Stockholm, Sweden: Norstedt Tryckeri AB, 1994).

79. For a discussion of the importance of the informal sector in the labor market and employment opportunity within the context of developing countries see: J. B. Rosser and E. Ahmed, "Income Inequality and the Informal Economy in Transition Economies," *Journal of Comparative Economics* (Vol. 28, 2000), pp. 156-171; K. Hart, "Informal Income Opportunities and Urban Employment in Ghana," *The Journal of Modern African Studies* (Vol. 11, No. 1, 1973), pp. 61-89.

80. S. V. Sethuraman, *The Urban Informal Sector in Developing Countries: Employment, Poverty and Environment* (ILO: Geneva, 1981).

81. For a comprehensive understanding of the concept of the informal sector, see Edgar, L. Feige, "Defining and Estimating Underground and Informal Economies: The New Institutional Economics Approach," *World Development* (Vol. 18, No. 7, 1990), pp. 989-1002; H. C. Haan and N. Serriere, *Training for work in the informal sector: Fresh evidence from West and Central Africa* (ILO, Turin, Italy, 2002); See also P. B. Simon, "Informal Responses to Crisis of Urban Employment: An Investigation into the Structure and Relevance of Small-Scale Informal Retailing in Kaduna in Nigeria," *Regional Studies* (Vol. 32, No. 6,), pp. 547-557; E. C. Okorji, "Women and Rural Development: Strategies for Sustaining Women's Contribution in Rural Households of Anambra State, Nigeria," Working Paper 66, *Women and International Development* (June, 1988); Jacques Charmes, "African Women in Food Processing: A Contribution of the National Economy," *Paper Prepared for the International Development Research Centre* (IDRC, December, 2000).

82. E. Ghersi, "The Informal Economy in Latin America," *Cato Journal* (Vol. 17, No. 1, Spring/Summer, 1997), pp. 99-108.

83. See Friedrich Schneider, "The Shadow Economies of Western Europe," *Journal of the Institute of Economic Affairs* (Vol. 17, No. 3, 1997), pp. 42-8; Friedrich Schneider, "Measuring the Size and Development of the Shadow Economy. Can the Causes be

found and the Obstacles be Overcome?" In Brandstaetter Hermann, and Werner Guth, eds., *Essays on Economic Psychology* (Berlin: Springer Publishing Co., 1994), pp. 193-212; Alejandro Portes and Richard Schauffler, "Competing Perspectives on the Latin America Informal Sector," *Population and Development Review* (Vol. 19, No. 1, March 1993), pp. 33-60. See also Jacques Charmes, "Street Vendors: A major component of the Informal Sector, but one of the Most Difficult to Capture and Measure," *Paper prepared for the United Nations Statistics Division on Umbrella Gender Statistics Programme and presented at the Delhi Group Meeting on Informal Sector Statistics* (Ankara, April, 1998).

84. Edgar L Feige, Ibid, 991; See also: De Soto, *The Other Path* (New York: Harper & Row, 1989); Alejandro Portes and Richard Schauffler, Ibid, pp. 33-60.
85. H. C. Haan and N. Serriere, Ibid.
86. See Enrique Ghersi, "The Informal Economy in Latin America," *Cato Journal,* (Vol. 17, No. 1, Spring/Summer, 1997), pp. 99-108.
87. See K. Hart, "Informal Income Opportunities and Urban Employment in Ghana," *The Journal of Modern African Studies* (Vol. 11, No. 1, 1973), pp. 61-89; For a detailed discussion of the arguments for and against the informal sector, see C. A. Rakowski, "Convergence and Divergence in the Informal Sector Debate; A Focus on Latin America," *World Development* (Vol. 22, 1994), pp. 501-516 and Geoffrey Nwaka, "The Urban Informal Sector in Nigeria," *Global Urban Development Magazine* (Vol. 1, No. 1, May 2005).
88. For a discussion of the consequences of SAP on the informal sector, see Steele, W F. and L. M. Webster, "Small Enterprises under Adjustment in Ghana," *World Bank Technical Paper, Industry and Finance Series* (No. 138, Washington, DC, 1991).
89. For a discussion of how the informal sector comes into being as a result of bureaucratic regulation, see for example Lagos, Ricardo, "Barriers to Legality and their Costs for the Informal Sector," In J. Tokman, ed., *Beyond Regulation: the informal economy in Latin America (*Boulder, Co.: Lynne Rienner, 1992); See also the World Bank and the IFC, *Business 2004: Understanding Regulation* (World Bank and Oxford University Press: Washington, DC, 2004).
90. A discussion of the arguments against the informal sector can be found in C. A. Rakowski, Ibid. pp. 501-516 and Geoffrey Nwaka, Ibid.
91. ILO, "Facts on Child Labour", www.ilo.orgchildlabour. See also International Labor Organization, *A Future without Child Labor* (Geneva, Switzerland, 2002).
92. John Ogbor, Ibid.
93. See K. Hart, Ibid. pp. 61-89.
94. H. C. Haan and N. Serriere, Ibid.
95. Source: This case was written by Professor John Ogbor with the following additional sources: International Crisis Group, "Fuelling the Niger Delta Crisis", *Africa Report,* No. 118, 28 September 2006, http://www.crisisgroup.org/home/index.cfm; Stephanie Hanson, "MEND: The Niger Delta's Umbrella Militant Group," *Council on Foreign Relations, March* 22, 2007, http://www.cfr.org/publication/12920/mend.html; Michael Olugbode, "Niger Delta crisis: FG plans new taxes," *Thisday*, Wednesday, August 29, 2007; BBC, "Nigerian leaders stole $380bn," Friday, 20 October 2006,

http://news.bbc.co.uk/2/hi/africa/6069230.stm); Dorina Bekoe, "Strategies for Peace in the Niger Delta", *United States Institute of Peace*, December 2005, http://www.usip.org/pubs/usipeace_briefings/2005/1219_nigerdelta.html; Ibang Isine, "The Niger Delta as albatross," *The Punch* (Friday, May 30, 2008); Harris-okon Emmanuel, "When SPDC empowered indigenes of host communities," *Daily Independent* (Tuesday, August 12, 2008): Ibanga Isine, "Shell awarded $1bn contracts to Nigerian contractors," *Punch* (Tuesday, August 12, 2008); Ahamefula Ogbu, "95% Shell Staff are Nigerians," *Thisday* (Tuesday, August 12, 2008); *The Guardian*, July 31, 2008.

CHAPTER 5

1. Source: Basil Enwegbara, "The African Entrepreneur," *The Tech Online* (Vol. 122, No. 54, Nov. 8, 2002).
2. D. Harrison and C. Friedrich, *A combined method questionnaire /case study survey of 7 informal sector business types* (Harare: Friedrich Naumann Stiftung, 1994).
3. M. Harper and T. T. Soon, Small enterprises in developing countries: Case studies and conclusions, (London: Intermediate Technology, 1979).
4. John O. Okpara and Pamela Wynn, "Determinants of small business growth constraints in a sub-Saharan African economy," *SAM Advanced Management Journal* (March 22, 2007); Charles Tushabomwe-Kazooba, "Causes of Small Business failure in Uganda: A Case Study from Bushenyi and Mbarara Towns," *African Studies Quarterly* (Vol. 8, No. 4, 2006). Accessed on January 21, 2008 from: http://web.africa.ufl.edu]asq/v8/v8i4a3.htm; M. L. Harris and S. G. Gibson, "Determining the common problems of early growth of small businesses in Eastern North Carolina," *SAM Advanced Management Journal* (Vol. 71, No. 2, 2006), pp. 39-45; S. Eeden, S. Viviers and D. Venter, "An exploratory study of selected problems encountered by small businesses in a South African context," *Journal of African Business* (Vol. 5, No. 1, 2004), pp. 45-72; M. Goedhuys and L. Sleuwaegen, "Entrepreneurship and growth of Entrepreneurial firms in Cote d'Ivoire," *The Journal of Development Studies* (Vol. 36, No. 3, 20000), pp. 123-138; C. Mambula, "Perceptions of SME growth constraints in Nigeria," *Journal of Small Business Management* (Vol. 40, No. 1, 2002), pp. 58-65.
5. Moses, N. Kiggundu, "Entrepreneurs and entrepreneurship in Africa: What is known and what needs to be done," *Journal of Developmental Entrepreneurship* (Vol. 7, No. 3, 2002), pp. 239-258.
6. Ibid.
7. John O. Okpara and Pamela Wynn, Ibid.
8. Ibid.
9. Per Trulsson, *Strategies of entrepreneurship: Understanding industrial entrepreneurship and structural change in Northern Tanzania*, (Linkoping, Sweden, 1997).
10. Charles Tushabomwe-Kazooba, "Causes of Small Business Failure in Uganda: A Case Study from Bushenyi and Mbarara Town," *African Studies Quarterly, The Online Journal of African studies* (Vol. 8, No. 4 Summer 2006) (http://web.africa.ufl.edu/asq/v8i4a3).

11. Charles Tushabomwe-Kazooba, Ibid.
12. H. Wilier, "Industrial Entrepreneurship and the Human Factor: The Succession Problem in Nigeria," *Paper presented at the International Institute for Human Factor Development Conference* (Harare, Zimbabwe, 1996).
13. France Maphosa, "Leadership Succession: A Recalcitrant Problem in the indigenization of African economies, *Zambezia* (Vol. xxvi, No. ii, 1999), pp. 169-182.
14. Moribo Sam and Peter Kilby, "Succession-related mortality among small firms in Nigeria," *Journal of Entrepreneurship* (Vol. 7, No. 2), 133-151.
15. See H. Wilier, Ibid and Moses Kiggundu, 2002, Ibid.
16. See A. W. Obi, "Prospects for small-scale industries development under a structural adjustment programme: The case of Nigeria," *Africa Development* (Vol. 16, No. ii, 1991), pp. 33-53; B. E. Osaze, "International small enterprise review: Development programmes in Africa", *Management Forum* (Vol. 10, 1984), pp. 169-174; A. E. B. Perrigo, "Delegation and succession in the small firm," in Gorb, P. et. al. eds., *Small Business Perspectives* (London: Armstrong Publishing, 1981).
17. F. Maphosa, Ibid.
18. Ibid.
19. H. Wilier, Ibid.
20. F. Maphosa, Ibid.
21. Tom Forrest, *The Advance of African Capitalism: The Growth of Nigerian Private Enterprise* (London, Edinburgh University, 1994).
22. Volker Wild, *Profit Not for Profit Sake: History and Business Culture of African Entrepreneurs in Zimbabwe* (Harare: Baobab Books, 1997).
23. Ibid.
24. F. Maphosa, Ibid.
25. Monibo A. Sam, "Exploring the link between customary inheritance practice and discontinuity of indigenous enterprises in Nigeria," *Canadian Journal of African Studies* (Vol. 32, No. 2, 1998), pp. 349-377.
26. Volker Wild, Ibid.
27. J. Charmes, "Micro-enterprises in West Africa", In K. King & S. McGrath (Eds.), *Enterprise in Africa* (London: Intermediate Technology, 1999), pp. 71-82; D. C. Mead and C. Liedholm, "The dynamics of micro and small enterprises in developing countries," *World Development* (Vol. 26, No. 1, 1998), pp. 61-74.
28. Samuel K. Buame, *Entrepreneurship, a contextual perspective: discourses and praxis of entrepreneurial activities within the institutional context of Ghana* (Lund, Sweden: Lund University Press, 1996).
29. Moses N. Kiggundu, *Managing Organizations in developing countries: An operational and strategic approach* (West Hartford, CT: Kumerian Press, 1989); Monibo A. Sam, Ibid; Samuel Buame, Ibid.
30. Per Trulsson, 2002, Ibid.
31. Charles Tushabomwe-Kazooba, Ibid.
32. Geert Hofstede, *Culture's Consequences - International Differences in Work-Related Values* (Beverly Hills, CA: Sage Publications, 1980); Geert Hofstede, "Organizing for Cultural Diversity," *European Management Journal* (Vol. 7, No. 4, 1989), pp. 390-397; Geert Hofstede, *Cultures and Organizations: Software of the Mind* (London: McGraw-Hill, 1993); John O. Ogbor, *Organizational change within a cultural context: The*

interpretation of cross-culturally transferred organizational practices (Lund Sweden: Lund University Press, 1990). John. O. Ogbor and Johnnie Williams), "The Cross-Cultural Transfer of Management Practices: The Case for Creative Synthesis," Cross Cultural Management: An International *Journal (Vol. 10, No. 2, 2003)*, pp. 3-23; Terence Jackson, *Management and change in Africa: A cross-cultural perspective* (London: Routledge, 2004); Terence Jackson, *Managers' perceptions of organization in Africa: Evidence from South Africa and Zimbabwe* (Unpublished Manuscript, 2005); A. M. Jaeger, "The applicability of Western management techniques in developing countries: a cultural perspective," In A. M. Jaeger and R. N. Kanungo, (eds.), *Management in Developing Countries* (London: Routledge, 1990), pp. 131-145; Moses N. Kiggundu, "The challenges of management development in Sub-Saharan Africa," *Journal of Management Development* (Vol. 10, No. 6, 1991), pp. 32-47.

33. L. Mbigi, *Ubuntu: The African Dream in Management* (Randburg, South Africa: Knowledge Resources, 1997); L. Mbigi and J. Maree, *Ubuntu: The Spirit of African Transformational Management* (Randburg, South Africa: Knowledge Resources, 1995).

34. C. O. Nzelibe, "The evolution of African management thought," *International Studies of Management and Organization* (Vol. 16, No. 2, 1986), pp. 6-16.

35. John O. Ogbor, Ibid; Ogbor and Williams, *Ibid*; P. Blunt and M. L. Jones, *Managing Organizations in Africa* (Berlin: Walter de Gruyter, 1992); Kiggundu, 1989, Ibid.

36. This issue is extensively discussed in Terence Jackson, *Managers' perceptions of organization in Africa: Evidence from South Africa and Zimbabwe* (Unpublished manuscript, 2005); A. M. Jaeger, "The applicability of Western management techniques in developing countries: a cultural perspective," In A. M. Jaeger and R. N. Kanungo, Ibid; Moses N. Kiggundu, "The challenges of management development in Sub-Saharan Africa," *Journal of Management Development* (Vol. 10, No. 6, 1991), pp. 32-47.

37. J. P. O. de Sardan, "A moral economy of corruption in Africa?" *The Journal of Modern African Studies* (Vol. 37, No. 1, 1999), pp. 25-52.

38. Benjamin Ehigie and Olanrewaju Otukoya, "Antecedents of organization citizenship behavior in a government-owned enterprise in Nigeria," *European Journal of Organizational Psychology* (Vol. 14, No. 4, 2005), pp. 389-399.

39. Martin C. Euwema, "Leadership styles and group organizational citizenship behavior across cultures," *Journal of Organizational Behavior* (Vol. 28, No. 4 Oct. 2007), pp. 1035-1057.

40. John O. Ogbor, Ibid.

41. Terence Jackson, *Management and Change in Africa: A Cross-Cultural Perspective* (London: Routledge, 2004).

42. Moses Kiggundu, 1989, Ibid.

43. See F. Abudu, "Work attitudes of Africans, with special reference to Nigeria," *International Studies of Management and Organization* (Vol. 16, No. 2, 1986), pp. 17-36; Terence Jackson, Ibid.

44. Terence Jackson, *Management and Change in Africa*, Ibid.

45. Charles Tushabomwe-Kazooba, Ibid.

46. P. Langseth and R. Stapenhurst, "The Role of the National Integrity System in Fighting Corruption," *EDI Working Paper 400/144* (Washington D. C: The World Bank, 1997); R. A. LeVine, *Dreams and deeds: Achievement motivation in Nigeria*

(Chicago: University of Chicago Press, 1966); J. Pope, *Confronting Corruption: the Elements of a National Integrity System* (London: Transparent International, 2001).

47. Source: Audri Lanford and Jim Lanford, "Scam: The Nigerian Advance Fee Scheme," ScamBusters.org, www.scambusters.org/NigeriaFee.html (Accessed on March 24, 2008).
48. Akin Fadahunsi and Peter Rosa, "Entrepreneurship and Illegality Insights from the Nigerian cross-border Trade," *Journal of Business Venturing* (Vol. 17, No. 5, September 2002), pp. 397-429.
49. See Moses Kiggundu, 2002, Ibid.
50. For example, the World Bank has a web site for developing a sense of social responsibility, sound ethical judgment and corporate governance for entrepreneurs at www.gcgf.org.
51. Organization for Economic Cooperation and Development, *OECD, Principles of Corporate Governance* (Paris, France: 2004), p. 13. www.oecd.org/dataoecd/32/18/31557724.pdf (Accessed on May, 2, 2008).
52. Andrei Schleifer and Rober Vishny, "A Survey of Corporate Governance," *Journal of Finance* (Vol. 52, No. 2, 1997), pp. 737-783.
53. James D. Wolfensohn, *Financial Times* (21 June 1999).
54. Charles C. Okeahalam and Oludele A. Akinboade, "A review of Corporate Governance in Africa: Literature, Issues and Challenges," Paper prepared for the Global Corporate Governance Forum, 15, June 2003. www.gcgf.org/ifcext/cgf.nsf/attachments. (Accessed on April 25, 2008).
55. Ibid.
56. Ayisi Makatiani (2006), "Navigating the risks and opportunities of investing in African SMEs," www.amsco.org/resource/article. (Accessed on May 4, 2008).
57. Ibid.
58. Charles C. Okeahalam and Oludele A. Akinboade, Ibid.
59. Ibid.
60. Ibid.
61. Source: www.evancarmichael.com/African-Accounts, "Stock Market Development in Sub-Saharan Africa: Trends and Characteristics." (Accessed on April 23, 2008).
62. Source: Finance MapsofWorld.com, "Nigerian Stock Exchange," www.finance.mapsofworld.com/stock-market/nigeria-stock-exchange.html. (Accessed on May 6, 2008).
63. Per Trulsson, Ibid.
64 Charles Tushabomwe-Kazooba, Ibid.
65. Ibid.
66. Louise van Scheers and Simon Radipere, "Why are so many managers not managing?" *African Journal of Business Management* (July 2007), pp. 085-091.
67. William Cooley, Kenneth R. Gray and Jesse Lutabinga, "Small-scale manufacturing in Kenya," *Journal of Small Business Management* (Vol. 35, 1997), pp. 241-264.
68. Per Trulsson, "Constraints of growth-oriented enterprises in the southern and eastern African region," *Journal of Developmental Entrepreneurship* (Vol. 7, No. 3, 2002).
69. Charles Tushabomwe-Kazooba, Ibid.

70. Basil Enwegbara, "The African Entrepreneur," *The Tech Online* (Vol. 122, No. 54, Nov 8, 2002).
71. Enyinna Chuta, "Upgrading the managerial process of small entrepreneurs in West Africa," *Public Administration and Development* (Vol. 3, No. 3, 2006), pp 275-283.
72. Okpara and Wynn, Ibid.
73. Per Trulsson, (p. 167), Ibid.
74. This case is compiled from the following sources: Norimitsu Onishi, "Step Aside, L. A. and Bombay, for Nollywood," *New York Times* (September 16, 2002]; Steven Gray, "Nollywood Films' Popularity Rising Among Emigres," *Washington Post* (Saturday, November 8, 2003) p. E01; Neely Tucker, "Nollywood, in a starring Role," *Washington Post* (Saturday, February 5, 2005) p. C04; Tayo Aderinokun, "The Economics of Nigerian Film, Art and Business," *AfricaUpdate* (Vol. XI, No. 2, Spring, 2004); Nigerian Tribune, "Nollywood: Impossible to Ignore," http://www.tribune.com.ng/12102006. (Accessed on November 20, 2006); The Economist, "Nollywood dreams," July 27, 2006; Wikipedia, "Cinema of Nigeria," http://en.wikipedia.or/wiki/Nollywood. (Accessed October 21, 2006); iCommons, "A message from Nollywood: 'Just do it,'" http://iCommon.org/2006/05/12/. (Accessed on November 10, 2006); *The African Journal*, www.africacncl.org/AfricaJournal/A_Journal_Fall_2006 (Accessed on October 15, 2006); Research Nigeria, "Research Study of the Nigerian Movie Industry," Friday March 31, 2006. www.researchnigeria.blog.com. (Accessed on December 14, 2006); www.capefilcommission.co.za/newsarchive. (Accessed on November 14, 2006).

CHAPTER 6

1. A. A. Thompson, A. J. Strickland and J.E. Gamble, *Crafting and Executing Strategy: the Quest for Competitive Advantage* (New York, NY: McGraw-Hill, 2005), p. 3.
2. A. A. Thompson, A. J. Strickland and J.E. Gamble, *Crafting and Executing Strategy: the Quest for Competitive Advantage* (New York, NY: McGraw-Hill, 2007), p. 35.
3. For a detailed discussion, see Michael E. Porter, *Competitive Strategy: techniques for Analyzing Industries and Competitors* (New York, NY: Free Press, 1980) and A. A. Thompson, A.J Strickland and J.E Gamble, *Crafting and Executing Strategy: the Quest for Competitive Advantage* (New York, NY: McGraw-Hill, 2007).
4. K. J. Hatten and M. L. Hatten, "Strategic Groups, Asymmetrical Mobility Barriers, and Contestability," *Strategic Management Journal* (July-August 1987), p. 329.
5. The idea of strategic group has been discussed extensively in the literature of strategic management. For more recent and informed discussion, see for example, K. Cool and D. Schendel, "Performance Differences among Strategic Group Members," *Strategic Management Journal* (Vol. 14, 1988), pp. 207-233; and C. S. Galbraith, G. B. Merrill, and G. Morgan, "Bilateral Strategic Groups," *Strategic Management Journal* (Vol. 15, 1994) pp, 613-626.
6. C. W. L. Hill and G. R. Jones, *Strategic Management Theory: An Integrated Approach* (Boston, MA: Houghton Mifflin, 2001), p. 137.
7. Ibid.
8. See A. A. Thompson, A. J. Strickland and J. E. Gamble, Ibid. p. 7

9. See J. B. Barney, "Firm Resources and Sustained Competitive Advantage," *Journal of Management* (Vol. 17, 1991), pp. 99-120.
10. See Michael Porter, *Competitive Advantage*, see Chapter 7.
11. Source: *Daily Sunday*, March 5, 2005.
12. C. W. L. Hill and G. R. Jones, *Strategic Management Theory: An Integrated Approach* (Boston, MA: Houghton Mifflin, 2001), p. 138.
13. The discussion in this section is adapted from A. A. Thompson, A. J. Strickland and J.E. Gamble, (2005), pp. 34-36.
14. A. A. Thompson, J. E. Gamble and A. J. Strickland, *Strategy: Winning in the Marketplace* (New York: McGraw-Hill, 2006), p. 26.
15. Source: *BusinessDay*, "UAC of Nigeria Plc." www.businessdayonline.com/economic-watch/market-outlook/8792.html
    (Accessed on May 23, 2008).
16. Ibid.
17. The discussion in this section is taken from A. A. Thompson, A. J. Strickland and John E. Gamble, *Crafting and Executing Strategy: The Quest for Competitive Advantage* (New York, NY: McGraw-Hill, 2008), p. 13.
18. The case is prepared with materials from: *Newswatch* June 29, 1998;
    AfricanLoft, "Aliko Dangote – Nigerian Numero Uno Entrepreneur Speaks", http://www.africaloft.com/aliko-dangote;
    www.dangote-sugar.com/corporateinfo.php; Oluwatoyosi Ogunseye, "Dangote: A brand in transit," The Daily Sun, (Thursday, June, 3, 2004); Businessinafrica.net, "Dangote: Leading businessman and billionaire,"
     www.businessinafrica.net/leadership/988609.html.

CHAPTER 7

1. Derek F. Abell, *Defining the Business: The Starting Point of Strategic Planning* (Englewood Cliffs, N.J.: Prentice-Hall, 1980)
2. Ibid, p. 17.
3. Ibid. p. 17.
4. T. L. Wheelen and J. D. Hunger, *Strategic Management and Business Policy* (Upper Saddle River, New Jersey, Prentice Hall, 2002), p. 11.
5. Ibid.
6. George Steiner, *Strategic Planning: What Every Manager Must Know* (New York: the Free Press, 1979), p. 160.
7. Derek F. Abell, Ibid, p. 17.
8. Quoted in T. Zimmerer and N. Scarborough, *Essentials of Entrepreneurship and Small Business Management*, 3r ed. (Upper Saddle River, NJ: Prentice Hall, 2002), p. 72.
9. The discussion in this section is taken from Charles N. Toftoy & Joydeep Chatterjee, *The Value of Mission Statements for Small Businesses* (School of Business & Public Management, George Washington University, 2002).
10. J. Pearce and F. David, "Corporate Mission Statements: the Bottom Line, "Academy of Management Executive (Vol.1, No. 2, May, 1987), p. 110
11. Fred R. David, *Ibid*, p. 96.

12. For a detailed discussion, see C. Hills and G. Jones, *Strategic Management Theory: an Integrated Approach* (Boston, MA: Houghton Mifflin Company)
13. Ibid.
14. Source: *Tell* Magazine, No. 16, January 7, 2002, p. 26.

CHAPTER 8

1. For a detailed discussion of the evolution, growth and consolidation of the Nigerian banking industry, see Erastus Akingbola, "Consolidating the gains of financial sector reforms," *Nigerian Tribune* (Tue., 18th Dec. 2007).
2. See Charles W. L. Hill and Gareth R. Jones, *Strategic Management: An Integrated Approach* (Boston, MA: Houghton Mifflin, 2001) p. 80 and A.A. Thompson and A.J. Strickland, *Strategic Management: Concepts and Cases* (New York, NY: McGraw-Hill, 2003).
3. Thompson and Strickland, Ibid. pp. 73-102.
4. M. E. Porter, *Competitive Strategy* (New York, NY: Free Press, 1980).
5. A.A. Thompson and A.J. Strickland, Ibid. p. 78.
6. This summary of the forces driving competitive intensity is taken from M.E Porter, *Competitive Strategy: Techniques for Analyzing Industries and Competitors* (New York, NY: Free Press, 1980) pp. 7-29.
7. See Thomas Wheelen and David Hunger, *Strategic Management and Business Policy* (Upper Saddle River, NJ: Prentice Hall. 2002), pp.60-61.
8. See also Michael Porter, Ibid. pp. 17-21.
9. Michael Porter, *Competitive Strategy*.
10. See A. A. Thompson and A. J. Strickland, Ibid.
11. The discussion on industry driving-forces is taken from Arthur Thompson, A. J. Strickland and John E. Gamble, *Crafting and Executing Strategy: The Quest for Competitive Advantage* (New York, NY: McGraw-Hill, 2008), pp. 74-81
12. Ibid.
13. Ibid.
14. See T. Wheelen and D. Hunger, Ibid.
15. W. Jack Dunkan, Peter M. Ginter, and Linda E. Swayne," Competitive Advantage and Internal Organizational Assessment," *Academy of Management Executive*, Vol. 12, No. 3, 1998, pp. 6-16.
16. Michael Porter, *Competitive Advantage*.
17. For a detailed discussion, see Elaine Mosakowski, "Strategy Making under Causal Ambiguity: Conceptual Issues and Empirical Evidence," *Organization Science*, July-August 1997, pp. 414-423.
18. The materials presented here are adapted from Thompson and Strickland, p. 117-121.
19. Source: Reproduced by permission from the author: Uche Nworah. The Nigerian Fast-food Brands,
http://www.collegehandouts.com/files/Nigerian_Fast_Food_Brands.pdf
20. M. Awodun, An Assessment of Competitive Strategies and Growth Patterns of New Enterprises in Nigeria Using the Developing Economy Model. *Lagos Organization*

Review. (Volume 1, No. 1, June – August 2005); N. Duru (2003), "Hunger Busters Restaurant Invests N100m in Eateries", http://www.thisdayonline.com/archive/2003/11/26/20031126bus15.html;

A. P. Herbig, *Handbook of Cross – Cultural Marketing.* (New York: The International Business Press, 1998); M. Stewart, M (1996) *Keep the Right Customers.* (London: McGraw-Hill); St Elmo's slices its way into Africa http://www.restaurants.co.za/fullStory.asp?NewsId=68;
http://www.nigeriabusinessinfo.com/nigeria-fastfood220303.htm;
http://www.cia.gov/cia/publications/factbook/geos/ni.html;
http://www.worldfactsandfigures.com/countries/nigeria.php;
http://www.nafdacnigeria.org/flabterms.

CHAPTER 9

1. Arthur A. Thompson, A. J. Strickland, and John E. Gamble, *Crafting & Executing Strategy: The Quest for Competitive Advantage,* (New York, NY: McGraw-Hill, 2008), p. 7.
2. Michael E. Porter, *Competitive Advantage* (New York: Free Press, 1985)
3. Michael E. Porter, "What is Strategy", *Harvard Business Review* (74, No. 6 November-December 1996), pp. 61-71.
4. See N. Brodsky, (1998), "Size Matters," *INC.* (September 1998, pp. 31-32).
5. See Michael E. Porter, *Competitive Advantage* (New York, NY: Free Press, 1985), chaps. 3, 4, 5, 17, 14, and 15.
6. James Eze, "My most embarrassing moment? Day my former boss tongue-lashed me before my wife". *Daily Sun* Wednesday March 09, 2005.
7. E. A. Murray and J. F. Mahon, "Strategic Alliances: Gateway to the new Europe?" *Long Range Planning* (August 1993), p. 103.
8. See R. P. Lynch, (1989), *The Practical Guide to Joint Ventures and Corporate Alliances* (New York: John Wiley), p. 89-90.
9. For a comprehensive discussion of cooperative strategies, see R. M. Kanter, "Collaborative Advantage: the Art of Alliances, *Harvard Business Review* (July-August, 1994), pp. 96-108.
10. A. A. Thompson, A. J. Strickland and J. E. Gamble, J. E. *Crafting and Executing Strategy: The Quest for Competitive Advantage* (New York, NY: McGraw-Hill, 2005) p. 168.
11. Daily Sun, "Federal Palace Hotel rebrands, doubles profit." http://www.sunewsonline.com/webpages/news/businessnews/2004 (Retrieved Tuesday May 03, 2005).
12. T. L. Wheelen and J. D. Hunger, *Strategic Management and Business Policy* (Upper Saddle River, NJ: Prentice Hall, 2002), p. 124-125.
13. Daily Sun, "There is money in courier business one you can develop a good network." http://www.sunewsonline.com/webpages/features/enterprise/2004 (Accessed on March 14, 2005).
14. Michael E. Porter, *Competitive Advantage* (New York, NY: Free Press, 1985).

15. Source: John Ogbor, *Cases in Entrepreneurship and Strategic Management* (Houston, TX: Crown Education Books, 2007).

CHAPTER 10

1. Dictionary of Marketing Terms (2nd ed.), Edited by Peter D. Bennett (Chicago: American Marketing Association, 1995).
2. Philip Kotler, *Marketing Management* (Upper Saddle River, NJ: Prentice Hall, 2003) p. 9.
3. Jay Conrad Levinson, *Guerrilla Marketing: Secrets for Making Big Profits from Your Small Business* (Boston: Houghton Mifflin Company, 1984).
4. Jay Conrad Levinson and Seth Goodin, *The Guerrilla Marketing Handbook*, (Boston: Houghton Mifflin Company, 1994).
5. See T. W. Zimmerer and N. M. Scarborough, *Essentials of Entrepreneurship and Small Business Management* (Upper Saddle River, NJ: Prentice Hall, 2002), Chapter six.
6. Philip Kotler, *Marketing Management* (Upper Saddle River, NJ: Prentice Hall), 2003), p. 129.
7. Roberta Maynard, "New Directions in Marketing," *Nations Business* (July 1995), p. 26.
8. R. D Hisrich, M. P. Peters and D. A. Shepherd, *Entrepreneurship* (Boston, MA: McGraw-Hill, 2005), p. 222.
9. Ibid.
10. The discussion here is based on Philip Kotler's discussion of the market research process. Philip Kotler, *Marketing Management* (Upper Saddle River, NJ: Prentice Hall), 2003), pp. 279-303.
11. T. W. Zimmerer and N. M, *Scarborough, Essentials of Entrepreneurship and* Small *Business Management* (Upper Saddle River, NJ: Prentice Hall), p. 193.
12. Jay Conrad Levinson and Michael W. McLaughlin, *Guerrilla Marketing for Consultants* (Hoboken, NJ: John Wiley and Sons, 2005).
13. The discussion here is based on Zimmerer and Scarborough, Ibid, p. 184, and Philip Kotler, Ibid, chapter six.
14. Philip Kotler, Ibid, p. 308.
15. The discussion on positioning in this section is taken from: http://en.wikipedia.org/wiki/Positioning_(marketing); http://www.quickmba.com/marketing/ries-trout/positioning/
16. Bernd H. Schmitt, *Customer Experience Management* (New York, NY: Wiley, 2003), pp. 97-101.
17. See Steven Peterson and Peter Jaret, *Business Plans Kit* (New York, NY: Wiley, 2001).
18. Philip Kotler, Ibid.
19. Steven Peterson and Peter Jaret, *Business Plans Kit* (New York, NY: Wiley, 2001).
20. Festus Bamiyo, "Micro Scale Palm Kernel Crushing," *The Guardian*, (Saturday, May 29, 2004).
21. Source: John Ogbor, *Cases in Entrepreneurship and Strategic Management* (Houston, TX: Crown Education Books, 2007).

CHAPTER 11

1. France Maphosa, "Leadership Succession: A Recalcitrant Problem in the indigenization of African economies, *Zambezia* (Vol. xxvi, No. ii, 1999), pp. 169-182; Moribo Sam and Peter Kilby, "Succession-related mortality among small firms in Nigeria," *Journal of Entrepreneurship* (Vol. 7, No. 2), 133-151.
2. *The Guardian* (of Nigeria), Wednesday, May 1, 2002, p. 19.
3. From A. A. Thompson, A. J. Strickland, and J. E. Gamble, *Crafting and Executing Strategy: The Quest for Competitive Advantage* (Boston, MA: McGraw-Hill, 2005), p. 368.
4. Corporate culture is a subject worth studying on its own. For readers interested in the subject, read John Ogbor, Critical Theory and the hegemony of corporate culture, *Journal of Organizational Change Management* (Vol. 14, No. 6, October 2001), pp. 590-608.
5. Boris Yavitz, "Human Resources in Strategic Planning," in Eli Ginzberg (ed.), *Executive Talent: Developing and Keeping the Best People* (New York: Wiley, 1988), p. 34.
6. Gary Dessler, *Human Resource Management* (Upper Saddle River, New Jersey: Prentice Hall, 2003), p. 227
7. Nichole L. Torres, "Hire Learning: You can't Just Throw New Hires into the Workplace and Hope for the Best," *Entrepreneur* (November 2004), pp. 100-101.
8. Ibid, p. 104.
9. For a detailed discussion of this topic, see John R. Kimberly, Robert Miles, et al. *The Organizational Life Cycle* (San Francisco: Jossey-Bass, 1980).
10. See the classic work of Alfred D. Chandler, *Strategy and Structure* (Cambridge, MA: MIT Press, 1962).
11. See also Alfred D. Chandler, "Origins of the Organization Chart," *Harvard Business Review* (March-April 1988), pp. 156-157.
12. See J. Greenberg and Robert A. Baron, *Organization Behavior* (Upper Saddle River, NJ: Prentice Hall), pp. 218-219, and John Schermerhorn, *Management* (New York, NY: John Wiley and Sons), pp. 218-219.
13. *Entrepreneur* (November 2004) p. 98.
14. John R. Schermerhorn, *Management* 9ed. (Hoboken, NJ: John Wiley and Sons, 2008), p. 245.
15. Source: John Ogbor, *Cases in Entrepreneurship and Strategic Management* (Houston, TX: Crown Education Books, 2007).

CHAPTER 12

1. Charles Tushabomwe-Kazooba, "Causes of Small Business Failure in Uganda: A Case Study from Bushenyi and Mbarara Town," *African Studies Quarterly, The Online Journal of African studies* (Volume 8, No. 4 Summer 2006) (http://web.africa.ufl.edu/asq/v8i4a3).
2. See E. Aryeete and C. Udry, "The characteristics of informal financial markets in Sub-Saharan Africa, *Journal of African Economies* (Vol. 6, No. 1, 1997), Pp. 161-203; M. S. D. Bagachwa, "Financial integration and Development in Sub-Saharan Africa: A

Study of Informal Finance in Tanzania," Working Paper 79 (London: Overseas Development Institute, 1995).
3. Source, John O. Ogbor, *Cases in Entrepreneurship and Strategic Management,* (Houston, TX: Crown Educational Books, 2007).

CHAPTER 13

1. See Kathleen Allen, *Entrepreneurship for Dummies* (New York, NY: Wiley Publishing Inc., 2001), p. 207.
2. For an excellent discussion of the limited partnership, see W. K. Daugherty, "The Limited Partnership - A *Financing Vehicle," Journal of Small Business Management* (Vol. 18, No. 2, April, 1980), pp. 55-60.
3. H. N. Broom, J. G. Longenecker and C. W. Moore, *Small Business Management*, (Dallas, USA: South-Western Publishing Co., 1988) p. 172.
4. See James W. Carland and Larry White, "Valuing the Small Business," *Journal of Small Business Management* (Vol.18, No. 4, October, 1980), pp. 40-48.
5. See H. N. Broom, J. G. Longenecker, and C. W. Moore, Ibid. p. 67.
6. Ibid, p. 84.
7. Joan Gillman, *Business Plans That Work* (New York, NY: Adams Media Corporation, 2001), p. 30.
8. For details of the Sunshine Foundation, see *Newswatch*, May 17, 2004, p. 44.
9. Source: John O. Ogbor, *Cases in Entrepreneurship and Strategic Management* (Houston, TX: Crown Education Books, 2007).

CHAPTER 14

1. "Can Business Be Ethical" The Economist, April 22, 2000 (Business Special: "Doing well by doing good").
2. Peter John Opio, "Towards an Ethics of Business in Africa: Integrity and Competitiveness," http://www.fiuc.org/iaup/esap/publications/BusinessEthics.pdf (Accessed on March 21, 2008).
3. *The Guardian,* Business Section, October 16, 2004.
4. *KPMG, LLP,* 2000 Organizational Integrity Survey: A Summary, published by the KPMG Integrity Management Services Unit. See http://www.us.kpmg.com
5. A. T. Lawrence, J. Weber, and J. E. Post, *Business and Society: Stakeholders, Ethics, Public Policy* (Boston, MA: McGraw-Hill, 2005), p. 82.
6. Sarah Roberts, Justin Keble and David Brown. "The Business Case for Corporate Citizenship" (a study of the World Economic Forum) www.weforum.org/corporatecitizenship (Accessed on November 25, 2005), p. 3.
7. See Melissa S. Baucus and David A. Baucus, *Academy of Management Journal* 40 (1997), p. 129.
8. For an overview, see Francis Joseph Aguilar, *Managing Corporate Ethics* (New York: Oxford, 2003).
9. Steven N. Brenner and Earl A. Mollander, "Is the Ethics of Business Changing?" *Harvard Business Review* Vol. 55 (January-February 1977), p. 57.

10. For a discussion of business ethics, see John Ogbor, "Globalization Pedagogy from an Ethics Perspective," *Proceedings of the American Society of Business and Behavioral Sciences*, (Vol. 9, No. 1, 2002), pp. 33-42.
11. John R. Boatright, *Ethics and the Conduct of Business* (Upper Saddle River, NJ, 2003), p. 5.
12. See *The Guardian*, May 27, 2004, p. 88.
13. R. C. Solomon, *Ethics and Excellence* (Oxford: Oxford University Press, 1992), p. 47.
14. Arthur Thompson, A. Strickland and John Gamble, *Crafting and Executing Strategy: The Quest for Competitive Advantage* (Boston, MA: McGraw-Hill, 2008), pp. 436-437.
15. Ibid. p. 437.
16. *Marketing Definitions: A Glossary of Marketing Terms* (Chicago: American Marketing Association, 1960), p. 15.
17. See John B. Hinge, "Critics Call Cuts in Package Size Deceptive Move," *Wall Street Journal* 5 February 1991, B1.
18. See Tom. L. Beauchamp, "Manipulative Advertising," in *Ethical Theory and Business*, 4th ed., Tom L. Beauchamp and Norman E. Bowie, eds. (Upper Saddle River, NJ: Prentice Hall, 1993), pp. 475-83.
19. Ikenna Emewu, "Actually, Aba shoemakers send their products to Dubai and back with foreign labels," *Daily Sun*, Saturday, May 15, 2004.
20. William M. Pride and O. C. Ferrell, *Marketing: Basic Concepts and Decisions*, 10th ed. (Boston: Houghton Mifflin, 1997), p. 40.
21. See W. S. Sachs, "Corporate Advertising: Ends, Means, P0072oblems," *Public Relations Journal* (Vol. 37, November 1981), pp. 14-17.
22. See Bonnie Liebman, "Nouveau Junk Food: Consumers Swallow the Back-to-Nature Bunk," *Business and Society Review* (Vol. 51, Fall 1984), pp. 47-51.
23. John R. Boatright, Ibid. p. 290.
24. See Ed Timmerman and Brad Reid, "The Doctrine of Invited Misuse: A Societal Response to Marketing Promotion," *Journal of Macro Marketing* (Vol. 4 Fall 1984), pp. 40-80.
25. Archie B. Carroll and Ann K. Buchholtz, *Business and Society: Ethics and Stakeholder Management* (Mason, Ohio: South-Western, 2006).
26. Richard Edwards, *Rights at Work* (Washington, DC: The Brookings Institution, 1993), pp. 25-26.
27. Patricia H. Werhane, *Persons, Rights and Corporations* (Englewood Cliffs, NJ: Prentice Hall, 1985), p. 110.
28. David W. Ewing, *Freedom Inside the Organization: Bringing Civil Liberties to the Workplace* (New York: McGraw-Hill, 1977), p11.
29. David W. Ewing, *Justice on the Job: Resolving Grievances in the Nonunion Workplace* (Boston: Harvard Business School Press, 1989), p. 324.
30. See Charles W. L. Hill and R. Jones Gareth, *Strategic Management Theory: an Integrated Approach* (Boston, MA: Houghton Mifflin Company, 2001), p. 67.
31. Archie B. Carroll and Ann K. Buchholtz, Ibid, p. 494-495.
32. For a good review of the concept of whistleblowing, see Marcia P. Micelli and Janet P. Near, *Blowing the Whistle* (Lexington, MA: Lexington Book, 1992); see also Marcia

P. Micelli and Janet P. Near, "Whistleblowing: Reaping the Benefits," *Academy of Management Executive* (Vol. No. 8), pp. 65-72.

33. Ana Radelat, "When Blowing the Whistle Ruins Your Life," *Public Citizens* (September/October 1991), pp. 16-20.
34. Kenneth D. Walters, "Your Employees' Right to Blow the Whistle," *Harvard Business Review* (July-August 1975), pp. 161-162.
35. Michael Brody, "Listen to Your Whistle-Blower," *Fortune* (November 24, 1986), pp. 77-78
36. A. Vincente Montes, "Philosophical Considerations of a Top Manager", in G. Enderle *et al.* (eds.), *People in Corporation: Ethical Responsibility and Corporate Effectiveness* (Dordrecht: Kluwer Academic Publishers, 1990), p. 244.
37. The following account is based largely on the discussion and analysis provided by Ronald. R. Sims and Johannes Brinkmann, "Enron Ethics (Or: Culture Matters More than Codes)," *Journal of Business Ethics* (Vol. 45, No. 3, July 2003), pp. 244-252. Although the case deals with a large global corporation, the ethical issues involved are as relevant to the management of small businesses.
38. Keith Davis and Robert L. Blomstrom, *Business and Society: Environment and Responsibility, 3rd* ed. (New York: McGraw-Hill, 1975), p. 39.
39. Archie B. Carroll, "A Three-Dimensional Conceptual Model of Corporate Social Performance," *Academy of Management* Review (Vol. 4, No. 4, 1979), pp. 497-295).
40. Archie B. Carroll and Ann K. Buchholtz, Ibid, pp. 37-39
42. Ibid., p. 44
42. Ibid., p. 44
43. This definition is taken from R. Edward Freeman, *Strategic Management: a Stakeholder Approach* (Boston: Pitman, 1984), p. 25.
44. Mark Starik, "Is the Environment an Organizational Stakeholder? Naturally!" *International Association for Business and Society (IABS) 1993 Proceedings*, pp. 466-471.
45. Source: Eguono Odjeba, "Foreign exchange Malpractices: Why Perpetrators Cheat on Regulatory Authorities," *Vanguard* (Sunday, February 08, 2004).

INDEX

A

Aba Shoes, 566
Abell, Derek, 293
Abiodun Student Impressions (Nig.), 387
Academy of Management Journal, 554
Ade, Jab, 238
Adenuga, Michael, 67, 74-82
Adeyemi, Oluwole, 374
Adeyumo, Moses, 238
Aderinokun, Tayo, 244
African Growth and Opportunity Act (AGOA), 565
African Independent Television, 27, 453
African Rainbow Minerals, 42
African Village (see Ujamaa), 95
Ajayi and Osunde Consulting (Nig.) Ltd., 516
Ajayi, Wole, 516
Akande, Funmilayo, 51
Akara, 348
Akinboade, Oludele, 226
Akindele, S. T. 170
Akyüz, Yilmaz, 105
Amoral manager, 569
Ampah, Yaa Linda, 138
An Extra Hand Ltd., 464-466
Apple Computers Inc., 11, 38
Aoko, Anietie, 49
Arthur Andersen, 559
Arusha Declaration, 95
Assets, 492, and
    account receivable, 493
    cash, 493, current, 493
    fixed, 494
    inventories, 493
    investment portfolio, 493
    prepaid expenses, 494
ASEAN, 112
Authoritarian manager, 220
Authority relations, 220
Avis-Rent-a-Car, 288
Ayodele Slimmer's Club, 11, 309
Ayodele, Isaac, 11, 309

B

Baah, Anthony, 98
Babalola, Funke, 338
Babangida, Ibrahim, 108, 196
Balance sheet, 487, 504
Balogun, Ade, 404
Balogun, Ola, 238
Bamiyo, John, 448
Bank Directors Association of Nigeria, 593
Bankruptcy, 475-477
BATA, 180
BBC, 138
Bell, Alexandra Graham, 316
Blomstrom, Robert, 583
Board of advisors, 445
Boatright, John, 557
Bodibeng Technologies Incubator, 4
Bokassa, Jean-Bedel, 101
Brautigam, Deborah, 124
Breed Valley Municipality, 290
Bribery, see corruption, 169-171
    business/economic consequences, 170
    causes of, 170
    entrepreneurial development, 169
Brodsky, N, 369
Buame, Samuel, 68, 70, 218
Buchholtz, Ann, 576, 584
Budgeting, 503
Bureaucracy, 43, and bureaucratic
    bribery and corruption, 169
    colonial legacy
    culture, 471
Business
    definition of, 284, 288
Business environment, 251
Business ethics, 223, 555
    economic relations, 558
    questionable practices, 560
Business plan, 599
    business description, 611
    executive summary, 608-609
    financial plan, 624-626
    historical documentation, 626
    legal issues, 620
    industry analysis, 612-614
Business plan contd.
    market analysis, 612-614

marketing plan, 616-618
meaning, 600
objectives and goals, 609-610
organization plan, 618-619
outline of, 603
purpose, 600-602
sources of finance, 623
strategic plan, 614
supporting documents, 627
vision and mission of, 609
BusinessDay, 13, 36, 252, 366, 370
Business ideas, 44
   experience as source of, 45
BusyInternet Café, 3, 4, 5, 139
Buyer's leverage, 326

C

Capabilities see resource, 254
Cape Winelands, 289
Capital and financing, 511
Carnegie, Andrew, 6, 56
Carroll, Archie, 576, 583, 584
Cash flow, 510
Cash flow statement, 488
Center of gravity, 379
Central Bank of Nigeria
   Foreign exchange, 593
   Vision of, 289
Champion, The, 252
Chandaria Group, 90
Character and financing, 508
Chatterjee, Joydeep, 296
Chellarams, 90
Chuta, Enyinna, 231
Civil wars, 100
Clarke, Matthew, 138
Classique Magazine, 542
Codes of ethics, 553, 580
Colgan, Ann-Louise, 108
Collateral, 509
Colonial era:
   dependent colonial capitalism, 92
   economic development policies, 89
   economic environment of 89-93
   entrepreneurial development, 90-93
   pattern of economic development, 91
Colonialism, 90
Community volunteering, 429
Compaq, 6, 12, 14, 45, 375
Competence and financing, 512
Competitive advantage, 249, 257, 287

Competitive scope, 366
Coopers, Frederick, 92
Core competence, 257, 379
Corporate level strategies, 261-262
Corporate social responsibility
Corruption, 552
   (see bribery and corruption)
Creative destruction, 6
Credit environment, 154
Crisis of autonomy, 468
Crisis of leadership, 469
Crook, Clive, 98
Cultural environment
   entrepreneurship of, 145-153
Cultural value systems, 147 and
   entrepreneurial environment, 151
Culture
   achievement-oriented, 151
   ascriptive-oriented, 151, 220
   bureaucratic regulation, of
   collectivism, 220
   company, of a (organization culture)
   definition of, 146
   entrepreneurship and 146
   power distance, 220
   imitation of, 150, 213
   individualistic, 221
   innovation and 149
   legal system, 151
   long-term orientation, 149
   particularistic-orientation, 152, 220
   risk aversion and, 150
   short-term orientation, 149
   uncertainty avoidance, 148
   universalistic-orientation, 152, 220
Customer(s)
   groups, 286
   market segmentation, 409
   mission statement and, 293
   needs, 286
   surveys and questionnaires, 404

D

DAAL Communications Nigeria Ltd., 7, 27, 37, 40, 42, 285, 288
Dada, Idi Amin, 101, 168
Daily Sun, 47, 252, 254, 292, 295
Dana Air, 365
Dangote, Aliko, 40, 275, 441, 450
Dangote Group, 40, 71, 261, 275, 441, 451
Dantata, Sanusi, 46

Darwinian doctrine, 129
Davis, Mark, 3, 139
Davis, Keith, 583
de Tocqueville, Alexis, 10
Deceptive marketing practices, 565
Defensive tactics, 374
Dell Computers, 6, 7, 14, 375
Dell, Michael, 6, 7
Demographics, 49
Depreciation, 494, and
    expenses, 490
Digital divide, 176
Direct marketing, 427
Disraeli, Benjamin, 65
Distinctive competence, 254, 287, 332
Distribution channel, 375
Diversification, 451
Divisional structure, 468-470
Divisionalization, 470
Dokpesi, Raymond, 7, 27, 37, 40, 42, 456
Drucker, Peter, 3, 8, 11, 12, 20, 29
Due process, 570-571
Durban Auto Clusters, 125

E

East African Community, 116-117
Ebi, Ernest, 593
Econet, 36
ECOWAS, 11-116
Economic development
    colonial era in, 89-91
    post colonial era in, 94
Economic stagnation, 100
Economies of scale, 324
Edordu, C.C., 125
El Rufai, Mallam, 456
Elastic demand, 420
Employee constitutionalism, 571
Employee rights, 569
Enron, 559, 582
Entrepreneur
    characteristics, 35
    confidence, 40
    creative destruction, 6
    definition, 6
    functions, 5
    independence, 54
    Indian, 89-92
    Lebanese, 90
    motives, 51-66
    part-time, 54
    profile, 35
    strategist, as, 21
    tenacity, 38
    types of, 40
Entrepreneurial activities, 10
Entrepreneurial competence, 210
Entrepreneurial drawbacks, 66
Entrepreneurial education, 177
Entrepreneurial firms and ventures
    differences between small business,
    14, 21
Entrepreneurial rewards, 52-66
Entrepreneurial risks
Entrepreneurship, and
    changes in demographics, 49
    changes in industry structure, 51
    conditions of, 8
    corporate downsizing, 9
    definition, 6
    discourses of, 68
    factors driving, 8
    global economy, 8
    importance of in developing countries,
    21
    innovation, 5, 10
    management, and, 209
    management style, 455
    nature of, 3
    sources of ideas, 44
    value creation, 6
Entry strategies, 361
Environmental uncertainty, 314
Enwegbara, Basil, 209
Esusu, 158, 182
Ethical decision making, 571-575
Ethical issues in
    Employer-employee relations, 569
    marketing, 564
    packaging and labeling, 564
    production and delivery, 568
Ethical dilemma, 559
Ethical principles, 553
Ethical rationalizations, 559
Ethics, and
    code of, 556
    definition of, 553
    entrepreneur as person, 562
    entrepreneurial firm of, 562
    external environment, 563
    management ethics, 569
    managerial, 557

meaning of, 553
  personal values, 556
  sources of, 554
Ethics training, 575
Ettah, Larry, 13
Existing business, 529, and
  reasons for buying, 529
  reasons for selling, 530
  valuation of, 530-531
Exit plan, 474
Expropriation, 169

F

Factor endowment, 129
Fair treatment, 570
Fatalistic worldview, 148, 212
Financial constraints, 67
Financial environment, 154-163
Financial Institutions Training Centre, 542
Financial Management
  cash flow problems, 231
  challenges in SSA, 230
  cultural practices of, 230
  inadequate record keeping, 231
  ownership attitude, 230
Financial Standard, 252
Financial Times, 13, 370
First Atlantic Bank (Nig.), 290, 300
First Bank of Nigeria, 255, 289, 299
First movers, 257, 372
Five-forces model, 321-323
Flanking maneuver, 373
Folu, Ayeni, 350
Foreign exchange malpractices, 593
Formal financial sector, 154, 157
  enterprise financing, 157
Forrest, Tom, 46, 215
Franchise contract, 534
Franchisee, 534
Franchiser, 534
Franchising, 534
  advantages of, 535
  agreement, 371
  evaluation of, 538-540
  limitation of 537
Free publicity, 429
Friedman, Milton, 560
Frontal assault, 373
Functional level strategies
Functional structure, 467

G

Gambles, John E., 12, 251, 271, 326, 563
Gendered entrepreneurial practices, 152
George, Susan, 107
Gates, Bill, 11, 67
Geekcorps, 137
George, Steiner, 293
Ghana Enterprise Development-
  Commission, 16
Ghana investment Promotion Center
  130
Ghana National Board of -
  Small Scale Industry, 16
Ghana Statistical Services, 16
Ghersi, Enrique, 183
Giannini, Amadeo. P., 40, 59, 550
Gilman, Joan, 537
Globacom, 74-82
Global economy, 109-130
  competitive advantage, 128-29
  entrepreneurship, 109-130
  factor endowment, 129
  nation state, and 128
  regional trade blocs, 109
Globalization, 8, 109, 454
Goals, 303
Goodman, Jon, 37
Grameen Bank, 161
Gross profit, 490
Gross revenue, 489
Growth
  factors affecting, 447
  industries, 316
  managing, 218, 462
  strategies, 447
  within an industry, 449-450
Guardian The, 252, 254, 293, 365, 422
Guerrilla marketing, 396, 397, 399
Guerrilla warfare, 367, 374

H

Halfon, Ian, 358
Harper, M., 210
Herbig, Paul, 350
Hewlett, Bill, 304
Hewlett-Packard, 6, 14, 140, i62
High uncertainty avoidance, 148
Hisrich, Robert, D, 5, 42, 43
Hofstede, Geert, 147, 148, 149
Horizontal integration, 450

Human Resource Management, 219,
    443, 458
    policy, 458
    process, 458
Hunger Busters, 350

I

IBM, 6, 12, 14
Ibru (Organization) Group, 261, 443
Ibru, Michael, 7, 46, 67, 450
ICT
    obstacles facing development of, 122
    entrepreneurship, 4, 119-122
    problems and challenges, 176-178
Idowu, Mobolaji Samuel, 65
Ifediora, John, 170
Immoral manager, 569
Imoukhuede, Aigboje, 594
Impersonal loyalty, 220
Income statement, 487, 488
Indian immigrants, 90
Indigenous entrepreneurship, 165
Indigenization policy,
Industrial clusters 125
Industry, and
    competition, 321
    competitive structure of, 367
    consolidated, 318, 368-369
    cooperative, 369-371
    declining, 318
    definition of, 314
    driving forces, 326-331
    emerging, 316
    fragmented, 316, 367-368
    key success factors, 331
    life cycle of, 315-319
    mature, 317
Industry economic features, 320
Industry structure, 319
Inelastic demand, 420
Infodev, South Africa, 4
Informal financial sector, 158
Informal sector, 180
    change and continuity, 186-187
    ILO, 184
    main features of, 183
    role of, 184
    problems of, 184-186
    World Bank, 184
Infrastructural constraints, 179
Infrastructure, 171-180
    definition of, 171
    education, 178
    energy, 175
    entrepreneurship, and 173
    ICT, 176
    transport, 174
Innovation, 10
    creative, 11
    incremental, 448
    momentary, 20
    pioneer, 11
    product, 11
    process, 6
Institutionalization,
    informal sector of, 186
    illegality of 225
intangibles, 496
intermediaries, 376
International Monetary Fund, 155
Internationalization of
    entrepreneurship, 453
Internet and
    entrepreneurship, 3-4, 178
    value chain, 384
Island Catering Services, 336-340
Iyare's Furniture Limited, 481

J

J & N House of Beauty
Jackson, Terrence, 220
Jide's Interiors, 434-438
Jobs, Steve, 11
John Holt, 180
Johnson & Johnson, 301
Johnson H. Johnson, 61
Joint venture, 370
Joko's Moin Moin Business, 627-628

K

Kalabule, 70
Kenyan Indians, 91
Kiggundu, Moses, 68, 210, 225
Kilby, Peter, 214
Kofi Annan Centre of Excellence in ICT, 137
Kotler, Philip, 396, 407
KPMG, 552

L

Ladipo Designs, 377
Lagos Business School, 456
Lagos University Teaching Hospital
Late-movers
Leadership, 220
Lebanese immigrants, 90
    see Lebanese entrepreneurs, 90
Leonard, Wayne, 455
Levels of strategies
Levinson, Jay Conrad, 396
Liabilities, 492, 496, 497
Licensing agreement, 371
Life-styles, 49
Limited liability company, 527-528
Liquidation, 472
Living in Bondage, 237, 316
Location, 233
Lockwood, Matthew, 108
Logistics, 376
Love, Ade, 238
Lunch for the Office, 397-398, 408

M

Macroeconomic deficiencies, 156
Magendo, 70
Makatiani, Ayisi, 227
Makawa, James, 45
Management problems, and
    culture of imitation, 213
    failure to develop strategic plan, 212
    lack of training, 219
    organization problems, 213
    poor financial control, 230
    poor locational decisions, 233
    weak corporate governance, 226
    weak marketing efforts, 229
Managerial succession, 213
Manipulative marketing practices, 565
Maphosa, France, 215, 216
Mark Newspaper, 38
Market
    development, 447
    penetration, 447
    segmentation, 286
Market research, 400-406
    customer survey, 404
    focus group, 404
    networking, 405
    observation, 405
    primary data, 404
    secondary data, 404
Market segmentation, 409-411
Marketing
    challenges in SSA, 229
    definition of, 396
Marketing mix, 412
Mary Kay Cosmetics, 300
Masiyiwa, Strive, 36, 44
Master budget, 506
McClelland, David, 41, 146
McDonald's, 43, 59, 289, 347
Medaaz, Nigeria Ltd,
Michael Adenuga Group, 261
Michel, Samora, 92
Microcredit, 160
Microenterprise
    definition of, 15
Microfinance, 160
Microfinance institutions, 160
Microsoft, 11, 162
Millelium Business Center, 413
Mission Statements, 290-292, and
    components of, 297-300
    customer-oriented approach, 293
    nature of, 291
    product-oriented approach, 293
    small businesses of, 295
Mitchell, B. C, 71
Mofe-Damijo, May, 542
Montes, Vincete, 581
Moral manager, 569
Moribo, S, 214
Motivation,
    employee, 220
Motives, 51
Motsepe, Patrice, 42
Mr. Bigg's, 12, 51, 354, 257, 290, 292,
    299, 303, 316, 349-360, 365, 373, 399,
    423, 425, 447, 628
MTN. 290, 294, 299
Mugabe, Robert, 92, 167, 233
Multinational enterprises and
    entrepreneurship, 123
multisegmentation strategy, 411
Muokwue, Ifeanyi, 47
Mutual service arrangements, 370

N

NAFDAC, 357, 557
NAFTA, 111

Nation-state, 128-130, and
    competitive advantage, 129-130
    entrepreneurial development, 130
    factor endowment, 129
    globalization, 129-130
National Mirror, 252
Need for achievement, 41, 146
Net profit, 488, 491
Network, 450
Network structure, 472
NEPAD, 112
Newswatch, 45, 443
Niger Delta, 192
    ChevronTexaco, 193
    economic and business fallout, 197
    entrepreneurial development, 201
    environmental pollution, 585
    government initiatives, 198
    loss of foreign investments, 201
    MEND, 194
    microfinance, 201
    MOSOP, 193
    multinational oil corporations, 200
    NDPVF, 193
    Niger Delta Vigilantes, 193
    OMPADEC, 196
    political risk, 165
    politics of resource control. 195
    Royal Dutch/Shell, 193-201
Nigerian advanced fee fraud, 224
Nigerian banking industry, 313
Nigerian Banks, 156
Nigerian Electricity and Power Authority, 94
Nigerian fast food industry, 347-359
Nigerian Railway Corporation, 94
Nigerian Ports Authority, 94
Nkrumah, Kwame, 92, 95, 97-100
Nnebue, Kenneth, 237
Nollywood, 233-245, 375
Non-indigenous entrepreneurship, 166
Nonprofit organizations 541
Noyce, Robert, 44
Nwosu, Ogechika, Mildness, 61
Nwuche, John, 421
Nwuche's People's Library, 421
Nyerere, Julius, 92, 95

O

Obasanjo, Olusegun, 193, 347
Objectives, 303, and
    financial, 305,
    strategic, 305
Oceanic Bank, 290, 300-303,
Odetola, T, 46
Odeyemi, Abiola, 257
OECD, 226
Offensive tactics, 373
Ogbor, John O., 5, 129, 180, 556
Ogunaike, Bamidele, 546
Ogundare, Abiodun, 387-392
Ogunde, Herbert, 238
Ogunde, Taiwo, 52
Ogunlola, Tope, 397, 405
Ohmae, Kenichi, 8
Okeahalam, Charles, 226
Okpara, John, 71, 211
Oladipo, Taiwo, 377
Olagbaju, Stella, 627
Olajide, Dayo and Sade, 434
Ombudsman, 577-579
Omolayo, Biodun, 55
Onome Gift Shoppe, 488-496
Operating profit, 490
Opio, Peter John, 551
Opportunities, 212, 315, 339, 355
Organizational challenge, 213
Organizational chart, 463
Organizational culture, 455
    See corporate culture
Organizational life cycle, 462
    birth stage, 464
    entrepreneurial stage, 464
    death stage, 471
    growth stage, 466
    maturity stage, 468
Organizational structure, 463 and
    divisional structure, 469
    functional structure, 467
    network structure, 474
    simple structure, 464
Osunde, Lare, 516
Outsourcing, 473
Oviah, Jim, 35, 36, 456
Owner's equity, 497

P

Partnership, 524, and
    agency power, 526
    agreement, 525
    general, 526
    limited, 526
    termination of, 526
Patton, George, 20
People's Bank, 162
Performance efficiency, 362
Peters, Michael P., 5, 42, 43
Phillips, Onwu, 594
Place, 418
Political culture, 163
Political environment, 163
Political risk, 163-165
Political system, 165
Porter, Michael, 125, 321-323, 362, 364, 375, 378
Positioning, 421-425
    experiential, 423
    functional, 423
    symbolic, 423
Post Colonial era, 94
Price, 419
Product, 413
    differentiation, 37, 286
Product life cycle, 413-414
Professional Employer Organizations, 472
Professional management, 454
Pro forma, 504
Promise Restaurant, 290, 300
Promotion, 421-426
Promotional strategies, 426-430
Public Private Partnership, 161
Punch, 252, 28, 300

R

Rabiu, Isiyaku, 46
Radipere, Simon, 230
Rapley, John, 90
Rapu, Obi, 316
Rational planning, 212
Ray, Kroc, 43, 59
Recruitment, 460-462
Redeemed Christian Church of God, 371
Regulatory environment, 168

Resistance to change, 442
Resource, 254
    capabilities, 333, 334
    deficiency, 334, 335
Risks, 42
    career 42
    family, 42
    financial, 42
    psychic, 42
    rivalry, 321
RSCA, 158

S

Salami, Adebayo, 238
Salawudeen, Medina, 65
Savings and credit associations, 158
Schaefer, Brett, 169
Schmitt, Bernd, 423
Schooster, Frank, 139
Schumpeter, Joseph, 5
Self-directed team, 459
Service, 413
    characteristics of, 416
Sese Sekou, Mobutu, 168
Shell Petroleum Development Co., 162
Shepherd, Dean A., 5, 42, 43
Single-segmentation strategy, 411
Skills development, 177
Small Business Administration, 512
Small business
    definition of, 15
Small business owner, 21
Small and Medium Scale Enterprise-Development Agency, 130
Smith, J. W., 106
Social responsibility, 223, 583-585, and
    definition of, 586
  Sole proprietorship, 522-523
SADC, 11-118
Soon, T. T., 210
South Africa, 4
    economic building blocks, 87
    SEDA, 130
Stakeholder, and
    competitors, 588
    community, 588
    customers, 587
    definition of, 586
    distributors, 588
    employees, 587
    entrepreneurial firm of, 585

government, 587
  interest groups, 588
  managing relations, 588
  suppliers, 588
Starik, Mark, 586
Start-up Partners, 443-44
Steers Fast Food, 49
Strategic alliances, 369, 372
Strategic entrepreneur, 21
Strategic factors, 332
Strategic group, 252
Strategic intent, 289
Strategic planning, 211
Strategist, 20, 268
Strategy (ies), 250, and
  business level, 262-263
  corporate level, 261-262
  cost focus
  cost leadership, 362-364
  differentiation, 363-366
  defensive strategies, 372
  entrepreneurship, 249
  ethics, 583
  functional level, 263-264
  generic, 362
  low cost, 362-3
  offensive, 372
  operating level, 264-265
Strategy Management, 258 and
  process, 258
strengths, 315, 33, 334
Strickland, A. J., 12, 251, 271, 326, 563
Structural Adjustment Program
  conditionalities, 102
  criminality, 109
  deregulation, 103
  foreign exchange policy, 104
  IMF, 101
  impact of, 105
  import-dependent economy, 109
  interest rate policy, 103
  liberalization, 103
  privatization, 104
  unequal trade, 106
  World Bank, 101
Substitute products, 322
Succession
  age of founder and, 215
  delegation and, 214
  leadership and, 214
  traditional practices of, 216

Sustainable competitive advantage, 253
SWOT analysis, 332-345
Synergistic diversification, 451
Synergistic effect, 444

T
Tan, Celine, 107
Tantalizers, 350, 628
Tanzanian socialism, 95
Tastee Fried Chicken, 351
Taxes, 501
Tell Magazine, 45, 443
Tetrazzini, 350
Theory X, 221-222
Theory Y, 222
Thiam, Papa, 167
Thisday, 252
Thompson, Arthur, A. 12. 251, 271, 326, 563
Threats, 315, 339, 345
Tide, 252
Toftoy, Charles, 296
Torres, Nichole, 462
Tribune, 252
Trulsson, Per, 219, 231, 232
Tshikuku, Kabeya, 149, 165
Training and development, 462
Transport infrastructure, 174
Tushabomwe-Kazooba, Charles, 229

U
Ugbomah, Eddy, 238
Ujamaa, 95, 96
Uncertainty avoidance, 147
UNIDO, 566
Union Bank of Nigeria, 255
United African Company of Nigeria, 180, 257, 265, 289, 301, 303, 349, 365, 451, 469
United Bank for Africa, 255, 318
Universal moral values, 577
Unsegmented strategy, 411
Utomi, Pat, 35

V
Value chain, 13, 378, and
  activities, 381-383
  cost advantage, 380
  differentiation, 381
  technology, 381-382
Value chain partnership, 371

Values, 581, 589
Values-based organization, 589
Values statements, 302
Van Scheers, Louise, 230
Vernon, Ellis, 442
Vertical integration, 449
Virtual firms, 472
Vision of organizations, 288

W
Walt Disney Co., 38
Wal-Mart, 38-39
Walters, Kenneth, 577
Walton, Sam 38-39
Weak corporate governance, 225
Weak uncertainty avoidance, 148
Weaknesses, 315, 333-335
 253, 290-2

Weber, Max, 149
Werhane, Patricia, 570
Whistleblowing, 576
Wilier, H., 214
Winfrey, Oprah, 42, 61, 67
Winters, David, 41
Wolfensohn, James, D. 171, 226
Working capital, 497
Wynn, Pamela, 71, 211

Y
Yar' adua Musa, 196
Yunus, Muhammad, 161

Z
Zenith Bank, 36,

Made in the USA
Lexington, KY
09 June 2011